A People's History
of the United States

Also by Howard Zinn

La Guardia in Congress

The Southern Mystique

SNCC: The New Abolitionists

New Deal Thought (editor)

Vietnam: The Logic of Withdrawal

Disobedience and Democracy

The Politics of History

The Pentagon Papers: Critical Essays
    (editor, with Noam Chomsky)

Postwar America

Justice in Everyday Life

Declarations of Independence:
    Cross-Examining American Ideology

Failure to Quit: Reflections of an Optimistic Historian

You Can't Be Neutral on a Moving Train

A People's History of the United States: The Wall Charts

A People's History of the United States:
    1492–Present, Revised and Updated Edition

A People's History of the United States

Teaching Edition

Howard Zinn

Teaching Materials by
Kathy Emery

The New Press
New York

Library of Congress Cataloging-in-Publication Data
Zinn, Howard
    A people's history of the United States / Howard Zinn.
Teaching ed.
    P.   cm.
Includes bibliographical references and index.
ISBN 1-56584-366-5 (hc)
ISBN 1-56584-379-7 (pb)
1. United States—History. I. Title.
E178.1.Z56   1997
973—dc21 96-52532
CIP

Published in the United States by The New Press, New York
Distributed by W.W. Norton & Company, Inc., New York

The New Press was established in 1990 as a not-for-profit alternative to the large,
commercial publishing houses currently dominating the book publishing industry.
The New Press operates in the public interest rather than for private gain, and is committed
to publishing, in innovative ways, works of educational, cultural, and community value
that might not normally be commercially viable.

Book design by [sic]

Production management by Kim Waymer
Printed in the United States of America

9 8 7 6 5 4 3 2 1

To Noah
and his generation

Rise like lions after slumber
In unvanquishable number!
Shake your chains to earth, like dew
Which in sleep had fallen on you—
Ye are many, they are few!

PERCY BYSSHE SHELLEY

Why do you stand
    they were asked, and
        Why do you walk?

Because of the children, they said, and
    because of the heart, and
    because of the bread.

DANIEL BERRIGAN

Contents

Contents

Acknowledgments

To André Schriffrin and Ellen Reeves of the New Press, for imagining and undertaking this special edition.

To Kathy Emery, for her heroic work in enriching the book for high school students.

To my two original editors, for their incalculable help: Cynthia Merman of Harper & Row, and Roslyn Zinn.

To Rick Balkin, my literary agent, for provoking me to do the original "People's History."

To Hugh Van Dusen of HarperCollins, for wonderful help and support throughout the history of this book.

To *Akwesasne Notes*, Mohawk Nation, for the passage from Ila Abernathy's poem.

To Dodd, Mead, & Company, for the passage from "We Wear the Mask," from *The Complete Poems of Paul Laurence Dunbar*.

To Harper & Row, for "Incident," from *On These I Stand* by Countee Cullen. Copyright 1925 by Harper & Row, Publishers, Inc.; renewed 1953 by Ida M. Cullen.

Acknowledgments

To Alfred A. Knopf, Inc., for the passage from "I, Too,"
from *Selected Poems of Langston Hughes*.

To *The New Trail*, 1953 yearbook of the Phoenix Indian School,
Phoenix, Arizona, for the poem "It Is Not!"

To Random House, Inc., for the passage from Langston Hughes's
"Lenox Avenue Mural," from *The Panther and the Lash: Poems
of Our Time*.

To Esta Seaton, for her poem "Her Life," which first appeared in
The Ethnic American Woman by Edith Blicksilver,
Kendall/Hunt Publishing Company, 1978.

To Warner Bros., for the excerpt from "Brother, Can You Spare a Dime?"
Lyrics by Jay Gorney, music by E. Y. Harburg. © 1932 Warner Bros. Inc.
Copyright Renewed. All rights reserved. Used by permission.

Introduction

Kathy Emery

From the very first day I taught history, I have searched for ways to make the subject interesting and intellectually challenging to my students. Every year of my twenty years of teaching, I have been responsible for teaching an American history survey course. This meant having to deal with the issue of textbooks. I did not want my students to be bored. I believed that if my students learned to think for themselves and didn't learn to merely memorize the opinions of the adults in their lives, I could kill two birds with one stone – they would experience learning to think as an enjoyable and rewarding experience. But to accomplish this task, I had to expose my students to several points of view and then teach them the skills that would allow them to pick and choose among the different views. This involved teaching a process involving moral evaluation as well as rational analysis and explication data. At first, I used *The National Experience*[1]. I chose it because I hoped it would provide enough detail to challenge its general statements. But it was still only one point of view and did not allow for the range of debate that I was looking for. So I began assigning a different textbook to each student. This was an improvement over using just one interpretation of the past since the standard textbooks of American history differ somewhat in their interpretations of events and selection of data.[2]

After several years experimenting with using different textbooks, I was still not satisfied with results. The range of difference was still too small to provoke the degree of controversy I wanted to see in the classroom. I tried to expand the interpretive continuum with Grob and Billias' *Interpretations of American History*3. But, I had to spend too much time in the classroom dissecting each article so the students could understand the arguments and data. I was never able to make it to the twentieth century by the end of the school year. I kept experimenting with a variety of secondary sources as supplements to the textbook, always looking for the perfect fit. It was only when I discovered Howard Zinn's *People's History* that I found the solution to the problem I had posed myself so many years earlier. Zinn provides what no other textbook does: the human impact, the human cost of decisions made by politicians and businessmen. I had been asking my students to evaluate the decisions as a method to develop the student's critical thinking. But such an exercise was only partially successful. Students could not challenge very many generalizations made in the standard texts without a significant range of data at their disposal. Students needed this full range if they were truly to think for themselves. People can only form opinions based the information to which they have been exposed, With the data that Zinn provides, the range of interpretations is wide enough for students to really have a choice in what they know and, then, in what they believe.

For several years, I taught both Zinn and *The National Experience*, continually asking students to compare Blum's version of an event with Zinn's. Finally, I had material that allowed a student to establish an opinion that was truly hers and defend that opinion with historical details.4 The first chapter in Zinn's text is the most powerful and successful in teaching students to think critically. When reading this chapter, students supplied to support their evaluations were as diverse as the students' personalities.

I have also used secondary sources and films to supplement the readings in the two texts. Exposure to Zinn has the salutary effect of making students ask more questions than either Zinn or the standard textbooks can answer. An annotated bibliography of some of these sources can be found in Appendix C.

Every teacher needs to develop his or her own style and method. But no style or method can be created in a vacuum. I have provided methodological suggestions from which you may pick and choose, expand upon or reduce. These suggestions are to be found in two places: the questions at the end of each chapter and a set of general instructions for teaching a group paragraph which includes a suggested system of assessment (i.e. giving grades); my thoughts on the uses and abuses of extra credit; the role of geography in a history class; a useful approach to using the debate format in teaching content and critical thinking; and techniques for class discussion.

The question at the end of each chapter are of several kinds; some simply ask the reader to extract detail, while others demand greater skills apart from accumulating *knowledge* and gaining *comprehension*. Many questions ask students to *analyze* the text, select relevant data, *synthesize* that data into an answer, and then *evaluate* the answer. The higher order questions provoke the most interesting discussions since they demand that students begin to attach meaning to the data/detail.[5]

In the years I have been using history to teach critical thinking, I have discovered that moving back and forth between the concrete and the abstract (inherent in both deductive and inductive thinking) is a skill that needs to be explicitly taught. A few students are "naturals", but most need to be shown how it is done and they need a great deal of practice doing it. Constantly asking students to define the terms[6] of their questions and statements is a crucial first step in developing or examining an argument. That is why many of the questions after each chapter ask the reader to define the terms Zinn uses or certain terms the historical actors used. Those questions requiring analysis and synthesis also require that the terms of the question be fully understood.

To illustrate this point let me examine one of the questions from the chapter on Reconstruction. I ask: *After the Civil War, was the South reduced to colonial status?* Before a student even begins to look for an answer to this question, several of the terms need to be understood in a very concrete way; in particular the word "colonial". Depending on how one defines "colonial", the answer could be yes or it could be no. Which answer is correct? That depends on which definition of "colonial" is acceptable to the person attempting to answer the question. If the teacher and student share the same definitions then the teacher is more likely to approve of the student's answer. To define the essential terms of a question explicitly avoids misunderstanding and ensures a greater likelihood of success by the student.

A teacher might use the question "*Was the South reduced to colonial status after the Civil War?*" as a discussion question in class, as a topic for a group paragraph or written homework.Regardless of the actual form of an assignment, the process of completing each assignment needs to be taught (repeatedly and consistently throughout the year). Break the question down into its discrete terms. For example, "The South" –

Identify the states to which the question refers. "After the Civil War" - Identify the time period during which the South's "status" is being assessed. Then tackle the thornier problem of defining "colonial". For this, a dictionary can be useful. But better yet, use historical precedents in tandem with the dictionary. The American states used to be English colonies. What was their status in relation to England? (a politically dependant territory used as a source of raw materials and a market for manufactured goods?). *The Webster's Collegiate Dictionary* provides several choices of definitions for the word "colony". Which one best fits the historical context?

* a body of people living in a new territory but retaining ties with the parent state?
* a group of people institutionalized away from others?
* a dependent area or people controlled, dominated or exploited by a parent state?

Once the terms are defined so their applicability to a specified group of historical data is clear, students previously unable to complete the question on their own, will now be able to do so.

There are a few questions I have asked to which Zinn does not provide the answer. For example, after Chapter 9 in question 26, I ask: "Was the Georgia legislature successful in expelling its black members?" The text indicates that the legislature made the attempt. We don't know if the attempt was, in fact, successful. This is what students call a "trick" question. If the question is used to exhibit one-upmanship by the teacher, students have every right to feel resentful. Used appropriately, however, this kind of question can be used to teach the students to read carefully.

Another skill introduced and reinforced by some of the chapter questions is that of being able to categorize data (for the purposes of then synthesizing and evaluating into economic, political, social and cultural factors). Most standard texts keep discussion at the political level. Consequently, most students are not used to thinking in terms of economic and social causes and consequences. An important component of critical thinking is establishing relationships. Zinn's data and explanations provide a wonderful opportunity to teach students how to develop a socioeconomic analysis of political events. Zinn hopes that the development of such thinking about the past will lead to such thinking about the present. It does.

Notes

1. Blum, J., et al., *The National Experience*, Harcourt Brace Jovanovich, New York.

2. One of the most successful assignments emerged when I asked to students to discover what happened during Bacon's Rebellion (1676). See Appendix B for a bibliography of the textbooks I used, page references to passages covering the events surrounding Bacon's Rebellion and the questions I used to provoke debate.

3. Grob, G., and Billias, G. A., *Interpretations of American History*, The Free Press, New York.

4. I use the word "detail" instead of "evidence" or "fact" very consciously. The distinction between an interpretation and a "fact" is a slippery slope. To avoid having to constantly deal with what was fact and what was not in the classroom, I only made distinctions with my students in terms of levels of detail. I required them to support a topic sentence (a generalization) with the next level of detail, some of which could be considered fact while other kinds of detail were not fact but still qualified as evidence, It proved over the years to be a very practical choice of diction.

5. I borrowed these categories of types of questions from Bloom's Taxonomy. Please refer to Appendix D for more details on the nature of the taxonomy.

6. "Define your terms" was a mantra that I repeated often so that my students internalized it. Effective communication depends on the participants sharing the same definition of the key terms of the topic under discussion. To ensure those definitions are shared, they need to be made explicit at the very beginning of any argument or thesis presentation. A common mistake people make in developing an argument is changing the definitions of the terms *in medias res*; hence, the need to make this process explicit.

A People's History
of the United States

Chapter 1

Columbus, the Indians, and Human Progress

Arawak men and women, naked, tawny, and full of wonder, emerged from their villages onto the island's beaches and swam out to get a closer look at the strange big boat. When Columbus and his sailors came ashore, carrying swords, speaking oddly, the Arawaks ran to greet them, brought them food, water, gifts. He later wrote of this in his log:

> They...brought us parrots and balls of cotton and spears and many other things, which they exchanged for the glass beads and hawks' bells. They willingly traded everything they owned.... They were well-built, with good bodies and handsome features.... They do not bear arms, and do not know them, for I showed them a sword, they took it by the edge and cut themselves out of ignorance. They have no iron. Their spears are made of cane.... They would make fine servants.... With fifty men we could subjugate them all and make them do whatever we want.

These Arawaks of the Bahama Islands were much like Indians on the mainland, who were remarkable (European observers were to say again and again) for their hospitality, their belief in sharing. These traits did not stand out in Renaissance Europe, dominated as it was by the religion of popes, the government of kings, the frenzy for money that marked Western civilization and its first messenger to the Americas, Christopher Columbus.

Columbus wrote:

As soon as I arrived in the Indies, on the first Indies, on the first Island which I found, I took some of the natives by force in order that they might learn and might give me information of whatever there is in these parts.

The information that Columbus wanted most was: Where is the gold? He had persuaded the king and queen of Spain to finance an expedition to the lands, the wealth, he expected would be on the other side of the Atlantic—the Indies and Asia, gold and spices. For, like other informed people of his time, he knew the world was round and that he could sail west in order to get to the Far East.

Spain was recently unified, one of the new modern nation-states, like France, England, and Portugal. Spain's population, mostly poor peasants, worked for the nobility, who were 2 percent of the population and owned 95 percent of the land. Spain had tied itself to the Catholic Church, expelled all the Jews, driven out the Moors. Like other states of the modern world, Spain sought gold, which was becoming the new mark of wealth, more useful than land because it could buy anything.

There was gold in Asia, it was thought, and certainly silks and spices, for Marco Polo and others had brought back marvelous things from their overland expeditions centuries before. Now that the Turks had conquered Constantinople and the eastern Mediterranean, and controlled the land routes to Asia, a sea route was needed. Portuguese sailors were working their way around the southern tip of Africa. Spain decided to gamble on a long sail across an unknown ocean.

In return for bringing back gold and spices, Ferdinand and Isabella promised Columbus 10 percent of the profits, governorship over new-found lands, and the fame that would go with a new title: Admiral of the Ocean Sea. He was a merchant's clerk from the Italian city of Genoa, part-time weaver (the son of a skilled weaver), and expert sailor. He set out with three sailing ships, the largest of which was the *Santa María*, perhaps one hundred feet long, and thirty-nine crew members.

Columbus would never have made it to Asia, which was thousands of miles farther away than he had calculated, imagining a smaller world. He would have been doomed by that great expanse of sea. But he was lucky. One-fourth of the way there he came upon an unknown, uncharted land that lay between Europe and Asia—the Americas. It was early October 1492, thirty-three days since he and his crew had left the Canary Islands, off the Atlantic coast of Africa. Now they saw branches and sticks floating in the water. They saw flocks of birds. These were signs of land. Then, on

October 12, a sailor called Rodrigo saw the early morning moon shining on white sands, and cried out. It was an island in the Bahamas, the Caribbean sea. The first man to sight land was supposed to get a yearly pension of ten thousand maravedis for life, but Rodrigo never got it. Columbus claimed he had seen a light the evening before. He got the reward.

So, approaching land, they were met by the Arawak Indians, who swam out to greet them. The Arawaks lived in village communes, had a developed agriculture of corn, yams, cassava. They could spin and weave, but they had no horses or work animals. They had no iron, but they wore tiny gold ornaments in their ears.

This was to have enormous consequences: it led Columbus to take some of them aboard ship as prisoners because he insisted that they guide him to the source of the gold. He then sailed to what is now Cuba, then to Hispaniola (the island that today consists of Haiti and the Dominican Republic). There, bits of visible gold in the rivers, and a gold mask presented to Columbus by a local Indian chief, led to wild visions of gold fields.

On Hispaniola, out of timbers from the *Santa María*, which had run aground, Columbus built a fort, the first European military base in the Western Hemisphere. He called it Navidad (Christmas) and left thirty-nine crew members there, with instructions to find and store the gold. He took more Indian prisoners and put them aboard his two remaining ships. At one part of the island he got into a fight with Indians who refused to trade as many bows and arrows as he and his men wanted. Two Arawaks were run through with swords and bled to death. Then the *Niña* and the *Pinta* set sail for the Azores and Spain. When the weather turned cold, the Indian prisoners began to die.

Columbus's report to the royal court in Madrid was extravagant. He insisted he had reached Asia (it was Cuba) and an island off the coast of China (Hispaniola). His descriptions were part fact, part fiction:

> Hispaniola is a miracle. Mountains and hills, plains and pastures, are both fertile and beautiful...the harbors are unbelievably good and there are many wide rivers of which the majority contain gold.... There are many spices, and great mines of gold and other metals....

The Indians, Columbus reported, "are so naive and so free with their possessions that no one who has not witnessed them would believe it. When you ask for something they have, they never say no. To the contrary, they offer to share with anyone...." He concluded his report by asking for a little help from their Majesties, and in return he would bring them from his next voyage "as much gold as they need...and as many slaves as they ask." He was full of religious talk: "Thus the eternal God, our Lord, gives victory to those who follow His way over apparent impossibilities."

Because of Columbus's exaggerated report and promises, his second expedition was given seventeen ships and more than twelve hundred men. The aim was clear: slaves and gold. They went from island to island in the Caribbean, taking Indians as captives. But as word spread of the Europeans' intent they found more and more empty villages. On Haiti, they found that the sailors left behind at Fort Navidad had been killed in a battle with the Indians, after they had roamed the island in gangs looking for gold, taking women and children as slaves for sex and labor.

Now, from his base on Haiti, Columbus sent expedition after expedition into the interior. They found no gold fields, but had to fill up the ships returning to Spain with some kind of dividend. In the year 1495, they went on a great slave raid, rounded up fifteen hundred Arawak men, women, and children, put them in pens guarded by Spaniards and dogs, then picked the five hundred best specimens to load onto ships. Of those five hundred, two hundred died en route. The rest arrived alive in Spain and were put up for sale by the archdeacon of the town, who reported that, although the slaves were "naked as the day they were born," they showed "no more embarrassment than animals." Columbus later wrote: "Let us in the name of the Holy Trinity go on sending all the slaves that can be sold."

But too many of the slaves died in captivity. And so Columbus, desperate to pay back dividends to those who had invested, had to make good his promise to fill the ships with gold. In the province of Cicao on Haiti, where he and his men imagined huge gold fields to exist, they ordered all persons fourteen years or older to collect a certain quantity of gold every three months. When they brought it, they were given copper tokens to hang around their necks. Indians found without a copper token had their hands cut off and bled to death.

The Indians had been given an impossible task. The only gold around was bits of dust garnered from the streams. So they fled, were hunted down with dogs, and were killed.

Trying to put together an army of resistance, the Arawaks faced Spaniards who had armor, muskets, swords, and horses. When the Spaniards took prisoners, they hanged them or burned them to death. Among the Arawaks, mass suicides began, with cassava poison. Infants were killed to "save" them from the Spaniards. In two years, through murder, mutilation, or suicide, half of the two hundred fifty thousand Indians on Haiti were dead.

When it became clear that there was no gold left, the Indians were taken as slave labor on huge estates, known later as *encomiendas*. They were worked at a ferocious pace, and died by the thousands. By the year 1515, there were perhaps fifty thousand Indians left. By 1550, there were five hundred. A report of the year 1650 shows none of the original Arawaks or their descendants left on the island.

The chief source—and, on many matters, the only source—of information about what happened on the islands after Columbus came is Bartolomé de las Casas, who, as a young priest, participated in the conquest of Cuba. For a time he owned a plantation on which Indian slaves worked, but he gave that up and became a vehement critic of Spanish cruelty. Las Casas transcribed Columbus's journal and, in his fifties, began a multivolume *History of the Indies*.

Women in Indian society were treated so well as to startle the Spaniards. Las Casas describes sex relations:

> Marriage laws are nonexistent: men and women alike choose their mates and leave them as they please, without offense, jealousy or anger. They multiply in great abundance; pregnant women work to the last minute and give birth almost painlessly; up the next day, they bathe in the river and are as clean and healthy as before giving birth. If they tire of their men, they give themselves abortions with herbs that force stillbirths, covering their shameful parts with leaves or cotton cloth; although on the whole, Indian men and women look upon total nakedness with as much casualness as we look upon a man's head or at his hands.

The Indians, Las Casas says, "put no value on gold and other precious things. They lack all manner of commerce, neither buying nor selling, and rely exclusively on their natural environment for maintenance. They are extremely generous with their possessions and by the same token covet the possessions of their friends and expect the same degree of liberality...."

Las Casas tells about the treatment of the Indians by the Spaniards.

> Endless testimonies...prove the mild and pacific temperament of the natives.... But our work was to exasperate, ravage, kill, mangle and destroy; small wonder, then, if they tried to kill one of us now and then.... The admiral, it is true, was blind as those who came after him, and he was so anxious to please the King that he committed irreparable crimes against the Indians....

Total control led to total cruelty. The Spaniards "thought nothing of knifing Indians by tens and twenties and of cutting slices off them to test the sharpness of their blades." Las Casas tells how "two of these so-called Christians met two Indian boys one day, each carrying a parrot; they took the parrots and for fun beheaded the boys."

While the native men were sent many miles away to the mines, their wives remained to work the soil, forced into the excruciating job of digging and making thousands of hills for cassava plants.

> Thus husbands and wives were together only once every eight or ten months and when they met they were so exhausted and depressed on both sides...they ceased to procreate. As for the newly born, they died early because their mothers, overworked and famished, had no milk to nurse them, and for this reason, while I was in Cuba, 7,000 children died in three months. Some mothers even drowned their babies from sheer desperation.... In this way, husbands died in the mines, wives died at work, and children died from lack of milk...and in a short time this land which was so great, so powerful and fertile...was depopulated.... My eyes have seen these acts so foreign to human nature, and now I tremble as I write....

When he arrived on Hispaniola in 1508, Las Casas says, "there were 60,000 people living on this island, including the Indians; so that from 1494 to 1508, over three million people had perished from war, slavery, and the mines. Who in future generations will believe this?"

Thus began the history, five hundred years ago, of the European invasion of the Indian settlements in the Americas, a history of conquest, slavery, and death. But in the history books given to children in the United States, for generation after generation, it all starts with heroic adventure—there is no bloodshed—and Columbus Day is a celebration. Only in recent years do we see droplets of change.

Past the elementary and high schools, there have been only occasional hints of something else. Samuel Eliot Morison, the Harvard historian, was the most distinguished writer on Columbus, the author of a multivolume biography, and was himself a sailor who retraced Columbus's route across the Atlantic. In his popular book *Christopher Columbus, Mariner*, written in 1954, he tells about the enslavement and the killing: "The cruel policy initiated by Columbus and pursued by his successors resulted in complete genocide."

That is on one page, buried halfway into the telling of a grand romance. In the book's last paragraph, Morison sums up his view of Columbus:

He had his faults and his defects, but they were largely the defects of the qualities that made him great—his indomitable will, his superb faith in God and in his own mission as the Christ-bearer to lands beyond the seas, his stubborn persistence despite neglect, poverty and discouragement. But there was no flaw, no dark side to the most outstanding and essential of all his qualities—his seamanship.

One can lie outright about the past. Or one can omit facts which might lead to unacceptable conclusions. Morison does neither. He refuses to lie about Columbus. He does not omit the story of mass murder; indeed he describes it with the harshest word one can use: genocide.

But he does something else. He mentions the truth quickly and goes on to other things more important to him. Outright lying or quiet omission takes the risk of discovery, which, when made, might arouse the reader to rebel against the writer. To state the facts, however, and then to bury them in a mass of other information is to say to the reader with a certain infectious calm: yes, mass murder took place, but it's not that important—it should weigh very little in our final judgments; it should affect very little what we do in the world.

It is true that the historian cannot avoid emphasis of some facts and not of others. This is as natural to him as to the mapmaker, who, in order to produce a usable drawing for practical purposes, must first flatten and distort the shape of the earth, then choose out of the bewildering mass of geographic information those things needed for the purpose of this or that particular map.

My argument cannot be against selection, simplification, or emphasis, which are inevitable for both cartographers and historians. But the mapmaker's distortion is a technical necessity for a common purpose shared by all people who need maps. The historian's distortion is more than technical, it is ideological; it is released into a world of contending interests, where any chosen emphasis supports (whether the historian means to or not) some kind of interest, whether economic or political or racial or national or sexual.

Furthermore, this ideological interest is not openly expressed in the way a mapmaker's technical interest is obvious ("This is a Mercator projection for long-range navigation—for short-range, you'd better use a different projection"). No, it is presented as if all readers of history had a common interest that historians serve to the best of their ability.

To emphasize the heroism of Columbus and his successors as navigators and discoverers, and to deemphasize their genocide, is not a technical necessity but an ideological choice. It serves—unwittingly—to justify what was done.

My point is not that we must, in telling history, accuse, judge, condemn Columbus *in absentia*. It is too late for that; it would be a useless scholarly exercise in morality. But the easy acceptance of atrocities as a deplorable but necessary price to pay for progress (Hiroshima and Vietnam, to save Western civilization; Kronstadt and Hungary, to save socialism; nuclear proliferation, to save us all)—that is still with us. One reason these atrocities are still with us is that we have learned to bury them in a mass of other facts, as radioactive wastes are buried in containers in the earth.

The treatment of heroes (Columbus) and their victims (the Arawaks)—the quiet acceptance of conquest and murder in the name of progress—is only one aspect of a certain approach to history, in which the past is told from the point of view of governments, conquerors, diplomats, leaders. It is as if they, like Columbus, deserve universal acceptance, as if they—the Founding Fathers, Jackson, Lincoln, Wilson, Roosevelt, Kennedy, the leading members of Congress, the famous justices of the Supreme Court—represent the nation as a whole. The pretense is that there really is such a thing as "the United States," subject to occasional conflicts and quarrels, but fundamentally a community of people with common interests. It is as if there really is a "national interest" represented in the Constitution, in territorial expansion, in the laws passed by Congress, the decisions of the courts, the development of capitalism, the culture of education, and the mass media.

"History is the memory of states," wrote Henry Kissinger in his first book, *A World Restored*, in which he proceeded to tell the history of nineteenth-century Europe from the viewpoint of the leaders of Austria and England, ignoring the millions who suffered from those statesmen's policies. From his standpoint, the "peace" that Europe had before the French Revolution was "restored" by the diplomacy of a few national leaders. But for factory workers in England, farmers in France, people of color in Asia and Africa, women and children everywhere except in the upper classes, it was a world of conquest, violence, hunger, and exploitation—a world not restored but disintegrated.

My viewpoint, in telling the history of the United States, is different: that we must not accept the memory of states as our own. Nations are not communities and never have been. The history of any country, presented as the history of a family, conceals fierce conflicts of interest (sometimes exploding, most often repressed) between conquerors and conquered, masters and slaves, capitalists and workers, dominators and dominated in race and sex. And in such a world of conflict, a world of victims and executioners, it is the job of thinking people, as Albert Camus suggested, not to be on the side of the executioners.

Thus, in that inevitable taking of sides which comes from selection and emphasis in history, I prefer to try to tell the story of the discovery of America from the viewpoint of the Arawaks, of the Constitution from the standpoint of the slaves, of Andrew Jackson as seen by the Cherokees, of the Civil War as seen by the New York Irish, of the Mexican War as seen by the deserting soldiers of Scott's army, of the rise of industrialism as seen by the young women in the Lowell textile mills, of the Spanish-American War as seen by the Cubans, the conquest of the Philippines as seen by black soldiers on Luzon, the Gilded Age as seen by southern farmers, the First World War as seen by socialists, the Second World War as seen by pacifists, the New Deal as seen by blacks in Harlem, the postwar American empire as seen by peons in Latin America. And so on, to the limited extent that any one person, however he or she strains, can "see" history from the standpoint of others.

My point is not to grieve for the victims and denounce the executioners. Those tears, that anger, cast into the past, deplete our moral energy for the present. And the lines are not always clear. In the long run, the oppressor is also a victim. In the short run (and so far, human history has consisted only of short runs), the victims, themselves desperate and tainted with the culture that oppresses them, often turn on other victims.

Still, understanding the complexities, this book will be skeptical of governments and their attempts, through politics and culture, to ensnare ordinary people in a giant web of nationhood pretending to a common interest. I will try not to overlook the cruelties that victims inflict on one another as they are jammed together in the boxcars of the system. I don't want to romanticize them. But I do remember (in rough paraphrase) a statement I once read: "The cry of the poor is not always just, but if you don't listen to it, you will never know what justice is."

I don't want to invent victories for people's movements. But to think that history writing must aim simply to recapitulate the failures that dominate the past is to make historians collaborators in an endless cycle of defeat. If history is to be creative, to anticipate a possible future without denying the past, it should, I believe, emphasize new possibilities by disclosing those hidden episodes of the past when, even if in brief flashes, people showed their ability to resist, to join together, occasionally to win. I am supposing, or perhaps only hoping, that our future may be found in the past's fugitive moments of compassion rather than in its solid centuries of warfare.

That, being as blunt as I can, is my approach to the history of the United States. The reader may as well know that before going on.

What Columbus did to the Arawaks of the Bahamas, Cortés did to the Aztecs of Mexico, Pizarro to the Incas of Peru, and the English settlers of Virginia and Massachusetts to the Powhatans and the Pequots.

It seems there was a frenzy in the early capitalist states of Europe for gold, for slaves, for products of the soil, to pay the bondholders and stockholders of the expeditions, to finance the monarchical bureaucracies rising in Western Europe, to spur the growth of the new money economy rising out of feudalism, to participate in what Karl Marx would later call "the primitive accumulation of capital." These were the violent beginnings of an intricate system of technology, business, politics, and culture that would dominate the world for the next five centuries.

Jamestown, Virginia, the first permanent English setlement in the Americas, was set up inside the territory of an Indian confederacy, led by the chief, Powhatan. Powhatan watched the English settle on his people's land, but did not attack, maintaining a posture of coolness. When the English were going through their "starving time" in the winter of 1610, some of them ran off to join the Indians, where they would at least be fed. When the summer came, the governor of the colony sent a messenger to ask Powhatan to return the runaways, whereupon Powhatan, according to the English account, replied with "noe other than prowde and disdaynefull Answers." Some soldiers were therefore sent out "to take Revendge." They fell upon an Indian settlement, killed fifteen or sixteen Indians, burned the houses, cut down the corn growing around the village, took the queen of the tribe and her children into boats, then ended up throwing the children overboard "and shoteinge owtt their Braynes in the water." The queen was later taken off and stabbed to death.

Twelve years later, the Indians, alarmed as the English settlements kept growing in numbers, apparently decided to try to wipe them out for good. They went on a rampage and massacred 347 men, women, and children. From then on it was total war.

Not able to enslave the Indians, and not able to live with them, the English decided to exterminate them. According to historian Edmund

Morgan, "Within two or three years of the massacre the English had avenged the deaths of that day many times over."

In that first year of the white man in Virginia, 1607, Powhatan had addressed a plea to John Smith that turned out prophetic. How authentic it is may be in doubt, but it is so much like so many Indian statements that it may be taken as, if not the rough letter of that first plea, the exact spirit of it:

> I have seen two generations of my people die.... I know the difference between peace and war better than any man in my country. Why will you take by force what you may have quietly by love? Why will you destroy us who supply you with food? What can you get by war? Why are you jealous of us? We are unarmed, and willing to give you what you ask, if you come in a friendly manner, and not so simple as not to know that it is much better to eat good meat, sleep comfortably, live quietly with my wives and children, laugh and be merry with the English, and trade for their copper and hatchets, than to run away from them, and to lie cold in the woods, feed on acorns, roots and such trash, and be so hunted that I can neither eat nor sleep.

When the Pilgrims came to New England, they too were coming not to vacant land but to territory inhabited by tribes of Indians.

The Pequot Indians occupied what is now southern Connecticut and Rhode Island. The Puritans wanted them out of the way; they wanted their land. So, the war with the Pequots began. Massacres took place on both sides. The English developed a tactic of warfare used earlier by Cortés and later, in the twentieth century, even more systematically: deliberate attacks on noncombatants for the purpose of terrorizing the enemy.

So the English set fire to the wigwams of villages. William Bradford, in his *History of the Plymouth Plantation* written at the time, describes John Mason's raid on the Pequot village:

> Those that scaped the fire were slaine with the sword; some hewed to peeces, others rune throw with their rapiers, so as they were quickly dispatchte, and very few escaped. It was conceived they thus destroyed about 400 at this time. It was a fearful sight to see them thus frying in the fyer.

A footnote in Virgil Vogel's book *This Land Was Ours* (1972) says: "The official figure on the number of Pequots now in Connecticut is twenty-one persons."

For a while, the English tried softer tactics. But ultimately, it was back to annihilation. The Indian population of ten million that lived north of

Mexico when Columbus came would ultimately be reduced to less than a million. Huge numbers of Indians would die from diseases introduced by the whites.

Behind the English invasion of North America, behind their massacre of Indians, their deception, their brutality, was that special powerful drive born in civilizations based on private property. It was a morally ambiguous drive; the need for space, for land, was a real human need. But in conditions of scarcity, in a barbarous epoch of history ruled by competition, this human need was transformed into the murder of whole peoples.

Was all this bloodshed and deceit—from Columbus to Cortés, Pizarro, the Puritans—a necessity for the human race to progress from savagery to civilization?

If there *are* necessary sacrifices to be made for human progress, is it not essential to hold to the principle that those to be sacrificed must make the decision themselves? We can all decide to give up something of ours, but do we have the right to throw into the pyre the children of others, or even our own children, for a progress that is not nearly as clear or present as sickness or health, life or death?

Beyond all that, how certain are we that what was destroyed was inferior? Who were these people who came out on the beach and swam to bring presents to Columbus and his crew, who watched Cortés and Pizarro ride through their countryside, who peered out of the forests at the first white settlers of Virginia and Massachusetts?

Columbus called them Indians, because he miscalculated the size of the earth. In this book we too call them Indians, with some reluctance, because it happens too often that people are saddled with names given them by their conquerors.

Widely dispersed over the great land mass of the Americas, they numbered approximately seventy-five million people by the time Columbus came, perhaps twenty-five million in North America. Responding to the different environments of soil and climate, they developed hundreds of different tribal cultures, perhaps two thousand different languages. They perfected the art of agriculture and figured out how to grow maize (corn), which cannot grow by itself and must be planted, cultivated, fertilized, harvested, husked, and shelled. They ingeniously developed a variety of other vegetables and fruits, as well as peanuts and chocolate and tobacco and rubber.

On their own, the Indians were engaged in the great agricultural revolution that other peoples in Asia, Europe, and Africa were going through about the same time.

While many of the tribes remained nomadic hunters and food gatherers in wandering, egalitarian communes, others began to live in more settled communities where there was more food, larger populations, more divisions of labor among men and women, more surplus to feed chiefs and priests, more leisure time for artistic and social work, for building houses.

From the Adirondacks to the Great Lakes, in what is now Pennsylvania and upper New York, lived the most powerful of the northeastern tribes, the League of the Iroquois. In the villages of the Iroquois, land was owned in common and worked in common. Hunting was done together, and the catch was divided among the members of the village.

Women were important and respected in Iroquois society. The women tended the crops and took general charge of village affairs while the men were always hunting or fishing. As Gary B. Nash notes in his fascinating study of early America, *Red, White, and Black,* "Thus power was shared between the sexes and the European idea of male dominancy and female subordination in all things was conspicuously absent in Iroquois society."

Children in Iroquois society, while taught the cultural heritage of their people and solidarity with the tribe, were also taught to be independent, not to submit to overbearing authority.

All of this was in sharp contrast to European values as brought over by the first colonists, a society of rich and poor, controlled by priests, by governors, by male heads of families. Gary Nash describes Iroquois culture:

> No laws and ordinances, sheriffs and constables, judges and juries, or courts or jails—the apparatus of authority in European societies—were to be found in the northeast woodlands prior to European arrival. Yet boundaries of acceptable behavior were firmly set. Though priding themselves on the autonomous individual, the Iroquois maintained a strict sense of right and wrong.... He who stole another's food or acted invalourously in war was "shamed" by his people and ostracized from their company until he had atoned for his actions and demonstrated to their satisfaction that he had morally purified himself.

Not only the Iroquois but other Indian tribes behaved the same way.

So, Columbus and his successors were not coming into an empty wilderness, but into a world which in some places was as densely populated as Europe itself, where the culture was complex, where human relations were more egalitarian than in Europe, and where the relations among men, women, children, and nature were more beautifully worked out than perhaps any place in the world.

They were people without a written language, but with their own laws, their poetry, their history kept in memory and passed on, in an oral vocabulary more complex than Europe's, accompanied by song, dance, and ceremonial drama. They paid careful attention to the development of personality, intensity of will, independence and flexibility, passion and potency, to their partnership with one another and with nature.

John Collier, an American scholar who lived among Indians in the 1920s and 1930s in the American Southwest, said of their spirit: "Could we make it our own, there would be an eternally inexhaustible earth and a forever lasting peace."

Perhaps there is some romantic mythology in that. But even allowing for the imperfection of myths, it is enough to make us question, for that time and ours, the excuse of progress in the annihilation of races, and the telling of history from the standpoint of the conquerors and leaders of Western civilization.

Exercises

1. Before reading the chapter: Write down all that you think you know about Columbus, including myth as well as reality. Examples: Columbus sailed in 1492; people believed the earth was round; Columbus sailed on three ships.

    While or after reading the chapter: Write down passages in the text that either support or contradict each item generated by the assignment above, then identify those events and actions discussed in the text that had not been part of your thinking about Columbus originally.

2. After reading the first chapter, choose two adjectives that describe Columbus, two that describe the Spanish, two that describe the English, two for the Arawaks, and two for the Powhatans. You may use the same adjective for more than one group. *Do not feel confined to using only the adjectives listed.*

CRUEL	NAIVE	HONEST	GREEDY
GENEROUS	KIND	BRAVE	IGNORANT
CIVILIZED	ADVENTUROUS	PRIMITIVE	INFERIOR
PRACTICAL	INTELLIGENT	HEROIC	THOUGHTFUL
ARROGANT	LAZY	DEDICATED	

For each of the adjectives you choose:

    a. Write down the definition that best describes the applicable group.

    b. Write ten short sentences using the selected adjectives—one adjective for each sentence. For example:

       ★ The Spanish were generous.

       ★ Columbus was brave.

       ★ The Arawaks were generous.

    c. Then look for details/facts in the text that you think illustrate the definitions of the selected adjectives.

Important: In defining a word, you cannot use any part of that word in the definition. Furthermore, useful definitions for this exercise will be ones that do not employ the opposite of the word. An example of a useless definition would be: primitive = not civilized. The problem here is what does "civilized" mean? Not primitive? If you have a dictionary that gives you such circular definitions, go find a more detailed dictionary or use a thesaurus.

3.   Choose an infinitive to finish each of the sentences below.

    a. Use a dictionary to define the infinitive.

    b. Look for details/facts in the text that you think illustrate the definitions.

    The purpose of Columbus's voyage(s) was...

    The result of Columbus's voyage(s) was...

Some options: to civilize, to explore, to exploit, to conquer, to establish trade, to discover, to Christianize, to destroy, to convert, to destroy...

4.   Write down the five most important things Zinn says about Columbus (include page numbers). Write down the two most important things he says about the writing of history.

Compare your list with a classmate(s). Why are your lists different? What are the criteria you each used in making your choices? [This is a real brain-teaser.]

5. Was Columbus responsible for the behavior of his men?
    a. Identify what the soldiers' behaviors were.
    b. For each act, identify what Columbus could or could not have done to alter that behavior.

6. Compare Columbus's log entries with Las Casas's journal entries.
    a. Identify differences and similarities (e.g., how each describes the Arawaks).
    b. Identify topics the other did not discuss.
    c. What accounts for the differences? the similarities (their personalities, their goals, their job functions, their status in relation to the other Spaniards)?

7. Write a two-page story of Columbus that you would want read to a third-grade class at the point when the students are first being introduced to Columbus.

8. For each of the suggested phrases below that completes the sentence, identify the passage(s) in the book that either supports or challenges each assertion. Identify irrelevant phrases with NP (no passage applies). When choosing a relevant passage, note its page number and whether the passage supports, challenges, or doesn't apply.

    Zinn thinks that Morison....
    a. omits the truth.
    b. believes that all readers share a common interest.
    c. writes the kind of history that allows atrocities to continue to be committed.
    d. is critical of Columbus.
    e. idealizes Columbus.
    f. is as accurate as a mapmaker.
    g. allows his opinions of Columbus to select out only the positive.

h. buries the negative facts with positive facts.

i. omits the bloodshed.

9. If communities share common interests, did Columbus and Las Casas belong to the same community? If so, what are their common interests? (What was Columbus in the Caribbean for? Las Casas?) If not, what interests separate them into different communities? Did Las Casas have more in common with the Arawaks than he did with Columbus?

10. Zinn argues (p. 10) that most history texts pretend that there is such a thing as "The United States"—a community of people with common interests.

   a. What are the "communities" that Zinn identifies? What "interests" do you think these groups have in common? What "interests" do they not share? What "interests" of one group might be in opposition to an "interest" of another group?

   b. What do recent actions of the United States government reveal about the definition of the "national interest" or what the national priorities are? (Refer to Afterword: On the Clinton Presidency); p. 482, Military budget; p. 482, dropping bombs on Baghdad; p. 482, supporting other governments in power to foster U.S. trade; p. 484, North American Free Trade Agreement; p. 484, restoring Aristide to power; p. 484, increasing military spending while reducing spending on health care, education, child care, housing, and the environment; p. 485, maintaining the present tax structure.

   c. Identify the community that you belong to, your community's interests, and other communities that share your interests, as well as those communities that do not share or oppose your interests (possibilities: students, teachers, administrators, male, female, young, old, ethnic and racial identities, neighborhood, city, suburb). Do the policies of the United States government favor some communities over others?

11. Brainstorming from details:

   a. Choose a detailed description of an event from the text.

   b. Then write down a series of questions that knowledge of the event may enable one to answer.

   c. Choose two of the questions and answer them.

Example

    a. *detailed description of an event from the text:* on page 5, Columbus "got into a fight with Indians who refused to trade as many bows and arrows as he and his men wanted. Two [Indians] were run through with swords and bled to death."

    b. *a series of questions that knowledge of the above event may enable one to answer:* What does the above event reveal about Columbus's personality? about the purpose of the voyage? about Spanish culture? about Arawak culture? about the comparative military strength of the Spanish and Arawaks?

    c. *answers to two of the questions above:* The Spanish had military superiority—swords versus bows and arrows. Columbus wanted to dictate the terms of trade.

12. Hollywood Movies: Fact or Fiction? Much controversy has surrounded the making of the films *Mississippi Burning* and *JFK*. Many critics complain that when Americans see these films, they will believe falsely that the events and circumstances dramatized in these films accurately represent what happened during the periods in question. And for unstated reasons, this is wrong. The Left has criticized *Mississippi Burning* for leaving the impression that the FBI was honestly trying to help the civil rights advocates when "in fact" the FBI was aiding the KKK. Most of the mainstream media excoriated *JFK* for implying that John Kennedy's assassination was engineered by Lyndon Johnson. Several questions are begged by this criticism. Do fictional movies (as opposed to documentaries) have a responsibility to reflect history accurately? Or do they have poetic license with reality, as art claims to have, in order to make a point about universal truth? But, more to the point with regard to Columbus, is "history" accurate? If films are supposed to convey "accurate" history, who decides what is the official version of the past? In order to explore this issue in more depth:

    a. Watch a movie made about Columbus.

    b. Compare the content of the movie with Zinn's chapter about Columbus in addition to any other historical sources you may wish to consult (the more the better).

Possible points comparison: reasons for the voyage, Columbus's first perceptions of the native inhabitants, Spanish treatment of the native inhabitants, success of the voyage(s), failures of the voyage(s), degree of Columbus's navigational skills, Columbus's leadership skills, the nature of the reception of Columbus by the native inhabitants, the portrayal of native inhabitants.

    c. Respond to any of the questions raised in the introduction to this assignment above. For example:

- ★ Is the movie historically accurate?

- ★ Is the movie good art?

- ★ Does the movie have a thesis?

- ★ Does it address a universal truth?

- ★ What is the difference between history and art?
- ★ Is the difference merely one of style?

Chapter 2

Drawing the Color Line

There is not a country in world history in which racism has been more important, for so long a time, as the United States. And the problem of "the color line," as W. E. B. Du Bois put it, is still with us. So it is more than a purely historical question to ask: How did it start?—and an even more urgent question: How might it end? Or, to put it differently: Is it possible for whites and blacks to live together without hatred?

If history can help answer these questions, then the beginnings of slavery in North America—a continent where we can trace the coming of the first whites and the first blacks—might supply at least a few clues.

In the English colonies, slavery developed quickly into a regular institution, into the normal labor relation of blacks to whites. With it developed that special racial feeling—whether hatred, or contempt, or pity, or patronization—that accompanied the inferior position of blacks in America for the next 350 years: that combination of inferior status and derogatory thought we call racism.

Everything in the experience of the first white settlers acted as a pressure for the enslavement of blacks.

The Virginians of 1619 were desperate for labor, to grow enough food to stay alive. Among them were survivors from the winter of 1609–10, the "starving time," when, crazed for want of food, they roamed the woods for nuts and berries, dug up graves to eat the corpses, and died in batches until five hundred colonists were reduced to sixty.

They needed labor, to grow corn for subsistence, to grow tobacco for

23

export. They had just learned from the Indians how to grow tobacco, and in 1617 they sent off the first cargo to England. Finding that, like all pleasurable drugs tainted with moral disapproval, it brought a high price, the planters, despite their high religious talk, were not going to ask questions about something so profitable.

They couldn't force Indians to work for them, as Columbus had done. They were outnumbered, and while, with superior firearms, they could massacre Indians, they would face massacre in return. They could not capture them and keep them enslaved; the Indians were tough, resourceful, defiant, and at home in these woods, as the transplanted Englishmen were not.

There may have been a kind of frustrated rage at their own ineptitude, at the Indian superiority at taking care of themselves, that made the Virginians especially ready to become the masters of slaves. Edmund Morgan imagines their mood as he writes in his book *American Slavery, American Freedom*:

> If you were a colonist, you knew that your technology was superior to the Indians'. You knew that you were civilized, and they were savages.... But your superior technology had proved insufficient to extract anything. The Indians, keeping to themselves, laughed at your superior methods and lived from the land more abundantly and with less labor than you did.... And when your own people started deserting in order to live with them, it was too much.... So you killed the Indians, tortured them, burned their villages, burned their cornfields. It proved your superiority, in spite of your failures. And you gave similar treatment to any of your own people who succumbed to their savage ways of life. But you still did not grow much corn.

Black slaves were the answer. And it was natural to consider imported blacks as slaves, even if the institution of slavery would not be regularized and legalized for several decades. Because, by 1619, a million blacks had already been brought from Africa to South America and the Caribbean, to the Portuguese and Spanish colonies, to work as slaves. Fifty years before Columbus, the Portuguese took ten African blacks to Lisbon: this was the start of a regular trade in slaves. African blacks had been stamped as slave labor for a hundred years. So it would have been strange if those twenty blacks, who had been forcibly transported to Jamestown and sold as objects to settlers anxious for a steadfast source of labor, were considered as anything but slaves.

Their helplessness made enslavement easier. The Indians were on their own land. The whites were in their own European culture. The blacks had been torn from their land and culture, forced into a situation where the heritage of language, dress, custom, and family relations was bit by bit obliterated except for the remnants that blacks could hold on to by sheer, extraordinary persistence.

Was their culture inferior—and so subject to easy destruction? The African civilization was as advanced in its own way as that of Europe. In certain ways, it was more admirable; but it also included cruelties, hierarchical privilege, and the readiness to sacrifice human lives for religion or profit. It was a civilization of one hundred million people, using iron implements and skilled in farming. It had large urban centers and remarkable achievements in weaving, ceramics, and sculpture.

European travelers in the sixteenth century were impressed with the African kingdoms of Timbuktu and Mali, already stable and organized at a time when European states were just beginning to develop into modern nations.

Africa had a kind of feudalism, like Europe, based on agriculture, with hierarchies of lords and vassals. But African feudalism did not come, as did Europe's, out of the slave societies of Greece and Rome, which had destroyed ancient tribal life. In Africa, tribal life was still powerful, and some of its better features—a communal spirit, more kindness in law and punishment—still existed. And because the lords did not have the weapons that European lords had, they could not command obedience as easily.

In England, even as late as 1740, a child could be hanged for stealing a rag of cotton. But in the Congo, communal life persisted, the idea of private property was a strange one, and thefts were punished with fines or various degrees of servitude. A Congolese leader, told of the Portuguese legal codes, asked a Portuguese once, teasingly: "What is the penalty in Portugal for anyone who puts his feet on the ground?"

Slavery existed in the African states, and it was sometimes used by Europeans to justify their own slave trade. But, as Basil Davidson points out in *The African Slave Trade*, the "slaves" of Africa were more like the serfs of Europe—in other words, like most of the population of Europe. It was a harsh servitude, but they had rights that the slaves brought to America did not have, and they were "altogether different from the human cattle of the slave ships and the American plantations."

African slavery lacked two elements that made American slavery the most cruel form of slavery in history: the frenzy for limitless profit that comes from capitalistic agriculture; the reduction of the slave to less than human status by the use of racial hatred, with that relentless clarity based on color, where white was master, black was slave.

In fact, it was because they came from a settled culture, of tribal customs and family ties, of communal life and traditional ritual, that African blacks found themselves especially helpless when removed from this. They were captured in the interior (frequently by blacks caught up in the slave trade themselves), sold on the coast, then shoved into pens with blacks of other tribes, often speaking different languages.

The conditions of capture and sale were crushing affirmations to the black African of his helplessness in the face of superior force. The marches to the coast, sometimes for a thousand miles, with people shackled around the neck, under whip and gun, were death marches, in which two of every five blacks died. On the coast, they were kept in cages until they were picked and sold.

Then they were packed aboard the slave ships, in spaces not much bigger than coffins, chained together in the dark, wet slime of the ship's bottom, choking in the stench of their own excrement.

On one occasion, hearing a great noise from belowdecks where the blacks were chained together, the sailors opened the hatches and found the slaves in different stages of suffocation, many dead, some having killed others in desperate attempts to breathe. Slaves often jumped overboard to drown rather than continue their suffering. To one observer a slave deck was "so covered with blood and mucus that it resembled a slaughter-house."

Under these conditions, perhaps one of every three blacks transported overseas died, but the huge profits (often double the investment on one trip) made it worthwhile for the slave trader, and so the blacks were packed into the holds like fish.

First the Dutch, then the English, dominated the slave trade. (By 1795 Liverpool had more than a hundred ships carrying slaves and accounted for half of all the European slave trade.) Some Americans in New England entered the business, and in 1637 the first American slave ship, the *Desire*, sailed from Marblehead, Massachusetts. Its holds were partitioned into racks, two feet by six feet, with leg irons and bars.

By 1800, ten to fifteen million blacks had been transported as slaves to the Americas, representing perhaps one-third of those originally seized in Africa. It is roughly estimated that Africa lost fifty million human beings to death and slavery in those centuries we call the beginnings of modern Western civilization, at the hands of slave traders and plantation owners in western Europe and America, the countries deemed the most advanced in the world.

With all of this—the desperation of the Jamestown settlers for labor, the impossibility of using Indians and the difficulty of using whites, the availability of blacks offered in greater and greater numbers by profit-seeking dealers in human flesh, and with such blacks possible to control because they had just gone through an ordeal that, if it did not kill them, must have left them in a state of psychic and physical helplessness—is it any wonder that such blacks were ripe for enslavement?

And under these conditions, even if some blacks might have been considered servants, would blacks be treated the same as white servants?

The evidence, from the court records of colonial Virginia, shows that in 1630 a white man named Hugh Davis was ordered "to be soundly whipt...for abusing himself...by defiling his body in lying with a Negro." Ten years later, six servants and "a negro of Mr. Reynolds" started to run away. While the whites received lighter sentences, "Emanuel the Negro to receive thirty stripes and to be burnt in the cheek with the letter *R*, and to work in shackle one year or more as his master shall see cause."

This unequal treatment, this developing combination of contempt and oppression, feeling and action, which we call "racism"—was this the result of a "natural" antipathy of white against black? If racism can't be shown to be natural, then it is the result of certain conditions, and we are impelled to eliminate those conditions.

All the conditions for blacks and whites in seventeenth-century America were powerfully directed toward antagonism and mistreatment. Under such conditions even the slightest display of humanity between the races might be considered evidence of a basic human drive toward community.

In spite of preconceptions about blackness, which in the English language suggested something "foul...sinister" (*Oxford English Dictionary*), in spite of the special subordination of blacks in the Americas in the seventeenth century, there is evidence that where whites and blacks found themselves with common problems, common work, a common enemy in their master, they behaved toward one another as equals.

The swift growth of plantation slavery is easily traceable to something other than natural racial repugnance: the number of arriving whites, whether free or indentured servants (under four- to seven-year contracts), was not enough to meet the need of the plantations. By 1700, in Virginia, there were 6,000 slaves, one-twelfth of the population. By 1763, there were 170,000 slaves, about half the population.

From the beginning, the imported black men and women resisted their enslavement, under the most difficult conditions, under pain of mutilation and death. Only occasionally was there an organized insurrection. More often they showed their refusal to submit by running away. Even more often, they engaged in sabotage, slowdowns, and subtle forms of resistance which asserted, if only to themselves and their brothers and sisters, their dignity as human beings.

A Virginia statute of 1669 referred to "the obstinacy of many of them," and in 1680 the Assembly took note of slave meetings "under the pretense of feasts and brawls" which they considered of "dangerous consequence." In 1687, in the colony's Northern Neck, a plot was discovered in which slaves planned to kill all the whites in the area and escape during a mass funeral.

Slaves recently from Africa, still holding on to the heritage of their communal society, would run away in groups and try to establish villages of runaways out in the wilderness, on the frontier. Slaves born in America, on the other hand, were more likely to run off alone, and, with the skills they had learned on the plantation, try to pass as free men.

In the colonial papers of England, a 1729 report from the lieutenant governor of Virginia to the British Board of Trade tells how "a number of Negroes, about fifteen...formed a design to withdraw from their Master and to fix themselves in the fastnesses of the neighboring Mountains. They had found means to get into their possession some Arms and Ammunition, and they took along with them some Provisions, their Cloths, bedding and working Tools.... Tho' this attempt has happily been defeated, it ought nevertheless to awaken us into some effectual measures...."

In 1710, warning the Virginia Assembly, Governor Alexander Spotswood said:

> ...freedom wears a cap which can without a tongue, call together all those who long to shake off the fetters of slavery and as such an Insurrection would surely be attended with most dreadful consequences so I think we cannot be too early in providing against it, both by putting our selves in a better posture of defence and by making a law to prevent the consultations of those Negroes.

Indeed, considering the harshness of punishment for running away, that so many blacks did run away must be a sign of a powerful rebelliousness. All through the 1700s, the Virginia slave code read:

If the slave is apprehended…it shall…be lawful for the county court, to order such punishment for the said slave, either by dismembering, or in any other way…as they in their discretion shall think fit, for the reclaiming any such incorrigible slave, and terrifying others from the like practices….

Fear of slave revolt seems to have been a permanent fact of plantation life. William Byrd, a wealthy Virginia slaveholder, wrote in 1736:

We have already at least 10,000 men of these descendants of Ham, fit to bear arms, and these numbers increase every day, as well by birth as by importation. And in case there should arise a man of desperate fortune, he might with more advantage than Cataline kindle a servile war…and tinge our rivers wide as they are with blood.

It was an intricate and powerful system of control that the slave owners developed to maintain their labor supply and their way of life, a system both subtle and crude, involving every device that social orders employ for keeping power and wealth where they are.

The system was psychological and physical at the same time. The slaves were taught discipline, were impressed again and again with the idea of their own inferiority to "know their place," to see blackness as a sign of subordination, to be awed by the power of the master, to merge their interest with the master's, destroying their own individual needs. To accomplish this there was the discipline of hard labor, the breakup of the slave family, the lulling effects of religion (which sometimes led to "great mischief," as one slaveholder reported), the creation of disunity among slaves by separating them into field slaves and more privileged house slaves, and finally the power of law and the immediate power of the overseer to invoke whipping, burning, mutilation, and death.

Still, rebellions took place—not many, but enough to create constant fear among white planters.

A letter to London from South Carolina in 1720 reports:

I am now to acquaint you that very lately we have had a very wicked and barbarous plot of the designe of the negroes rising with a designe to destroy all the white people in the country and then to take Charles Town in full body but it pleased God it was discovered and many of them taken prisoners and some burnt and some hang'd and some banish'd.

Herbert Aptheker, who did detailed research on slave resistance in North America for his book *American Negro Slave Revolts*, found about 250 instances where a minimum of ten slaves joined in a revolt or conspiracy.

From time to time, whites were involved in the slave resistance. As early as 1663, indentured white servants and black slaves in Gloucester County, Virginia, formed a conspiracy to rebel and gain their freedom. The plot was betrayed, and ended with executions.

In New York in 1741, there were ten thousand whites in the city and two thousand black slaves. It had been a hard winter and the poor—slave and free—had suffered greatly. When mysterious fires broke out, blacks and whites were accused of conspiring together. Mass hysteria developed against the accused. After a trial full of lurid accusations by informers, and forced confessions, two white men and two white women were executed, eighteen slaves were hanged, and thirteen slaves were burned alive.

Only one fear was greater than the fear of black rebellion in the new American colonies. That was the fear that discontented whites would join black slaves to overthrow the existing order. In the early years of slavery, especially, before racism as a way of thinking was firmly ingrained, while white indentured servants were often treated as badly as black slaves, there was a possibility of cooperation.

And so, measures were taken. About the same time that slave codes, involving discipline and punishment, were passed by the Virginia Assembly. Edmund Morgan writes:

> Virginia's ruling class, having proclaimed that all white men were superior to black, went on to offer their social (but white) inferiors a number of benefits previously denied them. In 1705 a law was passed requiring masters to provide white servants whose indenture time was up with ten bushels of corn, thirty shillings, and a gun, while women servants were to get 15 bushels of corn and forty shillings. Also, the newly freed servants were to get 50 acres of land.

Morgan concludes: "Once the small planter felt less exploited by taxation and began to prosper a little, he became less turbulent, less dangerous, more respectable. He could begin to see his big neighbor not as an extortionist but as a powerful protector of their common interests."

We see now a complex web of historical threads to ensnare blacks for slavery in America: the desperation of starving settlers, the special helplessness of the displaced African, the powerful incentive of profit for slave trader and planter, the temptation of superior status for poor whites, the elaborate controls against escape and rebellion, the legal and social punishment of black and white collaboration.

The point is that the elements of this web are historical, not "natural."

This does not mean that they are easily disentangled and dismantled. It means only that there is a possibility for something else, under historical conditions not yet realized. And one of these conditions would be the elimination of that class exploitation which has made poor whites desperate for small gifts of status, and has prevented that unity of black and white necessary for joint rebellion and reconstruction.

Around 1700, the Virginia House of Burgesses declared:

> The Christian Servants in this country for the most part consists of the Worser Sort of the people of Europe. And since...such numbers of Irish and other Nations have been brought in of which a great many have been soldiers in the late wars that according to our present Circumstances we can hardly governe them and if they were fitted with Armes and had the Opertunity of meeting together by Musters we have just reason to fears they may rise upon us.

It was a kind of class consciousness, a class fear. There were things happening in early Virginia, and in the other colonies, to warrant it.

Exercises

1. Why did Virginians massacre Indians instead of enslaving them?

2. How does the answer to the above question explain the choice to import black slaves?

3. Why were Africans vulnerable to enslavement?

4. Page 27: "...where whites and blacks found themselves with common problems, common work, common enemy in their master, they behaved toward one another as equals."

   What were the "problems" that blacks and whites shared? What was the "work" that blacks and whites did? Was it the same? Did they work together? How did the "master" treat his indentured servant? How did the "master" treat his slave? To what degree was the treatment the same?

5. How do we know that slaves resisted their enslavement?

6. How do we know that indentured servants resisted their indentured condition?

7. How did the Virginia ruling class begin to drive a wedge between the white indentured servants and enslaved blacks?

8. Below are three versions of one essential question. Choose ONE of the three to answer.

   a. Zinn argues that racism is not natural but a product of human choice and historical circumstances. Given the forces that created racism, what choices need to be made to undo it?

   b. What were the historical forces that caused white plantation owners to choose black slaves as their labor source? Was it a "decision" to make a profit, or were Englishmen forced to do it? Would the Powhatans have accepted wages to labor in the fields of the plantation owners? Does that constitute a historical force?

   c. Zinn argues that racism is not natural. Does he mean that it is caused by human decisions or historical forces? Explain your answer by first defining the difference between historical forces and human decision. What is a "historical force"? Do such forces compel humans to make decisions they would otherwise not have made?

9. At what point in the chronology of American history is the topic of slavery covered in traditional American history texts? At what point is it covered in Zinn's text? How might you explain the difference in placement? (What are the purposes of including slavery in the traditional texts? What are the purposes for Zinn?)

Chapter 3

Persons of Mean
and Vile Condition

In 1676, seventy years after Virginia was founded, a hundred years before it supplied leadership for the American Revolution, that colony faced a rebellion of white frontiersmen, joined by slaves and servants, a rebellion so threatening that the governor had to flee the burning capital of Jamestown and England decided to send a thousand soldiers across the Atlantic, hoping to maintain order among forty thousand colonists. This was Bacon's Rebellion. After the uprising was suppressed, its leader, Nathaniel Bacon, dead and his associates hanged, was described in a Royal Commission report:

> He seduced the Vulgar and most ignorant people to believe (two thirds of each county being of that Sort) Soe that their whole hearts and hopes were set now upon Bacon. Next he charges the Governour as negligent and wicked, treacherous and incapable, the Lawes and Taxes as unjust and oppressive and cryes up absolute necessity of redress.

Bacon's Rebellion began with conflict over how to deal with the Indians, who were close by, on the western frontier, constantly threatening. Whites who had been ignored when huge land grants around Jamestown were given away had gone west to find land, and there they encountered Indians. Were those frontier Virginians resentful that the politicos and landed aristocrats who controlled the colony's government in Jamestown first pushed them westward into Indian territory and then seemed indecisive in fighting the Indians? That might explain the character of their rebellion, not easily classifiable as either antiaristocrat or anti-Indian, because it was both.

And the governor, William Berkeley, and his Jamestown crowd— were they more conciliatory to the Indians (they wooed certain of them as spies and allies) now that they had monopolized the land in the East, could use frontier whites as a buffer, and needed peace? The desperation of the government in suppressing the rebellion seemed to have a double motive: developing an Indian policy that would divide Indians in order to control them, and teaching the poor whites of Virginia that rebellion did not pay—by a show of superior force, by calling for troops from England itself, by mass hanging.

Times were hard in 1676. "There was genuine distress, genuine poverty.... All contemporary sources speak of the great mass of people as living in severe economic straits," writes Wilcomb Washburn, who, using British colonial records, has done an exhaustive study of Bacon's Rebellion.

Bacon himself had a good bit of land and was probably more enthusiastic about killing Indians than about redressing the grievances of the poor. But he became a symbol of mass resentment against the Virginia establishment and was elected in the spring of 1676 to the House of Burgesses. When he insisted on organizing armed detachments to fight the Indians, outside official control, Berkeley proclaimed him a rebel and had him captured, whereupon two thousand Virginians marched into Jamestown to support him. Berkeley let Bacon go, in return for an apology, but Bacon went off, gathered his militia, and began raiding the Indians.

Bacon's "Declaration of the People" of July 1676 shows a mixture of populist resentment against the rich and frontier hatred of the Indians. It indicted the Berkeley administration for unjust taxes, for putting favorites in high positions, for monopolizing the beaver trade, and for not protecting the western farmers from the Indians.

But in the fall, Bacon, aged twenty-nine, fell sick and died, because of, as a contemporary put it, "swarmes of Vermyn that bred in his body."

The rebellion didn't last long after that. A ship armed with thirty guns, cruising the York River, became the base for securing order, and its captain, Thomas Grantham, used force and deception to disarm the last rebel forces. Coming upon the chief garrison of the rebellion, he found four hundred armed Englishmen and Negroes, a mixture of freemen, servants, and slaves. He promised to pardon everyone, to give freedom to slaves and servants, but when they got into the boat, he trained his big guns on them, disarmed them, and eventually delivered the slaves and servants to their masters. The remaining garrisons were overcome one by one. Twenty-three rebel leaders were hanged.

It was a complex chain of oppression in Virginia. The Indians were plundered by white frontiersmen, who were taxed and controlled by the Jamestown elite. And the whole colony was being exploited by England, which bought the colonists' tobacco at prices it dictated and made one hundred thousand pounds a year for the king.

From the testimony of the governor himself, the rebellion against him had the overwhelming support of the Virginia population. A member of his council reported that the defection was "almost general" and laid it to "the Lewd dispositions of some Persons of desperate Fortunes" who had "the Vaine hopes of takeing the Countrey wholley out of his Majesty's handes into their owne." Another member of the Governor's Council, Richard Lee, noted that Bacon's Rebellion had started over Indian policy. But the "zealous inclination of the multitude" to support Bacon was due, he said, to "hopes of levelling."

"Leveling" meant equalizing the wealth. Leveling was to be behind countless actions of poor whites against the rich in all the English colonies, in the century and a half before the Revolution.

The servants who joined Bacon's Rebellion were part of a large underclass of miserably poor whites who came to the North American colonies from European cities whose governments were anxious to be rid of them. In England, the development of commerce and capitalism in the 1500s and 1600s, the enclosing of land for the production of wool, filled the cities with vagrant poor, and from the reign of Elizabeth on, laws were passed to punish them, imprison them in workhouses, or exile them.

In the 1600s and 1700s, by forced exile, by lures, promises, and lies, by kidnapping, by their urgent need to escape the living conditions of the home country, poor people wanting to go to America became commodities of profit for merchants, traders, ship captains, and eventually their masters in America.

After signing the indenture, in which the immigrants agreed to pay their cost of passage by working for a master for five or seven years, they were often imprisoned until the ship sailed, to make sure they did not run away. In the year 1619, the Virginia House of Burgesses, born that year as the first representative assembly in America (it was also the year of the first importation of black slaves), provided for the recording and enforcing of contracts between servants and masters. As in any contract between unequal powers, the parties appeared on paper as equals, but enforcement was far easier for master than for servant.

The voyage to America lasted eight, ten, or twelve weeks, and the servants were packed into ships with the same fanatic concern for profits that marked the slave ships. If the weather was bad, and the trip took too long, they ran out of food. Gottlieb Mittelberger, a musician, traveling from Germany to America around 1750, wrote about his voyage:

> During the journey the ship is full of pitiful signs of distress—smells, fumes, horrors, vomiting, various kinds of sea sickness, fever, dysentery, headaches, heat, constipation, boils, scurvy, cancer, mouth-rot, and similar afflictions, all of them caused by the age and the high salted state of the food, especially of the meat, as well as by the very bad and filthy water.... Add to all that shortage of food, hunger, thirst, frost, heat, dampness, fear, misery, vexation, and lamentation as well as other troubles.... On board our ship, on a day on which we had a great storm, a woman about to give birth and unable to deliver under the circumstances, was pushed through one of the portholes into the sea....

Indentured servants were bought and sold like slaves. An announcement in the *Virginia Gazette*, March 28, 1771, read:

> "Just arrived at Leedstown, the Ship Justitia, with about one Hundred Healthy Servants, Men Women & Boys.... The Sale will commence on Tuesday the 2nd of April."

Against the rosy accounts of better living standards in the Americas one must place many others, like one immigrant's letter from America: "Whoever is well off in Europe better remain there. Here is misery and distress, same as everywhere, and for certain persons and conditions incomparably more than in Europe."

Beatings and whippings were common. Servant women were raped. In Virginia in the 1660s, a master was convicted of raping two women servants. He also was known to beat his own wife and children; he had whipped and chained another servant until he died. The master was berated by the court, but specifically cleared on the rape charge, despite overwhelming evidence.

The master tried to control completely the sexual lives of the servants. It was in his economic interest to keep women servants from marrying or from having sexual relations, because childbearing would interfere with work. Benjamin Franklin, writing as "Poor Richard" in 1736, gave advice to his readers: "Let thy maidservant be faithful, strong, and homely."

Sometimes servants organized rebellions, but one did not find on the mainland the kind of large-scale conspiracies of servants that existed, for instance, on Barbados in the West Indies.

Despite the rarity of servants' rebellions, the threat was always there, and masters were fearful. After Bacon's Rebellion, two companies of English soldiers remained in Virginia to guard against future trouble, and their presence was defended in a report to the Lords of Trade and Plantation saying: "Virginia is at present poor and more populous than ever. There is great apprehension of a rising among the servants, owing to their great necessities and want of clothes; they may plunder the storehouses and ships."

Escape was easier than rebellion. "Numerous instances of mass desertions by white servants took place in the Southern colonies," reports Richard Morris (*Government and Labor in Early America*), on the basis of an inspection of colonial newspapers in the 1700s. "The atmosphere of seventeenth-century Virginia," he says, "was charged with plots and rumors of combinations of servants to run away."

The mechanism of control was formidable. Strangers had to show passports or certificates to prove they were freemen. Agreements among the colonies provided for the extradition of fugitive servants (these became the basis of the clause in the U.S. Constitution that persons "held to Service or Labor in one State...escaping into another... shall be delivered up...").

Sometimes, servants went on strike. One Maryland master complained to the Provincial Court in 1663 that his servants did "peremptorily and positively refuse to goe and doe their ordinary labor." The servants responded that they were fed only "Beanes and Bread" and they were "soe weake, wee are not able to perform the imploym'ts hee puts us uppon." They were given thirty lashes by the court.

More than half the colonists who came to the North American shores in the colonial period came as servants. They were mostly English in the seventeenth century, Irish and German in the eighteenth century. More and more, slaves replaced them, as they ran away to freedom or finished their time, but as late as 1755, white servants made up 10 percent of the population of Maryland.

What happened to these servants after they became free? There are cheerful accounts in which they rise to prosperity, becoming landowners and important figures. But Abbot Smith, after a careful study (*Colonists in Bondage*), concludes that colonial society "was not democratic and certainly not equalitarian; it was dominated by men who had money enough to make others work for them." And: "Few of these men were descended from indentured servants, and practically none had themselves been of this class."

It seems quite clear that class lines hardened through the colonial period; the distinction between rich and poor became sharper. By 1700 there were fifty rich families in Virginia, with wealth equivalent to fifty thousand pounds (a huge sum those days), who lived off the labor of black slaves and white servants, owned the plantations, sat on the governor's council, served as local magistrates. In Maryland, the settlers were ruled by a proprietor whose right of total control over the colony had been granted by the English king. Between 1650 and 1689 there were five revolts against the proprietor.

Carl Bridenbaugh's study of colonial cities, *Cities in the Wilderness*, reveals a clear-cut class system. He finds: "The leaders of early Boston were gentlemen of considerable wealth who, in association with the clergy, eagerly sought to preserve in America the social arrangements of the Mother Country."

At the very start of the Massachusetts Bay Colony in 1630, the governor, John Winthrop, had declared the philosophy of the rulers: "in all times some must be rich, some poore, some highe and eminent in power and dignitie; others meane and in subjection."

Rich merchants erected mansions; persons "of Qualitie" traveled in coaches or sedan chairs, had their portraits painted, wore periwigs, and filled themselves with rich food and Madeira. A petition came from the town of Deerfield in 1678 to the Massachusetts General Court: "You may be pleased to know that the very principle and best of the land; the best for soile; the best for situation; as laying in ye center and midle of the town: and as to quantity, nere half, belongs unto eight or nine proprietors...."

New York in the colonial period was like a feudal kingdom. The Dutch had set up a patroonship system along the Hudson River, with enormous landed estates, where the barons controlled completely the lives of their tenants. In 1689, many of the grievances of the poor were mixed up in the farmers' revolt of Jacob Leisler and his group. Leisler was hanged, and the parceling out of huge estates continued. Under Governor Benjamin Fletcher, three-fourths of the land in New York was granted to about thirty people. He gave a friend a half million acres for a token annual payment of thirty shillings.

In 1700, New York City church wardens had asked for funds from the common council because "the Crys of the poor and Impotent for want of Relief are Extreamly Grevious." In the 1730s, demand began to grow for institutions to contain the "many Beggarly people daily suffered to wander about the Streets."

A letter to Peter Zenger's New York *Journal* in 1737 described the poor street urchin of New York as "an Object in Human Shape, half starv'd with Cold, with Cloathes out at the Elbows, Knees through the Breeches, Hair standing on end.... From the age about four to Fourteen they spend their Days in the Streets...then they are put out as Apprentices, perhaps four, five, or six years...."

The colonies grew fast in the 1700s. English settlers were joined by Scotch-Irish and German immigrants. Black slaves were pouring in; they were 8 percent of the population in 1690; 21 percent in 1770. The population of the colonies was 250,000 in 1700; 1,600,000 by 1760. Agriculture was growing. Small manufacturing was developing. Shipping and trading were expanding. The big cities—Boston, New York, Philadelphia, and Charleston—were doubling and tripling in size.

Through all that growth, the upper class was getting most of the benefits and monopolized political power. In Boston, by 1770, the top 1 percent of property owners owned 44 percent of the wealth.

Everywhere the poor were struggling to stay alive, simply to keep from freezing in cold weather. All the cities built poorhouses in the 1730s, not just for old people, widows, crippled, and orphans, but for unemployed, war veterans, new immigrants. In New York, at midcentury, the city almshouse, built for one hundred poor, was housing over four hundred. A Philadelphia citizen wrote in 1748: "It is remarkable what an increase of the number of Beggars there is about this town this winter." In 1757, Boston officials spoke of "a great Number of Poor...who can scarcely procure from day to day daily Bread for themselves & Families."

The colonies, it seems, were societies of contending classes—a fact obscured by the emphasis, in traditional histories, on the external struggle against England, the unity of colonists in the Revolution. The country therefore was not "born free" but born slave and free, servant and master, tenant and landlord, poor and rich. As a result, the political authorities were opposed "frequently, vociferously, and sometimes violently," according to Gary Nash. "Outbreaks of disorder punctuated the last quarter of the seventeenth century, toppling established governments in Massachusetts, New York, Maryland, Virginia, and North Carolina."

Free white workers were better off than slaves or servants, but they still resented unfair treatment by the wealthier classes. A severe food shortage in Boston in 1713 brought a warning from town selectmen to the General Assembly of Massachusetts, saying that the "threatening scarcity of provisions" had led to such "extravagant prices that the necessities of the poor in the approaching winter must needs be very pressing." Andrew Belcher, a wealthy merchant, was exporting grain to the Caribbean because the profit was greater there. On May 19, two hundred people rioted on the Boston Common. They attacked Belcher's ships, broke into his warehouses looking for corn, and shot the lieutenant governor when he tried to interfere.

In the 1730s, in Boston, people protesting the high prices established by merchants demolished the public market in Dock Square while (as a conservative writer complained) "murmuring against the Government & the rich people." No one was arrested, after the demonstrators warned that arrests would bring "Five Hundred Men in Solemn League and Covenent" who would destroy other markets set up for the benefit of rich merchants.

Bostonians rioted also against impressment, in which men were drafted for naval service. They surrounded the house of the governor, beat up the sheriff, locked up a deputy sheriff, and stormed the townhouse where the General Court sat. The militia did not respond when called to put them down, and the governor fled. The crowd was condemned by a merchants' group as a "Riotous Tumultuous Assembly of Foreign Seamen, Servants, Negroes, and Other Persons of Mean and Vile Condition."

In New Jersey in the 1740s and 1750s, poor farmers occupying land, over which they and the landowners had rival claims, rioted when rents were demanded of them. In 1745, Samuel Baldwin, who had long lived on his land and who held an Indian title to it, was arrested for nonpayment of rent to the proprietor and taken to the Newark jail. A contemporary described what happened then: "The People in general, supposing the Design of the Proprietors was to ruin them...went to the Prison, opened the Door, took out Baldwin."

Through this period, England was fighting a series of wars (Queen Anne's War in the early 1700s, King George's War in the 1730s). Some merchants made fortunes from these wars, but for most people they meant higher taxes, unemployment, poverty. An anonymous pamphleteer in Massachusetts, writing angrily after King George's War, described the situation: "Poverty and Discontent appear in every Face (except the Countenances of the Rich) and dwell upon every Tongue." He spoke of a few men, fed by "Lust of Power, Lust of Fame, Lust of Money," who got rich during the war. "No Wonder such Men can build Ships, Houses, buy Farms, set up their Coaches, Chariots, live very splendidly, purchase

Fame, Posts of Honour." He called them "Birds of prey...Enemies to all Communities—wherever they live."

The forced service of seamen led to a riot against impressment in Boston in 1747. Then crowds turned against Thomas Hutchinson, a rich merchant and colonial official who had backed the governor in putting down the riot, and who also designed a currency plan for Massachusetts which seemed to discriminate against the poor. Hutchinson's house burned down, mysteriously, and a crowd gathered in the street, cursing Hutchinson and shouting, "Let it burn!"

By the years of the Revolutionary crisis, the 1760s, the wealthy elite that controlled the British colonies on the American mainland had 150 years of experience, had learned certain things about how to rule. They had various fears, but also had developed tactics to deal with what they feared.

With the problem of Indian hostility and the danger of slave revolts, the colonial elite had to consider the class anger of poor whites—servants, tenants, the city poor, the propertyless, the taxpayer, the soldier and sailor. As the colonies passed their hundredth year and went into the middle of the 1700s, as the gap between rich and poor widened, as violence and the threat of violence increased, the problem of control became more serious.

What if these different despised groups—the Indians, the slaves, the poor whites—should combine? Even before there were so many blacks, in the seventeenth century, there was, as Abbot Smith puts it, "a lively fear that servants would join with Negroes or Indians to overcome the small number of masters."

Bacon's Rebellion was instructive: to conciliate a diminishing Indian population at the expense of infuriating a coalition of white frontiersmen was very risky. Better to make war on the Indian, gain the support of the white, divert possible class conflict by turning poor whites against Indians for the security of the elite.

Might blacks and Indians combine against the white enemy? In the Carolinas, whites were outnumbered by black slaves and nearby Indian tribes; in the 1750s, twenty-five thousand whites faced forty thousand black slaves, with sixty thousand Creek, Cherokee, Choctaw, and Chickasaw Indians in the area.

The white rulers of the Carolinas seemed to be conscious of the need for a policy, as one of them put it, "to make Indians & Negros a checque upon each other lest by their Vastly Superior Numbers we should be crushed by one or the other." And so laws were passed prohibiting free blacks from traveling in Indian country. Treaties with Indian tribes contained clauses requiring the return of fugitive slaves. Governor Lyttle-town of South Carolina wrote in 1738: "It has always been the policy of this government to create an aversion in them [Indians] to Negroes."

Blacks ran away to Indian villages, and the Creeks and Cherokees harbored runaway slaves by the hundreds. Many of these were amalgamated into the Indian tribes, married, produced children. But the combination of harsh slave codes and bribes to the Indians to help put down black rebels kept things under control.

It was the potential combination of poor whites and blacks that caused the most fear among the wealthy white planters. If there had been the natural racial repugnance that some theorists have assumed, control would have been easier. But sexual attraction was powerful, across racial lines. In 1743, a grand jury in Charleston, South Carolina, denounced "The Too Common Practice of Criminal Conversation with Negro and other Slave Wenches in this Province."

What made Bacon's Rebellion especially fearsome for the rulers of Virginia was that black slaves and white servants joined forces. All through those early years, black and white slaves and servants ran away together, as shown both by the laws passed to stop this and the records of the courts. A letter from the southern colonies in 1682 complained of "no white men to superintend our negroes, or repress an insurrection of negroes...." A report to the English government in 1721 said that in South Carolina "black slaves have lately attempted and were very near succeeding in a new revolution...and therefore, it may be necessary... to propose some new law for encouraging the entertainment of more white servants in the future."

This fear may help explain why Parliament, in 1717, made transportation to the New World a legal punishment for crime. After that, tens of thousands of convicts could be sent to Virginia, Maryland, and other colonies.

Racism was becoming more and more practical. Edmund Morgan, on the basis of his careful study of slavery in Virginia, sees racism not as "natural" to black-white difference, but something coming out of class scorn, a realistic device for control. "If freemen with disappointed hopes should make common cause with slaves of desperate hope, the results might be worse than anything Bacon had done. The answer to the problem, obvious if unspoken and only gradually recognized, was racism, to separate dangerous free whites from dangerous black slaves by a screen of racial contempt."

42

There was still another control which became handy as the colonies grew, and which had crucial consequences for the continued rule of the elite throughout American history. Along with the very rich and the very poor, there developed a white middle class of small planters, independent farmers, city artisans, who, given small rewards for joining forces with merchants and planters, would be a solid buffer against black slaves, frontier Indians, and very poor whites.

While it was the rich who ruled Boston, there were political jobs available for the moderately well-off, as "cullers of staves," "measurer of Coal Baskets," "Fence Viewer." Aubrey Land found in Maryland a class of small planters who were not "the beneficiary" of the planting society as the rich were, but who had the distinction of being called planters, and who were "respectable citizens."

The *Pennsylvania Journal* wrote in 1756: "The people of this province are generally of the middling sort, and at present pretty much upon a level. They are chiefly industrious farmers, artificers or men in trade".... To call them "the people" was to omit black slaves, white servants, displaced Indians. And the term "middle class" concealed a fact long true about this country, that, as Richard Hofstadter said: "It was...a middle-class society governed for the most part by its upper classes."

Those upper classes, to rule, needed to make concessions to the middle class, without damage to their own wealth or power, at the expense of slaves, Indians, and poor whites. This bought loyalty. And to bind that loyalty with something more powerful even than material advantage, the ruling group found, in the 1760s and 1770s, a wonderfully useful device. That device was the language of liberty and equality, which could unite just enough whites to fight a revolution against England, without ending either slavery or inequality.

Exercises

1. What was the economic condition of Virginia in 1676?

2. What is the evidence that Bacon's Rebellion in 1676 "had the overwhelming support of the Virginia population"?

3. Why would a European man or woman sign an indenture? Was it a "choice" or were they compelled by "historical forces"?

4. Copy and fill in the chart below. Expand the chart by adding to the given criteria of comparison.

	AFRICAN SLAVE	INDENTURED SERVANT
I. PERIOD OF SERVITUDE		
II. CONDITIONS/RIGHTS DURING SERVITUDE		
III. CONDITIONS OF VOYAGE		
IV. REASONS FOR OR CAUSE OF SERVITUDE		
V. FORMS OF RESISTANCE		
VI. METHODS BY WHICH THEY WERE CONTROLLED		
VII.		
VIII.		

5. What happened when servants became free?

6. Which of the following is the most accurate characterization of the colonial economy, and WHY? Consider (without limiting yourself to) the following as criteria: closeness to actual event; how far removed from witnessing the event; degree of possibility of being an isolated event; degree of safety in generalizing from the specific; relevance of detail to question; how much the detail actually says about the entire colonial society.

   a. In Boston, by 1770, the top 1% of property owners owned 44% of the wealth.

   b. In New York [around 1750], the city almshouse, built for 100 poor, was housing over 400.

   c. In 1757, Boston officials spoke of "a great Number of Poor...who can scarcely procure from day to day daily Bread for themselves & Families."

   d. According to the present day historian Gary Nash, "Outbreaks of disorder punctuated the last quarter of the seventeenth century [1675–1700], toppling established governments in Massachusetts, New York, Maryland, Virginia, and North Carolina."

   e. In Boston in 1713, a town selectmen said that the "threatening scarcity of provisions" had led to such "extravagant prices that the necessities of the poor in the approaching winter must needs be very pressing."

   f. In New Jersey in 1745, Sam Baldwin was arrested for nonpayment of rent. "The People in general, supposing the Design of the Proprietors was to ruin them...went to the Prison, opened the Door, took out Baldwin."

7. What experiences besides economic deprivation or hardship might have caused colonists to resent their local or state governments?

8. What was the greatest threat to the elite's control over the colonists—a fear that was realized in Bacon's Rebellion? What tactics did the wealthy elite/rich rulers adopt to prevent another Bacon's Rebellion?

Activity: Reenact a Virginia Company stockholders meeting, in London, England, circa 1678.

Chapter 4

Tyranny Is Tyranny

Around 1776, certain important people in the English colonies made a discovery that would prove enormously useful for the next two hundred years. They found that by creating a nation, a symbol, a legal unity called the United States, they could take over land, profits, and political power from favorites of the British Empire. In the process, they could hold back a number of potential rebellions and create a consensus of popular support for the rule of a new, privileged leadership.

When we look at the American Revolution this way, it was a work of genius, and the Founding Fathers deserve the awed tribute they have received over the centuries. They created the most effective system of national control devised in modern times and showed future generations of leaders the advantages of combining paternalism with command.

Starting with Bacon's Rebellion in Virginia, by 1760 there had been eighteen uprisings aimed at overthrowing colonial governments. There had also been six black rebellions, from South Carolina to New York, and forty riots of various origins.

By this time also, there emerged, according to Jack Greene, "stable, coherent, effective and acknowledged local political and social elites." And by the 1760s, this local leadership saw the possibility of directing much of the rebellious energy against England and her local officials. It was not a conscious conspiracy, but an accumulation of tactical responses.

After 1763, with England victorious in the Seven Years' War (known in America as the French and Indian War), expelling France from North

America, ambitious colonial leaders were no longer threatened by the French. They now had only two rivals left: the English and the Indians. The British, wooing the Indians, had declared Indian lands beyond the Appalachians out of bounds to whites (the Proclamation of 1763). Perhaps, once the British were out of the way, the Indians could be dealt with. Again, not a conscious, forethought strategy by the colonial elite, but a growing awareness as events developed.

With the French defeated, the British government could turn its attention to tightening control over the colonies. It needed revenues to pay for the war and looked to the colonies for that. Also, the colonial trade had become more and more important to the British economy, and more profitable: it had amounted to about 500,000 pounds in 1700 but by 1770 was worth 2,800,000 pounds.

So, the American leadership was less desirous of English rule, the English more in need of the colonists' wealth. The elements for conflict were there.

The war with France had brought glory to the generals, death to the privates, wealth for the merchants, unemployment for the poor. There were twenty-five thousand people living in New York (there had been seven thousand in 1720) when the war ended. A newspaper editor wrote about the growing "Number of Beggers and wandering Poor" in the streets of the city. Letters in the papers questioned the distribution of wealth: "How often have our Streets been covered with Thousands of Barrels of Flour for trade, while our near Neighbors can hardly procure enough to make a Dumplin to satisfy hunger?"

Gary Nash's study of city tax lists shows that by the early 1770s, the top 5 percent of Boston's taxpayers controlled 49 percent of the city's taxable assets. In Philadelphia and New York, too, wealth was more and more concentrated. Court-recorded wills show that by 1750 the wealthiest people in the cities were leaving twenty thousand pounds (equivalent to about $2.5 million today).

In Boston, the lower classes began to use the town meeting to vent their grievances. The governor of Massachusetts had written that in these town meetings "the meanest Inhabitants...by their constant Attendance there generally are the majority and outvote the Gentlemen, Merchants, Substantial Traders and all the better part of the Inhabitants."

What seems to have happened in Boston is that certain lawyers, editors, and merchants of the upper classes, but excluded from the ruling circles close to England—men like James Otis and Samuel Adams—

organized a "Boston Caucus" and through their oratory and their writing "molded laboring-class opinion, called the 'mob' into action, and shaped its behaviour." This is Gary Nash's description of Otis, who, he says, "keenly aware of the declining fortunes and the resentment of ordinary townspeople, was mirroring as well as molding popular opinion."

We have here a forecast of the long history of American politics, the mobilization of lower-class energy by upper-class politicians, for their own purposes. This was not purely deception; it involved, in part, a genuine recognition of lower-class grievances, which helps to account for its effectiveness as a tactic over the centuries.

In 1762, Otis, speaking against the conservative rulers of the Massachusetts colony represented by Thomas Hutchinson, gave an example of the kind of rhetoric that a lawyer could use in mobilizing city mechanics and artisans:

> I am forced to get my living by the labour of my hand; and the sweat of my brow, as most of you are and obliged to go thro' good report and evil report, for bitter bread, earned under the frowns of some who have no natural or divine right to be above me, and entirely owe their grandeur and honor to grinding the faces of the poor....

Boston seems to have been full of class anger in those days. In 1763, in the Boston *Gazette*, someone wrote that "a few persons in power" were promoting political projects "for keeping the people poor in order to make them humble."

This accumulated sense of grievance against the rich in Boston may account for the explosiveness of mob action after the Stamp Act of 1765. Through this act, the British were taxing the colonial population to pay for the French war, in which colonists had suffered to expand the British Empire. That summer, a shoemaker named Ebenezer MacIntosh led a mob in destroying the house of a rich Boston merchant named Andrew Oliver. Two weeks later, the crowd turned to the home of Thomas Hutchinson, symbol of the rich elite who ruled the colonies in the name of England. They smashed up his house with axes, drank the wine in his wine cellar, and looted the house of its furniture and other objects. A report by colony officials to England said that this was part of a larger scheme in which the houses of fifteen rich people were to be destroyed, as part of "a War of Plunder, of general levelling and taking away the Distinction of rich and poor."

It was one of those moments in which fury against the rich went further than leaders like Otis wanted. Could class hatred be focused against

49

the pro-British elite, and deflected from the nationalist elite? In New York, that same year of the Boston house attacks, someone wrote to the New York *Gazette*, "Is it equitable that 99, rather 999, should suffer for the Extravagance or Grandeur of one, especially when it is considered that men frequently owe their Wealth to the impoverishment of their Neighbors?" The leaders of the Revolution would worry about keeping such sentiments within limits.

Mechanics were demanding political democracy in the colonial cities: open meetings of representative assemblies, public galleries in the legislative halls, and the publishing of roll-call votes, so that constituents could check on representatives. They wanted open-air meetings where the population could participate in making policy, more equitable taxes, price controls, and the election of mechanics and other ordinary people to government posts.

During elections for the 1776 convention to frame a constitution for Pennsylvania, a Privates Committee urged voters to oppose "great and overgrown rich men...they will be too apt to be framing distinctions in society." The Privates Committee drew up a bill of rights for the convention, including the statement that "an enormous proportion of property vested in a few individuals is dangerous to the rights, and destructive of the common happiness of mankind; and therefore every free state hath a right by its laws to discourage the possession of such property."

In the countryside, where most people lived, there was a similar conflict of poor against rich—which political leaders would use to mobilize the population against England, granting some benefits for the rebellious poor, and many more for themselves in the process. The tenant riots in New Jersey in the 1740s, the New York tenant uprisings of the 1750s and 1760s in the Hudson Valley, and the rebellion in northeastern New York that led to the carving of Vermont out of New York State were all more than sporadic rioting. They were long-lasting social movements, highly organized, involving the creation of countergovernments.

In North Carolina, a "Regulator Movement" of white farmers was organized against wealthy and corrupt officials in the period from 1766 to 1771, exactly those years when, in the cities of the Northeast, agitation was growing against the British, crowding out class issues. The Regulators referred to themselves as "poor Industrious peasants," as "labourers," "the wretched poor," "oppressed" by "rich and powerful...designing Monsters." They resented the tax system, which was especially burdensome on the poor, and the combination of merchants and lawyers who worked in the courts to collect debts from the harassed farmers. The Regulators did not represent servants or slaves, but they did speak for small owners, squatters, and tenants.

In Orange County, North Carolina, in the 1760s, the Regulators organized to prevent the collection of taxes and the confiscation of the property of tax delinquents. Officials said "an absolute Insurrection of a dangerous tendency has broke out in Orange County," and made military plans to suppress it. At one point seven hundred armed farmers forced the release of two arrested Regulator leaders. In another county, Anson, a local militia colonel complained of "the unparalleled tumults, Insurrections, and Commotions which at present distract this County." At one point a hundred men broke up the proceedings at a county court.

The result of all this was that the assembly passed some mild reform legislation, but also an act "to prevent riots and tumults," and the governor prepared to crush them militarily. In May of 1771 there was a decisive battle in which several thousand Regulators were defeated by a disciplined army using cannon. Six Regulators were hanged.

One consequence of this bitter conflict is that only a minority of the people in the Regulator counties seem to have participated as patriots in the Revolutionary War. Most of them probably remained neutral.

Fortunately for the Revolutionary movement, the key battles were being fought in the North, and here, in the cities, the colonial leaders had a divided white population; they could win over the mechanics, who were a kind of middle class, who had a stake in the fight against England, facing competition from English manufacturers. The biggest problem was to keep the propertyless people, who were unemployed and hungry in the crisis following the French war, under control.

In Boston, the economic grievances of the lowest classes mingled with anger against the British and exploded in mob violence. The leaders of the Independence movement wanted to use that mob energy against England, but also to contain it so that it would not demand too much from them.

A political group in Boston called the Loyal Nine—merchants, distillers, shipowners, and master craftsmen who opposed the Stamp Act—organized a procession in August 1765 to protest it. They put fifty master craftsmen at the head, but needed to mobilize shipworkers from the North End and mechanics and apprentices from the South End. Two or three thousand were in the procession (Negroes were excluded). They marched to the home of the stampmaster and burned his effigy. But after the "gentlemen" who organized the demonstration left, the crowd went further and destroyed some of the stampmaster's property.

Now a town meeting was called and the same leaders who had planned the demonstration denounced the violence and disavowed the actions of the crowd. And when the Stamp Act was repealed, due to overwhelming resistance, the conservative leaders severed their connections with the rioters. They held annual celebrations of the first anti–Stamp Act demonstration, to which they invited, according to Dirk Hoerder, not the rioters but "mainly upper and middle-class Bostonians, who traveled in coaches and carriages to Roxbury or Dorchester for opulent feasts."

When the British Parliament turned to its next attempt to tax the colonies, this time by a set of taxes which it hoped would not excite as much opposition, the colonial leaders organized boycotts. But, they stressed, "No Mobs or Tumults, let the Persons and Properties of your most inveterate Enemies be safe." Samuel Adams advised: "No Mobs—No Confusions—No Tumult." And James Otis said that "no possible circumstances, though ever so oppressive, could be supposed sufficient to justify private tumults and disorders...."

The quartering of troops by the British was directly hurtful to the sailors and other working people. After 1768, two thousand soldiers were quartered in Boston, and friction grew between the crowds and the soldiers. The soldiers began to take the jobs of working people when jobs were scarce, and on March 5, 1770, grievances of ropemakers against British soldiers taking their jobs led to a fight.

A crowd gathered in front of the customhouse and began provoking the soldiers, who fired and killed first Crispus Attucks, a mulatto worker, then others. This became known as the Boston Massacre. Feelings against the British mounted quickly at the acquittal of six of the British soldiers (two were punished by having their thumbs branded and were discharged from the army). The crowd at the massacre was described by John Adams, defense attorney for the British soldiers, as "a motley rabble of saucy boys, negroes, and molattoes, Irish teagues and outlandish jack tarrs." Perhaps ten thousand people marched in the funeral procession for the victims of the massacre, out of a total Boston population of sixteen thousand. This led England to remove the troops from Boston and try to quiet the situation.

Impressment—drafting colonists into military service—was the background of the massacre. There had been impressment riots through the 1760s in New York and in Newport, Rhode Island, where five hundred seamen, boys, and Negroes rioted. Six weeks before the Boston Massacre, there was a battle in New York of seamen against British soldiers taking their jobs, and one seaman was killed.

In the Boston Tea Party of December 1773 tea was seized from ships and dumped into Boston Harbor. The Boston Committee of Correspondence, formed a year before to organize anti-British actions, "controlled crowd action against the tea from the start," Dirk Hoerder says. The Tea Party led to the Coercive Acts by Parliament, virtually establishing martial law in Massachusetts, dissolving the colonial government, closing the port in Boston, and sending in troops. Mass meetings rose in opposition.

Pauline Maier, who studied the development of opposition to Britain in the decade before 1776 in her book *From Resistance to Revolution*, emphasizes the moderation of the leadership and, despite their desire for resistance, their "emphasis on order and restraint." She notes: "The officers and committee members of the Sons of Liberty were drawn almost entirely from the middle and upper classes of colonial society." Their aim, however, was to broaden their organization, to develop a mass base of wage earners.

In Virginia, it seemed clear to the educated gentry that something needed to be done to persuade the lower orders to join the revolutionary cause, to deflect their anger against England.

It was a problem for which the rhetorical talents of Patrick Henry were superbly fitted. He found language inspiring to all classes, specific enough in its listing of grievances to charge people with anger against the British, vague enough to avoid class conflict among the rebels, and stirring enough to build patriotic feeling for the resistance movement.

Tom Paine's *Common Sense*, which appeared in early 1776 and became the most popular pamphlet in the American colonies, did this. It made the first bold argument for independence, in words that any fairly literate person could understand: "Society in every state is a blessing, but Government even in its best state is but a necessary evil...."

Paine disposed of the idea of the divine right of kings by a pungent history of the British monarchy, going back to the Norman conquest of 1066, when William the Conqueror came over from France to set himself on the British throne: "A French bastard landing with an armed Banditti and establishing himself king of England against the consent of the natives, is in plain terms a very paltry rascally original. It certainly hath no divinity in it."

Paine dealt with the practical advantages of sticking to England or being separated:

> I challenge the warmest advocate for reconciliation to show a single advantage that this continent can reap by being connected with Great Britain. I repeat the challenge; not a single advantage is derived. Our corn will fetch its price in any market in Europe, and our imported goods must be paid for by them where we will....

As for the bad effects of the connection with England, Paine appealed to the colonists' memory of all the wars in which England had involved them, wars costly in lives and money. He built slowly to an emotional pitch: "Everything that is right or reasonable pleads for separation. The blood of the slain, the weeping voice of nature cries, 'TIS TIME TO PART'."

Common Sense went through twenty-five editions in 1776 and sold hundreds of thousands of copies. It is probable that almost every literate colonist either read it or knew about its content. Pamphleteering had become by this time the chief theater of debate about relations with England. From 1750 to 1776 four hundred pamphlets had appeared arguing one or another side of the Stamp Act or the Boston Massacre or the Tea Party or the general questions of disobedience to law, loyalty to government, rights and obligations.

Paine's pamphlet appealed to a wide range of colonial opinion angered by England. But it caused some tremors in aristocrats like John Adams, who were with the patriot cause but wanted to make sure it didn't go too far in the direction of democracy. Popular assemblies needed to be checked, Adams thought, because they were "productive of hasty results and absurd judgements."

Paine himself came out of "the lower orders" of England—a staymaker, tax official, teacher, poor emigrant to America. But once the Revolution was under way, Paine more and more made it clear that he was not for the crowd action of lower-class people—like those militia who in 1779 attacked the house of James Wilson. Wilson was a Revolutionary leader who opposed price controls and wanted a more conservative government than was given by the Pennsylvania Constitution of 1776. Paine became an associate of one of the wealthiest men in Pennsylvania, Robert Morris, and a supporter of Morris's creation, the Bank of North America.

Later, during the controversy over adopting the Constitution, Paine would once again represent urban artisans, who favored a strong central government. He seemed to believe that such a government could represent some great common interest. In this sense, he lent himself perfectly to the myth of the Revolution—that it was on behalf of a united people.

The Declaration of Independence brought that myth to its peak of eloquence. Each harsher measure of British control—the Proclamation of 1763, which forbade colonists to settle beyond the Appalachians, the Stamp Tax, the Townshend taxes, including the one on tea, the stationing of troops and the Boston Massacre, the closing of the port of Boston and the dissolution of the Massachusetts legislature—escalated colonial rebellion to the point of revolution. The colonists had responded with the Stamp Act Congress, the Sons of Liberty, the Committees of Correspondence, the Boston Tea Party, and finally, in 1774, the setting up of a Continental Congress—an illegal body, forerunner of a future independent government.

It was after the military clash at Lexington and Concord in April 1775, between colonial minutemen and British troops, that the Continental Congress decided on separation. They organized a small committee to draw up the Declaration of Independence, which Thomas Jefferson wrote. It was adopted by the Congress on July 2, and officially proclaimed July 4, 1776.

By this time there was already a powerful sentiment for independence. Resolutions adopted in North Carolina in May of 1776, and sent to the Continental Congress, declared independence of England, asserted that all British law was null and void, and urged military preparations. About the same time, the town of Malden, Massachusetts, responding to a request from the Massachusetts House of Representatives that all towns in the state declare their views on independence, had met in town meeting and unanimously called for independence: "...we therefore renounce with disdain our connexion with a kingdom of slaves; we bid a final adieu to Britain."

"When in the Course of human events, it becomes necessary for one people to dissolve the political bands...they should declare the causes...." This was the opening of the Declaration of Independence. Then, in its second paragraph, came a powerful philosophical statement:

> We hold these truths to be self-evident, that all men are created equal, that they are endowed by their Creator with certain unalienable Rights, that among these are Life, Liberty and the pursuit of Happiness. That to secure these rights, Governments are instituted among Men, deriving their just powers from the consent of the governed, that whenever any Form of Government becomes destructive of these ends, it is the Right of the People to alter or to abolish it, and to institute new Government....

It then went on to list grievances against the king, "a history of repeated injuries and usurpations, all having in direct object the establishment of an absolute Tyranny over these States." The list accused the king of dissolving colonial governments, controlling judges, sending "swarms of Officers to harass our people," sending in armies of occupation, cutting off colonial trade with other parts of the world, taxing the colonists without their consent, and waging war against them, "transporting large Armies of foreign Mercenaries to compleat the works of death, desolation and tyranny."

All this, the language of popular control over governments, the right of rebellion and revolution, indignation at political tyranny, economic burdens, and military attacks, was language well suited to unite large numbers of colonists and persuade even those who had grievances against one another to turn against England.

Some Americans were clearly omitted from this circle of united interest drawn by the Declaration of Independence: Indians, black slaves, women. Indeed, one paragraph of the Declaration charged the king with inciting slave rebellions and Indian attacks:

> He has excited domestic insurrections amongst us, and has endeavoured
> to bring on the inhabitants of our frontiers, the merciless Indian Sav-
> ages, whose known rule of warfare is an undistinguished destruction of
> all ages, sexes and conditions.

Twenty years before the Declaration, a proclamation of the legislature of Massachusetts of November 3, 1755, declared the Penobscot Indians "rebels, enemies and traitors" and provided a bounty: "For every scalp of a male Indian brought in...forty pounds. For every scalp of such female Indian or male Indian under the age of twelve years that shall be killed...twenty pounds...."

Thomas Jefferson had written a paragraph of the Declaration accusing the king of transporting slaves from Africa to the colonies and "suppressing every legislative attempt to prohibit or to restrain this execrable commerce." This seemed to express moral indignation against slavery and the slave trade (Jefferson's personal distaste for slavery must be put alongside the fact that he owned hundreds of slaves to the day he died). Behind it was the growing fear among Virginians and some other southerners about the growing number of black slaves in the colonies (20 percent of the total population) and the threat of slave revolts as the number of slaves increased.

Jefferson's paragraph was removed by the Continental Congress because slaveholders themselves disagreed about the desirability of ending the slave trade. So even that gesture toward the black slave was omitted from the American Revolution's great manifesto of freedom.

The use of the phrase "all men are created equal" was probably not a deliberate attempt to make a statement about women. It was just that women were beyond consideration as worthy of inclusion. They were politically invisible. Though practical needs gave women a certain authority in the home, on the farm, or in occupations such as midwifery, they were simply overlooked in any consideration of political rights, any notions of civic equality.

To say that the Declaration of Independence, even by its own language, was limited to life, liberty, and happiness for white males is not to denounce the makers and signers of the Declaration for holding the ideas expected of privileged males of the eighteenth century. Reformers and radicals, looking discontentedly at history, are often accused of expecting too much from a past political epoch—and sometimes they do. But the point of noting those outside the arc of human rights in the Declaration is not, centuries late and pointlessly, to denounce the moral failures of that time. It is to try to understand the way in which the Declaration functioned to mobilize certain groups of Americans, ignoring others. Surely, inspirational language to create a secure consensus is still used, in our time, to cover up serious conflicts of interest in that consensus, and to cover up, also, the omission of large parts of the human race.

The reality behind the words of the Declaration of Independence was that a rising class of important people needed to enlist on their side enough Americans to defeat England, without disturbing too much the relations of wealth and power that had developed over 150 years of colonial history. Indeed, 69 percent of the signers of the Declaration of Independence had held colonial office under England.

When the Declaration of Independence was read, with all its flaming radical language, from the town hall balcony in Boston, it was read by Thomas Crafts, a member of the Loyal Nine group, conservatives who had opposed militant action against the British. Four days after the reading, the Boston Committee of Correspondence ordered the townsmen to show up on the common for a military draft. The rich, it turned out, could avoid the draft by paying for substitutes; the poor had to serve. This led to rioting and shouting: "Tyranny is Tyranny let it come from whom it may."

Exercises

1. Before reading the chapter, make a time line which includes the following: the founding of Jamestown, Virginia; the passage of the first Navigation Act; Bacon's Rebellion; the French and Indian War; the Stamp Act; the Coercive Acts; the battles of Lexington and Concord; and the battle of Yorktown.

2. On page 47: What does Zinn mean by "… the advantages of combining paternalism with command"?

3. Zinn argues that "It was not a conscious conspiracy, but an accumulation of tactical responses." (p. 47) What is the difference between a "conscious conspiracy" and "tactical responses"?

4. Below are a series of arguments (a-k). For each argument, identify an example (detail/data) from the chapter that supports the argument (note: one example might be used to illustrate more than one of the arguments below, but try to find a different example for each argument):
    a. "…they [took] over land, profits, and political power from favorites of the British Empire."
    b. "…create a consensus of popular support for the rule of a new, privileged leadership."
    c. "…mirroring as well as molding popular opinion"
    d. "…mobilization of lower-class energy by upper-class politicians…"
    e. "…class hatred be focused against the pro-British elite…"
    f. "…class hatred be…deflected from the nationalist elite."
    g. "…they [won] over the mechanics…"
    h. "…[the local elites kept] the propertyless people…under control…[by using the] mob energy against England, but also [contained] it so that it would not demand too much from them."
    i. "…language…specific enough in its listing of grievances to charge people with anger against the British, vague enough to avoid class conflict among the rebels…"

j. "…language [to] persuade even those who had grievances against one another to turn against England."

k. "…without disturbing too much the relations of wealth and power that had developed over 150 years of colonial history."

5. *Research*: What role did each of the events listed below play in causing conflict between the colonial elites and England (or their representatives in America); the colonial people (lower orders) and colonial elites; OR the colonial people (lower orders) and England (or their representatives in America)?

[NOTE: You will have to go to texts other than Zinn for some of the answers.]

   a. French and Indian War

   b. growth of trade between England and its American colonies

   c. Proclamation Line of 1763

   d. "…six black rebellions…and forty riots" all occurring between 1676 and 1760

   e. Stamp Act of 1765

   f. mechanic's demand for political democracy in the cities

   g. Privates Committee's bill of rights

   h. tenant riots from the 1740s through the 1760s

   i. Regulator Movement

   j. Townshend Acts of 1767

   k. quartering of British troops in 1768

   l. impressment of sailors

   m. impounding of ships in admiralty courts under the specifications of the Sugar Act

   n. Tea Act of 1773

   o. Boston Port Act of 1773

   p. Massachusetts Government Act of 1774

6. Define the "lower orders" in terms of their:
   ★ percentage of community wealth controlled
   ★ occupations

        ★ political and economic interests
        ★ social labels/epithets

7. Define the "local political and social elite" in terms of their:
        ★ percentage of community wealth controlled
        ★ occupations
        ★ political and economic interests
        ★ social labels/epithets

8. *Debate Resolution*: The American Revolution was a war not for independence but consolidation.

Chapter 5

A Kind of Revolution

The American victory over the British army was made possible by the existence of an already-armed people. Just about every white male had a gun and could shoot. The Revolutionary leadership distrusted the mobs of poor. But they knew the Revolution had no appeal to slaves and Indians. They would have to woo the armed white population.

This was not easy. Yes, mechanics and sailors and some others were incensed against the British. But general enthusiasm for the war was not strong. John Shy, in his study of the Revolutionary army (*A People Numerous and Armed*), estimates that perhaps a fifth of the population was actively treasonous. John Adams had estimated a third opposed, a third in support, a third neutral.

The men who first joined the colonial militia were generally "hallmarks of respectability or at least of full citizenship" in their communities, Shy says. Excluded from the militia were friendly Indians, free Negroes, white servants, and free white men who had no stable home. But desperation led to the recruiting of the less respectable whites. Massachusetts and Virginia provided for drafting "strollers" (vagrants) into the militia. In fact, the military became a place of promise for the poor, who might rise in rank, acquire some money, and change their social status.

Here was the traditional device by which those in charge of any social order mobilize and discipline a recalcitrant population—offering the adventure and rewards of military service to get poor people to fight for a cause they may not see clearly as their own. A wounded American lieutenant at Bunker Hill, John Scott, told how he had joined the rebel forces:

I was a Shoemaker, & got my living by my Labor. When this Rebellion came on, I saw some of my Neighbors got into Commission, who were no better than myself. I was very ambitious, & did not like to see those Men above me. I was asked to enlist, as a private Soldier...I offered to enlist upon having a Lieutenants Commission; which was granted. I imagined myself now in a way of Promotion.

Scott was one of many Revolutionary fighters, usually of lower military ranks, from poor and obscure backgrounds. Shy's study of the Peterborough contingent shows that the prominent and substantial citizens of the town had served only briefly in the war. Other American towns show the same pattern. As Shy puts it: "Revolutionary America may have been a middle-class society, happier and more prosperous than any other in its time, but it contained a large and growing number of fairly poor people, and many of them did much of the actual fighting and suffering between 1775 and 1783: A very old story."

The military conflict itself, by dominating everything in its time, diminished other issues, made people choose sides in the one contest that was publicly important, forced people onto the side of the Revolution whose interest in independence was not at all obvious. War was making the ruling elite more secure against internal trouble.

Here, in the war for liberty, was conscription, as usual, cognizant of wealth. With the impressment riots against the British still remembered, impressment of seamen by the American navy was taking place by 1779. A Pennsylvania official said: "We cannot help observing how similar this Conduct is to that of the British Officers during our Subjection to Great Britain and are persuaded it will have the same unhappy effects viz. an estrangement of the Affections of the People from...Authority...which by an easy Progression will proceed to open Opposition...and bloodshed."

The Americans lost the first battles of the war: Bunker Hill, Brooklyn Heights, Harlem Heights, the Deep South; they won small battles at Trenton and Princeton, and then, in a turning point, a big battle at Saratoga, New York, in 1777. Washington's frozen army hung on at Valley Forge, Pennsylvania, while Benjamin Franklin negotiated an alliance with the French monarchy, which was anxious for revenge on England. The war turned to the South, where the British won victory after victory, until the Americans, aided by a large French army, with the French navy blocking off the British from supplies and reinforcements, won the final victory of the war at Yorktown, Virginia, in 1781.

Through all this, the suppressed conflicts between rich and poor among the Americans kept reappearing. The war, Eric Foner says, was "a time of immense profits for some colonists and terrible hardships for others."

In May 1779, the First Company of Philadelphia Artillery petitioned the Assembly about the troubles of "the midling and poor" and threatened violence against "those who are avariciously intent upon amassing wealth by the destruction of the more virtuous part of the community." In October came the "Fort Wilson riot," in which a militia group marched into the city and to the house of James Wilson, a wealthy lawyer and Revolutionary official who had opposed price controls and the democratic constitution adopted in Pennsylvania in 1776. The militia were driven away by a "silk stocking brigade" of well-off Philadelphia citizens.

The Continental Congress, which governed the colonies through the war, was dominated by rich men, linked together in factions and compacts by business and family connections. For instance, Richard Henry Lee of Virginia was connected with the Adamses of Massachusetts and the Shippens of Pennsylvania.

The Congress voted half-pay for life for those officers who stuck to the end. This ignored the common soldier, who was not getting paid, who was suffering in the cold, dying of sickness, watching the civilian profiteers get rich. On New Year's Day, 1781, the Pennsylvania troops near Morristown, New Jersey, perhaps emboldened by rum, dispersed their officers, killed one captain, wounded others, and were marching, fully armed, with cannon, toward the Continental Congress at Philadelphia.

George Washington handled it cautiously. A peace was negotiated, in which half the men were discharged; the other half got furloughs.

Shortly after this, a smaller mutiny took place in the New Jersey Line, involving two hundred men who defied their officers and started out for the state capital at Trenton. Now Washington was ready. Six hundred men, who themselves had been well fed and clothed, marched on the mutineers and surrounded and disarmed them. Three ringleaders were put on trial immediately, in the field. One was pardoned, and two were shot by firing squads made up of their friends, who wept as they pulled the triggers. It was "an example," Washington said.

Two years later, there was another mutiny in the Pennsylvania Line. The war was over and the army had disbanded, but eighty soldiers, demanding their pay, invaded the Continental Congress headquarters in Philadelphia and forced the members to flee across the river to Princeton— "ignominiously turned out of doors," as one historian sorrowfully wrote (John Fiske, *The Critical Period*), "by a handful of drunken mutineers."

What soldiers in the Revolution could do only rarely, rebel against their authorities, civilians could do much more easily. Ronald Hoffman says: "The Revolution plunged the states of Delaware, Maryland, North Carolina, South Carolina, Georgia, and, to a much lesser degree, Virginia into divisive civil conflicts that persisted during the entire period of struggle." The southern lower classes resisted being mobilized for the revolution. They saw themselves under the rule of a political elite, win or lose against the British.

With black slaves 20 percent of the population (and in some counties 50 percent), fear of slave revolts grew. George Washington had turned down the requests of blacks, seeking freedom, to fight in the Revolutionary army. So when the British military commander in Virginia, Lord Dunmore, promised freedom to Virginia slaves who joined his forces, this created consternation.

Even more unsettling was white rioting in Maryland against leading families supporting the Revolution, who were suspected of hoarding needed commodities. Despite this, Maryland authorities retained control. They made concessions, taxing land and slaves more heavily, letting debtors pay in paper money. It was a sacrifice by the upper class to maintain power, and it worked.

In the lower South, however, the general mood was to take no part in a war that seemed to have nothing for them. Washington's military commander there, Nathanael Greene, dealt with disloyalty by a policy of concessions to some, brutality to others. In a letter to Thomas Jefferson he described a raid by his troops on Loyalists. "They made a dreadful carnage of them, upwards of one hundred were killed and most of the rest cut to pieces. It has had a very happy effect on those disaffected persons of which there were too many in this country." In general, throughout the states, concessions were kept to a minimum. The new constitutions that were drawn up in all states from 1776 to 1780 were not much different from the old ones. Only Pennsylvania abolished property qualifications for voting and holding office.

One would look, in examining the Revolution's effect on class relations, at what happened to land confiscated from fleeing Loyalists. It was distributed in such a way as to give a double opportunity to the Revolutionary leaders: to enrich themselves and their friends, and to parcel out some land to small farmers to create a broad base of support for the new government. Indeed, this became characteristic of the new nation: finding itself possessed of enormous wealth, it could create the richest ruling class in history and still have enough for the middle classes to act as a buffer between the rich and the dispossessed.

Edmund Morgan sums up the class nature of the Revolution this way: "The fact that the lower ranks were involved in the contest should not obscure the fact that the contest itself was generally a struggle for office and power between members of an upper class: the new against the established."

Carl Degler says (*Out of Our Past*): "No new social class came to power through the door of the American revolution. The men who engineered the revolt were largely members of the colonial ruling class." George Washington was the richest man in America. John Hancock was a prosperous Boston merchant. Benjamin Franklin was a wealthy printer. And so on.

On the other hand, town mechanics, laborers, and seamen, as well as small farmers, were swept into "the people" by the rhetoric of the Revolution, by the camaraderie of military service, by the distribution of some land. Thus was created a substantial body of support, a national consensus, something that, even with the exclusion of ignored and oppressed people, could be called "America."

Staughton Lynd's close study of Dutchess County, New York, in the Revolutionary period corroborates this. There were tenant risings in 1766 against the huge feudal estates in New York. The Rensselaerwyck holding was a million acres. Tenants, claiming some of this land for themselves, unable to get satisfaction in the courts, turned to violence. In Poughkeepsie, seventeen hundred armed tenants closed the courts and broke open the jails. But the uprising was crushed.

Tenants became a threatening force in the midst of the war. Many stopped paying rent. The legislature, worried, passed a bill to confiscate Loyalist land and add four hundred new freeholders to the eighteen hundred already in the county. The new freeholders found that they had stopped being tenants, but were now mortgagees, paying back loans from banks instead of rent to landlords.

It seems that the rebellion against British rule allowed a certain group of the colonial elite to replace those loyal to England, give some benefits to small landholders, and leave poor white working people and tenant farmers in very much their old situation.

What did the Revolution mean to the native Americans, the Indians? They had been ignored by the fine words of the Declaration, had not been considered equal, certainly not in choosing those who would govern the

American territories in which they lived, nor in being able to pursue happiness as they had pursued it for centuries before the white Europeans arrived. Now, with the British out of the way, the Americans could begin the inexorable process of pushing the Indians off their lands, killing them if they resisted. In short, as Francis Jennings puts it, the white Americans were fighting against British imperial control in the East, and for their own imperialism in the West.

In New York, through intricate swindling, eight hundred thousand acres of Mohawk land were taken, ending the period of friendship between the Mohawks and the state. Chief Hendrick of the Mohawks is recorded speaking his bitterness to Gov. George Clinton and the provincial council of New York in 1753:

> Brother when we came here to relate our Grievances about our Lands, we expected to have something done for us, and we have told you that the Covenant Chain of our Forefathers was like to be broken, and brother you tell us that we shall be redressed at Albany, but we know them so well, we will not trust to them, for they [the Albany merchants] are no people but Devils so...as soon as we come home we will send up a Belt of Wampum to our Brothers the other 5 Nations to acquaint them the Covenant Chain is broken between you and us. So brother you are not to expect to hear of me any more, and Brother we desire to hear no more of you.

When the British fought the French for North America in the Seven Years' War, the Indians fought on the side of the French. The French were traders but not occupiers of Indian lands, while the British clearly coveted their hunting grounds and living space.

When that war ended in 1763, the French, ignoring their old allies, ceded to the British lands west of the Appalachians. The Indians therefore united to make war on the British western forts; this is called "Pontiac's Conspiracy" by the British, but "a liberation war for independence" in the words used by Francis Jennings. Under orders from the British general Jeffrey Amherst, the commander of Fort Pitts gave the attacking Indian chiefs, with whom he was negotiating, blankets from the smallpox hospital. It was a pioneering effort at what is now called biological warfare. An epidemic soon spread among the Indians.

Despite the burning of villages, the British could not destroy the will of the Indians, who continued guerrilla war. A peace was made, with the British agreeing to establish a line at the Appalachians, beyond which settlements would not encroach on Indian territory. This was the Royal

Proclamation of 1763, and it angered Americans (the original Virginia charter said its land went westward to the ocean). It helps to explain why most of the Indians fought for England during the Revolution. With their French allies, then their English allies, gone, the Indians faced a new land-coveting nation—alone.

With the eastern elite controlling the lands on the seaboard, the poor, seeking land, were forced to go West. They became a useful bulwark for the rich, because it was the frontiers people who were the first targets of the Indians.

The situation of black slaves as a result of the American Revolution was more complex. Thousands of blacks fought with the British. Five thousand were with the Revolutionaries.

In the northern states, the combination of blacks in the military, the lack of powerful economic need for slaves, and the rhetoric of Revolution led to the end of slavery—but very slowly. As late as 1810, thirty thousand blacks, one-fourth of the black population of the North, remained slaves. In 1840 there were still a thousand slaves in the North. In the upper South, there were more free Negroes than before, leading to more control legislation. In the lower South, slavery expanded with the growth of rice and cotton plantations.

What the Revolution did was to create space and opportunity for blacks to begin making demands of white society. Sometimes these demands came from the new, small black elites in Baltimore, Philadelphia, Richmond, and Savannah, sometimes from articulate and bold slaves. Pointing to the Declaration of Independence, blacks petitioned Congress and the state legislatures to abolish slavery, to give blacks equal rights. In 1780, seven blacks in Dartmouth, Massachusetts, petitioned the legislature for the right to vote, linking taxation to representation:

> ...we apprehend ourselves to be Aggreeved, in that while we are not allowed the Privilage of freemen of the State having no vote or Influence in the Election of those that Tax us yet many of our Colour (as is well known) have cheerfully Entered the field of Battle in the defense of the Common Cause and that (as we conceive) against a similar Exertion of Power (in Regard to taxation) too well known to need a recital in this place....

A black man, Benjamin Banneker, who taught himself mathematics and astronomy, accurately predicted a solar eclipse, and was appointed to plan the new city of Washington, wrote to Thomas Jefferson:

I suppose it is a truth too well attested to you, to need a proof here, that we are a race of beings, who have long labored under the abuse and censure of the world; that we have long been looked upon with an eye of contempt; and that we have long been considered rather as brutish than human, and scarcely capable of mental endowments.... I apprehend you will embrace every opportunity to eradicate that train of absurd and false ideas and opinions, which so generally prevails with respect to us; and that your sentiments are concurrent with mine, which are, that one universal Father hath given being to us all; and that he hath not only made us all of one flesh, but that he hath also, without partiality, afforded us all the same sensations and endowed us all with the same facilities....

Banneker asked Jefferson "to wean yourselves from those narrow prejudices which you have imbibed."

Jefferson tried his best, as an enlightened, thoughtful individual might. But the structure of American society, the power of the cotton plantation, the slave trade, the politics of unity between northern and southern elites, and the established culture of race prejudice in the colonies, as well as his own weaknesses—that combination of practical need and ideological fixation—kept Jefferson a slaveowner throughout his life.

The inferior position of blacks, the exclusion of Indians from the new society, the establishment of supremacy for the rich and powerful in the new nation—all this was already settled in the colonies by the time of the Revolution. With the English out of the way, it could now be put on paper, solidified, regularized, made legitimate, by the Constitution of the United States, drafted at a convention of Revolutionary leaders in Philadelphia.

To many Americans over the years, the Constitution drawn up in 1787 has seemed a work of genius put together by wise, humane men who created a legal framework for democracy and equality.

Another view of the Constitution was put forward early in the twentieth century by the historian Charles Beard (arousing anger and indignation, including a denunciatory editorial in the *New York Times*). In his book *An Economic Interpretation of the Constitution*, Beard studied the economic backgrounds and political ideas of the fifty-five men who gathered in Philadelphia in 1787 to draw up the Constitution. He found that a majority of them were lawyers by profession, that most of them were men of wealth, in land, slaves, manufacturing, or shipping, that half of them had money loaned out at interest, and that forty of the fifty-five held government bonds, according to the records of the Treasury Department.

Thus, Beard found that most of the makers of the Constitution had some direct economic interest in establishing a strong federal government:

the manufacturers needed protective tariffs; the moneylenders wanted to stop the use of paper money to pay off debts; the land speculators wanted protection as they invaded Indian lands; slaveowners needed federal security against slave revolts and runaways; bondholders wanted a government able to raise money by nationwide taxation, to pay off those bonds.

Four groups, Beard noted, were not represented in the Constitutional Convention: slaves, indentured servants, women, and men without property. And so the Constitution did not reflect the interests of those groups.

He wanted to make it clear that he did not think the Constitution was written merely to benefit the Founding Fathers personally. Rather, it was to benefit the groups the founders represented, the "economic interests they understood and felt in concrete, definite form through their own personal experience."

By 1787 there was not only a positive need for strong central government to protect the large economic interests, but also immediate fear of rebellion by discontented farmers. The chief event causing this fear was an uprising in the summer of 1786 in western Massachusetts, known as Shays's Rebellion.

In the western towns of Massachusetts there was resentment against the legislature in Boston. The new constitution of 1780 had raised the property qualifications for voting. No one could hold state office without being quite wealthy. Furthermore, the legislature was refusing to issue paper money, as had been done in some other states, such as Rhode Island, to make it easier for debt-ridden farmers to pay off their creditors.

Illegal conventions began to assemble in some of the western counties to organize opposition to the legislature. At one of these, a man named Plough Jogger spoke his mind:

> I have been greatly abused, have been obliged to do more than my part in the war; been loaded with class rates, town rates, province rates, Continental rates and all rates ...been pulled and hauled by sheriffs, constables and collectors, and had my cattle sold for less than they were worth....
> ...The great men are going to get all we have and I think it is time for us to rise and put a stop to it, and have no more courts, nor sheriffs, nor collectors nor lawyers....

There were going to be court proceedings in Hampshire County, in the towns of Northampton and Springfield, to seize the cattle of farmers who hadn't paid their debts, to take away their land, now full of grain and ready for harvest. And so, veterans of the Continental army, also aggrieved because they had been treated poorly on discharge—given certificates for future redemption instead of immediate cash—began to organize the farmers into squads and companies. One of these veterans was Luke Day, who arrived the morning of court with a fife-and-drum corps, still angry with the memory of being locked up in debtors' prison in the heat of the previous summer.

The sheriff looked to the local militia to defend the court against these armed farmers. But most of the militia was with Luke Day. The sheriff did manage to gather five hundred men, and the judges put on their black silk robes, waiting for the sheriff to protect their trip to the courthouse. But there at the courthouse steps, Luke Day stood with a petition, asserting the people's constitutional right to protest the unconstitutional acts of the General Court, asking the judges to adjourn until the General Court could act on behalf of the farmers. Standing with Luke Day were fifteen hundred armed farmers. The judges adjourned.

Shortly after, at courthouses in Worcester and Athol, farmers with guns prevented the courts from meeting to take away their property, and the militia were too sympathetic to the farmers, or too outnumbered, to act. In Concord, a fifty-year-old veteran of two wars, Job Shattuck, led a caravan of carts, wagons, horses, and oxen onto the town green, while a message was sent to the judges: "The voice of the People of this county is such that the court shall not enter this courthouse until such time as the People shall have redress of the grievances they labor under at the present." A county convention then suggested the judges adjourn, which they did.

At Great Barrington, a militia of a thousand faced a square crowded with armed men and boys. But the militia was split in its opinion, most favoring the crowd, which, after obtaining the chief justice's promise to adjourn his court until the General Court met, went back to the square, broke open the county jail, and set the debtors free. The chief justice, a country doctor, said: "I have never heard anybody point out a better way to have their grievances redressed than the people have taken."

The governor and the political leaders of Massachusetts became alarmed. Samuel Adams, once looked on as a radical leader in Boston, now insisted people act within the law. He said "British emissaries" were stirring up the farmers. People in the town of Greenwich responded: You in Boston have the money, and we don't. And didn't you act illegally yourselves in the Revolution? The insurgents were now being called Regulators. Their emblem was a sprig of hemlock.

The problem went beyond Massachusetts. In Rhode Island, the debtors had taken over the legislature and were issuing paper money. In

New Hampshire, several hundred men, in September of 1786, surrounded the legislature in Exeter, asking that taxes be returned and paper money issued; they dispersed only when military action was threatened.

Daniel Shays entered the scene in western Massachusetts. A poor farm hand when the Revolution broke out, he joined the Continental army, fought at Lexington, Bunker Hill, and Saratoga, and was wounded in action. In 1780, not being paid, he resigned from the army, went home, and soon found himself in court for nonpayment of debts. He also saw what was happening to others: a sick woman, unable to pay, had her bed taken from under her.

What brought Shays fully into the situation was that on September 19, the Supreme Judicial Court of Massachusetts indicted eleven leaders of the rebellion, including three of his friends, as "disorderly, riotous and seditious persons." Shays organized seven hundred armed farmers, most of them veterans of the war, and led them to Springfield. As they marched, their ranks grew. Some of the militia joined, and reinforcements began coming in from the countryside. The judges postponed hearings for a day, then adjourned the court.

Now the General Court, meeting in Boston, was told by Governor James Bowdoin to "vindicate the insulted dignity of government." The recent rebels against England, secure in office, were calling for law and order. Sam Adams helped draw up a riot act and a resolution suspending habeas corpus, to allow the authorities to keep people in jail without trial. At the same time, the legislature moved to make some concessions to the angry farmers, saying certain old taxes could now be paid in goods instead of money.

This didn't help. Confrontations between farmers and militia now multiplied. But the winter snows began to interfere with the farmers' trips to the courthouses. When Shays began marching a thousand men into Boston, a blizzard forced them back, and one of his men froze to death.

An army came into the field, led by Gen. Benjamin Lincoln, on money raised by Boston merchants. The rebels were outnumbered and on the run. Shays took refuge in Vermont, and his followers began to surrender. There were a few more deaths in battle, and then sporadic, disorganized, desperate acts of violence against authority: the burning of barns, the slaughter of a general's horses. One government soldier was killed in an eerie nighttime collision of two sleighs.

Captured rebels were put on trial in Northampton and six were sentenced to death. A note was left at the door of the high sheriff of Pittsfield:

"I understand that there is a number of my countrymen condemned to die because they fought for justice.... Prepare for death with speed, for your life or mine is short."

Thirty-three more rebels were put on trial and six more condemned to death. General Lincoln urged mercy and a Commission of Clemency, but Samuel Adams said: "In monarchy the crime of treason may admit of being pardoned or lightly punished, but the man who dares rebel against the laws of a republic ought to suffer death." Several hangings followed; some of the condemned were pardoned. Shays, in Vermont, was pardoned in 1788 and returned to Massachusetts, where he died, poor and obscure, in 1825.

It was Thomas Jefferson, in France as ambassador at the time of Shays's Rebellion, who spoke of such uprisings as healthy for society. In a letter to a friend he wrote: "I hold it that a little rebellion now and then is a good thing.... It is a medicine necessary for the sound health of government.... God forbid that we should ever be twenty years without such a rebellion.... The tree of liberty must be refreshed from time to time with the blood of patriots and tyrants. It is its natural manure."

But Jefferson was far from the scene. The political and economic elite of the country were not so tolerant. They worried that the example might spread. A veteran of Washington's army, Gen. Henry Knox, founded an organization of army veterans, "The Order of the Cincinnati." Knox wrote to Washington in late 1786 about Shays's Rebellion, and in doing so expressed the thoughts of many of the wealthy and powerful leaders of the country: "The people who are the insurgents feel at once their own poverty, compared with the opulent.... Their creed is 'That the property of the United States has been protected from the confiscations of Britain by the joint exertions of all, and therefore ought to be the common property of all.'"

Alexander Hamilton, an aide to Washington during the war, was one of the most forceful and astute leaders of the new aristocracy. He voiced his political philosophy:

> All communities divide themselves into the few and the many. The first are the rich and well-born, the other the mass of the people.... The people are turbulent and changing; they seldom judge or determine right. Give therefore to the first class a distinct permanent share in the government.... Nothing but a permanent body can check the imprudence of democracy....

At the Constitutional Convention, Hamilton suggested a president and Senate chosen for life. The Convention did not take his suggestion.

But neither did it provide for popular elections, except in the case of the House of Representatives, where the qualifications were set by the state legislatures (which required property holding for voting in almost every state), and excluded women, Indians, and slaves. The Constitution provided for senators to be elected by the state legislators, for the president to be elected by electors chosen by the state legislators, and for the Supreme Court to be appointed by the president.

The problem of democracy in the post-Revolutionary society was not, however, the Constitutional limitations on voting. It lay deeper, beyond the Constitution, in the division of society into rich and poor. For if some people had great wealth and great influence; if they had the land, the money, the newspapers, the church, the educational system—how could voting, however broad, cut into such power? There was still another problem: wasn't it the nature of representative government, even when most broadly based, to be conservative, to prevent tumultuous change?

It came time to ratify the Constitution, to submit to a vote in state conventions, with approval of nine of the thirteen required to ratify it. In New York, where debate over ratification was intense, a series of newspaper articles appeared, anonymously, and they tell us much about the nature of the Constitution. These articles, favoring adoption of the Constitution, were written by James Madison, Alexander Hamilton, and John Jay, and came to be known as the *Federalist Papers* (opponents of the Constitution became known as anti-Federalists).

In *Federalist Paper #10*, James Madison argued that representative government was needed to maintain peace in a society ridden by factional disputes. These disputes came from "the various and unequal distribution of property. Those who hold and those who are without property have ever formed distinct interests in society." The problem, he said, was how to control the factional struggles that came from inequalities in wealth. Minority factions could be controlled, he said, by the principle that decisions would be by vote of the majority.

So the real problem, according to Madison, was a majority faction, and here the solution was offered by the Constitution, to have "an extensive republic," that is, a large nation ranging over thirteen states, for then "it will be more difficult for all who feel it to discover their own strength, and to act in unison with each other...."

As part of his argument for a large republic to keep the peace, James Madison tells quite clearly, in *Federalist #10*, whose peace he wants to keep:

"A rage for paper money, for an abolition of debts, for an equal division of property, or for any other improper or wicked project, will be less apt to pervade the whole body of the Union than a particular member of it."

When economic interest is seen behind the political clauses of the Constitution, then the document becomes not simply the work of wise men trying to establish a decent and orderly society, but the work of certain groups trying to maintain their privileges, while giving just enough rights and liberties to enough of the people to ensure popular support.

In the new government, Madison would belong to one party (the Democrat-Republicans) along with Jefferson and Monroe. Hamilton would belong to the rival party (the Federalists) along with Washington and Adams. But both agreed—one a slaveholder from Virginia, the other a merchant from New York—on the aims of this new government they were establishing. In this they anticipated the tradition of fundamental agreement between the two "opposing" political parties in the American system. Hamilton wrote elsewhere in the *Federalist Papers* that the new Union would be able "to repress domestic faction and insurrection." He referred directly to Shays's Rebellion: "The tempestuous situation from which Massachusetts has scarcely emerged evinces that dangers of this kind are not merely speculative."

It was either Madison or Hamilton (the authorship of the individual papers is not always known) who in *Federalist Paper # 63* argued the necessity of a "well-constructed Senate" as "sometimes necessary as a defence to the people against their own temporary errors and delusions." And: "In these critical moments, how salutary will be the interference of some temperate and respectable body of citizens in order to check the misguided career, and to suspend the blow meditated by the people against themselves, until reason, justice, and truth can regain their authority over the public mind?"

The Constitution was a compromise between slaveholding interests of the South and moneyed interests of the North. For the purpose of uniting the thirteen states into one great market for commerce, the northern delegates wanted laws regulating interstate commerce and urged that such laws require only a majority of Congress to pass. The South agreed to this, in return for allowing the trade in slaves to continue for twenty years before being outlawed.

Charles Beard warned us that governments—including the government of the United States—are not neutral, that they represent the dominant economic interests, and that their constitutions are intended to serve these interests.

True, there were many property owners. But some people had much more than others. A few people had great amounts of property; many people (roughly, one-third) had small amounts; others had none.

Still, one-third was a considerable number of people who felt they had something at stake in the stability of a new government. This was a larger base of support for government than anywhere in the world at the end of the eighteenth century. In addition, the city mechanics had an important interest in a government that would protect their work from foreign competition.

This was especially true in New York. When the ninth and tenth states had ratified the Constitution, four thousand New York City mechanics marched with floats and banners to celebrate. Bakers, blacksmiths, brewers, ship joiners and shipwrights, coopers, cartmen, and tailors all marched. They required a government that would protect them against the British hats and shoes and other goods that were pouring into the colonies after the Revolution. As a result, the mechanics often supported wealthy conservatives at the ballot box.

The Constitution, then, illustrates the complexity of the American system: that it serves the interests of a wealthy elite, but also does enough for small property owners, for middle-income workers and farmers, to build a broad base of support. The slightly prosperous people who make up this base of support are buffers against the blacks, the Indians, and the very poor whites. They enable the elite to keep control with a minimum of coercion, a maximum of law—all made palatable by the fanfare of patriotism and unity.

The Constitution became even more acceptable to the public at large after the first Congress, responding to criticism, passed a series of amendments known as the Bill of Rights. These amendments seemed to make the new government a guardian of people's liberties: to speak, to publish, to worship, to petition, to assemble, to be tried fairly, to be secure at home against official intrusion. It was, therefore, perfectly designed to build popular backing for the new government. What was not made clear—it was a time when the language of freedom was new and its reality untested—was the shakiness of anyone's liberty when entrusted to a government of the rich and powerful.

Indeed, the same problem existed for the other provisions of the Constitution, such as the clause forbidding states to "impair the obligation of contract," or that giving Congress the power to tax the people and to appropriate money. They all sound benign and neutral until one asks: Tax whom, for what? Appropriate what, for whom?

To protect everyone's contracts seems like an act of fairness, of equal treatment, until one considers that contracts made between rich and poor, between employer and employee, landlord and tenant, creditor and debtor, generally favor the more powerful of the two parties. Thus, to protect these contracts is to put the great power of the government, its laws, courts, sheriffs, police, on the side of the privileged—and to do it not, as in premodern times, as an exercise of brute force against the weak but as a matter of law.

The First Amendment of the Bill of Rights shows that quality of interest hiding behind innocence. Passed in 1791 by Congress, it provided that "Congress shall make no law... abridging the freedom of speech, or of the press...." Yet, seven years after the First Amendment became part of the Constitution, Congress passed a law very clearly abridging the freedom of speech.

This was the Sedition Act of 1798, passed under John Adams's administration, at a time when Irishmen and Frenchmen in the United States were looked on as dangerous revolutionaries because of the recent French Revolution and the Irish rebellions. The Sedition Act made it a crime to say or write anything "false, scandalous and malicious" against the government, Congress, or the President, with intent to defame them, bring them into disrepute, or excite popular hatreds against them.

This act seemed to violate the First Amendment directly. Yet, it was enforced. Ten Americans were put in prison for utterances against the government, and every member of the Supreme Court between 1798 and 1800, sitting as an appellate judge, held it constitutional.

Despite the First Amendment, the British common law of "seditious libel" still ruled in America. This meant that while the government could not exercise "prior restraint"—that is, prevent an utterance or publication in advance—it could legally punish the speaker or writer afterward. Thus, Congress has a convenient legal basis for the laws it has enacted since that time, making certain kinds of speech a crime. And, since punishment after the fact is a strong deterrent to the exercise of free expression, the claim of "no prior restraint" itself is destroyed. This leaves the First Amendment much less than the stone wall of protection it seems at first glance.

Are the economic provisions in the Constitution enforced just as weakly? We have an instructive example almost immediately in Washington's first administration, when Congress's power to tax and appropriate money was immediately put to use by the secretary of the treasury, Alexander Hamilton.

Hamilton, believing that government must ally itself with the richest elements of society to make itself strong, proposed to Congress a series of laws, which it enacted, expressing this philosophy. The Bank of the United States was set up as a partnership between the government and certain banking interests. A tariff was passed to help the manufacturers. It was agreed to pay bondholders—most of the war bonds were now concentrated among a small group of wealthy people—the full value of their bonds. Tax laws were passed to raise money for this bond redemption.

One of these tax laws was the Whiskey Tax, which especially hurt small farmers who raised grain that they converted into whiskey and then sold. In 1794 the farmers of western Pennsylvania took up arms and rebelled against the collection of this tax. Secretary of the Treasury Hamilton led the troops to put them down. We see then, in the first years of the Constitution, that some of its provisions—even those paraded most flamboyantly (like the First Amendment)—might be treated lightly. Others (like the power to tax) would be powerfully enforced.

Still, the mythology around the Founding Fathers persists. Were they wise and just men trying to achieve a balance of power? In fact, they did not want a balance, except one which kept things as they were, a balance among the dominant forces at that time. They certainly did not want an equal balance between slaves and masters, propertyless and property holders, Indians and white.

As many as half the people were not even considered by the Founding Fathers. They were not mentioned in the Declaration of Independence, they were absent in the Constitution, they were invisible in the new political democracy. They were the women of early America.

Exercises

1. How much colonial opposition was there to British rule in 1776?

2. What motivated the colonial poor to fight the British?

3. Zinn argues that the American Revolutionary "War was making the ruling elite more secure against internal trouble" (p. 62). What evidence does Zinn provide to support this assertion?

4. The Battle of Saratoga (1777) brought the French into the war on the side of the Americans. Why was this result significant enough to make the Battle of Saratoga the "turning point" of the war?

5. Which of the following is the most appropriate thesis for this chapter?
   a. The Americans won the war only with help from the French.
   b. The war was a struggle for power between members of an upper class.
   c. Rich men ran the war
   d. General enthusiasm for the war was not strong.

   Defend your choice and give your reasons for having eliminated the rest.

6. What were the grievances of the American troops who mutinied or rebelled during the American Revolution?

7. What were the methods of control used by the Revolutionary elite to control disobedient and rebellious colonists?

8. How did farmers resist impoverishment?

9. Why did the Indians fight with the British against the colonial rebels?

10. How did blacks respond to the opportunities presented by the Revolutionary War? How effective were their responses?

11. Why did the author of "All men are created equal," Thomas Jefferson, remain a slaveholder all his life?

12. The U.S. Constitution was: (Defend your choice with detail.)

a. "a work of genius put together by wise, humane men who created a legal framework for democracy and equality"

b. a work of genius put together by rich men to benefit their economic interests

c. a work of genius which balances the interests of slaves, indentured servants, women, men without property, and men with property

d. a compromise between slaveholding interests of the South and monied interests of the North

e. all of the above

13. Who benefits most from a strong central government? How?

14. In the months preceding Shays's Rebellion, what were the grievances of western Massachusetts farmers? What were the state government's responses (both judicial and legislative) to the grievances of these farmers? What were the Boston merchants' responses to Shays's resistance?

15. Did Shays's Rebellion have the salutary effect of "refreshing the tree of liberty"? Explain your response.

16. Explain the difference between Jefferson's and Hamilton's attitudes toward popular participation in the decision-making process. If one were to look only at *Federalist Paper #10*, does Madison agree with Hamilton or Jefferson on this issue?

17. Did the U.S. Constitution define a democratic government? Is a democratic government possible in an economically polarized society?

18. Why did city mechanics in New York support wealthy conservatives in promoting the ratification of the U.S. Constitution? Is it surprising that they did?

19. Many historians argue that the U.S. Constitution creates a neutral, level playing field on which contestants prove their worth (that any inequality in wealth is not due to unfair rules but to unequal abilities). For what reasons does Zinn disagree with this interpretation?

20. Why did Congress pass the Whiskey Tax? How did small farmers who manufactured whiskey respond? What is the difference between the means by which Shays's Rebellion was defeated and the Whiskey Rebellion was defeated? What is the significance of the answer to the previous question?

21. *Draw a map* that includes the following: Boston; Springfield; Massachusetts; New York City; New York; Washington, D.C.; Pennsylvania; Saratoga; Yorktown; Philadelphia; Hudson River; Proclamation Line of 1763.

Chapter 6

The Intimately Oppressed

It is possible, reading standard histories, to forget half the population of the country. The explorers were men, the landholders and merchants men, the political leaders men, the military figures men. The very invisibility of women, the overlooking of women, is a sign of their submerged status.

In this invisibility they were something like black slaves (and thus slave women faced a double oppression). The biological uniqueness of women, like skin color and facial characteristics for Negroes, became a basis for treating them as inferiors. It seems that their physical characteristics became a convenience for men, who could use, exploit, and cherish someone who was at the same time servant, sex mate, companion, and bearer-teacher-warden of his children.

Because of that intimacy and long-term connection with children, there was a special patronization, which on occasion, especially in the face of a show of strength, could slip over into treatment as an equal. An oppression so private would turn out hard to uproot.

Earlier societies—in America and elsewhere—in which property was held in common and families were extensive and complicated, with aunts and uncles and grandmothers and grandfathers all living together, seemed to treat women more as equals than did the white societies that later overran them, bringing "civilization" and private property.

In the Zuñi tribes of the Southwest, for instance, extended families— large clans—were based on the woman, whose husband came to live with her family. It was assumed that women owned the houses, and the fields belonged to the clans, and the women had equal rights to what was produced. A woman was more secure because she was with her own family, and she could divorce the man when she wanted to, keeping their property.

It would be an exaggeration to say that women were treated equally with men; but they were treated with respect, and the communal nature of the society gave them a more important place. The puberty ceremony of the Sioux was such as to give pride to a young Sioux maiden:

> Walk the good road, my daughter, and the buffalo herds wide and dark as cloud shadows moving over the prairie will follow you.... Be dutiful, respectful, gentle and modest, my daughter. And proud walking. If the pride and the virtue of the women are lost, the spring will come but the buffalo trails will turn to grass. Be strong, with the warm, strong heart of the earth. No people goes down until their women are weak and dishonored....

The conditions under which white settlers came to America created various situations for women. Where the first settlements consisted almost entirely of men, women were imported as sex slaves, childbearers, companions. In 1619, the year that the first black slaves came to Virginia, ninety women arrived at Jamestown on one ship: "Agreeable persons, young and incorrupt...sold with their own consent to settlers as wives, the price to be the cost of their own transportation."

Many women came in those early years as indentured servants—often teenaged girls—and lived lives not much different from slaves, except that the term of service had an end. They were to be obedient to masters and mistresses. Sexual abuse by their masters was common. According to the authors of *America's Working Women* (Baxandall, Gordon, and Reverby): "They were poorly paid and often treated rudely and harshly, deprived of good food and privacy."

In 1756, Elizabeth Sprigs wrote to her father about her servitude: "What we unfortunate English People suffer here is beyond the probibility of you in England to Conceive, let it suffice that I one of the unhappy Number, am toiling almost Day and Night...with only this comfort that you Bitch you do not halfe enough...."

Of course these terrible conditions provoked resistance. For instance, the General Court of Connecticut in 1645 ordered that a certain "Susan C., for her rebellious carriage toward her mistress, to be sent to the house of correction and be kept to hard labor and coarse diet...."

Whatever horrors can be imagined in the transport of black slaves to America must be multiplied for black women, who were often one-third of the cargo. Slave traders reported:

I saw pregnant women give birth to babies while chained to corpses which our drunken overseers had not removed.... [p]acked spoon-fashion they often gave birth to children in the scalding perspiration from the human cargo.... On board the ship was a young negro woman chained to the deck, who had lost her senses soon after she was purchased and taken on board.

A woman named Linda Brent who escaped from slavery told of another burden:

But I now entered on my fifteenth year—a sad epoch in the life of a slave girl. My master began to whisper foul words in my ear. Young as I was, I could not remain ignorant of their import.... My master met me at every turn, reminding me that I belonged to him, and swearing by heaven and earth that he would compel me to submit to him. If I went out for a breath of fresh air, after a day of unwearied toil, his footsteps dogged me. If I knelt by my mother's grave, his dark shadow fell on me even there. The light heart which nature had given me became heavy with sad forebodings....

Even free white women, not brought as servants or slaves but as wives of the early settlers, faced special hardships. Eighteen married women came over on the Mayflower. Three were pregnant, and one of them gave birth to a dead child before they landed. Childbirth and sickness plagued the women; by the spring, only four of those eighteen women were still alive.

All women were burdened with ideas carried over from England. English law was summarized in a document of 1632 entitled "The Lawes Resolutions of Womens Rights": "In this consolidation which we call wedlock is a locking together. It is true, that man and wife are one person, but understand in what manner.... Her new self is her superior; her companion, her master...."

Julia Spruill describes the woman's legal situation in the colonial period: "The husband's control over the wife's person extended to the right of giving her chastisement.... But he was not entitled to inflict permanent injury or death on his wife...."

As for property: "Besides absolute possession of his wife's personal property and a life estate in her lands, the husband took any other income that might be hers. He collected wages earned by her labor.... Naturally it followed that the proceeds of the joint labor of husband and wife belonged to the husband."

For a woman to have a child out of wedlock was a crime, and colonial

court records are full of cases of women being arraigned for "bastardy"—
the father of the child untouched by the law and on the loose. A colonial
periodical of 1747 reproduced a speech "of Miss Polly Baker before a
Court of Judicature, at Connecticut near Boston in New England; where
she was prosecuted the fifth time for having a Bastard Child."

> ...I take the liberty to say, that I think this law, by which I am punished,
> both unreasonable in itself, and particularly severe with regard to
> me.... Abstracted from the law, I cannot conceive...what the nature of
> my offense is. I have brought five fine children into the world, at the
> risque of my life; I have maintained them well by my own industry,
> without burthening the township, and would have done it better, if it
> had not been for the heavy charges and fines I have paid.... [n]or has
> anyone the least cause of complaint against me, unless, perhaps, the
> ministers of justice, because I have had children without being married,
> by which they missed a wedding fee. But can this be a fault of mine?

The father's position in the family was expressed in *The Spectator*, an
influential periodical in America and England: "Nothing is more gratify-
ing to the mind of man than power or dominion.... I look upon my family
as a patriarchal sovereignty in which I am myself both king and priest."

A best-selling "pocket book," published in London, was widely read
in the American colonies in the 1700s. It was called *Advice to a Daughter*:
"You must first lay it down for a Foundation in general, That there is
Inequality in Sexes, and that for the better Oeconomy of the World; the
Men, who were to be the Law-givers, had the larger share of Reason
bestow'd upon them...."

Against this powerful education, it is remarkable that women nevertheless rebelled. Women rebels have always faced special disabilities: they
live under the daily eye of their master; and they are isolated one from the
other in households, thus missing the daily camaraderie that has given
heart to rebels of other oppressed groups.

Anne Hutchinson was a religious woman, mother of thirteen children,
and knowledgeable about healing with herbs. She defied the church fathers
in the early years of the Massachusetts Bay Colony by insisting that she,
and other ordinary people, could interpret the Bible for themselves.

She was put on trial twice: by the church for heresy, and by the government for challenging their authority. At her civil trial she was pregnant and
ill, but they did not allow her to sit down until she was close to collapse. At
her religious trial she was interrogated for weeks, and again she was sick,
but challenged her questioners with expert knowledge of the Bible and

remarkable eloquence. When finally she repented in writing, they were not satisfied. They said: "Her repentance is not in her countenance."

She was banished from the colony, and when she left for Rhode Island in 1638, thirty-five families followed her. Then she went to the shores of Long Island, where Indians who had been defrauded of their land thought she was one of their enemies; they killed her and her family. Twenty years later, the one person back in Massachusetts Bay who had spoken up for her during her trial, Mary Dyer, was hanged by the government of the colony, along with two other Quakers, for "rebellion, sedition, and presumptuous obtruding themselves."

It remained rare for women to participate openly in public affairs, although on the southern and western frontiers conditions made this occasionally possible.

During the Revolution, the necessities of war brought women out into public affairs. Women formed patriotic groups, carried out anti-British actions, wrote articles for independence. In 1777 there was a women's counterpart to the Boston Tea Party—a "coffee party," described by Abigail Adams in a letter to her husband John:

> One eminent, wealthy, stingy merchant (who is a bachelor) had a hogshead of coffee in his store, which he refused to sell the committee under six shillings per pound. A number of females, some say a hundred, some say more, assembled with a cart and trunks, marched down to the warehouse, and demanded the keys, which he refused to deliver. Upon which one of them seized him by his neck and tossed him into the cart. Upon his finding no quarter, he delivered the keys when they tipped up the cart and discharged him; then opened the warehouse, hoisted out the coffee themselves, put it into the trunks and drove off.... A large concourse of men stood amazed, silent spectators of the whole transaction.

It has been pointed out by women historians recently that the contributions of working-class women in the American Revolution have been mostly ignored, unlike the genteel wives of the leaders (Dolly Madison, Martha Washington, and Abigail Adams, for example). Margaret Corbin, called "Dirty Kate," Deborah Sampson Garnet, and "Molly Pitcher" were rough, lower-class women, prettified into ladies by historians. While poor women, in the last years of the fighting, went to army encampments, helped, and fought, they were represented later as prostitutes, whereas Martha Washington was given a special place in history books for visiting her husband at Valley Forge.

When feminist impulses are recorded, they are, almost always, the writings of privileged women who had some status from which to speak freely, more opportunity to write and have their writings recorded. Abigail Adams, even before the Declaration of Independence, in March of 1776, wrote to her husband:

> ...in the new code of laws which I suppose it will be necessary for you to make... [d]o not put such unlimited power in the hands of husbands. Remember, all men would be tyrants if they could. If particular care and attention are not paid to the ladies, we are determined to foment a rebellion, and will not hold ourselves bound to obey the laws in which we have no voice of representation.

Nevertheless, Jefferson underscored his phrase "all men are created equal" by his statement that American women would be "too wise to wrinkle their foreheads with politics." And after the Revolution, none of the new state constitutions granted women the right to vote, except for New Jersey, and that state rescinded the right in 1807. New York's constitution specifically disfranchised women by using the word "male."

Working-class women had no means of recording whatever sentiments of rebelliousness they may have felt at their subordination. Not only were they bearing children in great numbers, under great hardships, but they were working in the home. Around the time of the Declaration of Independence, four thousand women and children in Philadelphia were spinning at home for local plants under the "putting out" system. Women also were shopkeepers and innkeepers and engaged in many trades.

Ideas of female equality were in the air during and after the Revolution. Tom Paine spoke out for the equal rights of women. And the pioneering book of Mary Wollstonecraft in England, *A Vindication of the Rights of Women*, was reprinted in the United States shortly after the Revolutionary War. She wrote: "I wish to persuade women to endeavor to acquire strength, both of mind and body...."

Between the American Revolution and the Civil War, so many elements of American society were being transformed that changes were bound to take place in the situation of women. In preindustrial America, the practical need for women in a frontier society had produced some measure of equality; women worked at important jobs—publishing newspapers, managing tanneries, keeping taverns, engaging in skilled work. A grandmother, Martha Moore Ballard, on a farm in Maine in 1795, in twenty-five years as a midwife delivered more than a thousand babies.

Now, women were being pulled out of the house and into industrial life, while at the same time there was pressure for women to stay home where they were more easily controlled. The idea of "the woman's place," promulgated by men, was accepted by many women. It became important to develop a set of ideas, taught in church, in school, and in the family, to keep women in their place even as that place became more and more unsettled. The woman was expected to be pious. One female writer said: "Religion is just what woman needs. Without it she is ever restless or unhappy."

Sexual purity was to be the special virtue of a woman. The role began early, with adolescence. Obedience prepared the girl for submission to the first proper mate. Barbara Welter describes this:

> The assumption is twofold: the American female was supposed to be so infinitely lovable and provocative that a healthy male could barely control himself when in the same room with her, and the same girl, as she "comes out" of the cocoon of her family's protectiveness, is so palpitating with undirected affection [that]...she is required to exert the inner control of obedience. The combination forms a kind of societal chastity belt which is not unlocked until the marriage partner has arrived, and adolescence is formally over.

When Amelia Bloomer in 1851 suggested in her feminist publication that women wear a kind of short skirt and pants, to free themselves from the encumbrances of traditional dress, this was attacked in the popular women's literature. One story has a girl admiring the "bloomer" costume, but her professor admonishes her that they are "only one of the many manifestations of that wild spirit of socialism and agrarian radicalism which is at present so rife in our land."

The woman's job was to keep the home cheerful, maintain religion, be nurse, cook, cleaner, seamstress, flower arranger. A woman shouldn't read too much, and certain books should be avoided.

A sermon preached in 1808 in New York: "How interesting and important are the duties devolved on females as wives...the counsellor and friend of the husband; who makes it her daily study to lighten his cares, to soothe his sorrows, and to augment his joys...."

Women were also urged, especially since they had the job of educating children, to be patriotic. One women's magazine offered a prize to the woman who wrote the best essay on "How May an American Woman Best Show Her Patriotism."

The cult of domesticity for the woman was a way of pacifying her with a doctrine of "separate but equal"—giving her work equally as important as the man's, but separate and different. Inside that "equality" there was the fact that the woman did not choose her mate, and once her marriage took place, her life was determined. Marriage enchained, and children doubled the chains.

The "cult of true womanhood" could not completely erase what was visible as evidence of woman's subordinate status: she could not vote, could not own property; when she did work, her wages were one-fourth to one-half what men earned in the same job. Women were excluded from the professions of law and medicine, from colleges, from the ministry.

Putting all women into the same category—giving them all the same domestic sphere to cultivate—created a classification (by sex) that blurred the lines of class. However, forces were at work to keep raising the issue of class. Samuel Slater had introduced industrial spinning machinery in New England in 1789, and now there was a demand for young girls literally, "spinsters"—to work the spinning machinery in factories. In 1814, the power loom was introduced in Waltham, Massachusetts, and now all the operations needed to turn cotton fiber into cloth were under one roof. The new textile factories swiftly multiplied, with women 80 to 90 percent of their operatives—most of these women between fifteen and thirty.

Some of the earliest industrial strikes took place in these textile mills in the 1830s. Women's daily average earnings in 1836 were less than thirty-seven cents, and thousands earned twenty-five cents a day, working twelve to sixteen hours a day. In Pawtucket, Rhode Island, in 1824, came the first known strike of women factory workers; 202 women joined men in protesting a wage cut and longer hours, but they met separately. Four years later, women in Dover, New Hampshire, struck alone.

In Lowell, Massachusetts, in 1834, when a young woman was fired from her job, other girls left their looms, one of them then climbing the town pump and making, according to a newspaper report, "a flaming Mary Wollstonecraft speech on the rights of women and the iniquities of the 'moneyed aristocracy' which produced a powerful effect on her auditors and they determined to have their own way, if they died for it."

Several times in those strikes, women armed with sticks and stones broke through the wooden gates of a textile mill and stopped the looms.

Catharine Beecher, a woman reformer of the time, wrote about the factory system:

> I was there in mid-winter, and every morning I was awakened at five, by the bells calling to labor.... Then half an hour only allowed for dinner, from which the time for going and returning was deducted. Then back to the mills, to work till seven o'clock.... [I]t must be remembered that all the hours of labor are spent in rooms where oil lamps, together with

from 40 to 80 persons, are exhausting the healthful principle of the air...and where the air is loaded with particles of cotton thrown from thousands of cards, spindles, and looms.

And the life of upper-class women? Frances Trollope, an English-woman, wrote in her book *Domestic Manners of the Americans*:

Let me be permitted to describe the day of a Philadelphian lady of the first class.... She rises, and her first hour is spent in the scrupulously nice arrangement of her dress; she descends to her parlor, neat, stiff, and silent; her breakfast is brought in by her free black footman.... Twenty minutes before her carriage should appear, she retires to her chamber, as she calls it; shakes and folds up her still snow-white apron, smooths her rich dress, and...sets on her elegant bonnet...then walks downstairs, just at the moment that her free black coachman announces to her free black footman that the carriage waits. She steps into it, and gives the word: "Drive to the Dorcas Society."

At Lowell, the Female Labor Reform Association put out a series of "Factory Tracts." The first was entitled "Factory Life as It Is By an Operative" and spoke of the textile mill women as "nothing more nor less than slaves in every sense of the word! Slaves, to a system of labor which requires them to toil from five until seven o'clock, with one hour only to attend to the wants of nature—slaves to the will and requirements of the 'powers that be.'"

Around that time, the *New York Herald* carried a story about "700 females, generally of the most interesting state and appearance," meeting "in their endeavor to remedy the wrongs and oppressions under which they labor." The *Herald* editorialized: "we very much doubt whether it will terminate in much good to female labor of any description.... All combinations end in nothing."

Middle-class women, barred from higher education, began to monopolize the profession of primary-school teaching. As teachers, they read more, communicated more, and education itself became subversive of old ways of thinking. They began to write for magazines and newspapers, and started some ladies' publications. Literacy among women doubled between 1780 and 1840. Women became health reformers. They formed movements against double standards in sexual behavior and the victimization of prostitutes. They joined in religious organizations. Some of the most powerful of them joined the antislavery movement. So, by the time a clear feminist movement emerged in the 1840s, women had become practiced organizers, agitators, and speakers.

When Emma Willard addressed the New York legislature in 1819, she told them that the education of women "has been too exclusively directed to fit them for displaying to advantage the charms of youth and beauty." The problem, she said, was that "the taste of men, whatever it might happen to be, has been made into a standard for the formation of the female character." Reason and religion teach us, she said, that "we too are primary existences...not the satellites of men."

In 1821, Willard founded the Troy Female Seminary, the first recognized institution for the education of girls. She wrote later of how she upset people by teaching her students about the human body: "Mothers visiting a class at the Seminary in the early thirties were so shocked.... To preserve the modesty of the girls, and spare them too frequent agitation, heavy paper was pasted over the pages in their textbooks which depicted the human body."

Women struggled to enter the all-male professional schools. Elizabeth Blackwell got her medical degree in 1849, having overcome many rebuffs before being admitted to Geneva College. She then set up the New York Dispensary for Poor Women and Children "to give to poor women an opportunity of consulting physicians of their own sex." In her first annual report, she wrote:

> My first medical consultation was a curious experience. In a severe case of pneumonia in an elderly lady I called in consultation a kind-hearted physician of high standing.... This gentleman, after seeing the patient, went with me into the parlour. There he began to walk about the room in some agitation, exclaiming, "A most extraordinary case! Such a one never happened to me before; I really do not know what to do!" I listened in surprise and much perplexity, as it was a clear case of pneumonia and of no unusual degree of danger, until at last I discovered that his perplexity related to me, not to the patient, and to the propriety of consulting with a lady physician!

Oberlin College pioneered in the admission of women. But the first girl admitted to the theology school there, Antoinette Brown, who graduated in 1850, found that her name was left off the class list. With Lucy Stone, Oberlin found a formidable resister. She was active in the peace society and in antislavery work, taught colored students, and organized a debating club for girls. She was chosen to write the commencement address, then was told it would have to be read by a man. She refused to write it.

Lucy Stone began lecturing on women's rights in 1847 in a church in Gardner, Massachusetts, where her brother was a minister. She was tiny, weighed about one hundred pounds, was a marvelous speaker. As lecturer for the American Anti-Slavery Society, she was, at various times, deluged with cold water, sent reeling by a thrown book, and attacked by mobs.

When she married Henry Blackwell, they joined hands at their wedding and read a statement:

> ...we deem it a duty to declare that this act on our part implies no sanction of, nor promise of voluntary obedience to such of the present laws of marriage as refuse to recognize the wife as an independent, rational being, while they confer upon the husband an injurious and unnatural superiority....

She was one of the first to refuse to give up her name after marriage. She was "Mrs. Stone." When she refused to pay taxes because she was not represented in the government, officials took all her household goods in payment, even her baby's cradle.

After Amelia Bloomer, a postmistress in a small town in New York, developed the bloomer, women activists adopted it in place of the old whale-boned bodice, the corsets and petticoats. The Reverend John Todd (one of his many best-selling books gave advice to young men on the results of masturbation: "the mind is greatly deteriorated") commented on the new feminist mode of dress:

> Some have tried to become semi-men by putting on the Bloomer dress. Let me tell you in a word why it can never be done. It is this: woman, robed and folded in her long dress, is beautiful. She walks gracefully.... If she attempts to run, the charm is gone.... Take off the robes, and put on pants, and show the limbs, and grace and mystery are all gone.

Women, after becoming involved in other movements of reform—antislavery, temperance, dress styles, prison conditions—turned, emboldened and experienced, to their own situation. Angelina Grimké, a southern white woman who became a fierce speaker and organizer against slavery, saw that movement leading further:

> Let us all first wake up the nation to lift millions of slaves of both sexes from the dust, and turn them into men and then...it will be an easy matter to take millions of females from their knees and set them on their feet, or in other words transform them from babies into women.

Sarah Grimké, Angelina's sister, wrote:

During the early part of my life, my lot was cast among the butterflies of the fashionable world; and of this class of women, I am constrained to say, both from experience and observation, that their education is miserably deficient; that they are taught to regard marriage as the one thing needful, the only avenue to distinction....

She said:

All I ask of our brethren is that they will take their feet from off our necks, and permit us to stand upright on the ground which God has designed us to occupy.... To me it is perfectly clear that whatsoever it is morally right for a man to do, it is morally right for a woman to do.

Sarah could write with power; Angelina was the firebrand speaker. Once she spoke six nights in a row at the Boston Opera House. She was the first woman (in 1838) to address a committee of the Massachusetts state legislature on antislavery petitions. Her talk attracted a huge crowd, and a representative from Salem proposed that "a Committee be appointed to examine the foundations of the State House of Massachusetts to see whether it will bear another lecture from Miss Grimké!"

Speaking out on other issues prepared the way for speaking on the situation of women: Dorothea Dix, in 1843, addressed the legislature of Massachusetts on what she saw in the prisons and almshouses in the Boston area:

I tell what I have seen, painful and shocking as the details often are.... I proceed, gentlemen, briefly to call your attention to the present state of insane persons confined within this Commonwealth in cages, closets, cellars, stalls, pens; chained, naked, beaten with rods, and lashed into obedience!

Frances Wright was a writer, founder of a utopian community, immigrant from Scotland in 1824, a fighter for the emancipation of slaves and for birth control and sexual freedom. She wanted free public education for all children over two years of age in state-supported boarding schools. She expressed in America what the utopian socialist Charles Fourier had said in France, that the progress of civilization depended on the progress of women.

I shall venture the assertion, that, until women assume the place in society which good sense and good feeling alike assign to them, human improvement must advance but feebly.... men will ever rise or fall to the level of the other sex.... Until power is annihilated on one side, fear and obedience on the other, and both restored to their birthright—equality.

Women put in enormous work in antislavery societies all over the country, gathering thousands of petitions to Congress. In the course of this work, events were set in motion that carried the movement of women for their own equality racing alongside the movement against slavery. In 1840, a World Anti-Slavery Society Convention met in London. After a fierce argument, it was voted to exclude women, but it was agreed they could attend meetings in a curtained enclosure. The women sat in silent protest in the gallery, and William Lloyd Garrison, one abolitionist who had fought for the rights of women, sat with them.

It was at that time that Elizabeth Cady Stanton met Lucretia Mott and others, and began to lay the plans that led to the first Women's Rights Convention in history. It was held at Seneca Falls, New York, where Elizabeth Cady Stanton lived as a mother, a housewife, full of resentment at her condition, declaring: "A woman is a nobody. A wife is everything." She wrote later:

> My experiences at the World Anti-Slavery Convention, all I had read of the legal status of women, and the oppression I saw everywhere, together swept across my soul.... I could not see what to do or where to begin— my only thought was a public meeting for protest and discussion.

An announcement was put in the Seneca County Courier calling for a meeting to discuss the "rights of woman" the 19th and 20th of July. Three hundred women and some men came. A Declaration of Principles was signed at the end of the meeting by sixty-eight women and thirty-two men. It made use of the language and rhythm of the Declaration of Independence:

> When in the course of human events, it becomes necessary for one portion of the family of man to assume among the people of the earth a position different from that they have hitherto occupied...
>
> We hold these truths to be self-evident: that all men and women are created equal; that they are endowed by their Creator with certain inalienable rights; that among these are life, liberty and the pursuit of happiness....
>
> The history of mankind is a history of repeated injuries and usurpations on the part of man toward woman, having in direct object the establishment of an absolute tyranny over her. To prove this, let facts be submitted to a candid world....

Then came the list of grievances. And then a series of resolutions. Women's conventions in various parts of the country followed the one at Seneca Falls. At one of these, in 1851, an aged black woman, who had been born a slave in New York, tall, thin, wearing a gray dress and white turban, listened to some male ministers who had been dominating the discussion. This was Sojourner Truth. She rose to her feet and joined the indignation of her race to the indignation of her sex:

> That man over there says that woman needs to be helped into carriages and lifted over ditches.... Nobody ever helps me into carriages, or over mud-puddles or gives me any best place. And a'nt I a woman?
>
> Look at my arm! I have ploughed, and planted, and gathered into barns, and no man could head me! And a'nt I a woman?
>
> I would work as much and eat as much as a man, when I could get it, and bear the lash as well. And a'nt I a woman?
>
> I have borne thirteen children and seen em most all sold off to slavery, and when I cried out with my mother's grief, none but Jesus heard me! And a'nt I a woman?

Thus were women beginning to resist, in the 1830s and 1840s and 1850s, the attempt to keep them in their "woman's sphere." They were taking part in all sorts of movements, for prisoners, for the insane, for black slaves, and also for all women.

In the midst of these movements, there exploded, with the force of government and the authority of money, a quest for more land, an urge for national expansion.

Exercises

1. What effect does private property seem to have on the position of women in society?

2. How did European women manage to pay for their voyage to the American colonies?

3. How did masters exercise their control over female servants and slaves? How did husbands exercise control over their wives?

4. Was it better for a woman to be married or single in colonial America?

5. What was a fundamental obstacle preventing women from rebelling against their subordinate status?

6. Why was Anne Hutchinson banished from the Massachusetts Bay Colony?

7. Why was Mary Dyer hanged?

8. What role did American women play during the American Revolution?

9. What was Abigail Adams's argument in favor of giving women the vote? To whom did she make this argument?

10. What might one of Thomas Jefferson's reasons have been for excluding women from politics?

11. In the periods before, during, and after the American Revolution, what factors caused some women to demand greater rights for themselves (or their sex)?

12. Why would women editors of a women's magazine write a story discrediting the wearing of bloomers?

13. How did the proponents of the Cult of Domesticity (or the Cult of Womanhood) argue that the women's sphere was separate but equal? One aspect of the "Cult" defined the role of women as being as responsible for the moral fabric of her family. How might a middle class woman have used the ideology of being responsible for the moral fabric of her family to justify her involvement, outside the home, in the reform movements—abolition, peace, communitarianism, education, temperance?

14. What is the origin of the word "spinster"?

15. What evidence does Zinn provide to indicate that single women were perhaps lured to the factory by attractive wages and conditions only to see those wages and conditions deteriorate?

16. Did the emergence of an idle, educated, middle-class female population in the midst of politically charged reform movements lead to the first organized feminist movement? Explain your answer.

17. Why did middle-class women activists gravitate to the reform movements (antislavery, temperance, dress styles, prison conditions, peace, education, communitarianism)? How were the reform movements excellent training grounds from which to promote and pursue a women's rights movement?

18. Why was the World Anti-Slavery Society Convention of 1840 the birthplace of the women's rights movement?

19. Take a standard American history text and compare its treatment of the following points with the Zinn's teatment of them in this chapter. (If the traditional text does not address one of the points below, speculate as to why the text excluded it.)

    a. means by which women came to colonial America

    b. the unique experiences of indentured women (as distinct from indentured men)

    c. the different legal status of single and married women in colonial America

    d. the significance of Anne Hutchinson's story

    e. the role of women in the American Revolution

    f. Abigail Adams

    g. women's magazines

    h. "cult of true womanhood" ("cult of domesticity")

    i. the reasons why women became mill workers

    j. the experiences of women mill workers in the 1830s and 1840s

    k. Frances Wright

    l. Emma Willard

    m. Elizabeth Blackwell

    n. Lucy Stone, Lucretia Mott, Elizabeth Cady Stanton

    o. Sojourner Truth

    p. Sarah and Angelina Grimké

    q. Seneca Falls

What points does your chosen traditional text make about women (1619–1848) that Zinn leaves out?

Chapter 7

As Long as Grass Grows
or Water Runs

If women, of all the subordinate groups in a society dominated by rich white males, were closest to home (indeed, *in* the home), the most interior, then the Indians were the most foreign, the most exterior. Women, because they were so near and so needed, were dealt with more by patronization than by force. The Indian, not needed—indeed, an obstacle—could be dealt with by sheer force, except that sometimes the language of paternalism preceded the burning of villages.

And so, "Indian removal," as it has been politely called, cleared the land for white occupancy between the Appalachians and the Mississippi, cleared it for cotton in the South and grain in the North, for expansion, immigration, canals, railroads, new cities, and the building of a huge continental empire clear across to the Pacific Ocean. The cost in human life cannot be accurately measured, in suffering not even roughly measured. Most of the history books given to children pass quickly over it.

In the Revolutionary War, almost every important Indian nation fought on the side of the British. They knew that if the British, who had set a limit on the colonists' expansion westward, lost the war, there would be no holding back the Americans. Indeed, by the time Jefferson became president in 1800, there were 700,000 white settlers west of the mountains. Jefferson now committed the federal government to promote future removal of the Creek and the Cherokee from Georgia. Aggressive activity against the Indians mounted in the Indiana Territory under Gov. William Henry Harrison.

When Jefferson doubled the size of the nation by purchasing the Louisiana Territory from France in 1803—thus extending the western frontier from the Appalachians across the Mississippi to the Rocky Mountains—he proposed to Congress that Indians should be encouraged to settle down on smaller tracts and do farming. "Two measures are deemed expedient. First to encourage them to abandon hunting.... Secondly, to Multiply trading houses among them...leading them thus to agriculture, to manufactures, and civilization...."

Jefferson's talk of "agriculture... manufactures... civilization" is crucial. Indian removal was necessary for the opening of the vast American lands to agriculture, to commerce, to markets, to money, to the development of the modern capitalist economy. Land was indispensable for all this, and after the Revolution, huge tracts of land were bought up by rich speculators, including George Washington and Patrick Henry. John Donelson, a North Carolina surveyor, ended up with twenty thousand acres of land near what is now Chattanooga. His son-in-law made twenty-two trips out of Nashville in 1795 for land deals. This was Andrew Jackson.

Jackson was a land speculator, merchant, slave trader, and the most aggressive enemy of the Indians in early American history. He became a hero of the War of 1812, which was not (as often depicted in American textbooks) just a war against England for survival, but a war for the expansion of the new nation, into Florida, into Canada, into Indian territory.

Tecumseh, a Shawnee chief and noted orator, tried to unite the Indians against the white invasion. "The land," he said, "belongs to all, for the use of each...." Angered when fellow Indians were induced to cede a great tract of land to the United States government, in 1811 Tecumseh organized an Indian gathering of five thousand, on the bank of the Tallapoosa River in Alabama, and told them: "Let the white race perish. They seize your land; they corrupt your women, they trample on the ashes of your dead! Back whence they came, upon a trail of blood, they must be driven."

The Creek Indians occupied most of Georgia, Alabama, and Mississippi. In 1813 some of their warriors massacred 250 people at Fort Mims, whereupon Jackson's troops burned down a Creek village, killing men, women, children. Jackson established the tactic of promising rewards in land and plunder.

But among Jackson's men there were mutinies. They were tired of fighting and wanted to go home. Jackson wrote to his wife about "the once brave and patriotic volunteers...sunk...to mere whining, complaining, seditioners and mutineers...." When a seventeen-year-old soldier who had refused to clean up his food and threatened his officer with a gun was sentenced to death by a court-martial, Jackson turned down his plea and ordered the execution to proceed. He then walked out of earshot of the firing squad.

Jackson became a national hero when in 1814 he fought the Battle of Horseshoe Bend against a thousand Creeks and killed eight hundred of them, with few casualties on his side. His white troops had failed in a frontal attack on the Creeks, but the Cherokees with him, promised governmental friendship if they joined the war, swam the river, came up behind the Creeks, and won the battle for Jackson.

When the war ended, Jackson and friends of his began buying up the seized Creek lands. He got himself appointed treaty commissioner and dictated a treaty in 1814 which took away half the land of the Creek nation.

This treaty started something new and important. It granted Indians individual ownership of land, thus splitting Indian from Indian, breaking up communal landholding, bribing some with land, leaving others out—introducing the competition and conniving that marked the spirit of Western capitalism. It fitted well the old Jeffersonian idea of how to handle the Indians, by bringing them into "civilization."

From 1814 to 1824, in a series of treaties with the southern Indians, whites took over three-fourths of Alabama and Florida, one-third of Tennessee, one-fifth of Georgia and Mississippi, and parts of Kentucky and North Carolina. Jackson played a key role in those treaties, using bribery, deception, and force to get more and more land, and giving jobs to his friends and relatives.

These treaties, these land grabs, laid the basis for the cotton kingdom, the slave plantations. Jackson's work had brought the white settlements to the border of Florida, owned by Spain. Here were the villages of the Seminole Indians, where some escaped black slaves were taking refuge. Jackson began raids into Florida, arguing it was a sanctuary for escaped slaves and for marauding Indians. Florida, he said, was essential to the defense of the United States. It was that classic modern preface to a war of conquest.

Thus began the Seminole War of 1818, leading to the American acquisition of Florida. It appears on classroom maps politely as "Florida Purchase, 1819," but it came from Andrew Jackson's military campaign across the Florida border, burning Seminole villages, seizing Spanish forts, until Spain was "persuaded" to sell. He acted, he said, by the "immutable laws of self-defense."

Jackson then became governor of the Florida Territory. He was able now to give good business advice to friends and relatives. To a nephew, he suggested holding on to property in Pensacola. To a friend, a surgeon-general in the army, he suggested buying as many slaves as possible, because the price would soon rise.

Leaving his military post, he also gave advice to officers on how to deal with the high rate of desertion. (Poor whites—even if willing to give their lives at first—may have discovered the rewards of battle going to the rich.) Jackson suggested whipping for the first two attempts, and the third time, execution.

If you look through high school textbooks and elementary school textbooks in American history you will find Jackson the frontiersman, soldier, democrat, man of the people—not Jackson the slaveholder, land speculator, executioner of dissident soldiers, exterminator of Indians.

After Jackson was elected president in 1828 (following John Quincy Adams, who had followed Monroe, who had followed Madison, who had followed Jefferson), the two political parties were the Democrats and Whigs, who disagreed on banks and tariffs, but not on issues crucial for the white poor, the blacks, the Indians—although some white working people saw Jackson as their hero, because he opposed the rich man's bank.

Under Jackson, and the man he chose to succeed him, Martin Van Buren, seventy thousand Indians east of the Mississippi were forced westward. In New York, the Iroquois Confederation stayed. But the Sac and Fox Indians of Illinois were removed, after the Black Hawk War. When Chief Black Hawk was defeated and captured in 1832, he made a surrender speech:

> [Black Hawk] is now a prisoner to the white men.... He has done nothing for which an Indian ought to be ashamed. He has fought for his countrymen, the squaws and papooses, against white men, who came year after year, to cheat them and take away their lands.... The white men are bad schoolmasters; they carry false books, and deal in false actions; they smile in the face of the poor Indian to cheat him; they shake them by the hand to gain their confidence, to make them drunk, to deceive them, and ruin our wives....
>
> The white men do not scalp the head; but they do worse—they poison the heart.... Farewell, my nation!... Farewell to Black Hawk.

The removal of the Indians was explained by Lewis Cass, who served variously as secretary of war, governor of the Michigan Territory, minister to France, and a presidential candidate:

> A principle of progressive improvement seems almost inherent in human nature.... We are all striving in the career of life to acquire riches

of honor, or power, or some other object, whose possession is to realize the day dreams of our imaginations; and the aggregate of these efforts constitutes the advance of society. But there is little of this in the constitution of our savages.

Cass, pompous, pretentious, honored (Harvard gave him an honorary doctor of laws degree in 1836, at the height of Indian removal), took millions of acres from the Indians by treaty when he was governor of the Michigan Territory: "We must frequently promote their interest against their inclination.... A barbarous people, depending for subsistence upon the scanty and precarious supplies furnished by the chase, cannot live in contact with a civilized community."

If the Indians would only move to new lands across the Mississippi, Cass promised in 1825 at a treaty council with Shawnees and Cherokees, "The United States will never ask for your land there. This I promise you in the name of your great father, the President. That country he assigns to his red people, to be held by them and their children's children forever."

Everything in the Indian heritage spoke out against leaving their land. An old Choctaw chief said, responding, years before, to President Monroe's talk of removal: "I am sorry I cannot comply with the request of my father.... We wish to remain here, where we have grown up as the herbs of the woods; and do not wish to be transplanted into another soil." A Seminole chief had said to John Quincy Adams: "Here our navel strings were first cut and the blood from them sunk into the earth, and made the country dear to us."

Not all the Indians responded to the white officials' common designation of them as "children" and the president as "father." It was reported that when Tecumseh met with William Henry Harrison, Indian fighter and future president, the interpreter said: "Your father requests you to take a chair." Tecumseh replied: "My father! The sun is my father, and the earth is my mother; I will repose upon her bosom."

As soon as Jackson was elected president, Georgia, Alabama, and Mississippi began to pass laws to extend the states' rule over the Indians in their territory. Indian land was divided up, to be distributed by state lottery. Federal treaties and federal laws gave Congress, not the states, authority over the tribes. Jackson ignored this, and supported state action.

He had now found the right tactic. The Indians would not be "forced" to go west. But if they chose to stay they would have to abide by state laws, which destroyed their tribal and personal rights and made them subject to endless harassment and invasion by white settlers coveting their land. If they left, however, the federal government would give them financial support and promise them lands beyond the Mississippi. Jackson's instructions to an army major sent to talk to the Choctaws and Cherokees put it this way:

> Say to the chiefs and warriors that I am their friend...but they must, by removing from the limits of the States of Mississippi and Alabama and by being settled on the lands I offer them, put it in my power to be such—There, beyond the limits of any State, in possession of land of their own, which they shall possess as long as Grass grows or water runs. I am and will protect them and be their friend and father.

That phrase "as long as Grass grows or water runs" was to be recalled with bitterness by generations of Indians. (An Indian GI, veteran of Vietnam, testifying publicly in 1970 not only about the horror of the war but about his own maltreatment as an Indian, repeated that phrase and began to weep.)

As Jackson took office in 1829, gold was discovered in Cherokee territory in Georgia. Thousands of whites invaded, destroyed Indian property, staked out claims. Jackson ordered federal troops to remove them, but also ordered Indians as well as whites to stop mining. Then he removed the troops, the whites returned, and Jackson said he could not interfere with Georgia's authority. The white invaders seized land and stock, forced Indians to sign leases, beat up Indians who protested, sold alcohol to weaken resistance, and killed game that Indians needed for food.

Treaties made under pressure and by deception broke up Creek, Choctaw, and Chickasaw tribal lands into individual holdings, making each person a prey to contractors, speculators, and politicians. The Creeks and Choctaws remained on their individual plots, but great numbers of them were defrauded by land companies. According to one Georgia bank president, a stockholder in a land company, "Stealing is the order of the day."

The Creeks, defrauded of their land, short of money and food, refused to go west. Starving Creeks began raiding white farms, while Georgia militia and settlers attacked Indian settlements. Thus began the Second Creek War. One Alabama newspaper sympathetic to the Indians wrote: "The war with the Creeks is all humbug. It is a base and diabolical scheme, devised by interested men, to keep an ignorant race of people from maintaining their just rights, and to deprive them of the small remaining pittance placed under their control."

A Creek man more than a hundred years old, named Speckled Snake, reacted to Andrew Jackson's policy of removal:

Brothers! I have listened to many talks from our great white father. When he first came over the wide waters, he was but a little man...very little. His legs were cramped by sitting long in his big boat, and he begged for a little land to light his fire on.... But when the white man had warmed himself before the Indians' fire and filled himself with their hominy, he became very large. With a step he bestrode the mountains, and his feet covered the plains and the valleys. His hand grasped the eastern and the western sea, and his head rested on the moon. Then he became our Great Father. He loved his red children, and he said, "Get a little further, lest I tread on thee."

Dale Van Every, in his book *The Disinherited*, sums up what removal meant to the Indian:

The Indian was peculiarly susceptible to every sensory attribute of every natural feature of his surroundings. He lived in the open. He knew every marsh, glade, hill top, rock, spring, creek, as only the hunter can know them. He had never fully grasped the principle establishing private ownership of land as any more rational than private ownership of air but he loved the land with a deeper emotion than could any proprietor. He felt himself as much a part of it as the rocks and trees, the animals and birds. His homeland was holy ground, sanctified for him as the resting place of the bones of his ancestors and the natural shrine of his religion.

Just before Jackson became president, in the 1820s, after the tumult of the War of 1812 and the Creek War, the southern Indians and the whites had settled down, often very close to one another, and were living in peace in a natural environment that seemed to have enough for all of them. White men were allowed to visit the Indian communities and Indians often were guests in white homes. Frontier figures like Davy Crockett and Sam Houston came out of this setting, and both—unlike Jackson—became lifelong friends of the Indian.

The forces that led to removal did not come from the poor white frontiersmen who were neighbors of the Indians. They came from industrialization and commerce, the growth of populations, of railroads and cities, the rise in value of land, and the greed of businessmen. The Indians were to end up dead or exiled, the land speculators richer, the politicians more powerful. As for the poor white frontiersman, he played the part of a pawn, pushed into the first violent encounters, but soon dispensable.

With 17,000 Cherokees surrounded by 900,000 whites in Georgia, Alabama, and Tennessee, the Cherokees decided that survival required adaptation to the white man's world. They became farmers, blacksmiths, carpenters, masons, owners of property.

The Cherokees' language—heavily poetic, metaphorical, beautifully expressive, supplemented by dance, drama, and ritual—had always been a language of voice and gesture. Now their chief, Sequoyah, invented a written language, which thousands learned. The Cherokees' newly established Legislative Council voted money for a printing press, which on February 21, 1828, began publishing a newspaper, the *Cherokee Phoenix*, printed in both English and Sequoyah's Cherokee.

Before this, the Cherokees had, like Indian tribes in general, done without formal government. As Van Every puts it:

> The foundation principle of Indian government had always been the rejection of government. The freedom of the individual was regarded by practically all Indians north of Mexico as a canon infinitely more precious than the individual's duty to his community or nation. This anarchistic attitude ruled all behavior, beginning with the smallest social unit, the family. The Indian parent was constitutionally reluctant to discipline his children. Their every exhibition of self-will was accepted as a favorable indication of the development of maturing character....

There was an occasional assembling of a council, with a very loose and changing membership, whose decisions were not enforced except by the influence of public opinion. Now, surrounded by white society, all this began to change. The Cherokees even started to emulate the slave society around them: they owned more than a thousand slaves. They were beginning to resemble that "civilization" the white men spoke about. They even welcomed missionaries and Christianity. None of this made them more desirable than the land they lived on.

Jackson's 1829 message to Congress made his position clear: "I informed the Indians inhabiting parts of Georgia and Alabama that their attempt to establish an independent government would not be countenanced by the Executive of the United States, and advised them to emigrate beyond the Mississippi or submit to the laws of those States." Congress moved quickly to pass a removal bill. It did not mention force, but provided for helping the Indians to move. What it implied was that if they did not, they were without protection, without funds, and at the mercy of the states.

There were defenders of the Indians. Perhaps the most eloquent was Sen. Theodore Frelinghuysen of New Jersey, who told the Senate, debating removal: "We have crowded the tribes upon a few miserable acres on our southern frontier; it is all that is left to them of their once boundless forest: and still, like the horse-leech, our insatiated cupidity cries, give! give!... Sir...Do the obligations of justice change with the color of the skin?"

Now the pressures began on the tribes, one by one. The Choctaws did not want to leave, but fifty of their delegates were offered secret bribes of money and land, and the Treaty of Dancing Rabbit Creek was signed: Choctaw land east of the Mississippi was ceded to the United States in return for financial help in leaving. Whites, including liquor dealers and swindlers, came swarming onto their lands.

In late 1831, thirteen thousand Choctaws began the long journey west to a land and climate totally different from what they knew. They went on ox wagons, on horses, on foot, then to be ferried across the Mississippi River. The army was supposed to organize their trek but there was chaos. Food disappeared. Hunger came.

The first winter migration was one of the coldest on record, and people began to die of pneumonia. In the summer, a major cholera epidemic hit Mississippi, and Choctaws died by the hundreds. The seven thousand Choctaws left behind now refused to go, choosing subjugation over death. Many of their descendants still live in Mississippi.

As for the Cherokees, they faced a set of laws passed by Georgia: their lands were taken, their government abolished, all meetings prohibited. Cherokees advising others not to migrate were to be imprisoned. Cherokees could not testify in court against any white. Cherokees could not dig for the gold recently discovered on their land.

The Cherokee nation addressed a memorial to the nation, a public plea for justice:

> We are aware that some persons suppose it will be for our advantage to remove beyond the Mississippi. We think otherwise. Our people universally think otherwise.... We wish to remain on the land of our fathers.... The treaties with us, and laws of the United States made in pursuance of treaties, guarantee our residence and our privileges, and secure us against intruders. Our only request is, that these treaties may be fulfilled, and these laws executed....

Now they went beyond history, beyond law:

> We intreat those to whom the foregoing paragraphs are addressed, to remember the great law of love. "Do to others as ye would that others should do to you."...We pray them to remember that, for the sake of principle, their forefathers were compelled to leave, therefore driven from the old world, and that the winds of persecution wafted them over

the great waters and landed them on the shores of the new world, when the Indian was the sole lord and proprietor of these extensive domains— Let them remember in what way they were received by the savage of America, when power was in his hand.... Let them bring to remembrance all these facts, and they cannot, and we are sure, they will not fail to remember, and sympathize with us in these our trials and sufferings.

Jackson's response to this, in his second annual message to Congress in December 1830, was to point to the fact that the Choctaws and Chickasaws had already agreed to removal, and that "a speedy removal" of the rest would offer many advantages to everyone. He reiterated a familiar theme. "Toward the aborigines of the country no one can indulge a more friendly feeling than myself...." However: "The waves of population and civilization are rolling to the westward, and we now propose to acquire the countries occupied by the red men of the South and West by a fair exchange...."

Georgia passed a law making it a crime for a white person to stay in Indian territory without taking an oath to the state of Georgia. When the white missionaries in the Cherokee territory declared their sympathies openly for the Cherokees to stay, Georgia militia entered the territory in the spring of 1831 and arrested three of the missionaries, including Samuel Worcester. Refusing to swear allegiance to Georgia's laws, Worcester and Elizar Butler were sentenced to four years at hard labor. The Supreme Court ordered Worcester freed, but President Jackson refused to enforce the court order.

Jackson, reelected in 1832, now moved to speed up Indian removal. Most of the Choctaws and some of the Cherokees were gone, but there were still 22,000 Creeks in Alabama, 18,000 Cherokees in Georgia, and 5,000 Seminoles in Florida.

The Creeks had been fighting for their land ever since the years of Columbus, against Spaniards, English, French, and Americans. But by 1832 they had been reduced to a small area in Alabama, while the population of Alabama, growing fast, was now over 300,000. On the basis of extravagant promises from the federal government, Creek delegates in Washington signed the Treaty of Washington, agreeing to removal beyond the Mississippi. They gave up five million acres, with the provision that two million of these would go to individual Creeks, who could either sell or remain in Alabama with federal protection.

Almost immediately, the promises made in the treaty were broken. A white invasion of Creek lands began—looters, land seekers, defrauders, whiskey sellers, thugs—driving thousands of Creeks from their homes into the swamps and forests. The federal government did nothing. Instead it negotiated a new treaty providing for prompt emigration west, managed by the Creeks themselves, financed by the national government. An army colonel, dubious that this would work, wrote:

> They fear starvation on the route; and can it be otherwise, when many of them are nearly starving now.... You cannot have an idea of the deterioration which these Indians have undergone during the last two or three years, from a general state of comparative plenty to that of unqualified wretchedness and want.... They are brow beat, and cowed, and imposed upon, and depressed with the feeling that they have no adequate protection in the United States, and no capacity of self-protection in themselves.

Despite the hardships, the Creeks refused to budge, but by 1836, both state and federal officials decided they must go. Using as a pretext some attacks by desperate Creeks on white settlers, it was declared that the Creek nation, by making "war," had forfeited its treaty rights.

The army would now force it to migrate west. An army of eleven thousand was sent after them. The Creeks did not resist, no shots were fired, they surrendered. Those Creeks presumed by the army to be rebels or sympathizers were assembled, the men manacled and chained together to march westward under military guard, their women and children trailing after them. Creek communities were invaded by military detachments, the inhabitants driven to assembly points and marched westward in batches of two or three thousand. No talk of compensating them for land or property left behind.

Private contracts were made for the march, the same kind that had failed for the Choctaws. Again, delays and lack of food, shelter, clothing, blankets, medical attention. Again, old, rotting steamboats and ferries, crowded beyond capacity, taking them across the Mississippi. Starvation and sickness began to cause large numbers of deaths.

Eight hundred Creek men had volunteered to help the United States army fight the Seminoles in Florida in return for a promise that their families could remain in Alabama, protected by the federal government until the men returned. The promise was not kept. The Creek families were attacked by land-hungry white marauders—robbed, driven from their homes, women raped. Then the army, claiming it was for their safety, removed them from Creek country to a concentration camp on Mobile Bay. Hundreds died there from lack of food and from sickness.

When the warriors returned from the Seminole War, they and their families were hustled west. Moving through New Orleans, they encountered a yellow fever plague. They crossed the Mississippi—611 Indians crowded onto the aged steamer *Monmouth*. It went down in the Mississippi River and 311 people died, four of them the children of the Indian commander of the Creek volunteers in Florida.

The Choctaws and Chickasaws had quickly agreed to migrate. The Creeks were stubborn and had to be forced. The Cherokees were practicing a nonviolent resistance. One tribe—the Seminoles—decided to fight.

With Florida now belonging to the United States, Seminole territory was open to American land grabbers. In 1834 Seminole leaders were assembled and the U.S. Indian agent told them they must move west. The Seminoles replied:

> We were all made by the same Great Father, and are all alike His Children. We all came from the same Mother, and were suckled at the same breast. Therefore, we are brothers, and as brothers, should treat together in an amicable way.... If suddenly we tear our hearts from the homes around which they are twined, our heart-strings will snap.

When, in December 1835, the Seminoles were ordered to assemble for the journey, no one came. Instead, the Seminoles began a series of guerrilla attacks on white coastal settlements, all along the Florida perimeter, striking in surprise and in succession from the interior. They murdered white families, captured slaves, destroyed property.

One December day in 1835, a column of 110 soldiers was attacked by Seminoles, and all but three soldiers were killed. One of the survivors later told the story:

> It was 8 o'clock. Suddenly I heard a rifle shot...followed by a musket shot.... I had not time to think of the meaning of these shots, before a volley, as if from a thousand rifles, was poured in upon us from the front, and all along our left flank.... I could only see their heads and arms, peering out from the long grass, far and near, and from behind the pine trees....

It was the classic Indian tactic against a foe with superior firearms. Gen. George Washington had once given parting advice to one of his officers: "General St. Clair, in three words, beware of surprise.... [A]gain and again, General, beware of surprise."

Congress now appropriated money for a war against the Seminoles. Gen. Winfield Scott took charge, but his columns of troops, marching impressively into Seminole territory, found no one. They became tired of the mud, the swamps, the heat, the sickness, the hunger—the classic fatigue of a civilized army fighting people on their own land. In 1836, 103 commissioned officers resigned from the regular army, leaving only forty-six.

It was an eight-year war. It cost $20 million and 1,500 American lives. Finally, in the 1840s, the Seminoles began to get tired. They were a tiny group against a huge nation with great resources. They asked for truces. But when they went forward under truce flags, they were arrested, again and again. In 1837, their leader Osceola, under a flag of truce, had been seized and put in irons, then died of illness in prison. The war petered out.

Meanwhile the Cherokees had not fought back with arms, but had resisted in their own way. And so the government began to play Cherokee against Cherokee, the old game. The pressures built up on the Cherokee community—their newspaper suppressed, their government dissolved, the missionaries in jail, their land parceled among whites by the land lottery. In 1834, seven hundred Cherokees, weary of the struggle, agreed to go west; eighty-one died en route, including forty-five children—mostly from measles and cholera. Those who lived arrived at their destination across the Mississippi in the midst of a cholera epidemic and half of them died within a year. Now the Georgia whites stepped up their attacks to speed the removal.

In April 1838, Ralph Waldo Emerson addressed an open letter to President Van Buren, referring with indignation to the removal treaty with the Cherokees (signed behind the backs of an overwhelming majority of them) and asked what had happened to the sense of justice in America: "You, sir, will bring down that renowned chair in which you sit into infamy if your seal is set to this instrument of perfidy; and the name of this nation, hitherto the sweet omen of religion and liberty, will stink to the world."

Thirteen days before Emerson sent this letter, Martin Van Buren had ordered Maj. Gen. Winfield Scott into Cherokee territory to use whatever military force was required to move the Cherokees west. Five regiments of regulars and four thousand militia and volunteers began pouring into Cherokee country.

Some Cherokees had apparently given up on nonviolence: three chiefs who signed the Removal Treaty were found dead. But the seventeen thousand Cherokees were soon rounded up and crowded into stockades. On October 1, 1838, the first detachment set out in what was to be known as the Trail of Tears. As they moved westward, they began to die—of sickness, of drought, of the heat, of exposure. There were 645 wagons, and people marching alongside. Survivors, years later, told of halting at the edge of the Mississippi in the middle of winter, the river running full of ice, "hundreds of sick and dying penned up in wagons or stretched upon the ground." During confinement in the stockade or on the march westward four thousand Cherokees died.

In December 1838, President Van Buren spoke to Congress:

> It affords sincere pleasure to apprise the Congress of the entire removal of the Cherokee Nation of Indians to their new homes west of the Mississippi. The measures authorized by Congress at its last session have had the happiest effects.

Exercises

1. Why did almost every important Indian nation fight on the side of the British during the American Revolutionary War?

2. What was Jefferson's policy toward the Indians?

3. What prompted Tecumseh's rebellion?

4. How was the Battle of Horseshoe Bend won?

5. Why would demanding that Indians own private property make them more vulnerable to losing their land than if they continued to use the land in common?

6. What reasons did Jackson give to explain his invasion of Spanish-owned Florida? What resulted from the Seminole War of 1818?

7. How did President Jackson's Indian policy compare (in practice, rationale, and effect) to his predecessors'?

8. How did Jackson act unconstitutionally?

9. What caused the outbreak of the Second Creek War?

10. How did Speckled Snake describe the history of European-Indian relations? Do you agree with his synopsis? If not, how would you alter it?

11. If you went up to a Creek or Cherokee in the 1830s and asked if you could buy some of his or her land, what would he or she say to you?

12. Is there any parallel between Bacon's Rebellion and the Indian Wars preceeding the War of 1812 with respect to the dynamics among Indians, poor whites, and rich whites? If so, explain how the situations are parallel. If not, what factors are different enough so that there is no structural parallel?

13. What strategy(ies) did the Cherokees adopt to fight removal?

14. What position did Senator Frelinghuysen take regarding Indian removal? What action did Ralph Waldo Emerson take to oppose the removal of the Cherokees? Does Frelinghuysen remind you of Bartolomé de las Casas (chapter 1)? Why or why not? Does the existence of ineffective white opposition to Indian removal indicate that white Americans were swept away by historical forces? Why or why not?

15. What happened to the Choctaws after they signed their treaty of removal? Were the terms of the Treaty of Dancing Rabbit Creek observed by both sides?

16. Why did the Georgia militia arrest Sam Worcester and Elizar Butler? Were the actions of the militia consistent with the Supreme Court's interpretation of the U.S. Constitution? Why did it not matter whether the Supreme Court ruled in favor of or against the Cherokees?

17. By 1832, how long had the Creeks been defending their lands against the Europeans?

18. Place the following events in the order in which they usually happened:

   a. Indians appeal to federal government to enforce treaty that protected the integrity of Indian land.

   b. White settlers encroach on/invade Indian land.

   c. Federal government does nothing.

   d. On Indian land (by federal treaty) whites and Indians attack each other.

   e. Federal government orders Indians to move farther west.

   f. [Are any steps missing?]

   Why did this process repeat itself over and over again?

19. What were the conditions under which the Creeks moved west?

20. How did the Seminoles resist removal? How effective was the Seminole form of resistance?

21. If the Cherokee removal was so dreadful that it was to be known as the Trail of Tears, why did Van Buren feel that it had the "happiest effects?"

22. *Draw a map* that includes the following: Appalachians, Mississippi River, Rocky Mountains, Florida Territory, Tallapoosa River in Alabama, the state borders of Georgia, Mississippi, and Alabama, the location of the Battle of Horshoe Bend, the Trail of Tears.

23. *Debate Resolution*: Andrew Jackson's Indian policy represented a fundamental change from the Indian policies of previous U.S. presidents.

Chapter 8

We Take Nothing by Conquest, Thank God

Col. Ethan Allen Hitchcock, a professional soldier, graduate of the Military Academy, commander of the Third Infantry Regiment, a reader of Shakespeare, Chaucer, Hegel, Spinoza, wrote in his diary:

> Fort Jesup, La., June 30, 1845. Orders came last evening by express from Washington City directing General Taylor to move without any delay to...take up a position on the banks of or near the Rio Grande, and he is to expel any armed force of Mexicans who may cross that river. Bliss read the orders to me last evening hastily at tattoo. I have scarcely slept a wink, thinking of the needful preparations.... Violence leads to violence, and if this movement of ours does not lead to others and to bloodshed, I am much mistaken.

Hitchcock was not mistaken. Jefferson's Louisiana Purchase had doubled the territory of the United States, extending it to the Rocky Mountains. To the southwest was Mexico, which had won its independence in a revolutionary war against Spain in 1821. Mexico was then an even larger country than it is now, since it included what are now Texas, New Mexico, Utah, Nevada, Arizona, California, and part of Colorado. After agitation, and aid from the United States, Texas broke off from Mexico in 1836 and declared itself the "Lone Star Republic." In 1845, the U.S. Congress brought it into the Union as a state.

In the White House now was James Polk, a Democrat, an expansionist, who, on the night of his inauguration, confided to his secretary of the navy that one of his main objectives was the acquisition of California. His order to General Taylor to move troops to the Rio Grande was a challenge to the Mexicans. It was not at all clear that the Rio Grande was the southern boundary of Texas, although Texas had forced the defeated Mexican general Santa Anna to say so when he was a prisoner. The traditional border between Texas and Mexico had been the Nueces River, about 150 miles to the north, and both Mexico and the United States had recognized that as the border. However, Polk, encouraging the Texans to accept annexation, had assured them he would uphold their claims to the Rio Grande.

Ordering troops to the Rio Grande, into territory inhabited by Mexicans, was clearly a provocation. Taylor's army marched in parallel columns across the open prairie, scouts far ahead and on the flanks, a train of supplies following. Then, along a narrow road, through a belt of thick chaparral, they arrived, March 28, 1846, in cultivated fields and thatched-roof huts hurriedly abandoned by the Mexican occupants, who had fled across the river to the city of Matamoros. Taylor set up camp, began construction of a fort, and implanted his cannons facing the white houses of Matamoros, whose inhabitants stared curiously at the sight of an army on the banks of a quiet river.

The *Washington Union*, a newspaper expressing the position of President Polk and the Democratic party, had spoken early in 1845 on the meaning of Texas annexation: "Let the great measure of annexation be accomplished, and with it the questions of boundary and claims. For who can arrest the torrent that will pour onward to the West? The road to California will be open to us. Who will stay the march of our western people?"

It was shortly after that, in the summer of 1845, that John O'Sullivan, editor of the *Democratic Review*, used the phrase that became famous, saying it was "Our manifest destiny to overspread the continent allotted by Providence for the free development of our yearly multiplying millions." Yes, manifest destiny.

All that was needed in the spring of 1846 was a military incident to begin the war that Polk wanted. It came in April, when General Taylor's quartermaster, Colonel Cross, while riding up the Rio Grande, disappeared. His body was found eleven days later, his skull smashed by a heavy blow. It was assumed he had been killed by Mexican guerrillas crossing the river.

The next day (April 25), a patrol of Taylor's soldiers was surrounded and attacked by Mexicans, and wiped out: sixteen dead, others wounded, the rest captured. Taylor sent a dispatch to Polk: "Hostilities may now be considered as commenced."

The Mexicans had fired the first shot. But they had done what the American government wanted, according to Colonel Hitchcock, who wrote in his diary, even before those first incidents:

> I have said from the first that the United States are the aggressors.... We have not one particle of right to be here.... It looks as if the government sent a small force on purpose to bring on a war, so as to have a pretext for taking California and as much of this country as it chooses.... My heart is not in this business...but, as a military man, I am bound to execute orders.

On May 9, before news of any battles, Polk was suggesting to his cabinet a declaration of war. Polk recorded in his diary what he said to the cabinet meeting:

> I stated...that up to this time, as we knew, we had heard of no open act of aggression by the Mexican army, but that the danger was imminent that such acts would be committed. I said that in my opinion we had ample cause of war, and that it was impossible...that I could remain silent much longer...that the country was excited and impatient on the subject....

The country was not "excited and impatient." But the president was. When the dispatches arrived from General Taylor telling of casualties from the Mexican attack, Polk summoned the cabinet to hear the news, and they unanimously agreed he should ask for a declaration of war. Polk's message to Congress was indignant: "Mexico has passed the boundary of the United States, has invaded our territory and shed American blood upon the American soil...."

Congress then rushed to approve the war message. The bundles of official documents accompanying the war message, supposed to be evidence for Polk's statement, were not examined, but were tabled immediately by the House. Debate on the bill providing volunteers and money for the war was limited to two hours, and most of this was used up reading selected portions of the tabled documents, so that barely half an hour was left for discussion of the issues.

The Whig party also wanted California, but preferred to do it without war. Nevertheless, they would not deny men and money for the operation and so joined Democrats in voting overwhelmingly for the war resolution, 174 to 14. In the Senate there was debate, but it was limited to one day, and the war measure passed, 40 to 2, Whigs joining Democrats. John Quincy Adams of Massachusetts, who originally voted with "the stubborn 14," later voted for war appropriations.

Abraham Lincoln of Illinois was not yet in Congress when the war began, but after his election in 1846 he had occasion to vote and speak on the war. His "spot resolutions" became famous—he challenged Polk to specify the exact spot where American blood was shed "on the American soil." But he would not try to end the war by stopping funds for men and supplies. Speaking in the House on July 27, 1848, he said:

> If to say "the war was unnecessarily and unconstitutionally commenced by the President" be opposing the war, then the Whigs have very generally opposed it.... The marching an army into the midst of a peaceful Mexican settlement, frightening the inhabitants away, leaving their growing crops and other property to destruction, to you may appear a perfectly amiable, peaceful, unprovoking procedure; but it does not appear so to us.... But if, when the war had begun, and had become the cause of the country, the giving of our money and our blood, in common with yours, was support of the war, then it is not true that we have always opposed the war. With few individual exceptions, you have constantly had our votes here for all the necessary supplies....

A handful of antislavery Congressmen voted against all war measures, seeing the Mexican campaign as a means of extending the southern slave territory. One of these was Joshua Giddings of Ohio, a fiery speaker, physically powerful, who called it "an aggressive, unholy, and unjust war."

After Congress acted in May of 1846, there were rallies and demostrations for the war in New York, Baltimore, Indianapolis, Philadelphia,and many other places. Thousands rushed to volunteer for the army. The poet Walt Whitman wrote in the *Brooklyn Eagle* in the early days of the war: "Yes: Mexico must be thoroughly chastised!...Let our arms now be carried with a spirit which shall teach the world that, while we are not forward for a quarrel, America knows how to crush, as well as how to expand!"

Accompanying all this aggressiveness was the idea that the United States would be giving the blessings of liberty and democracy to more people. This was intermingled with ideas of racial superiority, longings for the beautiful lands of New Mexico and California, and thoughts of commercial enterprise across the Pacific. The *New York Herald* said, in 1847: "The universal Yankee nation can regenerate and disenthrall the people of Mexico in a few years; and we believe it is a part of our destiny to civilize that beautiful country."

The *Congressional Globe* of February 11, 1847, reported:

> Mr. Giles, of Maryland—I take it for granted, that we shall gain territory, and must gain territory, before we shut the gates of the temple of

Janus.... We must march from ocean to ocean.... We must march from Texas straight to the Pacific ocean, and be bounded only by its roaring wave.... It is the destiny of the white race, it is the destiny of the Anglo-Saxon race....

The American Anti-Slavery Society, on the other hand, said the war was "waged solely for the detestable and horrible purpose of extending and perpetuating American slavery throughout the vast territory of Mexico." A twenty-seven-year-old Boston poet and abolitionist, James Russell Lowell, began writing satirical poems in the *Boston Courier* (they were later collected as the *Biglow Papers*). In them, a New England farmer, Hosea Biglow, spoke, in his own dialect, on the war:

> Ez fer war, I call it murder,—
> —There you hev it plain an' flat;
> I don't want to go no furder
> —Than my Testyment fer that....
>
> They jest want this Californy
> —So's to lug new slave-states in
> To abuse ye, an' to scorn ye,
> —An' to plunder ye like sin.

The war had barely begun, the summer of 1846, when a writer, Henry David Thoreau, who lived in Concord, Massachusetts, refused to pay his Massachusetts poll tax, denouncing the Mexican war. He was put in jail and spent one night there. His friends, without his consent, paid his tax, and he was released. Two years later, he gave a lecture, "Resistance to Civil Government," which was then printed as an essay, "Civil Disobedience":

> It is not desirable to cultivate a respect for the law, so much as for the right.... Law never made men a whit more just; and, by means of their respect for it, even the well-disposed are daily made the agents of injustice. A common and natural result of an undue respect for law is, that you may see a file of soldiers...marching in admirable order over hill and dale to the wars, against their wills, ay, against their common sense and consciences, which makes it very steep marching indeed, and produces a palpitation of the heart.

His friend and fellow writer Ralph Waldo Emerson agreed, but thought it futile to protest. When Emerson visited Thoreau in jail and asked, "What are you doing in there?" it was reported that Thoreau replied, "What are you doing out there?"

The churches, for the most part, were either outspokenly for the war or timidly silent. The Reverend Theodore Parker, a Unitarian minister in Boston, combined eloquent criticism of the war with contempt for the Mexican people, whom he called "a wretched people; wretched in their origin, history, and character," who must eventually give way as the Indians did. Yes, the United States should expand, he said, but not by war, rather by the power of her ideas, the pressure of her commerce, by "the steady advance of a superior race, with superior ideas and a better civilization...."

The racism of Parker was widespread. Congressman Delano of Ohio, an antislavery Whig, opposed the war because he was afraid of Americans mingling with an inferior people who "embrace all shades of color.... a sad compound of Spanish, English, Indian, and negro bloods...and resulting, it is said, in the production of a slothful, ignorant race of beings."

As the war went on, opposition grew. The American Peace Society printed a newspaper, the *Advocate of Peace*, which published poems, speeches, petitions, sermons against the war, and eyewitness accounts of the degradation of army life and the horrors of battle. Considering the strenuous efforts of the nation's leaders to build patriotic support, the amount of open dissent and criticism was remarkable. Antiwar meetings took place in spite of attacks by patriotic mobs.

As the army moved closer to Mexico City, the antislavery newspaper *The Liberator* daringly declared its wishes for the defeat of the American forces: "Every lover of Freedom and humanity, throughout the world, must wish them [the Mexicans] the most triumphant success...."

Frederick Douglass, a former slave and an extraordinary speaker and writer, wrote in his Rochester newspaper the *North Star*, January 21, 1848, of "the present disgraceful, cruel, and iniquitous war with our sister republic. Mexico seems a doomed victim to Anglo Saxon cupidity and love of dominion." Douglass was scornful of the unwillingness of opponents of the war to take real action (even the abolitionists kept paying their taxes):

> No politician of any considerable distinction or eminence seems willing to hazard his popularity with his party...by an open and unqualified disapprobation of the war. None seem willing to take their stand for peace at all risks; and all seem willing that the war should be carried on, in some form or other.

Where was popular opinion? It is hard to say. After the first rush, enlistments began to dwindle. Historians of the Mexican war have talked easily about "the people" and "public opinion." Their evidence, however, is not from "the people" but from the newspapers, claiming to be the voice of the people. The *New York Herald* wrote in August 1845: "The multitude cry aloud for war." The *New York Morning News* said "young and ardent spirits that throng the cities...want but a direction to their restless energies, and their attention is already fixed on Mexico."

It is impossible to know the extent of popular support of the war. But there is evidence that many organized workingmen opposed the war. There were demonstrations of Irish workers in New York, Boston, and Lowell against the annexation of Texas. In May, when the war against Mexico began, New York workingmen called a meeting to oppose the war, and many Irish workers came. The meeting called the war a plot by slave owners and asked for the withdrawal of American troops from disputed territory. That year, a convention of the New England Workingmen's Association condemned the war and announced they would "not take up arms to sustain the Southern slaveholder in robbing one-fifth of our countrymen of their labor."

Some newspapers, at the very start of the war, protested. Horace Greeley wrote in the *New York Tribune*, May 12, 1846:

> We can easily defeat the armies of Mexico, slaughter them by thousands.... Who believes that a score of victories over Mexico, the "annexation" of half her provinces, will give us more Liberty, a purer Morality, a more prosperous Industry, than we now have?...Is not Life miserable enough, comes not Death soon enough, without resort to the hideous enginery of War?

What of those who fought the war—the soldiers who marched, sweated, got sick, died? The Mexican soldiers. The American soldiers. We know little of the reactions of Mexican soldiers. We know much more about the American army—volunteers, not conscripts, lured by money and opportunity for social advancement via promotion in the armed forces. Half of General Taylor's army were recent immigrants—Irish and German mostly. Their patriotism was not very strong. Indeed, many of them deserted to the Mexican side, enticed by money. Some enlisted in the Mexican army and formed their own battalion, the San Patricio (St. Patrick's) Battalion.

At first there seemed to be enthusiasm in the army, fired by pay and patriotism. Martial spirit was high in New York, where the legislature authorized the governor to call fifty thousand volunteers. Placards read "Mexico or Death." There was a mass meeting of twenty thousand people in Philadelphia. Three thousand volunteered in Ohio.

This initial spirit soon wore off. One young man wrote anonymously to the *Cambridge Chronicle*:

Neither have I the least idea of "joining" you, or in any way assisting the unjust war waging against Mexico. I have no wish to participate in such "glorious" butcheries of women and children as were displayed in the capture of Monterey, etc. Neither have I any desire to place myself under the dictation of a petty military tyrant, to every caprice of whose will I must yield implicit obedience. No sir-ee!...Human butchery has had its day.... And the time is rapidly approaching when the professional soldier will be placed on the same level as a bandit, the Bedouin, and the Thug.

There were extravagant promises and outright lies to build up the volunteer units. A man who wrote a history of the New York Volunteers declared: "Many enlisted for the sake of their families, having no employment, and having been offered 'three months' advance,' and were promised that they could leave part of their pay for their families to draw in their absence.... I boldly pronounce, that the whole Regiment was got up by fraud."

By late 1846, recruitment was falling off, so physical requirements were lowered, and anyone bringing in acceptable recruits would get two dollars a head. Even this didn't work. Congress in early 1847 authorized ten new regiments of regulars, to serve for the duration of the war, promising them one hundred acres of public land upon honorable discharge. But dissatisfaction continued.

And soon, the reality of battle came in upon the glory and the promises. On the Rio Grande before Matamoros, as a Mexican army of five thousand under General Arista faced Taylor's army of three thousand, the shells began to fly, and artilleryman Samuel French saw his first death in battle. John Weems describes it: "He happened to be staring at a man on horseback nearby when he saw a shot rip off the pommel of the saddle, tear through the man's body, and burst out with a crimson gush on the other side."

When the battle was over, five hundred Mexicans were dead or wounded. There were perhaps fifty American casualties. Weems describes the aftermath: "Night blanketed weary men who fell asleep where they dropped on the trampled prairie grass, while around them other prostrate men from both armies screamed and groaned in agony from wounds. By the eerie light of torches the surgeon's saw was going the livelong night."

Away from the battlefield, in the army camps, the romance of the recruiting posters was quickly forgotten. The Second Regiment of Mississippi Rifles, moving into New Orleans, was stricken by cold and sickness.

The regimental surgeon reported: "Six months after our regiment had entered the service we had sustained a loss of 167 by death, and 134 by discharges." The regiment was packed into the holds of transports, eight hundred men into three ships. The surgeon continued:

> The dark cloud of disease still hovered over us. The holds of the ships...were soon crowded with the sick. The effluvia was intolerable.... The sea became rough.... Through the long dark night the rolling ship would dash the sick man from side to side bruising his flesh upon the rough corners of his berth. The wild screams of the delirious, the lamentations of the sick, and the melancholy groans of the dying, kept up one continual scene of confusion.... Four weeks we were confined to the loathsome ships and before we had landed at the Brasos, we consigned twenty-eight of our men to the dark waves.

Meanwhile, by land and by sea, Anglo-American forces were moving into California. A young naval officer, after the long voyage around the southern cape of South America, and up the coast to Monterey in California, wrote in his diary:

> Asia...will be brought to our very doors. Population will flow into the fertile regions of California. The resources of the entire country...will be developed.... The public lands lying along the route [of railroads] will be changed from deserts into gardens, and a large population will be settled....

It was a separate war that went on in California, where Anglo-Americans raided Spanish settlements, stole horses, and declared California separated from Mexico—the "Bear Flag Republic." Indians lived there, and naval officer Revere gathered the Indian chiefs and spoke to them (as he later recalled):

> I have called you together to have a talk with you. The country you inhabit no longer belongs to Mexico, but to a mighty nation whose territory extends from the great ocean you have all seen or heard of, to another great ocean thousands of miles toward the rising sun.... Our armies are now in Mexico, and will soon conquer the whole country. But you have nothing to fear from us, if you do what is right...if you are faithful to your new rulers.... I hope you will alter your habits, and be industrious and frugal, and give up all the low vices which you practice.... We shall watch over you, and give you true liberty; but beware of sedition, lawlessness, and all other crimes, for the army which shields can assuredly punish, and it will reach you in your most retired hiding places.

General Kearney moved easily into New Mexico, and Santa Fe was taken without battle. An American staff officer described the reaction of the Mexican population to the U.S. army's entrance into the capital city:

> Our march into the city...was extremely warlike, with drawn sabres, and daggers in every look.... As the American flag was raised, and the cannon boomed its glorious national salute from the hill, the pent-up emotions of many of the women could be suppressed no longer...as the wail of grief arose above the din of our horses' tread, and reached our ears from the depth of the gloomy-looking buildings on every hand.

That was in August. In December, Mexicans in Taos, New Mexico, rebelled against American rule. The revolt was put down and arrests were made. But many of the rebels fled and carried on sporadic attacks, killing a number of Americans, then hiding in the mountains. The American army pursued, and in a final desperate battle, in which six to seven hundred rebels were engaged, 150 were killed, and it seemed the rebellion was now over.

In Los Angeles, too, there was a revolt. Mexicans forced the American garrison there to surrender in September 1846. The United States did not retake Los Angeles until January, after a bloody battle.

General Taylor had moved across the Rio Grande, occupied Matamoros, and now moved southward through Mexico. But his volunteers became more unruly on Mexican territory. Mexican villages were pillaged by drunken troops. Cases of rape began to multiply.

As the soldiers moved up the Rio Grande to Camargo, the heat became unbearable, the water impure, and sickness grew—diarrhea, dysentery, and other maladies—until a thousand were dead. At first the dead were buried to the sounds of the "Dead March" played by a military band. Then the number of dead was too great, and formal military funerals ceased. Southward to Monterey and another battle, where men and horses died in agony, and one officer described the ground as "slippery with...foam and blood."

The U.S. Navy bombarded Vera Cruz in an indiscriminate killing of civilians. One of the navy's shells hit the post office, another a surgical hospital. In two days, thirteen hundred shells were fired into the city, until it surrendered. A reporter for the *New Orleans Delta* wrote: "The Mexicans variously estimate their loss at from 500 to 1000 killed and wounded, but all agree that the loss among the soldiery is comparatively small and the destruction among the women and children is very great."

Colonel Hitchcock, coming into the city, wrote: "I shall never forget the horrible fire of our mortars...going with dreadful certainty...often in

the centre of private dwellings—it was awful. I shudder to think of it."
Still, Hitchcock, the dutiful soldier, wrote for General Scott "a sort of
address to the Mexican people" which was then printed in English and
Spanish by the tens of thousands saying "we have not a particle of ill-will
towards you...we are here for no earthly purpose except the hope of
obtaining a peace."

It was a war of the American elite against the Mexican elite, each side
exhorting, using, killing its own population as well as the other. The Mexican commander Santa Anna had crushed rebellion after rebellion, his
troops also raping and plundering after victory. When Col. Hitchcock and
Gen. Winfield Scott moved into Santa Anna's estate, they found its walls
full of ornate paintings. But half his army was dead or wounded.

General Scott moved toward the last battle—for Mexico City—with
ten thousand soldiers. They were not anxious for battle. Three days' march
from Mexico City, at Jalapa, seven of his eleven regiments evaporated, their
enlistment times up, the reality of battle and disease too much for them.

On the outskirts of Mexico City, at Churubusco, Mexican and American armies clashed for three hours and thousands died on both sides.
Among the Mexicans taken prisoner were sixty-nine U.S. Army deserters.

As often in war, battles were fought without point. After one such
engagement near Mexico City, with terrible casualties, a marine lieutenant
blamed Gen. Scott: "He had originated it in error and caused it to be
fought, with inadequate forces, for an object that had no existence."

In the final battle for Mexico City, Anglo-American troops took the
height of Chapultepec and entered the city of 200,000 people, General
Santa Anna having moved northward. This was September 1847. A Mexican merchant wrote to a friend about the bombardment of the city: "In
some cases whole blocks were destroyed and a great number of men,
women and children killed and wounded."

General Santa Anna fled to Huamantla, where another battle was
fought, and he had to flee again. An American infantry lieutenant wrote to
his parents what happened after an officer named Walker was killed in battle:

General Lane...told us to "avenge the death of the gallant Walker.... Grog shops were broken open first, and then, maddened with
liquor, every species of outrage was committed. Old women and girls
were stripped of their clothing—and many suffered still greater out-
rages. Men were shot by dozens...their property, churches, stores and
dwelling houses ransacked.... It made me for the first time ashamed of
my country.

One Pennsylvania volunteer, stationed at Matamoros late in the war, wrote:

> We are under very strict discipline here. Some of our officers are very good men but the balance of them are very tyrannical and brutal toward the men.... [T]onight on drill an officer laid a soldier's skull open with his sword.... But the time may come and that soon when officers and men will stand on equal footing.... A soldier's life is very disgusting.

On the night of August 15, 1847, volunteer regiments from Virginia, Mississippi, and North Carolina rebelled in northern Mexico against Col. Robert Treat Paine. Paine killed a mutineer, but two of his lieutenants refused to help him quell the mutiny. The rebels were ultimately exonerated in an attempt to keep the peace.

Desertion grew. In March 1847 the army reported over a thousand deserters. The total number of deserters during the war was 9,207 (5,331 regulars and 3,876 volunteers). Those who did not desert became harder and harder to manage. General Cushing referred to sixty-five such men in the First Regiment of the Massachusetts Infantry as "incorrigibly mutinous and insubordinate."

The glory of the victory was for the president and the generals, not the deserters, the dead, the wounded. The Massachusetts Volunteers had started with 630 men. They came home with three hundred dead, mostly from disease, and at the reception dinner on their return their commander, General Cushing, was hissed by his men.

As the veterans returned home, speculators immediately showed up to buy the land warrants given by the government. Many of the soldiers, desperate for money, sold their 160 acres for less than fifty dollars.

Mexico surrendered. There were calls among Americans to take all of Mexico. The Treaty of Guadalupe Hidalgo, signed February 1848, just took half. The Texas boundary was set at the Rio Grande; New Mexico and California were ceded. The United States paid Mexico $15 million, which led the *Whig Intelligencer* to conclude that "we take nothing by conquest.... Thank God."

Exercises

1. When did Mexico achieve independence from Spain?
   When did Texas become independent from Mexico?
   When did Texas become a state of the United States?
   When did the Mexican-American War begin?

2. Before President Polk's term, which river had the U.S. government recognized as the border between Mexico and Texas? Which river did Texas claim as its border with Mexico? Which river did Polk choose as the border? How did Polk's choice of the border allow the U.S. to provoke a war with Mexico?

3. What were the arguments that the news media used to support a war with Mexico?

4. What were Colonel Hitchcock's private thoughts concerning the war with Mexico? Why might he have not shared those thoughts with fellow officers and enlisted men?

5. By 1848, did Congressman Lincoln end up supporting the war?

6. Walt Whitman wrote that Mexico must be soundly punished. What did Mexico do that persuaded Whitman to demand that Mexico be "crushed"?

7. What role did race play in both the promotion of and opposition to the war?

8. The *New York Herald* believed that, in conquering Mexico, the United States would "civilize" it. What exactly do you think the *Herald* meant by "civilize"? What data lead you to your hypothesis?

   a. building factories and transform farmers into workers?

   b. convert Mexican Catholics into Protestants

   c. teach the Mexican better table manners

   d. importing slavery-based plantations

e. dividing Mexican provinces into states subjected to the rules laid down by the U.S. Constitution (those rules are as follows: each state has a constitutional convention to create a state constitution that must be submitted and accepted by the U.S. Congress before the state is admitted to the Union—can elect and send representatives to Congress)

f. having Mexicans of mixed Spanish/Indian descent ruled by Anglo-Saxon Protestants whose government would be more efficient and less corrupt than the Mexican government was in 1845

9. Who were the opponents of the war? How did they manifest (in word and deed) their opposition to the war? To what degree were their tactics effective? How could they have been more effective (what were the obstacles in the way of their success)?

10. How can the division over the Mexican-American War (1846–48) be seen as a prelude to the Civil War (1861–65)?

11. Apart from an increase in pay, why might an Irish-American soldier desert the U.S. Army and join the Mexican army?

12. Why did many of the American soldiers wish to stop fighting?

13. How strong was the Mexican/Indian resistance to U.S. military advances at each of the following points of contact: Santa Fe; Taos; Los Angeles; Camargo; Vera Cruz; Churubusca; Mexico City; Huatmantla? To what can you attribute the degree of strength or weakness of the resistance?

14. What evidence does Zinn provide to determine how widespread desertion was among American soldiers?

15. Many soldiers signed up to go to war in hopes of acquiring land. Why then did these same soldiers sell their hard-won 160-acre land warrants to land speculators?

16. What percentage of Mexico did the United States take/buy/acquire in the Treaty of Guadalupe Hidalgo? Was this a better or worse bargain than the Louisiana Purchase?

17. *Draw a map* that includes the following: the Mexican Cession; the state borders of California, Colorado, Nevada, Utah, New Mexico, Arizona, and Texas; Mexic;, the Rio Grande; the Nueces River; Washington, D.C.; the Louisiana Purchase; the Oregon Territory; the cities of Santa Fe, Taos, Los Angeles, Vera Cruz, and Mexico City.

18. *Debate Resolution*: The United States did not provoke a war with Mexico over minor issues.

Chapter 9

Slavery Without Submission, Emancipation Without Freedom

The United States government's support of slavery was based on an overpowering practicality. In 1790, a thousand tons of cotton were being produced every year in the South. By 1860, it was a million tons. In the same period, 500,000 slaves grew to 4 million. A system harried by slave rebellions and conspiracies (Gabriel Prosser, 1800; Denmark Vesey, 1822; Nat Turner, 1831) developed a network of controls in the southern states, backed by the laws, courts, armed forces, and race prejudice of the nation's political leaders.

It would take either a full-scale slave rebellion or a full-scale war to end such a deeply entrenched system. If a rebellion, it might get out of hand, and turn its ferocity beyond slavery to the most successful system of capitalist enrichment in the world. If a war, those who made the war would organize its consequences. Hence, it was Abraham Lincoln who freed the slaves, not John Brown. In 1859, John Brown was hanged, with federal complicity, for attempting to do by small-scale violence what Lincoln would do by large-scale violence several years later—end slavery.

With slavery abolished by order of the government—true, a government pushed hard to do so, by blacks, free and slave, and by white abolitionists—its end could be orchestrated so as to set limits to emancipation. Liberation from the top would go only so far as the interests of the dominant groups permitted. If carried further by the momentum of war, the rhetoric of a crusade, it could be pulled back to a safer position. Thus, while the ending of slavery led to a reconstruction of national politics and economics, it was not a radical reconstruction, but a safe one—in fact, a profitable one.

The plantation system, based on tobacco growing in Virginia, North Carolina, and Kentucky, and rice in South Carolina, expanded into lush new cotton lands in Georgia, Alabama, Mississippi—and needed more slaves. But slave importation became illegal in 1808. Therefore, "from the beginning, the law went unenforced," says John Hope Franklin (*From Slavery to Freedom*). "The long, unprotected coast, the certain markets, and the prospects of huge profits were too much for the American merchants and they yielded to the temptation...." He estimates that perhaps 250,000 slaves were imported illegally before the Civil War.

How can slavery be described? Perhaps not at all by those who have not experienced it. The 1932 edition of a best-selling textbook by two northern liberal historians saw slavery as perhaps the Negro's "necessary transition to civilization." Economists or cliometricians (statistical historians) have tried to assess slavery by estimating how much money was spent on slaves for food and medical care. But can this describe the reality of slavery as it was to a human being who lived inside it? Are the *conditions* of slavery as important as the *existence* of slavery?

John Little, a former slave, wrote:

> They say slaves are happy, because they laugh, and are merry. I myself and three or four others, have received two hundred lashes in the day, and had our feet in fetters; yet, at night, we would sing and dance, and make others laugh at the rattling of our chains. Happy men we must have been! We did it to keep down trouble, and to keep our hearts from being completely broken: that is as true as the gospel! Just look at it, —must not we have been very happy? Yet I have done it myself—I have cut capers in chains.

A record of deaths kept in a plantation journal (now in the University of North Carolina Archives) lists the ages and cause of death of all those who died on the plantation between 1850 and 1855. Of the thirty-two who died in that period, only four reached the age of sixty, four reached the age of fifty, seven died in their forties, seven died in their twenties or thirties, and nine died before they were five years old.

But can statistics record what it meant for families to be torn apart, when a master, for profit, sold a husband or a wife, a son or a daughter? In 1858, a slave named Abream Scriven was sold by his master, and wrote to his wife: "Give my love to my father and mother and tell them good Bye for me, and if we Shall not meet in this world I hope to meet in heaven."

Slave revolts in the United States were not as frequent or as large-scale as those in the Caribbean islands or in South America. Probably the largest slave revolt in the United States took place near New Orleans in 1811. Four to five hundred slaves gathered after a rising at the plantation of a Major Andry. Armed with cane knives, axes, and clubs, they wounded Andry, killed his son, and began marching from plantation to plantation, their numbers growing. They were attacked by U.S. army and militia forces; sixty-six were killed on the spot, and sixteen were tried and shot by a firing squad.

The conspiracy of Denmark Vesey, himself a free Negro, was thwarted before it could be carried out in 1822. The plan was to burn Charleston, South Carolina, then the sixth-largest city in the nation, and to initiate a general revolt of slaves in the area. Several witnesses said thousands of blacks were implicated in one way or another. Blacks had made about 250 pike heads and bayonets and over three hundred daggers, according to Herbert Aptheker's account. But the plan was betrayed, and thirty-five blacks, including Vesey, were hanged. The trial record itself, published in Charleston, was ordered destroyed soon after publication, as too dangerous for slaves to see.

In Southampton County, Virginia, in the summer of 1831, a slave named Nat Turner, claiming religious visions, gathered about seventy slaves, who went on a rampage from plantation to plantation, murdering at least fifty-five men, women, and children. They gathered supporters, but were captured as their ammunition ran out. Turner and perhaps eighteen others were hanged.

This threw the slaveholding South into a panic, and then into a determined effort to bolster the security of the slave system. After that, Virginia kept a militia force of 101,000, almost 10 percent of its total population. Rebellion, though rare, was a constant fear among slave owners.

Eugene Genovese, in his comprehensive study of slavery, *Roll, Jordan, Roll*, sees a record of "simultaneous accommodation and resistance to slavery." The resistance included stealing property, sabotage and slowness, killing overseers and masters, burning down plantation buildings, running away. Even the accommodation "breathed a critical spirit and disguised subversive actions."

Running away was much more realistic than armed insurrection. During the 1850s about a thousand slaves a year escaped into the North, Canada, and Mexico. Thousands ran away for short periods. And this despite the terror facing the runaway. The dogs used in tracking fugitives "bit, tore, mutilated, and if not pulled off in time, killed their prey," Genovese says.

Harriet Tubman, born into slavery, her head injured by an overseer when she was fifteen, made her way to freedom alone as a young woman, then became the most famous conductor on the Underground Railroad. She made nineteen dangerous trips back and forth, often disguised, escorting more than three hundred slaves to freedom, always carrying a pistol, telling the fugitives, "You'll be free or die." She expressed her philosophy: "There was one of two things I had a right to, liberty or death; if I could not have one, I would have the other; for no man should take me alive...."

One form of resistance was not to work so hard. W. E. B. Du Bois wrote, in *The Gift of Black Folk*:

> As a tropical product with a sensuous receptivity to the beauty of the world, he was not as easily reduced to be the mechanical draft-horse which the northern European laborer became.... [T]hus he was easily accused of laziness and driven as a slave when in truth he brought to modern manual labor a renewed valuation of life.

The instances where poor whites helped slaves were not frequent, but sufficient to show the need for setting one group against the other. Genovese says:

> The slaveholders...suspected that non-slaveholders would encourage slave disobedience and even rebellion, not so much out of sympathy for the blacks as out of hatred for the rich planters and resentment of their own poverty. White men sometimes were linked to slave insurrectionary plots, and each such incident rekindled fears.

This helps explain the stern police measures against whites who fraternized with blacks. In return, blacks helped whites in need. One black runaway told of a slave woman who had received fifty lashes of the whip for giving food to a white neighbor who was poor and sick.

When the Brunswick canal was built in Georgia, the black slaves and white Irish workers were segregated, the excuse being that they would do violence against one another. That may well have been true, but Fanny Kemble, the famous actress and wife of a planter, wrote in her journal:

> But the Irish are not only quarrelers, and rioters, and fighters, and drinkers, and despisers of niggers—they are a passionate, impulsive, warm-hearted, generous people.... [T]hey might actually take to sympathy with the slaves, and I leave you to judge of the possible consequences. You perceive, I am sure, that they can by no means be allowed to work together on the Brunswick Canal.

The need for slave control led to an ingenious device, paying poor whites—themselves so troublesome for two hundred years of southern history—to be overseers of black labor and therefore buffers for black hatred.

Religion was used by plantation owners for control.

As for black preachers, as Genovese puts it, "they had to speak a language defiant enough to hold the high-spirited among their flock but neither so inflammatory as to rouse them to battles they could not win nor so ominous as to arouse the ire of ruling powers." Practicality decided: "The slave communities counseled a strategy of patience, of acceptance of what could not be helped, of a dogged effort to keep the black community alive and healthy...."

It was once thought that slavery had destroyed the black family. But interviews with ex-slaves, done in the 1930s by the Federal Writers Project of the New Deal for the Library of Congress, told a different story, which George Rawick summarizes (*From Sundown to Sunup*): "The slave community acted like a generalized extended kinship system in which all adults looked after all children and there was little division between 'my children for whom I'm responsible' and 'your children for whom you're responsible.'...It was part and parcel, as we shall see, of the social process out of which came black pride, black identity, black culture, the black community, and black rebellion in America."

Old letters and records dug out by historian Herbert Gutman (*The Black Family in Slavery and Freedom*) show the stubborn resistance of the slave family to pressures of disintegration. A woman wrote to her son from whom she had been separated for twenty years: "I long to see you in my old age.... Now my dear son I pray you to come and see your dear old Mother.... I love you Cato you love your Mother—You are my only son...."

And a man wrote to his wife, sold away from him with their children: "Send me some of the children's hair in a separate paper with their names on the paper.... I had rather anything to had happened to me most than ever to have been parted from you and the children.... Laura I do love you the same...."

Also insisting on the strength of blacks even under slavery, Lawrence Levine (*Black Culture and Black Consciousness*) gives a picture of a rich culture among slaves, a complex mixture of adaptation and rebellion, through the creativity of stories and songs:

> We raise de wheat,
> Dey gib us de corn;
> We bake de bread,
> Dey gib us de crust,
> We sif de meal,
> Dey gib us de huss;
> We peel de meat,
> Dey gib us de skin;
> And dat's de way
> Dey take us in....

Spirituals often had double meanings. The lyrics "O Canaan, sweet Canaan, I am bound for the land of Canaan" often meant that slaves meant to get to the North, their Canaan. During the Civil War, slaves began to make up new spirituals with bolder messages: "Before I'd be a slave, I'd be buried in my grave, and go home to my Lord and be saved." And the spiritual "Many Thousand Go":

> No more peck o' corn for me, no more, no more,
> No more driver's lash for me, no more, no more....

While southern slaves held on, free blacks in the North (there were about 130,000 in 1830, about 200,000 in 1850) agitated for the abolition of slavery. In 1829, David Walker, son of a slave, but born free in North Carolina, moved to Boston, where he sold old clothes. The pamphlet he wrote and printed, *Walker's Appeal*, became widely known. It infuriated southern slaveholders; Georgia offered a reward of $10,000 to anyone who would deliver Walker alive, and $1,000 to anyone who would kill him. It is not hard to understand why when you read his *Appeal*. Blacks must fight for their freedom, he said:

> Let our enemies go on with their butcheries, and at once fill up their cup. Never make an attempt to gain our freedom or natural right...until you see your way clear—when that hour arrives and you move, be not afraid or dismayed.... God has been pleased to give us two eyes, two hands, two feet, and some sense in our heads as well as they. They have no more right to hold us in slavery than we have to hold them.... "Every dog must have its day," the American's is coming to an end.

One summer day in 1830, David Walker was found dead near the doorway of his shop in Boston.

Some born in slavery acted out the unfulfilled desire of millions. Frederick Douglass, a slave, sent to Baltimore to work as a servant and as a laborer in the shipyard, somehow learned to read and write, and at twenty-one, in the year 1838, escaped to the North, where he became the most famous black man of his time, as a lecturer, newspaper editor, and writer. In his autobiography, *Narrative of the Life of Frederick Douglass*, he recalled his first childhood thoughts about his condition:

> Why am I a slave? Why are some people slaves, and others masters? Was there ever a time when this was not so? How did the relation commence?
>
> Once, however, engaged in the inquiry, I was not very long in finding out the true solution of the matter. It was not color, but crime, not God, but man, that afforded the true explanation of the existence of slavery; nor was I long in finding out another important truth, viz: what man can make, man can unmake....
>
> I distinctly remember being, even then, most strongly impressed with the idea of being a free man some day. This cheering assurance was an inborn dream of my human nature—a constant menace to slavery—and one which all the powers of slavery were unable to silence or extinguish.

The Fugitive Slave Act passed in 1850 was a concession to the southern states in return for the admission of the Mexican war territories (California, especially) into the Union as nonslave states. The act made it easy for slave owners to recapture ex-slaves or simply to pick up blacks they claimed had run away. Northern blacks organized resistance to the Fugitive Slave Act, denouncing President Fillmore, who signed it, and Sen. Daniel Webster, who supported it. One of these was J. W. Loguen, son of a slave mother and her white owner. He had escaped to freedom on his master's horse, gone to college, and was now a minister in Syracuse, New York. He spoke to a meeting in that city in 1850:

> The time has come to change the tones of submission into tones of defiance—and to tell Mr. Fillmore and Mr. Webster, if they propose to execute this measure upon us, to send on their blood-hounds.... I received my freedom from Heaven, and with it came the command to defend my title to it.... I don't respect this law—I don't fear it—I won't obey it! It outlaws me, and I outlaw it....

The following year, in Syracuse, a runaway slave named Jerry was captured and put on trial. A crowd used crowbars and a battering ram to break into the courthouse, defying marshals with drawn guns, and set Jerry free.

Loguen made his home in Syracuse a major station on the Under-

ground Railroad. It was said that he helped fifteen hundred slaves on their
way to Canada. His memoir of slavery came to the attention of his former
owner, and she wrote to him, asking him either to return or to send her
$1,000 in compensation. Loguen's reply to her was printed in the aboli-
tionist newspaper, *The Liberator:*

> Mrs. Sarah Logue.... You say you have offers to buy me, and that you
> shall sell me if I do not send you $1000, and in the same breath and almost
> in the same sentence, you say, "You know we raised you as we did our
> own children." Woman, did you raise your own children for the market?
> Did you raise them for the whipping post? Did you raise them to be dri-
> ven off, bound to a coffle in chains?...Shame on you!...
>
> Have you got to learn that human rights are mutual and reciprocal,
> and if you take my liberty and life, you forfeit your own liberty and life?
> Before God and high heaven, is there a law for one man which is not a law
> for every other man?
>
> If you or any other speculator on my body and rights, wish to know
> how I regard my rights, they need but come here, and lay their hands on
> me to enslave me....
>
> Yours, etc. J. W. Loguen

Frederick Douglass knew that the shame of slavery was not just the
South's, that the whole nation was complicit in it. On the Fourth of July,
1852, he gave an Independence Day address:

> Fellow Citizens: What to the American slave is your Fourth of July? I
> answer, a day that reveals to him more than all other days of the year, the
> gross injustice and cruelty to which he is the constant victim. To him
> your celebration is a sham; your boasted liberty an unholy license; your
> national greatness, swelling vanity; your sounds of rejoicing are empty
> and heartless; your denunciation of tyrants, brass-fronted impudence;
> your shouts of liberty and equality, hollow mockery; your prayers and
> hymns, your sermons and thanksgivings, with all your religious parade
> and solemnity, are to him mere bombast, fraud, deception, impiety, and
> hypocrisy—a thin veil to cover up crimes which would disgrace a nation
> of savages. There is not a nation of the earth guilty of practices more
> shocking and bloody than are the people of these United States at this
> very hour.

Ten years after Nat Turner's rebellion, there was no sign of black
insurrection in the South. But that year, 1841, one incident took place
which kept alive the idea of rebellion. Slaves being transported on a ship,
the *Creole*, overpowered the crew, killed one of them, and sailed into the
British West Indies (where slavery had been abolished in 1833). England

refused to return the slaves (there was much agitation in England against American slavery), and this led to angry talk in Congress of war with England, encouraged by Secretary of State Daniel Webster. The *Colored People's Press* denounced Webster's "bullying position," and, recalling the Revolutionary War and the War of 1812, wrote: "If war be declared... Will we fight in defense of a government which denies us the most precious right of citizenship?..."

As the tension grew, North and South, blacks became more militant. Frederick Douglass spoke in 1853:

> Let me give you a word of the philosophy of reforms. The whole history of the progress of human liberty shows that all concessions yet made to her august claims have been born of struggle.... If there is no struggle there is no progress.... Power concedes nothing without a demand. It never did and it never will....

How ever-present was slavery in the minds of northern Negroes in the decades before the Civil War is shown by black children in a Cincinnati school, a private school financed by Negroes. The children were responding to the question "What do you think *most* about?" Only five answers remain in the records, and all refer to slavery. A seven-year-old child wrote: "I am sorrow to hear that the boat...went down with 200 poor slaves from up the river. Oh how sorrow I am to hear that, it grieves my heart so that I could faint in one minute."

White abolitionists did courageous and pioneering work, on the lecture platform, in newspapers, in the Underground Railroad. Black abolitionists, less publicized, were the backbone of the antislavery movement. Before Garrison published his famous *Liberator* in Boston in 1831, the first national convention of Negroes had been held, David Walker had already written his *Appeal*, and the black abolitionist magazine *Freedom's Journal* had appeared. Of *The Liberator*'s first twenty-five subscribers, most were black.

Blacks had to struggle constantly with the unconscious racism of white abolitionists. They also had to insist on their own independent voice. Douglass wrote for *The Liberator*, but in 1847 started his own newspaper in Rochester, the *North Star*, which led to a break with Garrison. In 1854, a conference of Negroes declared: "...it is emphatically our battle; no one else can fight it for us.... Our relations to the Anti-Slavery movement must be and are changed. Instead of depending upon it we must lead it."

Certain black women faced the triple hurdle—of being abolitionists in a slave society, of being black among white reformers, and of being women in a reform movement dominated by men. When Sojourner Truth rose to speak in 1853 in New York City at the Fourth National Woman's Rights Convention, it all came together. There was a hostile mob in the hall shouting, jeering, threatening. She said: "I know that it feels a kind o' hissin' and ticklin' like to see a colored woman get up and tell you about things, and Woman's Rights.... I am sittin' among you to watch; and every once and awhile I will come out and tell you what time of night it is...."

After Nat Turner's violent uprising and Virginia's bloody repression, the security system inside the South became tighter. Perhaps only an outsider could hope to launch a rebellion. It was such a person, a white man of ferocious courage and determination, John Brown, whose wild scheme it was to seize the federal arsenal at Harpers Ferry, Virginia, and then set off a revolt of slaves through the South.

Harriet Tubman, five feet tall, a veteran of countless secret missions piloting blacks out of slavery, was involved with John Brown and his plans. But sickness prevented her from joining him. Frederick Douglass too had met with Brown. He argued against the plan from the standpoint of its chances of success, but he admired the ailing man of sixty, tall, gaunt, white-haired.

Douglass was right; the plan would not work. The local militia, joined by a hundred marines under the command of Robert E. Lee, surrounded the insurgents. Although his men were dead or captured, John Brown refused to surrender: he barricaded himself in a small brick building near the gate of the armory. The troops battered down a door; a marine lieutenant moved in and struck Brown with his sword. Wounded, sick, he was interrogated. W. E. B. Du Bois, in his book *John Brown*, writes:

> Picture the situation: An old and blood-bespattered man, half-dead from the wounds inflicted but a few hours before; a man lying in the cold and dirt, without sleep for fifty-five nerve-wrecking hours, without food for nearly as long, with the dead bodies of his two sons almost before his eyes, the piled corpses of his seven slain comrades near and afar, a wife and a bereaved family listening in vain, and a Lost Cause, the dream of a lifetime, lying dead in his heart....

Lying there, interrogated by the governor of Virginia, Brown said: "You had better—all you people at the South—prepare yourselves for a settlement of this question.... You may dispose of me very easily—I am nearly disposed of now, but this question is still to be settled,—this Negro question, I mean; the end of that is not yet."

Ralph Waldo Emerson, not an activist himself, said of the execution of John Brown: "He will make the gallows holy as the cross."

Of the twenty-two men in John Brown's striking force, five were black. Two of these were killed on the spot, one escaped, and two were hanged by the authorities. Before his execution, John Copeland wrote to his parents: "Remember that if I must die I die in trying to liberate a few of my poor and oppressed people from my condition of servitude which God in his Holy Writ has hurled his most bitter denunciations against.... I am not terrified by the gallows."

John Brown was executed by the state of Virginia with the approval of the national government. It was the national government that, while weakly enforcing the law ending the slave trade, sternly enforced the laws providing for the return of fugitives to slavery. It was the national government that, in Andrew Jackson's administration, collaborated with the South to keep abolitionist literature out of the mails in the southern states. It was the Supreme Court of the United States that declared in 1857 that the slave Dred Scott could not sue for his freedom because he was not a person, but property.

Such a government would never accept an end to slavery by rebellion. It would end slavery only under conditions controlled by whites, and only when required by the political and economic needs of the business elite of the North. It was Abraham Lincoln who combined perfectly the needs of business, the political ambition of the new Republican party, and the rhetoric of humanitarianism. He would keep the abolition of slavery not at the top of his list of priorities, but close enough to the top so it could be pushed there temporarily by abolitionist pressures and by practical political advantage.

Lincoln could skillfully blend the interests of the very rich and the interests of the black at a moment in history when these interests met. And he could link these two with a growing section of Americans, the white, up-and-coming, economically ambitious, politically active middle class. As Richard Hofstadter puts it:

> Thoroughly middle class in his ideas, he spoke for those millions of Americans who had begun their lives as hired workers—as farm hands, clerks, teachers, mechanics, flatboat men, and rail-splitters—and had passed into the ranks of landed farmers, prosperous grocers, lawyers, merchants, physicians and politicians.

Lincoln could argue with lucidity and passion against slavery on moral grounds, while acting cautiously in practical politics. He believed "that the institution of slavery is founded on injustice and bad policy, but that the promulgation of abolition doctrines tends to increase rather than abate its evils."

Lincoln refused to denounce the Fugitive Slave Law publicly. He wrote to a friend: "I confess I hate to see the poor creatures hunted down... but I bite my lips and keep quiet." And when he did propose, in 1849, as a congressman, a resolution to abolish slavery in the District of Columbia, he accompanied this with a section requiring local authorities to arrest and return fugitive slaves coming into Washington. (This led Wendell Phillips, the Boston abolitionist, to refer to him years later as "that slavehound from Illinois.") He opposed slavery, but could not see blacks as equals, so a constant theme in his approach was to free the slaves and to send them back to Africa.

In his 1858 campaign in Illinois for the Senate against Stephen Douglas, Lincoln spoke differently depending on the views of his listeners (and also perhaps depending on how close it was to the election). Speaking in northern Illinois in July (in Chicago), he said:

> Let us discard all this quibbling about this man and the other man, this race and that race and the other race being inferior, and therefore they must be placed in an inferior position. Let us discard all these things, and unite as one people throughout this land, until we shall once more stand up declaring that all men are created equal.

Two months later in Charleston, in southern Illinois, Lincoln told his audience:

> I will say, then, that I am not, nor ever have been, in favor of bringing about in any way the social and political equality of the white and black races [applause]; that I am not, nor ever have been, in favor of making voters or jurors of negroes, nor of qualifying them to hold office, nor to intermarry with white people....
>
> And inasmuch as they cannot so live, while they do remain together there must be the position of superior and inferior, and I as much as any other man am in favor of having the superior position assigned to the white race.

Behind the secession of the South from the Union, after Lincoln was elected president in the fall of 1860 as candidate of the new Republican party, was a long series of policy clashes between South and North. The northern elite wanted economic expansion—free land, free labor, a free market, a high protective tariff for manufacturers, a bank of the United

States. The slave interests opposed all that; they saw Lincoln and the Republicans as making continuation of their pleasant and prosperous way of life impossible in the future.

So, when Lincoln was elected, seven southern states seceded from the Union. Lincoln initiated hostilities by trying to repossess the federal base at Fort Sumter, South Carolina, and four more states seceded. The Confederacy was formed; the Civil War was on.

Lincoln's first inaugural address, in March 1861, was conciliatory: "I have no purpose, directly or indirectly, to interfere with the institution of slavery in the States where it exists. I believe I have no lawful right to do so, and I have no inclination to do so." And with the war four months on, when Gen. John C. Frémont in Missouri declared martial law and said slaves of owners resisting the United States were to be free, Lincoln countermanded this order. He was anxious to hold in the Union the slave states of Maryland, Kentucky, Missouri, and Delaware.

It was only as the war grew more bitter, the casualties mounted, desperation to win heightened, and the criticism of the abolitionists threatened to unravel the tattered coalition behind Lincoln that he began to act against slavery. Hofstadter puts it this way: "Like a delicate barometer, he recorded the trend of pressures, and as the Radical pressure increased he moved toward the left."

Racism in the North was as entrenched as slavery in the South, and it would take the war to shake both. New York blacks could not vote unless they owned $250 in property (a qualification not applied to whites). A proposal to abolish this, put on the ballot in 1860, was defeated two to one.

Wendell Phillips, with all his criticism of Lincoln, recognized the possibilities in his election. Speaking at the Tremont Temple in Boston the day after the election, Phillips said:

> If the telegraph speaks truth, for the first time in our history the slave has chosen a President of the United States.... Not an Abolitionist, hardly an antislavery man, Mr. Lincoln consents to represent an antislavery idea. A pawn on the political chessboard, his value is in his position; with fair effort, we may soon change him for knight, bishop or queen, and sweep the board. [Applause.]

The spirit of Congress, even after the war began, was shown in a resolution it passed in the summer of 1861, with only a few dissenting votes: "...this war is not waged...for any purpose of...over-throwing or interfering with the rights of established institutions of those states, but...to preserve the Union."

141

The abolitionists stepped up their campaign. Emancipation petitions poured into Congress in 1861 and 1862. In May of that year, Wendell Phillips said: "Abraham Lincoln may not wish it; he cannot prevent it.... [T]he negro is the pebble in the cog-wheel, and the machine cannot go on until you get him out."

In July of 1862 Congress passed a Confiscation Act, which enabled the freeing of slaves of those fighting the Union. But this was not enforced by the Union generals, and Lincoln ignored the nonenforcement. Horace Greeley, editor of the *New York Tribune*, wrote an open letter to Lincoln warning him that his supporters were "sorely disappointed and deeply pained.... We require of you, as the first servant of the Republic, charged especially and preeminently with this duty, that you EXECUTE THE LAWS.... We think you are strangely and disastrously remiss...with regard to the emancipating provisions of the new Confiscation Act.... We think you are unduly influenced by the councils...of certain politicians hailing from the Border Slave States."

Greeley appealed to the practical need of winning the war. "We must have scouts, guides, spies, cooks, teamsters, diggers and choppers from the blacks of the South, whether we allow them to fight for us or not.... I entreat you to render a hearty and unequivocal obedience to the law of the land."

Lincoln replied to Greeley:

> Dear Sir: ...I have not meant to leave any one in doubt.... My paramount object in this struggle is to save the Union, and is not either to save or destroy Slavery. If I could save the Union without freeing any slave, I would do it; and if I could save it by freeing all the slaves, I would do it.... I have here stated my purpose according to my view of official duty, and I intend no modification of my oft-expressed personal wish that all men, everywhere, could be free.

When in September 1862 Lincoln issued his preliminary Emancipation Proclamation, it was a military move, giving the South four months to stop rebelling, threatening to emancipate their slaves if they continued to fight, promising to leave slavery untouched in states that came over to the North.

Thus, when the Emancipation Proclamation was issued January 1, 1863, it declared slaves free in those areas still fighting against the Union (which it listed very carefully), and said nothing about slaves behind Union lines.

Limited as it was, the Emancipation Proclamation spurred antislavery forces. By the summer of 1864, 400,000 signatures asking legislation to end slavery had been gathered and sent to Congress, something unprecedented in the history of the country. That April, the Senate had adopted the Thirteenth Amendment, declaring an end to slavery, and in January 1865, the House of Representatives followed.

With the proclamation, the Union army was open to blacks. And the more blacks entered the war, the more it appeared a war for their liberation. The more whites had to sacrifice, the more resentment there was, particularly among poor whites in the North, who were drafted by a law that allowed the rich to buy their way out of the draft for $300. And so the draft riots of 1863 took place, uprisings of angry whites in northern cities, their targets not the rich, far away, but the blacks, near at hand.

It was an orgy of death and violence. A black man in Detroit described what he saw: a mob, with kegs of beer on wagons, armed with clubs and bricks, marching through the city, attacking black men, women, children. He heard one man say: "If we are got to be killed up for Negroes then we will kill every one in this town."

The Civil War was one of the bloodiest in human history up to that time: 600,000 dead on both sides, in a population of 30 million—the equivalent, in the United States of 1990, with a population of 250 million, of 5 million dead. As the battles became more intense, as the bodies piled up, as war fatigue grew, and hundreds of thousands of slaves were deserting the plantations, 4 million blacks in the South became a great potential force for whichever side would use them.

Du Bois, in *Black Reconstruction*, pointed this out: "It was this plain alternative that brought Lee's sudden surrender. Either the South must make terms with its slaves, free them, use them to fight the North...or they could surrender to the North with the assumption that the North after the war must help them to defend slavery, as it had before. Black women played an important part in the war, especially toward the end. Sojourner Truth became recruiter of black troops for the Union army, as did Josephine St. Pierre Ruffin of Boston. Harriet Tubman raided plantations, leading black and white troops, and in one expedition freed 750 slaves.

It has been said that black acceptance of slavery is proved by the fact that during the Civil War, when there were opportunities for escape, most slaves stayed on the plantation. In fact, half a million ran away—about one in five, a high proportion when one considers that there was great difficulty in knowing where to go and how to live.

In 1865, a South Carolina planter wrote to the *New York Tribune*:

> ...the conduct of the Negro in the late crisis of our affairs has convinced me that we were all laboring under a delusion.... I believed that these people were content, happy, and attached to their masters. But events and reflection have caused me to change these positions.... If they were content, happy and attached to their masters, why did they desert him in the moment of his need and flock to an enemy, whom they did not know; and thus left their perhaps really good masters whom they did know from infancy?

The war produced no general rising of slaves, but in parts of Mississippi, Arkansas, and Kentucky, slaves destroyed plantations or took them over. Two hundred thousand blacks joined the army and navy, and thirty-eight thousand were killed. Historian James McPherson says: "Without their help, the North could not have won the war as soon as it did, and perhaps it could not have won at all."

What happened to blacks in the Union army and in the northern cities during the war gave some hint of how limited the emancipation would be, even with full victory over the Confederacy. Off-duty black soldiers were attacked in northern cities, as in Zanesville, Ohio, in February 1864, where cries were heard to "kill the nigger." Black soldiers were used for the heaviest and dirtiest work, digging trenches, hauling logs and cannon, loading ammunition, digging wells for white regiments. White privates received $13 a month; Negro privates received $10 a month. Finally, in June of 1864, Congress passed a law granting equal pay to Negro soldiers.

After a number of military defeats, the Confederate secretary of war, Judah Benjamin, wrote in late 1864 to a newspaper editor in Charleston: "It is well known that General Lee...is strongly in favor of our using the negroes for defense, and emancipating them, if necessary, for that purpose...." One general, indignant, wrote: "If slaves will make good soldiers, our whole theory of slavery is wrong."

By early 1865, the pressure had mounted, and in March, President Davis of the Confederacy signed a "Negro Soldier Law" authorizing the enlistment of slaves as soldiers, to be freed by consent of their owners and their state governments. But before it had any significant effect, the war was over.

Former slaves, interviewed by the Federal Writers' Project in the thirties, recalled the war's end. Susie Melton:

I was a young gal, about ten years old, and we done heard that Lincoln gonna turn the niggers free.... Was wintertime and mighty cold that night, but everybody commenced getting ready to leave. Didn't care nothin' about missus—was going to the Union lines. And all that night the niggers danced and sang right out in the cold. Next morning at day break we all started out with blankets and clothes and pots and pans and chickens piled on our backs.... And as the sun come up over the trees, the niggers started to singing:

> Sun, you be here and I'll be gone
> Sun, you be here and I'll be gone
> Sun, you be here and I'll be gone

Anna Woods recalled:

We wasn't there in Texas long when the soldiers marched in to tell us that we were free.... I remembers one woman. She jumped on a barrel and she shouted. She jumped off and she shouted. She jumped back on again and shouted some more. She kept that up for a long time, just jumping on a barrel and back off again.

Annie Mae Weathers said:

I remember hearing my pa say that when somebody came and hollered, "You niggers is free at last," say he just dropped his hoe and said in a queer voice, "Thank God for that."

The Federal Writers' Project recorded an ex-slave named Fannie Berry:

Niggers shoutin' and clappin' hands and singin'! Chillun runnin' all over the place beatin' time and yellin'! Everybody happy. Sho' did some celebratin'. Run to the kitchen and shout in the window: "Mammy, don't you cook no more. You's free! You's free!"

Many Negroes understood that their status after the war, whatever their situation legally, would depend on whether they owned the land they worked on or would be forced to be semislaves for others.

Abandoned plantations, however, were leased to former planters, and to white men of the North. As one colored newspaper said: "The slaves were made serfs and chained to the soil.... Such was the boasted freedom acquired by the colored man at the hands of the Yankee."

Under congressional policy approved by Lincoln, the property confiscated during the war under the Confiscation Act of July 1862 would revert to the heirs of the Confederate owners. Dr. John Rock, a black physician in

Boston, spoke at a meeting: "It is the slave who ought to be compensated. The property of the South is by right the property of the slave...."

In the South Carolina Sea Islands, out of 16,000 acres up for sale in March of 1863, freedmen who pooled their money were able to buy 2,000 acres, the rest being bought by northern investors and speculators. A freedman on the islands dictated a letter to a former teacher: "My Dear Young Missus: Do, my missus, tell Linkum dat we wants land—dis bery land dat is rich wid de sweat ob de face and de blood ob we back.... We could a bin buy all we want, but dey make de lots too big, and cut we out."

Ex-slave Thomas Hall told the Federal Writers' Project: "Lincoln got the praise for freeing us, but did he do it? He gave us freedom without giving us any chance to live to ourselve and we still had to depend on the southern white man for work, food, and clothing, and he held us out of necessity and want in a state of servitude but little better than slavery."

The American government had set out to fight the slave states in 1861, not to end slavery, but to retain the enormous national territory and market and resources. Yet, victory required a crusade, and the momentum of that crusade brought new forces into national politics: more blacks determined to make their freedom mean something; more whites—whether Freedman's Bureau officials, or teachers in the Sea Islands, or "carpetbaggers" with various mixtures of humanitarianism and personal ambition—concerned with racial equality.

There was also the powerful interest of the Republican party in maintaining control over the national government, with the prospect of southern black votes to accomplish this. Northern businessmen, seeing Republican policies as beneficial to them, went along for a while.

The result was that brief period after the Civil War in which southern Negroes voted, elected blacks to state legislatures and to Congress, introduced free and racially mixed public education to the South. A legal framework was constructed. The Thirteenth Amendment outlawed slavery: "Neither slavery nor involuntary servitude, except as a punishment for crime whereof the party shall have been duly convicted, shall exist within the United States, or any place subject to their jurisdiction." The Fourteenth Amendment repudiated the prewar Dred Scott decision by declaring that "all persons born or naturalized in the United States" were citizens. It also seemed to make a powerful statement for racial equality, severely limiting "states' rights":

> No State shall make or enforce any law which shall abridge the privileges or immunities of citizens of the United States; nor shall any State

deprive any person of life, liberty, or property, without due process of law; nor deny to any person within its jurisdiction the equal protection of the laws.

The Fifteenth Amendment said: "The right of citizens of the United States to vote shall not be denied or abridged by the United States or by any State on account of race, color, or previous condition of servitude."

Congress passed a number of laws in the late 1860s and early 1870s in the same spirit—laws making it a crime to deprive Negroes of their rights, requiring federal officials to enforce those rights, giving Negroes the right to enter contracts and buy property without discrimination. And the Civil Rights Act of 1875 outlawed the exclusion of Negroes from hotels, theaters, railroads, and other public accommodations.

With these laws, with the Union army in the South as protection, and a civilian army of officials in the Freedman's Bureau to help them, southern Negroes came forward, voted, formed political organizations, and expressed themselves forcefully on issues important to them.

They were hampered in this for several years by Andrew Johnson, the vice president under Lincoln, who became president when Lincoln was assassinated at the close of the war. Johnson vetoed bills to help Negroes; he made it easy for Confederate states to come back into the Union without guaranteeing equal rights to blacks. During his presidency, these returned southern states enacted "black codes," which made the freed slaves like serfs, still working the plantations.

Andrew Johnson clashed with senators and congressmen who, in some cases for reasons of justice, in others out of political calculation, supported equal rights and voting for the freedman. These members of Congress succeeded in impeaching Johnson in 1868, using as an excuse that he had violated some minor statute, but the Senate fell one vote short of the two-thirds required to remove him from office. In the presidential election of that year, Republican Ulysses Grant was elected, winning by 300,000 votes, with 700,000 Negroes voting, and so Johnson was out as an obstacle. Now the southern states could come back into the Union only by approving the new constitutional amendments.

Whatever northern politicians were doing to help their cause, southern blacks were determined to make the most of their freedom, in spite of their lack of land and resources. They began immediately asserting their independence of whites, forming their own churches, becoming politically active, strengthening their family ties, trying to educate their children.

Black voting in the period after 1869 resulted in two Negro members of the U.S. Senate (Hiram Revels and Blanche Bruce, both from Mississippi) and twenty congressmen. This list would dwindle rapidly after 1876; the last black left Congress in 1901.

Negroes were now elected to southern state legislatures, although in all these they were a minority except in the lower house of the South Carolina legislature. A great propaganda campaign was undertaken North and South (one which lasted well into the twentieth century, in the history textbooks of American schools) to show that blacks were inept, lazy, corrupt, and ruinous to the governments of the South when they were in office. Undoubtedly there was corruption, but one could hardly claim that blacks had invented political conniving, especially in the bizarre climate of financial finagling North and South after the Civil War.

It was true that the public debt of South Carolina, $7 million in 1865, went up to $29 million in 1873, but the new legislature introduced free public schools into the state for the first time. Not only were seventy thousand Negro children going to school by 1876 where none had gone before, but fifty thousand white children were going to school where only twenty thousand had attended in 1860.

A Columbia University scholar of the twentieth century, John Burgess, referred to Black Reconstruction as follows:

> In place of government by the most intelligent and virtuous part of the people for the benefit of the governed, here was government by the most ignorant and vicious part of the population.... A black skin means membership in a race of men which has never of itself succeeded in subjecting passion to reason; has never, therefore, created civilization of any kind.

One has to measure against those words the black leaders in the postwar South. For instance, Henry MacNeal Turner, who had escaped from peonage on a South Carolina plantation at the age of fifteen, taught himself to read and write, read law books while a messenger in a lawyer's office in Baltimore, and medical books while a handyman in a Baltimore medical school, served as chaplain to a Negro regiment, and then was elected to the first postwar legislature of Georgia.

In 1868, the Georgia legislature voted to expel all its Negro members—two senators, twenty-five representatives—and Turner spoke to the Georgia House of Representatives (a black woman graduate student at Atlanta University later brought his speech to light):

> Mr. Speaker: ...I am here to demand my rights, and to hurl thunderbolts at the men who would dare to cross the threshold of my manhood....

148

> The scene presented in this House, today, is one unparalleled.... Never, in the history of the world, has a man been arraigned before a body clothed with legislative, judicial or executive functions, charged with the offense of being of a darker hue than his fellowmen....
>
> The great question, sir is this: Am I a man? If I am such, I claim the rights of a man....
>
> Why, sir, we have worked in your fields, and garnered your harvests, for two hundred and fifty years! And what do we ask of you in return? Do we ask you for compensation for the sweat our fathers bore for you—for the tears you have caused, and the hearts you have broken, and the lives you have curtailed, and the blood you have spilled? Do we ask retaliation? We ask it not. We are willing to let the dead past bury its dead; but we ask you now for our RIGHTS....

Frances Ellen Watkins Harper, born free in Baltimore, self-supporting from the age of thirteen, working as a nursemaid, later as an abolitionist lecturer, reader of her own poetry, spoke all through the southern states after the war. She was a feminist, participant in the 1866 Woman's Rights Convention, and founder of the National Association of Colored Women. In the 1890s she wrote the first novel published by a black woman: *Iola Leroy, or Shadows Uplifted.*

Through all the struggles to gain equal rights for blacks, certain black women spoke out on their special situation. Sojourner Truth, at a meeting of the American Equal Rights Association, said:

> There is a great stir about colored men getting their rights, but not a word about the colored women; and if colored men get their rights, and not colored women theirs, you see the colored men will be masters over the women, and it will be just as bad as it was before. So I am for keeping the thing going while things are stirring; because if we wait till it is still, it will take a great while to get it going again....
>
> I am above eighty years old; it is about time for me to be going. I have been forty years a slave and forty years free, and would be here forty years more to have equal rights for all...

The constitutional amendments were passed, the laws for racial equality were passed, and the black man began to vote and to hold office. But so long as the Negro remained dependent on privileged whites for work, for the necessities of life, his vote could be bought or taken away by threat of force. Thus, laws calling for equal treatment became meaningless. While Union troops—including colored troops—remained in the

South, this process was delayed. But the balance of military powers began to change.

The southern white oligarchy used its economic power to organize the Ku Klux Klan and other terrorist groups. Northern politicians began to weigh the advantage of the political support of impoverished blacks— maintained in voting and office only by force—against the more stable situation of a South returned to white supremacy, accepting Republican dominance and business legislation. It was only a matter of time before blacks would be reduced once again to conditions not far from slavery.

Violence began almost immediately with the end of the war. In Memphis, Tennessee, in May of 1866, whites on a rampage of murder killed forty-six Negroes, most of them veterans of the Union army, as well as two white sympathizers. Five Negro women were raped. Ninety homes, twelve schools, and four churches were burned. In New Orleans, in the summer of 1866, another riot against blacks killed thirty-five Negroes and three whites.

The violence mounted through the late 1860s and early 1870s as the Ku Klux Klan organized raids, lynchings, beatings, burnings. For Kentucky alone, between 1867 and 1871, the National Archives lists 116 acts of violence. A sampling:

1. A mob visited Harrodsburg in Mercer County to take from jail a man name Robertson Nov. 14, 1867....
5. Sam Davis hung by a mob in Harrodsburg, May 28, 1868.
6. Wm. Pierce hung by a mob in Christian July 12, 1868.
7. Geo. Roger hung by a mob in Bradsfordville Martin County July 11, 1868....
10. Silas Woodford age sixty badly beaten by disguised mob....
109. Negro killed by Ku Klux Klan in Hay county January 14, 1871.

As white violence rose in the 1870s, the national government, even under President Grant, became less enthusiastic about defending blacks, and certainly not prepared to arm them. The Supreme Court played its gyroscopic role of pulling the other branches of government back to more conservative directions when they went too far. It began interpreting the Fourteenth Amendment—passed presumably for racial equality—in a way that made it impotent for this purpose.

In 1883, the Civil Rights Act of 1875, outlawing discrimination against Negroes using public facilities, was nullified by the Supreme Court, which said: "Individual invasion of individual rights is not the subject-matter of the amendment." The Fourteenth Amendment, it said, was aimed at state action only. "No state shall..."

A remarkable dissent was written by Supreme Court Justice John Harlan, himself a former slave owner in Kentucky, who said there was constitutional justification for banning private discrimination. He noted that the Thirteenth Amendment, which banned slavery, applied to individual plantation owners, not just the state. He then argued that discrimination was a badge of slavery and similarly outlawable. He pointed also to the first clause of the Fourteenth Amendment, saying that anyone born in the United States was a citizen, and to the clause in Article 4, Section 2, saying "the citizens of each State shall be entitled to all privileges and immunities of citizens in the several States."

Harlan was fighting a force greater than logic or justice; the mood of the Court reflected a new coalition of northern industrialists and southern businessmen-planters. The culmination of this mood came in the decision of 1896, *Plessy v. Ferguson*, when the Court ruled that a railroad could segregate black and white if the segregated facilities were equal. Harlan again dissented: "Our Constitution is color-blind...."

It was the year 1877 that spelled out clearly and dramatically what was happening. When the year opened, the presidential election of the past November was in bitter dispute. The Democratic candidate, Samuel Tilden, had 184 electoral votes and needed one more to be elected: his popular vote was greater by 250,000. The Republican candidate, Rutherford Hayes, had 166 electoral votes. Three states not yet counted had a total of 19 electoral votes; if Hayes could get all of those, he would have 185 and be president. This is what his managers proceeded to arrange. They made concessions to the Democratic party and the white South, including an agreement to remove Union troops from the South, the last military obstacle to the reestablishment of white supremacy there.

Northern political and economic interests needed powerful allies and stability in the face of national crisis. The country had been in economic depression since 1873, and by 1877 farmers and workers were beginning to rebel. As C. Vann Woodward puts it in his history of the 1877 Compromise, *Reunion and Reaction*:

> It was a depression year, the worst year of the severest depression yet experienced. In the East labor and the unemployed were in a bitter and violent temper.... Out West a tide of agrarian radicalism was rising.... From both East and West came threats against the elaborate structure of protective tariffs, national banks, railroad subsidies and monetary arrangements upon which the new economic order was founded.

It was a time for reconciliation between southern and northern elites. Woodward asks: "[C]ould the South be induced to combine with the Northern conservatives and become a prop instead of a menace to the new capitalist order?"

With billions of dollars' worth of slaves gone, the wealth of the old South was wiped out. They now looked to the national government for help: credit, subsidies, flood control projects. Woodward says: "By means of appropriations, subsidies, grants, and bonds such as Congress had so lavishly showered upon capitalist enterprise in the North, the South might yet mend its fortunes—or at any rate the fortunes of a privileged elite."

And so the deal was made. The proper committee was set up by both houses of Congress to decide where the electoral votes would go. The decision was: they belonged to Hayes, and he was now president. As Woodward sums it up:

> The Compromise of 1877 did not restore the old order in the South.... It did assure the dominant whites political autonomy and non-intervention in matters of race policy and promised them a share in the blessings of the new economic order. In return, the South became, in effect, a satellite of the dominant region....

The importance of the new capitalism in overturning what black power existed in the postwar South is affirmed by Horace Mann Bond's study of Alabama Reconstruction. It was an age of coal and power, and northern Alabama had both. "The bankers in Philadelphia and New York, and even in London and Paris, had known this for almost two decades. The only thing lacking was transportation." And so, in the mid-1870s, Bond notes, northern bankers began appearing in the directories of southern railroad lines. J. P. Morgan appears by 1875 as director for several lines in Alabama and Georgia.

In the year 1886, Henry Grady, an editor of the *Atlanta Constitution*, spoke at a dinner in New York. In the audience were J. P. Morgan, H. M. Flagler (an associate of John D. Rockefeller), Russell Sage, and Charles Tiffany. His talk was called "The New South" and his theme was: Let bygones be bygones; let us have a new era of peace and prosperity.

That same month, an article in the *New York Daily Tribune* told of "the leading coal and iron men of the South" visiting New York and leaving "thoroughly satisfied." The reason:

> The time for which they have been waiting for nearly twenty years, when Northern capitalists would be convinced not only of the safety but

of the immense profits to be gained from the investment of their money in developing the fabulously rich coal and iron resources of Alabama, Tennessee, and Georgia, has come at last.

The North, it must be recalled, did not have to undergo a revolution in its thinking to accept the subordination of the Negro. When the Civil War ended, nineteen of the twenty-four northern states did not allow blacks to vote.

By 1900, all the southern states, in new constitutions and new statutes, had written into law the disfranchisement and segregation of Negroes, and a *New York Times* editorial said: "Northern men...no longer denounce the suppression of the Negro vote.... The necessity of it under the supreme law of self-preservation is candidly recognized."

Those Negro leaders most accepted in white society, like the educator Booker T. Washington, a one-time White House guest of Theodore Roosevelt, urged Negro political passivity. Invited by the white organizers of the Cotton States and International Exposition in Atlanta in 1895 to speak, Washington urged the southern Negro to "cast down your bucket where you are"—that is, to stay in the South, to be farmers, mechanics, domestics, perhaps even to attain to the professions.

He urged white employers to hire Negroes rather than immigrants of "strange tongue and habits." Negroes, "without strikes and labor wars," were the "most patient, faithful, law-abiding and unresentful people that the world has seen." He said: "The wisest among my race understand that the agitation of questions of social equality is the extremest folly."

Perhaps Washington saw this as a necessary tactic of survival in a time of hangings and burnings of Negroes throughout the South. It was a low point for black people in America. Thomas Fortune, a young black editor of the *New York Globe*, testified before a Senate committee in 1883 about the situation of the Negro in the United States. He spoke of "widespread poverty," of government betrayal, of desperate Negro attempts to educate themselves.

The average wage of Negro farm laborers in the South was about fifty cents a day, Fortune said. He was usually paid in "orders," not money, which he could use only at a store controlled by the planter, "a system of fraud."

Fortune spoke of "the penitentiary system of the South, with its infamous chain-gang... the object being to terrorize the blacks and furnish victims for contractors, who purchase the labor of these wretches from the State for a song.... The white man who shoots a negro always goes free, while the negro who steals a hog is sent to the chain-gang for ten years."

Many Negroes fled. About six thousand black people left Texas, Louisiana, and Mississippi and migrated to Kansas to escape violence and poverty. "We have found no leader to trust but God overhead of us," one said. Those who remained in the South began to organize in self-defense all through the 1880s, in the face of over a hundred lynchings a year.

There were black leaders who thought Booker T. Washington wrong in advocating caution and moderation. John Hope, a young black man in Georgia, who heard Washington's Cotton Exposition speech, told students at a Negro college in Nashville, Tennessee: "If we are not striving for equality, in heaven's name for what are we living? I regard it as cowardly and dishonest for any of our colored men to tell white people or colored people that we are not struggling for equality...."

Another black man, who came to teach at Atlanta University, W. E. B. Du Bois, saw the late-nineteenth-century betrayal of the Negro as part of a larger happening in the United States, something happening not only to poor blacks but to poor whites. In *Black Reconstruction*, he saw this new capitalism as part of a process of exploitation and bribery taking place in all the "civilized" countries of the world: "Home labor in cultured lands, appeased and misled by a ballot whose power the dictatorship of vast capital strictly curtailed, was bribed by high wage and political office to unite in an exploitation of white, yellow, brown and black labor, in lesser lands...."

Was Du Bois right—that in that growth of American capitalism, before and after the Civil War, whites as well as blacks were in some sense becoming slaves?

Exercises

1. On what basis did the U.S. government support slavery?

2. What actions did the U.S. government take to support slavery? Do these actions support Zinn's assertion on p. 139 that "Such a government would never accept an end to slavery by rebellion"? Why would the white elite want to determine when and how slavery would end?

3. Page 130: "Are the *conditions* of slavery as important as the *existence* of slavery?" Why does Zinn ask this question?

4. Why would someone dance and laugh the evening of the morning he received two hundred lashes?

5. Was resistance to slavery more, as much, or less, effective than rebellion? Explain.

6. How were the following used as methods of controlling not only the slave population but poor whites as well?
    * force
    * segregation
    * religion
What is the evidence that it was dangerous to slave masters to allow poor whites and blacks to fraternize?

7. How did slaves manage to maintain a community? Why did they work so hard to do so?

8. How can you account for Harriet Tubman's success?
        a. She had no fear.
        b. She was a fanatic.
        c. She was lucky.
        d. She had lots of help.
        e. She wore a disguise.
        f. She was smart enough to get out and not return.
        g. She carried a revolver.

    Does Zinn give you enough information to answer this question? If yes, what is the data he provides? If not, what information do you need (what questions do you still need answers to) in order to answer this question with any degree of satisfaction?

9. Why was there a price on David Walker's head?

10. Why might Frederick Douglass have been "the most famous black man of his time"?

11. What was J. W. Loguen's argument against the Fugitive Slave Act of 1850?

12. What does Sarah Logue's proposal and Loguen's response reveal about how slave owners justified slavery?

13. Why would the United States even talk about going to war with England over the Creole?

14. How did the racism of white abolitionists reveal itself? How could a white person be both an abolitionist and a racist? Why would a racist be an abolitionist? (Was the institution of slavery undermining the free labor philosophy that allowed the northern elite to justify economic inequality of the factory system?)

15. What was the "the triple hurdle" that Sojourner Truth had to overcome?

16. How old was John Brown at the time he led the raid on Harper's Ferry? What did he hope to accomplish?

17. How does the picture of John Brown below compare to the one that Zinn paints? The incident described below takes place in Kansas, in 1856, two years before Brown's raid on Harper's Ferry. John Brown had recently declared "that something must be done to show these barbarians that we too have rights." They were headed for Pottawatomie Creek with broad swords.

> ...for the lanky Ohio farmer who proposed to meddle with the peculiar institution lived with strange fever-haunted dreams and felt an overwhelming compulsion to act on them. He was a rover, a ne'er-do-well, wholly ineffectual in everything he did save that he had the knack of drawing an entire nation after him on the road to unreasoning violence....
>
> They had taken up arms two or three days earlier, along with other men, in a dimly legal free-state militia company, to go to the defense of Lawrence [Kansas]...they got there too late, and all of the company but Brown and his chosen seven disbanded and went home. But Brown was obsessed....
>
> John Brown and his band [four of which were his sons] went stumping along through the night. They were in proslavery land

now, and any man they saw would be an enemy. They came to one lonely cabin, saw lamplight gleaming under the door, and pounded for admittance. There was a noise as if someone were cocking a gun and sliding the muzzle through a chink in the logs, and the men slipped away from there—it was not precisely open combat that they were looking for. They went on, and after a time they came to a cabin occupied by a family named Doyle.

The Doyles were poor whites from Tennessee. They had come to Kansas recently, and although they believed in slavery…they did not like to lie too close to it; it appears that they had migrated in order to get away from it. Brown hammered on the door. It was opened, and he ordered Doyle and Doyle's two grown sons to come outside. The three men obeyed, the door closed behind them, and Brown's band led the three away from the cabin. Then there were quick muffled sounds, brief cries, silence and stillness and darkness, and Brown and his followers went off down the road. In the morning the bodies of the three Doyles were found lying on the ground, fearfully mangled. They had been hacked to death with the [broad swords].... The father had been shot in the head.

Bruce Catton,
This Hallowed Ground, New York,
Simon and Shuster, 1961,
pp. 10–11.

18. Lincoln was able to speak to both sides of the slavery debate. Why did he feel compelled to speak to both sides, given his personal solution to the problem of slavery in America?

19. How did the northern elite's plans for economic expansion force the South into radical opposition?

20. According to Zinn, "Lincoln initiated hostilities by trying to repossess the federal base at Fort Sumter."

   a. Look at three or four other sources to compare the details of the Battle of Fort Sumter with Zinn's interpretation.

   b. Compare Lincoln's maneuvers surrounding the Fort Sumter battle with Polk's maneuvers in starting the Mexican-American War. What might you conclude from such a comparison?

21. Lincoln's goal in waging war on the South was to "preserve the Union" by subjugating the South of the northern capital's control. What series of events altered Lincoln's rhetoric to include emancipation as a goal of the war?

22. How was the Emancipation Proclamation a military tactic?

23. What evidence supports the thesis that the North could not have won without the help of American blacks?

24. After the South surrendered unconditionally, how did Congress dispose of the land confiscated during the war? Of what significance was this decision? (For example, what did it reveal about the congressional majority's belief about the future status of blacks in the United States?)

25. Given the data from Zinn, how would you characterize (good, bad, messy, progressive, regressive) the period of Reconstruction (1863–1877)? In your characterization, include a description of the role of the U.S. government and the southern states, the status of the freed slaves, and the actions of white racists.

26. In 1868, was the Georgia legislature successful in expelling its black members?

27. Why does Zinn choose to tell us about Frances Ellen Watkins Harper? What is the point?

28. Why does Zinn think that laws calling for equal treatment of blacks and whites were meaningless in practice? What other reforms would have had to accompany such laws for the laws to be meaningful in Zinn's eyes? Why? Do you agree?

29. What caused Republicans to abandon their defense of black rights? Discuss economic as well as political reasons.

30. In 1883, the Supreme Court declared the Civil Rights Act of 1875 unconstitutional. What was the majority argument? What was Justice Harlan's dissenting argument?

31. How does Horace Mann Bond's study of Alabama Reconstruction reveal that the ultimate result of the Civil War was to reduce the South to colonial status? [To help define "colonial status," one might think the relationship between Britain and her American colonies was as defined by the Navigation Acts. These acts were passed by the English Parliament starting in 1665.]

32. The editorial board of the *New York Times* wrote in 1900: "Northern men...no longer denounce the suppression of the Negro vote.... The necessity of it under the supreme law of self-preservation is candidly recognized" [page 153]. Why would allowing white southerners to deny blacks the right and ability to vote (often by violent means, including murder) contribute to the self-preservation of "northern men"?

33. How did blacks respond to the end of the U.S. government's military protection of black civil rights?

34. *Draw a map* that identifies the following: those states that voted for Lincoln, Douglas, Breckinridge, and Bell in the election of 1860.

35. *Debate Resolution*: The Civil War was fought to end slavery.

36. *Draw a map* for the year 1854 that includes the following: slave and free states; free territories; territories open to slavery as determined by the Kansas-Nebraska Act of 1854; territories open to slavery as determined by the Compromise of 1850; the Missouri Compromise (1820) line.

Chapter 10

The Other Civil War

The stories of class struggle in the nineteenth century are not usually found in textbooks on United States history. That struggle is most often obscured by the pretense of intense conflict between the major political parties, although both parties have represented the same dominant classes of the nation.

Andrew Jackson, who was elected president in 1828 and served for two terms, said he spoke for "the humble members of society—the farmer, mechanics and laborers." He certainly did not speak for the Indians being pushed off their lands, or for the slaves. But the tensions aroused by the developing factory system, the growing immigration, required that the government develop a mass base of support among whites. The myth of "Jacksonian Democracy" was designed to do just that.

It was the new politics of ambiguity—speaking for the lower and middle classes to get their support in times of rapid growth and potential turmoil. To give people a choice between two different parties and allow them, in a period of rebellion, to choose the slightly more democratic one was an ingenious mode of control.

The Jacksonian idea was to achieve stability and control by winning to the Democratic party "the middling interest, and especially...the substantial yeomanry of the country" by "prudent, judicious, well-considered reform." That is, reform that would not yield too much. These were the words of Robert Rantoul, a reformer, corporation lawyer, and Jacksonian Democrat. It was a forecast of the successful appeal of the Democratic party—and at times the Republican party—in the twentieth century.

America was developing with enormous speed and excitement. In 1790, fewer than a million Americans lived in cities; in 1840 the figure was 11 million. New York had 130,000 people in 1820, a million by 1860. And while the traveler Alexis de Tocqueville had expressed astonishment at "the general equality of condition among the people," his observation was not in accord with the facts.

In Philadelphia, working-class families lived fifty-five to a tenement, usually one room per family, with no garbage removal, no toilets, no fresh air or water. There was fresh water newly pumped from the Schuylkill River, but it was going to the homes of the rich.

In New York you could see the poor lying in the streets with the garbage. There were no sewers in the slums, and filthy water drained into yards and alleys, into the cellars where the poorest of the poor lived, bringing with it a typhoid epidemic in 1837, typhus in 1842. In the cholera epidemic of 1832, the rich fled the city; the poor stayed and died.

These poor could not be counted on as political allies of the government. But they were there—like slaves, or Indians—invisible ordinarily, a menace if they rose. There were more solid citizens, however, who might give steady support to the system—better-paid workers, landowning farmers. Also, there was the new urban white-collar worker, born in the rising commerce of the time, who would be wooed enough and paid enough to consider himself a member of the bourgeois class and to give support to that class in times of crisis.

The opening of the West was being helped by turnpikes, canals, railroads, the telegraph. Farms were becoming mechanized. Iron plows cut plowing time in half; by the 1850s John Deere Company was turning out ten thousand plows a year. Cyrus McCormick was making a thousand mechanical reapers a year in his factory in Chicago. A man with a sickle could cut half an acre of wheat in a day; with a reaper he could cut ten acres.

In an economic system not rationally planned for human need, but developing fitfully, chaotically out of the profit motive, there seemed to be no way to avoid recurrent booms and slumps. There was a depression in 1837, another in 1853. One way to achieve stability was to decrease competition, organize the businesses, move toward monopoly. In the mid-1850s, price agreements and mergers became frequent: the New York Central Railroad was a merger of many railroads. The American Brass Association was formed "to meet ruinous competition," it said. The Hampton County Cotton Spinners Association was organized to control prices, and so was the American Iron Association.

With industry requiring large amounts of capital, risks had to be minimized. State legislatures gave charters to corporations giving them legal rights to conduct business and raise money, without imperiling the personal fortunes of the owners and managers. Between 1790 and 1860, twenty-three hundred corporations were chartered.

The federal government, starting with Alexander Hamilton and the first Congress, had given vital help to the business interests, and this was now done on a much larger scale.

Railroad men traveled to Washington and to state capitals armed with money, shares of stock, free railroad passes. Between 1850 and 1857 they got 25 million acres of public land, free of charge, and millions of dollars in bonds—loans—from the state legislatures. In Wisconsin in 1856, the LaCrosse and Milwaukee Railroad got a million acres free by distributing about $900,000 in stocks and bonds to fifty-nine assemblymen, thirteen senators, and the governor. Two years later the railroad was bankrupt and the bonds were worthless.

In the East, mill owners had become powerful, and organized. By 1850, fifteen Boston families called the "Associates" controlled 20 percent of the cotton spindleage in the United States, 39 percent of insurance capital in Massachusetts, 40 percent of banking resources in Boston.

On the eve of the Civil War it was money and profit, not the movement against slavery, that was uppermost in the priorities of the men who ran the country. As Thomas Cochran and William Miller (*The Age of Enterprise*) put it:

> Webster was the hero of the North—not Emerson, Parker, Garrison, or Phillips; Webster the tariff man, the land speculator, the corporation lawyer, politician for the Boston Associates, inheritor of Hamilton's coronet. "The great object of government" said he "is the protection of property at home, and respect and renown abroad." For these he preached union; for these he surrendered the fugitive slave.

They wrote of the Boston rich:

> Living sumptuously on Beacon Hill, admired by their neighbors for their philanthropy and their patronage of art and culture, these men traded in State Street while overseers ran their factories, managers directed their railroads, agents sold their water power and real estate.

Ralph Waldo Emerson described Boston in those years: "There is a certain poor-smell in all the streets, in Beacon Street and Mount Vernon, as well as in the lawyers' offices, and the wharves, and the same meanness and sterility, and leave-all-hope-behind, as one finds in a boot manufacturer's premises." The preacher Theodore Parker told his congregation: "Money is this day the strongest power of the nation."

The attempts at political stability, at economic control, did not quite work. The new industrialism, the crowded cities, the long hours in the factories, the sudden economic crises leading to high prices and lost jobs, the lack of food and water, the freezing winters, the hot tenements in the summer, the epidemics of disease, the deaths of children—these led to sporadic reactions from the poor. Sometimes there were spontaneous, unorganized uprisings against the rich. Sometimes the anger was deflected into racial hatred for blacks, religious warfare against Catholics, nativist fury against immigrants. Sometimes it was organized into demonstrations and strikes.

The full extent of the working-class consciousness of those years—as of any years—is lost in history, but fragments remain and make us wonder how much of this always existed underneath the very practical silence of working people. In 1827 an "Address...before the Mechanics and Working Classes...of Philadelphia" was recorded, written by an "Unlettered Mechanic," probably a young shoemaker:

> We find ourselves oppressed on every hand—we labor hard in producing all the comforts of life for the enjoyment of others, while we ourselves obtain but a scanty portion, and even that in the present state of society depends on the will of employers.

Frances Wright of Scotland, an early feminist and utopian socialist, was invited by Philadelphia workingmen to speak on the Fourth of July, 1829, to one of the first citywide associations of labor unions in the United States. She asked if the Revolution had been fought "to crush down the sons and daughters of your country's industry under...neglect, poverty, vice, starvation, and disease...." She wondered if the new technology was not lowering the value of human labor, making people appendages to machines, crippling the minds and bodies of child laborers.

Later that year, George Henry Evans, a printer, editor of the *Workingman's Advocate*, wrote "The Working Men's Declaration of Independence." Among its list of "facts" submitted to "candid and impartial" fellow citizens:

> 1. The laws for levying taxes are...operating most oppressively on one class of society....
> 3. The laws for private incorporation are all partial...favoring one class of society to the expense of the other....

6. The laws...have deprived nine tenths of the members of the body politics, who are not wealthy, of the equal means to enjoy "life, liberty, and the pursuit of happiness."...The lien law in favor of the landlords against tenants...is one illustration among innumerable others.

Evans believed that "all on arriving at adult age are entitled to equal property."

A citywide "Trades' Union" in Boston in 1834, including mechanics from Charlestown and women shoe binders from Lynn, referred to the Declaration of Independence:

We hold...that laws which have a tendency to raise any peculiar class above their fellow citizens, by granting special privileges, are contrary to and in defiance of those primary principles....

Our public system of Education, which so liberally endows those seminaries of learning, which...are only accessible to the wealthy, while our common schools...are so illy provided for.... Thus even in child-hood the poor are apt to think themselves inferior....

Episodes of insurrection of that time have gone unrecorded in traditional histories. Such was the riot in Baltimore in the summer of 1835, when the Bank of Maryland collapsed and its depositors lost their savings. Convinced that a great fraud had taken place, a crowd gathered and began breaking the windows of officials associated with the bank. When the rioters destroyed a house, the militia attacked, killing some twenty people, wounding a hundred. The next evening, other houses were attacked.

During those years, trade unions were forming. The courts called them conspiracies to restrain trade and therefore illegal. A New York judge, levying fines against "a conspiracy" of tailors, said: "In this favored land of law and liberty, the road to advancement is open to all.... Every American knows that...he needs no artificial combination for his protection. They are of foreign origin and I am led to believe mainly upheld by foreigners."

A handbill was then circulated throughout the city:

THE RICH AGAINST THE POOR!

Judge Edwards, the tool of the aristocracy, against the people! Mechanics and working men! A deadly blow has been struck at your liberty!...They have established the precedent that workingmen have no right to regulate the price of labor, or, in other words, the rich are the only judges of the wants of the poor man.

At City Hall Park, twenty-seven thousand people gathered to denounce the court decision, and elected a Committee of Correspondence which organized, three months later, a convention of Mechanics, Farmers, and Working Men, elected by farmers and working people in various towns in New York State. The convention met in Utica, drew up a Declaration of Independence from existing political parties, and established an Equal Rights party.

Although they ran their own candidates for office, there was no great confidence in the ballot as a way of achieving change. One of the great orators of the movement, Seth Luther, told a Fourth of July rally: "We will try the ballot box first. If that will not effect our righteous purpose, the next and last resort is the cartridge box."

The crisis of 1837 led to rallies and meetings in many cities. The banks had suspended specie payments—refusing to pay hard money for the bank notes they had issued. Working people, already hard-pressed to buy food, found that the prices of flour, pork, coal became impossibly high. In Philadelphia, twenty thousand people assembled, and someone wrote to President Van Buren describing it:

> This afternoon, the largest public meeting I ever saw assembled in Independence Square. It was called by placards posted through the city yesterday and last night. It was projected and carried on entirely by the working classes; without consultation or cooperation with any of those who usually take the lead in such matters. The officers and speakers were of those classes.... It was directed against the banks.

In New York, members of the Equal Rights party (often called the Locofocos) announced a meeting: "Bread, Meat, Rent, and Fuel! Their prices must come down! The people will meet in the Park, rain or shine, at 4 o'clock, p.m. on Monday afternoon.... All friends of humanity determined to resist monopolists and extortioners are invited to attend." The *Commercial Register*, a New York newspaper, reported on the meeting and what followed:

> At 4 o'clock, a concourse of several thousands had convened in front of the City Hall.... One of these orators...directed the popular vengeance against Mr. Eli Hart. "Fellow citizens!'" he exclaimed, "Mr. Hart has now 53,000 barrels of flour in his store; let us go and offer him eight dollars a barrel, and if he does not take it..."
>
> A large body of the meeting moved off in the direction of Mr. Hart's store.... Barrels of flour, by dozens, fifties and hundreds were tumbled into the street from the doors, and thrown in rapid succession

from the windows.... About one thousand bushels of wheat, and four or five hundred barrels of flour, were thus wantonly and foolishly as well as wickedly destroyed. The most active of the destructionists were foreigners, but there were probably five hundred or a thousand others, standing by and abetting their incendiary labors.

Amidst the falling and bursting of the barrels and sacks of wheat, numbers of women were engaged, like the crones who strip the dead in battle, filling the boxes and baskets with which they were provided, and their aprons, with flour, and making off with it....

Night had now closed upon the scene, but the work of destruction did not cease until strong bodies of police arrived, followed, soon afterward, by detachments of troops....

This was the Flour Riot of 1837. During the crisis of that year, 50,000 persons (one-third of the working class) were without work in New York City alone, and 200,000 (of a population of 500,000) were living, as one observer put it, "in utter and hopeless distress."

There is no complete record of the meetings, riots, actions, organized and disorganized, violent and nonviolent, which took place in the mid-nineteenth century, as the country grew, as the cities became crowded, with working conditions bad, living conditions intolerable, with the economy in the hands of bankers, speculators, landlords, merchants.

In 1835, fifty different trades organized unions in Philadelphia, and there was a successful general strike of laborers, factory workers, bookbinders, jewelers, coal heavers, butchers, cabinet workers—for the ten-hour day.

Weavers in Philadelphia in the early 1840s—mostly Irish immigrants working at home for employers—struck for higher wages, attacked the homes of those refusing to strike, and destroyed their work. A sheriff's posse tried to arrest some strikers, but it was broken up by four hundred weavers armed with muskets and sticks.

Soon, however, antagonism developed between these Irish Catholic weavers and native-born Protestant skilled workers over issues of religion. In May 1844 there were Protestant-Catholic riots in Kensington, a suburb of Philadelphia. Middle-class politicians soon led each group into a different political party (the nativists into the American Republican party, the Irish into the Democratic party), party politics and religion now substituting for class conflict.

The result of all this, says David Montgomery, historian of the Kensington Riots, was the fragmentation of the Philadelphia working class. It "thereby created for historians the illusion of a society lacking in class conflict," while in reality the class conflicts of nineteenth-century America "were as fierce as any known to the industrial world."

The immigrants from Ireland, fleeing starvation there when the potato crop failed, were coming to America now, packed into old sailing ships. The stories of these ships differ only in detail from the accounts of the ships that earlier brought black slaves and later German, Italian, and Russian immigrants. This is a contemporary account of one ship arriving from Ireland in May 1847, detained at Grosse Isle on the Canadian border:

> Who can imagine the horrors of even the shortest passage in an emigrant ship crowded beyond its utmost capacity of stowage with unhappy beings of all ages, with fever raging in their midst...the crew sullen or brutal from very desperation, or paralyzed with terror of the plague—the miserable passengers in different stages of the disease; many dying, some dead;...the wails of children, the ravings of the delirious, the cries and groans of those in mortal agony!

How could these new Irish immigrants, themselves poor and despised, become sympathizers with the black slaves? Indeed, most working-class activists at this time ignored the plight of blacks. Ely Moore, a New York trade union leader elected to Congress, argued in the House of Representatives against receiving abolitionist petitions. Racist hostility became an easy substitute for class frustration.

On the other hand, a white shoemaker wrote in 1848 in the *Awl*, the newspaper of Lynn shoe factory workers:

> ...we are nothing but a standing army that keeps three million of our brethren in bondage.... Living under the shade of Bunker Hill monument, demanding in the name of humanity, our right, and withholding those rights from others because their skin is black! Is it any wonder that God in his righteous anger has punished us by forcing us to drink the bitter cup of degradation.

Another economic crisis came in 1857. The boom in railroads and manufacturing, the surge of immigration, the increased speculation in stocks and bonds, the stealing, corruption, manipulation, led to wild expansion and then crash. By October of that year, 200,000 were unemployed, and thousands of recent immigrants crowded into the eastern ports, hoping to work their way back to Europe.

In Newark, New Jersey, a rally of several thousand demanded the city give work to the unemployed. And in New York, fifteen thousand people met at Tompkins Square in downtown Manhattan. From there they marched to Wall Street and paraded around the Stock Exchange shouting: "We want work!" That summer, riots occurred in the slum areas of New York. A mob of five hundred attacked the police one day with pistols and bricks. There were parades of the unemployed, demanding bread and work, looting shops. In November, a crowd occupied City Hall, and the U.S. marines were brought in to drive them out.

Of the country's work force of 6 million in 1850, half a million were women: 330,000 worked as domestics; 55,000 were teachers. Of the 181,000 women in factories, half worked in textile mills.

They organized. Women struck by themselves for the first time in 1825. They were the United Tailoresses of New York, demanding higher wages. In 1828, the first strike of mill women on their own took place in Dover, New Hampshire, when several hundred women paraded with banners and flags. They were forced to return to the mill, their demands unmet, and their leaders were fired and blacklisted.

In Exeter, New Hampshire, women mill workers went on strike ("turned out," in the language of that day) because the overseer was setting the clocks back to get more time from them. Their strike succeeded in exacting a promise from the company that the overseers would set their watches right.

The "Lowell system," in which young girls would go to work in the mills and live in dormitories supervised by matrons, at first seemed beneficent, sociable, a welcome escape from household drudgery or domestic service. Lowell, Massachusetts, was the first town created for the textile mill industry; it was named after the wealthy and influential Lowell family. But the dormitories became prisonlike, controlled by rules and regulations. The supper (served after the women had risen at four in the morning and worked until seven thirty in the evening) often consisted merely of bread and gravy.

So the Lowell girls organized. They started their own newspapers. They protested against the weaving rooms, which were poorly lit, badly ventilated, impossibly hot in the summer, damp and cold in the winter. The young women organized a Factory Girls' Association, and fifteen hundred went on strike in 1836 against a raise in boardinghouse charges. Harriet Hanson was an eleven-year-old girl working in the mill. She later recalled:

> ...when the girls in my room stood irresolute, uncertain what to do...I, who began to think they would not go out, after all their talk, became impatient, and started on ahead, saying, with childish bravado, "I don't care what you do, *I* am going to turn out, whether anyone else does or

not," and I marched out, and was followed by the others. As I looked back at the long line that followed me, I was more proud than I have ever been since....

The strikers marched through the streets of Lowell, singing. They held out a month, but then their money ran out, they were evicted from the boardinghouses, and many of them went back to work. The leaders were fired, including Harriet Hanson's widowed mother, a matron in the boardinghouse, who was blamed for her child's going out on strike.

Resistance continued. Meanwhile, the girls tried to hold on to thoughts about fresh air, the country, a less harried way of life. One of them recalled:" In sweet June weather I would lean far out of the window, and try not to hear the unceasing clash of sound inside."

In 1835, twenty mills went on strike to reduce the workday from thirteen and a half hours to eleven hours, to get cash wages instead of company scrip, and to end fines for lateness. Fifteen hundred children and parents went out on strike, and it lasted six weeks. Strikebreakers were brought in, and some workers went back to work, but the strikers did win a twelve-hour day and nine hours on Saturday. That year and the next, there were 140 strikes in the eastern part of the United States.

The crisis that followed the 1837 panic stimulated the formation in 1845 of the Female Labor Reform Association in Lowell, which sent thousands of petitions to the Massachusetts legislature asking for a ten-hour day. But a legislative committee reported: "Your committee returned fully satisfied that the order, decorum, and general appearance of things in and around the mills could not be improved by any suggestion of theirs or by any act of the legislature." In the late 1840s, the New England farm women who worked in the mills began to leave them, as more and more Irish immigrants took their place.

In Paterson, New Jersey, the first of a series of mill strikes was started by children. When the company suddenly put off their dinner hour from noon to 1:00 P.M., the children marched off the job, their parents cheering them on. They were joined by other working people in the town—carpenters, masons, machinists—who turned the strike into a ten-hour-day struggle. After a week, however, with the threat of bringing in militia, the children returned to work, and their leaders were fired. Soon after, trying to prevent more trouble, the company restored the noon dinner hour.

It was the shoemakers of Lynn, Massachusetts, a factory town northeast of Boston, who started the largest strike to take place in the United States before the Civil War. Lynn had pioneered in the use of sewing machines in factories, replacing shoemaker artisans. The factory workers in Lynn, who began to organize in the 1830s, later started a militant newspaper, the *Awl*. In 1844, four years before Marx and Engels's *Communist Manifesto* appeared, the *Awl* wrote:

> The division of society into the producing and the non-producing classes, and the fact of the unequal distribution of value between the two, introduces us at once to another distinction—that of capital and labor.... labor now becomes a commodity.... [C]apital and labor stand opposed.

The economic crisis of 1857 brought the shoe business to a halt, and many workers in Lynn lost their jobs. There was already anger at machine stitching replacing shoemakers. Prices were up, wages were repeatedly cut, and by the fall of 1859 men were earning three dollars a week and women were earning one dollar a week, working sixteen hours a day.

In early 1860, three thousand shoemakers met in the Lyceum Hall in Lynn and began a strike on Washington's Birthday. In a week, strikes had begun in all the shoe towns of New England, with Mechanics Associations in twenty-five towns and twenty thousand shoeworkers on strike. Newspapers called it "The Revolution at the North," "The Rebellion Among the Workmen of New England," "Beginning of the Conflict Between Capital and Labor."

One thousand women and five thousand men marched through the streets of Lynn in a blizzard, carrying banners and American flags. A huge Ladies' Procession was organized, the women marching through streets high with snowdrifts, carrying signs: "American Ladies Will Not Be Slaves." Ten days after that, a procession of ten thousand striking workers, including delegations from Salem, Marblehead, and other towns, men and women, marched through Lynn, in what was the greatest demonstration of labor to take place in New England up to that time.

Police from Boston and militia were sent in to make sure strikers did not interfere with shipments of shoes to be finished out of the state. The strike processions went on, while city grocers and provisions dealers provided food for the strikers. The strike continued through March with morale high, but by April it was losing force. The manufacturers offered higher wages to bring the strikers back into the factories, but without recognizing the unions, so that workers still had to face the employer as individuals.

Their class spirit was fierce but, in the view of Alan Dawley, who studied the Lynn strike (*Class and Community,*) electoral politics drained the energies of the resisters into the channels of the system.

Class-consciousness was overwhelmed during the Civil War, both North and South, by military and political unity in the crisis of war. That unity was weaned by rhetoric and enforced by arms. It was a war proclaimed as a war for liberty, but working people would be attacked by soldiers if they dared to strike, Indians would be massacred in Colorado by the U.S. Army, and those daring to criticize Lincoln's policies would be put in jail without trial—perhaps thirty thousand political prisoners.

Still, there were signs, in both the North and South, of dissent from that unity—anger of poor against rich, rebellion against the dominant political and economic forces.

In the North, the war brought high prices for food and the necessities of life. Employers made excess profits while wages were kept low. There were strikes all over the country during the war. The headline in *Fincher's Trade Review* of November 21, 1863, "THE REVOLUTION IN NEW YORK," was an exaggeration, but the list of labor activities that followed it is impressive evidence of the hidden resentments of the poor during the war.

> The upheaval of the laboring masses in New York has startled the capitalists of that city and vicinity....
>
> The workmen on the iron clads are yet holding out against the contractors....
>
> The glass cutters demand 15 percent to present wages.
>
> Imperfect as we confess our list to be, there is enough to convince the reader that the social revolution now working its way through the land must succeed, if workingmen are only true to each other.
>
> The stage drivers, to the number of 800, are on a strike....
>
> The workingmen of Boston are not behind.... In addition to the strike at the Charlestown Navy Yard....
>
> The riggers are on a strike....
>
> At this writing it is rumored, says the *Boston Post*, that a general strike is contemplated among the workmen in the iron establishments at South Boston, and other parts of the city.

The war brought many women into shops and factories. In New York City, girls sewed umbrellas from six in the morning to midnight, earning three dollars a week, and there was a strike of women umbrella workers in New York and Brooklyn. In Providence, Rhode Island, a Ladies Cigar Makers Union was organized.

All together, by 1864, about 200,000 workers, men and women, were in trade unions, forming national unions in some of the trades, putting out labor newspapers.

Union troops were used to break strikes. Federal soldiers were sent to Cold Springs, New York, to end a strike at a gun works where workers wanted a wage increase. Striking machinists and tailors in St. Louis were forced back to work by the army.

White workers of the North were not enthusiastic about a war that seemed to be fought for the black slave, or for the capitalist, for anyone but them. They worked in semislave conditions themselves. They thought the war was profiting the new class of millionaires.

The Irish working people of New York, recent immigrants, poor, looked upon with contempt by native Americans, could hardly find sympathy for the black population of the city who competed with them for jobs as longshoremen, barbers, waiters, domestic servants. Blacks, pushed out of these jobs, often were used to break strikes. Then came the war, the draft, the chance of death. And the Conscription Act of 1863 provided that the rich could avoid military service: they could pay three hundred dollars or buy a substitute.

When recruiting for the army began in July 1863, a mob in New York wrecked the main recruiting station. Then, for three days, crowds of white workers marched through the city, destroying buildings, factories, streetcar lines, homes. The draft riots were complex—antiblack, antirich, anti-Republican. From an assault on draft headquarters, the rioters went on to attacks on wealthy homes, then to the murder of blacks. They set the city's colored orphan asylum on fire. They shot, burned, and hanged blacks they found in the streets. Many people were thrown into the rivers to drown.

On the fourth day, Union troops returning from the Battle of Gettysburg came into the city and stopped the rioting. Perhaps four hundred people were killed, perhaps a thousand. No exact figures have ever been given, but the number of lives lost was greater than in any other incident of domestic violence in American history.

There were antidraft riots—not so prolonged or bloody—in other northern cities: Newark, Troy, Boston, Toledo, Evansville. In Boston the dead were Irish workers attacking an armory, who were fired on by soldiers.

In the South, beneath the apparent unity of the white Confederacy, there was also conflict. Most whites—two-thirds of them—did not own slaves. A few thousand families made up the plantation elite.

Millions of southern whites were poor farmers, living in shacks or abandoned outhouses. Just before the Civil War, in Jackson, Mississippi, slaves working in a cotton factory received twenty cents a day for board, and white workers at the same factory received thirty cents.

Behind the rebel battle yells and the legendary spirit of the Confederate army, there was much reluctance to fight. The conscription law of the Confederacy too provided that the rich could avoid service. Did Confederate soldiers begin to suspect they were fighting for the privileges of an elite they could never belong to? In April 1863, there was a bread riot in Richmond. That summer, draft riots occurred in various southern cities. In September, a bread riot in Mobile, Alabama. Georgia Lee Tatum, in her study *Disloyalty in the Confederacy*, writes: "Before the end of the war, there was much disaffection in every state, and many of the disloyal had formed into bands—in some states into well-organized, active societies."

The Civil War was one of the first instances of modern warfare: deadly artillery shells, Gatling guns, bayonet charges—combining the indiscriminate killing of mechanized war with hand-to-hand combat. In one charge before Petersburg, Virginia, a regiment of 850 Maine soldiers lost 632 men in half an hour. It was a vast butchery, 623,000 dead on both sides, and 471,000 wounded—over a million dead and wounded in a country whose population was 30 million.

No wonder that desertions grew among southern soldiers as the war went on. As for the Union army, by the end of the war, 200,000 had deserted.

Still, 600,000 had volunteered for the Confederacy in 1861, and many in the Union army were volunteers. The psychology of patriotism, the lure of adventure, the aura of moral crusade created by political leaders, worked effectively to dim class resentments against the rich and powerful,and turn much of the anger against "the enemy." As Edmund Wilson put it in *Patriotic Gore* (written after World War II):

> We have seen, in our most recent wars, how a divided and arguing public opinion may be converted overnight into a national near-unanimity, an obedient flood of energy which will carry the young to destruction and overpower any effort to stem it.

Under the deafening noise of the war, Congress was passing and Lincoln was signing into law a whole series of acts to give business interests what they wanted, and what the agrarian South had blocked before secession. The Republican platform of 1860 had been a clear appeal to businessmen. Now Congress in 1861 passed the Morrill Tariff. This made foreign goods more expensive, allowed American manufacturers to raise their prices, and forced American consumers to pay more.

The following year a Homestead Act was passed. It gave 160 acres of western land, unoccupied and publicly owned, to anyone who would cultivate it for five years. Anyone willing to pay $1.25 an acre could buy a homestead. Few ordinary people had the $200 necessary to do this; speculators moved in and bought up much of the land. Homestead land added up to 50 million acres. But during the Civil War, over 100 million acres were given by Congress and the president to various railroads, free of charge. Congress also set up a national bank, putting the government into partnership with the banking interests, guaranteeing their profits.

With strikes spreading, employers pressed Congress for help. The Contract Labor Law of 1864 made it possible for companies to sign contracts with foreign workers whenever the workers pledged to give twelve months of their wages to pay the cost of emigration. This gave the employers during the Civil War not only very cheap labor, but strikebreakers.

In the thirty years leading up to the Civil War, the law was increasingly interpreted in the courts to suit the capitalist development of the country. Mill owners were given the legal right to destroy other people's property by flood to carry on their business. The law of "eminent domain" was used to take farmers' land and give it to canal companies or railroad companies as subsidies.

It was a time when the law did not even pretend to protect working people—as it would in the next century. Health and safety laws were either nonexistent or unenforced. In Lawrence, Massachusetts, in 1860, on a winter day, the Pemberton Mill collapsed, with nine hundred workers inside, mostly women. Eighty-eight died, and although there was evidence that the structure had never been adequate to support the heavy machinery inside, and that this was known to the construction engineer, a jury found "no evidence of criminal intent."

Morton Horwitz (*The Transformation of American Law*) sums up what happened in the courts of law by the time of the Civil War:

> By the middle of the nineteenth century the legal system had been reshaped to the advantage of men of commerce and industry at the expense of farmers, workers, consumers, and other less powerful groups within the society.... [I]t actively promoted a legal redistribution of wealth against the weakest groups in the society.

In premodern times, the maldistribution of wealth was accomplished by simple force. In modern times, exploitation is disguised—it is accomplished by law, which has the look of neutrality and fairness.

With the war over, the urgency of national unity slackened and ordinary people could turn more to their daily lives, their problems of survival. The disbanded armies now were in the streets, looking for work.

The cities to which the soldiers returned were death traps of typhus, tuberculosis, hunger, and fire. In New York, 100,000 people lived in the cellars of the slums; 12,000 women worked in houses of prostitution to keep from starving; the garbage, lying two feet deep in the streets, was alive with rats. In Philadelphia, while the rich got fresh water from the Schuylkill River, everyone else drank from the Delaware, into which 13 million gallons of sewage were dumped every day. In the Great Chicago Fire in 1871, the tenements fell so fast, one after another, that people said it sounded like an earthquake.

A movement for the eight-hour day began among working people after the war, helped by the formation of the first national federation of unions, the National Labor Union. A three-month strike of 100,000 workers in New York won the eight-hour day, and at a victory celebration in June 1872, 150,000 workers paraded through the city.

Women, brought into industry during the war, organized unions: cigarmakers, tailoresses, umbrella sewers, capmakers, printers, laundresses, shoeworkers. They formed the Daughters of St. Crispin, and succeeded in getting the Cigarmakers Union and the National Typographical Union to admit women for the first time.

The dangers of mill work intensified efforts to organize. Work often went on around the clock. At a mill in Providence, Rhode Island, fire broke out one night in 1866. There was panic among the six hundred workers, mostly women, and many jumped to their deaths from upper-story windows.

In Fall River, Massachusetts, women weavers formed a union independent of the men weavers. They refused to take a 10 percent wage cut that the men had accepted, struck against three mills, won the men's support, and brought to a halt 3,500 looms and 156,000 spindles, with 3,200 workers on strike. But their children needed food; they had to return to work, signing an "iron-clad oath" (later called a "yellow-dog contract") not to join a union.

Black workers at this time found the National Labor Union reluctant to organize them. So they formed their own unions and carried on their own strikes—like the levee workers in Mobile, Alabama, in 1867, Negro longshoremen in Charleston, dockworkers in Savannah. This probably stimulated the National Labor Union, at its 1869 convention, to resolve to organize women and Negroes, declaring that it recognized "neither color nor sex on the question of the rights of labor." A journalist wrote about the remarkable signs of racial unity at this convention:

When a native Mississippian and an ex-confederate officer, in addressing a convention, refers to a colored delegate who has preceded him as "the gentleman from Georgia"...when an ardent and Democratic partisan (from New York at that) declares with a rich Irish brogue that he asks for himself no privilege as a mechanic or as a citizen that he is not willing to concede to every other man, white or black...then one may indeed be warranted in asserting that time works curious changes....

Most unions, however, still kept Negroes out, or asked them to form their own locals.

The National Labor Union began to expend more and more of its energy on political issues, especially currency reform, a demand for the issuance of paper money: greenbacks. As it became less an organizer of labor struggles, and more a lobbyist with Congress, concerned with voting, it lost vitality.

Reform laws were being passed for the first time, and hopes were high. The Pennsylvania legislature in 1869 passed a mine safety act providing for the "regulation and ventilation of mines, and for the protection of the lives of the miners." It calmed anger but accomplished little.

In 1873, another economic crisis devastated the nation. The crisis was built into a system that was chaotic in its nature, in which only the very rich were secure. It was a system of periodic crisis—1837, 1857, 1873 (and later: 1893, 1907, 1919, 1929)—that wiped out small businesses and brought cold, hunger, and death to working people while the fortunes of the Astors, Vanderbilts, Rockefellers, Morgans, kept growing through war and peace, crisis and recovery. During the 1873 crisis, Andrew Carnegie was capturing the steel market, John D. Rockefeller was wiping out his competitors in oil.

"LABOR DEPRESSION IN BROOKLYN" was the headline in the *New York Herald* in November 1873. It listed closings and layoffs: a felt-skirt factory, a picture-frame factory, a glass-cutting establishment, a steelworks factory. And women's trades: milliners, dressmakers, shoe-binders.

The depression continued through the 1870s. During the first three months of 1874, ninety thousand workers, almost half of them women, had to sleep in police stations in New York. All over the country, people were evicted from their homes. Many roamed the cities looking for food. Desperate workers tried to get to Europe or to South America. In 1878, the SS *Metropolis*, filled with laborers, left the United States for South America and sank with all aboard.

Mass meetings and demonstrations of the unemployed took place all over the country. Unemployed councils were set up. A meeting in New York at Cooper Institute in late 1873 drew a huge crowd, overflowing into the streets. The meeting asked that before bills became law they should be approved by a public vote, that no individual should own more than $30,000; they asked for an eight-hour day.

In Chicago, twenty thousand unemployed marched through the streets to City Hall asking "bread for the needy, clothing for the naked, and houses for the homeless." Actions like this resulted in some relief for about ten thousand families.

In January 1874, in New York City, a huge parade of workers, kept by the police from approaching City Hall, went to Tompkins Square, and there were told by the police they couldn't have the meeting. They stayed, and the police attacked. One newspaper reported: "Police clubs rose and fell. Women and children ran screaming in all directions. Many of them were trampled underfoot in the stampede for the gates. In the street bystanders were ridden down and mercilessly clubbed by mounted officers."

It was a time when employers brought in recent immigrants—desperate for work, different from the strikers in language and culture—to break strikes. Italians were imported into the bituminous coal area around Pittsburgh in 1874 to replace striking miners. This led to the killing of three Italians, to trials in which jurors of the community exonerated the strikers, and bitter feelings between Italians and other organized workers.

The centennial year of 1876—one hundred years after the Declaration of Independence—brought forth a number of new declarations. Whites and blacks, separately, expressed their disillusionment. A "Negro Declaration of Independence" denounced the Republican party on which they had once depended to gain full freedom, and proposed independent political action by colored voters. And the Workingmen's party of Illinois, at a July 4 celebration organized by German socialists in Chicago, said in its Declaration of Independence:

> The present system has enabled capitalists to make laws in their own interests to the injury and oppression of the workers.
>
> It has made the name Democracy, for which our forefathers fought and died, a mockery and a shadow, by giving to property an unproportionate amount of representation and control over Legislation.
>
> It has enabled capitalists...to secure government aid, inland grants and money loans, to selfish railroad corporations, who, by monopoliz-

ing the means of transportation are enabled to swindle both the producer and the consumer....

It has presented to the world the absurd spectacle of a deadly civil war for the abolition of negro slavery while the majority of the white population, those who have created all the wealth of the nation, are compelled to suffer under a bondage infinitely more galling and humiliating....

We, therefore, the representatives of the workers of Chicago, in mass meeting assembled, do solemnly publish and declare...

That we are absolved from all allegiance to the existing political parties of this country, and that as free and independent producers we shall endeavor to acquire the full power to make our own laws, manage our own production, and govern ourselves.

In the year 1877, the country was in the depths of the depression. That summer, in the hot cities where poor families lived in cellars and drank infested water, the children became sick in large numbers. The *New York Times* wrote: "...already the cry of the dying children begins to be heard.... Soon, to judge from the past, there will be a thousand deaths of infants per week in the city." That first week in July, in Baltimore, where all liquid sewage ran through the streets, 139 babies died.

That year there came a series of tumultuous strikes by railroad workers in a dozen cities; they shook the nation as no labor conflict in its history had done.

It began with wage cuts on railroad after railroad, in tense situations of already low wages ($1.75 a day for brakemen working twelve hours), scheming and profiteering by the railroad companies, deaths and injuries among the workers—loss of hands, feet, fingers, the crushing of men between cars.

At the Baltimore & Ohio station in Martinsburg, West Virginia, workers determined to fight the wage cut went on strike, uncoupled the engines, ran them into the roundhouse, and announced no more trains would leave Martinsburg until the 10 percent cut was canceled.

Six hundred freight trains now jammed the yards at Martinsburg. The West Virginia governor applied to newly elected President Rutherford Hayes for federal troops. Much of the U.S. Army was tied up in Indian battles in the West. Congress had not appropriated money for the army yet, but J. P. Morgan, August Belmont, and other bankers now offered to lend money to pay army officers (but not enlisted men). Federal troops arrived in Martinsburg, and the freight cars began to move.

In Baltimore, a crowd of thousands sympathetic to the railroad strikers surrounded the armory of the National Guard. The crowd hurled rocks, and the soldiers came out, firing. The streets now became the scene of a moving, bloody battle. When the evening was over, ten men or boys were dead, more badly wounded, one soldier wounded. Half of the 120 troops quit and the rest went on to the train depot, where a crowd of two hundred smashed the engine of a passenger train, tore up tracks, and engaged the militia again in a running battle.

By now, fifteen thousand people surrounded the depot. Soon, three passenger cars, the station platform, and a locomotive were on fire. The governor asked for federal troops, and Hayes responded. Five hundred soldiers arrived and Baltimore quieted down.

The rebellion of the railroad workers now spread. Joseph Dacus, then editor of the St. Louis *Republican*, reported:

> Strikes were occurring almost every hour. The great State of Pennsylvania was in an uproar; New Jersey was afflicted by a paralyzing dread; New York was mustering an army of militia; Ohio was shaken from Lake Erie to the Ohio River; Indiana rested in a dreadful suspense. Illinois, and especially its great metropolis, Chicago, apparently hung on the verge of a vortex of confusion and tumult. St. Louis had already felt the effect of the premonitory shocks of the uprising....

The strike spread to Pittsburgh and the Pennsylvania Railroad. Railroad and local officials decided that the Pittsburgh militia would not kill their fellow townsmen, and urged that Philadelphia troops be called in. By now two thousand cars were idle in Pittsburgh. The Philadelphia troops came and began to clear the track. Rocks flew. Gunfire was exchanged between crowd and troops. At least ten people were killed, all workingmen, most of them not railroaders.

Now the whole city rose in anger. A crowd surrounded the troops, who moved into a roundhouse. Railroad cars were set afire, buildings began to burn, and finally the roundhouse itself, the troops marching out of it to safety. There was more gunfire, the Union Depot was set afire, thousands looted the freight cars. A huge grain elevator and a small section of the city went up in flames. In a few days, twenty-four people had been killed (including four soldiers). Seventy-nine buildings had been burned to the ground. Something like a general strike was developing in Pittsburgh: mill workers, car workers, miners, laborers, and the employees at the Carnegie steel plant.

The entire National Guard of Pennsylvania, nine thousand men, was called out. But many of the companies couldn't move, as strikers in other towns held up traffic. In Lebanon, Pennsylvania, one National Guard company mutinied and marched through an excited town. In Altoona, troops surrounded by rioters, immobilized by sabotaged engines, surrendered, stacked arms, fraternized with the crowd, and then were allowed to go home, to the accompaniment of singing by a quartet in an all-Negro militia company.

In Reading, Pennsylvania, the railroad was two months behind in paying wages, and two thousand people gathered. Men who had blackened their faces with coal dust set about methodically tearing up tracks, jamming switches, derailing cars, setting fire to cabooses and also to a railroad bridge.

A National Guard company arrived. The crowd threw stones, fired pistols. The soldiers fired into the crowd. Six men were killed. The crowd grew angrier, more menacing. A contingent of soldiers announced it would not fire, one soldier saying he would rather put a bullet through the president of Philadelphia & Reading Coal & Iron.

Meanwhile the leaders of the big railway brotherhoods, the Order of Railway Conductors, the Brotherhood of Locomotive Firemen, the Brotherhood of Engineers, disavowed the strike. There was talk in the press of "communistic ideas...widely entertained...by the workmen employed in mines and factories and by the railroads."

There was a Workingmen's party, with several thousand members in Chicago. Most of its members were immigrants from Germany and Bohemia. In the midst of the railroad strikes, that summer of 1877, it called a rally. Six thousand people came and demanded nationalization of the railroads. Albert Parsons gave a fiery speech. He was from Alabama, had fought in the Confederacy during the Civil War, married a brown-skinned woman of Spanish and Indian blood, worked as a typesetter, and was one of the best English-speaking orators the Workingmen's party had.

The next day, a crowd of young people, not especially connected with the rally of the evening before, began moving through the railroad yards, closed down the freights, went to the factories, called out the mill workers, the stockyard workers, the crewmen on the Lake Michigan ships, closed down the brickyards and lumberyards. That day also, Albert Parsons was fired from his job with the *Chicago Times* and declared blacklisted.

The police attacked the crowds. The press reported: "The sound of clubs falling on skulls was sickening for the first minute, until one grew accustomed to it. A rioter dropped at every whack, it seemed, for the ground was covered with them." Two companies of U.S. infantry arrived, joining National Guardsmen and Civil War veterans. Police fired into a surging crowd, and three men were killed.

The next day, an armed crowd of five thousand fought the police. The police fired again and again, and when it was over, and the dead were counted, they were, as usual, workingmen and boys, eighteen of them, their skulls smashed by clubs, their vital organs pierced by gunfire.

The one city where the Workingmen's party clearly led the rebellion was St. Louis, a city of flour mills, foundries, packing houses, machine shops, breweries, and railroads. Here, as elsewhere, there were wage cuts on the railroads. And here there were perhaps a thousand members of the Workingmen's party, many of them bakers, coopers, cabinetmakers, cigarmakers, brewery workers. The party was organized in four sections, by nationality: German, English, French, Bohemian.

All four sections took a ferry across the Mississippi to join a mass meeting of railroad men in East St. Louis. Railroaders in East St. Louis declared themselves on strike. The mayor of East St. Louis was a European immigrant, himself an active revolutionist as a youth, and railroad men's votes dominated the city.

In St. Louis, itself, the Workingmen's party called a mass meeting to which five thousand people came. They called for nationalization of the railroads, mines, and all industry.

At one of those meetings a black man spoke for those who worked on the steamboats and levees. He asked: "Will you stand to us regardless of color?" The crowd shouted back: "We will!"

Handbills calling for a general strike were soon all over the city. There was a march of four hundred Negro steamboat men and roustabouts along the river, six hundred factory workers carrying a banner: "No Monopoly— Workingmen's Rights." A great procession moved through the city, ending with a rally of ten thousand people listening to communist speakers.

In New York, several thousand gathered at Tompkins Square. The tone of the meeting was moderate, speaking of "a political revolution through the ballot box." And: "If you will unite, we may have here within five years a socialistic republic...." It was a peaceful meeting. It adjourned. The last words heard from the platform were: "Whatever we poor men may not have, we have free speech, and no one can take it from us." Then the police charged, using their clubs.

In St. Louis, as elsewhere, the momentum of the crowds, the meetings, the enthusiasm, could not be sustained. As they diminished, the police, militia, and federal troops moved in and the strike leaders were arrested, then fired from their jobs with the railroad.

When the great railroad strikes of 1877 were over, a hundred people were dead, a thousand people had gone to jail, 100,000 workers had gone on strike, and the strikes had roused into action countless unemployed in the cities. More than half the freight on the nation's 75,000 miles of track had stopped running at the height of the strikes.

The railroads made some concessions, withdrew some wage cuts, but also strengthened their "Coal and Iron Police." In a number of large cities, National Guard armories were built, with loopholes for guns.

In 1877, the same year blacks learned they did not have enough strength to make real the promise of equality in the Civil War, working people learned they were not united enough, not powerful enough, to defeat the combination of private capital and government power. But there was more to come.

Exercises

1. Make and fill in a graph like the one below to illustrate the rise in the total population of Americans living in cities from 1790–1840.

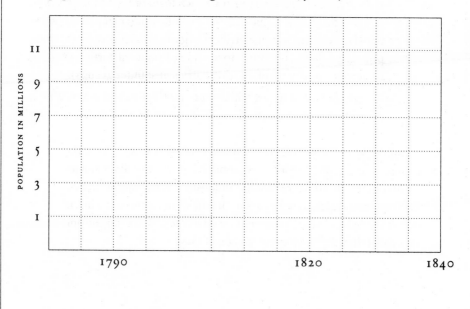

2. What factors contributed to the growth of monopolies before the Civil War?
   What are some examples of monopolies formed in the 1850s?

3. What role did the federal and state governments play in the creation of monopolies?

4. Define "working-class consciousness." Use the following documents to help you.

   * 1827 "Address...before the Mechanics and Working Classes...of Philadelphia"
   * 1829 Frances Wright's speech on July 4th
   * 1829 George Henry Evans's "The Working Men's Declaration of Independence"
   * 1834 Boston "Trades Union" document

5. The following questions refer to the time between c. 1830 and c. 1855.
   a. What were the different *forms* through which working people manifested their opposition to their political and economic position? Give *specific examples* to illustrate each form or type of opposition. (Types/forms can include any of the following: pamphlets/newspapers; demonstrations; strikes; organizations; meetings; riots; protests; debates; petitions; formation of political parties; creation of new political arms of existing parties or splinter groups).
   b. Of the above examples, which were ineffective and why? Which were effective? What effect did the form of protest have?

6. What do workers want (refer to questions a–l below)? Were the demands/requests of workers reasonable? If so, why did management object to these demands/requests? Why might managers/owners be led to believe that the incidents referred to in the questions below might represent a conspiracy? How might one argue that they did not represent a conspiracy?

a. Why did a crowd destroy the houses of bank officials in Maryland in 1835?

b. Why did the New York Tailors object to Judge Edwards's decision regarding the right of the Tailors to form a union?

c. What did the New York Locofocos want in 1837?

d. What did the trade unions in Philadelphia want in 1835?

e. What did the Irish weavers of Philadelphia want in the early 1840s?

f. What did several thousand people in Newark, New Jersey, want in 1857?

g. What did the United Tailoresses want in 1825?

h. What did the women mill workers in Exeter, New Hampshire, want in 1828?

i. What did the Lowell Girls want?

j. What did the Female Labor Reform Association of Lowell want in 1845?

k. What did the Paterson children want?

l. What did the shoemakers of Lynn, Massachusetts, want?

7. Did the Civil War (1861-1865) effectively end the growing division between capital and labor? Explain.

8. Why were there draft riots in 1863?

9. During the Civil War, northern congressmen, without the representatives from the seceded states, were able to pass legislation favorable to northern business interests. How do each of the following pieces of legislation favor the northern/western economic system (manufacturing/commerce/wage labor) over the southern system (plantation-agricultural/raw materials/slave labor):

a. Morrill Tariff (1861)

b. Homestead Act (1862)

c. Contract Labor Law (1864)

10. How did judges interpret the law in favor of those businessmen who wished to expand at the expense of others?

11. After the Civil War (post-1865), were the conditions of the urban poor the same, worse, or better than they had been before the Civil War (pre-1861)?

12. What types of work opened up to women as a result of the Civil War?

13. Why did the men of the National Labor Union vote to include blacks and women among their numbers in 1869?

14. After the Civil War (post-1865), local trade unions joined together into national organizations. How did the tactics of labor change as a result of this transformation?

15. What evidence does Zinn provide to illustrate the fact that economic crisis made workers adopt more radical tactics than they had used during periods of economic growth? Why would this happen?

16. How did the railroad strike of 1877 differ from other strikes described in this chapter? How was it similar? Did it represent a new stage in American labor history?

17. What does the title of this chapter mean? What is "The Other Civil War"?

18. *Debate Resolution*: Owners and government officials were not solely responsible for the violence that erupted surrounding labor disputes.

Chapter 11

Robber Barons and Rebels

In the year 1877, the signals were given for the rest of the century: the black would be put back; the strikes of white workers would not be tolerated; the industrial and political elites of North and South would take hold of the country and organize the greatest march of economic growth in human history. They would do it with the aid of, and at the expense of, black labor, white labor, Chinese labor, European immigrant labor, female labor, rewarding workers differently by race, sex, national origin, and social class, in such a way as to create separate levels of oppression—a skillful terracing to stabilize the pyramid of wealth.

Between the Civil War and 1900, steam and electricity replaced human muscle, iron replaced wood, and steel replaced iron (before the Bessemer process, iron was hardened into steel at the rate of three to five tons a day; now the same amount could be processed in fifteen minutes). Machines could now drive steel tools. Oil could lubricate machines and light homes, streets, factories. People and goods could move by railroad, propelled by steam along steel rails; by 1900 there were 193,000 miles of railroad. The telephone, the typewriter, and the adding machine speeded up the work of business.

Machines changed farming. Before the Civil War it took 61 hours of labor to produce an acre of wheat. By 1900, it took 3 hours, 19 minutes. Manufactured ice enabled the transport of food over long distances, and the industry of meatpacking was born.

Steam drove textile mill spindles; it drove sewing machines. It came from coal. Pneumatic drills now drilled deeper into the earth for coal. In 1860, 14 million tons of coal were mined; by 1884 it was 100 million tons. More coal meant more steel, because coal furnaces converted iron into steel; by 1880 a million tons of steel were being produced; by 1910, 25 million tons. By now electricity was beginning to replace steam. Electrical wire needed copper, of which 30,000 tons were produced in 1880; 500,000 tons by 1910.

To accomplish all this required ingenious inventors of new processes and new machines, clever organizers and administrators of the new corporations, a country rich with land and minerals, and a huge supply of human beings to do the back-breaking, unhealthful, and dangerous work. Immigrants would come from Europe and China to make the new labor force. Farmers unable to buy the new machinery or pay the new railroad rates would move to the cities. Between 1860 and 1914, New York grew from 850,000 to 4 million, Chicago from 110,000 to 2 million, Philadelphia from 650,000 to 1.5 million.

In some cases the inventor himself became the organizer of businesses—like Thomas Edison, inventor of electrical devices. In other cases, the businessman compiled other people's inventions, like Gustavus Swift, a Chicago butcher who put together the ice-cooled railway car with the ice-cooled warehouse to make the first national meatpacking company in 1885. James Duke used a new cigarette-rolling machine that could roll, paste, and cut tubes of tobacco into 100,000 cigarettes a day; in 1890 he combined the four biggest cigarette producers to form the American Tobacco Company.

While some multimillionaires started in poverty, most did not. A study of the origins of 303 textile, railroad, and steel executives of the 1870s showed that 90 percent came from middle- or upper-class families. The Horatio Alger stories of "rags to riches" were true for a few men, but mostly a myth, and a useful myth for control.

Most of the fortune building was done legally, with the collaboration of the government and the courts. Sometimes the collaboration had to be paid for. Thomas Edison promised New Jersey politicians $1,000 each in return for favorable legislation. Daniel Drew and Jay Gould spent $1 million to bribe the New York legislature to legalize their issue of $8 million in "watered stock" (stock not representing real value) on the Erie Railroad.

The first transcontinental railroad was built with blood, sweat, politics, and thievery, out of the meeting of the Union Pacific and Central Pacific railroads. The Central Pacific started on the West Coast going east;

it spent $200,000 in Washington on bribes to get 9 million acres of free land and $24 million in bonds, and paid $79 million, an overpayment of $36 million, to a construction company which really was its own. The construction was done by three thousand Irish and ten thousand Chinese, over a period of four years, working for one or two dollars a day.

The Union Pacific started in Nebraska going west. It had been given 12 million acres of free land and $27 million in government bonds. It created the Credit Mobilier company and gave them $94 million for construction when the actual cost was $44 million. Shares were sold cheaply to congressmen to prevent investigation. This was at the suggestion of Massachusetts Congressman Oakes Ames, a shovel manufacturer and director of Credit Mobilier, who said: "There is no difficulty in getting men to look after their own property." The Union Pacific used twenty thousand workers—war veterans and Irish immigrants, who laid five miles of track a day and died by the hundreds in the heat, the cold, and the battles with Indians opposing the invasion of their territory.

Both railroads used longer, twisting routes to get subsidies from towns they went through. In 1869, amid music and speeches, the two crooked lines met in Utah.

The wild fraud on the railroads led to more control of railroad finances by bankers, who wanted more stability. By the 1890s, most of the country's railway mileage was concentrated in six huge systems. Four of these were completely or partially controlled by the House of Morgan, and two others by the bankers Kuhn, Loeb, and Company.

There was a human cost to this exciting story of financial ingenuity. In the year 1889, records of the Interstate Commerce Commission showed that 22,000 railroad workers were killed or injured.

J. P. Morgan had started before the war, as the son of a banker who began selling stocks for the railroads for good commissions. During the Civil War he bought 5,000 rifles for $3.50 each from an army arsenal, and sold them to a general in the field for $22 each. The rifles were defective and would shoot off the thumbs of the soldiers using them. A congressional committee noted this in the small print of an obscure report, but a federal judge upheld the deal as the fulfillment of a valid legal contract.

Morgan had escaped military service in the Civil War by paying $300 to a substitute. So did John D. Rockefeller, Andrew Carnegie, Philip Armour, Jay Gould, and James Mellon. Mellon's father had written to him that "a man may be a patriot without risking his own life or sacrificing his health. There are plenty of lives less valuable."

While making his fortune, Morgan brought rationality and organization to the national economy. He kept the system stable. He said: "We do not want financial convulsions and have one thing one day and another thing another day." He linked railroads to one another, all of them to banks, banks to insurance companies. By 1900, he controlled 100,000 miles of railroad, half the country's mileage.

John D. Rockefeller started as a bookkeeper in Cleveland, became a merchant, accumulated money, and decided that, in the new industry of oil, who controlled the oil refineries controlled the industry. He bought his first oil refinery in 1862, and by 1870 set up Standard Oil Company of Ohio, made secret agreements with railroads to ship his oil with them if they gave him rebates—discounts—on their prices, and thus drove competitors out of business. One independent refiner said: "If we did not sell out.... we would be crushed out.... There was only one buyer on the market and we had to sell at their terms."

Andrew Carnegie was a telegraph clerk at seventeen, then secretary to the head of the Pennsylvania Railroad, then broker in Wall Street selling railroad bonds for huge commissions, and was soon a millionaire. He went to London in 1872, saw the new Bessemer method of producing steel, and returned to the United States to build a million dollar steel plant. Foreign competition was kept out by a high tariff conveniently set by Congress. By 1900 he was making $40 million a year, and that year, at a dinner party, he agreed to sell his steel company to J. P. Morgan. He scribbled the price on a note: $492,000,000.

Morgan then formed the U.S. Steel Corporation, combining Carnegie's corporation with others, and took a fee of $150 million for arranging the consolidation. How could dividends be paid to all those stockholders and bondholders? By making sure Congress passed tariffs keeping out foreign steel; by closing off competition and maintaining the price at $28 a ton; and by working 200,000 men twelve hours a day for wages that barely kept their families alive.

And so it went, in industry after industry—shrewd, efficient businessmen building empires, choking out competition, maintaining high prices, keeping wages low, using government subsidies. These industries were the first beneficiaries of the "welfare state." By the turn of the century, American Telephone and Telegraph had a monopoly of the nation's telephone system, International Harvester made 85 percent of all farm machinery, and in every other industry resources became concentrated, controlled.

The banks had interests in so many of these monopolies as to create an interlocking network of powerful corporation directors, each of whom sat on the boards of many other corporations. According to a Senate report of the early twentieth century, Morgan at his peak sat on the board of forty-eight corporations; Rockefeller, thirty-seven corporations.

Meanwhile, the government of the United States was behaving almost exactly as Karl Marx described a capitalist state: pretending neutrality to maintain order, but serving the interests of the rich. Not that the rich agreed among themselves; they had disputes over policies. But the purpose of the state was to settle upper-class disputes peacefully, control lower-class rebellion, and adopt policies that would further the long-range stability of the system. The arrangement between Democrats and Republicans to elect Rutherford Hayes in 1877 set the tone. Whether Democrats or Republicans won, national policy would not change in any important way.

When Grover Cleveland, a Democrat, ran for President in 1884, the general impression in the country was that he opposed the power of monopolies and corporations, and that the Republican party, whose candidate was James Blaine, stood for the wealthy. But when Cleveland defeated Blaine, Jay Gould wired him: "I feel…that the vast business interests of the country will be entirely safe in your hands." And he was right.

Cleveland himself assured industrialists that his election should not frighten them: "No harm shall come to any business interest as the result of administrative policy so long as I am President …a transfer of executive control from one party to another does not mean any serious disturbance of existing conditions."

The presidential election had avoided real issues. It took the usual form of election campaigns, concealing the basic similarity of the parties by dwelling on personalities, gossip, trivialities. Henry Adams, an astute literary commentator on that era, wrote to a friend about the election:

> We are here plunged in politics funnier than words can express. Very great issues are involved…. But the amusing thing is that no one talks about real interests. By common consent they agree to let these alone…. Instead of this the press is engaged in a most amusing dispute whether Mr. Cleveland had an illegitimate child and did or did not live with more than one mistress.

In 1887, with a huge surplus in the treasury, Cleveland vetoed a bill appropriating $100,000 to give relief to Texas farmers to help them buy seed grain during a drought. He said: "Federal aid in such cases…encourages the expectation of paternal care on the part of the government and weakens the sturdiness of our national character." But that same year,

Cleveland used his gold surplus to pay off wealthy bondholders at $28 above the $100 value of each bond—a gift of $45 million.

The chief reform of the Cleveland administration gives away the secret of reform legislation in America. The Interstate Commerce Act of 1887 was supposed to regulate the railroads on behalf of the consumers. But Richard Olney, a lawyer for the Boston & Maine and other railroads, and soon to be Cleveland's attorney general, told railroad officials who complained about the Interstate Commerce Commission that it would not be wise to abolish the commission "from a railroad point of view." He explained:

> The Commission...is or can be made, of great use to the railroads. It satisfies the popular clamor for a government supervision of railroads, at the same time that that supervision is almost entirely nominal.... The part of wisdom is not to destroy the Commission, but to utilize it.

Republican Benjamin Harrison, who succeeded Cleveland as president from 1889 to 1893, had been a lawyer for the railroads and had commanded a company of soldiers during the strike of 1877. Harrison's term also saw a gesture toward reform. The Sherman Anti-Trust Act, passed in 1890, made it illegal to form a "combination or conspiracy" to restrain trade in interstate or foreign commerce. Senator John Sherman, author of the act, explained the need to conciliate the critics of monopoly: "You must heed their appeal or be ready for the socialist, the communist, the nihilist. Society is now disturbed by forces never felt before...."

Cleveland, elected again in 1892, facing the agitation in the country caused by the panic and depression of 1893, used troops to break up "Coxey's Army," a demonstration of unemployed men who had come to Washington, and again to break up the national strike on the railroads the following year.

Meanwhile, the Supreme Court, despite its look of somber, black-robed fairness, was doing its bit for the ruling elite. How could it be independent, with its members chosen by the president and ratified by the Senate? How could it be neutral between rich and poor when its members were often former wealthy lawyers, and almost always came from the upper class? Early in the nineteenth century the Court laid the legal basis for a nationally regulated economy by establishing federal control over interstate commerce, and the legal basis for corporate capitalism by making the contract sacred.

In 1895 the Court interpreted the Sherman Anti-Trust Act so as to make it harmless.

Very soon after the Fourteenth Amendment became law, the Supreme Court began to demolish it as a protection for blacks, and to develop it as a protection for corporations. In 1886, the Court did away with 230 state laws that had been passed to regulate corporations. It declared that corporations were "persons" and their money was property protected by the due process clause of the Fourteenth Amendment. Of the Fourteenth Amendment cases brought before the Supreme Court between 1890 and 1910, nineteen dealt with the Negro, 288 dealt with corporations.

In 1893, Supreme Court Justice David J. Brewer, addressing the New York State Bar Association, said: "It is the unvarying law that the wealth of the community will be in the hands of the few...."

This was not just a whim of the 1880s and 1890s—it went back to the Founding Fathers, who had learned their law in the era of *Blackstone's Commentaries*, which said: "So great is the regard of the law for private property, that it will not authorize the least violation of it; no, not even for the common good of the whole community."

Control in modern times requires more than force, more than law. It requires that a population dangerously concentrated in cities and factories, whose lives are filled with cause for rebellion, be taught that all is right as it is. And so, the schools, the churches, the popular literature taught that to be rich was a sign of superiority, to be poor a sign of personal failure, and that the only way upward for a poor person was to climb into the ranks of the rich by extraordinary effort and extraordinary luck.

The rich, giving part of their enormous earnings to educational institutions, became known as philanthropists. Rockefeller was a donor to colleges all over the country and helped found the University of Chicago. Huntington, of the Central Pacific, gave money to two Negro colleges, Hampton Institute and Tuskegee Institute. Carnegie gave money to colleges and to public libraries. Johns Hopkins University was founded by a millionaire merchant, and millionaires Cornelius Vanderbilt, Ezra Cornell, James Duke, and Leland Stanford created universities in their own names.

These educational institutions did not encourage dissent; they trained the middlemen in the American system—the teachers, doctors, lawyers, administrators, engineers, technicians, politicians—those who would be paid to keep the system going, to be loyal buffers against trouble.

In the meantime, the spread of public school education enabled the learning of writing, reading, and arithmetic for a whole generation of workers, skilled and semiskilled, who would be the literate labor force of the new industrial age. It was important that these people learn obedience to authority. A journalist observer of the schools in the 1890s wrote: "The unkindly spirit of the teacher is strikingly apparent; the pupils, being completely subjugated to her will, are silent and motionless, the spiritual atmosphere of the classroom is damp and chilly."

This continued into the twentieth century, when William Bagley's *Classroom Management* became a standard teacher training text, reprinted thirty times. Bagley said: "One who studies educational theory aright can see in the mechanical routine of the classroom the educative forces that are slowly transforming the child from a little savage into a creature of law and order, fit for the life of civilized society."

It was in the middle and late nineteenth century that high schools developed as aids to the industrial system, that history was widely required in the curriculum to foster patriotism. Loyalty oaths, teacher certification, and the requirement of citizenship were introduced to control both the educational and the political quality of teachers. Also, in the latter part of the century, school officials—not teachers—were given control over textbooks. Laws passed by the states barred certain kinds of textbooks. Idaho and Montana, for instance, forbade textbooks propagating "political" doctrines.

Against this gigantic organization of knowledge and education for orthodoxy and obedience, there arose a literature of dissent and protest, which had to make its way from reader to reader against great obstacles. Henry George, a self-educated workingman from a poor Philadelphia family, who became a newspaperman and an economist, wrote a book that was published in 1879 and sold millions of copies, not only in the United States, but all over the world. His book *Progress and Poverty* argued that the basis of wealth was land, that this was becoming monopolized, and that a single tax on land, abolishing all others, would bring enough revenue to solve the problem of poverty and equalize wealth in the nation.

A different kind of challenge to the economic and social system was given by Edward Bellamy, a lawyer and writer from western Massachusetts, who wrote, in simple, intriguing language, a novel called *Looking Backward*, in which the author falls asleep and wakes up in the year 2000, to find a socialistic society in which people work and live cooperatively. *Looking Backward*, which described socialism vividly, lovingly, sold a million copies in a few years, and over a hundred groups were organized around the country to try to make the dream come true.

It seemed that despite the strenuous efforts of government, business, the church, the schools, to control their thinking, millions of Americans were ready to consider harsh criticism of the existing system, to contemplate other possible ways of living. They were helped in this by the great movements of workers and farmers that swept the country in the 1880s and 1890s. These movements went beyond the scattered strikes and tenants' struggles of the period 1830–1877. They were nationwide movements, more threatening than before to the ruling elite, more dangerously suggestive. It was a time when revolutionary organizations existed in major American cities, and revolutionary talk was in the air.

In the 1880s and 1890s, immigrants were pouring in from Europe at a faster rate than before. They all went through the harrowing ocean voyage of the poor. Now there were not so many Irish and German immigrants as Italians, Russians, Jews, Greeks—people from southern and eastern Europe, even more alien to native-born Anglo-Saxons than the earlier newcomers.

The immigration of these different ethnic groups contributed to the fragmentation of the working class. The Irish, still recalling the hatred against them when they arrived, began to get jobs with the new political machines that wanted their vote. Those who became policemen encountered the new Jewish immigrants. On July 30, 1902, New York's Jewish community held a mass funeral for an important rabbi, and a riot took place, led by Irish who resented Jews coming into their neighborhood.

There was desperate economic competition among the newcomers. By 1880, Chinese immigrants, brought in by the railroads to do the back-breaking labor at pitiful wages, numbered 75,000 in California, almost one-tenth of the population. They became the objects of continuous violence. The novelist Bret Harte wrote an obituary for a Chinese man named Wan Lee: "Dead, my revered friends, dead. Stoned to death in the streets of San Francisco, in the year of grace 1869 by a mob of halfgrown boys and Christian school children."

In Rock Springs, Wyoming, in the summer of 1885, whites attacked five hundred Chinese miners, massacring twenty-eight of them in cold blood.

A traffic in immigrant child laborers developed, either by contract with desperate parents in the home country or by kidnapping. The children were then supervised by "padrones" in a form of slavery, sometimes sent out as beggar musicians. Droves of them roamed the streets of New York and Philadelphia.

As the immigrants became naturalized citizens, they were brought into the American two-party system, invited to be loyal to one party or the other, their political energy thus siphoned into elections. An article in *L'Italia*, in November 1894, called for Italians to support the Republican party. Irish and Jewish leaders backed the Democrats.

There were 5.5 million immigrants in the 1880s, 4 million in the 1890s, creating a labor surplus that kept wages down. The immigrants were more controllable, more helpless than native workers; they were culturally displaced, at odds with one another, therefore useful as strikebreakers. Often their children worked, intensifying the problem of an oversized labor force and joblessness; in 1880 there were 1,118,000 children under sixteen (one out of six) at work in the United States.

Women immigrants became servants, prostitutes, housewives, factory workers, and sometimes rebels.

In 1884, women's assemblies of textile workers and hatmakers went on strike. The following year in New York, cloak and shirt makers, men and women (holding separate meetings but acting together), went on strike. The *New York World* called it "a revolt for bread and butter." They won higher wages and shorter hours.

That winter in Yonkers, a few women carpet weavers were fired for joining the Knights of Labor, and in the cold of February, twenty-five hundred women walked out and picketed the mill. The police attacked the picket line and arrested them, but a jury found them not guilty. A great dinner was held by working people in New York to honor them, with two thousand delegates from unions all over the city. The strike lasted six months, and the women won some of their demands, getting back their jobs, but without recognition of their union.

What was astonishing in so many of these struggles was not that the strikers did not win all that they wanted, but that, against such great odds, they dared to resist, and were not destroyed.

Perhaps it was the recognition that day-to-day combat was not enough, that fundamental change was needed, which stimulated the growth of revolutionary movements at this time. In 1883, an anarchist congress took place in Pittsburgh. It drew up a manifesto: "...All laws are directed against the working people.... The workers can therefore expect no help from any capitalistic party in their struggle against the existing system. They must achieve their liberation by their own efforts."

The manifesto asked "equal rights for all without distinction to sex or race." It quoted the *Communist Manifesto*: "Workmen of all lands, unite! You have nothing to lose but your chains; you have a world to win!"

In Chicago, the new International Working People's Association connected to the First International in Europe, had five thousand members, published newspapers in five languages, organized mass demonstrations and parades, and through its leadership in strikes was a powerful influence in the twenty-two unions that made up the Central Labor Union of Chicago. There were differences in theory among all these revolutionary groups, but the theorists were often brought together by the practical needs of labor struggles, and there were many in the mid-1880s.

By the spring of 1886, the movement for an eight-hour day had grown. On May 1, the American Federation of Labor, now five years old, called for nationwide strikes wherever the eight-hour day was refused. Terence Powderly, head of the Knights of Labor, opposed the strike, saying that employers and employees must first be educated on the eight-hour day, but assemblies of the Knights made plans to strike. The grand chief of the Brotherhood of Locomotive Engineers opposed the eight-hour day, saying "two hours less work means two hours more loafing about the corners and two hours more for drink," but railroad workers did not agree and supported the eight-hour movement.

So, 350,000 workers in 11,562 establishments all over the country went out on strike. In Detroit, 11,000 workers marched in an eight-hour parade. In New York, 25,000 formed a torchlight procession along Broadway. In Chicago, 40,000 struck, and 45,000 were granted a shorter working day to prevent them from striking. Every railroad in Chicago stopped running, and most of the industries in Chicago were paralyzed. The stockyards were closed down.

A "Citizens' Committee" of businessmen met daily to map strategy in Chicago. The state militia had been called out, the police were ready, and the *Chicago Mail* on May 1 asked that Albert Parsons and August Spies, the anarchist leaders of the International Working People's Association, be watched. "Keep them in view. Hold them personally responsible for any trouble that occurs. Make an example of them if trouble occurs."

Under the leadership of Parsons and Spies, the Central Labor Union, with twenty-two unions, had adopted a fiery resolution in the fall of 1885:

> Be it Resolved, That we urgently call upon the wage-earning class to arm itself in order to be able to put forth against their exploiters such an argument which alone can be effective: Violence, and further be it Resolved, that notwithstanding that we expect very little from the introduction of the eight-hour day, we firmly promise to assist our more backward brethren in this class struggle with all means and power at our disposal, so long as they will continue to show an open and resolute

front to our common oppressors, the aristocratic vagabonds and exploiters. Our war-cry is "Death to the foes of the human race."

On May 3, a series of events took place which were to put Parsons and Spies in exactly the position that the *Chicago Mail* had suggested ("Make an example of them if trouble occurs"). That day, in front of the McCormick Harvester Works, where strikers and sympathizers fought scabs, the police fired into a crowd of strikers running from the scene, wounded many of them, and killed four. Spies, enraged, went to the printing shop of the *Arbeiter-Zeitung* and printed a circular in both English and German:

> Revenge!
>   Workingmen, to Arms!!!
>   ...You have for years endured the most abject humiliations;...you have worked yourself to death...your Children you have sacrificed to the factory lord—in short: you have been miserable and obedient slaves all these years: Why? To satisfy the insatiable greed, to fill the coffers of your lazy thieving master? When you ask them now to lessen your burdens, he sends his bloodhounds out to shoot you, kill you!
>   ...To arms we call you, to arms!

A meeting was called for Haymarket Square on the evening of May 4, and about three thousand persons assembled. It was a quiet meeting, and as storm clouds gathered and the hour grew late, the crowd dwindled to a few hundred. A detachment of 180 policemen showed up, advanced on the speakers' platform, ordered the crowd to disperse. The speaker said the meeting was almost over. A bomb then exploded in the midst of the police, wounding sixty-six policemen, of whom seven later died. The police fired into the crowd, killing several people, wounding two hundred.

With no evidence on who threw the bomb, the police arrested eight anarchist leaders in Chicago. The *Chicago Journal* said: "Justice should be prompt in dealing with the arrested anarchists. The law regarding accessories to crime in this State is so plain that their trials will be short." Illinois law said that anyone inciting a murder was guilty of that murder. The evidence against the eight anarchists was their ideas, their literature; none had been at Haymarket that day except Fielden, who was speaking when the bomb exploded. A jury found them guilty, and they were sentenced to death. Their appeals were denied; the U.S. Supreme Court said it had no jurisdiction.

The event aroused international excitement. Meetings took place in France, Holland, Russia, Italy, Spain. In London a meeting of protest was sponsored by George Bernard Shaw, William Morris, and Peter Kropotkin, among others. Shaw had responded in his characteristic way to the turning down of an appeal by the eight members of the Illinois Supreme Court: "If the world must lose eight of its people, it can better afford to lose the eight members of the Illinois Supreme Court."

A year after the trial, four of the convicted anarchists—Albert Parsons, a printer, August Spies, an upholsterer, Adolph Fischer, and George Engel—were hanged. Louis Lingg, a twenty-one-year-old carpenter, blew himself up in his cell by exploding a dynamite tube in his mouth. Three remained in prison.

The executions aroused people all over the country. There was a funeral march of twenty-five thousand in Chicago.

While the immedite result was a suppression of the radical movement, the long-term effect was to keep alive the class anger of many, to inspire others—especially young people of that generation—to action in revolutionary causes. Sixty thousand signed petitions to the new governor of Illinois, John Peter Altgeld, who investigated the facts, denounced what had happened, and pardoned the three remaining prisoners. Year after year, all over the country, memorial meetings for the Haymarket martyrs were held; it is impossible to know the number of individuals whose political awakening—as with Emma Goldman and Alexander Berkman, long-time revolutionary stalwarts of the next generation—came from the Haymarket Affair.

Some of the energy of resentment in late 1886 was poured into the electoral campaign for mayor of New York that fall. Trade unions formed an Independent Labor party and nominated for mayor Henry George, the radical economist, whose *Progress and Poverty* had been read by tens of thousands of workers.

The Democrats nominated an iron manufacturer, Abram Hewitt, and the Republicans nominated Theodore Roosevelt. In a campaign of coercion and bribery, Hewitt was elected with 41 percent of the vote, George came second with more votes than Roosevelt. Roosevelt third with 27 percent of the vote. The *New York World* saw this as a signal:

> The deep-voiced protest conveyed in the 67,000 votes for Henry George against the combined power of both political parties, of Wall Street and the business interests, and of the public press should be a warning to the community to heed the demands of Labor so far as they are just and reasonable....

In other cities in the country too, labor candidates ran, electing a mayor in Milwaukee, and various local officials in Fort Worth, Texas; Eaton, Ohio; and Leadville, Colorado.

It seemed that the weight of Haymarket had not crushed the labor movement. The year 1886 became known to contemporaries as "the year of the great uprising of labor." From 1881 to 1885, strikes had averaged about 500 each year, involving perhaps 150,000 workers each year. In 1886 there were over 1,400 strikes, involving 500,000 workers. John Commons, in his *History of the Labor Movement in the United States*, saw in that:

> the signs of a great movement by the class of the unskilled, which had finally risen in rebellion.... The movement bore in every way the aspect of a social war. A frenzied hatred of labour for capital was shown in every important strike.... Extreme bitterness toward capital manifested itself in all the actions of the Knights of Labor, and wherever the leaders undertook to hold it within bounds, they were generally discarded by their followers....

Even among southern blacks, where all the military, political, and economic force of the southern states, with the acquiescence of the national government, was concentrated on keeping them docile and working, there were sporadic rebellions. In the cotton fields, blacks were dispersed in their work, but in the sugar fields, work was done in gangs, so there was opportunity for organized action.

By 1886, the Knights of Labor was organizing in the sugar fields. The black workers, unable to feed and clothe their families on their wages, often paid in store scrip, asked a dollar a day. The following year, in the fall, close to ten thousand sugar laborers went on strike, 90 percent of them Negroes and members of the Knights. The militia arrived and gun battles began.

Violence erupted in the town of Thibodaux, Louisiana, where hundreds of strikers, evicted from their plantation shacks, gathered, penniless and ragged, carrying their bed clothing and babies. Their refusal to work threatened the entire sugar crop, and martial law was declared in Thibodaux. Henry and George Cox, two Negro brothers, leaders in the Knights of Labor, were arrested, locked up, then taken from their cells, and never heard from again. On the night of November 22, shooting broke out, each side claiming the other was at fault; by noon the next day, thirty Negroes were dead or dying, and hundreds wounded. Two whites were wounded. A Negro newspaper in New Orleans wrote:

...Lame men and blind women shot; children and hoary-headed grand-sires ruthlessly swept down! The Negroes offered no resistance; they could not, as the killing was unexpected. Those of them not killed took to the woods, a majority of them finding refuge in this city.... Citizens of the United States killed by a mob directed by a State judge.... Laboring men seeking an advance in wages, treated as if they were dogs!...

Native-born poor whites were not doing well either. In the South, they were tenant farmers rather than landowners. In the southern cities, they were tenants, not homeowners. And the slums of the southern cities were among the worst, poor whites living like the blacks, on unpaved dirt streets "choked up with garbage, filth and mud," according to a report of one state board of health.

In the year 1891, miners of the Tennessee Coal Mine Company were asked to sign an "iron-clad contract": pledging no strikes, agreeing to get paid in scrip, and giving up the right to check the weight of the coal they mined (they were paid by the weight). They refused to sign and were evicted from their houses. Convicts were brought in to replace them.

On the night of October 31, 1891, a thousand armed miners took control of the mine area, set five hundred convicts free, and burned down the stockades in which the convicts were kept. The companies surrendered, agreeing not to use convicts, not to require the "iron-clad contract," and to let the miners check on the weight of the coal they mined.

The following year, there were more insurrections in Tennessee. Miners overpowered guards of the Tennessee Coal and Iron Company, burned the stockades, shipped the convicts to Nashville. Other unions in Tennessee came to their aid. An observer reported back to the Chattanooga Federation of Trades: "The entire district is as one over the main proposition, 'the convicts must go.' I counted 840 rifles on Monday as the miners passed.... Whites and Negroes are standing shoulder to shoulder."

That same year, in New Orleans, forty-two union locals, with over twenty thousand members, mostly white but including some blacks (there was one black on the strike committee), called a general strike, involving half the population of the city. Work in New Orleans came to a stop. After three days—with strikebreakers brought in, martial law, and the threat of militia—the strike ended with a compromise, gaining hours and wages but without recognition of the unions as bargaining agents.

The year 1892 saw strike struggles all over the country: besides the general strike in New Orleans and the coal miners' strike in Tennessee, there was a railroad switchmen's strike in Buffalo, New York, and a copper miners' strike in Coeur d'Alene, Idaho. The Coeur d'Alene strike was marked by gun battles between strikers and strikebreakers, and many deaths.

In early 1892, the Carnegie Steel plant at Homestead, Pennsylvania, just outside of Pittsburgh, was being managed by Henry Clay Frick while Carnegie was in Europe. Frick decided to reduce the workers' wages and break their union. He built a fence three miles long and twelve feet high around the steelworks and topped it with barbed wire, adding peepholes for rifles. When the workers did not accept the pay cut, Frick laid off the entire work force. The Pinkerton detective agency was hired to protect strikebreakers.

On the night of July 5, 1892, hundreds of Pinkerton guards boarded barges five miles down the river from Homestead and moved toward the plant, where ten thousand strikers and sympathizers waited. The crowd warned the Pinkertons not to step off the barge. A striker lay down on the gangplank, and when a Pinkerton man tried to shove him aside, he fired, wounding the detective in the thigh. In the gunfire that followed on both sides, seven workers were killed.

The Pinkertons had to retreat onto the barges. They were attacked from all sides, voted to surrender, and then were beaten by the enraged crowd. There were dead on both sides. For the next several days the strikers were in command of the area. Now the state went into action: the governor brought in the militia, armed with the latest rifles and Gatling guns, to protect the import of strikebreakers.

Strike leaders were charged with murder; 160 other strikers were tried for other crimes. All were acquitted by friendly juries. The strike held for four months, but the plant was producing steel with strikebreakers who were brought in, often in locked trains, not knowing their destination, not knowing a strike was on. The strikers, with no resources left, agreed to return to work, their leaders blacklisted.

In the midst of the Homestead strike, a young anarchist from New York named Alexander Berkman, in a plan prepared by anarchist friends in New York, including his lover Emma Goldman, came to Pittsburgh and entered the office of Henry Clay Frick, determined to kill him. Berkman's aim was poor; he wounded Frick and was overwhelmed, then was tried and found guilty of attempted murder.

He served fourteen years in the state penitentiary. His *Prison Memoirs of an Anarchist* gave a graphic description of the assassination attempt and of his years in prison, when he changed his mind about the usefulness of assassinations but remained a dedicated revolutionary. Emma Goldman's auto-biography, *Living My Life*, conveys the anger, the sense of injustice, the desire for a new kind of life, that grew among the young radicals of that day.

The year 1893 saw the biggest economic crisis in the country's history. After several decades of wild industrial growth, financial manipulation, uncontrolled speculation and profiteering, it all collapsed: 642 banks failed and 16,000 businesses closed down. Out of the labor force of 15 million, 3 million were unemployed. No state government voted relief, but mass demonstrations all over the country forced city governments to set up soup kitchens and give people work on streets or parks.

In New York City, in Union Square, Emma Goldman addressed a huge meeting of the unemployed and urged those whose children needed food to go into the stores and take it. She was arrested for "inciting to riot" and sentenced to two years in prison. In Chicago, it was estimated that 200,000 people were without work, the floors and stairways of City Hall and the police stations packed every night with homeless men trying to sleep.

The depression lasted for years and brought a wave of strikes throughout the country. The largest of these was the nationwide strike of railroad workers in 1894 that began at the Pullman Company in Illinois, just outside of Chicago.

Railroad work was one of the most dangerous jobs in America; over two thousand railroad workers were being killed each year, and thirty thousand injured. The *Locomotive Firemen's Magazine* said: "It comes to this: while railroad managers reduce their force and require men to do double duty, involving loss of rest and sleep...the accidents are chargeable to the greed of the corporation."

It was the Depression of 1893 that propelled Eugene Debs into a lifetime of action for unionism and socialism. He had worked on the railroads for four years until he was nineteen, but left when a friend was killed after falling under a locomotive. He read Edward Bellamy's *Looking Backward*; it deeply affected him.

In the midst of the economic crisis of 1893, a small group of railroad workers, including Debs, formed the American Railway Union, to unite all railway workers. Debs said: "It has been my life's desire to unify railroad employees and to eliminate the aristocracy of labor...and organize them so all will be on an equality...."

Debs wanted to include everyone, but blacks were kept out: at a convention in 1894, the provision in the constitution barring blacks was affirmed by a vote of 112 to 100. Later, Debs thought this might have had a crucial effect on the outcome of the Pullman strike, for black workers were in no mood to cooperate with the strikers.

In June 1894, workers at the Pullman Palace Car Company went on strike. They received immediate support from other unions in the Chicago area. The Pullman strikers appealed to a convention of the American Railway Union for support:

> Mr. President and Brothers of the American Railway Union. We struck at Pullman because we were without hope. We joined the American Railway Union because it gave us a glimmer of hope. Twenty thousand souls, men, women and little ones, have their eyes turned toward this convention today, straining eagerly through dark despondency for a glimmer of the heaven-sent message you alone can give us on this earth....
>
> You all must know that the proximate cause of our strike was the discharge of two members of our grievance committee.... Five reductions in wages.... Pullman, both the man and the town, is an ulcer on the body politic. He owns the houses, the schoolhouses, and churches of God in the town he gave his once humble name....

The American Railway Union responded. It asked its members all over the country not to handle Pullman cars. Since virtually all passenger trains had Pullman cars, this amounted to a boycott of all trains—a nationwide strike. Soon all traffic on the twenty-four railroad lines leading out of Chicago had come to a halt. Workers derailed freight cars, blocked tracks, pulled engineers off trains if they refused to cooperate.

The General Managers Association, representing the railroad owners, agreed to pay two thousand deputies, sent in to break the strike. But the strike went on. The attorney general of the United States, Richard Olney, a former railroad lawyer, now got a court injunction against blocking trains, on the legal ground that the federal mails were being interfered with. When the strikers ignored the injunction, President Cleveland ordered federal troops to Chicago. On July 6, hundreds of cars were burned by strikers.

The following day, the state militia moved in. A crowd of five thousand gathered. Rocks were thrown at the militia, and the command was given to fire. The *Chicago Times* reported:

> The command to charge was given.... From that moment only bayonets were used.... A dozen men in the front line of rioters received bayonet wounds.... The police were not inclined to be merciful, and driving the mob against the barbed wires clubbed it unmercifully.... The ground

over which the fight had occurred was like a battlefield. The men shot by the troops and police lay about like logs....

In Chicago that day, thirteen people were killed, fifty-three seriously wounded, seven hundred arrested. Before the strike was over, perhaps thirty-four were dead. With fourteen thousand police, militia, troops in Chicago, the strike was crushed. Debs was arrested for contempt of court, for violating the injunction that said he could not do or say anything to carry on the strike.

Debs, in court, denied he was a socialist. But during his six months in prison, he studied socialism and talked to fellow prisoners who were socialists. Later he wrote: "I was to be baptized in Socialism in the roar of conflict...in the gleam of every bayonet and the flash of every rifle the class struggle was revealed...."

Two years after he came out of prison, Debs wrote in the *Railway Times*: "The issue is Socialism versus Capitalism. I am for Socialism because I am for humanity. We have been cursed with the reign of gold long enough. Money constitutes no proper basis of civilization. The time has come to regenerate society—we are on the eve of a universal change."

Thus, the eighties and nineties saw bursts of labor insurrection, more organized than the spontaneous strikes of 1877. There were now revolutionary movements influencing labor struggles, the ideas of socialism affecting labor leaders. Radical literature was appearing, speaking of fundamental changes, of new possibilities for living.

In this same period, those who worked on the land—farmers, North and South, black and white—were going far beyond the scattered tenant protests of the pre–Civil War years and creating the greatest movement of agrarian rebellion the country had ever seen.

Behind the despair so often registered in the farm country literature of that day, there must have been visions, from time to time, of a different way to live, as in a Hamlin Garland novel, *A Spoil of Office*, where the heroine speaks at a farmers' picnic:

> I see a time when the farmer will not need to live in a cabin on a lonely farm. I see the farmers coming together in groups. I see them with time to read, and time to visit with their fellows. I see them enjoying lectures in beautiful halls, erected in every village. I see them gather like the Saxons of old upon the green at evening to sing and dance. I see cities rising near them with schools, and churches, and concert halls and theaters. I see a day when the farmer will no longer be a drudge and his wife a bond slave, but happy men and women who will go singing to their pleasant tasks upon their fruitful farms.

Between 1860 and 1910, the U.S. Army, wiping out the Indian villages on the Great Plains, paved the way for the railroads to move in and take the best land. Then the farmers came for what was left. From 1860 to 1900 the population of the United States grew from 31 million to 75 million. The crowded cities of the East needed food, and the number of farms grew from 2 million to 6 million.

Farming became mechanized—steel plows, mowing machines, reapers, harvesters, improved cotton gins for pulling the fibers away from the seed, and, by the turn of the century, giant combines that cut the grain, threshed it, and put it in bags. In 1830 a bushel of wheat had taken three hours to produce. By 1900, it took ten minutes. Specialization developed by region: cotton and tobacco in the South, wheat and corn in the Midwest.

Land cost money, and machines cost money—so farmers had to borrow, hoping that the prices of their harvests would stay high, so they could pay the bank for the loan, the railroad for transportation, the grain merchant for handling their grain, the storage elevator for storing it. But they found the prices for their produce going down, and the prices of transportation and loans going up, because the individual farmer could not control the price of his grain, while the monopolist railroad and the monopolist banker could charge what they liked.

The farmers who could not pay saw their homes and land taken away. They became tenants. By 1880, 25 percent of all farms were rented by tenants, and the number kept rising. Many did not even have money to rent and became farm laborers; by 1900 there were 4.5 million farm laborers in the country. It was the fate that awaited every farmer who couldn't pay his debts.

Could the squeezed and desperate farmer turn to the government for help?

The government was helping the bankers and hurting the farmers; it kept the amount of money—based on the gold supply—steady, while the population rose, so there was less and less money in circulation. The farmer had to pay off his debts in dollars that were harder to get. The bankers, getting the loans back, were getting dollars worth more than when they loaned them out—a kind of interest on top of interest. That is why so much of the talk of farmers' movements in those days had to do with putting more money in circulation—by printing greenbacks (paper money for which there was no gold in the treasury) or by making silver a basis for issuing money.

It was in the South that the crop-lien system was most brutal. By this system the farmer would get the things he needed from the merchant: the use of the cotton gin at harvest time, whatever supplies were necessary. He didn't have money to pay, so the merchant would get a lien—a mortgage on his crop—on which the farmer might pay 25 percent interest. The farmer would owe more money every year until finally his farm was taken away and he became a tenant.

In the depths of the 1877 depression, a group of white farmers gathered together on a farm in Texas and formed the first "Farmers Alliance." In a few years, it was across the state. By 1886, 100,000 farmers had joined in two thousand suballiances. They began to offer alternatives to the old system: join the Alliance and form cooperatives; buy things together and get lower prices. They began putting their cotton together and selling it cooperatively—they called it "bulking."

In some states a Grange movement developed; it managed to get laws passed to help farmers. But the Grange, as one of its newspapers put it, "is essentially conservative...." It was a time of crisis, and the Grange was doing too little. It lost members, while the Farmers Alliance kept growing.

From the beginning, the Farmers Alliance showed sympathy with the growing labor movement. When Knights of Labor men went on strike against a steamship line in Galveston, Texas, a group of Alliance people in Texas passed a resolution:

> Whereas we see the unjust encroachments that the capitalists are making upon all the different departments of labor...we extend to the Knights of Labor our hearty sympathy in their manly struggle against monopolistic oppression and...we propose to stand by the Knights.

In the summer of 1886, in the town of Cleburne, Texas, near Dallas, the Alliance gathered and drew up the first document of the Populist movement, asking "such legislation as shall secure to our people freedom from the onerous and shameful abuses that the industrial classes are now suffering at the hands of arrogant capitalists and powerful corporations." They called for a national conference of all labor organizations and proposed regulation of railroad rates, heavy taxation of land held only for speculative purposes, and an increase in the money supply.

The Alliance kept growing. By early 1887, it had 200,000 members in three thousand suballiances. By 1892 farmer lecturers had gone into forty-three states and reached 2 million farm families. It was a drive based on the idea of cooperation, of farmers creating their own culture, their own political parties.

Organizers from Texas came to Georgia to form alliances, and in three years Georgia had 100,000 members in 134 of the 137 counties. In Tennessee, there were soon 125,000 members and 3,600 suballiances in 92 of the state's 96 counties. The Alliance moved into Mississippi "like a cyclone," someone said, and into Louisiana and North Carolina. Then northward into Kansas and the Dakotas, where thirty-five cooperative warehouses were set up.

Now there were 400,000 members in the National Farmers Alliance. And the conditions spurring the Alliance onward got worse. Corn that had brought $.45 a bushel in 1870 brought $.10 a bushel in 1889. In the South the situation was worse than anywhere—90 percent of the farmers lived on credit.

There was one victory along the way. Farmers were being charged too much for jute bags (to put cotton in), which were controlled by a trust. The Alliance farmers organized a boycott of jute, made their own bags out of cotton, and forced the jute manufacturers to start selling their bags at $.05 a yard instead of $.14.

There were Alliance experiments. In the Dakotas, a great cooperative insurance plan for farmers insured them against loss of their crops. Where the big insurance companies had asked $.50 an acre, the cooperative asked $.25 or less. It issued thirty thousand policies, covering 2 million acres.

The complexity of Populist belief was shown in one of its important leaders in Texas, Charles Macune. He was a radical in economics (antitrust, anticapitalist), a conservative in politics (against a new party independent of the Democrats), and a racist. Macune came forward with a plan that was to become central to the Populist platform—the "sub-Treasury" plan. The government would have its own warehouses where farmers would store produce and get certificates from this sub-Treasury. These would be greenbacks, and thus much more currency would be made available, not dependent on gold or silver, but based on the amount of farm produce.

Macune's sub-Treasury plan depended on the government. And since it would not be taken up by the two major parties, it meant (against Macune's own beliefs) organizing a third party. The Alliance went to work. In 1890 thirty-eight Alliance people were elected to Congress. In the South, the Alliance elected governors in Georgia and Texas. It took over the Democratic party in Georgia and won three-fourths of the seats in the Georgia state legislature, six of Georgia's ten U.S. congressmen.

Corporate power still dominated the political structure, but the Alliance was spreading new ideas and a new spirit. Now, as a political party, it became the People's party (or Populist party), and met in convention in 1890 in Topeka, Kansas. The great Populist orator from that state, Mary Ellen Lease, told an enthusiastic crowd:

> Wall Street owns the country. It is no longer a government of the people, by the people, and for the people, but a government of Wall Street, by Wall Street and for Wall Street.... We want the power to make loans direct from the government. We want the accursed foreclosure system wiped out.... We will stand by our homes and stay by our firesides by force if necessary, and we will not pay our debts to the loan-shark companies until the Government pays its debts to us. The people are at bay, let the bloodhounds of money who have dogged us thus far beware.

At the People's party national convention in 1892 in St. Louis, a platform was drawn up. The preamble was written by, and read to the assemblage by, another of the great orators of the movement, Ignatius Donnelly:

> We meet in the midst of a nation brought to the verge of moral, political and material ruin. Corruption dominates the ballot box, the legislatures, the Congress, and touches even the ermine of the bench. The people are demoralized.... The newspapers are subsidized or muzzled; public opinion silenced; business prostrate, our homes covered with mortgages, labor impoverished, and the land concentrating in the hands of capitalists.

A People's party nominating convention in Omaha in July of 1892 nominated James Weaver, an Iowa Populist and former general in the Union army, for president. The Populist movement was now tied to the voting system. Weaver got over a million votes, but lost.

The People's Party had the job of uniting diverse groups—northern Republicans and southern Democrats, urban workers and country farmers, black and white. A Colored Farmers National Alliance grew in the South and had perhaps a million members, but it was organized and led by whites. There were also black organizers, but it was not easy for them to persuade black farmers that, even if economic reforms were won, blacks would have equal access to them. Blacks had tied themselves to the Republican party, the party of Lincoln and civil rights laws.

There were whites who saw the need for racial unity. One Alabama newspaper wrote: "The white and colored Alliance are united in their war against trusts...."

Some Alliance blacks made similar calls for unity. A leader of the

Florida Colored Alliance said: "We are aware of the fact that the laboring colored man's interests and the laboring white man's interest are one and the same."

When the Texas People's party was founded in Dallas in the summer of 1891, it was interracial, and radical. There was blunt and vigorous debate among whites and blacks. A black delegate, active in the Knights of Labor, dissatisfied with vague statements about "equality," said:

> If we are equal, why does not the sheriff summon Negroes on juries? And why hang up the sign "Negro," in passenger cars. I want to tell my people what the People's Party is going to do. I want to tell them if it is going to work a black and white horse in the same field.

A white leader responded by urging there be a black delegate from every district in the state. "They are in the ditch just like we are."

Blacks and whites were in different situations. The blacks were mostly field hands, hired laborers; most white Alliance people were farm owners. When the Colored Alliance declared a strike in the cotton fields in 1891 for a dollar a day wages for cotton pickers, Leonidas Polk, head of the white Alliance, denounced it as hurting the Alliance farmer who would have to pay that wage.

There was some black-white unity at the ballot box in the South—resulting in a few blacks elected in North Carolina local elections. An Alabama white farmer wrote to a newspaper in 1892: "I wish to God that Uncle Sam could put bayonets around the ballot box in the black belt on the first Monday in August so that the Negro could get a fair vote." There were black delegates to third-party conventions in Georgia: two in 1892, twenty-four in 1894. The Arkansas People's party platform spoke for the "downtrodden, regardless of race."

Still, racism was strong, and the Democratic party played on this, winning many farmers from the Populist party. When white tenants, failing in the crop-lien system, were evicted from their land and replaced by blacks, race hatred intensified. Southern states were drawing up new constitutions, starting with Mississippi in 1890, to prevent blacks from voting by various devices, and to maintain ironclad segregation in every aspect of life.

The laws that took the vote away from blacks—poll taxes, literacy tests, property qualifications—also often ensured that poor whites would not vote. And the political leaders of the South knew this. At the constitutional convention in Alabama, one of the leaders said he wanted to take away the vote from "all those who are unfit and unqualified, and if the rule strikes a white man as well as a negro let him go."

Tom Watson, the Populist leader of Georgia, pleaded for racial unity: "You are kept apart that you may be separately fleeced of your earnings. You are made to hate each other because upon that hatred is rested the keystone of the arch of financial despotism which enslaves you both." Watson wanted black support for a white man's party, and later, when Watson found this support embarrassing and no longer useful, he became as eloquent in affirming racism as he had been in opposing it.

It was a time that illustrated the complexities of class and race conflict. Fifteen blacks were lynched during Watson's election campaign. And in Georgia after 1891 the Alliance-controlled legislature, Allen points out, "passed the largest number of anti-black bills ever enacted in a single year in Georgia history." And yet, in 1896, the Georgia state platform of the People's party denounced lynch law and terrorism, and asked the abolition of the convict lease system.

C. Vann Woodward points to the unique quality of the Populist experience in the South: "Never before or since have the two races in the South come so close together as they did during the Populist struggles."

The Populist movement also made a remarkable attempt to create a new and independent culture for the country's farmers. The Alliance Lecture Bureau reached all over the country; it had 35,000 lecturers. The Populists poured out books and pamphlets from their printing presses. Their aim was to educate farmers, revising the orthodox history, economics, and political theory.

The *National Economist*, a Populist magazine, had 100,000 readers. There were over a thousand Populist journals in the 1890s. Books written by Populist leaders, such as Henry Demarest Lloyd's *Wealth Against Commonwealth* and William Harvey Coin's *Financial School*, were widely read. The Populist movement profoundly affected Southern life.

There were only fitful, occasional connections between the farmer and labor movements. Neither spoke eloquently enough to the other's needs. And yet, there were signs of a common consciousness that might, under different circumstances, lead to a unified, ongoing movement.

Undoubtedly, Populists, along with most white Americans, had racism and nativism in their thinking. But part of it was that they simply did not think race as important as the economic system. Thus, the *Farmers' Alliance* said: "The people's party has sprung into existence not to make the black man free, but to emancipate all men...to gain for all industrial freedom, without which there can be no political freedom...."

The Populist movement failed, finally, to unite blacks and whites, city workers and country farmers. That, plus the lure of electoral politics, combined to destroy the Populist movement. Once allied with the Democratic party in supporting William Jennings Bryan for president in 1896, Populism would drown in a sea of Democratic politics. The pressure for electoral victory led Populism to make deals with the major parties in city after city. If the Democrats won, it would be absorbed. If the Democrats lost, it would disintegrate. Electoral politics brought into the top leadership the political brokers instead of the agrarian radicals.

There were those radical Populists who saw this. They said fusion with the Democrats to try to "win" would lose what they needed, an independent political movement. They said the much-ballyhooed free silver would not change anything fundamental in the capitalist system.

Henry Demarest Lloyd noted that the Bryan nomination was subsidized in part by Marcus Daly (of Anaconda Copper) and William Randolph Hearst (of the silver interests in the West). He saw through the rhetoric of Bryan that stirred the crowd of twenty thousand at the Democratic Convention. Lloyd wrote bitterly:

> The poor people are throwing up their hats in the air for those who promise to lead them out of the wilderness by way of the currency route.... The people are to be kept wandering forty years in the currency labyrinth, as they have for the last forty years been led up and down the tariff bill.

In the election of 1896, with the Populist movement enticed into the Democratic party, Bryan, the Democratic candidate, was defeated by William McKinley, for whom the corporations and the press mobilized, in the first massive use of money in an election campaign. Even the hint of Populism in the Democratic party, it seemed, could not be tolerated, and the big guns of the Establishment pulled out all their ammunition, to make sure.

It was a time, as election times have often been in the United States, to consolidate the system after years of protest and rebellion. The black was being kept under control in the South. The Indian was being driven off the western plains for good; on a cold winter day in 1890, U.S. army soldiers attacked Indians camped at Wounded Knee, South Dakota, and killed three hundred men, women, and children. It was the climax to four hundred years of violence that began with Columbus, establishing that this continent belonged to white men. But only to certain white men, because it was clear by 1896 that the state stood ready to crush labor strikes, by the law if possible, by force if necessary. And where a threatening mass movement developed, the two-party system stood ready to send out one of its columns to surround that movement and drain it of vitality.

And always, as a way of drowning class resentment in a flood of slogans for national unity, there was patriotism. McKinley had said, in a rare rhetorical connection between money and flag:

> ...this year is going to be a year of patriotism and devotion to country. I am glad to know that the people in every part of the country mean to be devoted to one flag, the glorious Stars and Stripes; that the people of this country mean to maintain the financial honor of the country as sacredly as they maintain the honor of the flag.

The supreme act of patriotism was war. Two years after McKinley became president, the United States declared war on Spain.

Exercises

1. What was the technology that transformed the work-place from 1865–1900? What economic and social effects did the new technology have on American society?

2. Why did it "take money to make money" during the period of rapid economic expansion after the Civil War? What are the implications of this for the potential for social mobility?

3. How many railroad workers were killed or injured in 1889? Why did so many workers die on the job?

4. How did J. P. Morgan justify his methods of doing business?

5. What methods did each of the following use to build his fortune?
   a. Morgan (banking, railroads, and steel)
   b. Rockefeller (oil)
   c. Carnegie (steel)

6. Are there any facts surrounding the presidential election of 1884 and its outcome (Cleveland defeats Blaine) that support Zinn's assertion that "Whether Democrats or Republicans won, national policy would not change in any important way." Do the policies or legislation during either of the two Cleveland administrations or Benjamin Harrison's administration support any or all parts of Zinn's statement above? How persuasive is Zinn on this point? Explain.

7. How does Zinn argue that the Supreme Court cannot possibly act in a neutral fashion? What is the argument against Zinn?

8. What definition of the "law" was Supreme Court Justice David Brewer using when he addressed the New York Sate Bar Association (all options below are quoted from Webster's New Collegiate Dictionary, 1981)?

    a. a binding custom or practice of a community

    b. a rule of conduct enforced by a controlling authority

    c. the revelation of the will of God

    d. a statement of an order or relation of phenomena that so far as is known is invariable under the given conditions

    e. the observed regularity of nature

What point was Brewer trying to make? What point is Zinn trying to make by including this quotation?

9. What role did philanthropy play in maintaining the status quo? How does this inform your understanding of the heated debate of the last fifteen years about whether the U.S. government should give grants to artists and scientists?

10. How did the educational system function as a tool to reproduce the system? In your experience, are today's educational structure, methods and content any different from they were in the late nineteenth century?

11. What was Henry George's solution to the unequal distribution of wealth? What was Edward Bellamy's? What evidence indicates that these ideas were popular at the time?

12. What was a primary obstacle to worker unity in the 1880s?

13. Why would employers want there to be large numbers of unemployed workers around? Why wouldn't employers want large numbers of unemployed workers?

14. What evidence exists that the Knights of Labor recruited women? Blacks?

15. Why was the IWPA a "powerful influence" within the Central Labor Union of Chicago? Why would a worker belong both to the IWPA and the CLU?

16. What was the major tactical disagreement between the AFL (American Federation of Labor) and the Knights in 1886?

17. How did business respond when the 1886 strike for the eight-hour day successfully "paralyzed most of the industries in Chicago?"

18. What is the most accurate way to refer to the events and their aftermath that occurred on the evening of May 4, 1886 at Haymarket Square in Chicago? Defend your rejections as well as your choice. Which would be the most neutral way to refer to the events and their aftermath (You may want to refer to a dictionary to help define the terms of the selections below as well as help you be clear as to the difference between accurate and neutral)?

    a. The Haymarket Riot

    b. The Haymarket Affair

    c. The Haymarket Persecution

    d. The Haymarket Demonstration

    e. The Haymarket Tragedy

    f. The Haymarket Travesty

    g. (your choice?)

19. How do standard American history textbooks refer to the events surrounding the incident at the Haymarket Square in 1886? Is there a consensus among these standard texts? Over what do they differ?

In what do they agree? How different are they from Zinn's version? How do you explain the differences?

20. Were the executions of Spies, Parsons, Fischer, and Engel a tactic on the part of business and government to damage the effectiveness of the labor movement? If it was, did it work?

21. What successes did the labor movement score in the 1880s and 1890s?

22. Why did the Thibodaux workers go on strike? Was the strike successful? What accounts for its success or lack of success?

23. What were the demands of the Tennessee coal miners in 1891?

24. *Debate Resolution*: The labor movement was more successful in the North and West than in the South.

25. What was Frick's strategy to break the steel-workers' union at the Homestead steel plant? Did the plan work? What is the evidence to support your answer?

26. What was the effect of the mass demonstrations that immediately followed the economic collapse beginning in 1893?

27. What role did Emma Goldman play in the labor history of the late nineteenth century?

28. Why were black workers reluctant to support the Pullman strike?

29. Why did the strike at the Pullman plant in Chicago become a nationwide strike?

30. On what pretext did the federal government side with the railroad owners?

31. When did Eugene Debs become a socialist? Why?

32. Why did the number of tenant families increase steadily through-out the post–Civil War period (post-1865)? What actions did the farmers take to oppose this trend?

33. Why did the Populists believe that Macune's sub-Treasury Plan was necessary? (What economic dynamic would the sub-Treasury plan have replaced?)

34. Why were the farmers not satisfied with only establishing coopera-tives? (Why did they feel a need to take control of the local and national governments?)

35. *Debate Resolution*: In the fight against monopolies, farmers ensured their failure by engaging in electoral politics.

36. How did the Democratic party use race to defeat the Populists in the South?

37. Zinn writes: "C. Vann Woodward points to the unique quality of the Populist experience in the South: 'Never before or since have the two races in the South come so close together as they did during the Populist struggles.'" (p. 211) How "close" was that?

38. Why would creating an alternative culture be a priority for both the Alliance and Populist movements? (How did Alliance and Populist teachings differ from the official teachings in the public school sys-tem?)

39. The farmers needed an expansion of currency as a practical, short-term solution to being constantly in debt. Their preferred solution was to issue paper currency based on the amount of grain produced. The final manifestation of this solution was Macune's sub-Treasury Plan. (See Lawrence Goodwyn, *The Populist Moment*, chapter one, section five for an explanation of Alliance currency theory.) How would the Democrat's slogan of "free silver" effectively lure the Populists away from the sub-Treasury plan? What was the minority Populist opposition argument against "free silver"?

40. During the period from 1865 to 1898, how did the political/economic elite

      a. contain the demands of blacks for equal rights?

      b. contain the demands of farmers and laborers for economic justice?

      c. respond to Indians' desires to be allowed to exist?

41. *Debate Resolution*: The Populist movement failed because it did not attempt to attract labor to its cause.

Chapter 12

The Empire and the People

Theodore Roosevelt wrote to a friend in the year 1897: "In strict confidence...I should welcome almost any war, for I think this country needs one."

The year of the massacre at Wounded Knee, 1890, it was officially declared by the Bureau of the Census that the internal frontier was closed. The profit system, with its natural tendency for expansion, had already begun to look overseas. The severe depression that began in 1893 strengthened an idea developing within the political and financial elite of the country: that overseas markets for American goods might relieve the problem of underconsumption at home and prevent the economic crises that in the 1890s brought class war.

And would not a foreign adventure deflect some of the rebellious energy that went into strikes and protest movements toward an external enemy? Would it not unite people with government, with the armed forces, instead of against them? This was probably not a conscious plan among most of the elite—but a natural development from the twin drives of capitalism and nationalism.

Expansion overseas was not a new idea. Even before the war against Mexico carried the United States to the Pacific, the Monroe Doctrine looked southward into and beyond the Caribbean. Issued in 1823 when the countries of Latin America were winning independence from Spanish control, it made plain to European nations that the United States considered Latin America its sphere of influence. Not long after, some Americans began thinking into the Pacific: of Hawaii, Japan, and the great markets of China.

There was more than thinking. A State Department list of 1962 (presented to a Senate committee to cite precedents for the use of armed force against Cuba) shows 103 interventions in the affairs of other countries between 1798 and 1895. A sampling from the list, with the exact description given by the State Department:

1852–53 · Argentina
Marines were landed and maintained in Buenos Aires to protect American interests during a revolution.

1853 · Nicaragua
to protect American lives and interests during political disturbances.

1853–54 · Japan
The "Opening of Japan" and the Perry Expedition. [The State Department does not give more details, but this involved the use of warships to force Japan to open its ports to the United States.]

1853–54 · Ryukyu and Bonin Islands
Commodore Perry on three visits before going to Japan and while waiting for a reply from Japan made a naval demonstration, landing marines twice, and secured a coaling concession from the ruler of Naha on Okinawa. He also demonstrated in the Bonin Islands. All to secure facilities for commerce.

1854 · Nicaragua
San Juan del Norte [Greytown was destroyed to avenge an insult to the American Minister to Nicaragua.]

1855 · Uruguay
U.S. and European naval forces landed to protect American interests during an attempted revolution in Montevideo.

1859 · China
For the protection of American interests in Shanghai.

1860 · Angola, Portuguese West Africa
To protect American lives and property at Kissembo when the natives became troublesome.

1893 · Hawaii
Ostensibly to protect American lives and property; actually to promote a provisional government under Sanford B. Dole. This action was disavowed by the United States.

1894 · Nicaragua
To protect American interests at Bluefields following a revolution.

Thus, by the 1890s, there had been much experience in overseas probes and interventions. The ideology of expansion was widespread in the upper circles of military men, politicians, businessmen—and even among some of the leaders of farmers' movements who thought foreign markets would help them.

Captain A. T. Mahan of the U.S. Navy, a popular propagandist for expansion, greatly influenced Theodore Roosevelt and other American leaders. The countries with the biggest navies would inherit the earth, he said. "Americans must now begin to look outward." Senator Henry Cabot Lodge of Massachusetts wrote in a magazine article:

> for the sake of our commercial supremacy in the Pacific we should control the Hawaiian islands...and when the Nicaraguan canal is built, the island of Cuba...will become a necessity.... The great nations are rapidly absorbing for their future expansion and their present defense all the waste places of the earth. It is a movement which makes for civilization and the advancement of the race. As one of the great nations of the world the United States must not fall out of the line of march.

A *Washington Post* editorial on the eve of the Spanish-American War: "A new consciousness seems to have come upon us—the consciousness of strength—and with it a new appetite, the yearning to show our strength.... The taste of Empire is in the mouth of the people even as the taste of blood in the jungle...."

Was that taste in the mouth of the people through some instinctive lust for aggression or some urgent self-interest? Or was it a taste (if indeed it existed) created, encouraged, advertised, and exaggerated by the millionaire press, the military, the government, the eager-to-please scholars of the time? Political scientist John Burgess of Columbia University said the Teutonic and Anglo-Saxon races were "particularly endowed with the capacity for establishing national states...they are entrusted...with the mission of conducting the political civilization of the modern world."

Several years before his election to the presidency, William McKinley said: "We want a foreign market for our surplus products." Senator Albert Beveridge of Indiana in early 1897 declared: "American factories are making more than the American people can use; American soil is producing more than they can consume. Fate has written our policy for us; the trade of the world must and shall be ours."

When the United States did not annex Hawaii in 1893 after some Americans (the combined missionary and pineapple interests of the Dole family) set up their own government, Theodore Roosevelt called this hesitancy "a crime against white civilization." And he told the Naval War College: "All the great masterful races have been fighting races.... No triumph of peace is quite so great as the supreme triumph of war."

William James, the philosopher, who became one of the leading anti-imperialists of his time, wrote about Roosevelt that he "gushes over war as the ideal condition of human society."

While it was true that in 1898, 90 percent of American products were sold at home, the 10 percent sold abroad amounted to a billion dollars. In 1885, the steel industry's publication *Age of Steel* wrote that the internal markets were insufficient and the overproduction of industrial products "should be relieved and prevented in the future by increased foreign trade."

Oil became a big export in the 1880s and 1890s: by 1891, the Rockefeller family's Standard Oil Company accounted for 90 percent of American exports of kerosene and controlled 70 percent of the world market. Oil was now second to cotton as the leading product sent overseas.

Expansion overseas might be especially appealing if it looked like an act of generosity—helping a rebellious group overthrow foreign rule—as in Cuba. By 1898, Cuban rebels had been fighting their Spanish conquerors for three years in an attempt to win independence. By that time, it was possible to create a national mood for intervention.

It seems that the business interests of the nation did not at first want military intervention in Cuba. American merchants did not need colonies or wars of conquest if they could just have free access to markets. This idea of an "open door" became the dominant theme of American foreign policy in the twentieth century. It was a more sophisticated approach to imperialism than the traditional empire-building of Europe. But if peaceful imperialism turned out to be impossible, military action might be needed.

For instance, in late 1897 and early 1898, with China weakened by a recent war with Japan, German military forces occupied the Chinese port of Tsingtao (Qingdao). Within the next few months, other European powers moved in on China, and the partition of China by the major imperialist powers was under way, with the United States left behind.

At this point, the *New York Journal of Commerce*, which had been advocating peaceful development of free trade, now urged old-fashioned military colonialism. It called for a canal across Central America, the acquisition of Hawaii, and a larger navy.

There was a similar turnabout in U.S. business attitudes on Cuba in 1898. Businessmen had been interested, from the start of the Cuban revolt against Spain, in the effect on commercial possibilities there. There already was a substantial economic interest in the island. Popular support of the Cuban revolution was based on the thought that they, like the Americans of 1776, were fighting a war for their own liberation. The United States government, however, the conservative product of another revolutionary war, had power and profit in mind as it observed the events in Cuba. Neither Cleveland, president during the first years of the Cuban revolt, nor McKinley, who followed, recognized the insurgents officially as belligerents; such legal recognition would have enabled the United States to give aid to the rebels without sending an army. But there may have been fear that the rebels would win on their own and keep the United States out.

There seems also to have been another kind of fear. The Cleveland administration said a Cuban victory might lead to "the establishment of a white and a black republic," since Cuba had a mixture of the two races. And the black republic might be dominant. This idea was expressed in 1896 in an article in *The Saturday Review* by a young and eloquent im-perialist, whose mother was American and whose father was English—Winston Churchill. He wrote that while Spanish rule was bad and the rebels had the support of the people, it would be better for Spain to keep control:

> A grave danger represents itself. Two-fifths of the insurgents in the field are negroes. These men...would, in the event of success, demand a predominant share in the government of the country...the result being, after years of fighting, another black republic.

The reference to "another" black republic meant Haiti, whose revolution against France in 1803 had led to the first nation run by blacks in the New World. The Spanish minister to the United States wrote to the U.S. secretary of state about Cuba:

> In this revolution, the negro element has the most important part. Not only the principal leaders are colored men, but at least eight-tenths of their supporters.... and the result of the war, if the Island can be declared independent, will be a secession of the black element and a black Republic.

In February 1898, the U.S. battleship *Maine*, in Havana harbor as a symbol of American interest in the Cuban events, was destroyed by a mysterious explosion and sank, with the loss of 268 men. No evidence was ever produced on the cause of the explosion, but excitement grew swiftly in the United States, and McKinley began to move in the direction of war.

At a certain point in that spring, both McKinley and the business community began to see that their object, to get Spain out of Cuba, could not be accomplished without war, and that their accompanying object, the securing of American military and economic influence in Cuba, could not be left to the Cuban rebels, but could be ensured only by U.S. intervention.

Before this, Congress had passed the Teller Amendment, pledging the United States not to annex Cuba. It was initiated and supported by those people who were interested in Cuban independence and opposed to American imperialism, and also by business people who saw the "open door" as sufficient and military intervention unnecessary. But by the spring of 1898, the business community had developed a hunger for action. The *Journal of Commerce* said: "The Teller amendment...must be interpreted in a sense somewhat different from that which its author intended it to bear."

There were special interests who would benefit directly from war. In Washington, it was reported that a "belligerent spirit" had infected the Navy Department, encouraged "by the contractors for projectiles, ordnance, ammunition and other supplies, who have thronged the department since the destruction of the Maine."

Russell Sage, the banker, said that if war came, "There is no question as to where the rich men stand." A survey of businessmen said that John Jacob Astor, William Rockefeller, and Thomas Fortune Ryan were "feeling militant." And J. P. Morgan believed further talk with Spain would accomplish nothing.

On March 25, a telegram arrived at the White House from an adviser to McKinley, saying: "Big corporations here now believe we will have war. Believe all would welcome it as relief to suspense."

Two days after getting this telegram, McKinley presented an ultimatum to Spain, demanding an armistice. He said nothing about independence for Cuba. A spokesman for the Cuban rebels, part of a group of Cubans in New York, interpreted this to mean the U.S. simply wanted to replace Spain. He responded:

> In the face of the present proposal of intervention without previous recognition of independence, it is necessary for us to go a step farther and say that we must and will regard such intervention as nothing less than a declaration of war by the United States against the Cuban revolutionists....

Indeed, when McKinley asked Congress for war on April 11, he did not recognize the rebels as belligerents or ask for Cuban independence. Still, when American forces moved into Cuba, the rebels welcomed them, hoping the Teller Amendment would guarantee Cuban independence.

Many histories of the Spanish-American War have said that "public opinion" in the United States led McKinley to declare war on Spain and send forces to Cuba. True, certain influential newspapers had been pushing hard, even hysterically. And many Americans, seeing the aim of intervention as Cuban independence—and with the Teller Amendment as guarantee of this intention—supported the idea. But would McKinley have gone to war because of the press and some portion of the public (we had no public opinion surveys at that time) without the urging of the business community? Several years after the Cuban war, the chief of the Bureau of Foreign Commerce of the Department of Commerce wrote about that period: "The Spanish-American War was but an incident of a general movement of expansion which had its roots in the changed environment of an industrial capacity far beyond our domestic powers of consumption."

American labor unions had sympathy for the Cuban rebels as soon as the insurrection against Spain began in 1895. But they opposed American expansionism.

When the explosion of the *Maine* in February led to excited calls for war in the press, the monthly journal of the International Association of Machinists agreed it was a terrible disaster, but it noted that the deaths of workers in industrial accidents drew no such national clamor. It pointed to the Lattimer Massacre of September 10, 1897, during a coal strike in Pennsylvania...when a sheriff and his deputies opened fire on marching miners, killing nineteen of them, most shot in the back, with no outcry in the press. The labor journal said that "the thousands of useful lives that are annually sacrificed to the Moloch of greed, the blood tribute paid by labor to capitalism, brings forth no shout for vengeance and reparation...."

Some unions, like the United Mine Workers, called for U.S. intervention after the sinking of the *Maine*. But most were against war. The treasurer of the American Longshoremen's Union, Bolton Hall, wrote "A Peace Appeal to Labor," which was widely circulated: "If there is a war, you will furnish the corpses and the taxes, and others will get the glory."

Socialists, with few exceptions (the Jewish *Daily Forward* was one), opposed the war. The *Appeal to Reason*, the major Socialist newspaper, said the movement for war was "a favorite method of rulers for keeping the people from redressing domestic wrongs." In the San Francisco *Voice of Labor* a Socialist wrote: "It is a terrible thing to think that the poor workers of this country should be sent to kill and wound the poor workers of Spain merely because a few leaders may incite them to do so."

But after war was declared most unions went along. Samuel Gompers called the war "glorious and righteous." It did bring more employment and higher wages, but also higher prices and higher taxes.

On May Day, 1898, the Socialist Labor party organized an antiwar parade in New York City, but the authorities would not allow it to take place, while a May Day parade called by the Jewish *Daily Forward*, urging Jewish workers to support the war, was permitted.

The prediction made by longshoreman Bolton Hall, of wartime corruption and profiteering, turned out to be remarkably accurate. Richard Morris's *Encyclopedia of American History* gives startling figures:

> Of the more than 274,000 officers and men who served in the army during the Spanish-American War and the period of demobilization, 5,462 died in the various theaters of operation and in camps in the U.S. Only 379 of the deaths were battle casualties, the remainder being attributed to disease and other causes.

The same figures are given by Walter Millis in his book *The Martial Spirit*. In the *Encyclopedia* they are given tersely, and without mention of the "embalmed beef" (an army general's term) sold to the army by the meatpackers—meat preserved with boric acid, nitrate of potash, and artificial coloring matter, but now rotten and putrid. Thousands of soldiers got food poisoning. There are no figures on how many of the five thousand noncombat deaths were caused by that.

The Spanish forces were defeated in three months, in what John Hay, the American secretary of state, later called a "splendid little war." The American military pretended that the Cuban rebel army did not exist. When the Spanish surrendered, no Cuban was allowed to confer on the surrender, or to sign it. Gen. William Shafter said no armed rebels could enter the capital city of Santiago, and told the Cuban rebel leader, Gen. Calixto Garcia, that not Cubans, but the old Spanish civil authorities, would remain in charge of the municipal offices in Santiago. Garcia wrote a letter of protest: "...when the question arises of appointing authorities in Santiago de Cuba...I cannot see but with the deepest regret that such authorities are not elected by the Cuban people, but are the same ones selected by the Queen of Spain...."

Along with the American army in Cuba came American capital.

The *Lumbermen's Review*, spokesman for the lumber industry, said in the midst of the war: "Cuba still possesses 10,000,000 acres of virgin forest abounding in valuable timber...nearly every foot of which would be saleable in the United States and bring high prices."

Americans began taking over railroad, mine, and sugar properties when the war ended. In a few years, $30 million of American capital was invested. United Fruit moved into the Cuban sugar industry. It bought 1.9 million acres of land for about $.20 an acre. The American Tobacco Company arrived. By the end of the occupation, in 1901, at least 80 percent of the export of Cuba's minerals were in American hands, mostly Bethlehem Steel.

During the military occupation a series of strikes took place. In September 1899, a gathering of thousands of workers in Havana launched a general strike for the eight-hour day. The American General William Ludlow ordered the mayor of Havana to arrest eleven strike leaders, and U.S. troops occupied railroad stations and docks. Police moved through the city breaking up meetings. But the economic activity of the city had come to a halt. Tobacco workers struck. Printers struck. Bakers went on strike. Hundreds of strikers were arrested, and then some of the imprisoned leaders were intimidated into calling for an end to the strike.

The United States did not annex Cuba. But a Cuban constitutional convention was told that the United States army would not leave Cuba until the Platt Amendment, passed by Congress in February 1901, was incorporated into the new Cuban Constitution. This amendment gave the United States "the right to intervene for the preservation of Cuban independence, the maintenance of a government adequate for the protection of life, property, and individual liberty...."

The Platt Amendment was now seen, not only by the radical and labor press, but by newspapers and groups all over the United States, as a betrayal of the idea of Cuban independence. A mass meeting of the American Anti-Imperialist League at Faneuil Hall in Boston denounced it, ex-governor George Boutwell saying: "In disregard of our pledge of freedom and sovereignty to Cuba we are imposing on that island conditions of colonial vassalage."

In Havana, a torchlight procession of fifteen thousand Cubans marched on the constitutional convention, urging them to reject the amendment. A black delegate from Santiago reported to the convention: "For the United States to reserve to itself the power to determine when this independence was threatened, and when, therefore, it should intervene to preserve it, is equivalent to handing over the keys to our house so that they can enter it at any time, whenever the desire seizes them, day or night, whether with good or evil design."

With this report, the convention overwhelmingly rejected the Platt Amendment.

Within the next three months, however, the pressure from the United

States, the military occupation, the refusal to allow the Cubans to set up their own government until they acquiesced, had its effect; the convention, after several refusals, adopted the Platt Amendment. Gen. Leonard Wood wrote in 1901 to Theodore Roosevelt: "There is, of course, little or no independence left Cuba under the Platt Amendment."

Cuba was not an outright colony, but it was now in the American sphere. However, the Spanish-American War did lead to a number of direct annexations by the United States. Puerto Rico, a neighbor of Cuba in the Caribbean, belonging to Spain, was taken over by U.S. military forces. The Hawaiian Islands, one-third of the way across the Pacific, which had already been penetrated by American missionaries and pineapple plantation owners, and had been described by American officials as "a ripe pear ready to be plucked," was annexed by joint resolution of Congress in July of 1898. Around the same time, Wake Island, twenty-three hundred miles west of Hawaii, on the route to Japan, was occupied. And Guam, the Spanish possession in the Pacific, almost all the way to the Philippines, was taken. In December of 1898, the peace treaty was signed with Spain, officially turning over to the United States, Guam, Puerto Rico, and the Philippines, for a payment of $20 million.

There was heated argument in the United States about whether or not to take the Philippines. As one story has it, President McKinley told a group of ministers visiting the White House how he came to his decision:

> I walked the floor of the White House night after night until midnight; and I am not ashamed to tell you, gentlemen, that I went down on my knees and prayed Almighty God for light and guidance more than one night. And one night late it came to me this way—I don't know how it was, but it came:
>
> That we could not give them back to Spain—that would be cowardly and dishonorable.
>
> That we could not leave them to themselves—they were unfit for self-government—and they would soon have anarchy and misrule over there worse than Spain's was; and
>
> That there was nothing left for us to do but to take them all and to educate the Filipinos, and uplift and civilize and Christianize them, and by God's grace do the very best we could by them, as our fellow men for whom Christ also died. And then I went to bed and went to sleep and slept soundly.

The Filipinos did not get the same message from God. In February 1899, they rose in revolt against American rule, as they had rebelled several times against the Spanish. Emilio Aguinaldo, a Filipino leader, now became leader of the *insurrectos* fighting the United States. He proposed Filipino independence within a U.S. protectorate, but this was rejected.

It took the United States three years to crush the rebellion, using seventy thousand troops—four times as many as were landed in Cuba—and thousands of battle casualties, many times more than in Cuba. It was a harsh war. For the Filipinos the death rate was enormous from battle casualties and from disease.

The taste of empire was on the lips of politicians and business interests throughout the country now. Racism, paternalism, and talk of money mingled with talk of destiny and civilization. In the Senate, Albert Beveridge spoke, January 9, 1900, for the dominant economic and political interests of the country:

> Mr. President, the times call for candor. The Philippines are ours forever…. And just beyond the Philippines are China's illimitable markets. We will not retreat from either…. We will not renounce our part in the mission of our race, trustee, under God, of the civilization of the world…. It has been charged that our conduct of the war has been cruel. Senators, it has been the reverse…. Senators must remember that we are not dealing with Americans or Europeans. We are dealing with Orientals.

The fighting with the rebels began, McKinley said, when the insurgents attacked American forces. But later, American soldiers testified that the United States had fired the first shot. After the war, an army officer speaking in Boston's Faneuil Hall said his colonel had given him orders to provoke a conflict with the insurgents.

William James, the Harvard philosopher, was part of a movement of prominent American businessmen, politicians, and intellectuals who formed the Anti-Imperialist League in 1898 and carried on a long campaign to educate the American public about the horrors of the Philippine war and the evils of imperialism.

The Anti-Imperialist League published the letters of soldiers doing duty in the Philippines. A captain from Kansas wrote: "Caloocan was supposed to contain 17,000 inhabitants. The Twentieth Kansas swept through it, and now Caloocan contains not one living native." A volunteer from the state of Washington wrote: "Our fighting blood was up, and we all wanted to kill 'niggers.'"

It was a time of intense racism in the United States. In the years between 1889 and 1903, on the average, every week, two Negroes were lynched by mobs—hanged, burned, mutilated. The Filipinos were brown-skinned, physically identifiable, strange-speaking and strange-looking to Americans. To the usual indiscriminate brutality of war was thus added the factor of racial hostility.

In November 1901, the Manila correspondent of the *Philadelphia Ledger* reported: "...our men have been relentless, have killed to exterminate men, women, children, prisoners and captives, active insurgents and suspected people from lads of ten up, the idea prevailing that the Filipino as such was little better than a dog...."

Secretary of War Elihu Root responded to the charges of brutality: "The war in the Philippines has been conducted by the American army with scrupulous regard for the rules of civilized warfare...with self-restraint and with humanity never surpassed."

In Manila, a marine named Littletown Waller, a major, was accused of shooting eleven defenseless Filipinos, without trial, on the island of Samar. Other marine officers described his testimony: "The major said that General Smith instructed him to kill and burn...that it was no time to take prisoners, and that he was to make Samar a howling wilderness. Major Waller asked General Smith to define the age limit for killing, and he replied 'Everything over ten.'"

Mark Twain commented on the Philippine war: "We have pacified some thousands of the islanders and buried them; destroyed their fields; burned their villages, and turned their widows and orphans out-of-doors.... And so, by these Providences of God—and the phrase is the government's, not mine—we are a World Power."

American firepower was overwhelmingly superior to anything the Filipino rebels could put together. In the very first battle, Admiral Dewey steamed up the Pasig River and fired 500-pound shells into the Filipino trenches. Dead Filipinos were piled so high that the Americans used their bodies for breastworks. A British witness said: "This is not war; it is simply massacre and murderous butchery." He was wrong; it was war.

For the rebels to hold out against such odds for years meant that they had the support of the population. Gen. Arthur MacArthur, commander of the Filipino war, said: "I believed that Aguinaldo's troops represented only a faction. I did not like to believe that the whole population of Luzon—the native population, that is—was opposed to us." But he said he was "reluctantly compelled" to believe this because the guerrilla tactics of the Filipino army "depended upon almost complete unity of action of the entire native population."

Despite the growing evidence of brutality and the work of the Anti-Imperialist League, some of the trade unions in the United States supported imperial expansion. But the *Carpenters' Journal* asked: "How much better off are the workingmen of England through all its colonial possessions?"

When the treaty for annexation of the Philippines was up for debate in Congress in early 1899, the Central Labor Unions of Boston and New York opposed it. There was a mass meeting in New York against annexation. The Anti-Imperialist League circulated more than a million pieces of literature against taking the Philippines. While the League was organized and dominated by intellectuals and business people, a large part of its half-million members were working-class people, including women and blacks. Locals of the League held meetings all over the country. The campaign against the treaty was a powerful one, and when the Senate did ratify it, it was by one vote.

The mixed reactions of labor to the war—lured by economic advantage, yet repelled by capitalist expansion and violence—ensured that labor could not unite either to stop the war or to conduct class war against the system at home.

The reactions of black soldiers to the war were also mixed: there was the simple need to get ahead in a society where opportunities for success were denied the black man, and the military life gave such possibilities. There was race pride, the need to show that blacks were as courageous, as patriotic, as anyone else. And yet, there was with all this the consciousness of a brutal war, fought against colored people, a counterpart of the violence committed against black people in the United States.

Black soldiers encamped in Tampa, Florida, ran into bitter race hatred by white inhabitants there. A race riot began when drunken white soldiers used a Negro child as a target to show their marksmanship; Negro soldiers retaliated, and then the streets "ran red with negro blood," according to press dispatches.

The chaplain of a black regiment wrote to the *Cleveland Gazette* of black veterans of the Cuban war "unkindly and sneeringly received" in Kansas City, Missouri. He said that "these black boys, heroes of our country, were not allowed to stand at the counters of restaurants and eat a sandwich and drink a cup of coffee, while the white soldiers were welcomed and invited to sit down at the tables and eat free of cost."

But it was the Filipino situation that aroused many blacks in the United States to militant opposition to the war. The senior bishop of the African Methodist Episcopal Church, Henry M. Turner, called the campaign in the Philippines "an unholy war of conquest" and referred to the Filipinos as "sable patriots."

There were four black regiments on duty in the Philippines. Many of the black soldiers established rapport with the brown-skinned natives on the islands, and were angered by the term "nigger" used by white troops to describe the Filipinos. An "unusually large number" of black troops deserted during the Philippines campaign.

From the Philippines, William Simms wrote: "I was struck by a question a little Filipino boy asked me, which ran about this way: 'Why does the American Negro come...to fight us where we are much a friend to him and have not done anything to him. Why don't you fight those people in America who burn Negroes...?'"

A black infantryman named William Fulbright wrote from Manila in June 1901 to the editor of a paper in Indianapolis: "This struggle on the islands has been naught but a gigantic scheme of robbery and oppression."

Back home, while the war against the Filipinos was going on, a group of Massachusetts Negroes addressed a message to President McKinley:

> We...have resolved to address ourselves to you in an open letter, notwithstanding your extraordinary, your incomprehensible silence on the subject of our wrongs....
>
> ...you have seen our sufferings, witnessed from your high place our awful wrongs and miseries, and yet you have at no time and on no occasion opened your lips on our behalf....
>
> With one accord, with an anxiety that wrenched our hearts with cruel hopes and fears, the Colored people of the United States turned to you when Wilmington, North Carolina was held for two dreadful days and nights in the clutch of a bloody revolution; when Negroes, guilty of no crime except the color of their skin and a desire to exercise the rights of their American citizenship, were butchered like dogs in the streets of that ill-fated town...for want of federal aid, which you would not and did not furnish....
>
> And when you made your Southern tour a little later, and we saw how cunningly you catered to Southern race prejudice.... How you preached patience, industry, moderation to your long-suffering black fellow citizens, and patriotism, jingoism and imperialism to your white ones....

The "patience, industry, and moderation" preached to blacks, the "patriotism" preached to whites, did not fully sink in. In the first years of the twentieth century, despite all the demonstrated power of the state, large numbers of blacks, whites, men, women became impatient, immoderate, unpatriotic.

Exercises

1. Why might Teddy Roosevelt have thought that the U.S. needed a war in 1897?

2. In what sense was expansion overseas "not a new idea"? If it was not new, then why did it not begin until 1898?

3. How many times did the U.S. government intervene in the affairs of other countries between 1798 and 1895?

4. Senator Henry Cabot Lodge believed that the United States needed to control the balance of trade in the Pacific. Which island and countries did he believe were key acquisitions toward attaining such a goal?

5. Senator Albert Beveridge argued in 1897 that "the trade of the world must and shall be ours". What might his motivations and reasons have been for making such a statement?

6. The ideology justifying American aggression in 1846-48 was similar to or different from the same ideology of 1896?

7. U.S. business interests favored an "open door" policy over the conquest of colonies. From this point of view, what were the pros and cons of intervening in the Cuban revolt that began in 1895? Why did intervention ultimately win out?

8. How did the Cuban rebels react to McKinley's ultimatum to Spain?

9. What were labor's arguments against going to war with Spain? Why did most unions not oppose the war once it was declared?

10. During the Spanish-American War, what was the ratio of American soldiers who died in battle to those who died from disease or other causes?

11. How long did hostilities last between the United States and Spain once they began in 1898?

12. Why were the Cuban rebel leaders shut out of the negotiations for peace?

13. What did the American victory in the Spanish-American War allow American business to accomplish in Cuba? What role did the U.S. military occupation force play in the relationship between American investors and Cuban workers?

14. Was the Teller Amendment honored by the U.S. government?

15. How did the Filipinos respond to the U.S. decision to take over their country?

16. How did Beveridge justify American cruelty toward the Filipinos in 1900? Why did the U.S. government resort to such brutality? (Consider the following when answering the previous question: race relations in the United States; the Filipino population's relationship to the guerrillas; and the U.S. government's goals of the Spanish-American War).

17. What explains the heavy opposition to the passage of the Treaty of Annexation? (For example, why was it ratified by only one vote?)

18. According to an open letter to President McKinley by "a group of Massachusetts Negroes," what was the federal government's response when whites attacked and murdered blacks for two days in Wilmington, North Carolina?

19. *Debate Resolution*: The United States consciously provoked a war with Spain in order to acquire colonies from Spain.

20. *Draw a map* that identifies the following: the boundaries of the United States as of 1896; Hawaii; the Philippines; Cuba; Puerto Rico, and Guam.

Chapter 13

The Socialist Challenge

War and jingoism might postpone, but could not fully suppress, the class anger the came from the realities of ordinary life. As the twentieth century opened, that anger reemerged. Emma Goldman, the anarchist and feminist, whose political consciousness was shaped by factory work, the Haymarket executions, the Homestead strike, the long prison term of her lover and comrade, Alexander Berkman, the depression of the 1890s, the strike struggles of New York, her own imprisonment on Blackwell's Island, spoke at a meeting some years after the Spanish-American War:

> How our hearts burned with indignation against the atrocious Spaniards!...But when the smoke was over, the dead buried, and the cost of the war came back to the people in an increase in the price of commodities and rent—that is, when we sobered up from our patriotic spree—it suddenly dawned on us that the cause of the Spanish-American war was the price of sugar.... that the lives, blood and money of the American people were used to protect the interests of the American capitalists.

Mark Twain was neither an anarchist nor a radical. By 1900, at sixty-five, he was a world-acclaimed writer of funny-serious-American-to-the-bone stories. He watched the United States and other Western countries go about the world and wrote in the *New York Herald* as the century began: "I bring you the stately matron named Christendom, returning bedraggled, besmirched, and dishonored from pirate raids in Kiao-Chou, Manchuria, South Africa, and the Philippines, with her soul full of meanness, her pocket full of boodle, and her mouth full of pious hypocrisies."

There were writers of the early twentieth century who spoke for socialism, who criticized the capitalist system harshly. These were not obscure pamphleteers, but among the most famous of American literary figures, whose books were read by millions: Upton Sinclair, Jack London, Theodore Dreiser, Frank Norris.

Upton Sinclair's novel *The Jungle*, published in 1906, brought the conditions in the meatpacking plants of Chicago to the shocked attention of the whole country and stimulated demand for laws regulating the meat industry. But also, through the story of an immigrant laborer, Jurgis Rudkus, it spoke of socialism, of how beautiful life might be if people cooperatively owned and worked and shared the riches of the earth. *The Jungle* was first published in the Socialist newspaper *Appeal to Reason*; it was then read by millions as a book, and was translated into seventeen languages.

One of the influences on Upton Sinclair's thinking was a book, *People of the Abyss*, by Jack London. London was a member of the Socialist party. He had come out of the slums of San Francisco, the child of an unwed mother. He had been a newsboy, a cannery worker, a sailor, a fisherman, had worked in a jute mill and a laundry, hoboed the railroads to the East Coast, been clubbed by a policeman on the streets of New York and arrested for vagrancy in Niagara Falls, watched men beaten and tortured in jail, pirated oysters in San Francisco Bay, read Flaubert, Tolstoy, Melville, and the *Communist Manifesto*, preached socialism in the Alaskan gold camps in the winter of 1896, sailed two thousand miles back through the Bering Sea, and became a world-famous writer of adventure books. In 1906, he wrote his novel *The Iron Heel*, with its warning of a fascist America, its ideal of a socialist brotherhood of man. In the course of it, through his characters, he indicts the system.

> In the face of the facts that modern man lives more wretchedly than the cave-man, and that his producing power is a thousand times greater than that of the cave-man, no other conclusion is possible than that the capitalist class has mismanaged...criminally and selfishly mismanaged.

And with this attack, the vision: "Let us not destroy those wonderful machines that produce efficiently and cheaply. Let us control them. Let us profit by their efficiency and cheapness. Let us run them for ourselves. That, gentleman, is socialism...."

It was a time when even a self-exiled literary figure living in Europe and not prone to political statements—the novelist Henry James—could tour the United States in 1904 and see the country as a "huge Rappacini garden, rank with each variety of the poison-plant of the money passion."

"Muckrakers," who raked up the mud and the muck, contributed to the atmosphere of dissent by simply telling what they saw. Some of the new mass-circulation magazines, ironically enough in the interest of profit, printed their articles: Ida Tarbell's exposure of the Standard Oil Company; Lincoln Steffens's stories of corruption in the major American cities.

By 1900, neither the patriotism of the war nor the absorption of energy in elections could disguise the troubles of the system. The process of business concentration had gone forward; the control by bankers had become clearer. As technology developed and corporations became larger, they needed more capital, and it was the bankers who had this capital. By 1904, more than a thousand railroad leins had been consolidated into six great combinations, each allied with either Morgan or Rockefeller interests.

Morgan had always wanted regularity, stability, predictability. But even Morgan and his associates were not in complete control of such a system. In 1907, there was a panic, financial collapse, and crisis. True, the very big businesses were not hurt, but profits after 1907 were not as high as capitalists wanted, industry was not expanding as fast as it might, and industrialists began to look for ways to cut costs.

One way was Taylorism. Frederick W. Taylor had been a steel company foreman who closely analyzed every job in the mill and worked out a system of finely detailed division of labor, increased mechanization, and piecework wage systems, to increase production and profits. The purpose of Taylorism was to make workers interchangeable, able to do the simple tasks that the new division of labor required—like standard parts divested of individuality and humanity, bought and sold as commodities.

It was a system well fitted for the new auto industry. In 1909, Ford sold 10,607 autos; in 1913, 168,000; in 1914, 248,000 (45 percent of all autos produced). The profit: $30 million.

With immigrants a larger proportion of the labor force, Taylorism, with its simplified unskilled jobs, became more feasible. In New York City, the new immigrants went to work in the sweatshops. The poet Edwin Markham wrote in *Cosmopolitan* magazine, January 1907:

> In unaired rooms, mothers and fathers sew by day and by night. Those in the home sweatshop must work cheaper than those in the factory sweatshops.... And the children are called in from play to drive and drudge beside their elders....
>
> Is it not a cruel civilization that allows little hearts and little shoulders to strain under these grown-up responsibilities, while in the same city, a pet cur is jeweled and pampered and aired on a fine lady's velvet lap on the beautiful boulevards?

The city became a battlefield. On August 10, 1905, the *New York Tribune* reported that a strike at Federman's bakery on the Lower East Side led to violence when Federman used scab labor to continue producing:

> Strikers or their sympathizers wrecked the bake shop of Philip Federman at No. 183 Orchard Street early last night amid scenes of the most tumultuous excitement. Policemen smashed heads right and left with their nightsticks after two of their number had been roughly dealt with by the mob....

There were five hundred garment factories in New York. A woman later recalled the conditions of work:

> In these disease-breeding holes we, the youngsters together with the men and women toiled from seventy and eighty hours a week! Saturdays and Sundays included!... A sign would go up on Saturday afternoon: "If you don't come in on Sunday, you need not come in on Monday."...Children's dreams of a day off shattered. We wept, for after all, we were only children....

At the Triangle Shirtwaist Company, in the winter of 1909, women organized and decided to strike. Soon they were walking the picket line in the cold, knowing they could not win while the other factories were operating. A mass meeting was called of workers in the other shops, and Clara Lemlich, in her teens, an eloquent speaker, still bearing the signs of her recent beating on the picket line, stood up: "'I offer a resolution that a general strike be declared now!" The meeting went wild; they voted to strike.

Pauline Newman, one of the strikers, recalled years later the beginning of the general strike:

> Thousands upon thousands left the factories from every side, all of them walking down toward Union Square. It was November, the cold winter was just around the corner, we had no fur coats to keep warm, and yet there was the spirit that led us on and on until we got to some hall....
>
> I can see the young people, mostly women, walking down and not caring what might happen...the hunger, cold, loneliness.... They just didn't care on that particular day; that was their day.

The union had hoped three thousand would join the strike. Twenty thousand walked out. Every day a thousand new members joined the union, the International Ladies Garment Workers Union, which before this had few women. Colored women were active in the strike, which went on through the winter, against police, against scabs, against arrests and prison. In more than three hundred shops, workers won their demands. Women now became officials in the union. Pauline Newman again:

> We tried to educate ourselves. I would invite the girls to my rooms, and we took turns reading poetry in English to improve our understanding of the language. One of our favorites was Percy Bysshe Shelley's "Mask of Anarchy."...
>
> "Rise like lions after slumber
> In unvanquishable number!
> Shake your chains to earth, like dew
> Which in sleep had fallen on you—
> Ye are many, they are few!"

The conditions in the factories did not change much. On the afternoon of March 25, 1911, a fire at the Triangle Shirtwaist Company that began in a rag bin swept through the eighth, ninth, and tenth floors, too high for fire ladders to reach. The fire chief of New York had said that his ladders could reach only to the seventh floor. But half of New York's 500,000 workers spent all day, perhaps twelve hours, above the seventh floor. The laws said factory doors had to open outward. But at the Triangle Company the doors opened in. The law said the doors could not be locked during working hours, but at the Triangle Company doors were usually locked so the company could keep track of the employees. And so, trapped, the young women were burned to death at their worktables, or jammed against the locked exit door, or leaped to their deaths down the elevator shafts. The *New York World* reported:

> ...screaming men and women and boys and girls crowded out on the many window ledges and threw themselves into the streets far below. They jumped with their clothing ablaze.... [P]itiable companionships formed in the instant of death—girls who placed their arms around each other as they leaped.

When it was over, 146 Triangle workers, mostly women, were burned or crushed to death. There was a memorial parade down Broadway, and 100,000 marched.

There were more fires. And accidents. According to a report of the Commission on Industrial Relations, in 1914, 35,000 workers were killed in industrial accidents and 700,000 injured.

Unionization was growing, but the American Federation of Labor was an exclusive union—almost all male, almost all white, almost all skilled workers. By 1910, women were one-fifth of the labor force, but only one in a hundred belonged to a union. Black workers in 1910 made one-third of the earnings of white workers. They too were kept out of the AFL.

In the reality of struggle, rank-and-file workers overcame these separations from time to time. Mary McDowell told of the formation of a women's union in the Chicago stockyards: "It was a dramatic occasion on that evening, when an Irish girl at the door called out—'A Colored sister asks admission. What shall I do with her?' And the answer came from the Irish young woman in the chair—'Admit her, of course, and let all of you give her a hearty welcome!'"

In New Orleans in 1907 a general strike on the levees, involving ten thousand workers (longshoremen, teamsters, freight handlers), lasted twenty days, blacks and whites standing together.

But these were exceptions. In general, the Negro was kept out of the trade union movement. W. E. B. Du Bois wrote in 1913: "The net result of all this has been to convince the American Negro that his greatest enemy is not the employer who robs him, but his fellow white workingman."

Racism was practical for the AFL. The exclusion of women and foreigners was also practical. These were mostly unskilled workers, and the AFL, by monopolizing the supply of skilled workers, could win better conditions for them, leaving the majority of workers in the cold.

AFL officials drew larger salaries, hobnobbed with employers, even moved in high society. They were protected from criticism by tightly controlled meetings and by "goon" squads—hired toughs originally used against strikebreakers but after a while used to intimidate and beat up opponents inside the union.

In this situation—terrible conditions of labor, exclusivity in union organization—working people wanting radical change, seeing the root of misery in the capitalist system, moved toward a new kind of labor union. One morning in June 1905, there met in a hall in Chicago a convention of two hundred socialists, anarchists, and radical trade unionists from all over the United States. They were forming the IWW—the Industrial Workers of the World. Big Bill Haywood, a leader of the Western Federation of Miners, recalled in his autobiography that he picked up a piece of board that lay on the platform and used it for a gavel to open the convention:

> Fellow workers.... This is the Continental Congress of the working-class. We are here to confederate the workers of this country into a working-class movement that shall have for its purpose the emancipation of the working-class from the slave bondage of capitalism....

On the speakers' platform with Haywood were Eugene Debs, leader of the Socialist party, and Mother Mary Jones, a seventy-five-year-old white-haired woman who was an organizer for the United Mine Workers of America. The convention drew up a constitution, whose preamble said:

> The working class and the employing class have nothing in common. There can be no peace so long as hunger and want are found among millions of working people and the few, who make up the employing class, have all the good things of life.
>
> Between these two classes a struggle must go on until all the toilers come together on the political as well as on the industrial field, and take and hold that which they produce by their labor, through an economic organization of the working class without affiliation with any political party....

The IWW (or "Wobblies," as they came to be called, for reasons not really clear) aimed at organizing all workers in any industry into "One Big Union," undivided by sex, race, or skills. They argued against making contracts with the employer, because this had so often prevented workers from striking on their own, or in sympathy with other strikers, and thus turned union people into strikebreakers. Negotiations by leaders for contracts replaced continuous struggle by the rank and file, the Wobblies believed. They spoke of "direct action":

> Direct action means industrial action directly by, for, and of the workers themselves, without the treacherous aid of labor misleaders or scheming politicians. A strike that is initiated, controlled, and settled by the workers directly affected is direct action.... Direct action is industrial democracy.

The IWW people were militant, courageous. In McKees Rocks, Pennsylvania, they led a strike of six thousand workers in 1909 against an affiliate of the U.S. Steel Company, defied the state troopers. They promised to take a trooper's life for every worker killed (in one gun battle four strikers and three troopers were killed), and managed to keep picketing the factories until the strike was won.

The idea of anarcho-syndicalism was developing strongly in Spain and Italy and France at this time—that the workers would take power, not by seizing the state machinery in an armed rebellion, but by bringing the economic system to a halt in a general strike, then taking it over to use for the good of all. IWW organizer Joseph Ettor said:

> If the workers of the world want to win, all they have to do is recognize their own solidarity. They have nothing to do but fold their arms and the world will stop. The workers are more powerful with their hands in their pockets than all the property of the capitalists....

It was an immensely powerful idea. In the ten exciting years after its birth, the IWW became a threat to the capitalist class, exactly when capitalist growth was enormous and profits huge. The IWW never had more than five to ten thousand enrolled members at any one time; people came and went, and perhaps a hundred thousand were members at one time or another. But their energy, their persistence, their inspiration to others, their ability to mobilize thousands at one place, one time, made them an influence on the country far beyond their numbers. They traveled everywhere (many were unemployed or migrant workers); they organized, wrote, spoke, sang, spread their message and their spirit.

They were attacked with all the weapons the system could put together: the newspapers, the courts, the police, the army, mob violence. Local authorities passed laws to stop them from speaking; the IWW defied these laws. In Missoula, Montana, a lumber and mining area, hundreds of Wobblies arrived by boxcar after some had been prevented from speaking. They were arrested one after another until they clogged the jails and the courts, and finally forced the town to repeal its antispeech ordinance.

In Spokane, Washington, in 1909, an ordinance was passed to stop street meetings, and an IWW organizer who insisted on speaking was arrested. Thousands of Wobblies marched into the center of town to speak. One by one they spoke and were arrested, until six hundred were in jail. Jail conditions were brutal, and several men died in their cells, but the IWW won the right to speak.

In San Diego, Jack White, a Wobbly arrested in a free-speech fight in 1912, sentenced to six months in the county jail on a bread and water diet, was asked if he had anything to say to the court. A stenographer recorded what he said:

> I have sat in your court room day after day and have seen members of my class pass before this, the so-called bar of justice. I have seen you, Judge Sloane, and others of your kind, send them to prison because they dared to infringe upon the sacred rights of property. You have become blind and deaf to the rights of man to pursue life and happiness, and you have crushed those rights so that the sacred right of property shall be preserved. Then you tell me to respect the law. I do not. I did violate the law, as I will violate every one of your laws and still come before you and say, "To hell with the courts."...

There were also beatings, tarrings and featherings, defeats. One IWW member, John Stone, tells of being released from the jail at San Diego at midnight with another IWW man and forced into an automobile, taken out of the city, beaten with blackjacks. In 1917, the year the United States entered World War I—vigilantes in Montana seized IWW organizer Frank Little, tortured him, and hanged him, leaving his body dangling from a railroad trestle.

Joe Hill, an IWW organizer, wrote dozens of songs—biting, funny, class-conscious, inspiring. He became a legend in his time and after. His song "The Preacher and the Slave" had a favorite IWW target, the church:

> Long-haired preachers come out every night,
> Try to tell you what's wrong and what's right;
> But when asked how 'bout something to eat
> They will answer with voices so sweet:
> —You will eat, bye and bye,
> —In that glorious land above the sky;
> —Work and pray, live on hay,
> —You'll get pie in the sky when you die.

His song "Rebel Girl" was inspired by the strike of women at the textile mills in Lawrence, Massachusetts, and especially by the IWW leader of that strike, Elizabeth Gurley Flynn:

> There are blue-blooded queens and princesses,
> Who have charms made of diamonds and pearl,
> But the only and Thoroughbred Lady
> Is the Rebel Girl.

In November 1915, Joe Hill was accused of killing a grocer in Salt Lake City, Utah, in a robbery. There was no direct evidence presented to the court that he had committed the murder, but there were enough pieces of evidence to persuade a jury to find him guilty. The case became known throughout the world, and ten thousand letters went to the governor in protest, but with machine guns guarding the entrance to the prison, Joe Hill was executed by a firing squad. He had written Bill Haywood just before this: "Don't waste any time in mourning. Organize."

The IWW became involved in a set of dramatic events in the year 1912, in Lawrence, Massachusetts, where the American Woolen Company owned four mills. The work force were immigrant families—Portuguese, French-Canadian, English, Irish, Russian, Italian, Syrian, Lithuanian, German, Polish, Belgian—who lived in crowded, flammable wooden tenements. The average wage was $8.76 a week. A woman physician in Lawrence, Dr. Elizabeth Shapleigh, wrote: "A considerable number of the boys and girls die within the first two or three years after beginning work...thirty-six out of every 100 of all the men and women who work in the mill die before or by the time they are twenty-five years of age."

It was in January, midwinter, when pay envelopes distributed to weavers at one of the mills—Polish women—showed that their wages, already too low to feed their families, had been reduced. They stopped their looms and walked out of the mill. The next day, five thousand workers at another mill quit work, marched to still another mill, rushed the gates, shut off the power to the looms, and called on the other workers to leave. Soon ten thousand workers were on strike.

A telegram went to Joseph Ettor, a twenty-six-year-old Italian, an IWW leader in New York, to come to Lawrence to help conduct the strike. A committee of fifty was set up, representing every nationality among the workers, to make the important decisions.

The IWW organized mass meetings and parades. The strikers had to supply food and fuel for 50,000 people (the entire population of Lawrence was 86,000); soup kitchens were set up, and money began arriving from all over the country—from trade unions, IWW locals, socialist groups, individuals.

The mayor called out the local militia; the governor ordered out the state police. A parade of strikers was attacked by police a few weeks after the strike began. This led to rioting all that day. In the evening, a striker, Anna LoPizzo, was shot and killed. Witnesses said a policeman did it, but the authorities arrested Joseph Ettor and another IWW organizer who had come to Lawrence, a poet named Arturo Giovanitti. Neither was at the scene of the shooting, but the charge was that "Joseph Ettor and Arturo Giovanitti did incite, procure, and counsel or command the said person whose name is not known to commit the said murder."

Martial law was declared, and citizens were forbidden to talk on the street. Thirty-six strikers were arrested, many sentenced to a year in prison. On Tuesday, January 30, a young Syrian striker, John Ramy, was bayoneted to death. But the strikers were still out, and the mills were not working. Ettor said: "Bayonets cannot weave cloth."

In February, the strikers began mass picketing, seven thousand to ten thousand pickets in an endless chain. But their food was running out and the children were hungry. It was proposed by the New York *Call*, a Socialist newspaper, that the children of strikers be sent to sympathetic families in other cities to take care of them while the strike lasted. In three days, the *Call* got four hundred letters offering to take children. The IWW and the Socialist party began to organize the children's exodus, taking applications from families who wanted them, arranging medical exams for the youngsters.

On February 10, over a hundred children, aged four to fourteen, left Lawrence for New York City. They were greeted at Grand Central Station by five thousand Italian Socialists singing the "Marseillaise" and the "Internationale." The following week, another hundred children came to New York, and thirty-five to Barre, Vermont. It was becoming clear: if the children were taken care of, the strikers could stay out, for their spirit was high. The city officials in Lawrence, citing a statute on child neglect, said no more children would be permitted to leave Lawrence.

Despite the city edict, a group of forty children assembled on February 24 to go to Philadelphia. The railroad station was filled with police, and the scene that followed was described to congressmen by a member of the Women's Committee of Philadelphia: "When the time approached to depart, the children arranged in a long line, two by two, in orderly procession, with their parents near at hand, were about to make their way to the train when the police closed in on us with their clubs, beating right and left...."

A week after that, women returning from a meeting were surrounded by police and clubbed; one pregnant woman was carried unconscious to a hospital and gave birth to a dead child. Still, the strikers held out, continuing to march and sing.

The American Woolen Company decided to give in. It offered raises of 5 to 11 percent (the strikers insisted that the largest increases go to the lowest-paid), time and a quarter for overtime, and no discrimination against those who had struck. On March 14, 1912, ten thousand strikers gathered on the Lawrence Common and, with Bill Haywood presiding, voted to end the strike.

Ettor and Giovanitti went on trial. Support for them had been mounting all over the country. There were parades in New York and Boston; on September 30, fifteen thousand Lawrence workers struck for twenty-four hours to show their support for the two men. A jury found Ettor and Giovanitti not guilty, and that afternoon, ten thousand people assembled in Lawrence to celebrate.

The IWW took its slogan "One Big Union" seriously. Women, foreigners, black workers, the lowliest and most unskilled of workers, were included when a factory or mine was organized.

In 1900 there were 500,000 women office workers—in 1870 there had been 19,000. Women were switchboard operators, store workers, nurses. Half a million were teachers. The teachers formed a Teachers League that fought against the automatic firing of women who became pregnant. The following "Rules for Female Teachers" were posted by the school board of one town in Massachusetts:

1. Do not get married.
2. Do not leave town at any time without permission of the school board.
3. Do not keep company with men.
4. Be home between the hours of 8 p.m. and 6 a.m.
5. Do not loiter downtown in ice cream stores.
6. Do not smoke.
7. Do not get into a carriage with any man except your father or brother.
8. Do not dress in bright colors.
9. Do not dye your hair.
10. Do not wear any dress more than two inches above the ankle.

In 1909, the handbook of the Women's Trade Union Industrial League wrote about women in steam laundries: "How would you like to iron a shirt a minute? Think of standing at a mangle just above the wash-room with the hot steam pouring up through the floor for 10, 12, 14 and sometimes 17 hours a day! The Laundry Workers Union...in one city reduced this long day to 9 hours, and has increased the wages 50 percent."

Around the turn of the century, strike struggles were multiplying—in the 1890s there had been about a thousand strikes a year; by 1904 there were four thousand strikes a year. Law and military force again and again took the side of the rich. It was a time when hundreds of thousands of Americans began to think of socialism.

Debs wrote in 1904, three years after the formation of the Socialist party:

> The "pure and simple" trades union of the past does not answer the requirements of today.... The members of a trades union should be taught...that the labor movement means more, infinitely more, than a paltry increase in wages and the strike necessary to secure it; that...its higher object is to overthrow the capitalist system of private ownership of the tools of labor, abolish wage-slavery and achieve the freedom of the whole working class and, in fact, of all mankind....

Eugene Debs had become a Socialist while in jail in the Pullman strike. Now he was the spokesman of a party that made him its presidential candidate five times. The party at one time had 100,000 members, and 1,200 office holders in 340 municipalities. Its main newspaper, *Appeal to Reason*, for which Debs wrote, had half a million subscribers, and there were many other Socialist newspapers around the country, so that, all together, perhaps a million people read the Socialist press.

Socialism moved out of the small circles of city immigrants—Jewish and German socialists speaking their own languages—and became American. The strongest Socialist state organization was in Oklahoma, which in 1914 had twelve thousand dues-paying members (more than New York State), and elected over a hundred Socialists to local office, including six to the Oklahoma state legislature. There were fifty-five weekly Socialist newspapers in Oklahoma, Texas, Louisiana, Arkansas, and summer encampments that drew thousands of people.

Socialist women were active in the feminist movement of the early 1900s. According to Kate Richards O'Hare, the Socialist leader from Oklahoma, New York women socialists were superbly organized. During the 1915 campaign in New York for a referendum on women's suffrage, in one day at the climax of the campaign, they distributed 60,000 English leaflets, 50,000 Yiddish leaflets, sold 2,500 one-cent books and 1,500 five-cent books, put up 40,000 stickers, and held 100 meetings.

But were there problems of women that went beyond politics and economics, that would not be solved automatically by a socialist system? Once the economic base of sexual oppression was corrected, would equality follow? Battling for the vote, or for anything less than revolutionary change—was that pointless? The argument became sharper as the women's movement of the early twentieth century grew, as women spoke out more, organized, protested, paraded—for the vote, and for recognition as equals in every sphere, including sexual relations and marriage.

When Susan Anthony, at eighty, went to hear Eugene Debs speak (twenty-five years before, he had gone to hear her speak, and they had not met since then), they clasped hands warmly, then had a brief exchange. She said, laughing: "Give us suffrage, and we'll give you socialism." Debs replied: "Give us socialism and we'll give you suffrage."

There were women who insisted on uniting the two aims of socialism and feminism, like Crystal Eastman, who imagined new ways of men and women living together and retaining their independence, different from traditional marriage. She was a socialist, but wrote once that a woman "knows that the whole of woman's slavery is not summed up in the profit system, nor her complete emancipation assured by the downfall of capitalism."

In the first fifteen years of the twentieth century, there were more women in the labor force, more with experience in labor struggles. Some middle-class women, conscious of women's oppression and wanting to do something, were going to college and becoming aware of themselves as not just housewives.

They were defying the culture of mass magazines, which were spreading the message of woman as companion, wife, homemaker. Some of these femininists married; some did not. All struggled with the problem of relations with men, like Margaret Sanger, pioneer of birth control education, who suffered a nervous breakdown inside an apparently happy but confining marriage; she had to leave husband and children to make a career for herself and feel whole again. Sanger had written in *Woman and the New Race*: "No woman can call herself free who does not own and control her own body. No woman can call herself free until she can choose conscientiously whether she will or will not be a mother."

It was a complicated problem. Kate Richards O'Hare, for example, believed in the home, but thought socialism would make that better. On the other hand, Elizabeth Gurley Flynn wrote in her autobiography, *Rebel Girl*: "A domestic life and possibly a large family had no attraction for me.... I wanted to speak and write, to travel, to meet people, to see places, to organize for the I.W.W. I saw no reason why I, as a woman, should give up my work for this...."

While some women in this time were radicals, socialists, anarchists, an even larger number were involved in the campaign for suffrage. Veterans of trade union struggles joined the suffrage movement, like Rose Schneiderman of the Garment Workers. At a Cooper Union meeting in New York, she replied to a politician who said that women, given the vote, would lose their femininity:

> Women in the laundries...stand for thirteen or fourteen hours in the terrible steam and heat with their hands in hot starch. Surely these women won't lose any more of their beauty and charm by putting a ballot in a ballot box once a year than they are likely to lose standing in foundries or laundries all year round.

Every spring in New York, the parades for women's suffrage kept growing. In 1912, a news report:

All along Fifth Avenue from Washington Square, where the parade formed, to 57th Street, where it disbanded, were gathered thousands of men and women of New York. They blocked every cross street on the line of march. Many were inclined to laugh and jeer, but none did. The sight of the impressive column of women striding five abreast up the middle of the street stifled all thought of ridicule.... women doctors, women lawyers...women architects, women artists, actresses and sculptors; women waitresses, domestics; a huge division of industrial workers...all marched with an intensity and purpose that astonished the crowds that lined the streets.

Some women radicals were skeptical. Emma Goldman, the anarchist and feminist, spoke her mind forcefully, as always, on the subject of women's suffrage:

> Our modern fetish is universal suffrage.... There is no reason whatever to assume that woman, in her climb to emancipation, has been, or will be, helped by the ballot.... Her development, her freedom, her independence, must come from and through herself. First, by asserting herself as a personality. Second, by refusing the right to anyone over her body; by refusing to bear children, unless she wants them; by refusing to be a servant to God, the State, society, the husband, the family, etc. by making her life simpler, but deeper and richer.... Only that, and not the ballot, will set woman free....

And Helen Keller, writing in 1911 to a suffragist in England: "Our democracy is but a name. We vote? What does that mean? It means that we choose between two bodies of real, though not avowed, autocrats. We choose between Tweedledum and Tweedledee.... You ask for votes for women.... Have your men with their millions of votes freed themselves from this injustice?"

Blind, deaf, Hellen Keller fought with her spirit, her pen. When she became active and openly socialist, the *Brooklyn Eagle*, which had previously treated her as a heroine, wrote that "her mistakes spring out of the manifest limitations of her development." Her response was not accepted by the *Eagle*, but printed in the New York *Call*. She wrote that when once she met the editor of the *Brooklyn Eagle* he complimented her lavishly. "But now that I have come out for socialism he reminds me and the public that I am blind and deaf and especially liable to error...." She added:

> Oh, ridiculous Brooklyn *Eagle*! What an ungallant bird it is! Socially blind and deaf, it defends an intolerable system, a system that is the cause of much of the physical blindness and deafness which we are trying to

prevent.... The *Eagle* and I are at war. I hate the system which it represents.... When it fights back, let it fight fair.... It is not fair fighting or
good argument to remind me and others that I cannot see or hear. I can
read. I can read all the socialist books I have time for in English, German
and French. If the editor of the Brooklyn *Eagle* should read some of
them, he might be a wiser man, and make a better newspaper. If I ever
contribute to the Socialist movement the book that I sometimes dream
of, I know what I shall name it: Industrial Blindness and Social Deafness.

Mother Jones did not seem especially interested in the feminist movement. But she organized textile workers and miners, as well as their wives
and children. One of her many feats was the organization of a children's
march to Washington to demand the end of child labor (as the twentieth
century opened, 284,000 children between the ages of ten and fifteen
worked in mines, mills, factories). She described this:

> In the spring of 1903, I went to Kensington, Pennsylvania, where sev-
> enty-five thousand textile workers were on strike. Of this number at least
> ten thousand were little children. The workers were striking for more
> pay and shorter hours. Every day little children came into Union Head-
> quarters, some with their hands off, some with the thumb missing, some
> with their fingers off at the knuckle. They were stooped little things,
> round shouldered and skinny....
>
> I asked some of the parents if they would let me have their little boys
> and girls for a week or ten days, promising to bring them back safe and
> sound.... A man named Sweeny was marshall.... A few men and women
> went with me.... The children carried knapsacks on their backs in which
> was a knife and fork, a tin cup and plate.... One little fellow had a drum
> and another had a fife.... We carried banners that said:..."We want time
> to play."...

Black women faced double oppression. A Negro nurse wrote to a
newspaper in 1912:

> We poor colored women wage-earners in the South are fighting a terrible
> battle.... On the one hand, we are assailed by black men, who should be
> our natural protectors; and, whether in the cook kitchen, at the washtub,
> over the sewing machine, behind the baby carriage, or at the ironing
> board, we are but little more than pack horses, beasts of burden, slaves!...

In this early part of the twentieth century, labeled by generations of
white scholars as "the Progressive period," lynchings were reported every
week; it was the low point for Negroes, North and South, "the nadir," as
Rayford Logan, a black historian, put it. In 1910 there were 10 million

Negroes in the United States, and 9 million of them were in the South.

The government of the United States (between 1901 and 1921, the presidents were Theodore Roosevelt, William Howard Taft, and Woodrow Wilson)—whether Republican or Democrat—watched Negroes being lynched, observed murderous riots against blacks in Statesboro, Georgia, Brownsville, Texas, and Atlanta, Georgia, and did nothing.

There were Negroes in the Socialist party, but the Socialist party did not go much out of its way to act on the race question.

Blacks began to organize. W.E.B. Du Bois, teaching in Atlanta, Georgia, in 1905, sent out a letter to Negro leaders throughout the country, calling them to a conference just across the Canadian border from Buffalo, near Niagara Falls. It was the start of the "Niagara Movement."

Du Bois, born in Massachusetts, the first black to receive a Ph.D. degree from Harvard University (1895), had just written and published his poetic, powerful book *The Souls of Black Folk*. Du Bois was a Socialist sympathizer, although only briefly a party member.

One of his associates in calling the Niagara meeting was William Monroe Trotter, a young black man in Boston, of militant views, who edited a weekly newspaper, the *Guardian*. In it he attacked the moderate ideas of Booker T. Washington. When, in the summer of 1903, Washington spoke to an audience of two thousand at a Boston church, Trotter and his supporters prepared nine provocative questions, which caused a commotion and led to fistfights. Trotter and a friend were arrested. This may have added to the spirit of indignation which led Du Bois to spearhead the Niagara meeting. The tone of the Niagara group was strong:

> We refuse to allow the impression to remain that the Negro-American assents to inferiority, is submissive under oppression and apologetic before insults. Through helplessness we may submit, but the voice of protest of ten million Americans must never cease to assail the ears of their fellows so long as America is unjust.

A race riot in Springfield, Illinois, prompted the formation of the National Association for the Advancement of Colored People in 1910. Whites dominated the leadership of the new organization; Du Bois was the only black officer. He was also the first editor of the NAACP periodical *The Crisis*. The NAACP concentrated on legal action and education, but Du Bois represented in it that spirit which was embodied in the Niagara movement's declaration: "Persistent manly agitation is the way to liberty."

What was clear in this period to blacks, to feminists, to labor organizers and socialists, was that they could not count on the national government. True, this was the "Progressive Period," the start of the Age of Reform; but it was a reluctant reform, aimed at quieting the popular risings, not making fundamental changes.

What gave it the name "Progressive" was that new laws were passed. Under Theodore Roosevelt, there was the Meat Inspection Act, the Hepburn Act to regulate railroads and pipelines, a Pure Food and Drug Act. Under Taft, the Mann-Elkins Act put telephone and telegraph systems under the regulation of the Interstate Commerce Commission. In Woodrow Wilson's presidency, the Federal Trade Commission was introduced to control the growth of monopolies, and the Federal Reserve Act to regulate the country's money and banking system. Under Taft were proposed the Sixteenth Amendment to the Constitution, allowing a graduated income tax, and the Seventeenth Amendment, providing for the election of senators directly by popular vote instead of by the state legislatures, as the original Constitution provided. Also at this time, a number of states passed laws regulating wages and hours, providing for safety inspection of factories and compensation for injured workmen.

Undoubtedly, ordinary people benefited to some extent from these changes. The system was rich, productive, complex; it could give enough of a share of its riches to enough of the working class to create a protective shield between the bottom and the top of the society. A study of immigrants in New York between 1905 and 1915 finds that 32 percent of Italians and Jews rose out of the manual class to higher levels (although not to *much* higher levels).

But it was also true that many Italian immigrants did not find the opportunities inviting enough for them to stay. In one four-year period, seventy-three Italians left New York for every one hundred that arrived. Still, enough Italians became construction workers, enough Jews became businessmen and professionals, to create a middle-class cushion for class conflict.

Fundamental conditions did not change, however, for the vast majority of tenant farmers, factory workers, slum dwellers, miners, farm laborers, working men and women, black and white.

The new emphasis on strong government aimed to stabilize a system that benefited the upper classes. For instance, Theodore Roosevelt made a reputation for himself as a "trust-buster," but two of J. P. Morgan's men— Elbert Gary, chairman of U.S. Steel, and George Perkins, who would later become a campaigner for Roosevelt, arranged private negotiations with the president to make sure the "trust-busting" would not go too far.

The *Banker's Magazine* wrote in 1901: "As the business of the country has learned the secret of combination, it is gradually subverting the power of the politician and rendering him subservient to its purposes...."

By 1904, 318 trusts, with capital of more than seven billion dollars, controlled 40 percent of U.S. manufacturing.

Roosevelt's advisers were industrialists and bankers. Responding to his worried brother-in-law writing from Wall Street, Roosevelt replied: "I intend to be most conservative, but in the interests of the corporations themselves and above all in the interests of the country."

Roosevelt supported the regulatory Hepburn Act because he feared something worse. He wrote to Henry Cabot Lodge that the railroad lobbyists who opposed the bill "are very short-sighted not to understand that to beat it means to increase the movement for government ownership of the railroads."

The controls were constructed skillfully. In 1900, a man named Ralph Easley, a Republican and conservative, a schoolteacher and journalist, organized the National Civic Federation. Its aim was to get better relations between capital and labor. Its officers were mostly big businessmen, and important national politicians, but its first vice president, for a long time, was Samuel Gompers of the AFL.

The NCF wanted a more sophisticated approach to trade unions, seeing them as an inevitable reality, therefore wanting to come to agreements with them rather than fight with them: better to deal with a conservative union than face a militant one.

Many businessmen did not want even the puny reforms proposed by the Civic Federation—but the Federation's approach represented the sophistication and authority of the modern state, determined to do what was best for the capitalist class as a whole, even if this irritated some capitalists. The new approach was concerned with the long-range stability of the system, even at the cost, sometimes, of short-term profits.

Thus, the Federation drew up a model workmen's compensation bill in 1910, and the following year twelve states passed laws for compensation or accident insurance. When the Supreme Court said that year that New York's workmen's compensation law was unconstitutional because it deprived corporations of property without due process of law, Theodore Roosevelt was angry. Such decisions, he said, added "immensely to the strength of the Socialist Party." By 1920, forty-two states had workmen's compensation laws.

In this period, cities also put through reforms, many of them giving power to city councils instead of mayors, or hiring city managers. The idea was more efficiency, more stability.

The Progressive movement, whether led by honest reformers such as Senator Robert La Follette of Wisconsin or disguised conservatives like Roosevelt (who was the Progressive party candidate for president in 1912), seemed to understand it was fending off socialism. The *Milwaukee Journal*, a Progressive organ, said the conservatives "fight socialism blindly...while the Progressives fight it intelligently and seek to remedy the abuses and conditions upon which it thrives."

The Socialist movement was growing. Easley talked of "the menace of Socialism as evidenced by its growth in the colleges, churches, newspapers." In 1910, Victor Berger became the first member of the Socialist party elected to Congress; in 1911, seventy-three Socialist mayors were elected, and twelve hundred lesser officials in 340 cities and towns. The press spoke of "The Rising Tide of Socialism."

Did the Progressive reforms succeed in doing what they intended— stabilize the capitalist system by repairing its worst defects, blunt the edge of the Socialist movement, restore some measure of class peace in a time of increasingly bitter clashes between capital and labor? To some extent, perhaps. But the Socialist party continued to grow. The IWW continued to agitate. And shortly after Woodrow Wilson took office there began in Colorado one of the most bitter and violent struggles between workers and corporate capital in the history of the country.

This was the Colorado coal strike that began in September 1913 and culminated in the "Ludlow Massacre" of April 1914. Eleven thousand miners in southern Colorado, mostly foreign-born—Greeks, Italians, Serbs—worked for the Colorado Fuel & Iron Corporation, which was owned by the Rockefeller family. Aroused by the murder of one of their organizers, they went on strike against low pay, dangerous conditions, and feudal domination of their lives in towns completely controlled by the mining companies.

Mother Jones, at this time an organizer for the United Mine Workers, came into the area, fired up the miners with her oratory, and helped them in those critical first months of the strike, until she was arrested, kept in a dungeonlike cell, and then forcibly expelled from the state.

When the strike began, the miners were immediately evicted from their shacks in the mining towns. Aided by the United Mine Workers Union, they set up tents in the nearby hills and carried on the strike, the picketing, from these tent colonies. The gunmen hired by the Rockefeller interests—the Baldwin-Felts Detective Agency—using Gatling guns and rifles, raided the tent colonies.

The death list of miners grew, but they hung on, drove back an armored train in a gun battle, fought to keep out strikebreakers. With the miners resisting, refusing to give in, the mines not able to operate, the Colorado governor (referred to by a Rockefeller mine manager as "our little cowboy governor") called out the National Guard, with the Rockefellers supplying the guards' wages.

The miners at first thought the guard was sent to protect them, and greeted its arrivals with flags and cheers. They soon found out the guard was there to destroy the strike. The guard brought strikebreakers in under the cover of night, not telling them there was a strike. Guardsmen beat miners, arrested them by the hundreds, rode down with their horses parades of women in the streets of Trinidad, the central town in the area. And still the miners refused to give in. When they lasted through the cold winter of 1913–1914, it became clear that extraordinary measures would be needed to break the strike.

In April 1914, two National Guard companies were stationed in the hills overlooking the largest tent colony of strikers, the one at Ludlow, housing a thousand men, women, children. On the morning of April 20, a machine-gun attack began on the tents. The miners fired back. Their leader, a Greek named Lou Tikas, was lured up into the hills to discuss a truce, then shot to death by a company of National Guardsmen. The women and children dug pits beneath the tents to escape the gunfire. At dusk, the guard moved down from the hills with torches, set fire to the tents, and the families fled into the hills; thirteen people were killed by gunfire.

The following day, a telephone linesman going through the ruins of Ludlow tent colony lifted an iron cot covering a pit in one of the tents and found the charred, twisted bodies of eleven children and two women. This became known as the Ludlow Massacre.

The news spread quickly over the country. In Denver, the United Mine Workers issued a "Call to Arms"—"Gather together for defensive purposes all arms and ammunition legally available." Three hundred armed strikers marched from other tent colonies into the Ludlow area, cut telephone and telegraph wires, and prepared for battle. Railroad workers refused to take soldiers from Trinidad to Ludlow. At Colorado Springs, three hundred union miners walked off their jobs and headed for the Trinidad district, carrying revolvers, rifles, shotguns.

In Trinidad itself, miners attended a funeral service for the twenty-six dead at Ludlow, then walked from the funeral to a nearby building, where arms were stacked for them. They picked up rifles and moved into the hills, destroying mines, killing mine guards, exploding mine shafts. The press reported that "the hills in every direction seem suddenly to be alive with men."

In Denver, eighty-two soldiers in a company on a troop train headed for Trinidad refused to go. The press reported: "The men declared they would not engage in the shooting of women and children. They hissed the 350 men who did start and shouted imprecations at them."

Five thousand people demonstrated in the rain on the lawn in front of the state capital at Denver asking that the National Guard officers at Ludlow be tried for murder, denouncing the governor as an accessory. The Denver Cigar Makers Union voted to send five hundred armed men to Ludlow and Trinidad. Women in the United Garment Workers Union in Denver announced four hundred of their members had volunteered as nurses to help the strikers.

All over the country there were meetings, demonstrations. Pickets marched in front of the Rockefeller office at 26 Broadway, New York City. A minister protested in front of the church where Rockefeller sometimes gave sermons, and was clubbed by the police.

The *New York Times* carried an editorial on the events in Colorado, which were now attracting international attention. The *Times* emphasis was not on the atrocity that had occurred, but on the mistake in tactics that had been made. Its editorial on the Ludlow Massacre began: "Somebody blundered...." Two days later, with the miners armed and in the hills of the mine district, the *Times* wrote: "With the deadliest weapons of civilization in the hands of savage-minded men, there can be no telling to what lengths the war in Colorado will go unless it is quelled by force.... The President should turn his attention form Mexico long enough to take stern measures in Colorado."

The governor of Colorado asked for federal troops to restore order, and Woodrow Wilson complied. This accomplished, the strike petered out. Congressional committees came in and took thousands of pages of testimony. The union had not won recognition. Sixty-six men, women, and children had been killed. Not one militiaman or mine guard had been indicted for crime.

Still, Colorado had been a scene of ferocious class conflict, whose emotional repercussions had rolled through the entire country. Whatever legislation had been passed, whatever liberal reforms were on the books, whatever investigations were undertaken and words of regret and conciliation uttered, the threat of class rebellion was clearly still there in the industrial conditions of the United States, in the undeterred spirit of rebellion among working people.

The *Times* had referred to Mexico. On the morning that the bodies were discovered in the tent pit at Ludlow, American warships were attacking Vera Cruz, a city on the coast of Mexico—bombarding it, occupying it, leaving a hundred Mexicans dead—because Mexico had arrested American sailors and refused to apologize to the United States with a twenty-one-gun salute.

Could patriotic fervor and the military spirit cover up class struggle? Unemployment, hard times, were growing in 1914. Could guns divert attention and create some national consensus against an external enemy? It surely was a coincidence—the bombardment of Vera Cruz, the attack on the Ludlow colony. Or perhaps it was, as someone once described human history, "the natural selection of accidents." Perhaps the affair in Mexico was an instinctual response of the system for its own survival, to create a unity of fighting purpose among a people torn by internal conflict.

The bombardment of Vera Cruz was a small incident. But in four months the First World War would begin in Europe.

Exercises

1. Why is the suffrage movement included in a chapter called "The Socialist Challenge"?

2. Emma Goldman argued that "the cause of the Spanish-American war was the price of sugar..." How could that be?

3. In a letter to the *New York Herald* in 1900 characterizing the U.S. government's conduct of the Spanish-American War, Mark Twain refers to the U.S. as "Christendom." Why? Why does he refer to battles as "pirate raids"? How might the war have had the effect of filling America's "soul full of meanness"?

4. What was the topic of Upton Sinclair's 1906 novel, *The Jungle*? What might have accounted for its popularity?

5. For Jack London, what details/evidence/facts may have led him to the conclusion that the "capitalist class has mismanaged…criminally and selfishly mismanaged"?

6. Of the following, who cannot be considered a muckraker? Explain your rejections as well as your choice.

    a. Ida Tarbell

    b. Lincoln Steffens

    c. Henry Frick

    d. Upton Sinclair

    Are there other muckrakers whom Zinn mentions who are not in the list above? Explain.

7. How was Taylorism a response to the concerns of big business (concerns raised by the financial collapse of 1907)?

8. Which of the following was not a year that marked the beginning of an economic collapse (panic or depression)?

    a. 1819

    b. 1857

    c. 1873

    d. 1907

    e. 1837

    f. 1861

    g. 1893

    h. 1929

9. What would be the best word to describe the economic cycle of ups and downs in American history? Spasmodic? Cyclical? Sporadic? Fitful? Predictable?

10. Why did Clara Lemlich call for a general strike? (What is a general strike, and how does it differ from other kinds of strikes?)

11. Why was it particularly impressive that the shirtwaist workers went on strike at the time that they did?

12. How did working-class culture sustain strikers?

13. Why did 146 Triangle Shirtwaist Company workers die in the fire of 1911?

14. What reasons/factors might explain the following disparities?

    a. In 1910, women were 20 percent of the labor force but 1 percent of union members.

    b. In 1910, black workers made 33 percent of the earnings of white workers.

15. Why did the AFL leadership consider discrimination a practical tactic?

16. How did the leadership of the IWW differ from that of the AFL? Does the difference in membership between the IWW and AFL explain the difference in tactics and goals between the two organizations? If not, then what does explain the difference in tactics and goals between the AFL and the IWW?

17. "...the IWW became a threat to the capitalist class, exactly when capitalist growth was enormous and profits huge." Is this a coincidence? Defend your answer.

18. Discuss the First Amendment in relation to the laws that the Wobblies were fighting against with their "free speech" tactics.

19. Why do you think that Joe Hill's trial became known throughout the world?

20. What were Dr. Shapleigh's concerns about the living conditions of the Lawrence workers?

21. What event precipitated the walkout that led to the Lawrence strike of 1912?

22. What role did the IWW play in the Lawrence strike, and why? What role did the government play in the Lawrence strike, and why? What role would you have liked to play in the Lawrence strike, and why?

23. Why did the managers of the American Woolen Company finally decide to begin negotiations with the strikers?

24. Why did school boards want their female teachers to be single and celibate?

25. In 1909, what accomplishments did the Laundry Workers Union claim?

26. Why were workers attracted to socialism? Why did businessmen find socialism the greatest of threats (A threat to what)? Why would women workers be skeptical of socialism? Why would they be skeptical of feminism? Why would black workers be skeptical of socialism? Why would skilled workers be antagonistic to socialism? Is socialism as a theory inherently (by definition) discriminatory?

27. What opinions did Crystal Eastman, Margaret Sanger, and Elizabeth Gurley Flynn share?

28. How did Rose Schneiderman expose as hypocrisy the antisuffrage argument that voting would make women unfeminine?

29. Why was Helen Keller a socialist but not a suffragist?

30. What irony did Helen Keller invoke in her response to the *Brooklyn Eagle*?

31. Why did Mother Jones work so hard to end child labor?

32. If William Trotter's actions in a Boston church in 1903 reveal him to be a "radical militant," then what is the definition of a "radical militant"? Did the NAACP promise to be a militant organization?

33. For each group below, explain how a Progressive piece of legislation, policy, or amendment benefited that group. Were any of the groups helped more than others? Were any left out?

    a. farmers
    b. skilled labor
    c. small businesses

d. manufacturers

e. consumers

f. unskilled labor

g. blacks

h. monopolies

i. women

34. How was the approach NCF's to preserving the status quo more sophisticated than that of the courts?

35. What were the electoral gains that the Socialist party made in 1911?

36. Why might the Rockefellers want to buy coal mines?

37. Why did the coal strike at Ludlow "culminate" in a "massacre"?

38. From 1854–6, Kansas was engulfed essentially in a civil war between pro- and antislavery forces. From September 1913 to April 1914, Colorado was similarly engulfed in violence that the *New York Times* referred to at the time as "the war in Colorado." Standard history books refer to the violence in Kansas as "Bleeding Kansas." Why do standard history books not apply a similar epithet to the violence in Colorado?

39. If the 26 (or so) deaths at Ludlow on April 20, 1914, were called the "Ludlow Massacre," why not also refer to the deaths of 146 women in the Triangle fire of 1911 as the "Triangle Massacre" (were they not also murdered)?

40. *Draw a map* that includes the following: Boston; Lawrence, Massachusetts; Patterson, New Jersey; New York City; Denver and Trinidad, Colorado; Pennsylvania; Montana; Utah; Chicago; Oklahoma.

41. *Debate Resolution*: The Socialists responded more constructively to the needs of workers than the AFL or Knights of Labor did.

42. *Debate Resolution*: Progressive legislation was intended, and successfully worked, as a safety valve for the American political economy.

Chapter 14

War Is the Health of the State

"War is the health of the state," the radical writer Randolph Bourne said, in the midst of the First World War. Indeed, as the nations of Europe went to war in 1914, the governments flourished, patriotism bloomed, class struggle was stilled, and young men died in frightful numbers on the battlefields—often for a hundred yards of land, a line of trenches.

In the United States, not yet in the war, there was worry about the health of the state. Socialism was growing. The IWW seemed to be everywhere. Class conflict was intense. In the summer of 1916, during a Preparedness Day parade in San Francisco, a bomb exploded, killing nine people; two local radicals, Tom Mooney and Warren Billings, were arrested and would spend twenty years in prison. Shortly after that Senator James Wadsworth of New York suggested compulsory military training for all males, to avert the danger that "these people of ours shall be divided into classes." Rather: "We must let our young men know that they owe some responsibility to this country."

The supreme fulfillment of that responsibility was taking place in Europe. Ten million were to die on the battlefield; twenty million were to die of hunger and disease related to the war. And no one since that day has been able to show that the war brought any gain for humanity that would be worth one human life. The rhetoric of the socialists, that it was an "imperialist war," now seems moderate and hardly arguable. The advanced capitalist countries of Europe were fighting over boundaries, colonies, spheres of influence; they were competing for Alsace-Lorraine, the Balkans, Africa, the Middle East.

The war came shortly after the opening of the twentieth century, in the midst of exultation (perhaps only among the elite in the Western world) about progress and modernization. The killing started very fast, and on a large scale. In the first Battle of the Marne, the British and French succeeded in blocking the German advance on Paris. Each side had 500,000 casualties. In August 1914, a volunteer for the British army had to be 5 feet 8 inches to enlist. By October, the requirement was lowered to 5 feet 5 inches. That month there were thirty thousand casualties, and then one could be 5 feet 3. In the first three months of war, almost the entire original British army was wiped out.

For three years the battle lines remained virtually stationary in France. Each side would push forward, then back, then forward again—for a few yards, a few miles, while the corpses piled up. In 1916 the Germans tried to break through at Verdun; the British and French counterattacked along the Seine, moved forward a few miles, and lost 600,000 men. One day, the Ninth Battalion of the King's Own Yorkshire Light Infantry launched an attack with eight hundred men. Twenty-four hours later, there were eighty-four left.

Back home, the British were not told of the slaughter. The same thing was happening on the German side; as Erich Maria Remarque wrote in his great novel, on days when men by the thousands were being blown apart by machine guns and shells, the official dispatches announced "All Quiet on the Western Front."

In July 1916, British General Douglas Haig ordered eleven divisions of English soldiers to climb out of their trenches and move toward the German lines. The six German divisions opened up with their machine guns. Of the 110,000 who attacked, 20,000 were killed, 40,000 more wounded—all those bodies strewn on no-man's-land, the ghostly territory between the contending trenches. On January 1, 1917, Haig was promoted to field marshal. What happened that summer is described tersely in William Langer's *An Encyclopedia of World History*:

> Haig proceeded hopefully to the main offensive. The third battle of Ypres was a series of 8 heavy attacks, carried through in driving rain and fought over ground water-logged and muddy. No break-through was effected, and the total gain was about 5 miles of territory...and cost the British about 400,000 men.

The people of France and Britain were not told the extent of the casualties. When, in the last year of the war, the Germans attacked ferociously on the Somme, and left 300,000 British soldiers dead or wounded, London newspapers printed the following:

> How the Civilian May Help in this Crisis.
> Be cheerful....
> Write encouragingly to friends at the front....
> Don't think you know better than Haig.

Into this pit of death and deception came the United States, in the spring of 1917. Mutinies were beginning to occur in the French army. Soon, out of 112 divisions, 68 would have mutinies; 629 men would be tried and condemned, 50 shot by firing squads. American troops were badly needed.

President Woodrow Wilson had promised that the United States would stay neutral in the war: "There is such a thing as a nation being too proud to fight." But in April of 1917, the Germans had announced they would have their submarines sink any ship bringing supplies to their enemies; and they had sunk a number of merchant vessels. Wilson now said he must stand by the right of Americans to travel on merchant ships in the war zone.

It was unrealistic to expect that the Germans should treat the United States as neutral in the war when the U.S. had been shipping great amounts of war materials to Germany's enemies. In early 1915, the British liner *Lusitania* was torpedoed and sunk by a German submarine. She sank in eighteen minutes, and 1,198 people died, including 124 Americans.

The United States claimed the *Lusitania* carried an innocent cargo, and therefore the torpedoing was a monstrous German atrocity. Actually, the *Lusitania* was heavily armed: it carried thousands of cases of ammunition. Her manifests were falsified to hide this fact, and the British and American governments lied about the cargo.

In 1914 a serious recession had begun in the United States. But by 1915, war orders for the Allies (mostly England) had stimulated the economy, and by April 1917 more than $2 billion worth of goods had been sold to the Allies. American prosperity was now tied to England's war.

Prosperity depended much on foreign markets, it was believed by the leaders of the country. Early in his presidency, Woodrow Wilson described his aim as "an open door to the world," and in 1914 he said he supported "the righteous conquest of foreign markets."

With World War I, England became more and more a market for American goods and for loans at interest. J. P. Morgan and Company acted as agents for the Allies, and began lending money in such great amounts as to both make great profit and tie American finance closely to the interest of a British victory in the war against Germany.

The industrialists and the political leaders talked of prosperity as if it were classless, as if everyone gained from Morgan's loans. True, the war meant more production, more employment, but did the workers in the steel plants gain as much as U.S. Steel, which made $348 million in profit in 1916 alone? When the United States entered the war, it was the rich who took even more direct charge of the economy. Financier Bernard Baruch headed the War Industries Board, the most powerful of the wartime government agencies. Bankers, railroad men, and industrialists dominated these agencies.

A remarkably perceptive article on the nature of the First World War appeared in May 1915 in the *Atlantic Monthly*. Written by W. E. B. Du Bois, it was titled "The African Roots of War." It was a war for empire, he said. Germany and the Allies were fighting for the gold and diamonds of South Africa, the cocoa of Angola and Nigeria, the rubber and ivory of the Congo, the palm oil of the West Coast. Yes, the average citizen of England, France, Germany, the United States, had a higher standard of living than before. But: "Whence comes this new wealth?...It comes primarily from the darker nations of the world—Asia and Africa, South and Central America, the West Indies, and the islands of the South Seas."

Du Bois saw the ingenuity of capitalism in uniting exploiter and exploited—creating a safety valve for explosive class conflict. "It is no longer simply the merchant prince, or the aristocratic monopoly, or even the employing class, that is exploiting the world: it is the nation, a new democratic nation composed of united capital and labor."

The United States fitted that idea of Du Bois. American capitalism needed international rivalry—and periodic war—to create an artificial community of interest between rich and poor, supplanting the genuine community of interest among the poor which showed itself in sporadic movements. A national consensus for war was needed, and the government quickly moved to create such a consensus.

That there was no spontaneous urge to fight is suggested by the strong measures taken: a draft of young men, an elaborate propaganda campaign throughout the country, and harsh punishment for those who refused to get in line.

Despite the rousing words of Wilson about a war "to end all wars" and "to make the world safe for democracy," Americans did not rush to enlist. A million men were needed, but in the first six weeks after the declaration of war only 73,000 volunteered. Congress voted overwhelmingly for a draft.

George Creel, a veteran newspaperman, became the government's official propagandist for the war; he set up the Committee on Public Information to persuade Americans the war was right. It sponsored 75,000 speakers, who gave 750,000 four-minute speeches in 5,000 American cities and towns. It was a massive effort to excite a reluctant public.

The day after Congress declared war, the Socialist party met in emergency convention in St. Louis and called the declaration "a crime against the people of the United States." In the summer of 1917, Socialist antiwar meetings in Minnesota drew large crowds—five thousand, ten thousand, twenty thousand farmers—protesting the war, the draft, profiteering. The *Akron Beacon-Journal*, a conservative newspaper in Ohio, said that "were an election to come now a mighty tide of socialism would inundate the Middle West." It said the country had "never embarked upon a more unpopular war."

In the municipal elections of 1917, against the tide of propaganda and patriotism, the Socialists made remarkable gains. Their candidate for mayor of New York, Morris Hillquit, got 22 percent of the vote, five times the normal Socialist vote there. Ten Socialists were elected to the New York State legislature. In Chicago, the party vote went from 3.6 percent in 1915 to 34.7 percent in 1917. In Buffalo, it went from 2.6 percent to 30.2 percent. And although some prominent Socialists—Jack London, Upton Sinclair, Clarence Darrow—became prowar after the U.S. entered, most Socialists continued their opposition.

Congress passed, and Wilson signed, in June of 1917, the Espionage Act. From its title one would suppose it was an act against spying. However, it had a clause that provided penalties up to twenty years in prison for "Whoever, when the United States is at war, shall wilfully cause or attempt to cause insubordination, disloyalty, mutiny, or refusal of duty in the military or naval forces of the United States, or shall wilfully obstruct the recruiting or enlistment service of the U.S...." The act was used to imprison Americans who spoke or wrote against the war.

Two months after the law passed, a Socialist named Charles Schenck was arrested in Philadelphia for printing and distributing fifteen thousand leaflets that denounced the draft law and the war. Conscription, it said, was "a monstrous deed against humanity in the interests of the financiers of Wall Street." Schenck was indicted, tried, found guilty, and sentenced to six months in jail for violating the Espionage Act. (It turned out to be one of the shortest sentences given in such cases.) Schenck appealed, arguing that the act, by prosecuting speech and writing, violated the First Amendment: "Congress shall make no law…abridging the freedom of speech, or of the press…."

The Supreme Court's decision was unanimous and was written by its most famous liberal, Oliver Wendell Holmes. Was Schenck protected by the First Amendment? Holmes said:

> The most stringent protection of free speech would not protect a man in falsely shouting fire in a theatre and causing a panic…. The question in every case is whether the words used are used in such circumstances and are of such a nature as to create a clear and present danger that they will bring about the substantive evils that Congress has a right to prevent.

Holmes's analogy was clever and attractive. Few people would think free speech should be conferred on someone shouting fire in a theater and causing a panic. But did that example fit criticism of the war? Was not the war itself a "clear and present danger," indeed, more clear and more present and more dangerous to life than any argument against it?

The case of Eugene Debs soon came before the Supreme Court. In June of 1918, Debs visited three Socialists who were in prison for opposing the draft, and then spoke, across the street from the jail, to an audience he kept enthralled for two hours. He was one of the country's great orators, and was interrupted again and again by laughter and applause.

> They tell us that we live in a great free republic; that our institutions are democratic; that we are a free and self-governing people. That is too much, even for a joke….
>
> Wars throughout history have been waged for conquest and plunder…. And that is war in a nutshell. The master class has always declared the wars; the subject class has always fought the battles….

Debs was arrested for violating the Espionage Act. There were draft-age youths in his audience, and his words would "obstruct the recruiting or enlistment service."

His words were intended to do much more than that:

> Yes, in good time we are going to sweep into power in this nation and throughout the world. We are going to destroy all enslaving and degrading capitalist institutions and re-create them as free and humanizing institutions…. The sun of Socialism is rising…. In due time the hour will strike and this great cause triumphant…will proclaim the emancipation of the working class and the brotherhood of all mankind. [Thunderous and prolonged applause.]

Debs refused at his trial to take the stand in his defense, or to call a witness on his behalf. He denied nothing about what he said. But before the jury began its deliberations, he spoke to them:

> I have been accused of obstructing the war. I admit it. Gentlemen, I abhor war. I would oppose war if I stood alone.... I have sympathy with the suffering, struggling people everywhere. It does not make any difference under what flag they were born, or where they live....

The jury found him guilty of violating the Espionage Act. Debs addressed the judge before sentencing:

> Your honor, years ago I recognized my kinship with all living beings, and I made up my mind that I was not one bit better than the meanest on earth. I said then, and I say now, that while there is a lower class, I am in it; while there is a criminal element, I am of it; while there is a soul in prison, I am not free.

The judge denounced those "who would strike the sword from the hand of this nation while she is engaged in defending herself against a foreign and brutal power." He sentenced Debs to ten years in prison.

Debs's appeal was not heard by the Supreme Court until 1919. The war was over. Oliver Wendell Holmes, for a unanimous court, affirmed Debs's guilt. Holmes said Debs was implying "that the working men are not concerned in the war." Thus, Holmes said, the "natural and intended effect" of Debs's speech would be to obstruct recruiting.

President Wilson refused to pardon Debs, who spent thirty-two months in prison. In 1921, at the age of sixty-six, he was released by President Warren Harding.

About nine hundred people went to prison under the Espionage Act. The press cooperated with the government, intensifying the atmosphere of fear for possible opponents of the war. The *Literary Digest* asked its readers "to clip and send to us any editorial utterances they encounter which seem to them seditious or treasonable." The *New York Times* carried an editorial: "It is the duty of every good citizen to communicate to proper authorities any evidence of sedition that comes to his notice."

In the summer of 1917, the American Defense Society was formed. The *New York Herald* reported: "More than one hundred men enrolled yesterday in the American Vigilante Patrol at the offices of the American Defense Society.... The Patrol was formed to put an end to seditious street oratory."

The Department of Justice sponsored an American Protective League, which by June of 1917 had units in six hundred cities and towns, a membership of nearly 100,000. The press reported that their members were "the leading men in their communities...bankers...railroad men...hotel men." The League intercepted mail, broke into homes and offices, claimed to find three million cases of "disloyalty."

Creel's Committee on Public Information advertised that people should "report the man who spreads pessimistic stories. Report him to the Department of Justice." In 1918, the attorney general said: "It is safe to say that never in its history has this country been so thoroughly policed."

Why these huge efforts? On August 1, 1917, the *New York Herald* reported that in New York City ninety of the first hundred draftees claimed exemption. In Minnesota, headlines in the *Minneapolis Journal* of August 6 and 7 read: "DRAFT OPPOSITION FAST SPREADING IN STATE," and "CONSCRIPTS GIVE FALSE ADDRESSES." In Florida, two Negro farm hands went into the woods with a shotgun and mutilated themselves to avoid the draft: one blew off four fingers of his hand; the other shot off his arm below the elbow.

Senator Thomas Hardwick of Georgia said: "there was undoubtedly general and widespread opposition on the part of many thousands...to the enactment of the draft law. Numerous and largely attended mass meetings held in every part of the State protested against it...." Ultimately, over 330,000 men were classified as draft evaders.

In Oklahoma, the Socialist party and the IWW had been active among tenant farmers and sharecroppers who formed a "Working Class Union." A march on Washington was planned for draft objectors throughout the country. But before the Union could carry out its plans, its members were rounded up and arrested, and soon 450 individuals accused of rebellion were in the state penitentiary. Leaders were given three to ten years in jail, others sixty days to two years.

On July 1, 1917, radicals organized a parade in Boston against the war, with banners:

> Is this a Popular War, Why Conscription?
> Who Stole Panama? Who Crushed Haiti?
> We Demand Peace.

The New York *Call* said eight thousand people marched, including "4000 members of the Central Labor Union, 2000 members of the Lettish Socialist Organizations, 1500 Lithuanians, Jewish members of cloak trades, and other branches of the party." The parade was attacked by soldiers and sailors, on orders from their officers.

The Post Office Department began taking away the mailing privileges of newspapers and magazines that printed antiwar articles. *The Masses*, a socialist magazine of politics, literature, and art, was banned from the mails. It had carried an editorial by Max Eastman in the summer of 1917, saying, among other things: "For what specific purposes are you shipping our bodies, and the bodies of our sons, to Europe? For my part, I do not recognize the right of a government to draft me to a war whose purposes I do not believe in."

In Los Angeles, a film was shown that dealt with the American Revolution and depicted British atrocities against the colonists. It was called *The Spirit of '76*. The man who made the film was prosecuted under the Espionage Act because, the judge said, the film tended "to question the good faith of our ally, Great Britain." He was sentenced to ten years in prison. The case was officially listed as *U.S. v. Spirit of '76*.

Schools and universities discouraged opposition to the war. At Columbia University, J. McKeen Cattell, a psychologist, a long-time critic of the Board of Trustees' control of the university, and an opponent of the war, was fired. A week later, in protest, the famous historian Charles Beard resigned from the Columbia faculty.

In Congress, a few voices spoke out against the war. The first woman in the House of Representatives, Jeannette Rankin, did not respond when her name was called in the roll call on the declaration of war. On the next roll call she stood up: "I want to stand by my country, but I cannot vote for war. I vote No." A popular song of the time was: "I Didn't Raise My Boy to Be a Soldier." It was overwhelmed, however, by songs like "Over There," "It's a Grand Old Flag," and "Johnny Get Your Gun."

Socialist Kate Richards O'Hare was sentenced to five years in the Missouri state penitentiary. In prison she continued to fight. When she and fellow prisoners protested the lack of air, because the window above the cell block was kept shut, she was pulled out in the corridor by guards for punishment. In her hand she was carrying a book of poems, and as she was dragged out she flung the book up at the window and broke it, the fresh air streaming in, her fellow prisoners cheering.

Emma Goldman and her fellow anarchist Alexander Berkman were sentenced to prison for opposing the draft. She said to the jury: "Verily, poor as we are in democracy how can we give of it to the world?"

The IWW newspaper, the *Industrial Worker*, just before the declaration of war, had written: "Capitalists of America, we will fight against you, not for you!" The war now gave the government its opportunity to destroy the radical union.

In early September 1917, Department of Justice agents made simultaneous raids on forty-eight IWW meeting halls across the country, seizing correspondence and literature that would become courtroom evidence. In April of 1918, 101 IWW leaders went on trial for conspiring to hinder the draft and encourage desertion. One Wobbly man told the court:

> You ask me why the I.W.W. is not patriotic to the United States. If you were a bum without a blanket; if you had left your wife and kids when you went west for a job, and had never located them since; if your job had never kept you long enough in a place to qualify you to vote; if every person who represented law and order and the nation beat you up, railroaded you to jail, and the good Christian people cheered and told them to go to it, how in hell do you expect a man to be patriotic? This war is a business man's war and we don't see why we should go out and get shot in order to save the lovely state of affairs that we now enjoy.

The jury found them all guilty. The judge sentenced Haywood and fourteen others to twenty years in prison; thirty-three were given ten years, the rest shorter sentences. The IWW was shattered. Haywood jumped bail and fled to revolutionary Russia, where he remained until his death ten years later.

The war ended in November 1918. Fifty thousand American soldiers had died, and it did not take long, even in the case of patriots, for bitterness and disillusionment to spread through the country. This was reflected in the literature of the postwar decade. Ernest Hemingway would write *A Farewell to Arms*. Years later a college student named Irwin Shaw would write a play, *Bury the Dead*. And a Hollywood screenwriter named Dalton Trumbo would write a powerful and chilling antiwar novel about a torso and brain left alive on the battlefield of World War I, *Johnny Got His Gun*. Ford Madox Ford wrote *No More Parades*. John Dos Passos, in his novel *1919*, wrote of the death of John Doe:

> In the tarpaper morgue at Chalons-sur-Marne in the reek of chloride of lime and the dead, they picked out the pine box that held all that was left of...John Doe....
> and draped the Old Glory over it
> and the bugler played taps
> and Mr. Harding prayed to God and the diplomats and the generals
> and the admirals and the brass hats and the politicians and the hand-

somely dressed ladies out of the society column of the Washington Post stood up solemn

and thought how beautiful sad Old Glory God's Country it was to have the bugler play taps and the three volleys made their ears ring.

Where his chest ought to have been they pinned the Congressional Medal....

With all the wartime jailings, the intimidation, the drive for national unity, when the war was over, the Establishment still feared socialism. There seemed to be a need again, in the face of revolutionary challenge, for the twin tactics of reform and repression.

The first was suggested by George L. Record, one of Wilson's friends, who wrote to him in early 1919 that something would have to be done for economic democracy, "to meet this menace of socialism." He said: "You should become the real leader of the radical forces in America, and present to the country a constructive program of fundamental reform, which shall be an alternative to the program presented by the socialists, and the Bolsheviki...."

That summer of 1919, Wilson's adviser Joseph Tumulty reminded him that the conflict between the Republicans and Democrats was unimportant compared with that which threatened them both: "In this era of industrial and social unrest both parties are in disrepute with the average man...."

In the summer of 1919, a bomb exploded in front of the home of Wilson's attorney general, A. Mitchell Palmer. Six months later, Palmer carried out the first of his mass raids on aliens—immigrants who were not citizens. A law passed by Congress near the end of the war provided for the deportation of aliens who opposed organized government or advocated the destruction of property. Palmer's men, on December 21, 1919, picked up 249 aliens of Russian birth (including Emma Goldman and Alexander Berkman), put them on a transport, and deported them to what had become Soviet Russia.

In January 1920, four thousand persons were rounded up all over the country, held in seclusion for long periods of time, brought into secret hearings, and ordered deported. In Boston, Department of Justice agents, aided by local police, arrested six hundred people by raiding meeting halls or by invading their homes in the early morning. They were handcuffed in pairs and marched through the streets in chains.

In the spring of 1920, a typesetter and anarchist named Andrea Salsedo was arrested in New York by FBI agents and held for eight weeks in the FBI offices on the fourteenth floor of the Park Row Building, not allowed to contact family or friends or lawyers. Then his crushed body was found on the pavement below the building and the FBI said he had committed suicide by jumping from the fourteenth floor window.

Two friends of Salsedo, anarchists and workingmen in the Boston area, having just learned of his death, began carrying guns. They were arrested on a streetcar in Brockton, Massachusetts, and charged with a holdup and murder that had taken place two weeks before at a shoe factory. These were Nicola Sacco and Bartolomeo Vanzetti.

They went on trial, were found guilty, and spent seven years in jail while appeals went on, and while all over the country and the world, people became involved in their case. The trial record and the surrounding circumstances suggested that Sacco and Vanzetti were sentenced to death because they were anarchists and foreigners. In August 1927, as police broke up marches and picket lines with arrests and beatings, and troops surrounded the prison, they were electrocuted.

Sacco's last message to his son Dante, in his painfully learned English was a message to millions of others in the years to come:

> So, Son, instead of crying, be strong, so as to be able to comfort your mother…take her for a long walk in the quiet country, gathering wild flowers here and there…. But remember always, Dante, in the play of happiness, don't you use all for yourself only…. [H]elp the persecuted and the victim because they are your better friends…. In this struggle of life you will find more and love and you will be loved.

There had been reforms. The patriotic fervor of war had been invoked. The courts and jails had been used to reinforce the idea that certain ideas, certain kinds of resistance, could not be tolerated. And still, even from the cells of the condemned, the message was going out: the class war was still on in that supposedly classless society, the United States. Through the twenties and the thirties, it was still on.

Exercises

1. When did World War I begin? When did the United States enter World War I?

2. How many Europeans died during World War I? How many Americans?

3. Why can World War I be called a war of attrition?

4. What was so ironic about the title of Remarque's famous book about World War I?

5. Why were American troops "badly needed" by the French and British governments?

6. Why did the British and U.S. governments lie about the cargo that the *Lusitania* carried in 1915?

7. How was America's interest and participation in World War I an extension of the same foreign policy rationale behind the government's decision to wage war on Spain in 1898? (Would DuBois agree?)

8. According to Zinn, once the United States declared war on Germany "a national consensus for war was needed, and the government quickly moved to create such a consensus." What actions did the government take to create consensus?

9. Did the U.S. government's decision to enter World War I cause an increase in popularity of socialism in America, or did socialism's popularity merely coincide with America's participation in the war? (In other words, did the conditions created by the war compel people to become socialists whereas in a time of peace they would not have?)

10. Was advocating socialism during the war equivalent to falsely shouting "fire" in a crowed theater?

11. What were the methods employed by the different levels of government and private citizens to inhibit criticism of America's participation in World War I?

12. What were the reasons to oppose America's involvement in WWI? What were the reasons to support the war?

13. How did WWI shatter the IWW?

14. What is the evidence for Zinn's argument that "when the war was over, the Establishment still feared socialism"?

15. *Debate Resolution*: A government needs to silence dissent when it is at war. Consider the following when defending or disagreeing with the resolution: purpose of war; quantity and quality of dissent; method of expression of dissent; threat to government's war aims by such dissent; threat to lives of soldiers by dissent; threat to civil rights at the time and for the future.

Chapter 15

Self-help in Hard Times

The war was hardly over, it was February 1919, the IWW leadership was in jail, but the IWW idea of the general strike became reality for five days in Seattle, Washington, when a walkout of 100,000 working people brought the city to a halt.

It began with thirty-five thousand shipyard workers striking for a wage increase. They appealed for support to the Seattle Central Labor Council, which recommended a citywide strike, and in two weeks 110 locals—mostly American Federation of Labor, only a few IWW—voted to strike. The rank and file of each striking local elected three members to a General Strike Committee, and on February 6, 1919, at 10:00 A.M., the strike began.

The city now stopped functioning, except for activities organized by the strikers to provide essential needs. Firemen agreed to stay on the job. Laundry workers handled only hospital laundry. Vehicles authorized to move carried signs "Exempted by the General Strike Committee." Thirty-five neighborhood milk stations were set up.

A Labor War Veteran's Guard was organized to keep the peace. On the blackboard at one of its headquarters was written: "The purpose of this organization is to preserve law and order without the use of force. No volunteer will have any police power or be allowed to carry weapons of any sort, but to use persuasion only." During the strike, crime in the city decreased.

The mayor swore in twenty-four hundred special deputies, many of them students at the University of Washington. Almost a thousand sailors and marines were brought into the city by the U.S. government. The general strike ended after five days, according to the General Strike Committee because of pressure from the international officers of the various unions, as well as the difficulties of living in a shut-down city.

The strike had been peaceful. But when it was over, there were raids and arrests: on the Socialist party headquarters, on a printing plant. Thirty-nine members of the IWW were jailed as "ring-leaders of anarchy."

Why such a reaction to the general strike, to the organizing of the Wobblies? A statement by the mayor of Seattle suggests that the Establishment feared not just the strike itself but what it symbolized. He said: "The general strike, as practiced in Seattle, is of itself the weapon of revolution, all the more dangerous because quiet. To succeed, it must suspend everything; stop the entire life stream of a community.... That is to say, it puts the government out of operation."

Furthermore, the Seattle general strike took place in the midst of a wave of postwar rebellions all over the world. A writer in *The Nation* commented that year:

> The most extraordinary phenomenon of the present time...is the unprecedented revolt of the rank and file....
>
> In Russia it has dethroned the Czar.... In Korea and India and Egypt and Ireland it keeps up an unyielding resistance to political tyranny. In England it brought about the railway strike, against the judgement of the men's own executives. In New York, it brought about the longshoremen's strike and kept the men out in defiance of union officials, and caused the upheaval in the printing trade, which the international officers, even though the employers worked hand in glove with them, were completely unable to control.
>
> The common man...losing faith in the old leadership, has experienced a new access of self-confidence....

In the year 1919, 350,000 steelworkers went on strike; 120,000 textile workers struck in New England and New Jersey, and 30,000 silk workers struck in Paterson, New Jersey. In Boston the police went out on strike, and in New York City cigarmakers, shirtmakers, carpenters, bakers, teamsters, and barbers were out on strike. In Chicago, the press reported, "More strikes and lockouts accompany the mid-summer heat than ever known before at any one time." Five thousand workers at International Harvester and five thousand city workers were in the streets.

When the twenties began, however, the situation seemed under control. The IWW was destroyed, the Socialist party falling apart. The strikes were beaten down by force, and the economy was doing just well enough for just enough people to prevent mass rebellion.

Congress, in the twenties, put an end to the dangerous, turbulent flood of immigrants (14 million between 1900 and 1920) by passing laws setting immigration quotas: the quotas favored Anglo-Saxons, kept out black and yellow people, limited severely the coming of Latins, Slavs, Jews. No African country could send more than one hundred people; one hundred was the limit for China.

The Ku Klux Klan was revived in the 1920s, and it spread into the North. By 1924 it had 4.5 million members. The NAACP seemed helpless in the face of mob violence and race hatred everywhere. The impossibility of the black person's ever being considered equal in white America was the theme of the nationalist movement led in the 1920s by Marcus Garvey. He preached black pride, racial separation, and a return to Africa, which to him held the only hope for black unity and survival. But Garvey's movement, inspiring as it was to some blacks, could not make much headway against the powerful white supremacy currents of the postwar decade.

There was some truth to the standard picture of the twenties as a time of prosperity and fun—the Jazz Age, the Roaring Twenties. Unemployment was down, from 4,270,000 in 1921 to a little over 2 million in 1927. The general level of wages for workers rose. Some farmers made a lot of money. The 40 percent of all families who made over $2,000 a year could buy new gadgets: autos, radios, refrigerators. Millions of people were not doing badly—and they could shut out of the picture the others—the tenant farmers, black and white, the immigrant families in the big cities either without work or not making enough to get the basic necessities.

But prosperity was concentrated at the top. One-tenth of one percent of the families at the top received as much income as 42 percent of the families at the bottom. Every year in the 1920s, about 25,000 workers were killed on the job and 100,000 permanently disabled. Two million people in New York City lived in tenements condemned as firetraps.

Sinclair Lewis captured the false sense of prosperity, the shallow pleasure of the new gadgets for the middle classes, in his novel *Babbitt*.

Women had finally, after long agitation, won the right to vote in 1920 with the pasage of the Nineteenth Amendment, but voting was still a middle-class and upper-class activity, and these women divided along orthodox party lines as other voters did.

Few political figures spoke out for the poor of the twenties. One was

Fiorello La Guardia, a congressman from a district of poor immigrants in East Harlem (who ran, oddly, on both Socialist and Republican tickets). Receiving desperate letters from his constituents, La Guardia wrote to the secretary of agriculture about the high price of meat and received a pamphlet on how to use meat economically. La Guardia wrote back: "I asked for help and you send me a bulletin.... Your bulletins...are of no use to the tenement dwellers of this great city.... What we want is the help of your department on the meat profiteers who are keeping the hard-working people of this city from obtaining proper nourishment."

During the presidencies of Harding and Coolidge in the twenties, the secretary of the treasury was Andrew Mellon, one of the richest men in America. In 1923, Congress was presented with the "Mellon Plan," calling for what looked like a general reduction of income taxes, except that the top income brackets would have their tax rates lowered from 50 percent to 25 percent, while the lowest-income group would have theirs lowered from 4 percent to 3 percent.

A few congressmen from working-class districts spoke against the bill, such as William P. Connery of Massachusetts: "When I see a provision in this Mellon tax bill which is going to save Mr. Mellon himself $800,000 on his income tax and his brother $600,000 on his, I cannot give it my support."

The Mellon Plan passed. In 1928, La Guardia toured the poorer districts of New York and said: "I confess I was not prepared for what I actually saw. It seemed almost incredible that such conditions of poverty could really exist."

Buried in the general news of prosperity in the twenties were, from time to time, stories of bitter labor struggles. In 1922, coal miners and railroad men went on strike. That same year, a textile strike in Rhode Island among Italian and Portuguese workers failed, but class feelings were awakened and some of the strikers joined radical movements.

After the war, with the Socialist party weakened, a Communist party was organized, and Communists were involved in many labor struggles. They played a leading part in the great textile strike that spread through the Carolinas and Tennessee in the spring of 1929. The mill owners had moved to the South to escape unions, to find more subservient workers among the poor whites. But these workers rebelled against the long hours, the low pay. They particularly resented the "stretch-out"—an intensification of work.

In Gastonia, North Carolina, workers joined a new union, the

National Textile Workers Union, led by Communists, which admitted both blacks and whites to membership. When some of them were fired, half of the two thousand workers went out on strike. An atmosphere of anti-Communism and racism built up and violence began. Textile strikes began to spread across South Carolina.

One by one the various strikes were settled, with some gains, but not at Gastonia. There, with the textile workers living in a tent colony and refusing to renounce the Communists in their leadership, the strike went on. But strikebreakers were brought in and the mills kept operating. Desperation grew; there were violent clashes with the police.

One dark night, the chief of police was killed in a gun battle and sixteen strikers and sympathizers were indicted for murder, including Fred Beal, a Communist party organizer. Ultimately seven were tried and given sentences of from five to twenty years. They were released on bail, and left the state; the Communists escaped to Soviet Russia. Through all the defeats, the beatings, the murders, however, it was the beginning of textile mill unionism in the South.

The stock market crash of 1929, which marked the beginning of the Great Depression of the United States, came directly from wild speculation that collapsed and brought the whole economy down with it. But, as John Galbraith said in his study of that event (*The Great Crash*), behind that speculation was the fact that "the economy was fundamentally unsound." He pointed to very unhealthy corporate and banking structures, an unsound foreign trade, much economic misinformation, and the "bad distribution of income" (the highest 5 percent of the population received about one-third of all personal income).

A socialist critic would go further and say that the capitalist system was by its nature unsound: a system driven by the one overriding motive of corporate profit and therefore unstable, unpredictable, and blind to human needs. The result of all that: permanent depression for many of its people, and periodic crises for almost everybody. Capitalism, despite its attempts at self-reform, its organization for better control, was still in 1929 a sick and undependable system.

After the crash, the economy was stunned, barely moving. Over five thousand banks closed and huge numbers of businesses, unable to get money, closed too. Those that continued laid off employees and cut the wages of those who remained, again and again. Industrial production fell by 50 percent, and by 1933 perhaps 15 million (no one knew exactly)— one-fourth or one-third of the labor force—were out of work.

Clearly, those responsible for organizing the economy did not know what had happened, were baffled by it, refused to recognize it, and found reasons other than the failure of the system. Herbert Hoover had said, not long before the crash: "We in America today are nearer to the final triumph over poverty than ever before in the history of any land." Henry Ford, in March 1931, said the crisis was here because "the average man won't really do a day's work unless he is caught and cannot get out of it. There is plenty of work to do if people would do it." A few weeks later he laid off seventy-five thousand workers.

There were millions of tons of food around, but it was not profitable to transport it, to sell it. Warehouses were full of clothing, but people could not afford it. There were lots of houses, but they stayed empty because people couldn't pay the rent, had been evicted, and now lived in shacks in quickly formed "Hoovervilles" built on garbage dumps.

Brief glimpses of reality in the newspapers could have been multiplied by the millions: A *New York Times* story in early 1932:

> After vainly trying to get a stay of dispossession until January 15 from his apartment at 46 Hancock Street in Brooklyn, yesterday, Peter J. Cornell, 48 years old, a former roofing contractor out of work and penniless, fell dead in the arms of his wife.
>
> A doctor gave the cause of his death as heart disease, and the police said it had at least partly been caused by the bitter disappointment of a long day's fruitless attempt to prevent himself and his family being put out on the street....
>
> Cornell owed $5 in rent in arrears and $39 for January which his landlord required in advance. Failure to produce the money resulted in a dispossess order being served on the family yesterday and to take effect at the end of the week.
>
> After vainly seeking assistance elsewhere, he was told during the day by the Home Relief Bureau that it would have no funds with which to help him until January 15.

A tenement dweller on 113th Street in East Harlem wrote to Congressman La Guardia in Washington:

> You know my condition is bad. I used to get pension from the government and they stopped. It is now nearly seven months I am out of work. I hope you will try to do something for me.... I have four children who are in need of clothes and food.... My daughter who is eight is very ill and not recovering. My rent is due two months and I am afraid of being put out.

In Oklahoma, the farmers found their farms sold under the auctioneer's hammer, their farms turning to dust, the tractors coming in and taking over. John Steinbeck, in his novel of the depression, *The Grapes of Wrath*, describes what happened: "And the dispossessed, the migrants, flowed into California, two hundred and fifty thousand, and three hundred thousand. Behind them new tractors were going on the land and the tenants were being forced off. And new waves were on the way, new waves of the dispossessed and the homeless, hard, intent, and dangerous...."

These people were becoming "dangerous," as Steinbeck said. The spirit of rebellion was growing. Newspaper reports of things happening around the country tell the story:

England, Arkansas, January 3, 1931. Some 500 farmers, most of them white men and many of them armed, marched on the business section of this town.... Shouting that they must have food for themselves and their families, the invaders announced their intention to take it from the stores unless it were provided from some other source without cost.

Detroit, July 9, 1931. An incipient riot by 500 unemployed men turned out of the city lodging house for lack of funds was quelled by police reserves in Cadillac Square tonight....

Indiana Harbor, Indiana, August 5, 1931. Fifteen hundred jobless men stormed the plant of the Fruit Growers Express Company here, demanding that they be given jobs to keep from starving. The company's answer was to call the city police, who routed the jobless with menacing clubs.

Chicago, April 1, 1932. Five hundred school children, most with haggard faces and in tattered clothes, paraded through Chicago's downtown section to the Board of Education offices to demand that the school system provide them with food.

Boston, June 3, 1932. Twenty-five hungry children raided a buffet lunch set up for Spanish War veterans during a Boston parade. Two automobile-loads of police were called to drive them away.

New York, January 21, 1933. Several hundred jobless surrounded a restaurant just off Union Square today demanding they be fed without charge....

Seattle, February 16, 1933. A two-day siege of the County-City Building, occupied by an army of about 5,000 unemployed, was ended early tonight, deputy sheriffs and police evicting the demonstrators after nearly two hours of efforts.

Yip Harburg, the songwriter, had to write a song for the show *Americana*. He wrote "Brother, Can You Spare a Dime."

283

Once in khaki suits,
Gee, we looked swell,
Full of that Yankee Doodle-de-dum.
Half a million boots went sloggin' through Hell,
I was the kid with the drum.
Say, don't you remember, they called me Al—
It was Al all the time.
Say, don't you remember I'm your pal—
Brother, can you spare a dime.

The anger of the veteran of the First World War, now without work, his family hungry, led to the march of the Bonus Army to Washington in the spring and summer of 1932. War veterans, holding government bonus certificates that were due years in the future, demanded that Congress pay off on them now, when the money was desperately needed. And so they began to move to Washington from all over the country, with wives and children or alone. They came in broken-down old autos, stealing rides on freight trains, or hitchhiking.

More than twenty thousand came. Most camped across the Potomac River from the Capitol on Anacostia Flats where, as John Dos Passos wrote, "the men are sleeping in little lean-tos built out of old newspapers, cardboard boxes, packing crates, bits of tin or tarpaper roofing...."

President Hoover ordered the army to evict them. Four troops of cavalry, four companies of infantry, a machine gun squadron, and six tanks assembled near the White House. Gen. Douglas MacArthur was in charge of the operation, Maj. Dwight Eisenhower his aide. George S. Patton was one of the officers. MacArthur led his troops down Pennsylvania Avenue, used tear gas to clear veterans out of the old buildings, and set the buildings on fire.

Then the army moved across the bridge to Anacostia. Thousands of veterans, wives, children, began to run as the tear gas spread. The soldiers set fire to some of the huts, and soon the whole encampment was ablaze. When it was all over, two veterans had been shot to death, an eleven-week-old baby had died, an eight-year-old boy was partially blinded by gas, two police had fractured skulls, and a thousand veterans were injured by gas.

The hard, hard times, the inaction of the government in helping, the action of the government in dispersing war veterans—all had their effect on the election of November 1932. Democratic party candidate Franklin D. Roosevelt defeated Herbert Hoover overwhelmingly, took office in the spring of 1933, and began a program of reform legislation which became famous as the "New Deal." When a small veterans' march on Washington took place early in his administration, he greeted them and provided coffee; they met with one of his aides and went home. It was a sign of Roosevelt's approach.

The Roosevelt reforms went far beyond previous legislation. By giving help to people in need, they would meet two pressing needs: to reorganize capitalism in such a way as to overcome the crisis and stabilize the system; also, to head off the alarming growth of spontaneous rebellion in the early years of the Roosevelt administration—organization of tenants and the unemployed, movements of self-help, general strikes in several cities.

That first objective—to stabilize the system for its own protection—was most obvious in the major law of Roosevelt's first months in office, the National Recovery Act (NRA). It was designed to take control of the economy through a series of codes agreed on by management, labor, and the government, fixing prices and wages, limiting competition. From the first, the NRA was dominated by big businesses and served their interests. But where organized labor was strong, the NRA made some concessions to working people.

After the NRA had been operating for two years, the Supreme Court declared it unconstitutional, claiming it gave too much power to the president.

Also passed in the first months of the new administration, the AAA (Agricultural Adjustment Administration) was an attempt to organize agriculture. It favored the larger farmers as the NRA favored big business.

The TVA (Tennessee Valley Authority) was an unusual entrance of government into business—a government-owned network of dams and hydroelectric plants to control floods and produce electric power in the Tennessee Valley. It gave jobs to the unemployed, helped the consumer with lower electric rates, and in some respect deserved the accusation that it was "socialistic."

But the New Deal's organization of the economy was aimed mainly at stabilizing the economy, and secondly at giving enough help to the lower classes to keep them from turning a rebellion into a real revolution.

That rebellion was real when Roosevelt took office. Desperate people were not waiting for the government to help them; they were helping themselves, acting directly. All over the country, people organized spontaneously to stop evictions. In New York, in Chicago, in other cities—when word spread that someone was being evicted, a crowd would gather; the police would remove the furniture from the house, put it out in the street, and the crowd would bring the furniture back. The Communist party was active in organizing Workers Alliance groups in the cities. Mrs. Willye Jeffries, a black woman, told Studs Terkel about evictions:

> A lot of 'em was put out. They'd call and have the bailiffs come and sit them out, and as soon as they'd leave, we would put 'em back where they came out.... Take that stuff right on back up there. The men would connect those lights and go to the hardware and get gas pipe, and connect that stove back. Put the furniture back just like you had it, so it don't look like you been out the door.

Unemployed Councils were formed all over the country. One journalist described them:

> I find it is no secret that Communists organize Unemployed Councils in most cities and usually lead them, but the councils are organized democratically and the majority rules.... The Council's weapon is democratic force of numbers, and their function is to prevent evictions of the destitute, or if evicted to bring pressure to bear on the Relief Commission to find a new home; if an unemployed worker has his gas or his water turned off because he can't pay for it, to see the proper authorities; to see that the unemployed who are shoeless and clothesless get both; to eliminate through publicity and pressure discriminations between Negroes and white persons, or against the foreign born, in matters of relief...to march people down to relief headquarters and demand they be fed and clothed. Finally to provide legal defense for all unemployed arrested for joining parades, hunger marches, or attending union meetings.

People organized to help themselves, since business and government were not helping them in 1931 and 1932. In Seattle, the fishermen's union caught fish and exchanged them with people who picked fruit and vegetables, and those who cut wood exchanged that. By the end of 1932, there were 330 self-help organizations in thirty-seven states, with over 300,000 members. By early 1933, they seem to have collapsed; they were attempting too big a job in an economy that was more and more a shambles.

Perhaps the most remarkable example of self-help took place in the coal district of Pennsylvania, where teams of unemployed miners dug small mines on company property, mined coal, trucked it to cities, and sold it below the commercial rate. By 1934, "bootleg" coal was being produced by twenty thousand men using four thousand vehicles. When attempts were made to prosecute, local juries would not convict, local jailors would not imprison.

These were simple actions, taken out of practical need, but they had revolutionary possibilities. By taking direct action to meet their needs, working people were showing, without calling it that, a powerful class consciousness.

Were the New Dealers—Roosevelt and his advisers, the businessmen who supported him—also class-conscious? Did they understand that measures must be quickly taken, in 1933 and 1934, to give jobs, food baskets, relief, to prevent workers from concluding that their problems could be solved only by themselves? Perhaps, like the workers' class consciousness, it was a set of actions arising not from held theory, but from instinctive practical necessity.

It may have been such a consciousness that led to the legislation introduced in Congress in early 1934 to regulate labor disputes. The bill provided elections for union representation, a board to settle problems and handle grievances. Was this not exactly the kind of legislation to do away with the idea that the problems of the workers can be solved only by themselves? Big business thought it was too helpful to labor and opposed it. Roosevelt was cool to it. But in the year 1934 a series of labor outbursts suggested the need for legislative action.

A million and a half workers in different industries went on strike in 1934. That spring and summer, longshoremen on the West Coast, in a rank-and-file insurrection against their own union leadership as well as against the shippers, held a convention, demanded the abolition of the shape-up (a kind of early morning slave market where work gangs were chosen for the day), and went out on strike.

Two thousand miles of Pacific coastline were quickly tied up. The teamsters cooperated, refusing to truck cargo to the piers, and maritime workers joined the strike. When the police moved in to open the piers, the strikers resisted en masse, and two were killed by police gunfire. A mass funeral procession for the strikers brought together tens of thousands of supporters. And then a general strike was called in San Francisco, with 130,000 workers out, the city immobilized.

Five hundred special police were sworn in and forty-five hundred National Guardsmen assembled, with infantry, machine gun, tank and artillery units. The *Los Angeles Times* wrote:

> The situation in San Francisco is not correctly described by the phrase "general strike." What is actually in progress there is an insurrection, a Communist-inspired and led revolt against organized government. There is but one thing to be done—put down the revolt with any force necessary.

The pressure became too strong. There were the troops. There was the AFL pushing to end the strike. The longshoremen accepted a compromise settlement. But they had shown the potential of a general strike.

That same summer of 1934, a strike of teamsters in Minneapolis was supported by other working people, and soon nothing was moving in the city except milk, ice, and coal trucks given exemptions by the strikers. Farmers drove their products into town and sold them directly to the people in the city. The police attacked and two strikers were killed. Fifty thousand people attended a mass funeral. There was an enormous protest meeting and a march on City Hall. After a month, the employers gave in to the teamsters' demands.

In the fall of that same year, 1934, came the largest strike of all—325,000 textile workers in the South. They left the mills and set up flying squadrons in trucks and autos to move through the strike areas, picketing, battling guards, entering the mills, unbelting machinery. Here too, as in the other cases, the strike impetus came from the rank and file, against a reluctant union leadership at the top. The *New York Times* said: "The grave danger of the situation is that it will get completely out of the hands of the leaders."

Again, the machinery of the state was set in motion. Deputies and armed strikebreakers in South Carolina fired on pickets, killing seven, wounding twenty others. But the strike was spreading to New England. In Lowell, Massachusetts, twenty-five hundred textile workers rioted; in Saylesville, Rhode Island, a crowd of five thousand people defied state troopers who were armed with machine guns, and shut down the textile mill. In Woonsocket, Rhode Island, two thousand people, aroused because someone had been shot and killed by the National Guard, stormed through the town and closed the mill.

By September 18, 421,000 textile workers were on strike throughout the country. There were mass arrests, organizers were beaten, and the death toll rose to thirteen. Roosevelt now stepped in and set up a board of mediation, and the union called off the strike.

In the rural South, too, organizing took place, often stimulated by Communists, but nourished by the grievances of poor whites and blacks who were tenant farmers or farm laborers, always in economic difficulties but hit even harder by the depression. The Southern Tenant Farmers Union started in Arkansas, with black and white sharecroppers, and spread to other areas.

Roosevelt's AAA was not helping the poorest of farmers; in fact by encouraging farmers to plant less, it forced tenants and sharecroppers to leave the land. By 1935, of 6.8 million farmers, 2.8 million were tenants. The average income of a sharecropper was $312 a year. Farm laborers, moving from farm to farm, area to area, no land of their own, in 1933 were earning about $300 a year.

Black farmers were the worst off, and some were attracted to the strangers who began appearing in their area during the depression, suggesting they organize. Nate Shaw recalls, in Theodore Rosengarten's remarkable interview (*All God's Dangers*):

> And durin of the pressure years, a union begin to operate in this country, called it the Sharecroppers Union—that was a nice name, I thought...and I knowed what was goin on was a turnabout on the southern man, white and colored; it was somethin unusual. And I heard about it bein a organization for the poor class of people—that's just what I wanted to get into, too. I wanted to know the secrets of it enough that I could become in the knowledge of it....

Nate Shaw told of what happened when a black farmer who hadn't paid his debts was about to be dispossessed:

> The deputy said, "I'm goin to take all old Virgil Jones got this mornin."...
> I begged him not to do it, begged him. "You'll dispossess him of bein able to feed his family."

Nate Shaw, trying to stop a deputy sheriff from dispossessing a fellow farmer who hadn't paid his debts, was shot and wounded. Shaw then got his gun and fired back. He was arrested in late 1932, and served twelve years in an Alabama prison. His story is a tiny piece of the great unrecorded drama of the southern poor in those years of the Sharecroppers Union. Years after his release from prison, Nate Shaw spoke his mind on color and class:

> O, it's plain as your hand. The poor white man and the poor black man is sittin in the same saddle today—big dudes done branched em off that way. The control of a man, the controllin power, is in the hands of the rich man.... That class is standin together and the poor white man is out there on the colored list—I've caught that: ways and actions a heap of times speaks louder than words....

Hosea Hudson, a black man from rural Georgia, at the age of ten a plowhand, later an iron worker in Birmingham, was aroused by the case of the Scottsboro Boys in 1931 (nine black youths accused of raping two white girls and convicted on flimsy evidence by all-white juries). That year he joined the Communist party. In 1932 and 1933, he organized unemployed blacks in Birmingham. He recalls:

> Block committees would meet every week, had a regular meeting. We talked about the welfare question, what was happening, we read the *Daily Worker* and the *Southern Worker* to see what was going on about unemployed relief, what people doing in Cleveland…struggles in Chicago…or we talk about the latest developments in the Scottsboro case. We kept up, we was on top, so people always wanted to come cause we had something different to tell them every time.

In 1934 and 1935 hundreds of thousands of workers, left out of the tightly controlled, exclusive unions of the American Federation of Labor, began organizing in the new mass production industries—auto, rubber, packinghouse. The AFL could not ignore them; it set up a Committee for Industrial Organization to organize these workers outside of craft lines, by industry, all workers in a plant belonging to one union. This committee, headed by John Lewis, then broke away and became the CIO—the Congress of Industrial Organizations.

But it was rank-and-file strikes and insurgencies that pushed the union leadership, AFL and CIO, into action. A new kind of tactic began among rubber workers in Akron, Ohio, in the early thirties—the sit-down strike. The workers stayed in the plant instead of walking out, and this had clear advantages: they were directly blocking the use of strikebreakers; they did not have to act through union officials but were in direct control of the situation themselves; they did not have to walk outside in the cold and rain, but had shelter; they were not isolated, as in their work, or on the picket line; they were thousands under one roof, free to talk to one another, to form a community of struggle.

The idea spread through 1936. In December of that year began the longest sit-down strike of all, at Fisher Body plant #1 in Flint, Michigan. It started when two brothers were fired, and it lasted until February 1937. For forty days there was a community of two thousand strikers. "It was like war," one said. "The guys with me became my buddies." Committees organized recreation, information, classes, a postal service, sanitation. Courts were set up to deal with those who didn't take their turn washing dishes or who threw rubbish or smoked where it was prohibited or brought in liquor. The "punishment" consisted of extra duties; the ultimate punishment was expulsion from the plant. A restaurant owner across the street prepared three meals a day for two thousand strikers. There were classes in parliamentary procedure, public speaking, history of the labor movement. Graduate students at the University of Michigan gave courses in journalism and creative writing.

There were injunctions, but a procession of five thousand armed workers encircled the plant and there was no attempt to enforce the injunction. Police attacked with tear gas and the workers fought back with firehoses. Thirteen strikers were wounded by gunfire, but the police were driven back. The governor called out the National Guard. By this time the strike had spread to other General Motors plants. Finally there was a settlement, a six-month contract, leaving many questions unsettled but recognizing that from now on, the company would have to deal not with individuals but with a union.

In 1936 there were forty-eight sit-down strikes. In 1937 there were 477: electrical workers in St. Louis; shirt workers in Pulaski, Tennessee; broom workers in Pueblo, Colorado; trash collectors in Bridgeport, Connecticut; gravediggers in New Jersey; seventeen blind workers at the New York Guild for the Jewish Blind; prisoners in an Illinois penitentiary; and even thirty members of a National Guard company who had served in the Fisher Body sit-down, and now sat down themselves because they had not been paid.

The sit-downs were especially dangerous to the system because they were not controlled by the regular union leadership.

It was to stabilize the system in the face of labor unrest that the Wagner Act of 1935, setting up the National Labor Relations Board, had been passed. The wave of strikes in 1936, 1937, and 1938 made the need even more pressing. In Chicago, on Memorial Day, 1937, a strike at Republic Steel brought the police out, firing at a mass picket line of strikers, killing ten of them. Autopsies showed the bullets had hit the workers in the back as they were running away: this was the Memorial Day Massacre. But Republic Steel was organized, and so was Ford Motor Company, and the other huge plants in steel, auto, rubber, meatpacking, the electrical industry.

The Wagner Act was challenged by a steel corporation in the courts, but the Supreme Court found it constitutional—that the government could regulate interstate commerce, and that strikes hurt interstate commerce. From the trade unions' point of view, the new law was an aid to union organizing. From the government's point of view it was an aid to the stability of commerce.

Unions were not wanted by employers, but they were more controllable—more stabilizing for the system than the wildcat strikes, the factory occupations by the rank and file. In the spring of 1937, a *New York Times* article carried the headline "Unauthorized Sit-Downs Fought by CIO Unions."

Thus, two sophisticated ways of controlling direct labor action developed in the mid-thirties. First, the National Labor Relations Board would give unions legal status, listen to them, settling certain of their grievances. Thus it could moderate labor rebellion by channeling energy into elections—just as the constitutional system channeled possibly troublesome energy into voting. The NLRB would set limits in economic conflict as voting did in political conflict. And second, the workers' organization itself, the union, even a militant and aggressive union like the CIO, would channel the workers' insurrectionary energy into contracts, negotiations, union meetings, and try to minimize strikes, in order to build large, influential, even respectable organizations.

The history of those years seems to support the argument of Richard Cloward and Frances Piven, in their book *Poor People's Movements*, that labor won most during its spontaneous uprisings, before the unions were recognized or well organized: "Factory workers had their greatest influence, and were able to exact their most substantial concessions from government, during the Great Depression, in the years before they were organized into unions. Their power during the Depression was not rooted in organization, but in disruption."

Union membership rose enormously in the forties, during the Second World War (the CIO and AFL had over six million members each by 1945), but its power was less than before—its gains from the use of strikes kept getting whittled down. The members appointed to the NLRB were less sympathetic to labor, the Supreme Court declared sit-downs to be illegal, and state governments were passing laws to hamper strikes, picketing, boycotts.

The coming of World War II weakened the old labor militancy of the thirties because the war economy created millions of new jobs at higher wages. The New Deal had succeeded only in reducing unemployment from thirteen million to nine million. It was the war that put almost everyone to work, and the war did something else: patriotism, the push for unity of all classes against enemies overseas, made it harder to mobilize anger against the corporations. During the war, the CIO and AFL pledged to call no strikes.

Still, the grievances of workers were such—wartime "controls" meant their wages were being controlled better than prices—that they felt impelled to engage in many wildcat strikes: there were more strikes in 1944 than in any previous year in American history.

The thirties and forties showed more clearly than before the dilemma of working people in the United States. The system responded to workers' rebellions by finding new forms of control—internal control by their own organizations as well as outside control by law and force. But along with the new controls came new concessions. These concessions didn't solve basic problems; for many people they solved nothing. But they helped enough people to create an atmosphere of progress and improvement, to restore some faith in the system.

The minimum wage of 1938, which established the forty-hour week and outlawed child labor, left many people out of its provisions and set very low minimum wages (twenty-five cents an hour the first year). But it was enough to dull the edge of resentment. Housing was built for only a small percentage of the people who needed it, but the sight of federally subsidized housing projects, playgrounds, vermin-free apartments, replacing dilapidated tenements, was refreshing. The TVA suggested exciting possibilities for regional planning to give jobs, improve areas, and provide cheap power, with local instead of national control. The Social Security Act gave retirement benefits and unemployment insurance, and matched state funds for mothers and dependent children—but it excluded farmers, domestic workers, and old people, and offered no health insurance. Corporations were much more secure.

The New Deal gave federal money to put thousands of writers, artists, actors, and musicians to work—in a Federal Theatre Project, a Federal Writers Project, a Federal Art Project: murals were painted on public buildings; plays were put on for working-class audiences who had never seen a play; hundreds of books and pamphlets were written and published. People heard a symphony for the first time. It was an exciting flowering of arts for the people, such as had never happened before in American history, and which has not been duplicated since. But in 1939, with the country more stable and the New Deal reform impulse weakened, programs to subsidize the arts were eliminated.

When the New Deal was over, capitalism remained intact. The rich still controlled the nation's wealth, as well as its laws, courts, police, newspapers, churches, colleges. Enough help had been given to enough people to make Roosevelt a hero to millions, but the same system that had brought depression and crisis—the system of waste, of inequality, of concern for profit over human need—remained.

For black people, the New Deal was psychologically encouraging (Mrs. Roosevelt was sympathetic; some blacks got posts in the administration), but most blacks were ignored by the New Deal programs. As tenant farmers, as farm laborers, as migrants, as domestic workers, they didn't qualify for unemployment insurance, minimum wages, social security, or farm subsidies. Roosevelt, careful not to offend southern white politicians whose political support he needed, did not push a bill against lynching. Blacks and whites were segregated in the armed forces.

And black workers were discriminated against in getting jobs. They were the last hired, the first fired. Only when A. Philip Randolph, head of the Sleeping-Car Porters Union, threatened a massive march on Washington in 1941 would Roosevelt agree to sign an executive order establishing a Fair Employment Practices Committee. But the FEPC had no enforcement powers and changed little.

Black Harlem, with all the New Deal reforms, remained as it was. There 350,000 people lived, 233 persons per acre compared with 133 for the rest of Manhattan. In twenty-five years, its population had multiplied six times. Ten thousand families lived in rat-infested cellars and basements. Tuberculosis was common. Perhaps half of the married women worked as domestics. They traveled to the Bronx and gathered on street corners—"slave markets," they were called—to be hired. Prostitution crept in. In Harlem Hospital in 1932, proportionately twice as many people died as in Bellevue Hospital, which was in the white area downtown.

On March 19, 1935, even as the New Deal reforms were being passed, Harlem exploded. Ten thousand Negroes swept through the streets, destroying the property of white merchants. Seven hundred policemen moved in and brought order. Two blacks were killed.

In the mid-thirties, a young black poet named Langston Hughes wrote a poem, "Let America Be America Again":

> ...I am the poor white, fooled and pushed apart,
> I am the Negro bearing slavery's scars.
> I am the red man driven from the land,
> I am the immigrant clutching the hope I seek—
> And finding only the same old stupid plan.
> Of dog eat dog, of mighty crush the weak....
>
> O, let America be America again—
> The land that never has been yet—

To white Americans of the thirties, however, North and South, blacks were invisible. Only the radicals made an attempt to break the racial barriers: Socialists, Trotskyists, Communists most of all. The CIO, influenced by the Communists, was organizing blacks in the mass production industries. Blacks were still being used as strikebreakers, but now there were also attempts to bring blacks and whites together against their common enemy.

There was no great feminist movement in the thirties. But many women became involved in the labor organizing of those years. A Minnesota poet, Meridel LeSeuer, was thirty-four when the great teamsters' strike tied up Minneapolis in 1934. She became active in it, and later described her experiences:

> I have never been in a strike before.... The truth is I was afraid.... "Do you need any help?" I said eagerly.... We kept on pouring thousands of cups of coffee, feeding thousands of men...I saw them taking men out of cars and putting them on the hospital cots, on the floor.... Tuesday, the day of the funeral, one thousand more militia were massed downtown. It was over ninety in the shade. I went to the funeral parlors and thousands of men and women were massed there waiting in the terrific sun. I went over and stood near them. I didn't know whether I could march. I didn't like marching in parades.... Three women drew me in. "We want all to march," they said gently. "Come with us."...

Sylvia Woods spoke to Alice and Staughton Lynd years later about her experiences in the thirties as a laundry worker and union organizer:

> You have to tell people things they can see. Then they'll say, "Oh, I never thought of that" or "I have never seen it like that."...Like Tennessee. He hated black people. A poor sharecropper.... He danced with a black woman.... So I have seen people change. This is the faith you've got to have in people.

Many Americans began to change their thinking in those days of crisis and rebellion. In Europe, Hitler was on the march. Across the Pacific, Japan was invading China. The Western empires were being threatened by new ones. For the United States, war was not far off.

Exercises

1. Why did the Seattle general strike end after five days?

2. What did the Seattle general strike symbolize to the business and government elite?

3. Why were there so many strikes directly after the end of World War I?

4. Why is the depiction of the 1920s as prosperous and "roaring" a misleading one?

5. Why might working-class women not celebrate the passage of the Nineteenth Amendment?

6. How did Fiorella La Guardia behave differently from other political figures in the 1920s?

7. Would you have voted for the Mellon Plan? Why or why not?

8. Why was a communist party not organized in the United States until after 1919? (Why did socialism not emerge in America until after the Civil War?)

9. Why did mill owners move their factories to the South in the 1920s?

10. What was Galbraith's explanation of the American economy collapse in 1929? What was the socialist's explanation? What was Henry Ford's? What information, in addition to what Zinn provides, would you want to have in order to decide which theory to support?

11. What percentage of the workforce was laid off during the Great Depression? What happened to these workers?

12. What series of historical events did Steinbeck's *Grapes of Wrath* chronicle?

13. What was the direct action or grassroots political activity that the hungry and homeless engaged in as a response to their condition during the depression? What was their cultural response? Their electoral response?

14. What were the demands of the Bonus Army? What was Hoover's response to those demands? How might Hoover have handled the situation differently?

15. What evidence does Zinn use (and how does he use it) to support his argument that the New Deal legislation was intended "to reorganize capitalism in such a way as to overcome the crisis and stabilize the system; also, to head off the alarming growth of spontaneous rebellion...." Include (but do not necessarily limit yourself to) the following in your answer: NRA; AAA; Wagner Act; Minimum Wage Act of 1938; Social Security Act; WPA (theater, writer, and arts projects); and FEPC.

16. Was the purpose of the Unemployment Council consistent with the structure of its organization?

17. Does Zinn believe that workers and capitalists were consciously acting according to the interests of their class?

18. Why would the AFL work hard to end the longshoremen-inspired general strike of 1934?

19. "The grave danger of the situation is that it will get completely out of the hands of the leaders." To whom was this possibility so dangerous, and why?

20. According to Hosea Hudson, why did people want to attend block committee meetings?

21. What led to the creation of the CIO (Congress of Industrial Organizations)?

22. What were the tactical advantages of the sit-down strike over a

walkout? What were the disadvantages?

23. How were the workers able to sustain the strike in Flint, Michigan, for three winter months?

24. Did World War II function to weaken labor's strength in the same way World War I did?

25. What is Langston Hughes's argument in the section of his poem "Let America Be America Again," quoted by Zinn?

26. *Debate Resolution*: The more government does, the less people do to help themselves.

27. *Debate Resolution*: Communists were anti-American.

28. *Draw a map* which includes the following: Seattle, Oklahoma; California; Arkansas; Gastonia, North Carolina; Washington, D.C.; the area controlled by the TVA; Detroit; Chicago; San Francisco; Flint, Michigan; Akron, Ohio; Harlem.

Chapter 16

A People's War?

By certain evidence, World War II was the most popular war the United States had ever fought. Never had a greater proportion of the country participated in a war: 18 million served in the armed forces, 10 million overseas; 25 million workers gave of their pay envelope regularly for war bonds. But could this be considered a manufactured support, since all the power of the nation—not only of the government, but the press, the church, and even the chief radical organizations—was behind the calls for all-out war? Was there an undercurrent of reluctance; were there unpublicized signs of resistance?

It was a war against an enemy of unspeakable evil. Hitler's Germany was extending totalitarianism, racism, militarism, and overt aggressive warfare beyond what an already cynical world had experienced. And yet, did the governments conducting this war—England, the United States, the Soviet Union—represent something significantly different, so that their victory would be a blow to imperialism, racism, totalitarianism, militarism, in the world?

Would the behavior of the United States during the war—in military action abroad, in treatment of minorities at home—be in keeping with a "people's war"? Would the country's wartime policies respect the rights of ordinary people everywhere to life, liberty, and the pursuit of happiness? And would postwar America, in its policies at home and overseas, exemplify the values for which the war was supposed to have been fought?

These questions deserve thought. At the time of World War II, the atmosphere was too dense with war fervor to permit them to be aired.

For the United States to step forward as a defender of helpless countries matched its image in American high school history textbooks, but not its record in world affairs. It had instigated a war with Mexico and taken half of that country. It had pretended to help Cuba win freedom from Spain, and then planted itself in Cuba with a military base, investments, and rights of intervention. It had seized Hawaii, Puerto Rico, and Guam, and fought a brutal war to subjugate the Filipinos. It had "opened" Japan to its trade with gunboats and threats. It had declared an "Open Door" policy in China as a means of assuring that the United States would have opportunities equal to other imperial powers in exploiting China. It had sent troops to Peking with other nations, to assert Western supremacy in China, and kept them there for over thirty years.

While demanding an open door in China, it had insisted (with the Monroe Doctrine and many military interventions) on a "closed door" in Latin America—that is, closed to everyone but the United States. It had engineered a revolution against Colombia and created the "independent" state of Panama in order to build and control the canal. It sent five thousand marines to Nicaragua in 1926 to counter a revolution, and kept a force there for seven years. It intervened in the Dominican Republic for the fourth time in 1916 and kept troops there for eight years. It intervened for the second time in Haiti in 1915 and kept troops there for nineteen years. Between 1900 and 1933, the United States intervened in Cuba four times, in Nicaragua twice, in Panama six times, in Guatemala once, in Honduras seven times. By 1924 the finances of half of the twenty Latin American states were being directed to some extent by the United States. By 1935, over half of U.S. steel and cotton exports were being sold in Latin America.

Just before World War I ended, in 1918, an American force of seven thousand landed at Vladivostok as part of an Allied intervention in Russia, and remained until early 1920. Five thousand more troops were landed at Archangel, another Russian port, also as part of an Allied expeditionary force, and stayed for almost a year. The State Department told Congress: "All these operations were to offset effects of the Bolshevik revolution in Russia."

In short, if the entrance of the United States into World War II was (as so many Americans believed at the time, observing the Nazi invasions) to defend the principle of nonintervention in the affairs of other countries, the nation's record cast doubt on its ability to uphold that principle.

What seemed clear at the time was that the United States was a

democracy with certain liberties, while Germany was a dictatorship perse-
cuting its Jewish minority, imprisoning dissidents, whatever their religion,
while proclaiming the supremacy of the Nordic "race." However, blacks,
looking at anti-Semitism in Germany, might not see their own situation in
the U.S. as much different. And the United States had done little about
Hitler's policies of persecution. Indeed, it had joined England and France
in appeasing Hitler throughout the thirties. Roosevelt and his secretary of
state, Cordell Hull, were hesitant to criticize publicly Hitler's anti-Semitic
policies; when a resolution was introduced in the Senate in January 1934
asking the Senate and the president to express "surprise and pain" at what
the Germans were doing to the Jews and to ask restoration of Jewish
rights, the State Department made sure the resolution was buried.

When Mussolini's Italy invaded Ethiopia in 1935, the U.S. declared an
embargo on munitions but let American businesses send oil to Italy in
huge quantities, which was essential to Italy's carrying on the war. When a
Fascist rebellion took place in Spain in 1936 against the elected socialist-
liberal government, the Roosevelt administration sponsored a neutrality
act that had the effect of shutting off help to the Spanish government while
Hitler and Mussolini gave critical aid to Franco.

Was this simply poor judgment, an unfortunate error? Or was it the
logical policy of a government whose main interest was not stopping Fascism but advancing the imperial interests of the United States? For those
interests, in the thirties, an anti-Soviet policy seemed best. Later, when
Japan and Germany threatened U.S. world interests, a pro-Soviet, anti-
Nazi policy became preferable. Roosevelt was as much concerned to end
the oppression of Jews as Lincoln was to end slavery during the Civil War;
their priority in policy (whatever their personal compassion for victims of
persecution) was not minority rights, but national power.

It was not Hitler's attacks on the Jews that brought the United States
into World War II, any more than the enslavement of four million blacks
brought Civil War in 1861. Italy's attack on Ethiopia, Hitler's invasion of
Austria, his takeover of Czechoslovakia, his attack on Poland—none of
those events caused the United States to enter the war, although Roosevelt
did begin to give important aid to England.

What brought the United States fully into the war was the Japanese
attack on the American naval base at Pearl Harbor, Hawaii, on December
7, 1941. Surely it was not the humane concern for Japan's bombing of
civilians that led to Roosevelt's outraged call for war—Japan's attack on
China in 1937, her bombing of civilians at Nanking, had not provoked the

United States to war. It was the Japanese attack on a link in the American Pacific empire that did it.

So long as Japan remained a well-behaved member of that imperial club of Great Powers who—in keeping with the open-door policy—were sharing the exploitation of China, the United States did not object. It had exchanged notes with Japan in 1917 saying "the Government of the United States recognizes that Japan has special interests in China." In 1928, according to Akira Iriye (*After Imperialism*), American consuls in China supported the coming of Japanese troops. It was when Japan threatened potential U.S. markets by its attempted takeover of China, but especially as it moved toward the tin, rubber, and oil of Southeast Asia, that the United States became alarmed and took those measures which led to the Japanese attack: a total embargo on scrap iron, a total embargo on oil in the summer of 1941.

Once joined with England and Russia in the war (Germany and Italy declared war on the United States right after Pearl Harbor), did the behavior of the United States show that her war aims were humanitarian, or centered on power and profit? Was she fighting the war to end the control by some nations over others or to make sure the controlling nations were friends of the United States?

In August 1941, Roosevelt and Churchill met off the coast of Newfoundland and released to the world the Atlantic Charter, setting forth noble goals for the postwar world, saying their countries "seek no aggrandizement, territorial or other," and that they respected "the right of all peoples to choose the form of government under which they will live." The charter was celebrated as declaring the right of nations to self-determination.

Two weeks before the Atlantic Charter, however, the acting U.S. secretary of state, Sumner Welles, had assured the French government that they could keep their empire intact after the end of the war. In late 1942, Roosevelt's personal representative assured French General Henri Giraud: "It is thoroughly understood that French sovereignty will be re-established as soon as possible throughout all the territory, metropolitan or colonial, over which flew the French flag in 1939."

In the headlines were the battles and troop movements: the invasion of North Africa in 1942, Italy in 1943, the massive, dramatic cross-Channel invasion of German-occupied France in 1944, the bitter battles as Germany was pushed back toward and over her frontiers, the increasing bombardment by the British and American air forces. And, at the same time, the Russian victories over the Nazi armies (the Russians, by the time of the cross-Channel invasion, had driven the Germans out of Russia, and were engaging 80 percent of the German troops). In the Pacific, in 1943 and 1944, there was the island-by-island move of American forces toward Japan, finding closer and closer bases for the thunderous bombardment of Japanese cities.

Quietly, behind the headlines in battles and bombings, American diplomats and businessmen worked hard to make sure that when the war ended, American economic power would be second to none in the world. United States business would penetrate areas that up to this time had been dominated by England. The open-door policy of equal access would be extended from Asia to Europe, meaning that the United States intended to push England aside and move in.

That is what happened to the Middle East and its oil. Saudi Arabia was the largest oil pool in the Middle East. Its king, Ibn Saud, was a guest of President Roosevelt on a U.S. cruiser in early 1945.

Roosevelt then wrote to Ibn Saud, promising the United States would not change its Palestine policy without consulting the Arabs. In later years, the concern for oil would constantly compete with political concern for the Jewish state in the Middle East, but at this point, oil seemed more important.

With British imperial power collapsing during World War II, the United States was ready to move in. Before the war was over, the administration was planning the outlines of the new international economic order, based on partnership between government and big business.

The poet Archibald MacLeish, then an assistant secretary of state, spoke critically of what he saw in the postwar world: "As things are now going, the peace we will make, the peace we seem to be making, will be a peace of oil, a peace of gold, a peace of shipping, a peace, in brief...without moral purpose or human interest...."

During the war, England and the United States set up the International Monetary Fund to regulate international exchanges of currency; voting would be proportional to capital contributed, so American dominance would be assured. The International Bank for Reconstruction and Development was set up, supposedly to help reconstruct war-destroyed areas, but one of its first objectives was, in its own words, "to promote foreign investment."

The economic aid countries would need after the war was already seen in political terms: Averell Harriman, ambassador to Russia, said in early 1944: "Economic assistance is one of the most effective weapons at our disposal to influence European political events in the direction we desire...."

The creation of the United Nations during the war was presented to the world as international cooperation to prevent future wars. But the U.N. was dominated by the Western imperial countries—the United States, England, and France—and a new imperial power, with military bases and powerful influence in Eastern Europe—the Soviet Union. An important conservative Republican senator, Arthur Vandenburg, wrote in his diary about the United Nations Charter:

> The striking thing about it is that it is so conservative from a nationalist standpoint. It is based virtually on a four-power alliance.... This is anything but a wild-eyed internationalist dream of a world State.... I am deeply impressed (and surprised) to find Hull so carefully guarding our American veto in his scheme of things.

The plight of Jews in German-occupied Europe, which many people thought was at the heart of the war against the Axis, was not a chief concern of Roosevelt. Henry Feingold's research (*The Politics of Rescue*) shows that, while the Jews were being put in camps and the process of annihilation was beginning that would end in the horrifying extermination of six million Jews and millions of non-Jews, Roosevelt failed to take steps that might have saved thousands of lives. He did not see it as a high priority; he left it to the State Department, and in the State Department anti-Semitism and a cold bureaucracy became obstacles to action.

Was the war being fought to establish that Hitler was wrong in his ideas of white Nordic supremacy over "inferior" races? The United States' armed forces were segregated by race. When troops were jammed onto the *Queen Mary* in early 1945 to go to combat duty in the European theater, the blacks were stowed down in the depths of the ship near the engine room, as far as possible from the fresh air of the deck, in a bizarre reminder of the slave voyages of old.

The Red Cross, with government approval, separated the blood donations of black and white. It was, ironically, a black physician named Charles Drew who developed the blood-bank system. He was put in charge of the wartime donations, and then fired when he tried to end blood segregation. Despite the urgent need for wartime labor, blacks were still being discriminated against for jobs. A spokesman for a West Coast aviation plant said: "The Negro will be considered only as janitors and in other similar capacities.... Regardless of their training as aircraft workers, we will not employ them." Roosevelt never did anything to enforce the orders of the Fair Employment Practices Commission he had set up.

The Fascist nations were notorious in their insistence that the woman's place was in the home. Yet, the war against Fascism, although it utilized women in defense industries where they were desperately needed, took no special steps to change the subordinate role of women. The War Manpower Commission, despite the large numbers of women in war work, kept women off its policymaking bodies. A report of the Women's Bureau of the Department of Labor, by its director, Mary Anderson, said the War Manpower Commission had "doubts and uneasiness" about "what was then regarded as a developing attitude of militancy or a crusading spirit on the part of women leaders...."

In one of its policies, the United States came close to direct duplication of Fascism. This was in its treatment of the Japanese-Americans living on the West Coast. After the Pearl Harbor attack, anti-Japanese hysteria spread in the government. One congressman said: "I'm for catching every Japanese in America, Alaska and Hawaii now and putting them in concentration camps.... Damn them! Let's get rid of them!"

Franklin D. Roosevelt did not share this frenzy, but he calmly signed Executive Order 9066, in February 1942, giving the army the power, without warrants or indictments or hearings, to arrest every Japanese-American on the West Coast—110,000 men, women, and children—to take them from their homes, transport them to camps far into the interior, and keep them there under prison conditions. Three-fourths of these were *Nisei*—children born in the United States of Japanese parents and therefore American citizens. The other fourth—the *Issei*, born in Japan—were barred by law from becoming citizens. In 1944 the Supreme Court upheld the forced evacuation on the grounds of military necessity.

The Japanese remained in those camps for over three years. There were strikes, petitions, mass meetings, refusal to sign loyalty oaths, riots aginst the camp authorities. The Japanese Michi Weglyn was a young girl when her family experienced evacuation and detention. She tells(*Years of Infamy*) of bungling in the evacuation, of misery, but also of resistance.

It was a war waged by a government whose chief beneficiary—despite volumes of reforms—was a wealthy elite. By 1941 three-fourths of the value of military contracts were handled by fifty-six large corporations. Of $1 billion spent on scientific research in industry, $400 million went to ten large corporations.

Although twelve million workers were organized in the CIO and

AFL, labor was in a subordinate position. Labor-management committees were set up in five thousand factories, as a gesture toward industrial democracy, but they acted mostly as disciplinary groups for absentee workers, and devices for increasing production.

Despite the overwhelming atmosphere of patriotism and total dedication to winning the war, despite the no-strike pledges of the AFL and CIO, many of the nation's workers, frustrated by the freezing of wages while business profits rocketed skyward, went on strike. During the war, there were 14,000 strikes, involving 6,770,000 workers, more than in any comparable period in American history. In 1944 alone, a million workers were on strike, in the mines, in the steel mills, in the auto and transportation equipment industries. When the war ended, the strikes continued in record numbers—3 million on strike in the first half of 1946.

Beneath the noise of enthusiastic patriotism, there were many people who thought war was wrong, even in the circumstances of Fascist aggression. Out of 10 million drafted for the armed forces during World War II, only 43,000 refused to fight. Many more did not show up for the draft at all. The government lists about 350,000 cases of draft evasion. And this in the face of an American community almost unanimously for the war.

The literature that followed World War II, James Jones's *From Here to Eternity*, Joseph Heller's *Catch-22*, and Norman Mailer's *The Naked and the Dead*, captured the GI anger against the army "brass." In *The Naked and the Dead*, the soldiers talk in battle, and one of them says: "The only thing wrong with this Army is it never lost a war."

> Toglio was shocked. "You think we ought to lose this one?"
> Red found himself carried away. "What have I against the goddam Japs? You think I care if they keep this fuggin jungle? What's it to me if Cummings gets another star?"
> "General Cummings, he's a good man," Martinez said.
> "There ain't a good officer in the world," Red stated.

There seemed to be widespread indifference, even hostility, on the part of the Negro community to the war despite the attempts of Negro newspapers and Negro leaders to mobilize black sentiment. A black journalist wrote: "The Negro...is angry, resentful, and utterly apathetic about the war. 'Fight for what?' he is asking."

A student at a Negro college told his teacher: "The Army jim-crows us. The Navy lets us serve only as messmen. The Red Cross refuses our blood. Employers and labor unions shut us out. Lynchings continue. We are disenfranchised, jim-crowed, spat upon. What more could Hitler do than that?"

NAACP leader Walter White repeated this to a black audience of several thousand people in the Midwest, thinking they would disapprove, but instead, as he recalled: "To my surprise and dismay the audience burst into such applause that it took me some thirty or forty seconds to quiet it."

But there was no organized Negro opposition to the war. In fact, there was little organized opposition from any source. The Communist party was enthusiastically in support. The Socialist party was divided, unable to make a clear statement one way or the other.

A few small anarchist and pacifist groups refused to back the war. The Women's International League for Peace and Freedom said: "…war between nations or classes or races cannot permanently settle conflicts or heal the wounds that brought them into being." The *Catholic Worker* wrote: "We are still pacifists.…"

The difficulty of merely calling for "peace" in a world of capitalism, Fascism, Communism—dynamic ideologies, aggressive actions—troubled some pacifists. They began to speak of "revolutionary nonviolence." A. J. Muste of the Fellowship of Reconciliation said that the world was in the midst of a revolution, and those against violence must take revolutionary action, but without violence. A movement of revolutionary pacifism would have to "make effective contacts with oppressed and minority groups such as Negroes, share-croppers, industrial workers."

Only one organized socialist group opposed the war unequivocally. This was the Socialist Workers Party. In Minneapolis in 1943, eighteen members of the party were convicted for violating the Smith Act, which made it a crime to join any group that advocated "the overthrow of government by force and violence." They were sentenced to prison terms, and the Supreme Court refused to review their case.

A few voices continued to insist that the real war was inside each nation: Dwight Macdonald's wartime magazine *Politics* presented, in early 1945, an article by the French worker-philosopher Simone Weil:

> Whether the mask is labelled Fascism, Democracy, or Dictatorship of the Proletariat, our great adversary remains the Apparatus—the bureaucracy, the police, the military.… [T]he worst betrayal will always be to subordinate ourselves to this Apparatus, and to trample underfoot, in its service, all human values in ourselves and in others.

Still, the vast bulk of the American population was mobilized, in the army, and in civilian life, to fight the war, and the atmosphere of war enveloped more and more Americans. Public opinion polls show large majorities of soldiers favoring the draft for the postwar period. Hatred against the enemy, against the Japanese particularly, became widespread. Racism was clearly at work. *Time* magazine, reporting the battle of Iwo Jima, said: "The ordinary unreasoning Jap is ignorant. Perhaps he is human. Nothing...indicates it."

So, there was a mass base of support for what became the heaviest bombardment of civilians ever undertaken in any war: the aerial attacks on German and Japanese cities.

Italy had bombed cities in the Ethiopian war; Italy and Germany had bombed civilians in the Spanish civil war; at the start of World War II German planes dropped bombs on Rotterdam in Holland, Coventry in England, and elsewhere. Roosevelt had described these as "inhuman barbarism that has profoundly shocked the conscience of humanity."

These German bombings were very small compared with the British and American bombings of German cities. In January 1943 the Allies met at Casablanca and agreed on large-scale air attacks to achieve "the destruction and dislocation of the German military, industrial and economic system and the undermining of the morale of the German people to the point where their capacity for armed resistance is fatally weakened."

And so, the saturation bombing of German cities began—with thousand-plane raids on Cologne, Essen, Frankfurt, Hamburg. The English flew at night with no pretense of aiming at "military" targets; the Americans flew in the daytime and pretended precision, but bombing from high altitudes made that impossible. The climax of this terror bombing was the bombing of Dresden in early 1945, in which the tremendous heat generated by the bombs created a vacuum into which fire leaped swiftly in a great firestorm through the city. More than 100,000 died in Dresden.

The bombing of Japanese cities continued the strategy of saturation bombing to destroy civilian morale; one nighttime firebombing of Tokyo took 80,000 lives. And then, on August 6, 1945, came the lone American plane in the sky over Hiroshima, dropping the first atomic bomb, leaving perhaps 100,000 Japanese dead, and tens of thousands more slowly dying from radiation poisoning. Twelve U.S. navy fliers in the Hiroshima city jail were killed in the bombing, a fact that the U.S. government has never officially acknowledged. Three days later, a second atomic bomb was dropped on the city of Nagasaki, with perhaps 50,000 killed.

The justification for these atrocities was that this would end the war quickly, making an invasion of Japan unnecessary. Such an invasion would cost a huge number of lives, the government said—a million, according to Secretary of State Byrnes; half a million, Truman claimed was the figure given him by Gen. George Marshall. These estimates of invasion losses were not realistic and seem to have been pulled out of the air to justify bombings that, as their effects became known, horrified more and more people.

Japan, by August 1945, was in desperate shape and ready to surrender. *New York Times* military analyst Hanson Baldwin wrote, shortly after the war: "The enemy, in a military sense, was in a hopeless strategic position by the time the Potsdam demand for unconditional surrender was made on July 26. Such then, was the situation when we wiped out Hiroshima and Nagasaki. Need we have done it? No one can, of course, be positive, but the answer is almost certainly negative."

The United States Strategic Bombing Survey, set up by the War Department in 1944 to study the results of aerial attacks in the war, interviewed hundreds of Japanese civilian and military leaders after Japan surrendered, and reported just after the war: "...certainly prior to 31 December 1945, and in all probability prior to 1 November 1945, Japan would have surrendered even if the atomic bombs had not been dropped, even if Russia had not entered the war, and even if no invasion had been planned or contemplated."

But could American leaders have known this in August 1945? The answer is, clearly, yes. The Japanese code had been broken, and Japan's messages were being intercepted. It was known the Japanese had instructed their ambassador in Moscow to work on peace negotiations with the Allies. On July 13, Foreign Minister Shigenori Togo wired his ambassador in Moscow: "Unconditional surrender is the only obstacle to peace...."

If only the Americans had not insisted on unconditional surrender—that is, if they were willing to accept one condition to the surrender, that the emperor, a holy figure to the Japanese, remain in place—the Japanese would have agreed to stop the war. (In fact, when the war ended, the emperor was allowed to remain.)

Why did the United States not take that small step to save both American and Japanese lives? Was it because too much money and effort had been invested in the atomic bomb not to drop it? Or was it, as British scientist P. M. S. Blackett suggested (*Fear, War, and the Bomb*) that the United States was anxious to drop the bomb before the Russians entered the war against Japan?

The Russians had secretly agreed (they were officially not at war with Japan) they would come into the war ninety days after the end of the European war. That turned out to be May 8, and so, on August 8, the Russians were due to declare war on Japan. But by then the big bomb had been dropped, and the next day a second one would be dropped on Nagasaki; the Japanese would surrender to the United States, not the Russians, and the United States would be the occupier of postwar Japan. A diary entry for July 28, 1945, by Secretary of the Navy James Forrestal, described Secretary of State James F. Byrnes as "most anxious to get the Japanese affair over with before the Russians got in."

Truman had said, "The world will note that the first atomic bomb was dropped on Hiroshima, a military base. That was because we wished in this first attack to avoid, insofar as possible, the killing of civilians." It was a preposterous statement. Those 100,000 killed in Hiroshima were almost all civilians. The U.S. Strategic Bombing Survey said in its official report: "Hiroshima and Nagasaki were chosen as targets because of their concentration of activities and population."

The dropping of the second bomb on Nagasaki seems to have been scheduled in advance, and no one has ever been able to explain why it was dropped. Was it because this was a plutonium bomb whereas the Hiroshima bomb was a uranium bomb? Were the dead and irradiated of Nagasaki victims of a scientific experiment? Among the Nagasaki dead were probably American prisoners of war. An army report warned of this, but the plan remained unchanged.

True, the war then ended quickly. Italy had been defeated a year earlier. Germany had recently surrendered, crushed primarily by the armies of the Soviet Union on the Eastern Front, aided by the Allied armies on the West. Now Japan surrendered. The Fascist powers were destroyed.

But what about fascism—as idea, as reality? Were its essential elements—militarism, racism, imperialism—now gone? Or were they absorbed into the already poisoned bones of the victors?

The victors were the Soviet Union and the United States (also England, France, and Nationalist China, but they were weak). Both these countries now went to work, under the cover of "socialism" on one side, and "democracy" on the other, to carve out their own empires of influence. They proceeded to share and contest with one another the domination of the world, to build military machines far greater than the Fascist countries had built, to control the destinies of more countries than Hitler, Mussolini, and Japan had been able to do.

They also acted to control their own populations, each country with its own techniques—crude in the Soviet Union, sophisticated in the United States—to make their rule secure.

The war brought big gains in corporate profits, but it also brought higher prices for farmers, higher wages, enough prosperity for enough of the population to assure against the rebellions that so threatened the thirties.

It was an old lesson learned by governments: that war solves problems of control. Charles E. Wilson, the president of General Electric Corporation, was so happy about the wartime situation that he suggested a continuing alliance between business and the military for "a permanent war economy."

That is what happened. The American public was war-weary, but the Truman administration (Roosevelt had died in April 1945) worked to create an atmosphere of crisis and cold war. True, the rivalry with the Soviet Union was real—that country, which had come out of the war with its economy wrecked and 20 million people dead, was making an astounding comeback, rebuilding its industry, regaining military strength. The Truman administration, however, presented the Soviet Union as not just a rival but an immediate threat.

In a series of moves abroad and at home, it established a climate of fear—a hysteria about Communism—which would steeply escalate the military budget and stimulate the economy with war-related orders. This combination of policies would permit more aggressive actions abroad, more repressive actions at home.

Revolutionary movements in Europe and Asia were described to the American public as examples of Soviet expansionism—thus recalling the indignation against Hitler's aggressions.

In Greece, under a right-wing dictatorship, opponents of the regime were jailed, and trade union leaders removed. A left-wing guerrilla movement began to grow. Great Britain said it could not handle the rebellion and asked the United States to come in. As a State Department officer said later: "Great Britain had within the hour handed the job of world leadership...to the United States."

The United States responded with the Truman Doctrine, the name given to a speech Truman gave to Congress in the spring of 1947, in which he asked for $400 million in military and economic aid to Greece and Turkey. Truman said the U.S. must help "free peoples who are resisting attempted subjugation by armed minorities or by outside pressures." The rhetoric was about freedom, but the U.S. was concerned about Greece's proximity to Middle East oil.

With U.S. military aid, the rebellion was defeated by 1949. United States economic and military aid continued to the Greek government.

Investment capital from Esso, Dow Chemical, Chrysler, and other U.S. corporations flowed into Greece. But illiteracy, poverty, and starvation remained widespread there. The U.S. had succeeded in keeping in power a brutal military dictatorship.

In China, a revolution was already under way when World War II ended, led by a Communist movement with enormous mass support. A Red Army, which had fought against the Japanese, now fought to oust the corrupt dictatorship of Chiang Kai-shek, which was supported by the United States but which, according to the State Department's own white paper on China, had lost the confidence of its own troops and its own people. In January 1949, Chinese Communist forces moved into Peking, the civil war was over, and China was in the hands of a revolutionary movement, the closest thing, in the long history of that ancient country, to a people's government, independent of outside control.

The United States was trying, in the postwar decade, to create a national consensus of conservatives and liberals, Republicans and Democrats, around the policies of cold war and anti-Communism. Such a coalition could best be created by a liberal Democratic president, whose aggressive policy abroad would be supported by conservatives, and whose welfare programs at home (Truman's "Fair Deal") would be attractive to liberals. In 1950, there came an event that speeded the formation of the liberal-conservative consensus—Truman's undeclared war in Korea.

Korea, occupied by Japan for thirty-five years, was liberated from Japan after World War II and divided into North Korea, a socialist dictatorship, part of the Soviet sphere of influence, and South Korea, a right-wing dictatorship, in the American sphere. There had been threats back and forth between the two Koreas, and when on June 25, 1950, North Korean armies moved southward across the 38th parallel in an invasion of South Korea, the United Nations, dominated by the United States, asked its members to help "repel the armed attack." Truman ordered the American armed forces to help South Korea, and the American army became the U.N. army. Truman said: "A return to the rule of force in international affairs would have far-reaching effects. The United States will continue to uphold the rule of law."

The United States' response to "the rule of force" was to reduce Korea, North and South, to a shambles, in three years of bombing and shelling. Napalm was dropped, and a BBC journalist described the result: "In front of us a curious figure was standing, a little crouched, legs straddled, arms held out from his sides. He had no eyes, and the whole of his body, nearly all of which was visible through tatters of burnt rags, was covered with a hard black crust speckled with yellow pus...."

Perhaps two million Koreans, North and South, were killed in the Korean war, all in the name of opposing "the rule of force."

The U.N. resolution had called for action "to repel the armed attack and to restore peace and security in the area." But the American armies, after pushing the North Koreans back across the 38th parallel, advanced all the way up through North Korea to the Yalu River, on the border of China—which provoked the Chinese into entering the war. The Chinese then swept southward and the war was stalemated at the 38th parallel until peace negotiations restored, in 1953, the old boundary between North and South.

The Korean war mobilized liberal opinion behind the war and the president. It created the kind of coalition that was needed to sustain a policy of intervention abroad, militarization of the economy at home. This meant trouble for those who stayed outside the coalition as radical critics.

The left had become very influential in the hard times of the thirties, and during the war against Fascism. The actual membership of the Communist party was not large—fewer than 100,000 probably—but it was a potent force in trade unions numbering millions of members, in the arts, and among countless Americans who may have been led by the failure of the capitalist system in the thirties to look favorably on communism and socialism. Thus, if the Establishment, after World War II, was to make capitalism more secure in the country, and to build a consensus of support for the American Empire, it had to weaken and isolate the left.

Two weeks after presenting to the country the Truman Doctrine for Greece and Turkey, Truman issued, on March 22, 1947, Executive Order 9835, initiating a program to search out any "infiltration of disloyal persons" in the U.S. government. In the next five years, some six million government employees were investigated. About five hundred were fired for "questionable loyalty."

World events right after the war made it easier to build up public support for the anti-Communist crusade at home. In 1948, the Communist party in Czechoslovakia ousted non-Communists from the government and established their own rule. The Soviet Union that year blockaded Berlin, which was a jointly occupied city isolated inside the Soviet sphere of East Germany, forcing the United States to airlift supplies into Berlin. In 1949, there was the Communist victory in China, and in that year also, the Soviet Union exploded its first atomic bomb. In 1950 the Korean war began. These were all portrayed to the public as signs of a world Communist conspiracy.

All over the world, colonial peoples demanding independence were rebelling: in Indochina against the French; in Indonesia against the Dutch; in the Philippines against the United States. In Africa there were rumblings of discontent in the form of strikes, in French West Africa, Kenya, South Africa.

So it was not just Soviet expansion that was threatening to the United States government and to American business interests. In fact, China, Korea, Indochina, and the Philippines represented local Communist movements, not Russian fomentation. It was a general wave of anti-imperialist insurrection, which the United States wanted to defeat. This would require national unity, for militarization of the budget, for the suppression of domestic opposition to such a foreign policy.

In this atmosphere, Senator Joseph McCarthy of Wisconsin could go even further than Truman. As chairman of the Permanent Investigations Sub-Committee of the Senate Committee on Government Operations, he claimed that the State Department employed hundreds of Communists, a claim for which he had no evidence. He investigated the State Department's information program, its Voice of America, and its overseas libraries, which included books by people whom McCarthy considered Communists.

The State Department reacted in panic, issuing a stream of directives to its library centers across the world. Forty books were removed, including *The Selected Works of Thomas Jefferson*, edited by Philip Foner, and *The Children's Hour*, by Lillian Hellman. Some books were burned.

McCarthy became bolder. In the spring of 1954 he began hearings to investigate supposed subversives in the military. When he began attacking generals for not being hard enough on suspected Communists, he antagonized Republicans as well as Democrats, and in December 1954, the Senate voted overwhelmingly to censure him for "conduct...unbecoming a Member of the United States Senate."

At the very time the Senate was censuring McCarthy, liberals as well as conservatives in Congress were putting through a whole series of anti-Communist bills. Liberal Hubert Humphrey introduced a proposal to make the Communist party illegal, saying: "I do not intend to be a half patriot." Lyndon Johnson, as Senate minority leader, worked to pass the censure resolution on McCarthy but also to keep it within the narrow bounds of "conduct...unbecoming a Member of the United States Senate" rather than questioning McCarthy's anti-Communism.

John F. Kennedy, as senator, didn't speak out against McCarthy (he was absent when the censure vote was taken and never said how he would have voted). McCarthy's insistence that Communism had won in China because of softness on Communism in the American government was close to Kennedy's own view, expressed in the House of Representatives, January 1949, when the Chinese Communists took over Peking. Kennedy said:

> So concerned were our diplomats and their advisers, the Lattimores and the Fairbanks [both scholars in the field of Chinese history, Owen Lattimore a favorite target of McCarthy, John Fairbank, a Harvard professor], with the imperfection of the democratic system in China...that they lost sight of our tremendous stake in a non-Communist China.... This House must now assume the responsibility of preventing the onrushing tide of Communism from engulfing all of Asia.

Liberal Senators Hubert Humphrey and Herbert Lehman proposed the setting up of detention centers (really, concentration camps) for suspected subversives, who, when the president declared an "internal security emergency," would be held without trial. This was added to the Republicans' Internal Security Act, which called for the registration of "Communist organizations," and the proposed camps were set up, ready for use. (In 1968, a time of general disillusionment with anti-Communism, this law was repealed.)

Truman's executive order on loyalty in 1947 required the Department of Justice to draw up a list of organizations it decided were "totalitarian, fascist, communist or subversive...or as seeking to alter the form of government of the United States by unconstitutional means." Not only membership in, but also "sympathetic association" with, any organization on the attorney general's list would be considered in determining disloyalty. By 1954, there were hundreds of groups on this list.

The Truman administration initiated a series of prosecutions that intensified the nation's anti-Communist mood. The most important of these was the case of Julius and Ethel Rosenberg in the summer of 1950.

The Rosenbergs were charged with espionage. The major evidence was supplied by a few people who had already confessed to being spies and were either in prison or under indictment. David Greenglass, the brother of Ethel Rosenberg, was the key witness. He had been a machinist at the Manhattan Project laboratory at Los Alamos, New Mexico, in 1944–1945 when the atomic bomb was being made there, and testified that Julius Rosenberg had asked him to get information for the Russians.

Harry Gold, a chemist, already serving a thirty-year sentence in another espionage case, came out of jail to corroborate Greenglass's testimony. He had never met the Rosenbergs, but said a Soviet embassy official gave him half of a Jello box top and told him to contact Greenglass, saying, "I come from Julius." Gold said he took the sketches Greenglass had drawn from memory and gave them to the Russian official.

There were troubling aspects to all this. Did Gold cooperate in return for early release from prison? After serving fifteen years of his thirty-year sentence, he was paroled. Did Greenglass—under indictment at the time he testified—also know that his life depended on his cooperation? He was given fifteen years, served half of it, and was released. How reliable was Gold's testimony? It turned out that he had been prepared for the Rosenberg case by four hundred hours of interviews with the FBI. It also turned out that Gold was a frequent and highly imaginative liar.

The Rosenbergs' connection with the Communist party was an important factor in the trial. The jury found them guilty, and Judge Irving Kaufman pronounced sentence, saying they were responsible for the deaths of fifty thousand American soldiers in Korea. He sentenced them both to die in the electric chair.

Morton Sobell was also on trial as a co-conspirator with the Rosenbergs. The chief witness against him was an old friend, the best man at his wedding, a man who was facing possible perjury charges by the federal government for lying about his political past. The case against Sobell seemed so weak that Sobell's lawyer decided there was no need to present a defense. But the jury found Sobell guilty, and Kaufman sentenced him to thirty years in prison. He was sent to Alcatraz, parole was repeatedly denied, and he spent nineteen years in various prisons before he was released.

FBI documents subpoenaed in the 1970s showed that Judge Kaufman had conferred with the prosecutors secretly about the sentences he would give in the case. Another document shows that Chief Justice Fred Vinson of the Supreme Court secretly assured the U.S. attorney general that if any Supreme Court justice gave a stay of execution, he would immediately call a full court session and override it.

There had been a worldwide campaign of protest. Albert Einstein, whose letter to Roosevelt early in the war had initiated work on the atomic bomb, appealed for the Rosenbergs, as did Jean-Paul Sartre, Pablo Picasso, and the sister of Bartolomeo Vanzetti. There was an appeal to President Truman, just before he left office in the spring of 1953. It was turned down. Then, another appeal to the new president, Dwight Eisenhower, was also turned down.

At the last moment, Justice William O. Douglas granted a stay of execution. Chief Justice Vinson sent out special jets to bring the vacationing justices back to Washington from various parts of the country. They canceled Douglas's stay in time for the Rosenbergs to be executed June 19, 1953.

In that same period of the early fifties, the House Un-American Activities Committee was interrogating Americans about their Communist connections, holding them in contempt if they refused to answer, distributing millions of pamphlets to the American public: "One Hundred Things You Should Know About Communism" ("Where can Communists be found? Everywhere"). Liberals often criticized the committee, but in Congress, liberals and conservatives alike voted to fund it year after year.

It was Truman's Justice Department that prosecuted the leaders of the Communist party under the Smith Act, charging them with conspiring to teach and advocate the overthrow of the government by force and violence. The evidence consisted mostly of the fact that the Communists were distributing Marxist-Leninist literature, which the prosecution contended called for violent revolution. There was certainly not evidence of any immediate danger of violent revolution by the Communist party. But the Supreme Court, led by Truman's appointee, Chief Justice Vinson, stretched the old doctrine of the "clear and present danger" by saying there was a clear and present conspiracy to make a revolution at some convenient time. And so, the top leadership of the Communist party was put in prison.

The whole culture was permeated with anti-Communism. An FBI informer's story about his exploits as a Communist who became an FBI agent—"I Led Three Lives"—was serialized in five hundred newspapers and put on television. Hollywood movies had titles like *I Married a Communist* and *I Was a Communist for the FBI*. Between 1948 and 1954, more than forty anti-Communist films came out of Hollywood.

Young and old were taught that anti-Communism was heroic. A comic strip hero, Captain America, said: "Beware, commies, spies, traitors, and foreign agents! Captain America, with all loyal, free men behind him, is looking for you...." And in the fifties, schoolchildren all over the country participated in air raid drills in which a Soviet attack on America was signaled by sirens: the children had to crouch under their desks until it was "all clear."

It was an atmosphere in which the government could get mass support for a policy of rearmament. The system, so shaken in the thirties, had learned that war production could bring stability and high profits. By

1960, the military budget was $45.8 billion—49.7 percent of the budget. That year John F. Kennedy was elected president, and he immediately moved to increase military spending.

Based on a series of invented scares about Soviet military buildups, a false "bomber gap" and a false "missile gap," the United States added to its nuclear aresenal until it had overwhelming nuclear superiority. It had the equivalent, in nuclear weapons, of 1,500 Hiroshima-size atomic bombs, far more than enough to destroy every major city in the world. To deliver these bombs, the United States had more than 50 intercontinental ballistic missiles, 80 missiles on nuclear submarines, 90 missiles on stations overseas, 1,700 bombers capable of reaching the Soviet Union, 300 fighter-bombers on aircraft carriers, able to carry atomic weapons, and 1,000 land-based supersonic fighters able to carry atomic bombs.

The Soviet Union was obviously behind—it had between fifty and a hundred intercontinental ballistic missiles and fewer than two hundred long-range bombers. But the U.S. military budget kept mounting, the hysteria kept growing, the profits of corporations getting defense contracts multiplied, and employment and wages moved ahead just enough to keep a substantial number of Americans dependent on war industries for their living.

Meanwhile, the United States, giving economic aid to certain countries, was creating a network of American corporate control over the globe, and building its political influence over the countries it aided. The Marshall Plan of 1948, which gave $16 billion in economic aid to Western European countries in four years, had an economic aim: to build up markets for American exports.

The Marshall Plan also had a political motive. The Communist parties of Italy and France were strong, and the United States decided to use pressure and money to keep Communists out of the cabinets of those countries.

From 1952 on, foreign aid was more and more obviously designed to build up military power in non-Communist countries. When John F. Kennedy took office, he launched the Alliance for Progress, a program of help for Latin America, emphasizing social reform to better the lives of people. But it turned out to be mostly military aid to keep in power right-wing dictatorships and enable them to stave off revolutions.

From military aid, it was a short step to military intervention. After Iran, in 1953, nationalized its oil industry, the CIA organized its overthrow. In Guatemala, in 1954, a legally elected government, the most democratic Guatemala had ever had, was overthrown by an invasion force of mercenaries trained by the CIA at military bases in Honduras and Nicaragua and supported by four American fighter planes flown by American pilots.

The Guatemalan president, Jacobo Arbenz, was a left-of-center Socialist; four of the fifty-six seats in the Congress were held by Communists. What was most unsettling to American business interests was that Arbenz had expropriated 234,000 acres of land owned by United Fruit, offering compensation that United Fruit called "unacceptable." Col. Castillo Armas, put in power by the U.S. plan, had received military training at Fort Leavenworth, Kansas. He gave the land back to United Fruit, abolished the tax on interest and dividends to foreign investors, eliminated the secret ballot, and jailed thousands of political critics.

In 1958, the Eisenhower government sent thousands of marines to Lebanon to make sure the pro-American government there was not toppled by a revolution, and to keep an armed presence in that oil-rich area.

The Democrat-Republican, liberal-conservative agreement to prevent or overthrow revolutionary governments whenever possible—whether Communist, Socialist, or anti-United Fruit—became most evident in Cuba. Cuba's military dictator, Fulgencio Batista, had the support of the United States for many years. U.S. business interests dominated the Cuban economy, controlling 80 to 100 percent of Cuba's utilities, mines, cattle ranches, and oil refineries, 40 percent of the sugar industry, and 50 percent of the public railways.

Fidel Castro's tiny guerrilla force fought from the jungles and mountains against Batista's army, drawing more and more popular support, then came out of the mountains and marched across the country to Havana. The Batista government fell apart on New Year's Day 1959.

In power, Castro moved to set up a nationwide system of education, of housing, of land distribution to landless peasants. The government confiscated over a million acres of land from three American companies, including United Fruit.

Cuba needed money to finance its programs, but the International Monetary Fund, dominated by the United States, would not loan money to Cuba because Cuba would not accept its "stabilization" conditions, which seemed to undermine the revolutionary program that had begun. When Cuba now signed a trade agreement with the Soviet Union, American-owned oil companies in Cuba refused to refine crude oil that came from the Soviet Union. Castro seized these companies. The United States cut down on its sugar buying from Cuba, on which Cuba's economy depended, and the Soviet Union immediately agreed to buy all the 700,000 tons of sugar that the United States would not buy.

In the spring of 1960, President Eisenhower secretly authorized the Central Intelligence Agency to arm and train anti-Castro Cuban exiles in Guatemala for a future invasion of Cuba. When John F. Kennedy took office he moved ahead with the plans, and on April 17, 1961, the CIA-trained force, with some Americans participating, landed at the Bay of Pigs on the south shore of Cuba, 90 miles from Havana. They expected to stimulate a general rising against Castro. But it was a popular regime. There was no rising. In three days, the CIA forces were crushed by Castro's army.

The whole Bay of Pigs affair was accompanied by hypocrisy and lying. The invasion was a violation of a treaty the U.S. had signed, the Charter of the Organization of American States, which reads: "No state or group of states has the right to intervene, directly or indirectly, for any reason whatever, in the internal or external affairs of any other state."

Four days before the invasion—because there had been press reports of secret bases and CIA training for invaders—President Kennedy told a press conference: "...there will not be, under any conditions, any intervention in Cuba by United States armed forces." True, the landing force was Cuban, but it was all organized by the United States, and American war planes, including American pilots, were involved; Kennedy had approved the use of unmarked navy jets in the invasion. Four American pilots of those planes were killed, and their families were not told the truth about how those men died.

Certain important news publications cooperated with the Kennedy administration in deceiving the American public on the Cuban invasion: *The New Republic* was about to print an article on the CIA training of Cuban exiles, a few weeks before the invasion. Kennedy asked that the article not be printed, and *The New Republic* went along. So did the *New York Times*.

Around 1960, the fifteen-year effort since the end of World War II to break up the Communist-radical upsurge of the New Deal and wartime years seemed successful. The Communist party was in disarray—its leaders in jail, its membership shrunken, its influence in the trade union movement very small. The trade union movement itself had become more controlled, more conservative. The military budget was taking half of the national budget, but the public was accepting this.

The radiation from the testing of nuclear weapons had dangerous possibilities for human health, but the public was not aware of that. The Atomic Energy Commission insisted that the deadly effects of atomic tests were exaggerated, and an article in 1955 in the *Reader's Digest* (the largest-circulation magazine in the United States) said: "The scare stories about this country's atomic tests are simply not justified."

In the mid-fifties, there was a flurry of enthusiasm for air-raid shelters; the public was being told these would keep them safe from atomic blasts. A political scientist named Henry Kissinger wrote a book published in 1957 in which he said: "With proper tactics, nuclear war need not be as destructive as it appears...."

The country was on a permanent war economy which had big pockets of poverty, but there were enough people at work, making enough money, to keep things quiet. The distribution of wealth remained unequal. In 1953, 1.6 percent of the adult population owned more than 80 percent of the corporate stock and nearly 90 percent of the corporate bonds. About 200 giant corporations out of 200,000 corporations—one-tenth of one percent of all corporations—controlled about 60 percent of the manufacturing wealth of the nation.

When John F. Kennedy presented his budget to the nation after his first year in office, it was clear that there would be no major change in the distribution of income. *New York Times* columnist James Reston summed up Kennedy's budget messages as avoiding any "ambitious frontal attack on the unemployment problem." Reston said: "He agreed to a tax break for business investment in plant expansion and modernization. He is not spoiling for a fight with the Southern conservatives over civil rights. He has been urging the unions to keep wage demands down.... During these twelve months the President has moved over into the decisive middle ground of American politics...."

On this middle ground, all seemed secure. Nothing had to be done for blacks. Nothing had to be done to change the economic structure. An aggressive foreign policy could continue. The country seemed under control. And then, in the 1960s, came a series of explosive rebellions in every area of American life, which showed that all the system's estimates of security and success were wrong.

Exercises

1. How does the U.S. government's "record in world affairs" prior to 1941 indicate that U.S. involvement in World War II promised not to be an effective blow to "imperialism, racism, totalitarianism, militarism, in the world"?

2. How do standard American history textbooks explain Roosevelt's reluctance to stop Japanese and German aggression? How does Zinn? Which interpretation do you find most persuasive, and why?

3. Why did the U.S. government promise the French that their "sovereignty will be reestablished as soon as possible throughout all the territory, metropolitan or colonial, over which flew the French flag in 1939" when two weeks later the U.S. government promised "the right of all peoples to choose the form of government under which they will live"?

4. Why did Roosevelt promise that "the United States would not change its Palestine policy without consulting the Arabs"?

5. How did the United States ensure that it would control the international exchange rates after World War II?

6. The International Bank for Reconstruction expected to rebuild war-destroyed areas with foreign investment. After World War II, which was the only country that had money to invest? (Hint: which was the only country fighting in World War II that did not fight on its own soil?)

7. How did the structure of the U.N. allow it to be controlled by the United States, England, and France?

8. How does Zinn explain Roosevelt's failure to "take steps" that might have saved thousands of people from dying in Nazi concentration camps?

9. During World War II, women replaced men as factory workers. Why might this result in "a developing attitude of militancy or a crusading spirit," as observed by the Women's Bureau of the Department of Labor?

10. If an economic motive could be attributed to the signing of Executive Order 9066, what might it be?

11. Why were there so many strikes by U.S. workers during World War II?

12. According to the character Red in Mailer's *The Naked and the Dead*, why were U.S. GIs dying in the jungles of the Pacific Islands? What experiences might Red have had before and during the war that would lead him to feel this way?

13. Why is it ironic that eigthteen leaders of the only organization that was explicitly pacifist were sent to prison for violating the Smith Act?

14. Why were most American blacks unenthusiastic and even unsupportive of the United States' participation in World War II?

15. Why did the Allies engage in saturation bombing of enemy civilians when Roosevelt had already labeled such actions as "inhuman barbarism"?

16. If the atomic bombing of Hiroshima and Nagasaki was not necessary to force Japan to surrender, why was it done?

17. Why did Truman claim, "The world will note that the first atomic bomb was dropped on Hiroshima, a military base. That was because we wished in this first attack to avoid, insofar as possible, the killing of civilians"?

18. Why were there so many strikes following the end of World War II?

19. How does "a permanent war economy" solve the "problems of control"?

20. How did the Truman Doctrine convince Americans that the U.S. government should support fascism in Greece?

21. Is the rationale for American involvement in the Korean War contradicted by its actions during the war?

22. How did the Korean War contribute to the forging of a liberal/conservative consensus?

23. Is there any difference between Executive Order 9835 and the expulsion of non-communists in the Czech government in 1948?

24. How did the U.S. government portray the independence movements of the Indochinese, Indonesians, Africans, and Filipinos to the American public?

25. For what was Joe McCarthy censured?

26. What point is Zinn making by revealing the positions that Lyndon Johnson, Hubert Humphrey, and John Kennedy took regarding the government's anti-communist strategy of the late 1940s and early 1950s?

27. Why would such figures as Einstein, Sartre, and Picasso take such a passionate interest in the fate of the Rosenbergs (is it reminiscent of Mark Twain's concerns for Aquinaldo and his Filipino guerrillas)?

28. What role did the House Un-American Activities Committee (HUAC) play in forging the consensus behind American foreign policy after World War II?

29. What was America's foreign policy after World War II?

30. What evidence was there that American communists were advocating the violent overthrow of the government?

31. After 1960, how did the U.S. nuclear arsenal compare to the Soviets'?

32. What was the economic goal of the Marshall Plan? What was the political goal?

33. Why did U.S. foreign policy support right-wing dictatorships? (Why did the United States overthrow democratically elected governments, e.g., in Guatemala in 1954?)

34. Was Fidel Castro an agent of Soviet expansion? How so? How not?

35. What measures did the U.S. government take to keep the Bay of Pigs invasion secret from the American public? Why did the U.S. government plot to overthrow Castro with such secrecy?

36. According to James Reston, what were Kennedy's budgetary goals for his administration? What conclusions does Zinn draw from this?

37. *Debate Resolution*: The United States entered World War II to expand its own empire.

38. *Draw a map* that identifies all the countries of Central America in relationship to the United States.

39. *Draw a map* depicting the World War II period (1939–1945) that includes the following: Allied nations; neutral nations; Axis powers; area of maximum Axis control.

40. *Draw a map* of Europe, North Africa, and the Middle East (1955) which identifies the following: NATO members; CENTO members; the Arab League; those countries that were under the control of the Soviet Union.

Chapter 17

"Or Does It Explode?"

The black revolt of the 1950s and 1960s—North and South—came as a surprise. But perhaps it should not have. The memory of oppressed people is one thing that cannot be taken away, and for such people, with such memories, revolt is always an inch below the surface. For blacks in the United States, there was the memory of slavery, and after that of segregation, lynching, humiliation. And it was not just a memory but a living presence—part of the daily lives of blacks in generation after generation.

In the 1930s, Langston Hughes wrote a poem, "Lenox Avenue Mural":

> What happens to a dream deferred?
> Does it dry up
> like a raisin in the sun?
> Or fester like a sore—
> And then run?
> Does it stink like rotten meat?
> Or crust and sugar over—
> like a syrupy sweet?
>
> Maybe it just sags like a heavy load.
>
> Or does it explode?

In a society of complex controls, both crude and refined, secret thoughts can often be found in the arts, and so it was in black society. Perhaps the blues, however pathetic, concealed anger; and the jazz, however joyful, portended rebellion. And then the poetry, the thoughts no longer so secret. In the 1920s, Claude McKay, one of the figures of what came to be called the "Harlem Renaissance," wrote a poem that Henry Cabot Lodge put in the *Congressional Record* as an example of dangerous currents among young blacks:

> If we must die, let it not be like hogs
> Hunted and penned in an inglorious spot....
> Like men we'll face the murderous cowardly pack,
> Pressed to the wall, dying, but fighting back!

Countee Cullen's poem "Incident" evoked memories—all different, all the same—out of every black American's childhood:

> Once riding in Old Baltimore,
> Heart-filled, head-filled with glee,
> I saw a Baltimorean
> Keep looking straight at me.
>
> Now I was eight and very small,
> And he was no whit bigger,
> And so I smiled, but he poked out
> His tongue, and called me, "Nigger."
>
> I saw the whole of Baltimore
> From May until December;
> Of all the things that happened there
> That's all that I remember.

By the 1940s there was Richard Wright, a gifted novelist, a black man. His autobiography of 1937, *Black Boy*, told how he was prodded to fight another black boy for the amusement of white men. *Black Boy* expressed unashamedly every humiliation, but also the inner defiance:

> The white South said that it knew "niggers," and I was what the white South called a "nigger." Well, the white South had never known me— never known what I thought, what I felt.... It had never occurred to me that I was in any way an inferior being. And no word that I had ever heard fall from the lips of southern white men had ever made me really doubt the worth of my own humanity.

It was all there in the poetry, the prose, the music, sometimes masked, sometimes unmistakably clear—the signs of a people unbeaten, waiting, hot, coiled.

In *Black Boy*, Wright told about the training of black children in America to keep them silent. But also:

How do Negroes feel about the way they have to live? How do they discuss it when alone among themselves? I think this question can be answered in a single sentence. A friend of mine who ran an elevator once told me:

"Lawd, man! Ef it wuzn't fer them polices 'n' them ol' lynch mobs, there wouldn't be nothin' but uproar down here!"

Despite the police and the lynch mobs, black people in the South resisted. The Communist party was active, playing an important role in the defense of the "Scottsboro Boys," nine young black men falsely accused of rape in Alabama.

In Georgia, in 1932, a nineteen-year-old black youth named Angelo Herndon, whose father died of miner's pneumonia, who had worked in mines as a boy in Kentucky, joined the Unemployment Council organized by the Communist party in Birmingham and then joined the party. He wrote later:

All my life I'd been sweated and stepped-on and Jim-Crowed. I lay on my belly in the mines for a few dollars a week...and rode behind the "Colored" signs on streetcars, as though there was something disgusting about me. I heard myself called "nigger" and "darky" and I had to say "Yes, sir" to every white man, whether he had my respect or not.

I had always detested it, but I had never known that anything could be done about it. And here, all of a sudden, I had found organizations in which Negroes and whites sat together, and worked together, and knew no difference of race or color....

Herndon became a Communist party organizer in Atlanta. He and his fellow Communists organized block committees of unemployment councils in 1932, which got rent relief for needy people. They organized a demonstration to which a thousand people came, six hundred of them white, and the next day the city voted $6,000 in relief to the jobless. But soon after that Herndon was arrested, held incommunicado, and charged with violating a Georgia statute against insurrection. He recalled his trial:

The state of Georgia displayed the literature that had been taken from my room, and read passages of it to the jury. They questioned me in great detail. Did I believe that the bosses and government ought to pay insurance to unemployed workers? That Negroes should have complete equality with white people? Did I feel that the working-class could run the mills and mines and government? That it wasn't necessary to have bosses at all?

"I told them I believed all of that—and more....

Herndon was convicted and spent five years in prison until in 1937 the Supreme Court ruled unconstitutional the Georgia statute under which he was found guilty. It was men like him who represented to the Establishment a dangerous militancy among blacks, made more dangerous when linked with the Communist Party.

There were other important black people connected to the Communist party: Benjamin Davis, the black lawyer who defended Herndon at his trial; nationally renowned men such as singer and actor Paul Robeson and writer and scholar W. E. B. Du Bois.

The black militant mood, flashing here and there in the thirties, was reduced to a subsurface simmering during World War II, when the nation on the one hand denounced racism, and on the other hand maintained segregation in the armed forces and kept blacks in low-paying jobs. When the war ended, a new element entered the racial balance in the United States— the enormous, unprecedented upsurge of black and yellow people in Africa and Asia.

President Harry Truman had to reckon with this, especially as the cold war rivalry with the Soviet Union began. Action on the race question was needed, not just to calm a black population at home emboldened by war promises, frustrated by the basic sameness of their condition. It was needed to overcome in the nonwhite world the accusation that the United States was a racist society. What Du Bois had said long ago, unnoticed, now loomed large in 1945: "The problem of the 20th century is the problem of the color line."

Truman, in late 1946, appointed a Committee on Civil Rights, which recommended that there be a permanent Commission on Civil Rights, that Congress pass laws against lynching and to stop voting discrimination, and suggested new laws to end racial discrimination in jobs.

Truman's committee was blunt about its motivation. Yes, it said, there was "moral reason," but there was also an "economic reason"—discrimination was costly to the country, wasteful of its talent. And, perhaps most important, there was an international reason: "Our position in the postwar world is so vital to the future that our smallest actions have far-reaching effects.... We cannot escape the fact that our civil rights record has been an issue in world politics."

The United States was out in the world now in a way it had never been. The stakes were large—world supremacy. And, as Truman's committee said: "...our smallest actions have far-reaching effects."

And so the United States went ahead to take small actions, hoping they would have large effects. Congress did not move to enact the legislation asked for by the Committee on Civil Rights. But Truman—four months before the presidential election of 1948, and challenged from the left in that election by Progressive party candidate Henry Wallace—issued an executive order directing that the armed forces, segregated in World War II, institute policies of racial equality "as rapidly as possible." The order may have been prompted not only by the election but by the need to maintain black morale in the armed forces, as the possibility of war grew. It took over a decade to complete the desegregation in the military.

Truman could have issued executive orders in other areas, but did not. The Fourteenth and Fifteenth Amendments, plus the set of laws passed in the late 1860s and early 1870s, gave the president enough authority to wipe out racial discrimination. The Constitution demanded that the president execute the laws, but no president had used that power. Neither did Truman.

When courageous southern blacks confronted the Supreme Court in a series of suits against racial segregation in the schools, the Court finally, in 1954, struck down the "separate but equal" doctrine that it had defended since the 1890s. In *Brown v. Board of Education* the Court said the separation of schoolchildren "generates a feeling of inferiority...that may affect their hearts and minds in a way unlikely ever to be undone." In the field of public education, it said, "the doctrine of 'separate but equal' has no place."

The Court did not insist on immediate change: a year later it said that segregated facilities should be integrated "with all deliberate speed." By 1965, ten years after the "all deliberate speed" guideline, more than 75 percent of the school districts in the South remained segregated.

Still, it was a dramatic decision—and the message went around the world in 1954 that the American government had outlawed segregation. In the United States too, for those not thinking about the customary gap between word and fact, it was an exhilarating sign of change.

What to others seemed rapid progress to blacks was apparently not enough. In the early 1960s black people rose in rebellion all over the South. And in the late 1960s they were engaging in wild insurrection in a hundred northern cities. It was all a surprise to those without that deep memory of slavery, that everyday presence of humiliation, registered in the poetry, the music, the occasional outbursts of anger, the more frequent sullen silences. Part of that memory was of words uttered by politicians, laws passed, decisions made, which turned out to be meaningless.

For such a people, with such a memory, and such daily recapitulation of history, revolt was always minutes away, in a timing mechanism which no one had set, but which might go off with some unpredictable set of events. Those events came, at the end of 1955, in the capital city of Alabama—Montgomery—when Mrs. Rosa Parks, a forty-three-year-old seamstress who had been active in the NAACP, decided to sit down in the "white" section of a bus and was arrested: "Well...I was quite tired after spending a full day working. I handle and work on clothing that white people wear.... That didn't come in my mind but this is what I wanted to know: when and how would we ever determine our rights as human beings?...

Montgomery blacks called a mass meeting. They voted to boycott all city buses. Car pools were organized to take Negroes to work; most people walked. The city retaliated by indicting one hundred leaders of the boy- cott, and sent many to jail. White segregationists turned to violence. Bombs exploded in four Negro churches. A shotgun blast was fired through the front door of the home of Dr. Martin Luther King Jr., the twenty-seven-year-old Atlanta-born minister who was one of the leaders of the boycott. King's home was bombed. But the black people of Mont- gomery persisted, and in November 1956, the Supreme Court outlawed segregation on local bus lines.

Montgomery was the beginning. It forecast the style and mood of the vast protest movement that would sweep the South in the next ten years: emotional church meetings, Christian hymns adapted to current battles, references to lost American ideals, the commitment to nonviolence, the willingness to struggle and sacrifice.

At a mass meeting in Montgomery during the boycott, Martin Luther King gave a preview of the oratory that would soon inspire millions of peo- ple to demand racial justice. He said the protest was not merely over buses but over things that "go deep down into the archives of history." He said:

> We have known humiliation, we have known abusive language, we have been plunged into the abyss of oppression. And we decided to raise up only with the weapon of protest.... We must use the weapon of love. We must have compassion and understanding for those who hate us.

King's stress on love and nonviolence was powerfully effective in building a sympathetic following throughout the nation, among whites as well as blacks. But there were blacks who thought the message naive, that while there were misguided people who might be won over by love, there were others who would have to be bitterly fought. Two years after the Montgomery boycott, in Monroe, North Carolina, an ex-marine named

Robert Williams, the president of the local NAACP, became known for his view that blacks should defend themselves against violence, with guns if necessary. When local Klansmen attacked the home of one of the leaders of the Monroe NAACP, Williams and other blacks, armed with rifles, fired back. The Klan left. (The Klan was being challenged now with its own tactic of violence; a Klan raid on an Indian community in North Carolina was repelled by Indians firing rifles.)

Still, in the years that followed, southern blacks stressed nonviolence. On February 1, 1960, four freshmen at a Negro college in Greensboro, North Carolina, decided to sit down at the Woolworth's lunch counter downtown, where only whites ate. They were refused service, but would not leave, and returned, joined by others, day after day.

In the next two weeks, sit-ins spread to fifteen cities in five southern states.

In his Harlem apartment in New York, a young Negro teacher of mathematics named Bob Moses saw a photo in the newspapers of the Greensboro sit-inners. "The students in that picture had a certain look on their faces, sort of sullen, angry, determined. Before, the Negro in the South had always looked on the defensive, cringing. This time they were taking the initiative. They were kids my age, and I knew this had something to do with my own life."

There was violence against the sit-inners. But in the next twelve months, more than fifty thousand people, mostly black, some white, participated in demonstrations of one kind or another in a hundred cities, and over thirty-six hundred people were put in jail. But by the end of 1960, lunch counters were open to blacks in Greensboro and many other places.

In the spring of 1961, a group of whites and blacks boarded a bus in Washington, D.C., traveling together, headed for New Orleans. These were the first of the Freedom Riders, trying to break the pattern of segregation in interstate travel. Such segregation had long been illegal, but the federal government never enforced the law in the South; the president now was John F. Kennedy, but he too seemed cautious about the race question, concerned about the support of southern white leaders of the Democratic party.

The buses never got to New Orleans. In South Carolina, riders were beaten. In Alabama, a bus was set afire. Freedom Riders were attacked with fists and iron bars. The southern police did not interfere with any of this violence, nor did the federal government. FBI agents watched, took notes, did nothing.

At this point, veterans of the sit-ins, who had recently formed the Student Nonviolent Coordinating Committee (SNCC), dedicated to nonviolent but militant action for equal rights, organized another Freedom Ride, from Nashville to Birmingham. Before they started out, they called the Department of Justice in Washington, D.C., to ask for protection, but were rebuffed. As Ruby Doris Smith, a Spelman College student reported: "...the Justice Department said no, they couldn't protect anyone, but if something happened, they would investigate. You know how they do...."

The racially mixed SNCC Freedom Riders were arrested in Birmingham, Alabama, spent a night in jail, were taken to the Tennessee border by police, made their way back to Birmingham, took a bus to Montgomery, and there were attacked by whites with fists and clubs, in a bloody scene. They resumed their trip, to Jackson, Mississippi.

By this time the Freedom Riders were in the news all over the world, and the government was anxious to prevent further violence. Attorney General Robert Kennedy, instead of insisting on their right to travel without being arrested, agreed to the Freedom Riders' being arrested in Jackson, in return for Mississippi police protection against possible mob violence. The Freedom Riders in jail resisted, protested, sang, demanded their rights.

In Albany, Georgia, a small Deep South town where the atmosphere of slavery still lingered, mass demonstrations took place in the winter of 1961 and again in 1962. Of twenty-two thousand black people in Albany, over a thousand went to jail for marching, assembling, to protest segregation and discrimination. Here, as in all the demonstrations that would sweep over the South, little black children participated—a new generation was learning to act. The Albany police chief, after one of the mass arrests, was taking the names of prisoners lined up before his desk. He looked up and saw a Negro boy about nine years old. "What's your name?" The boy looked straight at him and said: "Freedom, Freedom."

In Birmingham in 1963, thousands of blacks went into the streets, facing police clubs, tear gas, dogs, high-powered water hoses. And meanwhile, all over the Deep South, the young people of SNCC, mostly black, a few white, were moving into communities in Georgia, Alabama, Mississippi, Arkansas. Joined by local black people, they were organizing, to register people to vote, to protest against racism, to build up courage against violence.

As the summer of 1964 approached, SNCC and other civil rights groups working together in Mississippi, and facing increasing violence, decided to call upon young people from other parts of the country for help. They hoped that would bring attention to the situation in Mississippi. Again and again in Mississippi and elsewhere, the FBI had stood by, lawyers for the Justice Department had stood by, while civil rights workers were beaten and jailed, while federal laws were violated.

On the eve of the "Mississippi Summer," in early June 1964, the civil rights movement rented a theater near the White House, and a busload of black Mississippians traveled to Washington to testify publicly about the daily violence, the dangers facing the volunteers coming into Mississippi. Constitutional lawyers testified that the national government had the legal power to give protection against such violence. The transcript of this testimony was given to President Johnson and Attorney General Kennedy, accompanied by a request for a protective federal presence during the Mississippi Summer. There was no response.

Twelve days after the public hearing, three civil rights workers, James Chaney, a young black Mississippian, and two white volunteers, Andrew Goodman and Michael Schwerner, were arrested in Philadelphia, Mississippi, released from jail late at night, then seized, beaten with chains, and shot to death. Ultimately, an informer's testimony led to jail sentences for the sheriff and deputy sheriff and others. That came too late. The Mississippi murders had taken place after the repeated refusal of the national government, under Kennedy and Johnson, and every other president, to defend blacks against violence.

Dissatisfaction with the national government intensified. Later that summer, during the Democratic National Convention in Washington, blacks from Mississippi asked to be seated as part of the state delegation to represent the 40 percent of the state's population who were black. They were turned down by the liberal Democratic leadership, including vice presidential candidate Hubert Humphrey.

Congress began reacting to the black revolt, the turmoil, the world publicity. Civil rights laws were passed in 1957, 1960, and 1964. They promised much, on voting equality, on employment equality, but were enforced poorly or ignored. In 1965, President Johnson sponsored and Congress passed an even stronger Voting Rights Law, this time ensuring on-the-spot federal protection of the right to register and vote. The effect on Negro voting in the South was dramatic. In 1952, a million southern blacks (20 percent of those eligible) registered to vote. In 1964 the number was 2 million—40 percent. By 1968, it was 3 million, 60 percent—the same percentage as white voters.

The federal government was trying—without making fundamental changes—to control an explosive situation, to channel anger into the traditional cooling mechanism of the ballot box, the polite petition, the officially endorsed quiet gathering. When black civil rights leaders planned a huge march on Washington in the summer of 1963 to protest the failure of the nation to solve the race problem, it was quickly embraced by President Kennedy and other national leaders, and turned into a friendly assemblage.

Martin Luther King's speech there thrilled 200,000 black and white Americans—"I have a dream…." It was magnificent oratory, but without the anger that many blacks felt. When John Lewis, a young Alabama-born SNCC leader, much arrested, much beaten, tried to introduce a stronger note of outrage at the meeting, he was censored by the leaders of the march, who insisted he omit certain sentences critical of the national government and urging militant action.

Eighteen days after the Washington gathering, almost as if in deliberate contempt for its moderation, a bomb exploded in the basement of a black church in Birmingham and four girls attending a Sunday school class were killed. President Kennedy had praised the "deep fervor and quiet dignity" of the march, but the black militant Malcolm X was probably closer to the mood of the black community. Speaking in Detroit two months after the march on Washington and the Birmingham bombing, Malcolm X said, in his powerful, icy-clear, rhythmic style:

> The Negroes were out there in the streets. They were talking about how they were going to march on Washington…. That they were going to march on Washington, march on the Senate, march on the White House, march on the Congress, and tie it up, bring it to a halt, not let the government proceed.
>
> It was the grass roots out there in the street. It scared the white man to death, scared the white power structure in Washington, D.C. to death….
>
> This is what they did with the march on Washington. They joined it…became part of it, took it over…. It became a picnic, a circus. Nothing but a circus, with clowns and all…. It was a takeover…they told those Negroes what time to hit town, where to stop, what signs to carry, what song to sing, what speech they could make, and what speech they couldn't make, and then told them to get out of town by sundown.

But the black could not be easily brought into "the democratic coalition" when bombs kept exploding in churches, when new "civil rights" laws did not change the root condition of black people. In the spring of

1963, the rate of unemployment for whites was 4.8 percent. For nonwhites it was 12.1 percent. According to government estimates, one-fifth of the white population was below the poverty line, and one-half of the black population was below that line. The civil rights bills emphasized voting, but voting was not a fundamental solution to racism or poverty. In Harlem, blacks who had voted for years still lived in rat-infested slums.

In precisely those years when civil rights legislation coming out of Congress reached its peak, 1964 and 1965, there were black outbreaks in every part of the country.

In August 1965, just as Lyndon Johnson was signing into law the strong Voting Rights Act, providing for federal registration of black voters to ensure their protection, the black ghetto in Watts, Los Angeles, erupted in the most violent urban outbreak since World War II. It was provoked by the forcible arrest of a young Negro driver, the clubbing of a bystander by police, the seizure of a young black woman falsely accused of spitting on the police. There was rioting in the streets, looting and fire-bombing of stores. Police and National Guardsmen were called in; they used their guns. Thirty-four people were killed, most of them black, hundreds injured, four thousand arrested.

In the summer of 1966, there were more outbreaks, with rock throwing, looting, and fire bombings by Chicago blacks and wild shootings by the National Guard; three blacks were killed, one a thirteen-year-old boy, another a fourteen-year-old pregnant girl. In cleveland, the National Guard was summoned to stop a commotion in the black community; four Negroes were shot to death, two by troopers, two by white civilians.

It seemed clear by now that the nonviolence of the southern movement, perhaps tactically necessary in the southern atmosphere, and effective because it could be used to appeal to national opinion against the segregationist South, was not enough to deal with the entrenched problems of poverty in the black ghetto. In 1910, 90 percent of Negroes lived in the South. But by 1965, mechanical cotton pickers harvested 81 percent of Mississippi Delta cotton. Between 1940 and 1970, 4 million blacks left the country for the city. By 1965, 80 percent of blacks lived in cities and 50 percent of the black people lived in the North.

In 1967, in the black ghettos of the country, came the greatest urban riots of American history. According to the report of the National Advisory Committee on Urban Disorders there were eight major uprisings, thirty-three "serious but not major" outbreaks, and 123 "minor" disorders. Eighty-three died of gunfire, mostly in Newark and Detroit. "The overwhelming majority of the persons killed or injured in all the disorders were Negro civilians."

The "typical rioter," according to the commission, was a young, high school dropout but "nevertheless, somewhat better educated than his non-rioting Negro neighbor" and "usually underemployed or employed in a menial job." He was "proud of his race, extremely hostile to both whites and middle-class Negroes and, although informed about politics, highly distrustful of the political system." The report blamed "white racism" for the disorders, and identified the ingredients of the "explosive mixture which has been accumulating in our cities since the end of World War II":

> Pervasive discrimination and segregation in employment, education, and housing...growing concentrations of impoverished Negroes in our major cities, creating a growing crisis of deteriorating facilities and services and unmet human needs....
>
> A new mood has sprung up among Negroes, particularly the young, in which self-esteem and enhanced racial pride are replacing apathy and submission to the "system."

But the commission report itself was a standard device of the system when facing rebellion: set up an investigating committee, issue a report; the words of the report, however strong, will have a soothing effect.

That didn't completely work either. "Black Power" was the new slogan—an expression of distrust of any "progress" given or conceded by whites, a rejection of paternalism. Malcolm X was the most eloquent spokesman for this. After he was assassinated as he spoke on a public platform in February 1965, in a plan whose origins are still obscure, he became the martyr of this movement. Hundreds of thousands read his autobiography. He was more influential in death than during his lifetime.

Martin Luther King, though still respected, was being replaced now by new heroes: Huey Newton of the Black Panthers, for instance. The Panthers had guns; they said blacks should defend themselves.

Malcolm X in late 1964 had spoken to black students from Mississippi visiting Harlem:

> You'll get freedom by letting your enemy know that you'll do anything to get your freedom; then you'll get it. It's the only way you'll get it. When you get that kind of attitude, they'll label you as a "crazy Negro," or they'll call you a "crazy nigger"—they don't say Negro. Or they'll call you an extremist or a subversive, or seditious, or a red or a radical. But when you stay radical long enough and get enough people to be like you, you'll get your freedom.

Martin Luther King himself became more and more concerned about problems untouched by civil rights laws—problems coming out of poverty. In the spring of 1968, he began speaking out, against the advice of some Negro leaders who feared losing friends in Washington, against the war in Vietnam. He connected war and poverty: "We are spending all of this money for death and destruction, and not nearly enough money for life and constructive development."

King now became a chief target of the FBI, which tapped his private phone conversations, sent him fake letters, threatened him, blackmailed him, and even suggested once in an anonymous letter that he commit suicide. FBI internal memos discussed finding a black leader to replace King. As a Senate report on the FBI said in 1976, the FBI tried "to destroy Dr. Martin Luther King."

King was turning his attention to troublesome questions. He planned a "Poor People's Encampment" on Washington, this time without the paternal approval of the president. And he went to Memphis, Tennessee, to support a strike of garbage workers in that city. There, standing on a balcony outside his hotel room, he was shot to death by an unseen marksman. The Poor People's Encampment went on, and then it was broken up by police action, just as the World War I veterans' Bonus Army of 1932 was dispersed.

The killing of King brought new urban outbreaks all over the country, in which thirty-nine people were killed, thirty-five of them black. Evidence was piling up that even with all of the civil rights laws now on the books, the courts would not protect blacks against violence and injustice. For instance:

> In Jackson, Mississippi, in the spring of 1970, on the campus of Jackson State College, a Negro college, police laid down a twenty-eight-second barrage of gunfire, using shotguns, rifles, and a submachine gun. Four hundred bullets or pieces of buckshot struck the girls' dormitory, and two black students were killed. A local grand jury found the attack "justified" and U.S. District Court Judge Harold Cox (a Kennedy appointee) declared that students who engage in civil disorders "must expect to be injured or killed."
>
> In Boston in April 1970, a policeman shot and killed an unarmed black man, a patient in a ward in the Boston City Hospital, firing five shots after the black man snapped a towel at him. The chief judge of the municipal court of Boston exonerated the policeman.

Such incidents were endlessly repeated in the history of the country, coming randomly but persistently out of a racism deep in the institutions, the mind of the country. But there was something else—a planned pattern of violence against militant black organizers, carried on by the police and the Federal Bureau of Investigation.

On December 4, 1969, a little before five in the morning, a squad of Chicago police, armed with a submachine gun and shotguns, raided an apartment where Black Panthers lived. They fired at least eight-two and perhaps two hundred rounds into the apartment, killing twenty-one-year-old Black Panther leader Fred Hampton as he lay in his bed, and another Black Panther, Mark Clark. Years later, it was discovered in a court proceeding that the FBI had an informer among the Panthers, and that he had given the police a floor plan of the apartment, including a sketch of where Fred Hampton slept.

Was the government turning to murder and terror because the concessions—the legislation, the speeches, the intonation of the civil rights hymn "We Shall Overcome" by President Lyndon Johnson—were not working? Between 1956 and 1971 the FBI concluded a massive Counterintelligence Program (known as COINTELPRO) that took 295 actions against black groups. Black militancy seemed stubbornly resistant to destruction.

Was there fear that blacks would turn their attention from the controllable field of voting to the more dangerous arena of wealth and poverty—of class conflict? In 1966, seventy poor black people in Greenville, Mississippi, occupied an unused air force barracks, until they were evicted by the military. A local woman, Mrs. Unita Blackwell, said: "I feel that the federal government have proven that it don't care about poor people.... We're tired of it so we're going to build for ourselves, because we don't have a government that represents us."

The new emphasis was more dangerous than civil rights, because it created the possibility of blacks and whites uniting on the issue of class exploitation. Back in November 1963, A. Philip Randolph had spoken to an AFL-CIO convention about the civil rights movement, and foreseen its direction: "The Negro's protest today is but the first rumbling of the 'under-class.' As the Negro has taken to the streets, so will the unemployed of all races take to the streets."

Attempts began to do with blacks what had been done historically with whites—to lure a small number into the system with economic enticements. There was talk of "black capitalism." Leaders of the

NAACP and CORE were invited to the White House. Chase Manhattan Bank and the Rockefeller family (controllers of Chase) took a special interest in developing "black capitalism." There was a small amount of change and a lot of publicity. There were more black faces in the newspapers and on television, creating an impression of change—and siphoning off into the mainstream a small but significant number of black leaders.

Some new black voices spoke against this. Robert Allen (*Black Awakening in Capitalist America*) wrote: "If the community as a whole is to benefit.... Black business firms must be treated and operated as social property, belonging to the general black community, not as the private property of individual or limited groups of individuals...."

A black woman, Patricia Robinson, in a pamphlet distributed in Boston in 1970 (*Poor Black Woman*), said the black woman "allies herself with the have-nots in the wider world and their revolutionary struggles." She said the poor black woman "has begun to question aggressive male domination and the class society which enforces it, capitalism."

The system was working hard, by the late sixties and early seventies, to contain the frightening explosiveness of the black upsurge. Blacks were voting in large numbers in the South, and in the 1968 Democratic Convention three blacks were admitted into the Mississippi delegation. By 1977, more than 2,000 blacks held office in eleven southern states (in 1965 the number was 72). There were 2 Congressman, 11 state senators, 95 state representatives, 267 county commissioners, 76 mayors, 824 city council members, 18 sheriffs or chiefs of police, 508 school board members.

It was a dramatic advance. But blacks, with 20 percent of the South's population, still held less than 3 percent of the elective offices. A *New York Times* reporter, analyzing the new situation in 1977, pointed out that even where blacks held important city offices: "Whites almost always retain economic power." After Maynard Jackson, a black, became mayor of Atlanta, "the white business establishment continued to exert its influence."

Those blacks in the South who could afford to go to downtown restaurants and hotels were no longer barred because of their race. More blacks could go to colleges and universities, to law schools and medical schools. Northern cities were busing children back and forth in an attempt to create racially mixed schools, despite the racial segregation in housing. None of this, however, was halting what Frances Piven and Richard Cloward (*Poor People's Movements*) called "the destruction of the black lower class"—the unemployment, the deterioration of the ghetto, the rising crime, drug addiction, violence.

In the summer of 1977, the Department of Labor reported that the rate of unemployment among black youths was 34.8 percent. Despite the new opportunities for a small number of blacks, blacks were twice as likely to die of diabetes; seven times as likely to be victims of homicidal violence rising out of the poverty and despair of the ghetto.

Statistics did not tell the whole story. Racism, always a national fact, not just a southern one, emerged in northern cities, as the federal government made concessions to poor blacks in a way that pitted them against poor whites for resources made scarce by the system. Blacks, freed from slavery to take their place under capitalism, had long been forced into conflict with whites for scarce jobs. Now, with desegregation in housing, blacks tried to move into neighborhoods where whites, themselves poor, crowded, troubled, could find in them a target for their anger.

In Boston, the busing of black children to white schools, and whites to black schools, set off a wave of white neighborhood violence. The use of busing to integrate schools—sponsored by the government and the courts in response to the black movement—was an ingenious concession to protest. It had the effect of pushing poor whites and poor blacks into competition for the miserable, inadequate schools that the system provided for all the poor.

Was the black population—hemmed into the ghetto, divided by the growth of a middle class, decimated by poverty, attacked by the government, driven into conflict with whites—under control? Surely, in the mid-seventies, there was no great black movement under way. Yet, a new black consciousness had been born and was still alive.

Would a new black movement go beyond the limits of the civil rights actions of the sixties, beyond the spontaneous urban riots of the seventies, beyond separatism to a coalition of white and black in a historic new alliance? There was no way of knowing this. As Langston Hughes said, what happens to a dream deferred? Does it dry up? Or does it explode?

Exercises

1. Why do you suppose Henry Cabot Lodge put McKay's poem in the *Congressional Record*?

2. How does Countee Cullen's poem "Incident" capture the complex and indelible psychological impact of racism?

3. Why were many whites surprised by the black revolt of the 1950s and 1960s?

4. Why did Herndon join the Communist party? For what action(s) did he spend five years in prison?

5. Why did Truman and his advisers feel a need to "act on the race question" immediately following World War II? What evidence exists to support Zinn's answer to this question?

6. What actions did Truman's administration take "on the race question"? What actions did they not take?

7. In what way did the 1954 Brown decision by the Supreme Court mark a departure from its previous course? In what way did it not?

8. How did the Montgomery bus boycott begin? What was the end result of the boycott?

9. What were the successful tactics and tools used in the Montgomery boycott that were used in similarly successive struggles?

10. What was the key strategy that King contributed to the civil rights movement of the 1950s and 1960s?

11. What event led to sit-ins in fifteen cities and five states? What was the purpose of the sit-ins?

12. What was the final result of the sit-ins?

13. What was the goal of the Freedom Riders? How were they able to achieve that goal?

14. What are the differences and similarities between SNCC and the IWW? Consider the following when answering: goals; tactics; strategies; tools; media response; government response (local, state, and federal); membership; degree of success.

15. What point is Zinn making by retelling the murders of Goodman and Schwerner?

16. Compare the degree of success or failure of the civil rights movement and the Populist movement. Consider: legislation passed; effectiveness of legislation; difference between stated goals and accomplished goals; effect on the dominant culture of the United States.

17. How did the Voting Rights Law of 1965 differ from previous laws?

18. In 1968, only 60 percent of those eligible to vote were registered. What is the significance of being a registered voter? of not being registered? If 30 percent of registered voters voted in the presidential election of 1968, what then is the percentage of total voters who voted?

19. Why did the U.S. government choose to enforce voting to the exclusion of other means to end racism in the United States? Why did the U.S. governmnt later choose busing as another area to enforce? What laws were on the books by the end of the 1960s that were not being enforced by the government?

20. What compromises did civil rights leaders make in order to have federal approval of the 1963 March on Washington? Why do you think they felt that federal approval was worth such compromises?

21. What did Malcolm X think of the 1963 march?

22. What do you think Zinn means by this: "...but voting was not a fundamental solution to racism or poverty?"

23. How did the Watts riot begin? How did it end?

24. How did the National Advisory Committee on Urban Disorders explain the explosion of violence that followed the Watts riot of 1965?

25. Why did the Black Panthers have guns? (Compare Zinn's answer with standard American history texts).

26. Why did King speak out against the war in Vietnam? Why did he not speak out against the war earlier than he did?

27. How did the government respond to King's shift in focus from civil rights to poverty? How can one explain the government's response?

28. Judge Harold Cox exonerated the police who killed two students at Jackson State College by declaring that those who participated in protest demonstrations "must expect to be injured or killed." Why is it important for the government to have such a principle established?

29. Were Fred Hampton and Mark Clark murdered? Defend your answer and establish the argument against your answer. What further detail (in addition to that which Zinn provides) would help make one argument stronger than the other?

30. What were the goals of "black capitalists"? What strategies did they adopt to achieve these goals?

31. In 1977, what percentage of elective offices were held by blacks in the South? Did this represent progress? Progress toward what goal? Whose goal? (Keep in mind that "goal" means an end or stopping point.)

32. How was "busing" an "ingenious concession to protest"? Did it contribute to deferring the dream?

33. *Debate Resolution*: Voting does affects neither social nor economic change.

34. *Draw a map* that identifies the following: Montgomery and Birmingham, Alabama; Jackson and Philadelphia, Mississippi; Greensboro, North Carolina; Watts (Los Angeles); Detroit; Chicago.

Chapter 18

The Impossible Victory: Vietnam

From 1964 to 1972, the wealthiest and most powerful nation in the history of the world made a maximum military effort, with everything short of atomic bombs, to defeat a nationalist revolutionary movement in a tiny, peasant country—and failed. When the United States fought in Vietnam, it was organized modern technology versus organized human beings, and the human beings won.

In the course of that war, there developed in the United States the greatest antiwar movement the nation had ever experienced, a movement that played a critical part in bringing the war to an end. It was another startling fact of the sixties.

In the fall of 1945 Japan, defeated, was forced to leave Indochina, the former French colony it had occupied at the start of the war. In the meantime, a revolutionary movement had grown there, determined to end colonial control and to achieve a new life for the peasants of Indochina. Led by a Communist named Ho Chi Minh, the revolutionists fought against the Japanese, and when they were gone held a spectacular celebration in Hanoi in late 1945, with a million people in the streets, and issued a Declaration of Independence.

Their declaration borrowed from the Declaration of the Rights of Man and the Citizen, in the French Revolution, and from the American Declaration of Independence, and began: "All men are created equal. They are endowed by their Creator with certain inalienable rights; among these are Life, Liberty, and the pursuit of Happiness." Just as the Americans in 1776 had listed their grievances against the English king, the Vietnamese listed their complaints against French rule:

> They have enforced inhuman laws.... They have built more prisons than schools. They have mercilessly slain our patriots, they have drowned uprisings in rivers of blood. They have fettered public opinion.... They have robbed us of our rice fields, our mines, our forests, and our raw materials....

The U.S. Defense Department study of the Vietnam war, intended to be "top secret" but released to the public by Daniel Ellsberg and Anthony Russo in the famous *Pentagon Papers* case, described Ho Chi Minh's work:

> ...Ho had built the Viet Minh into the only Vietnam-wide political organization capable of effective resistance to either the Japanese or the French. He was the only Vietnamese wartime leader with a national following, and he assured himself wider fealty among the Vietnamese people when in August–September, 1945, he overthrew the Japanese... established the Democratic Republic of Vietnam, and staged receptions for in-coming allied occupation forces.... For a few weeks in September, 1945, Vietnam was—for the first and only time in its modern history—free of foreign domination, and united from north to south under Ho Chi Minh....

The Western powers were already at work to change this. England occupied the southern part of Indochina and then turned it back to the French. Nationalist China (this was under Chiang Kai-shek, before the Communist revolution) occupied the northern part of Indochina, and the United States persuaded it to turn that back to the French. As Ho Chi Minh told an American journalist: "We apparently stand quite alone.... We shall have to depend on ourselves."

Between October 1945 and February 1946, Ho Chi Minh wrote eight letters to President Truman, reminding him of the self-determination promises of the Atlantic Charter. One of the letters was sent both to Truman and to the United Nations:

> I wish to invite attention of your Excellency for strictly humanitarian reasons to following matter. Two million Vietnamese died of starvation during winter of 1944 and spring 1945 because of starvation policy of French who seized and stored until it rotted all available rice.... Three-fourths of cultivated land was flooded in summer 1945, which was followed by a severe drought; of normal harvest five-sixths was lost .... Many people are starving.... Unless great world powers and international relief organizations bring us immediate assistance we face imminent catastrophe....

Truman never replied.

In October of 1946, the French bombarded Haiphong, a port in northern Vietnam, and there began the eight-year war between the Vietminh movement and the French over who would rule Vietnam. After the Communist victory in China in 1949 and the Korean war the following year, the United States began giving large amounts of military aid to the French. By 1954, the United States had given 300,000 small arms and machine guns, enough to equip the entire French army in Indochina, and $1 billion; all together, the U.S. was financing 80 percent of the French war effort.

Why was the United States doing this? To the public, the word was that the United States was helping to stop Communism in Asia, but there was not much public discussion.

A secret memo of the National Security Council in June 1952 also pointed to the chain of U.S. military bases along the coast of China, the Philippines, Taiwan, Japan, South Korea:

> Communist control of all of Southeast Asia would render the U.S. position in the Pacific offshore island chain precarious and would seriously jeopardize fundamental U.S. security interests in the Far East.... Southeast Asia, especially Malaya and Indonesia, is the principal world source of natural rubber and tin, and a producer of petroleum and other strategically important commodities....

It was also noted that Japan depended on the rice of Southeast Asia, and Communist victory there would "make it extremely difficult to prevent Japan's eventual accommodation to communism."

In 1953, a congressional study mission reported: "The area of Indochina is immensely wealthy in rice, rubber, coal and iron ore. Its position makes it a strategic key to the rest of Southeast Asia." That year, a State Department memorandum said that: "If the French actually decided to withdraw, the U.S. would have to consider most seriously whether to take over in this area."

In 1954, the French, having been unable to win Vietnamese popular support, which was overwhelmingly behind Ho Chi Minh and the revolutionary movement, had to withdraw.

An international assemblage at Geneva presided over the peace agreement between the French and the Vietminh. It was agreed that the French would temporarily withdraw into the southern part of Vietnam, that the Vietminh would remain in the north, and that an election would take place in two years in a unified Vietnam to enable the Vietnamese to choose their own government.

The United States moved quickly to prevent the unification and to establish South Vietnam as an American sphere. It set up in Saigon as head of the government a former Vietnamese official named Ngo Dinh Diem, who had recently been living in New Jersey, and encouraged him not to hold the scheduled elections for unification. As the *Pentagon Papers* put it: "South Viet Nam was essentially the creation of the United States."

The Diem regime became increasingly unpopular. Diem was a Catholic, and most Vietnamese were Buddhists; Diem was close to the land-lords, and this was a country of peasants. His pretenses at land reform left things basically as they were. He replaced locally selected provincial chiefs with his own men, appointed in Saigon. Diem imprisoned more and more Vietnamese who criticized the regime for corruption, for lack of reform.

Opposition grew quickly in the countryside, where Diem's apparatus could not reach well, and around 1958 guerrilla activities began against the regime. The Communist regime in Hanoi gave aid, encouragement, and sent people south—most of them southerners who had gone north after the Geneva accords—to support the guerrilla movement.

In 1960, the National Liberation Front was formed in the South. It united the various strands of opposition to the regime; its strength came from South Vietnamese peasants, who saw it as a way of changing their daily lives. A U.S. government analyst named Douglas Pike, in his book *Viet Cong*, based on interviews with rebels and captured documents, tried to give a realistic assessment of what the United States faced:

> In the 2561 villages of South Vietnam, the National Liberation Front created a host of nation-wide socio-political organizations in a country where mass organizations…were virtually nonexistent…. Aside from the NLF there had never been a truly mass-based political party in South Vietnam.

Pike wrote: "The Communists have brought to the villages of South Vietnam significant social change and have done so largely by means of the communication process." That is, they were organizers much more than they were warriors. "What struck me most forcibly about the NLF was its totality as a social revolution first and as a war second…. [T]he purpose of this vast organizational effort was…to restructure the social order of the village and train the villages to control themselves."

Pike estimated that the NLF membership by early 1962 stood at around 300,000. The *Pentagon Papers* said of this period: "Only the Viet Cong had any real support and influence on a broad base in the countryside."

When Kennedy took office in early 1961 he continued the policies of

Truman and Eisenhower in Southeast Asia. Almost immediately, he approved a secret plan for various military actions in Vietnam and Laos, including the "dispatch of agents to North Vietnam" to engage in "sabotage and light harassment," according to the *Pentagon Papers*. Back in 1956, he had spoken of "the amazing success of President Diem" and said of Diem's Vietnam: "Her political liberty is an inspiration."

One day in June 1963, a Buddhist monk sat down in the public square in Saigon and set himself afire. More Buddhist monks began committing suicide by fire to dramatize their opposition to the Diem regime. Diem's police raided the Buddhist pagodas and temples, wounded thirty monks, arrested fourteen hundred people, and closed down the pagodas. There were demonstrations in the city. The police fired, killing nine people. Then, in Hué, the ancient capital, ten thousand demonstrated in protest.

Under the Geneva Accords, the United States was permitted to have 685 military advisers in southern Vietnam. Eisenhower secretly sent several thousand. Under Kennedy, the figure rose to sixteen thousand, and some of them began to take part in combat operations. Diem was losing. Most of the South Vietnam countryside was now controlled by local villagers organized by the NLF.

Diem was becoming an embarrassment, an obstacle to effective control over Vietnam. Some Vietnamese generals began plotting to overthrow his regime, staying in touch with a CIA man named Lucien Conein. Conein met secretly with American Ambassador Henry Cabot Lodge, who was enthusiastically for the coup. Lodge reported to Kennedy's assistant, McGeorge Bundy, on October 25 (*Pentagon Papers*): "I have personally approved each meeting between General Tran Van Don and Conein who has carried out my orders in each instance explicitly." Kennedy seemed hesitant, but no move was made to warn Diem. Indeed, just before the coup, and just after he had been in touch through Conein with the plotters, Lodge spent a weekend with Diem at a seaside resort. When, on November 1, 1963, the generals attacked the presidential palace, Diem phoned Ambassador Lodge for help, and Lodge replied: "I have heard the shooting, but am not acquainted with all the facts." He told Diem to phone him if he could do anything for his physical safety.

That was the last conversation any American had with Diem. He fled the palace, but he and his brother were apprehended by the plotters, taken out in a truck, and executed.

Earlier in 1963, Kennedy's undersecretary of state, U. Alexis Johnson, was speaking before the Economic Club of Detroit: "What is the attraction that Southeast Asia has exerted for centuries on the great powers flanking it on all sides?"...The countries of Southeast Asia produce rich exportable surpluses such as rice, rubber, teak, corn, tin, spices, oil, and many others...."

This was not the language used by President Kennedy, who explained the U.S. aim in Vietnam as stopping Communism and promoting freedom.

Three weeks after the execution of Diem, Kennedy himself was assassinated, and his Vice President, Lyndon Johnson, took office.

The generals who succeeded Diem could not suppress the National Liberation Front. Gen. Maxwell Taylor reported in late 1964: "Not only do the Viet-Cong units have the recuperative powers of the phoenix, but they have an amazing ability to maintain morale."

In early August 1964, President Johnson used a murky set of events in the Gulf of Tonkin, off the coast of North Vietnam, to launch full-scale war on Vietnam. Johnson and Secretary of Defense Robert McNamara told the American public there was an attack by North Vietnamese torpedo boats on American destroyers. "While on routine patrol in international waters," McNamara said, "The U.S. destroyer *Maddox* underwent an unprovoked attack."

It later turned out that the Gulf of Tonkin episode was a fake, that the highest American officials had lied to the public. In fact, the CIA had engaged in a secret operation attacking North Vietnamese coastal installations—so if there had been an attack it would not have been "unprovoked." It was not a "routine patrol," because the *Maddox* was on a special electronic spying mission. And it was not in international waters but in Vietnamese territorial waters. It turned out that no torpedoes were fired at the *Maddox*, as McNamara said. Another reported attack on another destroyer, two nights later, which Johnson called "open aggression on the high seas," seems also to have been an invention.

At the time of the incident, Secretary of State Rusk was questioned on NBC television about why the tiny country of Vietnam would attack the United States. Rusk replied: "Their very processes of logic are different. So that it's very difficult to enter into each other's minds across that great ideological gulf."

The Tonkin "attack" brought a congressional resolution, passed unanimously in the House, and with only two dissenting votes in the Senate, giving Johnson the power to take military action as he saw fit in Southeast Asia. There was no congressional declaration of war, as the Constitution required.

The Supreme Court, supposed to be the watchdog of the Constitution, was asked by a number of petitioners in the course of the Vietnam war to declare the war unconstitutional. Again and again, it refused even to consider the issue.

Immediately after the Tonkin affair, American warplanes began bombarding North Vietnam. During 1965, over 200,000 American soldiers were sent to South Vietnam, and in 1966, 200,000 more. By early 1968, there were more than 500,000 American troops there, and the U.S. Air Force was dropping bombs at a rate unequaled in history. Tiny glimmerings of the massive human suffering under this bombardment came to the outside world. On June 5, 1965, the *New York Times* carried a dispatch from Saigon:

> As the Communists withdrew from Quangngai last Monday, United States jet bombers pounded the hills into which they were headed. Many Vietnamese—one estimate is as high as 500—were killed by the strikes. The American contention is that they were Vietcong soldiers. But three out of four patients seeking treatment in a Vietnamese hospital afterward for burns from napalm, or jellied gasoline, were village women.

On September 6, another press dispatch from Saigon:

> In another delta province there is a woman who has both arms burned off by napalm and her eyelids so badly burned that she cannot close them. When it is time for her to sleep her family puts a blanket over her head. The woman had two of her children killed in the air strike that maimed her. Few Americans appreciate what their nation is doing to South Vietnam with airpower...innocent civilians are dying every day in South Vietnam.

Large areas of South Vietnam were declared "free fire zones," which meant that all persons remaining within them—civilians, old people, children—were considered an enemy, and bombs were dropped at will. Villages suspected of harboring Viet Cong were subject to "search and destroy" missions—men of military age in the villages were killed, the homes were burned, the women, children, and old people were sent off to refugee camps.

The CIA in Vietnam, in a program called "Operation Phoenix," secretly, without trial, executed at least twenty thousand civilians in South Vietnam who were suspected of being members of the Communist underground.

After the war, the release of records of the International Red Cross showed that in South Vietnamese prison camps, where at the height of the war 65,000 to 70,000 people were held and often beaten and tortured, American advisers observed and sometimes participated. The Red Cross observers found continuing, systematic brutality at the two principal Vietnamese POW camps—at Phu Quoc and Qui Nhon, where American advisers were stationed.

By the end of the war, seven million tons of bombs had been dropped on Vietnam, Laos, and Cambodia—more than twice the amount of bombs dropped on Europe and Asia in World War II. In addition, poisonous sprays were dropped by planes to destroy trees and any kind of growth—an area the size of the state of Massachusetts was covered with such poison. Vietnamese mothers reported birth defects in their children. Yale biologists, using the same poison (2,4,5,T) on mice, reported defective mice born and said they had no reason to believe the effect on humans was different.

On March 16, 1968, a company of American soldiers went into the hamlet of My Lai 4, in Quang Ngai province. They rounded up the inhabitants, including old people and women with infants in their arms. These people were ordered into a ditch, where they were methodically shot to death by American soldiers. The testimony of James Dursi, a rifleman, at the later trial of Lieut. William Calley, was reported in the *New York Times*:

> Lieutenant Calley and a weeping rifleman named Paul D. Meadlo—the same soldier who had fed candy to the children before shooting them—pushed the prisoners into the ditch.... People were diving on top of each other; mothers were trying to protect their children.... Between 450 and 500 people—mostly women, children, and older men, were buried in mass graves.

The army tried to cover up what happened. But a letter began circulating from a GI named Ron Ridenhour, who had heard about the massacre. There were photos taken of the killing by an army photographer, Ronald Haeberle. Seymour Hersh, then working for an antiwar news agency in Southeast Asia called *Dispatch News Service*, wrote about it, but the American press did not pay any attention.

Several of the officers in the My Lai massacre were put on trial, but only Lieutenant Calley was found guilty. He was sentenced to life imprisonment, but his sentence was reduced twice; he served three years—Nixon ordered that he be under house arrest rather than a regular prison—and then was paroled. Thousands of Americans came to his defense. Part of it was in patriotic justification of his action as necessary against the "Communists." Part of it seems to have been a feeling that he was unjustly singled out in a war with many similar atrocities. Col. Oran Henderson, who had been charged with covering up the My Lai killings, told reporters in early 1971: "Every unit of brigade size has its My Lai hidden someplace."

Indeed, My Lai was unique only in its details. Hersh reported a letter sent by a GI to his family, and published in a local newspaper:

> Dear Mom and Dad:
> Today we went on a mission and I am not very proud of myself, my friends, or my country. We burned every hut in sight!...
> Everyone is crying, begging and praying that we don't separate them and take their husbands and fathers, sons and grandfathers. The women wail and moan.
> Then they watch in terror as we burn their homes, personal possessions and food. Yes, we burn all rice and shoot all livestock.

The unpopularity of the Saigon government explains the success of the National Liberation Front in infiltrating Saigon and other government-held towns in early 1968, without the people there warning the government. The NLF thus launched a surprise offensive (it was the time of "Tet," their New Year holiday) that carried them into the heart of Saigon, immobilized Tan San Nhut airfield, even occupied the American Embassy briefly. The offensive was beaten back, but it demonstrated that all the enormous firepower delivered on Vietnam by the United States had not destroyed the NLF, its morale, its popular support, its will to fight. It caused a reassessment in the American government, more doubts among the American people.

The heavy bombings were intended to destroy the will of ordinary Vietnamese to resist, as in the bombings of German and Japanese population centers in World War II—despite President Johnson's public insistence that only "military targets" were being bombed. The government was using language like "one more turn of the screw" to describe bombing. The CIA at one point in 1966 recommended a "bombing program of greater intensity," according to the *Pentagon Papers*, directed against, in the CIA's words, "the will of the regime as a target system."

Meanwhile, just across the border of Vietnam, in a neighboring country, Laos, where a right-wing government installed by the CIA faced a rebellion, one of the most beautiful areas in the world, the Plain of Jars, was being destroyed by bombing. This was not reported by the government or the press, but an American who lived in Laos, Fred Branfman, told the story in his book *Voices from the Plain of Jars*.

Over 25,000 attack sorties were flown against the Plain of Jars from May 1964 through September 1969; over 75,000 tons of bombs were dropped on it; on the ground, thousands were killed and wounded, tens of thousands driven underground, and the entire above-ground society leveled.

In September 1973, a former government official in Laos, Jerome Doolittle, wrote in the *New York Times*: "When I first arrived in Laos, I was instructed to answer all press questions about our massive and merciless bombing campaign in that tiny country with: 'At the request of the Royal Laotian Government, the United States is conducting unarmed reconnaissance flights.'...This was a lie. Every reporter to whom I told it knew it was a lie...."

By early 1968, the cruelty of the war began touching the conscience of many Americans. For many others, the problem was that the United States was unable to win the war, while 40,000 American soldiers were dead by this time, 250,000 wounded, with no end in sight. (The Vietnam casualties were many times this number.)

Lyndon Johnson had escalated a brutal war and failed to win it. His popularity was at an all-time low; he could not appear publicly without a demonstration against him and the war. The chant "LBJ, LBJ, how many kids did you kill today?" was heard in demonstrations throughout the country. In the spring of 1968 Johnson announced he would not run again for president, and that negotiations for peace would begin with the Vietnamese in Paris.

In the fall of 1968, Richard Nixon, pledging that he would get the United States out of Vietnam, was elected president. He began to withdraw troops; by February 1972, less than 150,000 were left. But the bombing continued. Nixon's policy was "Vietnamization"—the Saigon government, with Vietnamese ground troops, using American money and air power, would carry on the war. Nixon was not ending the war; he was ending the most unpopular aspect of it, the involvement of American soldiers on the soil of a faraway country.

In the spring of 1970, Nixon and Secretary of State Henry Kissinger launched an invasion of Cambodia, after a long bombardment that the government never disclosed to the public. The invasion not only led to an outcry of protest in the United States, but it was also a military failure, and Congress resolved that Nixon could not use American troops in extending the war without congressional approval.

The following year, without American troops, the United States supported a South Vietnamese invasion of Laos. This too failed. In 1971, 800,000 tons of bombs were dropped by the United States on Laos, Cambodia, and Vietnam. Meantime, the Saigon military regime, headed by President Nguyen Van Thieu, the last of a long succession of Saigon chiefs of state, was keeping thousands of opponents in jail.

Some of the first signs of opposition in the United States to the Vietnam war came out of the civil rights movement—perhaps because the experience of black people with the government led them to distrust any claim that it was fighting for freedom. On the very day that Lyndon Johnson was telling the nation in early August 1964 about the Gulf of Tonkin incident, and announcing the bombing of North Vietnam, black and white activists were gathering near Philadelphia, Mississippi, at a memorial service for the three civil rights workers killed there that summer. One of the speakers pointed bitterly to Johnson's use of force in Asia, comparing it with the violence used against blacks in Mississippi.

In mid-1965, in McComb, Mississippi, young blacks who had just learned that a classmate of theirs was killed in Vietnam distributed a leaflet: "No Mississippi Negroes should be fighting in Viet Nam for the White man's freedom, until all the Negro People are free in Mississippi."

When Secretary of Defense Robert McNamara visited Mississippi and praised Senator John Stennis, a prominent racist, as a "man of very genuine greatness," white and black students marched in protest, with placards saying "In Memory of the Burned Children of Vietnam."

The Student Nonviolent Coordinating Committee declared in early 1966 that "the United States is pursuing an aggressive policy in violation of international law" and called for withdrawal from Vietnam. That summer, six members of SNCC were arrested for an invasion of an induction center in Atlanta. They were convicted and sentenced to several years in prison.

Around the same time, Julian Bond, a SNCC activist who had just been elected to the Georgia House of Representatives, spoke out against the war and the draft, and the House voted that he not be seated because his statements violated the Selective Service Act and "tend to bring discredit to the House." The Supreme Court restored Bond to his seat, saying he had the right to free expression under the First Amendment.

One of the great sports figures of the nation, Muhammad Ali, the black boxer and heavyweight champion, refused to serve in what he called a "white man's war"; boxing authorities took away his title as champion. Martin Luther King Jr. spoke out in 1967 at Riverside Church in New York:

Somehow this madness must cease. We must stop now. I speak as a child of God and brother to the suffering poor of Vietnam. I speak for those whose land is being laid waste, whose homes are being destroyed, whose culture is being subverted. I speak for the poor of America who are paying the double price of smashed hopes at home and death and corruption in Vietnam. I speak as a citizen of the world, for the world as it stands aghast at the path we have taken. I speak as an American to the leaders of my own nation. The great initiative in this war is ours. The initiative to stop it must be ours.

Young men began to refuse to register for the draft, refused to be inducted if called. As early as May 1964 the slogan "We Won't Go" was widely publicized. Some who had registered began publicly burning their draft cards to protest the war. In October of 1967 there were organized draft-card "turnins" all over the country; in San Francisco alone, three hundred draft cards were returned to the government. Just before a huge demonstration at the Pentagon that month, a sack of collected draft cards was presented to the Justice Department.

In May 1969 the Oakland induction center, where draftees reported from all of northern California, reported that of 4,400 men ordered to report for induction, 2,400 did not show up. In the first quarter of 1970 the Selective Service System, for the first time, could not meet its quota.

Early in the war, there had been two separate incidents, barely noticed by most Americans. On November 2, 1965, in front of the Pentagon in Washington, as thousands of employees were streaming out of the building in the late afternoon, Norman Morrison, a thirty-two-year-old pacifist, father of three, stood below the third-floor windows of Secretary of Defense Robert McNamara, doused himself with kerosene, and set himself afire, giving up his life in protest against the war. Also that year, in Detroit, an eighty-two-year-old woman named Alice Herz burned herself to death to make a statement against the horror of Indochina.

A remarkable change in sentiment took place. In early 1965, when the bombing of North Vietnam began, a hundred people gathered on the Boston Common to voice their indignation. On October 15, 1969, the number of people assembled on the Boston Common to protest the war was 100,000. Perhaps 2 million people across the nation gathered that day in towns and villages that had never seen an antiwar meeting.

By 1970, the Washington peace rallies were drawing hundreds of thousands of people. In 1971, twenty thousand came to Washington to commit civil disobedience, trying to tie up Washington traffic to express their revulsion against the killing still going on in Vietnam. Fourteen thousand of them were arrested, the largest mass arrest in American history.

Hundreds of volunteers in the Peace Corps spoke out against the war. In Chile, ninety-two volunteers defied the Peace Corps director and issued a circular denouncing the war. Eight hundred former members of the corps issued a statement of protest against what was happening in Vietnam.

The poet Robert Lowell, invited to a White House function, refused to come. Arthur Miller, also invited, sent a telegram to the White House: "When the guns boom, the arts die." Singer Eartha Kitt was invited to a luncheon on the White House lawn and shocked all those present by speaking out, in the presence of the president's wife, against the war. A teenager, called to the White House to accept a prize, came and criticized the war.

In London, two young Americans gate-crashed the American ambassador's elegant Fourth of July reception and called out a toast: "To all the dead and dying in Vietnam." They were carried out by guards. In the Pacific Ocean, two young American seamen hijacked an American munitions ship to divert its load of bombs from airbases in Thailand. For four days they took command of the ship and its crew, taking amphetamine pills to stay awake until the ship reached Cambodian waters.

Middle-class and professional people unaccustomed to activism began to speak up. In May 1970, the *New York Times* reported from Washington: "100 'ESTABLISHMENT' LAWYERS JOIN WAR PROTEST." Corporations began to wonder whether the war was going to hurt their long-range business interests; the *Wall Street Journal* began criticizing the continuation of the war.

As the war became more and more unpopular, people in or close to the government began to break out of the circle of assent. The most dramatic instance was the case of Daniel Ellsberg.

Ellsberg was a Harvard-trained economist, a former marine officer, employed by the RAND Corporation, which did special, often secret research for the U.S. government. Ellsberg helped write the Department of Defense history of the war in Vietnam and then decided to make the top-secret document public, with the aid of his friend, Anthony Russo, a former RAND Corporation man. The two had met in Saigon, where both had been affected, in different experiences, by direct sight of the war, and had become powerfully indignant at what the United States was doing to the people of Vietnam.

Ellsberg and Russo spent night after night, after hours, at a friend's advertising agency, duplicating the 7,000-page document. Then Ellsberg gave copies to various Congressmen and to the *New York Times*. In June 1971 the *Times* began printing selections from what came to be known as the *Pentagon Papers*. It created a national sensation.

The Nixon administration tried to get the Supreme Court to stop further publication, but the Court said this was "prior restraint" of the freedom of the press and thus unconstitutional. The government then indicted Ellsberg and Russo for violating the Espionage Act by releasing classified documents to unauthorized people; they faced long terms in prison if convicted. The judge, however, called off the trial during the jury deliberations, because the Watergate events unfolding at the time revealed unfair practices by the prosecution.

The antiwar movement, early in its growth, found a strange, new constituency: priests and nuns of the Catholic Church. Some of them had been aroused by the civil rights movement, others by their experiences in Latin America, where they saw poverty and injustice under governments supported by the United States. In the fall of 1967, Father Philip Berrigan (a Josephite priest who was a veteran of World War II), joined by artist Tom Lewis and friends David Eberhardt and James Mengel, went to the office of a draft board in Baltimore, Maryland, drenched the draft records with blood, and waited to be arrested. They were put on trial and sentenced to prison terms of two to six years.

The following May, Philip Berrigan—out on bail in the Baltimore case—was joined in a second action by his brother Daniel, a Jesuit priest who had visited North Vietnam and seen the effects of U.S. bombing. They and seven other people went into a draft board office in Catonsville, Maryland, removed records, and set them afire outside in the presence of reporters and onlookers. They were convicted and sentenced to prison, and became famous as the "Catonsville Nine."

Dan Berrigan wrote a "Meditation" at the time of the Catonsville incident:

> Our apologies, good friends, for the fracture of good order, the burning of paper instead of children.... We could not, so help us God, do otherwise.... The time is past when good men can remain silent, when obedience can segregate men from public risk, when the poor can die without defense.

When his appeals had been exhausted, and he was supposed to go to prison, Daniel Berrigan disappeared. He stayed underground for four months, writing poems, issuing statements, giving secret interviews, appearing suddenly in a Philadelphia church to give a sermon and then disappearing again, baffling the FBI, until an informer's interception of a letter disclosed his whereabouts and he was captured and imprisoned.

The effect of the war and of the bold action of some priests and nuns was to crack the traditional conservatism of the Catholic community. On Moratorium Day 1969, at the Newton College of the Sacred Heart near Boston, a sanctuary of bucolic quiet and political silence, the great front door of the college displayed a huge painted red fist. At Boston College, a Catholic institution, six thousand people gathered that evening in the gymnasium to denounce the war.

Students, often spurred by the Students for a Democratic Society (SDS), were heavily involved in the early protests against the war. Even in the high schools, in the late sixties, there were five hundred underground newspapers. At the Brown University commencement in 1969, two-thirds of the graduating class turned their backs when Henry Kissinger stood up to address them.

The climax of protest came in the spring of 1970 when President Nixon ordered the invasion of Cambodia. At Kent State University in Ohio, on May 4, when students gathered to demonstrate against the war, National Guardsmen fired into the crowd. Four students were killed. One was paralyzed for life. Students at four hundred colleges and universities went on strike in protest. It was the largest general student strike in the history of the United States. During that school year of 1969–1970, the FBI listed 1,785 student demonstrations, including the occupation of 313 buildings.

The commencement day ceremonies after the Kent State killings were unlike any the nation had ever seen. From Amherst, Massachusetts, came this newspaper report on the 100th Commencement of the University of Massachusetts: "Red fists of protest, white peace symbols, and blue doves were stenciled on black academic gowns, and nearly every other senior wore an armband representing a plea for peace."

Student protests against the ROTC (Reserve Officers Training Program) resulted in the canceling of those programs in over forty colleges and universities. The ROTC was depended on to supply half the officers in Vietnam. In September 1973, for the sixth straight month, the ROTC could not fulfill its quota.

The publicity given to the student protests created the impression that the opposition to the war came mostly from middle-class intellectuals. But in Dearborn, Michigan, an automobile manufacturing town, a poll as early as 1967 showed 41 percent of the population favored withdrawal from the Vietnam war. In late 1970, when a Gallup presented the statement: "The

United States should withdraw all troops from Vietnam by the end of next year," 65 percent of those questioned said Yes.

But the most surprising data were in a survey made by the University of Michigan. This showed that, throughout the Vietnam war, Americans with only a grade school education were much more strongly for withdrawal from the war than Americans with a college education. In June 1966, of people with a college education, 27 percent were for immediate withdrawal from Vietnam; of people with only a grade school education, 41 percent were for immediate withdrawal. By September 1970, both groups were more antiwar: 47 percent of the college educated were for withdrawal and 61 percent of grade school graduates.

All this was part of a general change in the entire population of the country. In August of 1965, 61 percent of the population thought the American involvement in Vietnam was not wrong. By May 1971 it was exactly reversed; 61 percent thought our involvement *was* wrong. Bruce Andrews, a Harvard student of public opinion, found that the people most opposed to the war were people over fifty, blacks, and women. He also noted that a study in the spring of 1964, when Vietnam was a minor issue in the newspapers, showed that 53 percent of college-educated people were willing to send troops to Vietnam, but only 33 percent of grade-school-educated people were so willing.

The capacity for independent judgment among ordinary Americans is probably best shown by the swift development of antiwar feeling among American GIs—volunteers and draftees who came mostly from lower-income groups. There had been, earlier in American history, instances of soldiers' disaffection from the war: isolated mutinies in the Revolutionary War, refusal of reenlistment in the midst of hostilities in the Mexican war, desertion and conscientious objection in World War I and World War II. But Vietnam produced opposition by soldiers and veterans on a scale, and with a fervor, never seen before.

It began with isolated protests. As early as June 1965, Richard Steinke, a West Point graduate in Vietnam, refused to board an aircraft taking him to a remote Vietnamese village. "The Vietnamese war," he said, "is not worth a single American life." Steinke was court-martialed and dismissed from the service. The following year, three army privates, one black, one Puerto Rican, one Lithuanian-Italian—all poor—refused to embark for Vietnam, denouncing the war as "immoral, illegal, and unjust." They were court-martialed and imprisoned.

The individual acts multiplied. A black private in Oakland refused to board a troop plane to Vietnam, although he faced eleven years at hard labor. A navy nurse, Lieut. Susan Schnall, was court-martialed for marching in a peace demonstration while in uniform, and for dropping antiwar leaflets from a plane on navy installations. In Norfolk, Virginia, a sailor refused to train fighter pilots because he said the war was immoral. An army lieutenant was arrested in Washington, D.C., in early 1968 for picketing the White House with a sign that said: "120,000 American Casualties—Why?" Two black marines, George Daniels and William Harvey, were given long prison sentences (Daniels, six years, Harvey, ten years, both later reduced) for talking to other black marines against the war.

As the war went on, desertions from the armed forces mounted. Thousands went to Western Europe—France, Sweden, Holland. Most deserters crossed into Canada; some estimates were 50,000, others 100,000. Some stayed in the United States. A few openly defied the military authorities by taking "sanctuary" in churches, where, surrounded by antiwar friends and sympathizers, they waited for capture and court-martial. At Boston University, a thousand students kept vigil for five days and nights in the chapel, supporting an eighteen-year-old deserter, Ray Kroll. Then he was seized by federal agents.

The GI antiwar movement became more organized. Near Fort Jackson, South Carolina, the first "GI coffeehouse" was set up, a place where soldiers could get coffee and doughnuts, find antiwar literature, and talk freely with others. It was called the UFO, and lasted for several years before it was declared a "public nuisance" and closed by court action. But other GI coffeehouses sprang up in half a dozen other places across the country. An antiwar "bookstore" was opened near Fort Devens, Massachusetts, and another one at the Newport, Rhode Island, naval base.

Underground newspapers sprang up at military bases across the country; by 1970 more than fifty were circulating. Mixed with feeling against the war was resentment at the cruelty, the dehumanization, of military life.

The dissidence spread to the war front itself. When the great Moratorium Day demonstrations were taking place in October 1969 in the United States, some GIs in Vietnam wore black armbands to show their support. A news photographer reported that in a platoon on patrol near Da Nang, about half of the men were wearing black armbands. The French newspaper *Le Monde* reported: "A common sight is the black soldier, with his left fist clenched in defiance of a war he has never considered his own."

Veterans back from Vietnam formed a group called Vietnam Veterans

Against the War. In December 1970, hundreds of them went to Detroit to what was called the "Winter Soldier" investigations, to testify publicly about atrocities they had participated in or seen in Vietnam, committed by Americans against Vietnamese. In April 1971 more than a thousand of them went to Washington, D.C., to demonstrate against the war. One by one, they went up to a wire fence around the Capitol, threw over the fence the medals they had won in Vietnam, and made brief statements about the war, sometimes emotionally, sometimes in icy, bitter calm.

In the summer of 1970, twenty-eight commissioned officers of the military, including some veterans of Vietnam, saying they represented about 250 other officers, announced formation of the Concerned Officers Movement against the war. During the fierce bombings of Hanoi and Haiphong, around Christmas 1972, came the first defiance of B-52 pilots who refused to fly those missions.

But most of the antiwar action came from ordinary GIs, and most of these came from lower-income groups—white, black, Native American, Chinese.

A twenty-year-old New York City Chinese-American named Sam Choy enlisted at seventeen in the army, was sent to Vietnam, was made a cook, and found himself the target of abuse by fellow GIs, who called him "Chink" and "gook" (the term for the Vietnamese) and said he looked like the enemy. One day he took a rifle and fired warning shots at his tormenters. Choy was taken by military police, beaten, court-martialed, sentenced to eighteen months of hard labor at Fort Leavenworth. "They beat me up every day, like a time clock.... One thing: I want to tell all the Chinese kids that the army made me sick. They made me so sick that I can't stand it."

Altogether, about 563,000 GIs received less than honorable discharges. In the year 1973, one of every five discharges was "less than honorable," indicating something less than dutiful obedience to the military. Deserters doubled from 47,000 in 1967 to 89,000 in 1971.

One of those who stayed, fought, but then turned against the war was Ron Kovic. His father worked in a supermarket on Long Island. In 1963, at the age of seventeen, he enlisted in the marines. Two years later, in Vietnam, at the age of nineteen, his spine was shattered by shellfire. Paralyzed from the waist down, he was put in a wheelchair. Back in the States, he observed the brutal treatment of wounded veterans in the veterans' hospitals, thought more and more about the war, and joined the Vietnam Veterans Against the War. He went to demonstrations to speak against the war.

One evening Kovic heard actor Donald Sutherland read from the post–World War I novel by Dalton Trumbo, *Johnny Got His Gun*, about a soldier whose limbs and face were shot away by gunfire, a thinking torso who invented a way of communicating with the outside world and then beat out a message so powerful it could not be heard without trembling. "Sutherland began to read the passage and something I will never forget swept over me. It was as if someone was speaking for everything I ever went through in the hospital.... I began to shake and I remember there were tears in my eyes."

Kovic demonstrated against the war, and described his arrest in his book *Born on the Fourth of July*:

> "What's your name?" the officer behind the desk says.
> "Ron Kovic," I say. "Occupation, Vietnam veteran against the war."
> "What?" he says sarcastically, looking down at me.
> "I'm a Vietnam veteran against the war," I almost shout back.
> "You should have died over there," he says. He turns to his assistant.
> "I'd like to take this guy and throw him off the roof."

Kovic and the other veterans drove to Miami to the Republican National Convention in 1972, went into the Convention Hall, wheeled themselves down the aisles, and as Nixon began his acceptance speech shouted, "Stop the bombing! Stop the war!" Delegates cursed them: "Traitor!" and Secret Service men hustled them out of the hall.

In the fall of 1973, with no victory in sight and North Vietnamese troops entrenched in various parts of the South, the United States agreed to accept a settlement that would withdraw American troops and leave the revolutionary troops where they were, until a new elected government would be set up including Communist and non-Communist elements. But the Saigon government refused to agree, and the United States decided to make one final attempt to bludgeon the North Vietnamese into submission. It sent waves of B-52s over Hanoi and Haiphong, destroying homes and hospitals, killing unknown numbers of civilians. The attack did not work. Many of the B-52s were shot down, there was angry protest all over the world—and Kissinger went back to Paris and signed very much the same peace agreement that had been agreed on before.

The United States withdrew its forces, continuing to give aid to the Saigon government, but when the North Vietnamese launched attacks in early 1975 against the major cities in South Vietnam, the government collapsed. In late April 1975, North Vietnamese troops entered Saigon. The American embassy staff fled, along with many Vietnamese who feared

Communist rule, and the long war in Vietnam was over. Saigon was renamed Ho Chi Minh City, and both parts of Vietnam were unified as the Democratic Republic of Vietnam.

Traditional history portrays the end of wars as coming from the initiatives of leaders—negotiations in Paris or Brussels or Geneva or Versailles—just as it often finds the coming of war a response to the demand of "the people." The Vietnam war gave clear evidence that it was only after the intervention in Cambodia ended, and only after the nationwide campus uproar over the invasion, that Congress passed a resolution declaring that American troops should not be sent into Cambodia without its approval.

It was not until late 1973, when American troops had finally been removed from Vietnam, that Congress passed a bill limiting the power of the president to make war without congressional consent; even there, in that "War Powers Resolution," the president could make war for sixty days on his own without a congressional declaration.

The administration tried to persuade the American people that the war was ending because of its decision to negotiate a peace—not because it was losing the war, not because of the powerful antiwar movement in the United States. But the government's own secret memoranda all through the war testify to its sensitivity at each stage about "public opinion" in the United States and abroad. The data is in the *Pentagon Papers*.

Assistant Secretary of Defense John McNaughton's memo of early 1966 suggested destruction of locks and dams to create mass starvation, because "strikes at population targets," would "create a counterproductive wave of revulsion abroad and at home." He warned:

> There may be a limit beyond which many Americans and much of the world will not permit the United States to go. The picture of the world's greatest superpower killing or seriously injuring 1000 non-combatants a week, while trying to pound a tiny backward nation into submission, on an issue whose merits are hotly disputed, is not a pretty one.

In the spring of 1968, with the sudden and scary Tet offensive of the National Liberation Front, General Westmoreland asked President Johnson to send him 200,000 more troops on top of the 525,000 already there. Johnson asked a small group of "action officers" in the Pentagon to advise him on this. They studied the situation and concluded that 200,000 troops would not strengthen the Saigon government because: "The Saigon leadership shows no signs of a willingness—let alone an ability—to attract the necessary loyalty or support of the people." Furthermore, the report said, sending troops would mean mobilizing reserves, increasing the military budget. There would be more U.S. casualties, more taxes. And:

> This growing disaffection accompanied as it certainly will be, by increased defiance of the draft and growing unrest in the cities because of the belief that we are neglecting domestic problems, runs great risks of provoking a domestic crisis of unprecedented proportions.

The "growing unrest in the cities" must have been a reference to the black uprisings that had taken place in 1967—and showed the link, whether blacks deliberately made it or not—between the war abroad and poverty at home.

When Nixon took office, he too tried to persuade the public that protest would not affect him. But he almost went berserk when one lone pacifist picketed the White House. The frenzy of Nixon's actions against dissidents—plans for burglaries, wiretapping, mail openings—suggests the importance of the antiwar movement in the minds of national leaders.

One sign that the ideas of the antiwar movement had taken hold in the American public was that juries became more reluctant to convict antiwar protesters, and local judges too were treating them differently.

The last group of draft board raiders, the "Camden 28," were priests, nuns, and laypeople who raided a draft board in Camden, New Jersey, in August 1971. They were acquitted by the jury on all counts. When the verdict was in, one of the jurors, a fifty-three-old black taxi driver from Atlantic City named Samuel Braithwaite, who had spent eleven years in the army, left a letter for the defendants:

> To you...I say, well done. Well done for trying to heal the sick irresponsible men, men who were chosen by the people to govern and lead them. These men, who failed the people, by raining death and destruction on a hapless country.... You went out to do your part while your brothers remained in their ivory towers watching...and hopefully some day in the near future, peace and harmony may reign to people of all nations.

Vietnam was the first clear defeat to the global American empire formed after World War II. It was administered by revolutionary peasants abroad, and by an astonishing movement of protest at home.

Back on September 26, 1969, President Richard Nixon, noting the growing antiwar activity all over the country, announced that "under no circumstance will I be affected whatever by it." But nine years later, in his *Memoirs*, he admitted that the antiwar movement caused him to drop plans for an intensification of the war: "Although publicly I continued to ignore the raging antiwar controversy...I knew, however, that after all the protests and the Moratorium, American public opinion would be seriously divided by any military escalation of the war." It was a rare presidential admission of the power of public protest.

From a long-range viewpoint, something perhaps even more important had happened. The rebellion at home was spreading beyond the issue of war in Vietnam.

Exercises

1. How were "organized human beings" able to defeat "organized modern technology"? Is it surprising to you that they did? Why or why not?

2. What were the Vietnamese complaints against French rule as itemized in their 1945 Declaration of Independence in 1945 and in Ho Chi Minh's letters to Truman?

3. How did the U.S. Department of Defense internally account for Ho Chi Minh's widespread popular support? What was the public account?

4. Why did the United States finance 80 percent of the French war effort in Indochina? Did the public reason differ from the reason circulated internally?

5. What did the 1954 Geneva Peace Accord stipulate? Why did the United States agree to elections and then prevent elections from occurring?

6. Why was the Diem regime unpopular with the South Vietnamese?

7. What constituted the fundamental strength of the National Liberation Front (NLF)?

8. Can you draw any parallels between the political activity of the NLF in the villages of South Vietnam and the American Communist party's work with American labor? What about between the NLF and the Farmer's Alliance?

9. What was Kennedy's policy toward Vietnam? How was such policy consistent with his policy toward Cuba?

10. Why did Vietnamese Buddhists immolate themselves? Were the Buddhist self-immolations an effective tactic? (Were American self-immolations equally effective?)

11. Why did Kennedy not warn Diem of the impending coup?

12. How did the Johnson administration persuade Congress to give the president the freedom to wage war on Vietnam?

13. Why might U.S newspaper accounts of the U.S. bombings of Vietnam cause American readers to question the reasons behind U.S. involvement in the war?

14. What did the U.S. military hope to achieve by increasing the number of and size of the bombs dropped on Vietnam—"one more turn of the screw"?

15. Why did the United States adopt the tactic of "free fire zones"?

16. What were "search and destroy" missions? What was their purpose?

17. What was "Operation Phoenix"? Why were the American people kept ignorant of its existence?

18. If Chuck Norris or Sylvester Stallone were to make a movie about a rescue from a South Vietnamese prison camp, what might the plot summary be?

19. What does napalm do? Why use it rather than conventional bombs?

20. What does the poison "2,4,5,T" do? Why use it?

21. In what way was the American attack on My Lai 4 a "search and destroy" mission?

22. Why was the U.S. military surprised by the Tet Offensive? What did the NLF accomplish by the offensive?

23. Why did the U.S. press not report the saturation bombing of the Plain of Jars?

24. What did the majority of voting Americans want their president to do about the Vietnam war in 1968? Did Nixon respond to this opinion when elected?

25. Was Nixon's order to invade Cambodia a tactical error in his pursuit of control over American foreign policy?

26. What were the connections that civil rights activists made between American domestic policies and American pursuit of war in Vietnam?

27. What methods did the U.S. government use in its attempt to silence domestic critics of the Vietnam war?

28. What methods did Americans use to hamper the U.S. government's pursuit of war in Vietnam?

29. What were the *Pentagon Papers*? Why did the government want to keep them secret? Why was Ellsberg not jailed for releasing classified material?

30. What experiences initially radicalized those who were to become antiwar priests and nuns?

31. Did the government respond to antiwar protesters differently than the Black Panthers or the Wobblies?

32. What event precipitated the largest general student strike in American history? What is a "general student strike"?

33. Why was the media coverage of the Vietnam war protests biased toward middle-class intellectuals (academic, religious and civic leaders)?

34. "Americans with only a grade school education were much more strongly for withdrawal from the war than Americans with a college education." What might explain this? What evidence is there that might support this statement?

35. "But Vietnam produced opposition by soldiers and veterans on a scale and with a fervor never seen before." Why?

36. What need was being satisfied by underground newspapers? "Bookstores"? "Coffeehouses"?

37. What was being described (testified to) by the speakers at the "Winter Soldier" investigations?

38. What was Sam Choy's experience in the army?

39. Why did the North Vietnamese refuse to sign the peace accord offered by the U.S government in the fall of 1973?

40. At what point did the Vietnam war end?

41. What evidence and arguments does Zinn give to support his thesis that the U.S. involvement in Vietnam was not a response to the demands of the American (or even South Vietnamese) people? What is the evidence that the end of the war did not end at the initiative of the leaders?

42. According to McNaughton's memo, what prevented the U.S. government from perpetrating even greater horrors on the Vietnamese population than they did?

43. After the Tet Offensive, why did Johnson refuse Westmoreland's request for 200,000 troops?

44. The Catonsville Nine were convicted in 1968. The Camden 28 were acquitted in 1971. How does Zinn account for the different verdicts?

45. *Debate Resolution*: U.S. government conduct of the Vietnam war revealed that America is not a democracy.

46. *Draw a map* of Southeast Asia and identify the following: North and South Vietnam; the Demilitarized Zone (DMZ;, Saigon; Hanoi, Cambodia; Laos; the border between China and North Vietnam.

Chapter 19

Surprises

Helen Keller had said in 1911: "We vote? What does that mean?" And Emma Goldman around the same time: "Our modern fetish is universal suffrage." After 1920, women were voting, as men did, and their subordinate condition had hardly changed.

Robert and Helen Lynd, studying Muncie, Indiana (*Middletown*), in the late twenties, noted the importance of good looks and dress in the assessment of women. Also, they found that when men spoke frankly among themselves they were "likely to speak of women as creatures purer and morally better than men but as relatively impractical, emotional, unstable, given to prejudice, easily hurt, and largely incapable of facing facts or doing hard thinking."

It seems that women have best been able to make their first escape from the prison of wifeliness, motherhood, femininity, housework, beautification, isolation, when their services have been desperately needed—whether in industry, or in war, or in social movements. Each time practicality pulled the woman out of her prison—in a kind of work-parole program—the attempt was made to push her back once the need was over, and this led to women's struggle for change.

World War II had brought more women than ever before out of the home into work. By 1960, 36 percent of all women sixteen and older—23 million women—worked for paid wages. But there were nursery schools for the children of only 2 percent of working mothers. The median income of the working woman was about one-third that of the man. And attitudes toward women did not seem to have changed much since the twenties.

In the civil rights movement of the sixties, the signs of a collective stirring began to appear. Women took the place they customarily took in social movements, in the front lines—as privates, not generals. Ella Baker, a veteran fighter from Harlem, now organizing in the South, knew the pattern: "I knew from the beginning that as a woman, an older woman in a group of ministers who are accustomed to having women largely as supporters, there was no place for me to have come into a leadership role."

Nevertheless, women played a crucial role in those early dangerous years of organizing in the South, and were looked on with admiration. Women of all ages demonstrated, went to jail. Mrs. Fannie Lou Hamer, a sharecropper in Ruleville, Mississippi, became legendary as organizer and speaker. She sang hymns; she walked picket lines with her familiar limp (as a child she contracted polio). She roused people to excitement at mass meetings: "I'm sick an' tired o' bein' sick an' tired!"

Around the same time, white, middle-class, professional women were beginning to speak up. A pioneering, early book, strong and influential, was Betty Friedan's *The Feminine Mystique*. "Just what was the problem that has no name? What were the words women used when they tried to express it? Sometimes a woman would say 'I feel empty somehow... incomplete.' Or she would say, 'I feel as if I don't exist.'"

Friedan wrote out of her experience as a middle-class housewife, but what she spoke about touched something inside all women. The "mystique" that Friedan spoke of was the image of the woman as mother, as wife, living through her husband, through her children, giving up her own dreams for that. She concluded: "The only way for a woman, as for a man, to find herself, to know herself as a person, is by creative work of her own."

In the summer of 1964, in McComb, Mississippi, at a Freedom House (a civil rights headquarters where people worked and lived together) the women went on strike against the men who wanted them to cook and make beds while the men went around in cars organizing. The stirring that Friedan spoke of was true of women everywhere, it seemed.

By 1969, women were 40 percent of the entire labor force of the United States, but a substantial number of these were secretaries, cleaning women, elementary school teachers, saleswomen, waitresses, and nurses. One out of every three working women had a husband earning less than $5,000 a year.

What of the women who didn't have jobs? They worked very hard, at home, but this wasn't looked on as work, because in a capitalist society (or perhaps in any modern society where things and people are bought and sold for money), if work is not paid for, not given a money value, it is considered valueless.

The women who worked in the typical "woman's job"—secretary, receptionist, typist, salesperson, cleaning woman, nurse—were treated to the full range of humiliations that men in subordinate positions faced at work, plus another set of humiliations stemming from being a woman: gibes at their mental processes, sexual jokes and aggression, invisibility except as sexual objects, cold demands for more efficiency.

But times were changing. Around 1967, women in the various movements—civil rights, Students for a Democratic Society, antiwar groups—began meeting as women, and in early 1968, at a women's antiwar meeting in Washington, hundreds of women carrying torches paraded to the Arlington National Cemetery and staged "The Burial of Traditional Womanhood."

In the fall of 1968, a group called Radical Women attracted national attention when they protested the selection of Miss America, which they called "an image that oppresses women." They all threw bras, girdles, curlers, false eyelashes, wigs, and other things they called "women's garbage" into a Freedom Trash Can. A sheep was crowned Miss America. More important, people were beginning to speak of "Women's Liberation."

Poor women, black women, expressed the universal problem of women in their own way. In 1964 Robert Coles (*Children of Crisis*) interviewed a black woman from the South recently moved to Boston, who spoke of the desperation of her life, the difficulty of finding happiness: "To me, having a baby inside me is the only time I'm really alive."

Without talking specifically about their problems as women, many women, among the poor, did as they had always done, quietly organized neighborhood people to right injustices, to get needed services. In the mid-1960s, ten thousand black people in a community in Atlanta called Vine City joined together to help one another: they set up a thrift shop, a nursery, a medical clinic, monthly family suppers, a newspaper, a family counseling service. One of the organizers, Helen Howard, told about it:

> The way we got this playground: we blocked off the street, wouldn't let anything come through. We wouldn't let the trolley bus come through. The whole neighborhood was in it. Took record players and danced; it went on for a week. We didn't get arrested, they was too many of us. So then the city put up this playground for the kids....

In 1970, Dorothy Bolden, a laundry worker in Atlanta and mother of six, told why in 1968 she began organizing women doing house-work, into the National Domestic Workers Union. She said: "I think women should have a voice in making decisions in their community for betterment."

Women tennis players organized. A woman fought to be a jockey, won her case, became the first woman jockey. Women artists picketed the Whitney Museum, charging sex discrimination in a sculptors' show. Women journalists picketed the Gridiron Club in Washington, which excluded women. By the start of 1974, women's studies programs existed at seventy-eight institutions, and about two thousand courses on women were being offered at about five hundred campuses.

Women's magazines and newspapers began appearing, locally and nationally, and books on women's history and the movement came out in such numbers that some bookstores had special sections for them. The very jokes on television, some sympathetic, some caustic, showed how national was the effect of the movement. Certain television commercials, which women felt humiliated them, were eliminated after protest.

In 1967, after lobbying by women's groups, President Johnson signed an executive order banning sex discrimination in federally connected employment, and in the years that followed, women's groups demanded that this be enforced. Over a thousand suits were initiated by NOW (National Organization for Women, formed in 1966) against U.S. corporations, charging sex discrimination.

The right to abortion became a major issue. Before 1970, about a million abortions were done every year, of which only about ten thousand were legal. Perhaps a third of the women having illegal abortions— mostly poor people—had to be hospitalized for complications. How many thousands died as a result of these illegal abortions no one really knows. But the illegalization of abortion clearly worked against the poor, for the rich could manage either to have their baby or to have their abortion under safe conditions.

Court actions to do away with the laws against abortions were begun in over twenty states between 1968 and 1970. In the spring of 1969 a Harris poll showed that 64 percent of those polled thought the decision on abortion was a private matter.

Finally, in early 1973, the Supreme Court decided (*Roe v. Wade, Doe v. Bolton*) that the state could prohibit abortions only in the last three months of pregnancy, that it could regulate abortion for health purposes during the second three months of pregnancy, and during the first three months, a woman and her doctor had the right to decide.

There was a push for child care centers, and although women did not succeed in getting much help from government, thousands of cooperative child care centers were set up.

Women also began to speak openly, for the first time, about the problem of rape. Each year, fifty thousand rapes were reported and many more were unreported. Women began taking self-defense courses. There were protests against the way police treated women, interrogated them, insulted them, when women filed rape charges.

Many women were active in trying to get a Constitutional amendment, ERA (Equal Rights Amendment), passed by enough states. But it seemed clear that even if it became law, it would not be enough, that what women had accomplished had come through organization, action, protest. Even where the law was helpful it was helpful only if backed by action. Shirley Chisholm, a black congresswoman, said:

> The law cannot do it for us. We must do it for ourselves. Women in this country must become revolutionaries. We must refuse to accept the old, the traditional roles and stereotypes.... We must replace the old, negative thoughts about our femininity with positive thoughts and positive action....

Perhaps the most profound effect of the women's movement of the sixties—beyond the actual victories on abortion, in job equality—was called "consciousness raising," often done in "women's groups," which met in homes all across the country. This meant the rethinking of roles, the rejection of inferiority, the confidence in self, a bond of sisterhood, a new solidarity of mother and daughter.

For the first time, the sheer biological uniqueness of women was openly discussed. One of the most influential books to appear in the early seventies was a book assembled by eleven women in the Boston Women's Health Book Collective called *Our Bodies, Ourselves*. It contained an enormous amount of practical information, on women's anatomy, on sexuality and sexual relationships, on lesbianism, on nutrition and health, on rape, self-defense, venereal disease, birth control, abortion, pregnancy, childbirth, and menopause.

More important even than the information, the charts, the photos, the candid exploration of the previously unmentioned, was the mood of exuberance throughout the book, the enjoyment of the body, the happiness with the newfound understanding, the new sisterhood with young women, middle-aged women, older women.

The fight began, many women were saying, with the body, which seemed to be the beginning of the exploitation of women—as sex plaything (weak and incompetent), as pregnant woman (helpless), as middle-aged woman (no longer considered beautiful), as older woman (to be ignored, set aside). A biological prison had been created by men and society. As Adrienne Rich said (*Of Woman Born*): "Women are controlled by lashing us to our bodies."

Rich discussed the training of passivity in women. Generations of schoolgirls were raised on *Little Women*, where Jo is told by her mother: "I am angry nearly every day of my life, Jo; but I have learned not to show it; and I still hope to learn not to feel it, though it may take me another forty years to do so."

Male doctors used instruments to bring out children, replacing the sensitive hands of midwives, in the era of "anesthetized, technologized childbirth." Rich said childbirth should be a source of physical and emotional joy.

For many women the question was immediate: how to eliminate hunger, suffering, subordination, humiliation, in the here and now. A woman named Johnnie Tillmon wrote in 1972:

> I'm a woman. I'm a black woman. I'm a poor woman. I'm a fat woman. I'm a middle-aged woman. And I'm on welfare.... I have raised six children.... I grew up in Arkansas...worked there for fifteen years in a laundry...moved to California.... In 1963 I got too sick to work anymore. Friends helped me to go on welfare....
>
> Welfare's like a traffic accident. It can happen to anybody, but especially it happens to women. And that is why welfare is a women's issue. For a lot of middle-class women in this country, Women's Liberation is a matter of concern. For women on welfare it's a matter of survival.

She and other welfare mothers organized a National Welfare Rights Organization. They urged that women be paid for their work—housekeeping, child rearing. "No woman can be liberated, until all women get off their knees."

In the problem of women was the germ of a solution, not only for their oppression, but for everybody's. The control of women in society was ingeniously effective. It was not done directly by the state. Instead, the family was used—men to control women, women to control children, all to be preoccupied with one another, to do violence to one another when things weren't going right. Why could this not be turned around? Could women liberating themselves, children freeing themselves, men and women beginning to understand one another, find the source of their common oppression outside rather than in one another?

Perhaps then they could create nuggets of strength in their own relationships, millions of pockets of insurrection. They could revolutionize thought and behavior in exactly that seclusion of family privacy which the system had counted on to do its work of control and indoctrination. And together, instead of at odds—male, female, parents, children—they could undertake the changing of society itself.

It was a time of uprisings. If there could be rebellion inside that most subtle and complex of prisons—the family—it was reasonable that there be rebellions in the most brutal and obvious of prisons: the penitentiary system itself. In the sixties and early seventies, those rebellions multiplied. They also took on an unprecedented political character and the ferocity of class war, coming to a climax at Attica, New York, in September of 1971.

The prison had arisen in the United States as an attempt at Quaker reform, to replace mutilation, hanging, exile. The prison was intended, through isolation, to produce repentence and salvation, but prisoners went insane and died in that isolation. By mid-nineteenth century, the prison was based on hard labor, along with various punishments: sweat boxes, iron yokes, solitary. The approach was summed up by the warden at the Ossining, New York, penitentiary: "In order to reform a criminal you must first break his spirit." That approach persisted.

There had always been prison riots. A wave of them in the 1920s ended with a riot at Clinton, New York, a prison of sixteen hundred inmates, which was suppressed with three prisoners killed. Between 1950 and 1953 more than fifty major riots occurred in American prisons. In the early 1960s, prisoners on a work gang in Georgia smashing rocks used the same sledgehammers to break their legs, to call attention to their situation of daily brutality.

In November 1970, in Folsom prison in California, a work stoppage began which became the longest prison strike in the history of the United States. Most of the two thousand four hundred prisoners held out in their cells for nineteen days, without food, in the face of threats and intimidation. The strike was broken with a combination of force and deception, and four of the prisoners were sent on a fourteen-hour ride to another

379

prison, shackled and naked on the floor of a van. One of the rebels wrote: "...the spirit of awareness has grown.... The seed has been planted...."

The prisons in the United States had long been an extreme reflection of the American system itself: the stark life differences between rich and poor, the racism, the use of victims against one another, the lack of resources of the underclass to speak out, the endless "reforms" that changed little. Dostoyevsky once said: "The degree of civilization in a society can be judged by entering its prisons."

It had long been true, and prisoners knew this better than anyone, that the poorer you were the more likely you were to end up in jail. This was not just because the poor committed more crimes. In fact, they did. The rich did not have to commit crimes to get what they wanted; the laws were on their side. But when the rich did commit crimes, they often were not prosecuted, and if they were they could get out on bail, hire clever lawyers, get better treatment from judges. Somehow, the jails ended up disproportionately full of poor black people.

In 1969, there were 502 convictions for tax fraud. Such cases, called "white-collar crimes," usually involve people with a good deal of money. Of those convicted, 20 percent ended up in jail. The fraud averaged $190,000 per case; their sentences averaged seven months. That same year, for burglary and auto theft (crimes of the poor) 60 percent ended up in prison. The auto thefts averaged $992; the sentences averaged eighteen months. The burglaries averaged $321; the sentences averaged thirty-three months.

Judges had enormous discretion in the handing out of sentences. In Oregon, of thirty-three men convicted of violating the draft law, eighteen were put on probation. In southern Texas, of sixteen men violating the same law, none was put on probation, and in southern Mississippi, every defendant was convicted and given the maximum of five years. In one part of the country (New England), the average sentence for all crimes was eleven months; in another part (the South), it was seventy-eight months. But it wasn't simply a matter of North and South. In New York City, one judge handling 673 persons brought before him for public drunkenness (all poor; the rich get drunk behind closed doors) discharged 531 of them. Another judge, handling 566 persons on the same charge, discharged one person.

With such power in the hands of the courts, the poor, the black, the odd, the homosexual, the hippie, the radical are not likely to get equal treatment before judges who are almost uniformly white, upper-middle-class, orthodox.

Anyone trying to describe the reality of prison falters. A man in Walpole prison in Massachusetts wrote:

> Every program that we get is used as a weapon against us. The right to go to school, to go to church, to have visitors, to write, to go to the movies. They all end up being weapons of punishment. None of the programs are ours. Everything is treated as a privilege that can be taken away from us. The result is insecurity—a frustration that keeps eating away at you.

Another Walpole prisoner:

> I haven't eaten in the mess hall for four years. I just couldn't take it any more. You'd go into the serving line in the morning and 100 or 200 cockroaches would go running away from the trays. The trays were grimy and the food was raw or had dirt or maggots in it. Many a night I'd go hungry, living on peanut butter and sandwiches.

Communication with the outside world was difficult. Guards would tear up letters. Others would be intercepted and read.

The families suffered. One prisoner reported: "During the last lockup my four-year-old son sneaked off into the yard and picked me a flower. A guard in the tower called the warden's office and a deputy came in with the State Police at his side. He announced that if any child went into the yard and picked another flower, all visits would be terminated."

The prison rebellions of the late sixties and early seventies had a distinctly different character than the earlier ones. The prisoners in the Queens House of Detention referred to themselves as "revolutionaries." All over the country, prisoners were obviously affected by the turmoil in the country, the black revolt, the youth upsurge, the antiwar movement.

The events of those years underlined what prisoners already sensed—that whatever crimes they had committed, the greatest crimes were being committed by the authorities who maintained the prisons, by the government of the United States. The law was being broken daily by the president, sending bombers to kill, sending men to be killed, outside the Constitution, outside the "highest law of the land." State and local officials were violating the civil rights of black people, which was against the law, and were not being prosecuted for it.

Literature about the black movement, books on the war, began to seep into the prisons. The example set in the streets by blacks, by antiwar demonstrators, was exhilarating—against a lawless system, defiance was the only answer.

It was a system that sentenced Martin Sostre, a fifty-two-year-old black man running an Afro-Asian bookstore in Buffalo, New York, to twenty-five to thirty years in prison for allegedly selling $15 worth of heroin to an informer who later recanted his testimony. The recantation did not free Sostre—he could find no court, including the Supreme Court of the United States, to revoke the judgment. He spent eight years in prison, was beaten ten times by guards, spent three years in solitary confinement, battling and defying the authorities all the way until his release. Such injustice deserved only rebellion.

There had always been political prisoners—people sent to jail for belonging to radical movements, for opposing war. But now a new kind of political prisoner appeared—the man, or woman, convicted of an ordinary crime, who, in prison, became awakened politically. Some prisoners began making connections between their personal ordeal and the social system. They then turned not to individual rebellion but to collective action. They became concerned—amid an environment whose brutality demanded concentration on one's own safety, an atmosphere of cruel rivalry—for the rights, the safety of others.

George Jackson was one of these new political prisoners. In Soledad prison, California, on an indeterminate sentence for a $70 robbery, having already served ten years of it, Jackson became a revolutionary.

His book *Soledad Brother* became one of the most widely read books of black militancy in the United States—by prisoners, by black people, by white people—perhaps this ensured he would not last. He knew what might happen: "Born to a premature death, a menial, subsistence-wage worker, odd-job man, the cleaner, the caught, the man under hatches, without bail—that's me, the colonial victim. Anyone who can pass the civil service examination today can kill me tomorrow...with complete immunity."

In August 1971 he was shot in the back by guards at San Quentin prison while he was allegedly trying to escape. Shortly after Jackson's death, there was a chain of rebellions around the country.

The most direct effect of the George Jackson murder was the rebellion at Attica prison in September 1971—a rebellion that came from long, deep grievances, but that was raised to boiling point by the news about George Jackson. Attica was surrounded by a thirty-foot wall, two feet thick, with fourteen gun towers. Fifty-four percent of the inmates were black; 100 percent of the guards were white. Prisoners spent fourteen to sixteen hours a day in their cells, their mail was read, their reading material restricted, their visits from families conducted through a mesh screen, their medical care disgraceful, their parole system inequitable, racism everywhere.

When Attica prisoners were up for parole, the average time of their hearing, including the reading of the file and deliberation among the three members of the parole board, was 5.9 minutes. Then the decision was handed out, with no explanation.

At Attica, an inmate-instructed sociology class became a forum for ideas about change. Then there was a series of organized protest efforts, and an inmate manifesto setting forth a series of moderate demands, culminating in a day of protest over the killing of George Jackson at San Quentin, during which few inmates ate at lunch and dinner and many wore black armbands.

On September 9, 1971, a series of conflicts between prisoners and guards ended with a group of inmates breaking through a gate with a defective weld and taking over one of the four prison yards, with forty guards as hostages. Then followed five days in which the prisoners set up a remarkable community in the yard.

A group of citizen-observers, invited by the prisoners, included *New York Times* columnist Tom Wicker, who wrote (*A Time to Die*): "The racial harmony that prevailed among the prisoners—it was absolutely astonishing."

After five days, the state lost patience. Governor Nelson Rockefeller approved a military attack on the prison. National Guardsmen, prison guards, and local police went in with automatic rifles, carbines, and submachine guns in a full-scale assault on the prisoners, who had no firearms. Thirty-one prisoners were killed.

The first stories given the press by prison authorities said that nine guards held hostage had their throats slashed by the prisoners during the attack. The official autopsies almost immediately showed this to be false: the nine guards died in the same hail of bullets that killed the prisoners.

In the weeks and months after Attica, the authorities were taking preventive action to break up organizing efforts among the prisoners. But prisoners continued to demand change, trying to get prisoners to care for one another, to take the hatred and anger of individual rebellion and turn it into collective effort for change. On the outside, something new was also happening, the development of prison support groups all over the country, the building of a body of literature about prisons. There were more studies of crime and punishment, a growing movement for the abolition of prisons on the ground that they did not prevent crime or cure it, but expanded it. Alternatives were discussed: community houses in the short run (except for the incorrigibly violent); guaranteed minimum economic security, in the long run.

The prisoners were thinking about issues beyond prison, victims other than themselves and their friends. In Walpole prison a statement asking for American withdrawal from Vietnam was circulated; it was signed by every single prisoner—an amazing organizing feat by a handful of inmates. One Thanksgiving day there, most of the prisoners, not only in Walpole but in three other prisons, refused to eat the special holiday meal, saying they wanted to bring attention to the hungry all over the United States.

Prisoners worked laboriously on lawsuits, and some victories were won in the courts. The publicity around Attica, the community of support, had its effect. Although the Attica rebels were indicted on heavy charges and faced double and triple life terms, the charges were finally dropped. But in general, the courts declared their unwillingness to enter the closed, controlled world of the prison, and so the prisoners remained as they had been so long, on their own.

In 1978 the Supreme Court ruled that the news media do not have guaranteed rights of access to jails and prisons. It ruled also that prison authorities could forbid inmates to speak to one another, assemble, or spread literature about the formation of a prisoners' union.

It became clear—and prisoners seemed to know this from the start—that their condition would not be changed by law, but by protest, organization, resistance, the creation of their own culture, their own literature, the building of links with people on the outside. There were more outsiders now who knew about prisons. Tens of thousands of Americans had spent time behind bars in the civil rights and antiwar movements. They had learned about the prison system and could hardly forget their experiences. There was a basis now for breaking through the long isolation of the prisoners from the community and finding support there. In the mid-seventies, this was beginning to happen.

It was a time of upsurge. Women, guarded in their very homes, rebelled. Prisoners, put out of sight and behind bars, rebelled. The greatest surprise was still to come.

It was thought that the Indians, once the only occupants of the continent, then pushed back and annihilated by the white invaders, would not be heard from again. In the last days of the year 1890, shortly after Christmas, the last massacre of Indians took place at Pine Ridge, South Dakota, near Wounded Knee Creek. When it was over, between 200 and 300 of the original 350 men, women, and children were dead. The twenty-five soldiers who died were mostly hit by their own shrapnel or bullets, since the Indians had only a few guns.

The Indian tribes, attacked, subdued, starved out, had been divided up by putting them on reservations where they lived in poverty. In 1887, an Allotment Act tried to break up the reservations into small plots of land owned by individual Indians, to turn them into American-type small farmers—but much of this land was taken by white speculators, and the reservations remained.

Then, during the New Deal, with a friend of the Indians, John Collier, in charge of the Bureau of Indian Affairs, there was an attempt to restore tribal life. But in the decades that followed, no fundamental change took place. Many Indians stayed on the impoverished reservations. The younger ones often left. An Indian anthropologist said: "An Indian reservation is the most complete colonial system in the world that I know about."

For a time, the disappearance or amalgamation of the Indians seemed inevitable—only 300,000 were left at the turn of the century, from the original million or more in the area of the United States. But then the population began to grow again, as if a plant left to die refused to do so, began to flourish. By 1960 there were 800,000 Indians, half on reservations, half in towns all over the country.

The autobiographies of Indians show their refusal to be absorbed by the white man's culture. One wrote:

> Oh, yes, I went to the white man's schools. I learned to read from school books, newspapers, and the Bible. But in time I found that these were not enough. Civilized people depend too much on man-made printed pages. I turn to the Great Spirit's book which is the whole of his creation....

Chief Luther Standing Bear, in his 1933 autobiography, *From the Land of the Spotted Eagle*, wrote:

> True, the white man brought great change. But the varied fruits of his civilization, though highly colored and inviting, are sickening and deadening. And if it be the part of civilization to maim, rob, and thwart, then what is progress?
>
> I am going to venture that the man who sat on the ground in his tipi meditating on life and its meaning, accepting the kinship of all creatures, and acknowledging unity with the universe of things, was infusing into his being the true essence of civilization....

As the civil rights and antiwar movements developed in the 1960s, Indians were already gathering their energy for resistance, thinking about how to change their situation, beginning to organize.

Indians began to approach the United States government on an embarrassing topic: treaties. The United States government had signed more than four hundred treaties with Indians and violated every single one. For instance, back in George Washington's administration, a treaty was signed with the Iroquois of New York: "The United States acknowledge all the land within the aforementioned boundaries to be the property of the Seneka nation...." But in the early sixties, under President Kennedy, the United States ignored the treaty and built a dam on this land, flooding most of the Seneca reservation.

Resistance was already taking shape in various parts of the country. In the state of Washington, there was an old treaty taking land from the Indians but leaving them fishing rights. This became unpopular as the white population grew and wanted the fishing areas exclusively for themselves. When state courts closed river areas to Indian fishermen, in 1964, Indians had "fish-ins" on the Nisqually River, in defiance of the court orders, and went to jail, hoping to publicize their protest.

Some of the Indians involved in the fish-ins were veterans of the Vietnam war. One was Sid Mills, who was arrested in a fish-in at Frank's Landing on the Nisqually River in Washington on October 13, 1968. He made a statement: "I am a Yakima and Cherokee Indian, and a man. For two years and four months, I've been a soldier in the United States Army. I served in combat in Vietnam—until critically wounded.... I hereby renounce further obligation in service or duty to the United States Army."

Indians fought back not only with physical resistance, but also with the artifacts of white culture—books, words, newspapers. In 1968, members of the Mohawk Nation at Akwesasne, on the St. Lawrence River between the United States and Canada, began a remarkable newspaper, *Akwesasne Notes*, with news, editorials, poetry, all flaming with the spirit of defiance. Mixed in with all that was an irrepressible humor. Vine Deloria Jr. wrote:

> Every now and then I am impressed with the thinking of the non-Indian. I was in Cleveland last year and got to talking with a non-Indian about American history. He said that he was really sorry about what had happened to Indians, but: "After all, what did you do with the land when you had it?" I didn't understand him until later when I discovered that the Cuyahoga River running through Cleveland is inflammable. So

many combustible pollutants are dumped into the river that the inhabitants have to take special precautions during the summer to avoid setting
it on fire. How many Indians could have thought of creating an inflam-
mable river?

In 1969, November 9, there took place a dramatic event which
focused attention on Indian grievances as nothing else had. On that day,
before dawn, seventy-eight Indians landed on Alcatraz Island in San Francisco Bay and occupied the island. Alcatraz was an abandoned federal
prison, a hated and terrible place nicknamed "The Rock."

This time, it was different. The group was led by Richard Oakes, a
Mohawk who directed Indian Studies at San Francisco State College, and
Grace Thorpe, a Sac and Fox Indian, daughter of Jim Thorpe, the famous
Indian college football star and Olympic runner, jumper, hurdler. More
Indians landed, and by the end of November nearly six hundred of them,
representing more than fifty tribes, were living on Alcatraz.

They called themselves "Indians of All Tribes" and issued a proclamation, "We Hold the Rock." In it they offered to buy Alcatraz in glass
beads and red cloth, the price paid Indians for Manhattan Island over three
hundred years earlier. They announced they would make the island a center for Native American Studies for Ecology: "We will work to de-pollute
the air and waters of the Bay Area...restore fish and animal life...."

In the months that followed, the government cut off telephones, electricity, and water to Alcatraz Island. Many of the Indians had to leave, but
others insisted on staying. A year later they were still there, and they sent
out a message to "our brothers and sisters of all races and tongues upon
our Earth Mother":

> We are still holding the Island of Alcatraz in the true names of Freedom,
> Justice and Equality, because you, our brothers and sisters of this earth,
> have lent support to our just cause.
>
> We have learned that violence breeds only more violence and we
> therefore have carried on our occupation of Alcatraz in a peaceful man-
> ner, hoping that the government of these United States will also act
> accordingly....
>
> We are Indians Of All Tribes! WE HOLD THE ROCK!

Six months later, federal forces invaded the island and physically
removed the Indians living there.

In the late 1960s, the Peabody Coal Company began strip mining on
Navajo land in New Mexico—a ruthless excavation of the topsoil. The
company pointed to a "contract" signed with some Navajos. It was remi-

niscent of the "treaties" signed with some Indians in the past that took away all Indian land.

One hundred and fifty Navajos met in the spring of 1969 to declare that the strip mining would pollute the water and the air, destroy the grazing land for livestock, use up their scarce water resources. An elderly Navajo woman, one of the organizers of the meeting, said, "Peabody's monsters are digging up the heart of our mother earth, our sacred mountain, and we also feel the pains.... I have lived here for years and I'm not about to move."

The Hopi Indians were also affected by the Peabody operations. They wrote to President Nixon in protest: "Today the sacred lands where the Hopi live are being desecrated by men who seek coal and water from our soil that they may create more power for the whiteman's cities.... The Great Spirit said not to allow this to happen.... The Great Spirit said not to take from the Earth—not to destroy living things...."

In the fall of 1970, a magazine called *La Raza,* one of the countless local publications coming out of the movements of those years to supply information ignored in the regular media, told about the Pit River Indians of northern California. Sixty Pit Indians occupied land they said belonged to them; they defied the Forest Services when ordered to leave. But 150 marshals came, with machine guns, shotguns, rifles, pistols, riot sticks, Mace, dogs, chains, manacles.

One of the Indians, Darryl Wilson, wrote: "The old people were frightened. The young questioned bravery. The small children were like a deer that has been shot by the thunder stick. Hearts beat fast as though a race was just run in the heat of summer."

The marshals began swinging their riot sticks, and blood started flowing. Wilson grabbed one marshal's club, was thrown down, manacled, and while lying face down on the ground was struck behind the head several times. A sixty-six-year-old man was beaten to unconsciousness. A white reporter was arrested, his wife beaten. They were all thrown into trucks and taken away, charged with assaulting state and federal officers and cutting trees—but not with trespassing, which might have brought into question the ownership of the land. When the episode was all over, they were still defiant.

Indians who had been in the Vietnam war made connections. At the "Winter Soldier Investigations" in Detroit, where Vietnam veterans testified about their experiences, an Oklahoma Indian named Evan Haney told about his:

The same massacres happened to the Indians 100 years ago. Germ warfare was used then. They put smallpox in the Indians' blankets.... I got to know the Vietnamese people and I learned they were just like us.... What we are doing is destroying ourselves and the world.

...Though 50 percent of the children at the country school I attended in Oklahoma were Indians, nothing in school, on television, or on the radio taught anything about Indian culture. There were no books on Indian history, not even in the library.... But I knew something was wrong. I started reading and learning my own culture....

Indians began to do something about their "own destruction"—the annihilation of their culture. In 1969, at the First Convocation of American Indian Scholars, Indians spoke indignantly of either the ignoring or the insulting of Indians in textbooks given to little children all over the United States. That year the Indian Historian Press was founded. It evaluated four hundred textbooks in elementary and secondary schools and found that not one of them gave an accurate depiction of the Indian.

Other Americans were beginning to pay attention, to rethink their own learning. The first motion pictures attempting to redress the history of the Indian appeared: one was *Little Big Man*, based on a novel by Thomas Berger. More and more books appeared on Indian history, until a whole new literature came into existence. Teachers became sensitive to the old stereotypes, threw away the old textbooks, started using new material. One elementary school student wrote to the publisher of one of his schoolbooks:

> Dear Editor,
> I don't like your book called The Cruise of Christopher Columbus. I didn't like it because you said some things about Indians that weren't true.... Another thing I didn't like was on page 69, it says that Christopher Columbus invited the Indians to Spain, but what really happened was that he stole them!
>
> censearly,
> Raymond Miranda

On Thanksgiving Day 1970, at the annual celebration of the landing of the Pilgrims, the authorities decided to do something different: invite an Indian to make the celebratory speech. They found a Wampanoag Indian named Frank James and asked him to speak. But when they saw the speech he was about to deliver, they decided they did not want it. His speech, not heard at Plymouth, Massachusetts, on that occasion, said, in part: "I speak to you as a Man—a Wampanoag Man.... It is with mixed emotions that I stand here to share my thoughts.... The Pilgrims had hardly explored the shores of Cape Cod four days before they had robbed the graves of my ancestors, and stolen their corn, wheat, and beans.... Our spirit refuses to die.... We stand tall and proud and before too many moons pass we'll right the wrongs we have allowed to happen to us...."

In March of 1973 came a powerful affirmation that the Indians of North America were still alive. On the site of the 1890 massacre, on Pine Ridge reservation, several hundred Oglala Sioux and friends returned to the village of Wounded Knee to occupy it as a symbol of the demand for Indian land, Indian rights.

Within hours, more than two hundred FBI agents, federal marshals, and police of the Bureau of Indian Affairs surrounded and blockaded the town. They had armored vehicles, automatic rifles, machine guns, grenade launchers, and gas shells, and soon began firing.

After the siege began, food supplies became short. Indians in Michigan sent food via a plane that landed inside the encampment. The next day FBI agents arrested the pilot and a doctor from Michigan who had hired the plane. In Nevada, eleven Indians were arrested for taking food, clothing, and medical supplies to South Dakota. In mid-April three more planes dropped twelve hundred pounds of food, but as people scrambled to gather it up, a government helicopter appeared overhead and fired down on them while groundfire came from all sides. Frank Clearwater, an Indian man lying on a cot inside a church, was hit by a bullet. When his wife accompanied him to a hospital, she was arrested and jailed. Clearwater died.

There were more gun battles, another death. Finally, a negotiated peace was signed, in which both sides agreed to disarm. The siege ended and 120 occupiers were arrested.

The Indians had held out for seventy-one days, creating a marvelous community inside the besieged territory. Communal kitchens were set up, a health clinic, and hospital. A Navajo Vietnam veteran:

> There's a tremendous amount of coolness considering that we're out-gunned.... But people stay because they believe; they have a cause. That's why we lost in Viet Nam, cause there was no cause. We were fighting a rich man's war, for the rich man.... In Wounded Knee, we're doing pretty damn good, morale-wise. Because we can still laugh.

Messages of support had come to Wounded Knee from Australia, Finland, Germany, Italy, Japan, England. One message came from some of the Attica brothers, two of whom were Indians: "You fight for our Earth Mother and Her Children. Our spirits fight with you!" Wallace Black Elk replied: "Little Wounded Knee is turned into a giant world."

After Wounded Knee, in spite of the deaths, the trials, the use of the police and courts to try to break the movement, the Native American movement continued. *Akwesasne Notes* continued to publish. On its poetry page, late autumn, 1976, appeared poems reflecting the spirit of the times. Ila Abernathy wrote:

> I am grass growing and the shearer of grass,
> I am the willow and the splitter of laths,
>
> *   *   *
>
> I am the burr in your conscience:
> acknowledge me.

In the sixties and seventies, it was not just a women's movement, a prisoner's movement, an Indian movement. There was general revolt against oppressive, artificial, previously unquestioned ways of living. It touched every aspect of personal life: childbirth, childhood, love, sex, marriage, dress, music, art, sports, language, food, housing, religion, literature, death, schools.

Sexual behavior went through startling changes. Premarital sex was no longer a matter for silence. Men and women lived together outside of marriage, and struggled for words to describe the other person when introduced: "I want you to meet my...friend." Married couples candidly spoke of their affairs, and books appeared discussing "open marriage." Masturbation could be talked about openly, even approvingly. Homosexuality was no longer concealed. "Gay" men and "gay" women—lesbians—organized to combat discrimination against them, to give themselves a sense of community, to overcome shame and isolation.

All this was reflected in the literature and in the mass media. A new literature appeared to teach men and women how sexual fulfillment could be attained. The movies now did not hesitate to show nudity. The language of sex became more common both in literature and in ordinary conversation. All this was connected with new living arrangements. Especially among young people, communal living arrangements flourished.

In the cultural change of the sixties there was greater informality. For women it was a continuation of the historic feminist movement's insistence on discarding of "feminine," hampering clothes. Many women stopped wearing bras. The restrictive "girdle"—almost a uniform of the forties and fifties—became rare. Young men and women dressed more nearly alike, in jeans, in discarded army uniforms. Men stopped wearing neckties, women of all ages wore pants more often—unspoken homage to Amelia Bloomer.

There was a new popular music of protest. Pete Seeger had been singing protest songs since the forties, but now he came into his own, his audiences much larger. Bob Dylan and Joan Baez, singing not only protest songs, but songs reflecting the new abandon, the new culture, became popular idols. A middle-aged woman on the West Coast, Malvina Reynolds, wrote and sang songs that fit her socialist thinking and her libertarian spirit, as well as her critique of the modern commercial culture. Everybody now, she sang, lived in "little boxes" and they "all came out just the same."

Bob Dylan was a phenomenon unto himself: powerful songs of protest, personal songs of freedom and self-expression. In an angry song, "Masters of War," he hopes that one day they will die and he will follow their casket "in the pale afternoon." "A Hard Rain's A-Gonna Fall" recounts the terrible stories of the last decades, of starvation and war, and tears, and dead ponies, and poisoned waters, and damp, dirty prisons— "It's a hard rain's a-gonna fall." Dylan sang a bitter antiwar song, "With God on Our Side," and one about the killer of the black activist Medgar Evers, "Only a Pawn in Their Game." He offered a challenge to the old, hope to the new, for "The Times They Are A-Changin'."

The Catholic upsurge against the war was part of a general revolt in side the Catholic Church, which had for so long been a bulwark of conservatism, tied to racism, jingoism, war. Priests and nuns resigned from the church, opened their lives to sex, got married and had children—sometimes without bothering to leave the church officially. True, there was still enormous popularity for the old-time religious revivalists, and Billy Graham commanded the obedience of millions, but now there were small swift currents against the mainstream.

With the loss of faith in big powers—business, government, religion—there arose a stronger belief in self, whether individual or collective. The experts in all fields were now looked at skeptically: the belief grew that people could figure out for themselves what to eat, how to live their lives, how to be healthy. There was suspicion of the medical industry and campaigns against chemical preservatives, valueless foods, advertising. By now the scientific evidence of the evils of smoking—cancer, heart disease—was so powerful that the government barred advertising of cigarettes on television and in newspapers.

Traditional education began to be reexamined. The schools had taught whole generations the values of patriotism, of obeying authority, and had perpetuated ignorance, even contempt for people of other nations, races, Native Americans, women. Not just the content of education was challenged, but the style—the formality, the bureaucracy, the insistence on subordination to authority. This made only a small dent in the formidable national system of orthodox education, but it was reflected in a new generation of teachers all over the country, and a new literature to sustain them.

Never in American history had more movements for change been concentrated in so short a span of years. But the system in the course of two centuries had learned a good deal about the control of people. In the mid-seventies, it went to work.

Exercises

1. "By 1960, 36 percent of all women sixteen and older—23 million women—worked for paid wages. But there were nursery schools for the children of only 2 percent of working mothers." What is the point of pairing these two statistics together?

2. How did World War II cause the modern feminist movement?

3. Why did women in the civil rights, student, and antiwar movements become feminists? (Are there any parallels to the radicalization of feminists in the 1840s?)

4. "The only way for a woman, as for a man, to find herself, to know herself as a person, is by creative work of her own." Why would a working-class woman not be inspired to become a feminist by such a statement?

5. By 1969, "One out of every three working women had a husband earning less than $5,000 a year." What is the significance of this fact?

6. What was the double bind that working women were in?

7. Why might Radical Women call "bras, girdles, curlers, false eye-lashes, wigs and other things" "women's garbage"?

8. Why would a woman say, "To me, having a baby inside me is the only time I'm really alive"?

9. According to Helen Howard, how did the people of Vine City get their government to build a playground for their kids? Why were petitions insufficient? (Is this incident a microcosm of the struggle between the American people and their government over Vietnam? Explain your answer.)

10. Why could women not seek legal action before 1967 if they had been discriminated against because they were women?

11. Why is abortion perceived as a feminist issue and not a medical or civil rights issue? (What is a feminist issue? Is it different from a human rights or civil rights issue?)

12. Match the evidence with the interpretation.

> Women organized to gain some control over their work lives.
>
> Women fought to enter occupations previously denied them.
>
> Women fought to be judged by their work and not by their sex.
>
> Women fought to gain credibility for their own culture.

> a. A woman fought to be a jockey.
>
> b. Women tennis players organized.
>
> c. Women journalists picketed the Gridiron Club in Washington.
>
> d. Dorothy Bolden organized women into the National Domestic Workers Union.
>
> e. Women's history became a legitimate academic field of study.
>
> f. Women successfully protested for the elimination of certain television commercials humiliating to women.
>
> g. Feminists established the NOW Legal and Education Defense Fund.
>
> h. The National Welfare Rights Organization was founded.

13. "Women are controlled by lashing us to our bodies." What might Adrienne Rich have meant by this?

14. "Welfare's like a traffic accident." What did Johnnie Tillmon mean by this?

15. "In the problem of women was the germ of a solution." Could this be applied to other groups as well?

16. How does "breaking his spirit" reform a criminal?

17. "In the early 1960s, prisoners on a work gang in Georgia smashing rocks used the same sledgehammers to break their legs, to call attention to their situation of daily brutality." What might these acts of "brutality" have been?

18. Why did prisoners go on strike, fast, and riot?

19. "...[T]he poorer you were the more likely you were to end up in jail." With what evidence does Zinn support this argument?

20. "There had always been prison riots...the prison rebellions of the late sixties and early seventies had a distinctly different character than the earlier ones." Why?

21. How was George Jackson an example of a new kind of political prisoner?

22. What was it like to be a prisoner in Attica in 1971?

23. What incident provoked the Attica rebellion? How did the rebellion end?

24. How can you account for the racial harmony among prisoners ,given the discriminatory manner in which they were treated?

25. What did the Supreme Court determine in 1978 regarding prisoners and their ability to communicate with the outside world? What lesson did prisoners draw from this decision?

26. Why was the emergence of the American Indian Movement (AIM) a surprise to whites?

27. How did Chief Luther Standing Bear's testimony in 1933 explain many Indians' refusal to adopt the dominant culture as their own?

28. In the 1960s, by what methods did Indians assert their treaty rights?

29. How can you explain the difference between the state's response to the Attica rebels and the Indians who occupied Alcatraz?

30. What happened at Pit River, California, in 1970?

31. What parallels did Evan Haney make between the U.S. government treatment of Indians and the treatment of the Vietnamese?

32. Of what importance was the founding of the Indian Historian Press?

33. Why was the government's response to the occupation of Wounded Knee different from its response to the Attica rebellion?

34. How did the sexual revolution manifest itself?

35. What effect did the sixties have on the role of "the expert" in American society? What professions were specifically affected and how?

36. *Debate Resolution*: In the 1960s and 1970s, free speech didn't exist in the United States.

Chapter 20

The Seventies: Under Control?

In the early seventies, the system seemed out of control—it could not hold the loyalty of the public. As early as 1970, according to the University of Michigan's Survey Research Center, "trust in government" was low in every section of the population. And there was a significant difference by class. Of professional people, 40 percent had "low" political trust in the government; of unskilled blue-collar workers, 66 percent had "low" trust.

Public opinion surveys in 1971—after seven years of intervention in Vietnam—showed an unwillingness to come to the aid of other countries, even those in our own hemisphere, assuming they were attacked by Communist-backed forces. As for Thailand, if it were under Communist attack, only 12 percent of whites and 4 percent of nonwhites would send troops.

The Survey Research Center of the University of Michigan had been posing the question: "Is the government run by a few big interests looking out for themselves?" The answer in 1964 had been "yes" from 26 percent of those polled; by 1972 the answer was "yes" from 53 percent of those polled.

More voters than ever before refused to identify themselves as either Democrats or Republicans. Back in 1940, 20 percent of those polled called themselves "independents." In 1974, 34 percent called themselves "independents."

The courts, the juries, and even judges were not behaving as usual. Juries were acquitting radicals: Angela Davis, an acknowledged Communist, was acquitted by an all-white jury on the West Coast. Black Panthers, whom the government had tried in every way to malign and destroy, were freed by juries in several trials. A judge in western Massachusetts threw out a case against a young activist, Sam Lovejoy, who had toppled a five-hundred-foot tower erected by a utility company trying to set up a nuclear plant. In Washington, D.C., in August 1973, a Superior Court judge refused to sentence six men charged with unlawful entry who had stepped from a White House tour line to protest the bombing of Cambodia.

Undoubtedly, much of this national mood of hostility to government and business came out of the Vietnam war, its 58,000 American deaths, its moral shame, its exposure of government lies and atrocities. On top of this came the political disgrace of the Nixon administration in the scandals that came to be known by the one-word label "Watergate," and which led to the historic resignation from the presidency—the first in American history—of Richard Nixon in August 1974.

The Watergate story began during the presidential campaign in June of 1972, when five burglars, carrying wiretapping and photo equipment, were caught in the act of breaking into the offices of the Democratic National Committee, in the Watergate apartment complex of Washington, D.C. One of the five, James McCord Jr., worked for the Nixon campaign; he was "security" officer for the Committee to Re-elect the President (CREEP). Another of the five had an address book in which was listed the name of E. Howard Hunt, and Hunt's address was listed as the White House. He was assistant to Charles Colson, who was special counsel to President Nixon.

Both McCord and Hunt had worked for many years for the CIA. Hunt had been the CIA man in charge of the invasion of Cuba in 1961, and three of the Watergate burglars were veterans of the invasion. McCord, as CREEP security man, worked for the chief of CREEP, John Mitchell, the attorney general of the United States.

Thus, due to an unforeseen arrest by police unaware of the high-level connections of the burglars, information was out to the public before anyone could stop it, linking the burglars to important officials in Nixon's campaign committee, to the CIA, and to Nixon's attorney general. Mitchell denied any connection with the burglary, and Nixon, in a press conference five days after the event, said "the White House has had no involvement whatever in this particular incident."

What followed the next year, after a grand jury in September indicted the Watergate burglars—plus Howard Hunt and G. Gordon Liddy—was that, one after another, lesser officials of the Nixon administration, fearing prosecution, began to talk. They gave information in judicial proceedings, to a Senate investigating committee, to the press. They implicated not only John Mitchell, but Robert Haldeman and John Ehrlichman, Nixon's highest White House aides, and finally Richard Nixon himself—in not only the Watergate burglaries, but a whole series of illegal actions against political opponents and antiwar activists. Nixon and his aides lied again and again as they tried to cover up their involvement.

These are a few of the facts that came out in the various testimonies:

1. "Attorney-General John Mitchell controlled a secret fund of $350,000 to $700,000—to be used against the Democratic Party—for forging letters, leaking alse news items to the press, stealing campaign files."

2. Gulf Oil Corporation, ITT (International Telephone and Telegraph), American Airlines, and other huge American corporations had made illegal contributions, running into millions of dollars, to the Nixon campaign.

3. In September 1971, shortly after the *New York Times* printed Daniel Ellsberg's copies of the top-secret *Pentagon Papers*, the administration planned and carried out—Howard Hunt and Gordon Liddy themselves doing it—the burglary of the office of Ellsberg's psychiatrist, looking for Ellsberg's records.

4. After the Watergate burglars were caught, Nixon secretly pledged to give them executive clemency if they were imprisoned, and suggested that up to a million dollars be given them to keep them quiet. In fact, $450,000 was given to them, on Ehrlichman's orders.

5. It turned out that certain material had disappeared from FBI files—material from a series of illegal wiretaps ordered by Henry Kissinger, placed on the telephones of four journalists and thirteen government officials—and was in the White House safe of Nixon's adviser John Ehrlichman.

6. One of the Watergate burglars, Bernard Barker, told the Senate committee that he had also been involved in a plan to physically attack Daniel Ellsberg while Ellsberg spoke at an antiwar rally in Washington.

7. A witness told the Senate committee that President Nixon had tapes of all personal conversations and phone conversations at the White House. Nixon at first refused to turn over the tapes, and when he finally did, they had been tampered with: eighteen and a half minutes of one tape had been erased.

8. In the midst of all this, Nixon's vice president, Spiro Agnew, was indicted in Maryland for receiving bribes from Maryland contractors in return for political favors, and resigned from the vice presidency in October 1973. Nixon appointed Congressman Gerald Ford to take Agnew's place.

9. Nixon had illegally taken—with the aid of a bit of forgery—a $576,000 tax deduction for some of his papers.

10. It was disclosed that for over a year in 1969–1970 the U.S. had engaged in a secret, massive bombing of Cambodia, which it kept from the American public and even from Congress.

It was a swift and sudden fall. In the November 1972 presidential election, Nixon and Agnew had won 60 percent of the popular vote and carried every state except Massachusetts, defeating an antiwar candidate, Senator George McGovern. By June of 1973 a Gallup poll showed 67 percent of those polled thought Nixon was involved in the Watergate break-in or lied to cover up.

Early in 1974, a House committee drew up a bill of impeachment to present it to a full House. Nixon's advisers told him it would pass the House by the required majority and then the Senate would vote the necessary two-thirds majority to remove him from office. A leading financier said: "Right now, 90% of Wall Street would cheer if Nixon resigns." On August 8, 1974, Nixon resigned.

Gerald Ford, taking Nixon's office, said: "Our long national nightmare is over." Newspapers, whether they had been for or against Nixon, liberal or conservative, celebrated the successful, peaceful culmination of the Watergate crisis. "The system is working," said *New York Times* columnist Anthony Lewis.

No respectable American newspaper said what was said by Claude Julien, editor of *Le Monde Diplomatique* in September 1974. "The elimination of Mr. Richard Nixon leaves intact all the mechanisms and all the false values which permitted the Watergate scandal." Julien noted that Nixon's secretary of state, Henry Kissinger, would remain at his post—in other words, that Nixon's foreign policy would continue.

Months after Julien wrote this, it was disclosed that top Democratic and Republican leaders in the House of Representatives had given secret assurance to Nixon that if he resigned they would not support criminal proceedings against him. The *New York Times*'s articles that reported on Wall Street's hope for Nixon's resignation quoted one Wall Street financier as saying that if Nixon resigned: "What we will have is the same play with different players."

In the charges brought by the House Committee on Impeachment against Nixon, it stayed clear of Nixon's dealings with powerful corporations; it did not mention the bombing of Cambodia. It concentrated on things peculiar to Nixon, not on fundamental policies continuous among American presidents, at home and abroad.

The word was out: get rid of Nixon, but keep the system. Theodore Sorensen, who had been an adviser to President Kennedy, wrote at the time of Watergate: "The underlying causes of the gross misconduct in our law-enforcement system now being revealed are largely personal, not institutional. Some structural changes are needed. All the rotten apples should be thrown out. But save the barrel."

Indeed, the barrel was saved. Nixon's foreign policy remained. The government's connections to corporate interests remained. Ford's closest friends in Washington were corporate lobbyists. One of Ford's first acts was to pardon Nixon, thus saving him from possible criminal proceedings and allowing him to retire with a huge pension in California.

The televised Senate committee hearings on Watergate stopped suddenly before the subject of corporate connections was reached. It was typical of the selective coverage of important events by the television industry: bizarre shenanigans like the Watergate burglary were given full treatment, while instances of ongoing practice—the My Lai massacre, the secret bombing of Cambodia, the work of the FBI and CIA—were given the most fleeting attention. Dirty tricks against the Socialist Workers party, the Black Panthers, other radical groups, could only be found in a few newspapers. The whole nation heard the details of the quick break-in at the Watergate apartment; there was never a similar television hearing on the long-term break-in in Vietnam.

Corporate influence on the White House is a permanent fact of the American system. Many of these corporations gave money to both sides, so that whichever won they would have friends in the administration. Chrysler Corporation urged its executives to "support the party and candidate of their choice," and then collected the checks from them and delivered the checks to Republican or Democratic campaign committees.

International Telephone and Telegraph was an old hand at giving money on both sides. A senior vice president of ITT was quoted by one of his assistants as saying the board of directors "have it set up to 'butter' both sides so we'll be in good position whoever wins." And in 1970, an

ITT director, John McCone, who also had been head of the CIA, told Henry Kissinger, secretary of state, and Richard Helms, CIA director, that ITT was willing to give $1 million to help the U.S. government in its plans to overthrow the Allende government in Chile.

In 1971 ITT planned to take over the $1.5 billion Hartford Fire Insurance Company—the largest merger in corporate history. The antitrust division of the Justice Department moved to prosecute ITT for violating the antitrust laws. However, the prosecution did not take place and ITT was allowed to merge with Hartford. It was all settled out of court, in a secret arrangement in which ITT agreed to donate $400,000 to the Republican party.

Whether Nixon or Ford or any Republican or Democrat was president, the system would work pretty much the same way.

Even in the most diligent of investigations in the Watergate affair, that of Archibald Cox, a special prosecutor later fired by Nixon, the corporations got off easy. American Airlines, which admitted making illegal contributions to the Nixon campaign, was fined $5,000; Goodyear was fined $5,000; 3M Corporation was fined $3,000. A Goodyear official was fined $1,000; a 3M official was fined $500. The *New York Times* (October 20, 1973) reported:

> Mr. Cox charged them only with the misdemeanor of making illegal contributions. The misdemeanor, under the law, involved "nonwillful" contributions. The felony count, involving willful contributions, is punishable by a fine of $10,000 and/or a two-year jail term; the misdemeanor by a $1000 fine and/or a one-year jail term.
>
> Asked at the courthouse here how the two executives—who had admitted making the payments—could be charged with making non-willing contributions, Mr. McBride [Cox's staff] replied: "That's a legal question which frankly baffles me as well."

With Gerald Ford in office, the long continuity in American policy was maintained. He continued Nixon's policy of aid to the Saigon regime, apparently still hoping that the Thieu government would remain stable. But in the spring of 1975, everything that radical critics of American policy in Vietnam had been saying—that without American troops, the Saigon government's lack of popular support would be revealed—came true. An offensive by North Vietnamese troops, left in the South by terms of the 1973 truce, swept through town after town. On April 29, 1975, the North Vietnamese moved into Saigon, and the war was over.

Most of the Establishment had already—despite Ford and a few stalwarts—given up on Vietnam. What they worried about was the readiness of the American public now to support other military actions overseas. There were trouble signs in the months before the defeat in Vietnam. In early 1975 Senator John C. Culver of Iowa was unhappy that Americans would not fight for Korea: "He said that Vietnam had taken a mighty toll on the national will of the American people."

In March 1975 a Catholic organization, making a survey of American attitudes on abortion, learned other things. To the statement: "The people running this country (government, political, church and civic leaders) don't tell us the truth," more than 83 percent agreed.

New York Times international correspondent C. L. Sulzberger, a consistent supporter of government cold-war foreign policy, wrote: "There must be something seriously wrong with the way we present ourselves these days." The problem, according to Sulzberger, was not the United States' behavior, but the way this behavior was presented to the world.

In April 1975, Secretary of State Kissinger, invited to be commencement speaker at the University of Michigan, was faced with petitions protesting the invitation, because of Kissinger's role in the Vietnam War. Also a countercommencement program was planned. He withdrew. It was a low time for the administration. Vietnam was "lost" (the assumption was that it was "ours" to lose), and Kissinger was quoted (by *Washington Post* columnist Tom Braden): "The U.S. must carry out some act somewhere in the world which shows its determination to continue to be a world power."

The following month came the *Mayaguez* affair.

The *Mayaguez* was an American cargo ship sailing from South Vietnam to Thailand in mid-May 1975, just three weeks after the victory of the revolutionary forces in Vietnam. When it came close to an island in Cambodia, where a revolutionary regime had just taken power, the ship was stopped by the Cambodians, taken to a port at a nearby island, and the crew removed to the mainland. The crew later described their treatment as courteous.

President Ford sent a message to the Cambodian government to release the ship and crew, and when thirty-six hours had elapsed and there was no response he began military operations—U.S. planes bombed Cambodian ships. They strafed the very boat that was taking the American sailors to the mainland.

The men had been detained on a Monday morning. On Wednesday evening the Cambodians released them, putting them on a fishing boat headed for the American fleet. That afternoon, knowing the seamen had been taken off Tang Island, Ford nevertheless ordered a marine assault on Tang Island.

The marines met unexpectedly tough resistance, and of two hundred invaders, one-third were soon dead or wounded. (This exceeded the casualty rate in the World War II invasion of Iwo Jima.) Five of eleven helicopters in the invasion force were blown up or disabled. Also, twenty-three Americans were killed in a helicopter crash over Thailand on their way to participate in the action, a fact the government tried to keep secret.

Altogether, forty-one Americans were killed in the military actions ordered by Ford. There were thirty-nine sailors on the *Mayaguez*. Why the rush to bomb, strafe, attack? Why, even after the ship and crew were recovered, did Ford order American planes to bomb the Cambodian mainland, with untold Cambodian casualties?

The answer to this came soon: it was necessary to show the world that giant America, defeated by tiny Vietnam, was still powerful and resolute. The *New York Times* reported on May 16, 1975:

> Administration officials, including Secretary of State Henry Kissinger and Secretary of Defense James Schlesinger were said to have been eager to find some dramatic means of underscoring President Ford's stated intention to "maintain our leadership on a world-wide basis." The occasion came with the capture of the vessel.... Administration officials...made it clear that they welcomed the opportunity....

But why would the prestigious *Times* columnist James Reston, a strong critic of Nixon and Watergate, call the *Mayaguez* operation "melodramatic and successful"? And why would the *New York Times*, which had criticized the Vietnam war, talk about the "admirable efficiency" of the operation?

What seemed to be happening was that the Establishment—Republicans, Democrats, newspapers, television—was closing ranks behind Ford and Kissinger, and behind the idea that American authority must be asserted everywhere in the world.

Congress at this time behaved much as it had done in the early years of the Vietnam war, like a flock of sheep. Back in 1973, in a mood of fatigue and disgust with the Vietnam war, Congress had passed a War Powers Act that required the president, before taking military action, to consult with Congress. In the *Mayaguez* affair, Ford ignored this—he had several aides make phone calls to eighteen congressmen to inform them that military action was under way. Only a few members of Congress protested.

It was a complex process of consolidation that the system undertook in 1975. It included old-type military actions, like the *Mayaguez* affair, to assert authority in the world and at home. There was also a need to satisfy a disillusioned public that the system was criticizing and correcting itself. The standard way was to conduct publicized investigations that found specific culprits but left the system intact. Watergate had made both the FBI and the CIA look bad—breaking the laws they were sworn to uphold, cooperating with Nixon in his burglary jobs and illegal wiretapping. In 1975, congressional committees in the House and Senate began investigations of the FBI and CIA.

The CIA inquiry disclosed that the CIA had gone beyond its original mission of gathering intelligence and was conducting secret operations of all kinds. For instance, back in the 1950s, it had administered the drug LSD to unsuspecting Americans to test its effects: one American scientist, given such a dose by a CIA agent, leaped from a New York hotel window to his death in the 1950s.

The CIA had also been involved in assassination plots against Castro of Cuba and other heads of state. It had introduced African swine fever virus into Cuba in 1971, bringing disease and then slaughter to 500,000 pigs. A CIA operative told a reporter he delivered the virus from an army base in the Canal Zone to anti-Castro Cubans.

It was also learned from the investigation that the CIA—with the collusion of a secret Committee of Forty headed by Henry Kissinger—had worked to "destabilize" the Chilean government headed by Salvador Allende, a Marxist who had been elected president in one of the rare free elections in Latin America. ITT, with large interests in Cuba, played a part in this operation.

The investigation of the FBI disclosed many years of illegal actions to disrupt and destroy radical groups and left-wing groups of all kinds. The FBI had sent forged letters, engaged in burglaries (it admitted to ninety-two between 1960 and 1966), opened mail illegally, and, in the case of Black Panther leader Fred Hampton, seems to have conspired in murder.

Valuable information came out of the investigations, but it was just enough, and in just the right way—moderate press coverage, little television coverage, thick books of reports with limited readership—to give the impression of an honest society correcting itself.

The investigations themselves revealed the limits of government willingness to probe into such activities. The Church Committee, set up by the Senate, submitted its findings on the CIA to the CIA to see if there was material that the agency wanted omitted.

The Pike Committee, set up in the House of Representatives, made no such agreement with the CIA or FBI, and when it issued its final report, the same House that had authorized its investigation voted to keep the report secret. When the report was leaked via a CBS newscaster, Daniel Schorr, to the *Village Voice* in New York, it was never printed by the important newspapers in the country—the *Times,* the *Washington Post,* or others. Schorr was suspended by CBS. It was another instance of cooperation between the mass media and the government in instances of "national security."

The Church Committee uncovered CIA operations to secretly influence the minds of Americans:

> "The CIA is now using several hundred American academics (administrators, faculty members, graduate students engaged in teaching) who, in addition to providing leads and, on occasion, making introductions for intelligence purposes, write books and other material to be used for propaganda purposes abroad.... These academics are located in over 100 American colleges, universities and related institutions." The committee found that more than a thousand books were produced, subsidized, or sponsored by the CIA before the end of 1967.

The resignation of Nixon, the succession of Ford, the exposure of bad deeds by the FBI and CIA—all aimed to regain the badly damaged confidence of the American people. However, even with these strenuous efforts, there were still many signs in the American public of suspicion, even hostility, to the leaders of government, military, big business.

That July the Lou Harris poll, looking at the public's confidence in the government from 1966 to 1975, reported that confidence in the military during that period had dropped from 62 percent to 29 percent, in business from 55 percent to 18 percent, in both president and Congress from 42 percent to 13 percent.

Perhaps much of the general dissatisfaction was due to the economic state of most Americans. Inflation and unemployment had been rising steadily since 1973. In the fall of 1975 a *New York Times* survey of 1,559 persons, and interviews with sixty families in twelve cities, showed "a substantial decline in optimism about the future." Even higher-income people, the survey found, "are not as optimistic now as they were in past years, indicating that discontent is moving up from the lower middle-income to higher economic levels." Government statistics suggested the reasons. The unemployment rate, which had been 5.6 percent in 1974, had risen to 8.3 percent in 1975, and the number of people who had exhausted their unemployment benefits increased from 2 million in 1974 to 4.3 million in 1975.

Government figures, however, generally underestimated the amount of poverty, set the "legally" poor level too low, and underestimated the amount of unemployment. For instance, if 16.6 percent of the population averaged six months of unemployment during 1975, or 33.2 percent averaged three months of unemployment, the "average annual figure" given by the government was 8.3 percent, which sounded better.

In the year 1976, with a presidential election approaching, there was worry among the Establishment about the public's faith in the system. William Simon, secretary of the treasury under both Nixon and Ford (before then an investment banker earning over $2 million a year), spoke to a Business Council meeting in Hot Springs, Virginia: "Vietnam, Watergate, student unrest, shifting moral codes, the worst recession in a generation, and a number of other jarring cultural shocks have all combined to create a new climate of questions and doubt.... It all adds up to a general malaise, a society-wide crisis of institutional confidence...." Too often, Simon said, Americans "have been taught to distrust the very word profit and the profit motive that makes our prosperity possible, to somehow feel this system, that has done more to alleviate human suffering and privation than any other, is somehow cynical, selfish, and amoral." We must, Simon said, "get across the human side of capitalism."

As the United States prepared in 1976 to celebrate the bicentennial of the Declaration of Independence, a group of intellectuals and political leaders from Japan, the United States, and Western Europe, organized into "The Trilateral Commission," issued a report. It was entitled "The Governability of Democracies."

Samuel Huntington, a political science professor at Harvard University and long-time consultant to the White House on the war in Vietnam, wrote the part of the report that dealt with the United States. "In the sixties," Huntington wrote, there was a huge growth of citizen participation "in the forms of marches, demonstrations, protest movements, and 'cause' organizations." There were also "markedly higher levels of self-consciousness on the part of blacks, Indians, Chicanos, white ethnic groups, students and women, all of whom became mobilized and organized in new ways...." There was a "marked expansion of white-collar unionism," and all this added up to "a reassertion of equality as a goal in social, economic and political life."

The great demands in the sixties for equality, Huntington pointed out, had transformed the federal budget. In 1960 foreign affairs spending was 53.7 percent of the budget, and social spending was 22.3 percent of the budget. By 1974 social spending had risen to 31 percent. This seemed to reflect a change in public mood: in 1960 only 18 percent of the public said the government was spending too much on defense, but in 1969 this jumped to 52 percent.

Huntington was troubled by what he saw:

> The essence of the democratic surge of the 1960's was a general challenge to existing systems of authority, public and private. In one form or another, this challenge manifested itself in the family, the university, business, public and private associations, politics, the governmental bureaucracy, and the military services. People no longer felt the same obligation to obey those whom they had previously considered superior to themselves in age, rank, status, expertise, character, or talents.

All this, he said, "produced problems for the governability of democracy in the 1970's...."

Huntington further said that the president, to win the election, needed the support of a broad coalition of people. However: "The day after his election...[w]hat counts then is his ability to mobilize support from the leaders of key institutions in a society and government.... This coalition must include key people in Congress, the executive branch, and the private-sector 'Establishment.'" He gave examples:

> Truman made a point of bringing a substantial number of non-partisan soldiers, Republican bankers, and Wall Street lawyers into his Administration. He went to the existing sources of power in the country to get help he needed in ruling the country. Eisenhower in part inherited this coalition and was in part almost its creation.... Kennedy attempted to recreate a somewhat similar structure of alliances.

What worried Huntington was the loss in governmental authority. His conclusion was that there had developed "an excess of democracy," and he suggested "desirable limits to the extension of political democracy."

Huntington was reporting all this to an organization that was very important to the future of the United States. The Trilateral Commission was organized in early 1973 by David Rockefeller and Zbigniew Brzezinski. Rockefeller was an official of the Chase Manhattan Bank and a powerful financial figure in the United States and the world; Brzezinski, a Columbia University professor, specialized in international relations and was a consultant to the State Department.

The Trilateral Commission was set up to create greater unity among Japan, Western Europe, and the United States in the face of a much more complicated threat to tri-continental capitalism than a monolithic Communism: revolutionary movements in the Third World. These movements had directions of their own.

The Trilateral Commission wanted also to deal with another situation, that modern business now knew no national boundaries. In 1960 there were eight United States banks with foreign branches; in 1974 there were 129. The assets of these overseas branches amounted to $3.5 billion in 1960, $155 billion in 1974. The Trilateral Commission apparently saw itself as helping to create the necessary international links for the new multinational economy.

1976 was not only a presidential election year—it was the much-anticipated year of the bicentennial celebration—two hundred years after the Declaration of Independence. The great effort that went into the celebration suggests that it was seen as a way of restoring American patriotism, invoking the symbols of history to unite people and government and put aside the protest mood of the recent past.

But there did not seem to be great enthusiasm for it. When the 200th anniversary of the Boston Tea Party was celebrated in Boston, an enormous crowd turned out, not for the official celebration, but for the "People's Bi-Centennial" countercelebration, where packages marked "Gulf Oil" and "Exxon" were dumped into the Boston Harbor, to symbolize opposition to corporate power in America.

Exercises

1. What conclusion does Zinn draw from the results of the University of Michigan Survey Research Center's study of public opinion in 1970?

2. "The courts, the juries, and even judges were not behaving as usual." How is Zinn defining "usual"?

3. How were those who broke into the offices of the Democratic National Committee connected to Nixon's administration? What was the purpose of the break-in?

4. Why would Nixon have promised the Watergate burglars clemency and large sums of money if they were imprisoned?

5. Why would Hunt and Liddy have wanted to gain access to Daniel Ellsberg's psychiatric files? Why would Barker have been given the assignment to physically attack Ellsberg while Ellsberg would be making a speech?

6. Why would Kissinger want to tap the phones of certain journalists and government officials?

7. Why did Agnew resign?

8. When did the American people learn that the U.S. government was subjecting Cambodia to massive bombing attacks? When did the bombing actually begin?

9. Why did Nixon resign?

10. "The system is working." What did Anthony Lewis mean by this? Does Zinn agree with Lewis?

11. According to a Wall Street financier, if Nixon resigned, the U. S. would have "The same play with different players." What do you think he meant by "play"?

12. Why did ITT not care whether Democrats or Republicans won an election?

13. Why would ITT want to overthrow the Allende government in Chile?

14. Why are large corporations not inhibited about giving illegal campaign contributions?

15. How did C. L. Sulzberger explain the lack of popular support for American foreign policy in the 1970s? How does Zinn explain it?

16. What is the significance of the *Mayaguez* affair? Why did the *New York Times* commend the "admirable efficiency" of the operation?

17. Why did Watergate prompt in-depth investigations into the CIA and FBI? What did these investigations discover in terms of the degree to which these organizations had gone beyond their mandates? Why does Zinn call into question the sincerity of these investigations?

18. What other factors besides Vietnam and Watergate could be seen as contributing to American's loss of confidence in their business, political, and military leaders?

19. How are the government's annual figures for unemployment misleading? Which groups in society would be misled by these figures? Why would it be a good tactic for the government to mislead these groups in this way?

20. What did William Simon mean by "the human side of capitalism"?

21. Why might the federal government spend over half its budget on foreign affairs?

22. What effect did the revolts of the 1960s have on the percentage of the federal budget spent on the military? On social programs?

23. According to the Trilateral Commission, which of the following is necessary in order for a democratic government to govern?
     a. inequality
     b. equality
     c. a well-informed public
     d. the support of a broad coalition of people
     e. the support of the business and government leaders

24. According to Samuel Huntington, how much democracy is an "excess of democracy"?

25. What was the purpose of the Trilateral Commission?

26. *Debate Resolution*: Watergate was the result of a flawed president.

Chapter 21

Carter-Reagan-Bush:
The Bipartisan Consensus

Halfway through the twentieth century, the historian Richard Hofstadter, in his book *The American Political Tradition*, examined our important national leaders, from Jefferson and Jackson to Herbert Hoover and the two Roosevelts—Republicans and Democrats, liberals and conservatives. Hofstadter concluded that "the range of vision...in the major parties has always been bounded by the horizons of property and enterprise. ...They have accepted the economic virtues of capitalist culture.... That culture has been intensely nationalistic...."

Coming to the end of the century, observing its last twenty-five years, we have seen exactly that limited vision—a capitalistic encouragement of enormous fortunes alongside desperate poverty, a nationalistic acceptance of war and preparations for war. Governmental power swung from Republicans to Democrats and back again, but neither party showed itself capable of going beyond that vision.

After the disastrous war in Vietnam came the scandals of Watergate. There was a deepening economic insecurity for much of the population, along with environmental deterioration, and a growing culture of violence and family disarray. Clearly, such fundamental problems could not be solved without bold changes in the social and economic structure. But no major party candidates proposed such changes. The "American political tradition" held fast.

In recognition of this, perhaps only vaguely conscious of this, voters stayed away from the polls in large numbers, or voted without enthusiasm.

More and more they declared, if only by nonparticipation, their alienation from the political system. In 1960, 63 percent of those eligible to vote voted in the presidential election. By 1976, this figure had dropped to 53 percent. In a CBS News and *New York Times* survey, over half of the respondents said that public officials didn't care about people like them.

Electoral politics dominated the press and television screens, and the doings of presidents, members of Congress, Supreme Court justices, and other officials were treated as if they constituted the history of the country. Yet there was something artificial in all this, a straining to persuade a skeptical public that this was all, that they must rest their hopes for the future in Washington politicians.

A citizenry disillusioned with politics and with what pretended to be intelligent discussions of politics turned its attention (or had its attention turned) to entertainment, to gossip, to ten thousand schemes for self-help. Those at its margins became violent, finding scapegoats within one's group (as with poor-black on poor-black violence), or against other races, immigrants, demonized foreigners, welfare mothers, minor criminals (standing in for untouchable major criminals).

But there were other citizens, those who tried to hold on to ideas and ideals still remembered from the sixties and early seventies. Indeed, all across the country there was a part of the public unmentioned in the media, ignored by political leaders—energetically active in thousands of local groups around the country. These organized groups were campaigning for environmental protection or women's rights or decent health care (including anguished concern about AIDS) or housing for the homeless, or against military spending.

This activism was unlike that of the sixties, when the surge of protest against race segregation and war became an overwhelming national force. It struggled uphill, against callous political leaders, trying to reach fellow Americans most of whom saw little hope in either the politics of voting or the politics of protest.

The presidency of Jimmy Carter, covering the years 1977 to 1980, seemed an attempt by one part of the Establishment, that represented in the Democratic party, to recapture a disillusioned citizenry. But Carter, despite a few gestures toward black people and the poor, despite talk of "human rights" abroad, remained within the historic political boundaries of the American system, protecting corporate wealth and power, maintaining a huge military machine that drained the national wealth, allying the United States with right-wing tyrannies abroad.

His appeal was "populist"—that is, he appealed to various elements of American society who saw themselves beleaguered by the powerful and wealthy. Although he himself was a millionaire peanut grower, he presented himself as an ordinary American farmer. Although he had been a supporter of the Vietnam war until its end, he presented himself as a sympathizer with those who had been against the war, and he appealed to many of the young rebels of the sixties by his promise to cut the military budget.

In a much-publicized speech to lawyers, Carter spoke out against the use of the law to protect the rich. He appointed a black woman, Patricia Harris, as secretary of Housing and Urban Development, and a black civil rights veteran, Andrew Young, as ambassador to the United Nations. He gave the job of heading the domestic youth service corps to a young former antiwar activist, Sam Brown.

His most crucial appointments, however, were in keeping with the Trilateral Commission report of Harvard political scientist Samuel Huntington, which said that, whatever groups voted for a president, once elected "what counts then is his ability to mobilize support from the leaders of key institutions." Brzezinski, a traditional cold war intellectual, became Carter's national security adviser. His secretary of defense, Harold Brown, had, during the Vietnam war, according to the *Pentagon Papers,* "envisaged the elimination of virtually all the constraints under which the bombing then operated."

His other cabinet appointees had strong corporate connections. A financial writer wrote, not long after Carter's election: "So far, Mr. Carter's actions, commentary, and particularly his Cabinet appointments, have been highly reassuring to the business community." Veteran Washington correspondent Tom Wicker wrote: "The available evidence is that Mr. Carter so far is opting for Wall Street's confidence."

Carter did initiate more sophisticated policies toward governments that oppressed their own people. He used United Nations Ambassador Andrew Young to build up goodwill for the United States among the black African nations, and urged that South Africa liberalize its policies toward blacks. A peaceful settlement in South Africa was necessary for strategic reasons; South Africa was used for radar tracking systems. Also, it had important U.S. corporate investments and was a critical source of needed raw materials (diamonds, especially). Therefore, what the United States needed was a stable government in South Africa; the continued oppression of blacks might create civil war.

Under Carter, the United States continued to support, all over the world, regimes that engaged in imprisonment of dissenters, torture, and mass murder: in the Philippines, in Iran, in Nicaragua, and in Indonesia, where the inhabitants of East Timor were being annihilated in a campaign bordering on genocide.

The *New Republic* magazine, presumably on the liberal side of the Establishment, commented approvingly on the Carter policies: "...American foreign policy in the next four years will essentially extend the philosophies developed...in the Nixon-Ford years. This is not at all a negative prospect.... There should be continuity. It is part of history...."

Carter had presented himself as a friend of the movement against the war, but when Nixon mined Haiphong harbor and resumed bombing of North Vietnam in the spring of 1973, Carter urged that "we give President Nixon our backing and support—whether or not we agree with specific decisions." Once elected, Carter declined to give aid to Vietnam for reconstruction, despite the fact that the land had been devastated by American bombing. Asked about this at a press conference, Carter replied that there was no special obligation on the United States to do this because "the destruction was mutual." Considering that the United States had crossed half the globe with an enormous fleet of bombers and two million soldiers, and after eight years left a tiny nation with over a million dead and its land in ruins, this was an astounding statement.

The Carter administration clearly was trying to end the disillusionment of the American people after the Vietnam war by following foreign policies more palatable, less obviously aggressive. But on close examination, these more liberal policies were designed to leave intact the power and influence of American military and American business in the world.

The renegotiation of the Panama Canal treaty with the tiny Central American republic of Panama was an example. The canal saved American companies $1.5 billion a year in delivery costs, and the United States collected $150 million a year in tolls, out of which it paid the Panama government $2.3 million dollars, while maintaining fourteen military bases in the area.

Back in 1903 the United States had engineered a revolution against Colombia, set up the new tiny republic of Panama in Central America, and dictated a treaty giving the United States military bases, control of the Panama Canal, and sovereignty "in perpetuity." The Carter administration in 1977, responding to anti-American protests in Panama, and recognizing that the canal had lost military importance, decided to negotiate a new treaty which called for a gradual removal of U.S. bases.

Whatever Carter's sophistication in foreign policy, certain fundamentals operated in the late sixties and the seventies. American corporations were active all over the world on a scale never seen before. There were, by the early seventies, about three hundred U.S. corporations, including the seven largest banks, which earned 40 percent of their net profits outside the United States. They were called "multinationals," but actually 98 percent of their top executives were Americans. As a group, they now constituted the third-largest economy in the world, next to the United States and the Soviet Union.

The relationship of these global corporations with the poorer countries had long been an exploiting one, it was clear from U.S. Department of Commerce figures. Whereas U.S. corporations in Europe between 1950 and 1965 invested $8.1 billion and made $5.5 billion in profits, in Latin America they invested $3.8 billion and made $11.2 billion in profits, and in Africa they invested $5.2 billion and made $14.3 billion in profits.

It was the classical imperial situation, where the places with natural wealth became victims of more powerful nations whose power came from that seized wealth. American corporations depended on the poorer countries for 100 percent of their diamonds, coffee, platinum, mercury, natural rubber, and cobalt. They got 98 percent of their manganese from abroad, 90 percent of their chrome and aluminum. And 20 to 40 percent of certain imports (platinum, mercury, cobalt, chrome, manganese) came from Africa.

And yet the United States cultivated a reputation of being generous with its riches. Indeed, it had frequently given aid to disaster victims. This aid, however, often depended on political loyalty. In early 1975 the press carried a dispatch from Washington: "Secretary of State Henry A. Kissinger has formally initiated a policy of selecting for cutbacks in American aid those nations that have sided against the U.S. in votes in the United Nations. In some cases the cutbacks involve food and humanitarian relief."

Most aid was openly military, and by 1975, the United States exported $9.5 billion in arms. The Carter administration promised to end the sale of arms to repressive regimes, but when it took office the bulk of the sales continued.

And the military continued to take a huge share of the national budget. Carter's first budget proposed an increase of $10 billion for the military. Indeed, he proposed that the U.S. spend a trillion dollars in the next five years on its military forces. And the administration had just announced that the Department of Agriculture would save $25 million a year by no longer giving free second helpings of milk to 1.4 million needy schoolchildren who got free meals in school.

If Carter's job was to restore faith in the system, here was his greatest failure—solving the economic problems of the people. The price of food and the necessities of life continued to rise faster than wages were rising. For certain key groups in the population—young people, and especially young black people—the unemployment rate was 20 or 30 percent.

Carter opposed federal aid to poor people who needed abortions, and when it was pointed out to him that this was unfair, because rich women could get abortions with ease, he replied: "Well, as you know, there are many things in life that are not fair, that wealthy people can afford and poor people cannot."

Carter's "populism" was not visible in his administration's relationship to the oil and gas interests. It was part of Carter's "energy plan" to end price regulation of natural gas for the consumer. The largest producer of natural gas was Exxon Corporation, and the largest blocs of private stock in Exxon were owned by the Rockefeller family.

The fundamental facts of maldistribution of wealth in America were clearly not going to be affected by Carter's policies, any more than by previous administrations, whether conservative or liberal. In 1977, the top 10 percent of the American population had an income thirty times that of the bottom tenth; the top 1 percent of the nation owned 33 percent of the wealth. The richest 5 percent owned 83 percent of the personally owned corporate stock. The one hundred largest corporations paid an average of 26.9 percent in taxes, and the leading oil companies paid 5.8 percent in taxes (Internal Revenue Service figures for 1974). Indeed, 244 individuals who earned over $200,000 paid no taxes. Carter approved tax "reforms" in 1978 which benefited mainly the corporations.

American weaponry was used to support dictatorial regimes battling left-wing rebels abroad. Thus, Carter asked Congress in the spring of 1980 for $5.7 million in credits for the military junta fighting off a peasant rebellion in El Salvador. In the Philippines, after the 1978 National Assembly elections, President Ferdinand Marcos imprisoned ten of the twenty-one losing opposition candidates; many prisoners were tortured, many civilians were killed. Still, Carter urged Congress to give Marcos $300 million in military aid for the next five years.

In Nicaragua, the United States had helped maintain the Somoza dictatorship for decades. Misreading the basic weakness of that regime, and the popularity of the revolution against it, the Carter administration continued its support for Somoza until close to the regime's fall in 1979.

In Iran, toward the end of 1978, the long years of resentment against the Shah's dictatorship culminated in mass demonstrations. On September 8, 1978, hundreds of demonstrators were massacred by the Shah's troops. The next day, according to a UPI dispatch from Teheran, Carter affirmed his support for the Shah:

> Troops opened fire on demonstrators against the Shah for the third straight day yesterday and President Jimmy Carter telephoned the royal palace to express support for Shah Mohammad Reza Pahlevi, who faced the worst crisis of his 37-year reign. Nine members of parliament walked out on a speech by Iran's new premier, shouting that his hands were "stained with blood" in the crackdown on conservative Moslems and other protesters.

It was a popular, massive revolution, and the Shah fled. The Carter administration later accepted him into the country, presumably for medical treatment, and the anti-American feelings of the revolutionaries reached a high point. On November 4, 1979, the U.S. embassy in Teheran was taken over by student militants who, demanding that the Shah be returned to Iran for punishment, held fifty-two embassy employees hostage.

For the next fourteen months, with the hostages still held in the embassy compound, that issue took the forefront of foreign news in the United States and aroused powerful nationalist feelings. Politicians and the press played into a general hysteria. An Iranian-American girl who was slated to give a high school commencement address was removed from the program. The bumper sticker "Nuke Iran" appeared on autos all over the country.

It was a rare journalist bold enough to point out, as Alan Richman of the *Boston Globe* did when the fifty-two hostages were released alive and apparently well, that there was a certain lack of proportion in American reactions to this and other violations of human rights: "There were 52 of them, a number easy to comprehend.... They [the American hostages] spoke our language. There were 3000 people summarily shot in Guatemala last year who did not."

The hostages were still in captivity when Jimmy Carter faced Ronald Reagan in the election of 1980. That fact, and the economic distress felt by many, were largely responsible for Carter's defeat.

Reagan's victory, followed eight years later by the election of George

Bush, meant that another part of the Establishment, lacking even the faint liberalism of the Carter presidency, would be in charge. The policies would be more crass—cutting benefits to poor people, lowering taxes for the wealthy, increasing the military budget, filling the federal court system with conservative judges, actively working to destroy revolutionary movements in the Caribbean.

The dozen years of the Reagan-Bush presidency transformed the federal judiciary, never more than moderately liberal, into a predominantly conservative institution. By the fall of 1991, Reagan and Bush had filled more than half of the 837 federal judgeships, and appointed enough right-wing justices to transform the Supreme Court.

In the seventies, with liberal justices William Brennan and Thurgood Marshall in the lead, the Court had declared death penalties unconstitutional, had supported (in *Roe v. Wade*) the right of women to choose abortions, and had interpreted the civil rights law as permitting special attention to blacks and women to make up for past discrimination (affirmative action).

William Rehnquist, first named to the Supreme Court by Richard Nixon, was made chief justice by Ronald Reagan. In the Reagan-Bush years, the Rehnquist Court made a series of decisions that weakened *Roe v. Wade*, brought back the death penalty, reduced the rights of detainees against police powers, prevented doctors in federally supported family planning clinics from giving women information on abortions, and said that poor people could be forced to pay for public education (education was not "a fundamental right").

Justices William Brennan and Thurgood Marshall were the last of the Court's liberals. Old and ill, though reluctant to give up the fight, they retired. The final act to create a conservative Supreme Court was President Bush's nomination to replace Marshall. He chose a black conservative, Clarence Thomas. Despite dramatic testimony from a former colleague, a young black law professor named Anita Hill, that Thomas had sexually harassed her, Thomas was approved by the Senate and now the Supreme Court moved even more decisively to the right.

With conservative federal judges, with probusiness appointments to the National Labor Relations Board, judicial decisions and board findings weakened a labor movement already troubled by a decline in manufacturing. Workers who went out on strike found themselves with no legal protection. One of the first acts of the Reagan administration was to dismiss from their jobs, en masse, striking air traffic controllers. It was a warning to future strikers, and a sign of the weakness of a labor movement which in the thirties and forties had been a powerful force.

Corporate America became the greatest beneficiary of the Reagan-Bush years. In the sixties and seventies an important environmental movement had grown in the nation, horrified at the poisoning of the air, the seas and rivers, and the deaths of thousands each year as a result of work conditions. After a mine explosion in West Virginia killed seventy-eight miners in November 1968 there had been angry protest in the mine district, and Congress passed the Coal Mine Health and Safety Act of 1969. Nixon's secretary of labor spoke of "a new national passion, passion for environmental improvement."

The following year, yielding to strong demands from the labor movement and consumer groups, but also seeing it as an opportunity to win the support of working-class voters, President Nixon had signed the Occupational Safety and Health Act of 1970. This was an important piece of legislation, establishing a universal right to a safe and healthy workplace.

While President Jimmy Carter came into office praising the OSHA program, he was also eager to please the business community. He became an advocate of removing regulations on corporations and giving them more leeway, even if this was hurtful to labor and to consumers.

Under Reagan and Bush this concern for "the economy," which was a short-hand term for corporate profit, dominated any concern for workers or consumers. President Reagan proposed to replace tough enforcement of environmental laws by a "voluntary" approach. One of the first acts of his administration was to order the destruction of 100,000 government booklets pointing out the dangers of cotton dust to textile workers.

George Bush presented himself as the "environmental president," and pointed with pride to his signing of the Clean Air Act of 1990. But two years after that act was passed, it was seriously weakened by a new rule of the Environmental Protection Agency that allowed manufacturers to increase by 245 tons a year hazardous pollutants in the atmosphere.

The ecological crisis in the world had become so obviously serious that Pope John Paul II felt the need to rebuke the wealthy classes of the industrialized nations for creating that crisis: "Today, the dramatic threat of ecological breakdown is teaching us the extent to which greed and selfishness, both individual and collective, are contrary to the order of creation."

At international conferences to deal with the perils of global warming, the European Community and Japan proposed specific levels and timetables for carbon dioxide emissions, in which the United States was the leading culprit. But the U. S. opposed that.

Evidence became stronger by the late eighties that renewable energy sources (water, wind, sunlight) could produce more usable energy than nuclear plants, which were dangerous and expensive, and produced radioactive wastes that could not be safely disposed of. Yet the Reagan and Bush administrations made deep cuts (under Reagan, a 90 percent cut) in research into renewable energy possibilities.

In June 1992 more than a hundred countries participated in the Earth Summit environmental conference in Brazil. Statistics showed that the armed forces of the world were responsible for two-thirds of the gases that depleted the ozone layer. But when it was suggested that the Earth Summit consider the effects of the military on environmental degradation, the United States delegation objected and the suggestion was defeated.

Indeed, the preservation of a huge military establishment and the retention of profit levels of oil corporations appeared to be twin objectives of the Reagan-Bush administrations. Shortly after Ronald Reagan took office, twenty-three oil industry executives contributed $270,000 to redecorate the White House living quarters. According to the Associated Press:

> The solicitation drive...came four weeks after the President decontrolled oil prices, a decision worth $2 billion to the oil industry...Jack Hodges of Oklahoma City, owner of Core Oil and Gas Company, said: "The top man of this country ought to live in one of the top places. Mr. Reagan has helped the energy business."

While he built up the military (allocations of over a trillion dollars in his first four years in office), Reagan tried to pay for this with cuts in benefits for the poor. He also proposed tax cuts of $190 billion (most of this going to the wealthy). Reagan insisted the tax cuts would so stimulate the economy as to generate new revenue. But Department of Commerce figures showed that periods of lowered corporate taxes did not at all show higher capital investment, but a steep drop.

The human consequences of Reagan's budget cuts went deep. For instance, Social Security disability benefits were terminated for 350,000 people. A war hero of Vietnam, Roy Benavidez, who had been presented with the Congressional Medal of Honor by Reagan, was told by Social Security officials that the shrapnel pieces in his heart, arms, and leg did not prevent him from working. Appearing before a congressional committee, he denounced Reagan.

Unemployment grew in the Reagan years. In the year 1982, thirty million people were unemployed all or part of the year. One result was that over sixteen million Americans lost medical insurance, which was often tied to holding a job. In Michigan, where the unemployment rate was the highest in the country, the infant death rate began to rise in 1981.

New requirements eliminated free school lunches for more than one million poor children, who depended on the meal for as much as half of their daily nutrition. Soon a quarter of the nation's children—twelve million—were living in poverty.

Welfare became an object of attack: aid to single mothers with children through the AFDC (Aid to Families with Dependent Children) program, food stamps, health care for the poor through Medicaid. For most people on welfare (the benefits differed from state to state) this meant $500 to $700 a month in aid, leaving them well below the poverty level of about $900 a month. Black children were four times as likely as white children to grow up on welfare.

Early in the Reagan administration, responding to the argument that government aid was not needed, that private enterprise would take care of poverty, a mother wrote to her local newspaper:

> I am on Aid to Families with Dependent Children, and both my children are in school.... I have applied for jobs paying as little as $8000 a year. I work part-time in a library for $3.50 an hour; welfare reduces my allotment to compensate....
>
> So this is the great American dream my parents came to this country for: Work hard, get a good education, follow the rules, and you will be rich. I don't want to be rich. I just want to be able to feed my children and live with some semblance of dignity....

Democrats often joined Republicans in denouncing welfare programs. Both parties had strong connections to wealthy corporations. Kevin Phillips, a Republican analyst of national politics, wrote in 1990 that the Democratic party was "history's second-most enthusiastic capitalist party."

Yet the constant attacks on welfare by politicians did not succeed in eradicating a fundamental generosity felt by most Americans. A *New York Times*/CBS News poll conducted in early 1992 showed that public opinion on welfare changed depending on how the question was worded. If the word "welfare" was used, 44 percent of those questioned said too much was being spent on welfare. But when the question was about "assistance to the poor," only 13 percent thought too much was being spent, and 64 percent thought too little was being spent.

When government policy enriched the already rich, by lowering their taxes, it was not called welfare. This was not as obvious as the monthly checks to the poor; it most often took the form of generous changes in the tax system.

It was not the Republicans but the Democrats—the Kennedy-Johnson administrations—who, under the guise of "tax reform," first lowered the World War II–era rate of 91 percent on incomes over $400,000 a year to 70 percent. During the Carter administration (though over his objections) Democrats and Republicans in Congress joined to give even more tax breaks to the rich.

The Reagan administration, with the help of Democrats in Congress, lowered the tax rate on the very rich to 50 percent and in 1986 a coalition of Republicans and Democrats sponsored another "tax reform" bill that lowered the top rate to 28 percent. A schoolteacher, a factory worker, and a billionaire could all pay 28 percent. The idea of a "progressive" income in which the rich paid at higher rates than everyone else was now almost dead.

As a result of all the tax bills from 1978 to 1992, about $70 billion a year was lost in government revenue, so that in those thirteen years the wealthiest 1 percent of the country gained a trillion dollars.

Not only did the income tax become less progressive during the last decades of the century, but the Social Security tax became more *regressive*. That is, more and more was deducted from the salary checks of the poor and middle classes, but when salaries went over $50,000 no more was deducted. Someone earning $500,000 a year paid as much in social security taxes as someone making $50,000 a year.

The result of these higher payroll taxes was that three-fourths of all wage earners paid more each year through the Social Security tax than through the income tax. Embarrassingly for the Democratic party, which was supposed to be the party of the working class, those higher payroll taxes had been put in motion under the administration of Jimmy Carter.

In a two-party system, if *both* parties ignore public opinion, there is no place voters can turn. By 1984, when all those tax "reforms" had been put into effect by Democrats and Republicans, a public opinion survey by the Internal Revenue Service found that 80 percent of those polled agreed with the statement: "The present tax system benefits the rich and is unfair to the ordinary working man and woman."

By the end of the Reagan years, the gap between rich and poor in the United States had grown dramatically. Where in 1980, the chief executive officers (CEOs) of corporations made forty times as much in salary as the average factory worker, by 1989 they were making ninety-three times as much.

While everybody at the lower levels was doing worse, there were especially heavy losses for blacks, Hispanics, women, and the young. The general impoverishment of the lowest-income groups that took place in the Reagan-Bush years hit black families hardest, with their lack of resources to start with and with racial discrimination facing them in jobs. The victories of the civil rights movement had opened up spaces for some African-Americans, but left others far behind.

At the end of the eighties, at least a third of African-American families fell below the official poverty level, and black unemployment seemed fixed at two and a half times that of whites, with young blacks out of work at the rate of 30 to 40 percent. The life expectancy of blacks remained at least ten years lower than that of whites. In Detroit, Washington, and Baltimore, the mortality rate for black babies was higher than in Jamaica or Costa Rica.

Along with poverty came broken homes, family violence, street crime, drugs. In Washington, D.C., with a concentrated population of black poor within walking distance of the marbled buildings of the national government, 42 percent of young black men between the ages of eighteen and thirty-five were either in jail, or out on probation or parole. The crime rate among blacks, instead of being seen as a crying demand for the elimination of poverty, was used by politicians to call for the building of more prisons.

The 1954 Supreme Court decision in *Brown v. Board of Education* had begun the process of desegregating schools. But poverty kept black children in ghettos and many schools around the country remained segregated by race and class. Supreme Court decisions in the seventies determined that there need be no equalization of funds for poor school districts and rich school districts (*San Antonio Independent School District* v. *Rodriguez*) and that the busing of children need not take place between wealthy suburbs and inner cities (*Milliken.* v. *Bradley*).

To admirers of free enterprise and laissez-faire, those people were poor who did not work and produce, and so had themselves to blame for their poverty. They ignored the fact that women taking care of children on their own were working very hard indeed. They did not ask why babies who were not old enough to show their work skills should be penalized— to the point of death—for growing up in a poor family.

In the mid-eighties, a major scandal began to emerge in Washington. The deregulation of the savings and loan banks begun in the Carter administration had continued under Reagan, leading to risky investments that drained the assets of the banks, leaving them owing hundreds of billions of dollars to depositors, which the government had insured, and which taxpayers would now have to pay.

The enormous drain of money from the treasury for defense had once been declared by President Eisenhower to be a "theft" from human needs. But it was accepted by both parties. Jimmy Carter as president had proposed a $10 billion increase in the military budget, an enactment of exactly what Eisenhower had described. All of the huge military budgets of the post–World War II period, from Truman to Reagan and Bush, were approved overwhelmingly by both Democrats and Republicans.

The spending of trillions of dollars to build up nuclear and nonnuclear forces was justified by fears that the Soviet Union, also building up its military forces, would invade Western Europe. In 1984, the CIA admitted that it had exaggerated Soviet military expenditures. Harry Rositzke, who worked for the CIA for twenty-five years and was at one time CIA director of espionage operations against the Soviet Union, wrote in the 1980s: "In all of my years in government and since I have never seen an intelligence estimate that shows how it would be profitable to Soviet interests to invade Western Europe or to attack the United States."

However, the creation of such a fear in the public mind was useful in arguing for the building of frightful and superfluous weapons. For instance, the Trident submarine, which was capable of firing hundreds of nuclear warheads, cost $1.5 billion. That $1.5 billion was enough to finance a five-year program of child immunization around the world against deadly diseases, and prevent five million deaths.

One of the favorite military programs of the Reagan administration was the "Star Wars" program, in which billions were spent, supposedly to build a shield in space to stop enemy nuclear missiles in midair. But the first three tests of the technology failed. A fourth test was undertaken, with government funding for the program at stake, and there was another failure, but Reagan's secretary of defense, Caspar Weinberger, approved the faking of results to show that the test had succeeded.

When the Soviet Union began to disintegrate in 1989, and there was no longer the familiar "Soviet threat," the military budget was reduced somewhat, but still remained huge. A National Press Club survey showed that 59 percent of American voters wanted a 50 percent cut in defense spending over the next five years, but both parties continued to ignore the public they were supposed to represent.

In the summer of 1992, congressional Democrats and Republicans joined to vote against a transfer of funds from the military budget to human needs, and voted to spend $120 billion to "defend" Europe, which everyone acknowledged was no longer in danger—if it ever had been—from Soviet attack.

Ronald Reagan became president just after a revolution had taken place in Nicaragua, in which a popular Sandinista movement (named after the 1920s revolutionary hero Augusto Sandino) overthrew the corrupt Somoza dynasty (long supported by the United States). The Sandinistas, a coalition of Marxists, left-wing priests, and assorted nationalists, set about to give more land to the peasants and to spread education and health care among the poor.

The Reagan administration, seeing in this a "Communist" threat, but even more important, a challenge to the long U.S. control over governments in Central America, began immediately to work to overthrow the Sandinista government. It waged a secret war by having the CIA organize a counterrevolutionary force (the "Contras"), many of whose leaders were former leaders of the hated National Guard under Somoza.

The Contras seemed to have no popular support inside Nicaragua and so were based next door in Honduras, a very poor country dominated by the United States. From Honduras they moved across the border, raiding farms and villages, killing men, women and children, committing atrocities. A former colonel with the Contras, Edgar Chamorro, testified before the World Court:

> ...Many civilians were killed in cold blood. Many others were tortured, mutilated, raped, robbed, or otherwise abused.... When I agreed to join...I had hoped that it would be an organization of Nicaraguans.... [It] turned out to be an instrument of the U.S. government....

There was a reason for the secrecy of the U.S. actions in Nicaragua; public opinion surveys showed that the American public was opposed to military involvement there. In 1984, the CIA, using Latin American agents to conceal its involvement, put mines in the harbors of Nicaragua to blow up ships. When information leaked out, Secretary of Defense Weinberger lied to ABC news: "The United States is not mining the harbors of Nicaragua."

Later that year Congress, responding perhaps to public opinion and the memory of Vietnam, made it illegal for the United States to support "directly or indirectly, military or paramilitary operations in Nicaragua."

The Reagan administration decided to ignore this law and to find ways to fund the Contras secretly.

In 1986, a story appearing in a Beirut magazine created a sensation: that weapons had been sold by the United States to Iran (supposedly an enemy), that in return Iran had promised to release American hostages being held by extremist Muslims in Lebanon, and that profits from the weapons sale were being given to the Nicaraguan Contras to buy arms.

When asked about this at a press conference in November 1986, President Reagan told a number of lies and said that the purpose of the operation was to promote a dialogue with Iranian moderates. In reality, the purpose was a double one: to free hostages and get credit for that, and to help the Contras.

Out of the much-publicized "Contragate" scandal came no powerful critique of secrecy in government or of the erosion of democracy by actions taken in secret by a small group of men safe from the scrutiny of public opinion. The media, in a country priding itself on its level of education and information, kept the public informed only on the most superficial level.

The limits of Democratic party criticism of the affair were revealed by a leading Democrat, Senator Sam Nunn of Georgia, who, as the investigation was getting under way, said: "We must, all of us, help the President restore his credibility in foreign affairs."

It was clear that President Reagan and Vice President Bush were involved in what became known as the Iran-Contra Affair. But their underlings scrupulously kept them out of it, illustrating the familiar government device of "plausible denial," in which the top official, shielded by subordinates, can plausibly deny involvement.

Neither Reagan nor Bush were indicted. Rather, the congressional committee put the lesser culprits on the witness stand and several of them were indicted. One (Robert McFarlane, a former national security adviser to Reagan) attempted suicide. Another, Col. Oliver North, stood trial for lying to Congress, was found guilty, but on appeal the conviction was overturned on a legal technicality. Reagan retired in peace and Bush became the next president of the United States.

The Iran-Contra affair was only one of the many instances in which the government of the United States violated its own laws in pursuit of some desired goal in foreign policy.

Toward the end of the Vietnam war, in 1973, Congress, seeking to limit the presidential power that had been used so ruthlessly in Indochina, passed the War Powers Act, which said, "The President, in every possible instance, shall consult with Congress before introducing United States Armed Forces into hostilities or into situations where imminent involvement in hostilities is clearly indicated by the circumstances."

In the fall of 1982, President Reagan sent American marines into a dangerous situation in Lebanon, where a civil war was raging, again ignoring the requirements of the War Powers Act. The following year, over two hundred of those marines were killed when a bomb was exploded in their barracks by terrorists.

Shortly after that, in October 1983 (with some analysts concluding this was done to take attention away from the Lebanon disaster), Reagan sent U.S. forces to invade the tiny Caribbean island of Grenada. Again, Congress was notified, but not consulted. The reasons given to the American people for this invasion were that a recent coup that had taken place in Grenada put American citizens (students at a medical school on the island) in danger; and that the United States had received an urgent request from the Organization of Eastern Caribbean States to intervene.

An unusually pointed article in the *New York Times* on October 29, 1983, by correspondent Bernard Gwertzman demolished those reasons: "The formal request...was made...at the request of the United States. The wording of the...request, however, was drafted in Washington and conveyed to the Caribbean leaders by special American emissaries."

The real reason for the invasion, one high American official told Gwertzman, was that the United States should show (determined to overcome the sense of defeat in Vietnam) that it was a truly powerful nation: "What good are maneuvers and shows of force, if you never use it?"

The connection between U.S. military intervention and the promotion of capitalist enterprise had always been especially crass in the Caribbean. As for Grenada, an article in the *Wall Street Journal* eight years after the military invasion (October 29, 1991) spoke of "an invasion of banks" and noted that St. George's, the capital of Grenada, with 7,500 people, had 118 offshore banks, one for every 64 residents.

U.S. invasions were often justified to "protect" citizens, but when four churchwomen were killed by government-sponsored death squads in El Salvador in 1980, there was no U.S. intervention. Instead, military aid to the government, the training of death squads, continued.

The historic role of the United States in El Salvador, where 2 percent of the population owned 60 percent of the land, was to make sure governments were in power there that would support U.S. business interests, no matter how this impoverished the great majority of people. Popular rebellions that would threaten these business arrangements were to be opposed. When a popular uprising in 1932 threatened the military government, the United States sent a cruiser and two destroyers to stand by while the government massacred thirty thousand Salvadorans.

In February 1980 El Salvador's Catholic archbishop, Oscar Romero, sent a personal letter to President Carter, asking him to stop military aid to El Salvador. Not long before that, the National Guard and National Police had opened fire on a crowd of protesters in front of the Metropolitan Cathedral and killed twenty-four people. But the Carter administration continued the aid. The following month Archbishop Romero was assassinated.

There was mounting evidence that the assassination had been ordered by Roberto D'Aubuisson, a leader of the right wing. But D'Aubuisson had the protection of Nicolas Carranza, a deputy minister of defense, who at the time was receiving $90,000 a year from the CIA. And Elliot Abrams, ironically assistant secretary of state for human rights, declared that D'Aubuisson "was not involved in murder."

Congress was sufficiently embarrassed by the killings in El Salvador to require that before any more aid was given the president must certify that progress in human rights was taking place. Reagan did not take this seriously. Massacres took place, but certification and military aid continued. When Congress passed a law in 1983 to continue the requirement of certification, Reagan vetoed it.

The press was especially timid and obsequious during the Reagan years. When journalist Raymond Bonner continued to report on the atrocities in El Salvador, and on the U.S. role, the *New York Times* removed him from his assignment. Back in 1981 Bonner had reported on the massacre of hundreds of civilians in the town of El Mozote, by a battalion of soldiers trained by the United States. The Reagan administration scoffed at the account, but in 1992, a team of forensic anthropologists began unearthing skeletons from the site of the massacre, most of them children; the following year a U.N. commission confirmed the story of the massacre at El Mozote.

The Reagan administration, which did not appear at all offended by military juntas governing in Latin America (Guatemala, El Salvador, Chile) if they were "friendly" to the United States, became very upset when a tyranny was hostile, as was the government of Muammar Qaddafi in Libya. In 1986, when unknown terrorists bombed a discotheque in West Berlin, killing a U.S. serviceman, the White House immediately decided to retaliate. Qaddafi was probably responsible for various acts of terrorism over the years, but there was no real evidence that in this case he was to blame.

Planes were sent over the capital city of Tripoli with specific instructions to aim at Qaddafi's house. The bombs fell on a crowded city; perhaps a hundred people were killed. Qaddafi was not injured, but an adopted daughter of his was killed.

Early in the presidency of George Bush, there came the most dramatic developments on the international scene since the end of World War II. In the year 1989, with a dynamic new leader, Mikhail Gorbachev, at the head of the Soviet Union, the long suppressed dissatisfaction with "dictatorships of the proletariat" which had turned out to be dictatorships *over* the proletariat erupted all through the Soviet bloc.

There were mass demonstrations in the Soviet Union and in the countries of Eastern Europe which had been long dominated by the Soviet Union. East Germany agreed to unite with West Germany, and the wall separating East Berlin from West Berlin, long a symbol of the tight control of its citizens by East Germany, was dismantled in the presence of wildly exultant citizens of both Germanies. In Czechoslovakia, a new non-Communist government came into being, headed by a playwright and former imprisoned dissident named Vaclav Havel. In Poland, Bulgaria, Hungary, a new leadership emerged, promising freedom and democracy. And remarkably, all this took place without civil war, in response to overwhelming popular demand.

In the United States, the Republican party claimed that the hard-line policies of Reagan and the increase in military expenditures had brought down the Soviet Union. But former ambassador to the Soviet Union, George Kennan, wrote that "the general effect of cold war extremism was to delay rather than hasten the great change that overtook the Soviet Union by the end of the 1980s." These cold war policies were carried on at a frightful cost to the American people, Kennan said: "We paid with forty years of enormous and otherwise unnecessary military expenditures. We paid through the cultivation of nuclear weaponry to the point where the vast and useless nuclear arsenal had become (and remains today) a danger to the very environment of the planet...."

The sudden collapse of the Soviet Union left the political leadership of the United States unprepared. Several trillion dollars had been taken from American citizens in the form of taxes to maintain a huge nuclear and nonnuclear arsenal and military bases all over the world—all primarily justified by the "Soviet threat." Here then was an opportunity for the United States to reconstruct its foreign policy, and to free hundreds of billion dollars a year from the budget to be used for constructive, healthy projects.

But this did not happen. Along with exultation—"We have won the cold war"—came a kind of panic: "What can we do to maintain our military establishment?" The military budget remained huge. The chairman of the Joint Chiefs of Staff, Colin Powell, said: "I want to scare the hell out of the rest of the world. I don't say that in a bellicose way."

As if to prove that the gigantic military establishment was still necessary, the Bush administration, in its four-year term, launched two wars: a "small" one against Panama and a massive one against Iraq.

Panama's dictator, Gen. Manuel Noriega, was corrupt, brutal, authoritarian, but President Reagan and Vice President Bush had overlooked this because Noriega cooperated with the CIA in many ways. By 1987, however, Noriega's usefulness was over. His activities in the drug trade were in the open, and he became a convenient target. The Bush administration wanted to prove that the United States, apparently unable to destroy the Castro regime or the Sandinistas or the revolutionary movement in El Salvador, was still a power in the Caribbean.

Claiming that it wanted to bring Noriega to trial as a drug trafficker and also that it needed to protect U.S. citizens, the United States invaded Panama in December 1989, with twenty-six thousand troops.

It was a quick victory. Noriega was captured and brought to Florida to stand trial (where he was subsequently found guilty and sent to prison). But in the invasion, neighborhoods in Panama City were bombarded and hundreds, perhaps thousands, of civilians were killed. It was estimated that fourteen thousand were homeless.

A new president friendly to the United States was installed in Panama, but poverty and unemployment remained, and in 1992 the *New York Times* reported that the invasion and removal of Noriega "failed to stanch the flow of illicit narcotics through Panama."

The United States, however, succeeded in one of its aims—to reestablish its strong influence over Panama. Liberal Democrats (Senators John Kerry and Ted Kennedy of Massachusetts, and many others) declared their approval of the military action. The Democrats were being true to their historic role as supporters of military intervention; foreign policy remained bipartisan. They seemed determined to show they were as tough (or as ruthless) as the Republicans.

But the Panama operation was on too small a scale to accomplish what both the Reagan and Bush administrations badly wanted: to overcome the American public's abhorrence, since Vietnam, of foreign military interventions. Two years later, the Gulf War against Iraq presented such an opportunity. Iraq, under the brutal dictatorship of Saddam Hussein, had taken over its small but oil-rich neighbor, Kuwait, in August 1990.

George Bush needed something at this point to boost his popularity among American voters. The *Washington Post* reported in October: "Some observers in his own party worry that the president will be forced to initiate combat to prevent further erosion of his support at home."

On October 30, a secret decision was made for war against Iraq. The United Nations had responded to the invasion of Kuwait by establishing sanctions against Iraq. Secret CIA testimony to the Senate affirmed that Iraq's imports and exports had been reduced by more than 90 percent because of the sanctions. But Bush was determined. After the November elections brought gains for the Democrats in Congress, Bush doubled American military forces in the Gulf, to 500,000, creating what was now clearly an offensive force rather than a defensive one.

According to Elizabeth Drew, a writer for the *New Yorker*, Bush's aide John Sununu "was telling people that a short successful war would be pure political gold for the President and would guarantee his re-election." That and the long-time U.S. wish to have a decisive voice in the control of Middle East oil resources were the crucial elements in the decision to go to war against Iraq.

But those motives were not presented to the American public. It was told that the United States wanted to liberate Kuwait from Iraqi control. The major media dwelled on this as a reason for war, without noting that other countries had been invaded without the United States showing such concern (East Timor by Indonesia, Iran by Iraq, Lebanon by Israel, Mozambique by South Africa; to say nothing of countries invaded by the United States itself—Grenada, Panama).

The justification for war that seemed most compelling was that Iraq was on its way to building a nuclear bomb, but the evidence for this was very weak. Even if Iraq could build a bomb in a year or two, which was the most pessimistic estimate, it had no delivery system to send it anywhere. Besides, Israel already had nuclear weapons. And the United States had perhaps thirty thousand of them. The Bush administration was trying hard to develop a paranoia in the nation about an Iraqi bomb that did not yet exist.

Bush seemed set on war. There had been several chances to negotiate an Iraqi withdrawal from Kuwait right after the invasion, including an Iraqi proposal reported on August 29 by *Newsday* correspondent Knut Royce. But there was no response from the United States. When Secretary of State James Baker went to Geneva to meet with Iraqi foreign minister Tariq Aziz, the instruction from Bush was "no negotiations."

Despite months of exhortation from Washington about the dangers of Saddam Hussein, surveys showed that less than half of the public favored military action.

In January 1991, Bush, apparently feeling the need for support, asked Congress to give him the authority to make war. The debate in Congress was lively. (At one point, a Senate speech was interrupted by protesters in the balcony shouting: "No blood for oil!" The protesters were hustled out by guards.) The Senate voted for military action by only a few votes. The House supported the resolution by a larger majority. However, once Bush ordered the attack on Iraq, both houses, with just a few dissents, Democrats as well as Republicans, voted to "support the war and support the troops."

It was in mid-January 1991, after Saddam Hussein defied an ultimatum to leave Kuwait, that the U.S. launched its air war against Iraq. It was given the name Desert Storm. The government and the media had conjured up a picture of a formidable military power, but Iraq was far from that. The U.S. Air Force had total control of the air, and could bomb at will.

Not only that, U.S. officials had virtual total control of the airwaves. The American public was overwhelmed with television photos of "smart bombs" and confident statements that laser bombs were being guided with perfect precision to military targets. The major networks presented all of these claims without question or criticism.

This confidence in "smart bombs" sparing civilians may have contributed to a shift in public opinion, from being equally divided on going to war, to perhaps 85 percent support for the invasion. Perhaps more important in winning over public support was that once American military were engaged, it seemed to many people who had previously opposed military action that to criticize it now meant betraying the troops who were there. All over the nation yellow ribbons were displayed as a symbol of support for the forces in Iraq.

In fact, the public was being deceived about how "smart" the bombs being dropped on Iraqi towns were. After talking with former intelligence and air force officers, a correspondent for the *Boston Globe* reported that perhaps 40 percent of the laser-guided bombs dropped in Operation Desert Storm missed their targets. Reuters reported that the air raids on Iraq first used laser-guided bombs, but within a few weeks turned to B-52s, which carried conventional bombs, meaning more indiscriminate bombing.

John Lehman, secretary of the navy under President Reagan, estimated there had been thousands of civilian casualties. A Reuters dispatch from Iraq described the destruction of a seventy-three-room hotel in a town south of Baghdad, and quoted an Egyptian witness: "They hit the hotel, full of families, and then they came back to hit it again."

American reporters were kept from seeing the war close up, and their dispatches were subject to censorship. Apparently recalling how press reports of civilian casualties had affected public opinion during the Vietnam war, the U.S. government was taking no chances this time.

In mid-February, U.S. planes dropped bombs on an air raid shelter in Baghdad at four in the morning, killing 400 to 500 people. An Associated Press reporter who was one of few allowed to go to the site said: "Most of the recovered bodies were charred and mutilated beyond recognition. Some clearly were children." The Pentagon claimed it was a military target, but the AP reporter on the scene said: "No evidence of any military presence could be seen inside the wreckage." Other reporters who inspected the site agreed.

After the war, fifteen Washington news bureau chiefs complained in a joint statement that the Pentagon exercised "virtual total control...over the American press" during the Gulf War. But while it was happening, leading television news commentators behaved as if they were working for the United States government. When the Soviet government tried to negotiate an end to the war, bringing Iraq out of Kuwait before the ground war could get under way, top CBS correspondent, Lesley Stahl, asked another reporter: "Isn't this the nightmare scenario? Aren't the Soviets trying to stop us?"

The final stage of the war, barely six weeks after it had begun, was a ground assault that, like the air war, encountered virtually no resistance. With victory certain and the Iraqi army in full flight, U.S. planes kept bombing the retreating soldiers who clogged the highway out of Kuwait City. A reporter called the scene "a blazing hell...a gruesome testament.... To the east and west across the sand lay the bodies of those fleeing."

The human consequences of the war became shockingly clear after its end, when it was revealed that the bombings of Iraq had caused starvation, disease, and the deaths of tens of thousands of children. A Harvard medical team reporting in May said that child mortality had risen steeply, and that fifty-five thousand more children died in the first four months of the year (the war lasted from January 15 to February 28) than in a comparable period the year before.

The director of a pediatric hospital in Baghdad told a *New York Times* reporter that on the first night of the bombing campaign the electricity was knocked out: "Mothers grabbed their children out of incubators, took intravenous tubes out of their arms. Others were removed from oxygen tents and they ran to the basement, where there was no heat. I lost more than 40 prematures in the first 12 hours of the bombing."

Although in the course of the war Saddam Hussein had been depicted by U.S. officials and the press as another Hitler, the war ended short of a march into Baghdad, leaving Hussein in power. It seemed that the United States had wanted to weaken him, but not to eliminate him, in order to keep him as a balance against Iran. In the years before the Gulf War, the United States had sold arms to both Iran and Iraq, at different times favoring one or the other as part of the traditional "balance of power" strategy.

Therefore, as the war ended, the United States did not support Iraqi dissidents who wanted to overthrow the regime of Saddam Hussein. The *New York Times*: "President Bush has decided to let President Saddam Hussein put down rebellions in his country without American intervention rather than risk the splintering of Iraq...." This left the Kurdish minority, which was rebelling against Saddam Hussein, helpless. And anti-Hussein elements among the Iraqi majority were also left hanging.

The war provoked an ugly wave of anti-Arab racism in the United States, with Arab-Americans insulted or beaten or threatened with death. There were bumper stickers that said "I don't brake for Iraqis." An Arab-American businessman was beaten in Toledo, Ohio.

The Democratic party went along with the Bush administration. It was pleased with the results. It had some misgivings about civilian casualties. But it did not constitute an opposition.

President George Bush was satisfied. As the war ended, he declared on a radio broadcast: "The specter of Vietnam has been buried forever in the desert sands of the Arabian peninsula."

The Establishment press very much agreed. The two leading news magazines, *Time* and *Newsweek*, had special editions hailing the victory in the war, noting there had been only a few hundred American casualties.

They did not mention Iraqi casualties. A *New York Times* editorial said: "America's victory in the Persian Gulf war…provided special vindication for the U.S. Army, which brilliantly exploited its firepower and mobility and in the process erased memories of its grievous difficulties in Vietnam."

A black poet in Berkeley, California, June Jordan, had a different view: "I suggest to you it's a hit the same way that crack is, and it doesn't last long."

Exercises

1. If only 60 percent of voting age adults are registered to vote, what percentage voted in the presidential election of 1960? Of 1976?

2. How does Zinn characterize post-1960s activism?

3. How did Carter present himself to the voters during the presidential campaign of 1976?

4. How did Carter's cabinet appointments belie his populist campaign rhetoric?

5. Zinn refers to Carter's policy toward South Africa as "sophisticated." What does Zinn mean by this? Explain why you agree or disagree with Zinn's characterization of Carter's South African policy.

6. How did the United States acquire the Panama Canal? How could Reagan argue that Carter "lost" or "gave away" the canal? Why would the American people care?

7. What is a "multinational"? Which continent proved the most profitable for these multinationals to invest in? Which was the least profitable? How might you explain the differences in profitability?

8. What were the raw materials that American corporations needed to acquire from other countries? For what did these corporations need these materials? Why would support of repressive regimes guarantee that American corporations could purchase these raw materials at low prices?

9. Why did the United States make political loyalty a stipulation for foreign aid?

10. Why did Carter end federal price regulation of oil and gas?

11. Why support a military junta in El Salvador against a peasant rebellion?

12. How might Ferdinand Marcos have used $300 million in U.S. *military* aid? What was the United States getting in return for its generous aid to the Philippines?

13. What point was Alan Richman trying to make when calling attention to the number of American hostages in Iran and comparing them to the three thousand Guatamalans executed by their government the year before? (What is his implied critique of American foreign policy?)

14. What were Reagan's and Bush's lasting legacies?

15. What did the Supreme Court accomplish during the Reagan-Bush years?

16. What was the significance of Reagan's ability to end the air traffic controller's strike?

17. Anita Hill's testimony:
    a. supported the confirmation of Clarence Thomas to the Supreme Court.
    b. had such credibility with middle-class America that almost all businesses were compelled to adopt sexual harassment policies.
    c. proved that the Senate was composed primarily of men "who didn't get it."
    d. revealed a major defect in the Founding Fathers' decision to have only the Senate be required to confirm presidential appointments.

18. What event prompted the passage of the Coal Mine Health and Safety Act of 1969?

19. How did Reagan weaken OSHA (Occupational Safety and Health Act)?

20. In *Who Will Tell the People?* William Greider argues that legislation is passed to appease popular concerns. But legislation is written in such general terms that it allows the regulatory agencies to actually define how the law will be enforced. These regulatory agencies are appointed, not elected, positions and operate out of the public's eye. Yet their members are in constant contact with lobbyists from the very businesses that the regulatory agencies are to oversee. What evidence is there that the EPA might have been influenced by such lobbyists?

21. What position did the United States take at the 1992 Earth Summit in Brazil?

22. How much did the oil companies profit from Reagan's decision to lift the price controls on oil?

23. What were the effects of Reagan's tax cuts?

24. What was Reagan's rationale for his welfare position?

25. What specific programs did "welfare" constitute? Who were the primary recipients of welfare?

26. Why would middle-class taxpayers support "assistance to the poor" but not "welfare"? (Are "welfare" and "assistance to the poor" different?)

27. What was the tax rate on incomes over $400,000 in 1946? 1968? 1984? 1986?

28. How did changes in the Social Security tax fall more heavily on those earning below $50,000 than on those earning over $50,000?

29. How did the economic position of blacks in the 1980s testify to the enduring nature of racism?

30. How did Supreme Court decisions in the 1970s prevent most blacks from gaining access to decent education?

31. How much money did taxpayers lose in the savings and loan crisis?

32. Why did the CIA exaggerate Soviet military expenditures?

33. Zinn writes of a series of failed tests of the Star Wars technology: "…but Reagan's secretary of defense, Caspar Weinberger, approved the faking of results to show that the test had succeeded." Who was Weinberger's intended audience?

34. How many Trident submarines could the U.S. have built with the funds Congress authorized for the "defense of Europe"?

35. What parallels can you draw between U.S. government conduct of the Vietnam war and its war against the Sandinistas?

36. Why pass laws and not obey them? Why sign treaties and not honor them?

37. What was the purpose of the U.S. invasion of Grenada?

38. How did the U.S. government contribute to the stability of El Salvador's government?

39. Zinn writes: "Congress was sufficiently embarrassed by the killings in El Salvador…" "Embarrassed" in front of whom?

40. Explain the difference in the U.S. government's response to the deaths of the four American churchwomen in El Salvador (1980) and the death of a U.S. serviceman in West Berlin (1986).

41. Assess the validity of the following statement made by George Kennan as quoted by Zinn: "the general effect of cold war extremism was to delay rather than hasten the great change that overtook the Soviet Union by the end of the 1980s."

42. Why did Colin Powell "want to scare the hell out of the rest of the world"?

43. Explain the logic of the following argument: the invasion of Panama and the war against Iraq were the means "to prove that the gigantic military establishment was still necessary." In your explanation, be sure to elaborate on what *needs* the military establishment fills.

44. What were the most common reasons that the U.S. government (during the Carter-Reagan-Bush years) publicly gave for invading Caribbean countries:

    a. to protect American citizens

    b. to protect American business interests

    c. to prove American military superiority

    d. to prove the president's independence from Congress

    e. to protect human rights

45. Using the options from the previous question, what reasons did the U.S. government actually have for invading Caribbean countries?

46. Is there a difference between your answers to #44 and #45? Explain.

47. Did the Gulf War succeed in "overcoming the public's abhorrence of foreign military interventions"?

48. How was the U.S. government's role preceding and during the Gulf War consistent with its diplomatic and military actions since World War II? In what ways was it a departure? (To what degree does the Gulf War represent part of the "American Political Tradition"?)

49. How did Bush gain congressional approval to attack Iraq? How did his process compare to that of Johnson getting approval and cooperation from Congress to wage the Vietnam war?

50. Why did people who opposed U.S. military action become supporters of such action once the United States had attacked Iraq?

51. How did the media's role in Desert Storm differ from their role during the Vietnam war?

52. Why didn't the U.S. government remove Saddam Hussein from power?

53. Why were Arab-Americans often objects of attack during and after the Persian Gulf War?

54. June Jordan observed that the Persian Gulf War was "…a hit the same way that crack is, and it doesn't last long." Is this an accurate observation? Why is this a criticism of the Gulf War?

55. Why did the U.S. media virtually ignore the number of Iraqi war casualties while focusing on how few Americans died?

56. Was the "bipartisan consensus" of these years greater than in previous years? Evaluate in terms of the purpose of foreign policy; the tactics of foreign policy; domestic policy—goals, tactics, and methods of coping with dissent.

57. *Draw a world map* (circa 1980) on which you identify the following: Central America; South Africa; Brazil; Soviet Union; United States; Philippines; Vietnam; North and South Korea; Iran; Iraq; Kuwait. Include an enlarged insert of Central America and the Caribbean on which you identify: Grenada; Guatemala; Honduras; El Salvador; Nicaragua and Panama.

58. *Debate Resolution*: Carter represented an interruption of the "American Political Tradition".

Chapter 22

The Unreported Resistance

In the early 1990s, a writer for the *New Republic* magazine, reviewing with approval in the *New York Times* a book about the influence of dangerously unpatriotic elements among American intellectuals, warned his readers of the existence of "a permanent adversarial culture" in the United States.

It was an accurate observation. Despite the political consensus of Democrats and Republicans in Washington which set limits on American reform, making sure that capitalism was in place, that national military strength was maintained, that wealth and power remained in the hands of a few, there were millions of Americans, probably tens of millions, who refused, either actively or silently, to go along. Their activities were largely unreported by the media. They constituted this "permanent adversarial culture."

In the Carter years, a small but determined movement against nuclear arms began to grow. The pioneers were a tiny group of Christian pacifists who had been active against the Vietnam war (among them were a former priest, Philip Berrigan and his wife, Elizabeth McAlister, a former nun). Again and again, members of this group would be arrested for engaging in nonviolent acts of dramatic protest against nuclear war at the Pentagon and the White House—trespassing on forbidden areas, pouring their own blood on symbols of the war machine.

In 1980, small delegations of peace activists from all over the country maintained a series of demonstrations at the Pentagon, in which over a thousand people were arrested for acts of nonviolent civil disobedience.

Over the next decade, a national movement against nuclear weapons developed, from a small number of men and women willing to go to jail to make others stop and think to millions of Americans frightened at the thought of nuclear holocaust, indignant at the billions of dollars spent on weaponry while people were in need of life's necessities.

Even the very Middle American Pennsylvania jurors who convicted a group of protesters (called "The Plowshares Eight" for suggesting that, as the Bible said, swords should be turned into plowshares) showed remarkable sympathy with their actions. One juror, Mary Ann Ingram, said: "We...really didn't want to convict them on anything.... These people are not criminals. Here are people who are trying to do some good for the country. But the judge said nuclear power wasn't the issue."

Reagan's huge military budget was to provoke a national movement against nuclear weapons. In the election of 1980 that brought him into the presidency, local referenda in three districts in western Massachusetts permitted voters to say whether they believed in a mutual Soviet-American halt to testing, production, and deployment of all nuclear weapons, and wanted Congress to devote those funds instead to civilian use. Two peace groups had worked for months on the campaign and all three districts approved the resolution (94,000 to 65,000), even those that voted for Reagan as president. Similar referenda received majority votes between 1978 and 1981 in San Francisco, Berkeley, Oakland, Madison, and Detroit.

Women were in the forefront of the new antinuclear movement. Randall Forsberg, a young specialist in nuclear arms, organized the Council for a Nuclear Weapons Freeze, whose simple program—a mutual Soviet-American freeze on the production of new nuclear weapons—began to catch on throughout the country. Shortly after Reagan's election, two thousand women assembled in Washington, marched on the Pentagon, and surrounded it in a great circle, linking arms or stretching to hold the ends of brightly colored scarves. One hundred forty women were arrested for blocking the Pentagon entrance.

A small group of doctors began to organize meetings around the country to teach citizens the medical consequences of nuclear war. They were the core of the Physicians for Social Responsibility, and Dr. Helen Caldicott, the group's president, became one of the most powerful and eloquent national leaders of the movement.

At a national meeting of Catholic bishops early in the Reagan administration, the majority opposed any use of nuclear weapons. In November 1981, there were meetings on 151 college campuses around the country on the issue of nuclear war. And at local elections in Boston that month, a resolution calling for increased federal spending on social programs "by reducing the amount of our tax dollars spent on nuclear weapons and programs of foreign intervention" won a majority in every one of Boston's twenty-two wards, including both white and black working-class districts.

On June 12, 1982, the largest political demonstration in the history of the country took place in Central Park, New York City. Close to a million people gathered to express their determination to bring an end to the arms race.

Scientists who had worked on the atom bomb added their voices to the growing movement. George Kistiakowsky, a Harvard University chemistry professor who had worked on the first atomic bomb and later was science adviser to President Eisenhower, became a spokesman for the disarmament movement. His last public remarks, before his death from cancer at the age of eighty-two, were in an editorial for the *Bulletin of Atomic Scientists* in December 1982. "I tell you as my parting words: Forget the channels. There simply is not enough time left before the world explodes. Concentrate instead on organizing, with so many others of like mind, a mass movement for peace such as there has not been before."

By the spring of 1983, the nuclear freeze had been endorsed by 368 city and county councils across the country, by 444 town meetings and 17 state legislatures, and by the House of Representatives. A Harris poll at this time indicated that 79 percent of the population wanted a nuclear freeze agreement with the Soviet Union. Even among evangelical Christians—a group of 40 million people presumed to be conservative and pro-Reagan—a Gallup poll sampling showed 60 percent favoring a nuclear freeze.

A year after the great Central Park demonstration, there were over three thousand antiwar groups around the country. And the antinuclear feeling was being reflected in the culture—in books, magazine articles, plays, motion pictures. Jonathan Schell's impassioned book against the arms race, *The Fate of the Earth*, became a national best-seller. A documentary film on the arms race made in Canada was forbidden to enter the country by the Reagan administration, but a federal court ordered it admitted.

In less than three years, there had come about a remarkable change in public opinion. At the time of Reagan's election, nationalist feeling—drummed up by the recent hostage crisis in Iran and by the Russian invasion of Afghanistan—was strong; the University of Chicago's National

Opinion Research Center found that only 12 percent of those it polled thought too much was being spent on arms. But when it took another poll in the spring of 1982, that figure rose to 32 percent. And in the spring of 1983, a *New York Times*/CBS News poll found that the figure had risen again, to 48 percent.

Antimilitarist feeling expressed itself also in resistance to the draft. When President Jimmy Carter, responding to the Soviet Union's invasion of Afghanistan, called for the registration of young men for a military draft, more than 800,000 men (10 percent) failed to register. One mother wrote to the *New York Times*:

> To the Editor: Thirty-six years ago I stood in front of the crematorium. The ugliest force in the world had promised itself that I should be removed from the cycle of life—that I should never know the pleasure of giving life. With great guns and great hatred, this force thought itself the equal of the force of life.
>
> I survived the great guns, and with every smile of my son, they grow smaller. It is not for me, sir, to offer my son's blood as lubricant for the next generation of guns. I remove myself and my own from the cycle of death.
>
> ISABELLA LEITNER

William Beecher, a former Pentagon reporter, wrote in November 1981 that Reagan was "obviously concerned, even alarmed, by the mounting voices of discontent and suspicion over emerging U.S. nuclear strategy both in the streets of Europe and more recently on American campuses." Hoping to intimidate this opposition, the Reagan administration began to prosecute draft resisters. One of those facing prison was Benjamin Sasway, who cited U.S. military intervention in El Salvador as a good reason not to register for the draft.

Reagan's policy of giving military aid to the dictatorship of El Salvador was not accepted quietly around the nation. He had barely taken office when the following report appeared in the *Boston Globe*: "It was a scene reminiscent of the 1960s, a rally of students in Harvard Yard shouting antiwar slogans, a candlelight march through the streets of Cambridge.... 2000 persons, mostly students, gathered to protest U.S. involvement in El Salvador...."

During commencement exercises that spring of 1981 at Syracuse University, when Reagan's secretary of state, Alexander Haig, was given an honorary doctorate in "public service," two hundred students and faculty turned their backs on the presentation. The press reported, "Nearly every pause in Mr. Haig's fifteen-minute address was punctuated by chants: 'Human needs, not military greed!' 'Get out of El Salvador!' 'Washington guns killed American nuns!'"

The last slogan was a reference to the execution in the fall of 1980 of four American nuns by Salvadoran soldiers. Thousands of people in El Salvador were being murdered each year by "death squads" sponsored by a government armed by the United States, and the American public was beginning to pay attention.

Public opinion was simply ignored. A *New York Times*/CBS News poll in the spring of 1982 reported that only 16 percent of its sampling favored Reagan's program of sending military and economic aid to El Salvador.

There was much talk in the American press in the early eighties about the political cautiousness of a new generation of college students concerned mostly with their own careers. But when, at the Harvard commencement of June 1983, Mexican writer Carlos Fuentes criticized American intervention in Latin America, and said, "Because we are your true friends, we will not permit you to conduct yourselves in Latin American affairs as the Soviet Union conducts itself in Central European and Central Asian affairs," he was interrupted twenty times by applause and received a standing ovation when finished.

Among my own students at Boston University, I did not find the pervasive selfishness and unconcern with others that the media kept reporting, in deadening repetition, about the students of the eighties. One student wrote in his class journal: "I work in Roxbury [a black neighborhood]. I know the government doesn't work. Not for the people of Roxbury, and not for the people anywhere. It works for people with money."

Beyond the campuses, out in the country, there was opposition to government policy, not widely known. Over a thousand people in Tucson, Arizona, marched in a procession and attended a mass to commemorate the anniversary of the assassination of Archbishop Oscar Romero, who had spoken out against the Salvadoran death squads.

Over sixty thousand Americans signed "The Pledge of Resistance," promsing to take action of some sort, including civil disobedience, if Reagan moved to invade Nicaragua. When the president instituted a blockade of the tiny country to try to force its government out of power, there were demonstrations around the country. In Boston alone, 550 people were arrested protesting the blockade.

During Reagan's presidency, there were hundreds of actions against

his policies in South Africa. He obviously did not want to see the white ruling minority of South Africa displaced by the radical African National
Congress, which represented the black majority. But public opinion was
strong enough to cause Congress to legislate economic sanctions against
the South African government in 1986, overriding Reagan's veto.

Reagan's cuts in social services were felt on the local level and there
were angry reactions. In the spring and summer of 1981, residents of East
Boston took to the streets; for fifty-five nights they blocked major thor-
oughfares and the Sumner Tunnel during rush hour, in order to protest
cutbacks in funds for fire, police, and teachers. The police superintendent,
John Doyle, said: "Maybe these people are starting to take lessons from
the protests of the sixties and seventies." The *Boston Globe* reported: "The
demonstrators in East Boston were mostly middle-aged, middle- or working-class people who said they had never protested anything before."

The Reagan administration took away federal funds for the arts, suggesting that the performing arts seek help from private donors. In New
York, two historic Broadway theaters were razed to make way for a luxury
fifty-story hotel, after two hundred theater people demonstrated, picketing, reading plays and singing songs, refusing to disperse when ordered by
police. Some of the nation's best-known theater personalities were
arrested, including producer Joseph Papp, actresses Tammy Grimes,
Estelle Parsons, and Celeste Holm, actors Richard Gere and Michael
Moriarty.

The budget cuts spurred strikes across the country, often by groups
unaccustomed to striking. In the fall of 1982, United Press International
reported: "Angered by layoffs, salary cuts and uncertainty about job security, more schoolteachers throughout the country have decided to go on
strike. Teachers' strikes last week in seven states, from Rhode Island to
Washington, have idled more than 300,000 students."

Surveying a series of news events in the first week of January 1983,
David Nyhan of the *Boston Globe* wrote: "There is something brewing in the
land that bodes ill for those in Washington who ignore it. People have moved
from the frightened state to the angry stage and are acting out their frustra-
tions in ways that will test the fabric of civil order." He gave some examples:

> In Little Washington, Pennsylvania, in early 1983, when a 50-year-old
> computer science teacher who led a teachers' strike was sent to jail, 2000
> people demonstrated outside the jailhouse in his support, and the *Pitts-
> burgh Post-Gazette* called it "the largest crowd in Washington County
> since the 1794 Whiskey Rebellion."

When unemployed or bankrupt home owners in the Pittsburgh area could no longer make mortgage payments, and foreclosure sales were scheduled, 60 pickets jammed the courthouse to protest the auction, and Allegheny sheriff Eugene Coon halted the proceedings.

The foreclosure of a 320-acre wheat farm in Springfield, Colorado, was interrupted by 200 angry farmers, who had to be dispersed by tear gas and Mace.

When Reagan arrived in Pittsburgh in April 1983 to make a speech, three thousand people, many of them unemployed steelworkers, demonstrated against him, standing in the rain outside his hotel. Demonstrations by the unemployed were taking place in Detroit, Flint, Chicago, Cleveland, Los Angeles, Washington—over twenty cities in all.

Just around that time, Miami blacks rioted against police brutality; they were reacting against their general deprivation as well. The unemployment rate among young African-Americans had risen above 50 percent, and the Reagan administration's only response to poverty was to build more jails.

Reagan's policies clearly joined the two issues of disarmament and social welfare. It was guns versus children, and this was expressed dramatically by the head of the Children's Defense Fund, Marian Wright Edelman, in a commencement speech at the Milton Academy in Massachusetts in the summer of 1983:

> You are graduating into a nation and world teetering on the brink of moral and economic bankruptcy. Since 1980, our President and Congress have been turning our national plowshares into swords and been bringing good news to the rich at the expense of the poor.... Children are the major victims.

The repeated elections of Republican candidates, Reagan in 1980 and 1984, George Bush in 1988, were treated by the press with words like "landslide" and "overwhelming victory." They were ignoring the fact that roughly half the population, though eligible to vote, did not. Only 54 percent of the voting-age population voted, so that—of the total eligible to vote—27 percent voted for Reagan. For a second term, running against former vice president Walter Mondale, Reagan won 59 percent of the popular vote, but with half the electorate not voting, he had 29 percent of the voting population. In the 1988 election, with Vice President George Bush running against Democrat Michael Dukakis, Bush's 54 percent victory added up to 27 percent of the eligible voters.

When the people did speak about issues, in surveys of public opinion, they expressed beliefs to which neither the Republican nor Democratic parties paid attention. For instance, both parties, through the eighties and early nineties, kept strict limits on social programs for the poor, on the ground that this would require more taxes, and "the people" did not want higher taxes. This was certainly true as a general proposition, that Americans wanted to pay as little in taxes as possible. But when they were asked if they would be willing to pay higher taxes for specific purposes like health and education, they said yes, they would. For instance, a 1990 poll of Boston area voters showed that 54 percent of them would pay more taxes if that would go toward cleaning up the environment.

And when higher taxes were presented in class terms, rather than as a general proposal, people were quite clear. A *Wall Street Journal*/NBC News poll in December 1990 showed that 84 percent of the respondents favored a surtax on millionaires. Even though 51 percent of the respondents were in favor of *raising* the capital gains tax, neither major party favored that.

A Harris/Harvard School of Public Health poll of 1989 showed that most Americans (61 percent) favored a Canadian-type health system, in which the government was the single payer to doctors and hospitals, bypassing the insurance companies, and offering universal medical coverage to everyone. Neither the Democratic nor the Republican party adopted that as its program, although both insisted they wanted to "reform" the health system.

A survey by the Gordon Black Corporation for the National Press Club in 1992 found that 59 percent of all voters wanted a 50 percent cut in defense spending in five years. Neither of the major parties was willing to make major cuts in the military budget.

How the public felt about government aid to the poor seemed to depend on how the question was put. Both parties, and the media, talked incessantly about the "welfare" system, that it was not working, and the word "welfare" became a signal for opposition. When people were asked (a *New York Times*/CBS News poll of 1992) if more money should be allocated to welfare, only 23 percent agreed. But when the same people were asked, should the government help the poor, 64 percent said yes.

This was a recurring theme. When, at the height of the Reagan presidency, in 1987, people were asked if the government should guarantee food and shelter to needy people, 62 percent answered yes.

Clearly, there was something amiss with a political system, supposed to be democratic, in which the desires of the voters were repeatedly ignored. They could be ignored with impunity so long as the political system was dominated by two parties, both tied to corporate wealth, and not capable of dealing with a fundamental economic illness whose roots were deeper than any single presidency.

That illness came from a fact that was almost never talked about: that the United States was a class society, in which 1 percent of the population owned 33 percent of the wealth, with an underclass of 30 to 40 million people living in poverty. The social programs of the sixties—Medicare and Medicaid, food stamps, and so on—did not do much more than maintain the historic American maldistribution of resources.

While the Democrats would give more help to the poor than the Republicans, they were not capable (indeed, not really desirous) of seriously tampering with an economic system in which corporate profit comes before human need.

There was no important national movement for radical change, no social democratic (or democratic socialist) party such as existed in countries in Western Europe, Canada, and New Zealand. But there were a thousand signs of alienation, voices of protest, local actions in every part of the country to call attention to deep-felt grievances, to demand that some injustice be remedied.

For instance, the Citizens' Clearinghouse for Hazardous Wastes in Washington, D.C., which had been formed early in the Reagan administration by housewife and activist Lois Gibbs, reported that it was giving help to eight thousand local groups around the country.

In Seabrook, New Hampshire, there were years of persistent protest against a nuclear power plant that residents considered a danger to themselves and their families. Between 1977 and 1989, over thirty-five hundred people were arrested in these protests. Ultimately, the plant, plagued by financial problems and opposition, had to shut down.

Fear of nuclear accidents was intensified by disastrous events at Three Mile Island in Pennsylvania in 1979 and by an especially frightening calamity in Chernobyl in the Soviet Union in 1986. All of this was having an effect on the once-booming nuclear industry. By 1994, the Tennessee Valley Authority had stopped the construction of three nuclear plants, which the *New York Times* called "the symbolic death notice for the current generation of reactors in the United States."

In Minneapolis, Minnesota, thousands of people demonstrated year after year against the Honeywell Corporation's military contracts, and between 1982 and 1988 over eighteen hundred people were arrested.

Furthermore, when those who engaged in such civil disobedience were brought into court, they often found sympathetic support from juries, winning acquittals from ordinary citizens who seemed to understand that even if they had technically broken the law, they had done so in a good cause.

In 1984, a group of Vermont citizens (the "Winooski Forty-four") refused to leave the hallway outside a U.S. senator's office, protesting his votes to give arms to the Nicaraguan Contras. They were arrested, but at their trial they were treated sympathetically by the judge and acquitted by the jury.

At another trial shortly after, a number of people (including activist Abbie Hoffman and Amy Carter, daughter of former president Jimmy Carter) were charged with blocking CIA recruiters at the University of Massachusetts. They called to the witness stand ex-CIA agents who told the jury that the CIA had engaged in illegal and murderous activities all around the world. The jury acquitted them. The county district attorney, prosecuting the case, concluded: "Middle America doesn't want the CIA doing what they are doing."

In the South, while there was no great movement comparable to the civil rights movement of the sixties, there were hundreds of local groups organizing poor people, white and black. In North Carolina, Linda Stout, the daughter of a mill worker who had died of industrial poisons, coordinated a multiracial network of five hundred textile workers, farmers, maids—most of them low-income women of color—in the Piedmont Peace Project.

Back in the sixties, Chicano farmworkers, people of Mexican descent who came to work and live mostly in California and the southwestern states, rebelled against their feudal working conditions. They went out on strike and organized a national boycott of grapes, under the leadership of Cesar Chavez. Soon farmworkers were organizing in other parts of the country.

In the seventies and eighties, Latinos' struggles against poverty and discrimination continued. The Reagan years hit them hard, as it did poor people all over the country. By 1984, 42 percent of all Latino children and one-fourth of Latino families lived below the poverty line.

Copper miners in Arizona, mostly Mexican, went on strike against the Phelps-Dodge company after it cut wages, benefits, and safety measures in 1983. They were attacked by National Guardsmen and state troopers, by tear gas and helicopters, but held out for three years until a combination of governmental and corporate power finally defeated them.

There were victories too. In 1985, seventeen hundred cannery workers, most of them Mexican women, went on strike in Watsonville, California, and won a union contract with medical benefits. In 1990 workers who had been laid off from the Levi Strauss company in San Antonio because the company was moving to Costa Rica called a boycott, organized a hunger strike, and won concessions. In Los Angeles, Latino janitors went on strike in 1990 and despite police attacks, won recognition of their union, a pay raise, and sick benefits.

In New Mexico, Latinos fought for land and water rights against real estate developers who tried to throw them off land they had lived on for decades. In 1988 there was a confrontation, and the people organized an armed occupation, built bunkers for protection against attack, and won support from other communities in the Southwest; finally, a court ruled in their favor.

Abnormal rates of cancer for farmworkers in California aroused the Chicano community. Cesar Chavez of the United Farm Workers fasted for thirty-five days in 1988 to call attention to these conditions. There were now United Farm Workers unions in Texas, Arizona, and other states.

As the Latino population of the country kept growing, it soon matched the 12 percent of the population that was African-American and began to have a distinct effect on American culture. Much of its music, art, and drama was much more consciously political and satirical than mainstream culture.

The Border Arts workshop was formed in 1984 by artists and writers in San Diego and Tijuana, and its work dealt powerfully with issues of racism and injustice. In Northern California, Teatro Campesino and Teatro de la Esperanza performed for working people all over the country, turning schoolhouses, churches, and fields into theaters.

Latinos were especially conscious of the imperial role the United States had played in Mexico and the Caribbean, and many of them became militant critics of U.S. policy toward Nicaragua, El Salvador, and Cuba. In 1970 in Los Angeles a great anti–Vietnam war march was attacked by police, leaving three Chicanos dead.

When the Bush administration was preparing for war against Iraq in the summer of 1990, thousands of people in Los Angeles marched along the same route they had taken twenty years before, when they were protesting the Vietnam war. As Elizabeth Martinez wrote (*500 Years of Chicano History in Pictures*):

Before and during President Bush's war in the Persian Gulf many people—including Raza [literally "race"; a term adopted by Latino activists]—had doubts about it or were opposed. We had learned some lessons about wars started in the name of democracy that turned out to benefit only the rich and powerful. Raza mobilized to protest this war of mass murder, even faster than the U.S. war in Vietnam, though we could not stop it.

A new generation of lawyers, schooled in the sixties, constituted a small but socially conscious minority within the legal profession. They were in court defending the poor and the helpless, or bringing suit against powerful corporations. One law firm used its talent and energy to defend whistleblowers—men and women who were fired because they "blew the whistle" on corporate corruption that victimized the public.

The women's movement, which had managed to raise the consciousness of the whole nation on the issue of sexual equality, faced a powerful backlash in the eighties. The Supreme Court's defense of abortion rights in its 1973 *Roe v. Wade* decision aroused a pro-life movement that had strong supporters in Washington. Congress passed, and the Supreme Court later let stand, a law that eliminated federal medical benefits to help poor women pay for abortions. But the National Organization of Women and other groups remained strong; in 1989, a Washington rally for what had come to be known as the right to choose drew over 300,000 people. When, in 1994 and 1995, abortion clinics were attacked and several supporters murdered, the conflict became grimly intense.

The rights of gay and lesbian Americans had come vividly to the forefront in the seventies with radical changes in ideas about sexuality and freedom. The gay movement then became a visible presence in the nation, with parades, demonstrations, campaigns for the elimination of state statutes discriminating against homosexuals. One result was a growing literature about the hidden history of gay life in the United States and in Europe.

In 1994, there was a "Stonewall 25" march in Manhattan, which commemorated an event homosexuals regarded as a turning point: twenty-five years earlier, gay men fought back vigorously against a police raid on the Stonewall bar in Greenwich Village. In the early nineties, gay and lesbian groups campaigned more openly, more determinedly, against discrimination, and for more attention to the scourge of AIDS, which they claimed was being given only marginal attention by the national government.

The labor movement in the eighties and nineties was considerably weakened by the decline of manufacturing, by the flight of factories to other countries, by the hostility of the Reagan administration and its appointees on the National Labor Relations Board. Yet organizing continued, especially among white-collar workers and low-income people of color. The AFL-CIO put on hundreds of new organizers to work among Latinos, African-Americans, and Asian-Americans.

Rank-and-file workers in old, stagnant unions began to rebel. In 1991, the notoriously corrupt leadership of the powerful Teamsters Union was voted out of office by a reform slate. The new leadership immediately became a force in Washington and took the lead in working for independent political coalitions outside the two major parties. But the labor movement as a whole, much diminished, was struggling for survival.

Against the overwhelming power of corporate wealth and governmental authority, the spirit of resistance was kept alive in the early nineties, often by small-scale acts of courage and defiance. On the West Coast, a young activist named Keith McHenry and hundreds of others were arrested again and again for distributing free food to poor people without a license. They were part of a program called Food Not Bombs. More Food Not Bombs groups sprang up in communities around the country.

In 1992, a New York group interested in revising traditional ideas about American history received approval from the New York City Council to put up thirty metal plaques high on lampposts around the city. One of them, placed opposite the Morgan corporate headquarters identified the famous banker J. P. Morgan as a Civil War "draft dodger." In fact, Morgan had avoided the draft and profited in business deals with the government during the war. Another plaque, placed near the Stock Exchange, portrayed a suicide and carried the label "Advantage of an Unregulated Free Market."

The general disillusionment with government during the Vietnam years and the Watergate scandals, the exposure of anti-democratic actions by the FBI and the CIA, led to resignations from government and open criticism by former employees.

A number of former CIA officials left the agency and wrote books critical of its activities. John Stockwell, who had headed the CIA operation in Angola, resigned, wrote a book exposing the CIA's activities, and lectured all over the country about his experiences. David MacMichael, a historian and former CIA specialist, testified at trials on behalf of people who had protested government policy in Central America.

FBI agent Jack Ryan, a twenty-one-year veteran of the bureau, was fired when he refused to investigate peace groups. He was deprived of his pension and for some time had to live in a shelter for homeless people.

Sometimes the war in Vietnam, which had ended in 1975, came back to public attention in the eighties and nineties through people who had made dramatic turnabouts in their thinking. Charles Hutto, a U.S. soldier who had participated in the atrocity known as the My Lai massacre, in which a company of American soldiers shot to death women and children by the hundreds in a tiny Vietnamese village, told a reporter:

> I was nineteen years old, and I'd always been told to do what the grown-ups told me to do.... But now I'll tell my sons, if the government calls, to go, to serve their country, but to use their own judgment at times...to forget about authority...to use their own conscience. I wish somebody had told me that before I went to Vietnam. I didn't know. Now I don't think there should be even a thing called war...cause it messes up a person's mind.

It was this legacy of the Vietnam war—the feeling among a great majority of Americans that it was a terrible tragedy, a war that should not have been fought—that plagued the Reagan and Bush administrations, which still hoped to extend American power around the world.

In 1985, when George Bush was vice president, former defense secretary James Schlesinger had warned the Senate Foreign Relations Committee: "Vietnam brought a sea change in domestic attitudes...a breakdown in the political consensus behind foreign policy...."

When Bush became president, he was determined to overcome what came to be called the Vietnam syndrome—the resistance of the American people to a war desired by the Establishment. And so, he launched the air war against Iraq in mid-January 1991 with overwhelming force, so the war could be over quickly, before there was time for a national antiwar movement to develop.

The signs of a possible movement were there in the months of the prewar buildup. On Halloween, six hundred students marched through downtown Missoula, Montana, shouting "Hell no, we won't go!" In Shreveport, Louisiana, despite the *Shreveport Journal*'s front-page headline—POLL FAVORS MILITARY ACTION—the story was that 42 percent of the respondents thought the U.S. should "initiate force" and 41 percent said "wait and see."

The November 11, 1990, Veterans Parade in Boston was joined by a group called Veterans for Peace, carrying signs: "No More Vietnams. Bring 'Em Home Now" and "Oil and Blood Do Not Mix, Wage Peace."

The *Boston Globe* reported that "the protesters were greeted with respectful applause and, at some places, strong demonstrations of support by onlookers."

Perhaps the most famous Vietnam veteran, Ron Kovic, author of *Born on the Fourth of July*, made a thirty-second television speech as Bush moved toward war. In the appeal, broadcast on 200 television stations in 120 cities across the country, he asked all citizens to "stand up and speak out" against war. "How many more Americans coming home in wheelchairs—like me—will it take before we learn?"

Ten days before the bombing began, at a town meeting in Boulder, Colorado, with eight hundred people present, the question was put: "Do you support Bush's policy for war?" Only four people raised their hands. A few days before the war began, four thousand people in Santa Fe, New Mexico, blocked a four-lane highway for an hour, asking that there be no war. Residents said this was larger than any demonstration in the Vietnam era.

On the eve of war, six thousand people marched through Ann Arbor, Michigan, to ask for peace. On the night the war began, five thousand people gathered in San Francisco to denounce the war and formed a human chain around the Federal Building. Police broke the chain by swinging their clubs at the hands of the protesters. But the San Francisco Board of Supervisors passed a resolution declaring the city and county a sanctuary for those who for "moral, ethical or religious reasons cannot participate in war."

The night before Bush gave the order to launch the bombing, a seven-year-old girl in Lexington, Massachusetts, told her mother she wanted to write a letter to the president. Her mother suggested it was late and she should write the next day. "No, tonight," the girl said. She was still learning to write, so she dictated a letter:

> Dear President Bush. I don't like the way you are behaving. If you would make up your mind there won't be a war we won't have to have peace vigils. If you were in a war you wouldn't want to get hurt. What I'm saying is: I don't want any fighting to happen. Sincerely yours. Serena Kabat-Zinn

Once the war was on, and clearly irreversible, in an atmosphere charged with patriotic fervor (the president of the United Church of Christ spoke of "the steady drumbeat of war messages"), it was not surprising that a great majority of the country would declare its support.

Nevertheless, even with little time to organize, and with the war over very fast, there was an opposition—a minority for sure, but a determined one, and with the potential to grow. Compared to the first months of the military escalation in Vietnam, the movement against the Gulf War expanded with extraordinary speed and vigor.

That first week of the war, while it was clear most Americans were supporting Bush's action, tens of thousands of people took to the streets in protest, in towns and cities all over the country. In Athens, Ohio, over one hundred people were arrested, as they clashed with a prowar group. In Portland, Maine, five hundred marched wearing white arm bands or carrying white paper crosses with one word—"Why?"—written in red.

At the University of Georgia, seventy students opposed to the war held an all-night vigil, and in the Georgia Legislature, Representative Cynthia McKinnon made a speech attacking the bombing of Iraq, leading many of the other legislators to walk off the floor. She held her ground, and it seemed that there had been at least some change in thinking since Representative Julian Bond was expelled from the very same legislature for criticizing the war in Vietnam during the 1960s. At a junior high school in Newton, Massachusetts, 350 students marched to city hall to present a petition to the mayor declaring their opposition to the war in the Gulf.

In Ada, Oklahoma, while East Central Oklahoma State University was "adopting" two National Guard units, two young women sat quietly on top of the concrete entrance gate with signs that read "Teach Peace...Not War." One of them, Patricia Biggs, said: "I don't think we should be over there. I don't think it's about justice and liberty, I think it's about economics. The big oil corporations have a lot to do with what is going on over there.... We are risking people's lives for money."

Four days after the United States launched its air attack, seventy-five thousand people (the estimate of the Capitol Police) marched in Washington, rallying near the White House to denounce the war. In Southern California, Ron Kovic addressed six thousand people who chanted "Peace Now!" In Fayetteville, Arkansas, a group supporting military policy was confronted by the Northwest Arkansas Citizens Against War who marched, carrying a flag-draped coffin and a banner that read "Bring Them Home Alive."

Another disabled Vietnam veteran, a professor of history and political science at York College in Pennsylvania named Philip Avillo, wrote in a local newspaper: "Yes, we need to support our men and women under arms. But let's support them by bringing them home; not by condoning this barbarous, violent policy." In Salt Lake City, hundreds of demonstra-

tors, many with children, marched through the city's main streets chant-
ing antiwar slogans.

In Vermont, which had just elected Socialist Bernie Sanders to Congress, over two thousand demonstrators disrupted a speech by the governor at the state house, and in Burlington, Vermont's largest city, three
hundred protesters walked through the downtown area, asking shop owners to close their doors in solidarity.

On January 26, nine days after the beginning of the war, over 150,000
people marched through the streets of Washington, D.C., and listened to
speakers denounce the war, including the movie stars Susan Sarandon and
Tim Robbins. A woman from Oakland, California, held up the folded
American flag that was given to her when her husband was killed in Vietnam, saying: "I learned the hard way there is no glory in a folded flag."

Labor unions had supported the war in Vietnam for the most part, but
after the bombing started in the Gulf, eleven affiliates of the AFL-CIO,
including some of its more powerful unions—such as steel, auto, communications, chemical workers—spoke out against the war.

The black community was far less enthusiastic than the rest of the
country about what the U.S. Air Force was doing to Iraq. An ABC
News/*Washington Post* poll in early February, 1991, found that support for
the war was 84 percent among whites, but only 48 percent among African-
Americans.

When the war had been going on for a month, with Iraq devastated by
the incessant bombing, there were feelers from Saddam Hussein that Iraq
would withdraw from Kuwait if the United States would stop its attacks.
Bush rejected the idea, and a meeting of black leaders in New York
sharply criticized him, calling the war "an immoral and unspiritual diver-
sion…a blatant evasion of our domestic responsibilities."

In Selma, Alabama, which had been the scene of bloody police violence against civil rights marchers twenty-six years before, a meeting to
observe the anniversary of that "bloody Sunday" demanded that "our
troops be brought home alive to fight for justice at home."

The father of a twenty-one-year-old marine in the Persian Gulf, Alex
Molnar, wrote an angry open letter, published in the *New York Times*, to
President Bush:

> Where were you, Mr. President, when Iraq was killing its own people
> with poison gas? Why, until the recent crisis, was it business as usual with
> Saddam Hussein, the man you now call a Hitler? Is the American "way of
> life" that you say my son is risking his life for the continued "right" of

Americans to consume 25 to 30 percent of the world's oil?...I intend to support my son and his fellow soldiers by doing everything I can to oppose any offensive American military action in the Persian Gulf.

There were courageous individual acts by citizens, speaking out in spite of threats.

Peg Mullen, of Brownsville, Texas, whose son had been killed by "friendly fire" in Vietnam, organized a busload of mothers to protest in Washington, in spite of a warning that her house would be burned down if she persisted.

The actress Margot Kidder ("Lois Lane" in the *Superman* films), despite the risk to her career, spoke out eloquently against the war.

A basketball player for Seton Hall University in New Jersey refused to wear the American flag on his uniform, and when he became the object of derision for this, he left the team and the university, and returned to his native Italy.

More tragically, a Vietnam veteran in Los Angeles set fire to himself and died, to protest the war. And in Amherst, Massachusetts, a young man carrying a cardboard peace sign knelt on the town common, poured two cans of flammable fluid on himself, struck two matches, and died in the flames. Two hours later, students from nearby universities gathered on the common for a candlelight vigil, and placed peace signs at the site of death. One of the signs read, "Stop this crazy war."

There was no time, as there had been during the Vietnam conflict, for a large antiwar movement to develop in the military. But there were men and women who defied their commanders and refused to participate in the war.

When the first contingents of U.S. troops were being sent to Saudi Arabia, in August of 1990, Corp. Jeff Patterson, a twenty-two-year-old marine stationed in Hawaii, sat down on the runway of the airfield and refused to board a plane bound for Saudi Arabia. He asked to be discharged from the Marine Corps: "I object to the military use of force against any people, anywhere, any time."

Fourteen Marine Corps reservists at Camp Lejeune, North Carolina, filed for conscientious objector status, despite the prospect of a court-martial for desertion.

Corp. Yolanda Huet-Vaughn, a physician who was a captain in the Army Reserve Medical Corps, a mother of three young children, and a member of the Physicians for Social Responsibility, was called to active duty in December 1990, a month before the start of the war. She replied: "I am refusing orders to be an accomplice in what I consider an immoral, inhumane and unconstitutional act, namely an offensive military mobilization in the Middle East." She was court-martialed, convicted of desertion, and sentenced to two and a half years in prison.

Another soldier, Stephanie Atkinson of Murphysboro, Illinois, refused to report for active duty, saying she thought the U.S. military was in the Persian Gulf solely for economic reasons. She was first placed under house arrest, then given a discharge under "other than honorable conditions."

An army physician named Harlow Ballard, stationed at Fort Devens in Massachusetts, refused to follow an order to go to Saudi Arabia. "I would rather go to jail than support this war," he said. "I don't believe there is any such thing as a just war."

Over a thousand reservists declared themselves conscientious objectors. A twenty-three-year-old Marine Corps reservist named Rob Calabro was one of them. "My father tells me that he's ashamed of me, he screams at me that he's embarrassed by me. But I believe that killing people is morally wrong. I believe I'm serving my country more by being true to my conscience than by living a lie."

An information network sprang up during the Gulf War to tell what was not being told in the major media. There were alternative newspapers in many cities. There were over a hundred community radio stations, able to reach only a fraction of those tuned in to the major networks but the only sources, during the Gulf War, of critical analyses of the war.

After "victorious" wars there is almost always a sobering effect, as the war fervor wears off and citizens assess the costs and wonder what was gained. War fever was at its height in February 1991. In that month, when people being polled were reminded of the huge costs of the war, only 17 percent said the war was not worth it. Four months later, in June, the figure was 30 percent. In the months that followed, Bush's support in the nation dropped steeply, as economic conditions deteriorated. (And in 1992, with the war spirit evaporated, Bush went down to defeat.)

After the disintegration of the Soviet bloc began in 1989, there had been talk in the United States of a "peace dividend," the opportunity to take billions of dollars from the military budget and use it for human needs. The war in the Gulf became a convenient excuse for the government determined to stop such talk. A member of the Bush administration said: "We owe Saddam a favor. He saved us from the peace dividend."

In 1992, the limits of military victory became apparent during the

461

quincentennial celebrations of Columbus's arrival in the Western Hemisphere. Five hundred years ago Columbus and his fellow conquerors had wiped out the native population of Hispaniola. This was followed during the next four centuries by the methodical destruction of Indian tribes by the United States government as it marched across the continent. But now, there was a dramatic reaction.

The Indians—the Native Americans—had become a visible force since the sixties and seventies, and in 1992 were joined by other Americans to denounce the quincentennial celebrations. For the first time in all the years that the country had celebrated Columbus Day, there were nationwide protests against honoring a man who had kidnapped, enslaved, mutilated, murdered the natives who greeted his arrival with gifts and friendship.

In the summer of 1990, 350 Indians, representatives from all over the hemisphere, met in Quito, Ecuador, at the first intercontinental gathering of indigenous people in the Americas, to mobilize against the glorification of the Columbus conquest.

The movement grew. The largest ecumenical body in the United States, the National Council of Churches, called on Christians to refrain from celebrating the Columbus quincentennial, saying: "What represented newness of freedom, hope and opportunity for some was the occasion for oppression, degradation and genocide for others."

A newspaper called *Indigenous Thought* began publication in early 1991 to create a link among all the counter-Columbus quincentenary activities. It carried articles by Native Americans about current struggles over land stolen by treaty.

In Corpus Christi, Texas, Indians and Chicanos joined to protest the city's celebrations of the quincentennial. A woman named Angelina Mendez spoke for the Chicanos: "The Chicano nation, in solidarity with our Indian brothers and sisters to the north, come together with them on this day to denounce the atrocity the U.S. government proposes in reenacting the arrival of the Spanish, more specifically the arrival of Cristóbal Colón, to the shores of this land."

The Columbus controversy brought an extraordinary burst of educational and cultural activity. A professor at the University of California at San Diego, Deborah Small, put together an exhibit of over two hundred paintings on wood panels called "1492." She juxtaposed words from Columbus's diary with blown-up fragments from sixteenth-century engravings to dramatize the horrors that accompanied Columbus's arrival in the hemisphere. A reviewer wrote that "it does remind us, in the most vivid way, of how the coming of Western-style civilization to the New World doesn't provide us with a sunny tale."

When President Bush attacked Iraq in 1991, claiming that he was acting to end the Iraqi occupation of Kuwait, a group of Native Americans in Oregon distributed a biting and ironic "open letter": "Dear President Bush. Please send your assistance in freeing our small nation from occupation. This foreign force occupied our lands to steal our rich resources. As in your own words, the occupation and overthrow of one small nation…is one too many. Sincerely, An American Indian."

The publication *Rethinking Schools*, which represented socially conscious schoolteachers all over the country, printed a one-hundred-page book called *Rethinking Columbus*, featuring articles by Native Americans and others, a critical review of children's books on Columbus, a listing of resources for people wanting more information on Columbus, and more reading material on counter-quincentenary activities. In a few months, 200,000 copies of the book were sold.

A Portland, Oregon, teacher named Bill Bigelow, who helped put together *Rethinking Schools*, took a year off from his regular job to tour the country in 1992, giving workshops to other teachers, so that they could begin to tell those truths about the Columbus experience that were omitted from the traditional books and class curricula.

One of Bigelow's own students wrote: "It seemed to me as if the publishers had just printed up some 'glory story' that was supposed to make us feel more patriotic about our country…. They want us to look at our country as great and powerful and forever right…."

A student named Rebecca wrote: "Of course, the writers of the books probably think it's harmless enough—what does it matter who discovered America, really…. But the thought that I have been lied to all my life about this, and who knows what else, really makes me angry."

In Los Angeles, a high school student named Blake Lindsey went before the city council to argue against celebrating the quincentennial.

There were counter-Columbus activities all over the country. The protests, the dozens of new books that were appearing about Indian history, the discussions taking place all over the country, were bringing about an extraordinary transformation in the educational world. For generations, exactly the same story had been told all American schoolchildren about Columbus, a romantic, admiring story. Now, thousands of teachers around the country were beginning to tell that story differently.

This aroused anger among defenders of the old history, who derided what they called a movement for "political correctness" and "multiculturalism." They resented the critical treatment of Western expansion and imperialism, which they considered an attack on Western civilization. A philosopher named Allan Bloom, in *The Closing of the American Mind*, expressed horror at what the social movements of the sixties had done to change the educational atmosphere of American universities. "America tells one story: the unbroken, ineluctable progress of freedom and equality."

In the civil rights movement, black people disputed that claim of America's standing for "freedom and equality." The women's movement disputed that claim, too. And now, in 1992, Native Americans were pointing to the crimes of Western civilization against their ancestors. They were recalling the communitarian spirit of the Indians Columbus met and conquered, trying to tell the history of those millions of people who were here before Columbus, giving the lie to what a Harvard historian had called "the movement of European culture into the vacant wilderness of America."

As the United States entered the nineties, the political system, whether Democrats or Republicans were in power, remained in the control of those who had great wealth. The main instruments of information were also dominated by corporate wealth. The country was divided, though no mainstream political leader would speak of it, into classes of extreme wealth and extreme poverty, separated by an insecure and jeopardized middle class.

Yet, there was, unquestionably, though largely unreported, what a worried mainstream journalist had called "a permanent adversarial culture" which refused to surrender the possibility of a more equal, more humane society. If there was hope for the future of America, it lay in the promise of that refusal.

Exercises

1. What danger did an "adversarial culture" pose and to whom? Or, what would be the "dangerous" consequences of:

    a. spending less money on nuclear arms?

    b. not giving military aid to El Salvador?

    c. negotiating a nuclear freeze with Russia?

    d. maintaining the army as a volunteer outfit?

    e. not cutting funding for the arts? Fire? Police? Teachers?

    f. not instituting a blockade of Nicaragua?

    g. not "legislate[ing] economic sanctions against the South African government?

    h. not providing federally funded loans to help the unemployed keep their homes and farms?

    i. not providing a jobs program for displaced workers?

    j. not adopting a Canadian-style health care system?

2. What evidence is there of this "adversarial culture"? Is there any evidence that it is "permanent"?

3. Why would the following groups have taken a leadership role in the antinuclear movement: scientists; Catholics; physicians; women; college professors?

4. Why did the Reagan administration choose to prosecute draft resisters?

5. In 1983, what was the unemployment rate for African-Americans?

6. What percentage of the voting-age population voted for Reagan in 1980? 1984? For Bush in 1988? Why would the press call these elections "landslides"? (Look at the electoral college results.)

7. What percentage of the population (in the late 1980s and early 1990s):

a. wanted to pay more taxes?

b. would pay more taxes to clean up the environment?

c. wanted to place an extra tax on millionaires?

d. wanted to raise the capital gains tax? (What is a capital gains tax?)

e. wanted a Canadian-style health care system? (What kind of system is that?)

f. wanted a 50 percent cut in defense spending?

8. How can it be inferred from the opinion polls that the majority of Americans believe that welfare doesn't help the poor? Why might they think that? How could the government help the poor without providing welfare?

9. What point (argument/thesis) is Zinn trying to make by relating the following facts?

★ 8,000 local groups supported the Citizens' Clearinghouse for Hazardous Wastes.

★ 3,500 people were arrested in pursuit of shutting down Seabrook.

★ 1,800 people were arrested protesting Honeywell's military contracts.

★ the arrest of the Winooski Fourty-four when protesting against the arming of the Contras by the U.S. government.

★ the arrest of those protesting against on-campus CIA recruiting.

★ the frequent acquittals of those arrested in civil protests.

10. What point is Zinn trying to prove with the following details?

★ migrant farm-workers' strikes led by Cesar Chavez

★ three year Arizona copper mill strike

★ Watsonville cannery strike

★ hunger strike against Levi-Strauss

★ Los Angeles janitors' strike of 1990

★ New Mexico land and water rights fight

11. How did Latino-American culture differ from mainstream Anglo-American culture in the 1990s?

12. Zinn explains that one way to manipulate opinion is to frame the question in a certain way. Can you give examples from your own experience for which this has been true?

13. What was the status of each of the following in the 1980s and 1990s? What factors had the greatest impact on each of the following?

   a. legal profession

   b. women's movement

   c. labor movement

14. What argument is Zinn making with the information he provides for the following?

   a. Food Not Bombs

   b. thirty metal plaques "revising traditional ideas about American history"

   c. "open criticism by former employees" of the FBI and CIA

15. How does Zinn define the "Vietnam syndrome"? How might this differ from President Bush's or Colin Powell's definition of it?

16. What arguments did opponents make against U.S. involvement in a war against Iraq?

17. Why were the 1991 antiwar demonstrations in Shreveport, Boston, Santa Fe, Ann Arbor, and San Francisco surprising? Why were the ones in Athens, Ohio, on the campus of the University of Georgia, Newton, Massachussetts, Washington, D.C., and Portland, Maine, even more surprising?

18. In February, 1991, 84 percent of whites supported the war, while only 48 percent of African-Americans did. What might be the reasons for this rather large disparity?

19. Match the person with the action:

a. Rob Calabro

risked losing career   b. a Vietnam vet

risked losing life   c. Yolanda Huet-Vaughn

lost life   d. Peg Mullen

lost freedom   e. Margot Kidder

risked losing family   f. Harlow Ballard

g. a Seton Hall basketball player

h. Stephanie Atkinson

20. Why did the people named in the above question respond so differently from the rest of the American population to Bush's pursuit of war against Iraq? Which behaviors described above do you find admirable? Which do you not find admirable? Explain.

21. Why does "war fervor" wear off so quickly?

22. How did Saddam Hussein "save" the Bush administration from the "peace dividend"? (What was the "peace dividend" and why did the Bush administration want to be "saved" from it?)

23. What actions were taken to oppose the 500th year celebration of Columbus's landing on Hispaniola? What motivated those who dissented from celebrating? What motivated those who wished to celebrate the quincentennial?

24. *Debate Resolution*: Opposition to the U.S. government has been neither permanent nor systematic but highly volatile and sporadic.

25. *Debate Resolution*: The single-issue nature of the protests of the 1980s proves that there was no widespread opposition to the American system itself.

Chapter 23

The Coming Revolt
of the Guards

The title of this chapter is not a prediction, but a hope, which I will soon explain.

As for the title of this book, it is not quite accurate; a "people's history" promises more than any one person can fulfill, and it is the most difficult kind of history to recapture. I call it that anyway because, with all its limitations, it is a history disrespectful of governments and respectful of people's movements of resistance.

That makes it a biased account, one that leans in a certain direction. I am not troubled by that, because the mountain of history books under which we all stand leans so heavily in the other direction—so tremblingly respectful of states and statesmen and so disrespectful, by inattention, to people's movements—that we need some counterforce to avoid being crushed into submission.

All those histories of this country centered on the Founding Fathers and the presidents weigh oppressively on the capacity of the ordinary citizen to act. They suggest that in times of crisis we must look to someone to save us: in the Revolutionary crisis, the Founding Fathers; in the slavery crisis, Lincoln; in the Depression, Roosevelt; in the Vietnam-Watergate crisis, Carter. And that between occasional crises everything is all right, and it is sufficient for us to be restored to that normal state. They teach us that the supreme act of citizenship is to choose among saviors, by going into a voting booth every four years to choose between two white and well-off Anglo-Saxon males of inoffensive personality and orthodox opinions.

The idea of saviors has been built into the entire culture, beyond politics. We have learned to look to stars, leaders, experts in every field, thus surrendering our own strength, demeaning our own ability, obliterating our own selves. But from time to time, Americans reject that idea and rebel.

These rebellions, so far, have been contained. The American system is the most ingenious system of control in world history. With a country so rich in natural resources, talent, and labor power the system can afford to distribute just enough wealth to just enough people to limit discontent to a troublesome minority. It is a country so powerful, so big, so pleasing to so many of its citizens that it can afford to give freedom of dissent to the small number who are not pleased.

There is no system of control with more openings, apertures, leeways, flexibilities, rewards for the chosen, winning tickets in lotteries. There is none that disperses its controls more complexly through the voting system, the work situation, the church, the family, the school, the mass media—none more successful in mollifying opposition with reforms, isolating people from one another, creating patriotic loyalty.

One percent of the nation owns a third of the wealth. The rest of the wealth is distributed in such a way as to turn those in the 99 percent against one another: small property owners against the propertyless, black against white, native-born against foreign-born, intellectuals and professionals against the uneducated and unskilled. These groups have resented one another and warred against one another with such vehemence and violence as to obscure their common position as sharers of leftovers in a very wealthy country.

Against the reality of that desperate, bitter battle for resources made scarce by elite control, I am taking the liberty of uniting those 99 percent as "the people." I have been writing a history that attempts to represent their submerged, deflected, common interest. To emphasize the commonality of the 99 percent, to declare deep enmity of interest with the one percent, is to do exactly what the governments of the United States, and the wealthy elite allied to them—from the Founding Fathers to now—have tried their best to prevent. Madison feared a "majority faction" and hoped the new Constitution would control it. He and his colleagues began the Preamble to the Constitution with the words "We the people...," pretending that the new government stood for everyone, and hoping that this myth, accepted as fact, would ensure "domestic tranquillity."

The pretense continued over the generations, helped by all-embracing symbols, physical or verbal: the flag, patriotism, democracy, national interest, national defense, national security. The slogans were dug into the earth of American culture like a circle of covered wagons on the western plain, from inside of which the white, slightly privileged American could shoot to kill the enemy outside—Indians or blacks or foreigners or other whites too wretched to be allowed inside the circle. The managers of the caravan watched at a safe distance, and when the battle was over and the field strewn with dead on both sides, they would take over the land, and prepare another expedition, for another territory.

The scheme never worked perfectly. The Revolution and the Constitution, trying to bring stability by containing the class angers of the colonial period—while enslaving blacks, annihilating or displacing Indians—did not quite succeed, judging by the tenant uprisings, the slave revolts, the abolitionist agitation, the feminist upsurge, the Indian guerrilla warfare of the pre–Civil War years. After the Civil War, a new coalition of southern and northern elites developed, with southern whites and blacks of the lower classes occupied in racial conflict, native workers and immigrant workers clashing in the North, and the farmers dispersed over a big country, while the system of capitalism consolidated itself in industry and government. But there came rebellion among industrial workers and a great opposition movement among farmers.

At the turn of the century, the violent pacification of blacks and Indians and the use of elections and war to absorb and divert white rebels were not enough, in the conditions of modern industry, to prevent the great upsurge of socialism, the massive labor struggles, before the First World War. Neither that war nor the partial prosperity of the twenties, nor the apparent destruction of the socialist movement, could prevent, in the situation of economic crisis, another radical awakening, another labor upsurge in the thirties.

World War II created a new unity, followed by an apparently successful attempt, in the atmosphere of the cold war, to extinguish the strong radical temper of the war years. But then, surprisingly, came the surge of the sixties, from people thought long subdued or put out of sight—blacks, women, Native Americans, prisoners, soldiers—and a new radicalism, which threatened to spread widely in a population disillusioned by the Vietnam war and the politics of Watergate. The exile of Nixon, the celebration of the Bicentennial, the presidency of Carter, all aimed at restoration. But restoration to the old order was no solution to the uncertainty, the alienation, which was intensified in the Reagan-Bush years. The election of Clinton in 1992, carrying with it a vague promise of change, did not fulfill the expectations of the hopeful.

With such continuing malaise, it is very important for the Establishment—that uneasy club of business executives, generals, and politicos—to maintain the historic pretension of national unity, in which the government represents all the people, and the common enemy is overseas, not at home, where disasters of economics or war are unfortunate errors or tragic accidents, to be corrected by the members of the same club that brought the disasters. It is important for them also to make sure this artificial unity of highly privileged and slightly privileged is the only unity—that the 99 percent remain split in countless ways, and turn against one another to vent their angers.

How skillful to tax the middle class to pay for the relief of the poor, building resentment on top of humiliation! How adroit to bus poor black youngsters into poor white neighborhoods, in a violent exchange of impoverished schools, while the schools of the rich remain untouched and the wealth of the nation, doled out carefully where children need free milk, is drained for billion-dollar aircraft carriers. How ingenious to meet the demands of blacks and women for equality by giving them small special benefits, and setting them in competition with everyone else for jobs made scarce by an irrational, wasteful system. How wise to turn the fear and anger of the majority toward a class of criminals bred—by economic inequity—faster than they can be put away, deflecting attention from the huge thefts of national resources carried out within the law by men in executive offices.

But with all the controls of power and punishment, enticements and concessions, diversions and decoys, operating throughout the history of the country, the Establishment has been unable to keep itself secure from revolt. Every time it looked as if it had succeeded, the very people it thought seduced or subdued, stirred and rose. Blacks, cajoled by Supreme Court decisions and congressional statutes, rebelled. Women, wooed and ignored, romanticized and mistreated, rebelled. Indians, thought dead, reappeared, defiant. Young people, despite lures of career and comfort, defected. Working people, thought soothed by reforms, regulated by law, kept within bounds by their own unions, went on strike. Government intellectuals, pledged to secrecy, began giving away secrets. Priests turned from piety to protest.

To recall this is to remind people of what the Establishment would like them to forget—the enormous capacity of apparently helpless people to resist, of apparently contented people to demand change. To uncover such history is to find a powerful human impulse to assert one's humanity. It is to hold out, even in times of deep pessimism, the possibility of surprise.

True, to overestimate class consciousness, to exaggerate rebellion and its successes, would be misleading. It would not account for the fact that the world—not just the United States, but everywhere else—is still in the hands of the elites, that people's movements, although they show an infinite capacity for recurrence, have so far been either defeated or absorbed or perverted, that "socialist" revolutionists have betrayed socialism, that nationalist revolutions have led to new dictatorships.

But most histories understate revolt, overemphasize statesmanship, and thus encourage impotency among citizens. When we look closely at resistance movements, or even at isolated forms of rebellion, we discover that class consciousness, or any other awareness of injustice, has multiple levels. It has many ways of expression, many ways of revealing itself—open, subtle, direct, distorted. In a system of intimidation and control, people do not show how much they know, how deeply they feel, until their practical sense informs them they can do so without being destroyed.

History that keeps alive the memory of people's resistance suggests new definitions of power. By traditional definitions, whoever possesses military strength, wealth, command of official ideology, cultural control, has power. Measured by these standards, popular rebellion never looks strong enough to survive.

However, the unexpected victories—even temporary ones—of insurgents show the vulnerability of the supposedly powerful. In a highly developed society, the Establishment cannot survive without the obedience and loyalty of millions of people who are given small rewards to keep the system going: the soldiers and police, teachers and ministers, administrators and social workers, technicians and production workers, doctors, lawyers, nurses, transport and communications workers, garbagemen and firemen. These people—the employed, the somewhat privileged—are drawn into alliance with the elite. They become the guards of the system, buffers between the upper and lower classes. If they stop obeying, the system falls.

That will happen, I think, only when all of us who are slightly privileged and slightly uneasy begin to see that we are like the guards in the prison uprising at Attica—expendable; that the Establishment, whatever rewards it gives us, will also, if necessary to maintain its control, kill us.

Certain new facts may, in our time, emerge so clearly as to lead to general withdrawal of loyalty from the system. The new conditions of technology, economics, and war, in the atomic age, make it less and less possible for the guards of the system—the intellectuals, the homeowners, the taxpayers, the skilled workers, the professionals, the servants of government—to remain immune from the violence (physical and psychic) inflicted on the black, the poor, the criminal, the enemy overseas. The internationalization of the economy, the movement of refugees and illegal immigrants across borders, both make it more difficult for the people of the industrial countries to be oblivious to hunger and disease in the poor countries of the world.

All of us have become hostages in the new conditions of doomsday technology, runaway economics, global poisoning, uncontainable war. The atomic weapons, the invisible radiations, the economic anarchy, do not distinguish prisoners from guards, and those in charge will not be scrupulous in making distinctions. There is the unforgettable response of the U.S. high command to the news that American prisoners of war might be near Nagasaki: "Targets previously assigned for Centerboard remain unchanged."

There is evidence of growing dissatisfaction among the guards. We have known for some time that the poor and ignored were the nonvoters, alienated from a political system they felt didn't care about them, and about which they could do little. Now alienation has spread upward into families above the poverty line. These are white workers, neither rich nor poor, but angry over economic insecurity, unhappy with their work, worried about their neighborhoods, hostile to government—combining elements of racism with elements of class consciousness, contempt for the lower classes along with distrust for the elite, and thus open to solutions from any direction, right or left.

In the twenties there was a similar estrangement in the middle classes, which could have gone in various directions—the Ku Klux Klan had millions of members at that time—but in the thirties the work of an organized left wing mobilized much of this feeling into trade unions, farmers' unions, socialist movements. We may, in the coming years, be in a race for the mobilization of middle-class discontent.

The fact of that discontent is clear. The surveys since the early seventies show 70 to 80 percent of Americans distrustful of government, business, the military. This means the distrust goes beyond blacks, the poor, the radicals. It has spread among skilled workers, white-collar workers, professionals; for the first time in the nation's history, perhaps, both the lower classes and the middle classes, the prisoners and the guards, were disillusioned with the system.

There are other signs: the high rate of alcoholism, the high rate of divorce (from one of three marriages ending in divorce, the figure is climbing to one of two), of drug use and abuse, of nervous breakdowns and mental illness. Millions of people have been looking desperately for solutions to their sense of impotency, their loneliness, their frustration, their estrangement from other people, from the world, from their work, from themselves. They have been adopting new religions, joining self-help groups of all kinds. It is as if a whole nation were going through a critical point in its middle age, a life crisis of self-doubt, self-examination.

All this, at a time when the middle class is increasingly insecure economically. The system, in its irrationality, has been driven by profit to build steel skyscrapers for insurance companies while the cities decay, to spend billions for weapons of destruction and virtually nothing for children's playgrounds, to give huge incomes to men who make dangerous or useless things, and very little to artists, musicians, writers, actors. Capitalism has always been a failure for the lower classes. It is now beginning to fail for the middle classes.

The threat of unemployment, always inside the homes of the poor, has spread to white-collar workers, professionals. A college education is no longer a guarantee against joblessness, and a system that cannot offer a future to the young coming out of school is in deep trouble. If it happens only to the children of the poor, the problem is manageable; there are the jails. If it happens to the children of the middle class, things may get out of hand. The poor are accustomed to being squeezed and always short of money, but in recent years the middle classes, too, have begun to feel the press of high prices, high taxes.

In the seventies, eighties, and early nineties there was a dramatic, frightening increase in the number of crimes. It was not hard to understand, when one walked through any big city. There were the contrasts of wealth and poverty, the culture of possession, the frantic advertising. There was the fierce economic competition, in which the legal violence of the state and the legal robbery by the corporations were accompanied by the illegal crimes of the poor. Most crimes by far involved theft. A disproportionate number of prisoners in American jails were poor and nonwhite, with little education. Half were unemployed in the month prior to their arrest.

The most common and most publicized crimes have been the violent crimes of the young, the poor—a virtual terrorization in the big cities—in which the desperate or drug-addicted attack and rob the middle class, or even their fellow poor. A society so stratified by wealth and education lends itself naturally to envy and class anger.

The critical question in our time is whether the middle classes, so long led to believe that the solution for such crimes is more jails and more jail terms, may begin to see, by the sheer uncontrollability of crime, that the only prospect is an endless cycle of crime and punishment. They might then conclude that physical security for a working person in the city can come only when everyone in the city is working. And that would require a transformation of national priorities, a change in the system.

In recent decades, the fear of criminal assault has been joined by an even greater fear. Deaths from cancer began to multiply, and medical researchers seemed helpless to find the cause. It began to be evident that more and more of these deaths were coming from an environment poisoned by military experimentation and industrial greed. The water people drank, the air they breathed, the particles of dust from the buildings in which they worked, had been quietly contaminated over the years by a system so frantic for growth and profit that the safety and health of human beings had been ignored. A new and deadly scourge appeared, the AIDS virus, which spread with special rapidity among homosexuals and drug addicts.

In the early nineties, the false socialism of the Soviet system had failed. And the American system seemed out of control—a runaway capitalism, a runaway technology, a runaway militarism, a running away of government from the people it claimed to represent. Crime was out of control, cancer and AIDS were out of control. Prices and taxes and unemployment were out of control. The decay of cities and the breakdown of families were out of control. And people seemed to sense all this.

Perhaps much of the general distrust of government reported in recent years comes from a growing recognition of the truth of what the U.S. Air Force bombardier Yossarian said in the novel *Catch-22* to a friend who had just accused him of giving aid and comfort to the enemy: "The enemy is anybody who's going to get you killed, no matter which side he's on. And don't you forget that, because the longer you remember it the longer you might live." The next line in the novel is: "But Clevinger did forget, and now he was dead."

Let us imagine the prospect—for the first time in the nation's history—of a population united for fundamental change. Would the elite turn as so often before, to its ultimate weapon—foreign intervention—to unite the people with the Establishment, in war? It tried to do that in 1991, with the war against Iraq. But, that martial spirit did not last long.

With the Establishment's inability either to solve severe economic problems at home or to manufacture abroad a safety valve for domestic discontent, Americans might be ready to demand not just more tinkering, more reform laws, another reshuffling of the same deck, another New Deal, but radical change. Let us be utopian for a moment so that when we get realistic again it is not that "realism" so useful to the Establishment in its discouragement of action, that "realism" anchored to a certain kind of history empty of surprise. Let us imagine what radical change would require of us all.

The society's levers of powers would have to be taken away from those whose drives have led to the present state—the giant corporations, the military, and their politician collaborators. We would need—by a coordinated effort of local groups all over the country—to reconstruct the economy for both efficiency and justice, producing in a cooperative way what people need most. We would start on our neighborhoods, our cities, our workplaces. Work of some kind would be needed by everyone, including people now kept out of the work force—children, old people, "handicapped" people. Society could use the enormous energy now idle, the skills and talents now unused. Everyone could share the routine but necessary jobs for a few hours a day, and leave most of the time free for enjoyment, creativity, labors of love, and yet produce enough for an equal and ample distribution of goods. Certain basic things would be abundant enough to be taken out of the money system and be available—free—to everyone: food, housing, health care, education, transportation.

The great problem would be to work out a way of accomplishing this without a centralized bureaucracy, using not the incentives of prison and punishment, but those incentives of cooperation which spring from natural human desires, which in the past have been used by the state in times of war, but also by social movements that gave hints of how people might behave in different conditions. Decisions would be made by small groups of people in their workplaces, their neighborhoods—a network of cooperatives, in communication with one another, a neighborly socialism avoiding the class hierarchies of capitalism and the harsh dictatorships that have taken the name "socialist."

People in time, in friendly communities, might create a new, diversified, nonviolent culture, in which all forms of personal and group expression would be possible. Men and women, black and white, old and young, could then cherish their differences as positive attributes, not as reasons for domination. New values of cooperation and freedom might then show up in the relations of people, the upbringing of children.

To do all that, in the complex conditions of control in the United States, would require combining the energy of all previous movements in

American history—of labor insurgents, black rebels, Native Americans, women, young people—along with the new energy of an angry middle class. People would need to begin to transform their immediate environments—the workplace, the family, the school, the community—by a series of struggles against absentee authority, to give control of these places to the people who live and work there.

These struggles would involve all the tactics used at various times in the past by people's movements: demonstrations, marches, civil disobedience; strikes and boycotts and general strikes; direct action to redistribute wealth, to reconstruct institutions, to revamp relationships; creating—in music, literature, drama, all the arts, and all the areas of work and play in everyday life—a new culture of sharing, of respect, a new joy in the collaboration of people to help themselves and one another.

There would be many defeats. But when such a movement took hold in hundreds of thousands of places all over the country it would be impossible to suppress, because the very guards the system depends on to crush such a movement would be among the rebels. It would be a new kind of revolution, the only kind that could happen, I believe, in a country like the United States. It would take enormous energy, sacrifice, commitment, patience. But because it would be a process over time, starting without delay, there would be the immediate satisfactions that people have always found in the affectionate ties of groups striving together for a common goal.

All this takes us far from American history, into the realm of imagination. But not totally removed from history. There are at least glimpses in the past of such a possibility. In the sixties and seventies, for the first time, the Establishment failed to produce national unity and patriotic fervor in a war. There was a flood of cultural changes such as the country had never seen—in sex, family, personal relations—exactly those situations most difficult to control from the ordinary centers of power. And never before was there such a general withdrawal of confidence from so many elements of the political and economic system. In every period of history, people have found ways to help one another—even in the midst of a culture of competition and violence—if only for brief periods, to find joy in work, struggle, companionship, nature.

The prospect is for times of turmoil, struggle, but also inspiration. There is a chance that such a movement could succeed in doing what the system itself has never done—bring about great change with little violence. This is possible because the more of the 99 percent that begin to see themselves as sharing needs, the more the guards and the prisoners see their common interest, the more the Establishment becomes isolated, ineffectual. The elite's weapons, money, control of information would be useless in the face of a determined population. The servants of the system would refuse to work to continue the old, deadly order, and would begin using their time, their space—the very things given them by the system to keep them quiet—to dismantle that system while creating a new one.

The prisoners of the system will continue to rebel, as before, in ways that cannot be foreseen, at times that cannot be predicted. The new fact of our era is the chance that they may be joined by the guards. We readers and writers of books have been, for the most part, among the guards. If we understand that, and act on it, not only will life be more satisfying, right off, but our grandchildren, or our great grandchildren, might possibly see a different and marvelous world.

Exercises

1. How does Zinn defend his "bias"? Why does he feel he has to? Is his defense persuasive? Redundant? Not persuasive to you?

2. What does Zinn mean when he argues that "the idea of saviors has been built into the entire culture, beyond politics."? What are the important implications of this statement?

3. How has the "American System" been able to sustain a gross inequality of wealth and suppress or obviate dissent?

4. What specific divide and conquer tactics does Zinn cite as used by the Establishment in pursuit of its goal of controlling the other 99 percent of the American population?

5. In Zinn's summary of the ebb and flow of dissent, what are the major historical landmarks that he cites? What do these milestones represent?

6. Zinn argues: "To uncover [people's] history is to find a powerful human impulse to assert one's humanity." Having read and studied the previous chapters, have you felt this effect? (Have you had moments where you begin to "show how much [you] know, how deeply [you] feel"?)

7. How do "unexpected victories" redefine "power" as traditionally defined?

8. Why does Zinn think that the 1980s and 1990s, in hindsight, could prove to represent a unique period in American history?

9. What is Zinn's utopian vision of the future? How does he hope such a way of life would come about?

10. What historical evidence supports Zinn's vision of the future?

11. *Debate Resolution*: The middle class guard the poor for the rich.

Afterword

On the Clinton Presidency

In the presidential election of 1992, Democrat Bill Clinton, the young, personable governor of Arkansas, defeated Republican George Bush. Economic conditions in the country were deteriorating, and Clinton promised "change."

It was hardly an enthusiastic electorate (45 percent stayed away from the polls), and of those who voted, barely 43 percent voted for Clinton. Bush received 38 percent of the vote, and almost 20 percent of the voters deserted the major parties and voted for Texas billionaire Ross Perot, who promised a departure from traditional politics.

Clinton had been backed strongly by the Democratic Leadership Council, which wanted to move the Democratic party closer to the center. Its plan was to promise enough for blacks, women, and working people to keep their support, but to appeal to white conservative voters with a program of toughness on crime and a strong military.

Accordingly, Clinton made a few cabinet appointments that suggested support for labor and for social welfare programs. But his key appointments to the Treasury and Commerce Departments were wealthy corporate lawyers, and his foreign policy staff—secretary of defense, director of the CIA, national security adviser—were traditional players on the bipartisan cold war team.

Immediately after his election victory, Clinton said: "I want to reaffirm the essential continuity in American foreign policy." Indeed, on the eve of the election, he had made it plain that despite the end of the cold

481

war he would reduce the Bush military budget by only 5 percent. In office, he followed through on this, maintaining an arms budget of $262 billion.

Clinton was accepting a Republican premise, that the United States must be prepared to fight two regional wars at once. This, in spite of the statement made by Gen. Colin Powell, who, viewing the collapse of the Soviet Union, had told *Defense News* (April 8, 1991), "I'm running out of demons. I'm running out of villains. I'm down to Castro and Kim Il Sung." Bush's secretary of defense, Dick Cheney, hardly a dove, had said in 1992, "The threats have become remote, so remote they are difficult to discern."

After being in office two years, Clinton proposed even more money for the military. A *New York Times* dispatch from Washington (December 1, 1994) reported: "Trying to quiet Republican criticism that the military is underfinanced, president Clinton held a Rose Garden ceremony today to announce that he would seek a $25 billion increase in military spending over the next six years."

Clinton had been in office barely six months when he sent the air force to drop bombs on Baghdad, presumably in retaliation for an assassination plot against George Bush on the occasion of the former president's visit to Kuwait. The evidence for such a plot was very weak, coming as it did from the notoriously corrupt Kuwaiti police, and Clinton did not wait for the results of the trial supposed to take place in Kuwait of those accused of the plot. U.S. planes aiming, the government said, at "Intelligence Headquarters" bombed a suburban neighborhood, killing at least six people, including a prominent Iraqi artist and her husband. It turned out later that there was no significant damage, if any, to Iraqi intelligence facilities. The *New York Times* commented: "Mr. Clinton's sweeping statement was reminiscent of the assertions by President Bush and General Norman Schwarzkopf during the Persian Gulf War that later proved to be untrue."

Columnist Molly Ivins suggested that the purpose of the bombing of Baghdad—"sending a powerful message"—fit the definition of terrorism. "The maddening thing about terrorists is that they are indiscriminate in their acts of vengeance, or cries for attention, or whatever.... What is true for individuals...must also be true of nations."

Clinton's foreign policy had very much the traditional bipartisan emphasis on maintaining friendly relations with whatever governments were in power and promoting profitable trade arrangements with them, whatever their record in protecting human rights. Thus, aid to Indonesia continued, despite that country's record of mass murder (perhaps 200,000 killed out of a population of 700,000) in the invasion and occupation of East Timor.

A similar callousness with regard to human rights was shown in regard to the Clinton administration's bizarre approach to two nations both of which considered themselves "Communist." China had massacred protesting students in Beijing in 1989 and put dissenters in prison. Cuba had imprisoned critics of the regime, but had no bloody record of suppression as did Communist China and other governments in the world that received U.S. aid.

The U.S. continued to give China economic aid, and certain trade privileges ("most favored nation" status) for the sake of U.S. business interests. But the Clinton administration continued, and even extended, a blockade of Cuba, which deprived its population of food and medicine.

A concern for "stability" over morality seemed to motivate the Clinton administration in its relations with Russia. It insisted on firm support for the regime of Boris Yeltsin, even after Russia initiated a brutal invasion and bombardment of the outlying region of Chechnya, which wanted independence.

Both Clinton and Yeltsin, on the occasion of the death of Richard Nixon, expressed admiration for the man who had continued the war in Vietnam, violated his oath of office, and escaped criminal charges only because he was pardoned by his own vice president. Yeltsin called Nixon "one of the greatest politicians in the world," and Clinton said that Nixon, throughout his career, "remained a fierce advocate for freedom and democracy around the world."

Clinton's foreign economic policy was in keeping with the nation's history, in which both major parties were more concerned for corporate interests than for the rights of working people, here or abroad, and saw foreign aid as a political and economic tool more than as a humanitarian act.

The World Bank and the International Monetary Fund, both dominated by the United States, adopted a hard-nosed banker's approach to debt-ridden Third World countries. They insisted that these poor nations allocate a good part of their meager resources to repaying their loans to the rich countries, at the cost of cutting social services to their already desperate populations.

The emphasis in foreign economic policy was on "the market economy" and "privatization." This forced the people of former Soviet bloc countries to fend for themselves in a supposedly "free" economy, without the social benefits that they had received under the admittedly inefficient former regimes.

The concept of "free trade" became an important objective for the Clinton administration. It actively solicited the support of Republicans as well as Democrats in Congress in order to pass the North American Free Trade Agreement with Mexico. This removed obstacles for corporate capital and goods to move back and forth across the Mexican-U.S. border without restrictions.

Clinton's one impressive act in foreign policy was to put pressure on the military leaders of Haiti, who had deposed the democratically elected Jean-Bertrand Aristide in 1991, to accept Aristide back as president, and Haitians rejoiced. But this was coupled with suspicion because of the historic U.S. policy of supporting corrupt dictators in Haiti.

Clinton's domestic policies, as was traditional with Democratic candidates, were more attuned to the party's electoral supporters—black people, women, labor. But even his progressive measures were severely limited by his apparent desire to woo conservatives, his fear of offending corporate interests, and the limits set by huge expenditures for the military budget.

Clinton's economic program, at first announced as a job-creation program, was soon to change direction and concentrate on reduction of the deficit (under Reagan and Bush the national debt had grown to four trillion dollars). But this emphasis meant that there would be no bold program of expenditures for universal health care, for education, for child care, housing, the environment, the arts, or job creation.

Clinton's small gestures would not come close to what was needed in a nation where one-fourth of the children lived in poverty, where homeless people lived on the streets in every major city, where women could not look for work for lack of child care, where the air, the water, were deteriorating dangerously, where thirty-five million Americans—ten million of them children—were without health care.

The United States was the richest country in the world, with 5 percent of the earth's population, yet consuming 30 percent of what was produced worldwide. Wealth was polarized, with 1 percent of the population owning 35 percent of the wealth, approximately $5.7 trillion. In its poverty-ridden cities babies died at a higher rate than in almost every other industrialized country in the world. In one year, 1988, forty thousand babies died before their first birthday, with the mortality rate for African-American babies twice that for whites.

To bring about even a rough equality of opportunity would require a drastic redistribution of wealth, a huge expenditure of money for job creation, health, education, the environment. There were two possible sources to pay for this, and the Clinton administration was not inclined to use either one.

One source was the military budget. During the presidential campaign of 1992, Randall Forsberg, an expert on military expenditures, had suggested that: "A military budget of $60 billion, to be achieved over a number of years, would support a demilitarized U.S. foreign policy, appropriate to the needs and opportunities of the post–Cold War world." Thus, $200 billion a year could be saved for social purposes.

But the Clinton presidency, like all Republican and Democratic administrations before it, was not willing to renounce war as an instrument of national policy. The insistence on military predominance made it clear that this power was being maintained, and probably had always been maintained, not to confront the Soviet Union, but to intervene in Third World countries for economic and political advantage. And so no pressing human need at home would be allowed to interfere with this.

The other possible source to pay for social needs was the wealth of the superrich. The richest one percent of the country had gained over a trillion dollars in the past dozen years as a result of tax breaks. A "wealth tax" could retrieve that. In addition, a truly progressive income tax—going back to the post–World War II levels of 70 to 90 percent on very high incomes—could make perhaps a hundred billion dollars available for social programs. Thus, four or five hundred billion dollars could be made available, for a universal health system, for a full-employment program, for affordable housing, public transport, the arts, the environment.

The alternative to such a bold program was to continue as before, with minor help to the poor, allowing the cities to fester, offering no useful work for the young, creating a marginal population of idle, desperate people who turn to drugs and crime, constituting a threat to the physical security of the rest of the population.

To meet this situation, Democrats and Republicans united to pass a crime bill, to build more prisons, to lock up more of those desperate people, many of them young, many of them nonwhite. This was a gesture to those Americans who felt threatened by rising violent crime. And so, by 1994, the United States had more of its population in prison per capita—a million people—than any other country in the world.

If the Clinton administration and the Democratic Leadership Council hoped to win over moderate voters by moving away from bold social programs and emphasizing toughness on crime and a strong military, they failed. In the congressional elections of 1994, Republicans ousted Democrats in both House and Senate in sufficient numbers to give them a majority in both houses. They immediately proposed, in the name of escaping "big government," to dismantle the social programs that had been constructed over the years since the New Deal.

The victorious Republicans claimed a "mandate" from the people for their program. But it was hardly that. Only 37 percent of the electorate went to the polls, and slightly more than half of that had voted Republican. If anyone had a mandate, it was that 63 percent of the population which seemed alienated from a political process dominated by two unpopular major parties. (In 1988, a survey showed that two-thirds of the voters wanted candidates other than the Republican Bush or the Democrat Dukakis.)

Indeed, public opinion surveys in the eighties and early nineties indicated that Americans favored bold policies that neither Democrats nor Republicans were willing to put forward. These polls showed 61 percent support for a Canadian-type health system and 84 percent for a surtax on millionaires.

While both parties were speaking critically of "welfare" (as if the corporations, the banks, were not receiving enormous welfare from the government) a *New York Times*/CBS News poll in December 1994 found that 65 percent said that "it is the responsibility of government to take care of people who can't take care of themselves."

If democracy meant some recognition by government of the will of the people, it was clear by 1995 that this was not being fulfilled by either Republicans or Democrats. A *Los Angeles Times* survey of September 1994 found that: "Americans increasingly say they are willing to support a new party." This confirmed the Gordon Black poll of two years earlier in which 54 percent of those polled said they wanted "a new national reform party."

If historical experience taught anything, it was that a serious national crisis—such as existed in the United States in the mid-nineties, a crisis of poverty, drugs, violence, crime, alienation from politics, uncertainty for the future—would not be solved without some great social movement of the citizenry. Such a movement would need to join together the inspiration and commitment of the antislavery movement, the labor movement, the antiwar movement, the civil rights movement, the women's movement, the gay and lesbian movement, the environmental movement, to turn the nation in a new direction.

Sometime in 1992, the Republican party held a dinner to raise funds, in which individuals and corporations paid up to $400,000 to attend. A spokesman for President Bush, Marlin Fitzwater, told reporters: "It's buying access to the system, yes." When asked about people who didn't have so much money, he replied: "They have to demand access in other ways."

That may have been a clue to Americans wanting real change. They would have to demand access in their own way.

Exercises

1. What percentage is 43 percent of 45 percent? What is the implication of the answer to this question?

2. How do Clinton's campaign promises and cabinet appointments compare to Jimmy Carter's?

3. What was Dick Cheney's assessment of possible foreign threats to U.S. interests?

4. Why did Clinton bomb Baghdad?

5. Why did the United States support the regimes of China, Indonesia, and Russia but continue to try to bring down the rule of Castro in Cuba?

6. What policies have the World Bank and the IMF (International Monetary Fund) continued to impose on developing countries, including Russia?

7. What is the purpose of NAFTA (North American Free Trade Agreement)?

8. Why did Clinton's economic program change its focus from job creation to deficit reduction? Can't one do both?

9. If Clinton wanted to create real equality of opportunity, from where could he have gotten the money?

10. What did Clinton's crime bill accomplish?

11. How many people voted to give the Republicans control of Congress in 1994?

12. How do the wealthy gain "access" to the system? How do the middle class, working poor, and unemployed gain "access" to the system?

13. *Debate Resolution*: Clinton's election served as a palliative to the damages done by the Reagan tax cuts and deferral of the "peace dividend" just as Carter's presidency had served to ameliorate the damage done by Watergate.

Appendix A

Teaching Techniques

Kathy Emery

1. The Group Paragraph*

There are important reasons for teachers to present material in a variety of ways. To always have discussions or to always lecture eventually becomes tedious to students and to the teacher, regardless of how expertly the lecture or facilitating is done. Having students work in groups to write a paragraph not only brings variety into the classroom, but it simultaneously encourages cooperative and active learning. Yet many teachers avoid this technique or use it so sparingly that the behavior induced by the experience is never internalized by the student. I have found that, used with clearly stated goals and consistently enforced rules of behavior, the group paragraph is an invaluable tool in teaching, content, critical thinking, and cooperative learning.

Group paragraphs need to be assigned two to three times a month with the exact same rules and goals expected every time. Groups of four work best (but three and five can work too). One might alternate between allowing students to choose their own groups and assigning students to groups. Each group must have a recorder, who is assigned or volunteers to write out the group's answer to the given question. It is important to ensure that the same students are not always being recorders. Over the course of the school year the responsibility of the recorder should be

---

* The following kinds of questions are well suited for group paragraph work: those whose answers require detail from throughout a chapter; those whose answers require detail from more than one chapter; those whose answers require analysis, synthesis, or evaluation.

evenly divided among the students. The recorder writes the paragraph as it is composed verbally by the group. If someone else grabs the paragraph and writes a sentence, that is fine as long as the official recorder gets the paper back. If done on paper, the essay will be a rough draft, and hence the students should be encouraged to cross out and rearrange using stars, arrows, and the like. It is ideal if each group can compose its paragraph on a computer.

It is imperative that the teacher pose a controversial question that must be answered within a clearly defined time. I prefer to give students at least forty minutes to discuss a question that has several possible answers. The more students argue sincerely, the sharper their thinking will become. Since students must commit their answer to paper and know that their written statement will be assessed, they feel accountable, and it is accountability that creates an expectation to which students will rise. Hence, the time limit. Sometimes, students think they are finished early but they are not. I deal with early finishers by quickly reading their paragraph and making a few criticisms to get them back to work. I check whether the thesis is stated in the first sentence, whether the terms are defined, if there is detail, and if the detail is relevant to their thesis.

The choice of reading assignments in advance of the group paragraph is crucial. Students must have data with which to argue. And they need to have that data in front of them when they are collectively writing the paragraph. The question needs to involve interpreting the data. If they have just read a chapter on the first women factory workers in which the fate of single and married women was described, then one can successfully ask: "Was it better to be married or single?" This question has invariably led to wonderful arguments within a group since neither condition was attractive and there were pros and cons to each. When students ask if they have to make a definitive statement, I always insist that they do even when this is often unrealistic. Forcing them to have a clear-cut opinion clarifies their thinking. Once they have arrived at an opinion, they can then see how simplistic it is and want to go beyond it. Such a discussion is an important element of the exercise. One can't achieve more complexity without establishing a simple thesis first.

To focus the student's thinking, three rules need to be consistently enforced: (1) the paragraph (or page) must begin with a thesis statement that answers the question; (2) next, students must define the terms of the thesis. If the answer is single women had more freedom than married women, then it is crucial for the writers to define "freedom" as they argue

490

their data; (3) students must support their general statements with detail, that is, either "facts" or quotations from the text. The concept of what a "fact" is can be avoided by focusing instead on the distinction between generalizations and detail.

Selective intervention is necessary to foster cooperative behavior. As the students work, I walk around the classroom, pausing before each group, listening not for what is being said but for tone of voice and the number of voices involved. Students should feel a supervisory but not stifling presence. As long as the tone of the conversation is one of thoughtful or excited questioning and everyone in the group is at least paying attention if not speaking, then intervention is not necessary and one can go on to the next group. If there is an argument that has taken on a hostile tone, then I will pause and listen for a while to see if it is resolved. If it isn't, I will stop the group, comment on what I have observed and get the students to agree that the argument was going nowhere. Usually, arguments develop when both sides are using the same term but, unbeknownst to either, each defines the term differently. The problem is rarely solved if I tell a student that he or she wasn't listening to another student. One must define what that means. I often find that if I lead the students through the conversation by isolating each part of the argument, they can resolve the confusion themselves. Often, just by slowing down the argument, the students themselves will become more precise and listen to each other more carefully. Below is a typical exchange of the sort that needs teacher intervention.

LIYAH: The Puritans were democrats, they elected their officials.

CESAR: Yeah? Well, they were all brainwashed.

LIYAH: Not if they choose their leaders.

CESAR: The elections were rigged.

LIYAH: They had debates.

CESAR: Yeah, some debates they were!

LIYAH: Better debates than you have!

CESAR: If you would ever do your homework you might know something!

At this point they begin to raise their voices, and I decide to intervene.

TEACHER: Have you heard what Liyah said?

CESAR: Yes.

TEACHER: Can you tell her how she defined democracy in Puritan New England?

CESAR: She said that the Puritans were democrats because they elected their leaders.

TEACHER: What is your response to that?

CESAR: But the ministers told the congregation what to think.

TEACHER: Liyah, can you respond to that?

LIYAH: How could they tell them what to think if there were debates?

CESAR: What debates?

TEACHER: Can both of you look at last night's reading and find a reference to debates in the text?

LIYAH: It says here...

TEACHER: What page? (*I motion to Cesar to look at his copy of the text.*)

LIYAH: Page 34...that when John Philips [minister of Salem] denounced the Puritan ministers of Boston, Governor Winthrop went to his church and debated with him. Then the Salem congregation voted to continue to have Philips as their minister.

TEACHER: So, Cesar, was the Salem congregation brainwashed?

CESAR: It was a setup. Philips and Winthrop put on a show!

LIYAH: No they didn't.

TEACHER: Is there anything in the text that can allow us to say one way or the other?

CESAR: Huh?

TEACHER: What other detail besides what Liyah read to us just

> now might indicate that Philips and Winthrop were in
> cahoots?

CESAR: Nothing!

LIYAH: I don't know?

TEACHER: But Philips was denouncing Winthrop, why would he
denounce him to begin with?

CESAR: They fabricated it all to fool the congregation that there
were debates.

Textual support may not have been there, but at least the argument of the detail that was available was developed in a more sophisticated manner than before my intervention.

I like to point out to students, at that moment, that what resolved the dispute was referring to the details of the text. That is a theme I like to repeat over and over all year so that going to the text becomes an instinctive reaction when they disagree with each other. If their instinct is to go to the text, they then must figure out what they are looking for, which in turn encourages them to define their terms. Insisting that there must be textual support for anything that is said prevents shouting matches. Of course, this technique risks stifling brainstorming, although generally there is so little discipline in the students' thinking that this is not a real danger. One can spot those students who become intimidated by the need for detail despite their superior command of it. The teacher must encourage those students to speak more freely. Once students internalize these rules, they begin to demand that other students follow them. There will be more frustration but fewer shouting matches of "I'm right," "No. I'm right!"

When I have misread the situation and intervened and the students point that out, I apologize and withdraw quickly. There is no point in intervening unless one maintains the cooperation of the students. One can't teach them not to browbeat each other in discussion by browbeating them into appropriate behavior. Modeling their behavior is crucial to the success of the process. Every intervention must be one that solicits the students' agreement with one's observations. On the other hand, one cannot allow the students to pursue tangents. Knowing when to get involved and when to back off is the art of intervention (and only learned from experience, learning from one's mistakes).

It is important to be concrete and consistent when one interrupts the group dynamic. Without clear goals and parameters the students lose respect for the process. If students understand what the limits of their freedom are they are surprisingly cooperative in tackling any task one asks of them. The rules that should be clearly stated and repeated often are: (1) that everyone must participate in the creation of the paragraph; (2) there must be respect for each other's ideas at all times; (3) while discussing what to write, the students must consistently refer to the text; and (4) the paragraph must have a thesis statement in the first sentence supported by detail that is argued in terms of the thesis.

Too often students will make a laundry list of detail instead of explaining how the detail supports the topic sentence. It is in the "arguing" that the students are being analytical. To do this, the students need to break down the terms of the topic sentences into parts small enough so the detail fits snugly. In the first paragraph below, the details are *listed*. In the second paragraph, the information is beginning to be *argued*. The term "discover" is defined by those words in italics. Defining terms is crucial to the process of analysis or, in other words, arguing the detail.

> Columbus did not discover America. He landed on Hispaniola in 1492. Arawaks greeted him. Columbus took many of them as slaves. Those that were not taken back to Spain, were made to look for gold. Every Arawak was responsible for filling a hawk's bell full of gold each month. If an Arawak failed to do so, the Spanish cut his or her hands off...

> Columbus did not discover America. Hispaniola was *already inhabited* by the Arawaks. They had been living there for centuries. Columbus *took their land away from them* by enslaving them. The Arawaks, *instead of working for themselves*, were forced to find gold for the Spanish...

If one student in the group is consistently silent or, worse, not listening, then the teacher needs to intervene. One way to involve the student is merely to pick up the paper on which the recorder is writing and give it to the uninvolved student, announcing that you have just made him or her the recorder. That will force the inattentive person to be involved. Another tactic, which depends on the nature of the group dynamic, is to sit down with the students and confront them with the fact that one member of the group is not involved and ask why. If neither tactic works, then one can sit down with the group and participate in the discussion, occasionally asking the uninvolved student to answer a question or respond to a statement. If the student begins to answer, ask for textual support if it has not been provided. The other students sometimes will leap to the defense of a student who is being "picked on" by the teacher, thus creating group unity that did not exist before.

The way most schools are structured, the teacher is in the position of adversary, especially if student work is graded. One can use that normally destructive role in a constructive way by allowing and encouraging students to unite against it. The groups hand in their paragraphs at the end of the allotted time period. I found it effective to grade the paragraphs on a point system as opposed to letter grades. I gave two points for homework assignments, so I decided to make the paragraphs worth four points, grading them (on a scale 0, 1, 2, 3, 4) according to the degree to which they support their thesis.

I have discovered that it is fairly useless to write comments on student work unless the students rewrite their work. In order to make the comments useful and to simultaneously ease the individual's responsibility to the group, I make photocopies of each paragraph for every member of the group. With his or her own copy of the group paragraph, the student can choose to rewrite the paragraph individually or with any number of members of the group. I allow them to hand in rewrites as many times as they would like. Rewriting individually is an option, since group rewriting means giving up more class time. And, insisting that students rewrite together outside of class seems to be placing an unreasonable burden on them. Unfortunately, most students have very little free time during the school day.

When I first assign a group paragraph in the beginning of the year, many of the students balk at being given a grade that is dependent on the group. They argue that it is unfair to give an individual a group grade. By allowing them to rewrite the paragraph individually, I defuse this sense of outrage that has been bred into them by their lack of experience in the benefits of cooperative learning.

One can encourage students to rewrite by increasing the point value of the paragraph. If this is done, it should be done from the very beginning of the year. It is important to keep the criteria for assessment consistent throughout the year. I have increased the weight of the group paragraph during the year, but only after explaining why. Changing the criteria without making the change explicit and giving a reasonable explanation for the change makes students see the assignment as arbitrary. This perception undermines any incentive students have for doing the work.

If one can incorporate group writing throughout the year and clearly state and consistently enforce the parameters within which students must operate, then students will learn how to work in groups on their own. Ultimately, little supervision will be needed. Students eventually exhibit a sense of purpose without supervision when they have experienced highly structured group work on a regular basis.

II. The Grading System

One's grading system has a great deal to do with how much students learn from an assignment. The most detrimental aspect of "grades" is that they act to inhibit. Students become afraid of making mistakes, even though mistakes are a fundamental part of the learning process. Many of the chapter questions in Zinn will not be fully explored by the students, will not provoke creative and critical thinking unless the teacher has a grading system that does not penalize the students for coming up with "wrong" answers. I have always found it effective to have part of the student's final grade be based on percentage of work completed, ignoring whether that work was done "correctly" or not. If and when a teacher does grade an assignment, students will learn a great deal from the opportunity to rewrite the assignment (assuming that the grading criteria is explicit, concrete, and consistently adhered to).

III. Extra Credit

I have heard teachers say: "I don't believe in extra credit." I don't think extra credit is a matter of faith, but it is a useful tool. Students do not all learn at the same rate and at the same time. There are plenty of students in tenth grade who are not ready to read about Puritans or Columbus or the New Deal. The more choices students have in what they study, the more they are likely to learn. I like to use extra credit to encourage students to read the newspaper. I give them the option of finding an article that relates to an issue in the course. They must hand in a copy of the article (or cut out the original). They also must hand in a paragraph that summarizes the article and explains the connection they see between the article and an issue in any one of the issues that they have studied in the course. For a few students this has become an entire course in and of itself. It is part of my attempt to encourage students to see the connection between the past and the present.

If students wish to invent other kinds of extra credit assignments I encourage them to do so. As long as the assignment involves writing and making connections, I think it should be permitted. Some students need to find their own "hook" into history. By encouraging and rewarding creative extra credit assignments that are connected to the history, you are looking for that "hook." I have learned a great deal about how best to teach students from the students themselves. In a sense, I provide them with the structure that allows them to teach me how to teach them.

IV. Geography

Much has been made of students' lack of geographical knowledge and the need to remedy that. It certainly is important to know where the places are that one is reading about. But, again, what is important is only that which is relevant to the thesis. It is not particularly useful to know all the state capitals by heart. If students are asked to memorize the state capitals without being told the purpose of such work, then the lesson is meaningless to them.

Most of the chapter questions in Zinn have a geography question. Having the students actually draw freehand maps can get them into the habit of looking more closely at maps generally. Betty Edwards' *Drawing from the Right Side of the Brain* includes a chapter about how to teach yourself and others "contour drawing." As with all skills, the ability to draw a map takes practice. The first time you ask your students to draw a map, many will rebel, insisting that they can't draw. It would be a good idea to give them a lesson in contour drawing first. Or better yet, have an art teacher come into your class to give a lesson. Everyone can learn to draw. The benefits are manifold: students will have practice developing their right brain functions; they will have one more small piece of evidence that disciplines do not exist in isolation of each other; it will provide the naturally visual with some confidence building experiences; and it will provide a change of pace in what you do in the classroom every day.

In addition to having my students draw their own maps, whenever my class is in the midst of a discussion of a topic that involves geography, I will ask a student to get up from his or her seat, go to the relevant map on the wall of the classroom, and point out the places we have been discussing. It is very important for this process to be fun, even though it is serious work. If the topic were the Spanish-American War, for example, I would ask a student to point to the Philippines, Puerto Rico, Cuba, Guam, China, and Hawaii. As the student searches for Guam, say, encourage the class to help out, saying: "You are getting warmer" or "You are getting colder." That way the exercise seems less like learning geography than playing pin the tail on the donkey. Keep it light.

After the student has finished, I thank her and let her sit down. Then I call on another student (preferably one who was not paying attention) to perform the same task. I do this with several students, until they are able to find the places on the map without too much help from me or their peers. Then I explain (or better, ask a student to explain) the significance of the places. For example: "The Pacific islands were important stepping stones to China, and the United States was interested in developing coaling stations for its fleet, which would then be better able to protect U.S. trade with China." It is an informal, humorous, and painless way to learn geography, a method that allows more students to learn for a longer period of time than with traditional quizzes on paper. It eliminates that bad feeling of failing a quiz and the isolation that such activities engender. If one doesn't have a map on the wall, one can be drawn on the blackboard.

I often make the first geography "quiz" of the year into a game. I tell my students that there will be a quiz the next day on specific maps in their text. But, I don't tell them what kind of quiz. The students assume it will be like any other quiz they have ever had—a map and they must identify places on it. Instead, when they come to class the next day, I have drawn a map on the board. I explain that when I call a person's name and a geographical place, that person must go up to the board, take a piece of chalk and identify the place on the map with the chalk. Then, the student must sit down. The score will be based on how fast the student is able to get out of and return to his or her chair. I have a stopwatch and a list of names and places on my clipboard. I pretend to be serious and see for how long they will believe me. This serves two purposes. First, the students learn that teachers are capable of giving bizarre assignments and that students should regularly question the methods used by their teachers. Second, students learn that geography quizzes (and perhaps all quizzes) are a little silly.

v. Debates

I have provided at least one debate resolution per chapter, usually at the end of each chapter's questions.

I use the debate format as an additional change of pace in teaching students how to define terms and support their generalizations with detail. The structure I use is developed with this goal in mind. I divide the class in half. I usually ask the students to choose the side they wish to be on. If the students don't break themselves up evenly, I ask some students to switch sides so that the class is evenly divided. (It is always important to explain the purpose of your instructions.) Those who are asked to switch often complain. I explain to them that it is useful to have to argue a point of view that one does not hold. It helps one develop one's own argument better because then one understands the opposing argument much better. I usually give the class one night to prepare. I give them a resolution that is relevant to the previous night's reading or that night's reading. Before the debate begins, I explain the ground rules. The rules below are designed to encourage all students to speak. If they know they must participate eventually, then there is more incentive to listen and think. The rules alter the dynamic of class discussion in which a few students tend to monopolize the discussion.

1. Each student must speak once before anyone has a chance to speak twice. Those who have something to say before it is their turn need to take notes in order to remember what they want to say when it finally is their turn.

2. The two sides alternate turns. Two people on the same team may not speak sequentially.

3. Students must raise their hands if they wish to speak. I decide who speaks, giving preference to those students who do not readily participate in class discussion.

4. The only exception to rules 1 and 2 is if a student needs clarification of something that has just been said. In that case, then any student may ask for a "point of clarification." I will grant the floor to the student who asked the question. If the question and answer session turns into a cross-examination, I stop it. There is to be no cross-examination. (It takes too much time away from others who wish to speak.)

At the beginning of the year, I need to intervene in the debates frequently, by pointing out whether or not the detail is relevant or whether there is detail or not. I will even add rules to encourage the kind of quality that I want to see. For example, if the students are not using details from the reading, I might stipulate that no one may speak unless she incorporates a quotation from the text in support of what she is saying. Or, if students are consistently ignoring what the other team says, I might stipulate that no one may speak, except in response to what has already been said. If that doesn't work, I might further demand that the speaker name the student whose argument is being rebutted. I only resort to these rules, however, if there is a free flow of discussion that is devoid of analysis. As the teacher, one must always be sensitive to the fine line between inhibiting student participation and insisting that when students talk, they have something relevant and substantive to say. At times, I will even jump into the debate and help a student who is struggling with an argument and develop it for him or her. Or, I might jump into the debate and respond to an argument that needs to be challenged but is not being challenged by any student in the opposition.

The purpose of the debates is not to learn official debating skills and tactics but to create a situation in which the students must argue. Structured argument develops critical thinking. When I intervene in the debate I am doing so in order to encourage the students to define their terms and support their arguments with detail from the text. The informal debate format forces some students to speak who do not do so in a free-flowing class discussion. Of course, I don't "force" everyone to speak. If there are students who cannot, then I let them pass. Students who refuse to speak in tenth grade may end up as irrepressible orators in college. People develop at very different rates, and that needs acknowledgement in the flexibility of one's "system."

If the debate resolutions prove difficult for the students to work with, don't give up on the resolutions. Break down the process even further into smaller steps, assign one step at a time and build up their skills. The best place to start is defining the terms of the debate resolution. Then there is data collection. Depending on the skill level of your class, you might have to teach students how to find data , how to take notes, and how to skim. If individuals are having trouble, put them into groups. The important thing is to not give up. The assignment may take longer to complete than you expected, but it can be completed. In completing the assignment, students will develop crucial skills, not to mention the fact that they will actually remember the content past the next test.

vi. Class Discussion

When I first started to teach, a master teacher once advised me that to have a good class discussion, one must start off the class with a "big" question. The question was so big that one did not expect the students to have an answer for it until the end of the class period. One asked it in the beginning, so the students knew where the discussion was leading. After beginning class by asking the big question, one would immediately follow it up with sub questions that would lead students to develop different parts of an argument that would then be drawn together at the end of class to answer the big question. Any of the the the debate resolutions can function as the "big question." For example, "Was Watergate the result of a flawed president?" Never expect an immediate answer to such a "big" question. Have follow-up questions prepared in advance to explore different parts of the question.

- ★ What was Watergate?

- ★ Was is it only the burglary?

- ★ How long did the cover-up last?

- ★ Was Nixon flawed?

- ★ Did he make any mistakes during his presidency?

- ★ Were those mistakes the result of character defects?

- ★ Who else made mistakes during Nixon's administration?

- ★ Can we blame only Nixon? Or is the system at fault?

After exploring these follow-up questions, then one poses the "big" question again at the end of class. This provides structure to the class discussion, which is important if one wants to encourage students to become systematic in their thinking. One doesn't always have to rigidly adhere to the "big" question, but when students go off on tangents, it is important to identify them as such and then return to the original topic of conversation. Becoming self-conscious of what is relevant and what is not is crucial to the development of critical thinking. I had one student, recently, who was so right brained that she could rarely contribute to the topic at hand. I commissioned her as the "tangent police." She was so taken with her title that she became excellent at announcing to the class every time I ever went off on a tangent.

Another technique that I have found useful in developing critical thinking is to start class by asking the students to identify (by writing them down) the two most important "facts" from the previous night's reading. After most of the students are done, I ask students to volunteer their answers, defending why they think their choices are important. This allows for a discussion as to what determines "importance" (if it supports the author's thesis or if it supports a particular interest or axe that the student wants to grind). This makes everyone more self-conscious about how subjective the selection process is. It helps students develop a sense of what is important to them. It also allows for a discussion as to what a fact is and is not. After several classes devoted to this specific exercise, I found that my tenth-grade students began to appreciate the difference between a generalization and a piece of detail. "Columbus sailed for profit" is a generalization, while "His contract wasto receive 10% of the profits from the voyage" is detail. Most students need to be taught the distinction.

If students are particularly resistant to structured class discussion as described above, one can loosen them up in the following manner. Start a class out with what is usually the worst question you can ask: What did you think about the reading? Did you like it or not, why or why not? These questions are merely to get the students to speak. It is what you do with what they say that is crucial in getting a discussion going on the historical material.

TEACHER: How did you like the reading last night?

STUDENT: This reading sucked!

TEACHER: What does "sucked" mean?

STUDENT: It means "stinks."

TEACHER: In what way did it stink?

STUDENT: It was boring.

TEACHER: Why?

STUDENT: Because I fell asleep reading it.

TEACHER: What was it that put you to sleep?

STUDENT: Well, I didn't understand it.

TEACHER: Any of it?

STUDENT: Well, what did this guy mean when he said… [At this point you are off and running!]

VII. Using Drama in the Classroom

Gavin Bolton has written several books and offers workshops on how to use drama in the classroom. I highly recommend his techniques, since they provide one more teaching technique that contributes to variety in the classroom (as well as appealing to one of the variety of learning styles). He distinguishes between "forming" and "performing." "Forming" is for the benefit of the actors involved and not for the benefit of an audience.

Students divide up into pairs and act out just with each other conversations that might have happened between historical actors, such as between a factory girl and her foreman in 1840.

Role plays are very easy to develop on one's own. Put Columbus on trial. Have a news reporter interview, on live television, an indentured servant, a slave, a merchant, and a planter giving their opinions on the growing body of legislation governing servants and slaves in Virginia (c. 1832). Have the class turn into Congress and have them introduce bills addressing the role lobbyists play in the political process. The possibilities are endless.

VIII. Students Teaching Other Students

This is a principle I try to employ as much as possible. Students are teaching each other when they participate in group paragraphs, in dramatic exercises, debates, and class discussions. Yet they can do so in many other situations as well. I have my students actually go out and teach a class about Columbus to younger students. This gives the potentially arid assignment of creating a third-grade Columbus curriculum a tremendous amount of zip and excitement. Instead of the teacher lecturing, students individually or by groups can give oral reports. I know many teachers who don't want to do this because they feel that they can't cover enough material or that the students won't teach the material the way the teacher wants it taught. But these objections are based on the assumption that what the teacher says is what the students hear. This assumption needs to be more closely examined.

I used to lecture until I discovered that many of the students did not understand the material in the way I presented it. There were too many different learning styles among the students for me to match up with all of them. The students do not present material in the manner I would want them to, but they learn much more in the process than if I had presented the material my way.* Not only do they learn content but they undergo mental and emotional development. When student teachers return to their roles as students, they have had an experience that alters the dynamic of the classroom. The ex-student teachers, because they have had to wrestle with the preparation of a lesson, with the frustration of trying to make their peers pay attention to and understand what they were presenting, begin to feel more compassionate toward or connected with the teacher. Yet, at the same time, because they were in the teacher's shoes for a moment, they often become more critical of the teacher as well. Their consciences and consciousness are raised on many levels. This helps them to become more sophisticated thinkers. One student came back to visit me after he had gone to college and told me that one of the most important and memorable days in our American history course was the day that he was responsible for telling the story of the Cuban Missile Crisis. The first time he gave the report, he was confused. I made him do it again the next day. He had to go home that night and reread the text. The next day, he delivered a clear and accurate report. He had *gained ownership* over that story in a way he never would have had he merely read it in preparation for a traditional test or listened to a teacher present it. But, he was not impressed with the content he learned. He was impressed with the lesson it taught him about the most effective way to teach himself. He felt that lesson helped him succeed in college. He also felt very good about himself because he had been able to master material he had never thought himself capable of mastering before. Most students have grown passive and given up responsibility for their own learning after sitting through years of lectures. They need to be given the responsibility of teaching themselves and others in a situation in which they know they will be supported and encouraged but not bailed out.

*

Appendix B

Textbook Interpretations of Bacon's Rebellion (1676)

Kathy Emery

A typical assignment that I gave my students, when I used multiple text-books, involved a series of questions about a specific event. Below are a list of six textbooks that I have used in the classroom. You can achieve similar results with any set of textbooks. They differ inherently. The page numbers refer to those pages devoted to describing the events leading to and including Bacon's Rebellion. Also listed below are the questions I asked my students when the assigned event was Bacon's Rebellion. I have answered the first question—"What was Berkeley's Indian policy and his reasons for such a policy?"—to illustrate the degree to which the textbooks differ from one another.

Textbooks:

BAILEY and KENNEDY, *The American Pageant*, DC Heath and Co., Lexington, Massachusetts, 1983, pp. 13–14.

NASH AND JEFFREY, *The American People*, HarperCollins, N.Y., 1986, pp. 76–78.

NORTON ET AL., *A People and a Nation*, Houghton Mifflin, Boston, Massachusetts, 1986, p. 49.

UNGER, *These United States*, Little, Brown, Boston, Massachusetts, 1982, pp. 67–69.

Appendix B: Textbook Interpretations of Bacon's Rebellion (1676)

WEINSTEIN AND GATTELL, *Freedom and Crisis*, Random House, N.Y.,
1981, p. 49.

WILLIAMS AND FRIEDEL, *American History: A Survey*, Alfred Knopf,
N.Y., 1979, p. 43.

WILSON AND GILBERT, *The Pursuit of Liberty*, Alfred Knopf, N.Y.,
1984, pp. 39–55.

Questions for readings on Bacon's Rebellion:

★ What was Berkeley's Indian policy and his reasons for such a policy?

★ Why did the frontiersmen attack Indians?

★ Why did the frontiersmen attack Jamestown?

★ What event led Berkeley to declare Bacon a rebel?

★ Is there a hero in the story? If so, who is it and why?

★ Why did Bacon become a leader of the frontiersmen?

★ What is the historical significance of Bacon's Rebellion?

Analysis of question: What was Berkeley's Indian policy and
his reasons for such a policy?

I have retrieved information from each text that is relevant to the question of
Berkeley's policy toward the Indians and his reasons behind such a policy.

★ Bailey and Kennedy: Berkeley "...allegedly involved in the fur trade
with the Indians, was unwilling to antagonize them by fighting back."

★ Nash and Jeffreys: The 1646 treaty with the Powhatans forbade white
settlement beyond the territory north of the York river; "...stable
Indian relations suited the established planters." White settlers attacked
the Susquehannocks. When the Susquehannocks attacked white
encroachment on their land, Berkeley denounced the whites' subse-
quent retaliatory raid.

★ Norton et al.: Berkeley "...hoped to avoid setting off a major war like
that raging in New England."

Appendix B: Textbook Interpretations of Bacon's Rebellion (1676)

★ Unger: When violence broke out between Indians and white frontier settlers in 1675, Berkeley decided on defensive measures, ordering "whites to withdraw from areas near Indian land and locate behind a line of forts..." Berkeley "offered good pay to farmers to enroll as soldiers..." and he built frontier forts. But building forts meant higher taxes, and it increased the value of the wealthy estates on which they were to be built.

★ Weinstein and Gattell: "When Indian warfare broke out on the frontier," Berkeley "called for restraint."

★ Williams and Freidel: In 1644, Berkeley opened up the frontier to settlement, sending explorers and an army. The defeated Indians signed a treaty "ceding all the land between the York and James Rivers to the east of the fall line, and prohibiting white settlement to the west of that line." But, the ever increasing English population pushed into Indian territory, causing increasing number of violent clashes. "Berkeley preferred not to antagonize the Indians." He and his "associates were profiting from a large scale trade with them." Berkeley ordered the militia to guard the edge of the settlement.

★ Wilson and Gilbert: "Berkeley was outraged by the open murder of the Susquehannah chiefs." He "wanted a policy of peace and order that would protect the friendly tribes and the beaver trade. He also wanted Indian policy to rest in the hands of the government at Jamestown, not in the hands of hundreds of small planters scattered along the edges of the wilderness." Berkeley declared war on the Indians, formed a militia, and started to build forts. He ordered the militia to patrol between the forts. Any attack on the Indians needed the governor's permission. Berkeley wanted to distinguish between those Indians who were abiding by the rules of treaties and those who were not.

When one compares the different versions of Bacon's Rebellion, one is immediately struck by the difference in interpretation and kind of information provided. For example, Weinstein and Gattell define Berkeley's policy but not the reason behind it, while Norton identifies Berkeley's reasons but not his policy. Bailey and Kennedy cast doubt on Berkeley's involvement in the "fur trade," while Williams and Freidel state that Berkeley was profiting directly from such trade. Nash and Jefferies imply that Berkeley's Indian policy of restraint was morally grounded, while Wilson and Gilbert see constitutional and practical reasons for Berkeley's policy.

Is Berkeley using his position as governor to enrich himself and his cronies at the expense of poor frontiersmen? Or is Berkeley valiantly trying to negotiate peace between greedy frontiersmen and irate Indians? Depending on which text one reads, one either cannot answer these questions, or one can have a definite opinion one way or the other. It is in reading all six versions that a more complex, less simplistic answer is available. The real lesson here is that the more detail one has, the more likely one will be close to the truth of what happened. The process of sifting through different versions of the same event is the process that develops critical thinking. An open and healthy debate over these questions allows students to discover how to think for themselves and not rely on external opinions solely.

Appendix C

Additional Resources

Kathy Emery

The criteria I used in identifying the books, articles, and videos below are as follows: smooth diction; clear thesis; lots of detailed support explained clearly in terms of the thesis; challenges mainstream traditional version of American history; good supplementary reading to Zinn. There are, of course, many other titles that are useful. I only included those that I think are of the highest quality and the most useful in supporting the curriculum I have proposed.

Books

★ VERY READABLE
★★ CHALLENGING FOR HIGH SCHOOL STUDENTS
★★★ FOR TEACHER'S USE ONLY
★★★★ EXTRAORDINARY BUT DIFFICULT TO READ
   BECAUSE OF THE COMPLEXITY OF THE THESIS
   OR THE USE OF ESOTERIC JARGON

★ BELL, DERRICK, *Faces at the Bottom of the Well*, Basic Books, New York, 1992 (a series of disparate stories, some fact, some fiction, illustrating the complexities of modern day racism; readable, challenging, and provocative).

★ BROWN, DEE, *Bury My Heart At Wounded Knee*, Henry, Holt and Company, New York, 1991 (a graphic and gripping account of the brutal invasion of Europeans into Indian territory west of the Mississippi from 1860 until the final defeat in 1890).

★★ CATTON, BRUCE, *This Hallowed Ground*, Simon and Schuster, New York, 1961 (his abridged three-volume history of the Civil War).

★★★★ CHOMSKY, NOAM, *Year 501; The Conquest Continues*, South End Press, Boston, 1993 (a post World War II history of American foreign policy; an excellent companion to Ehrenreich's domestic study; makes explicit what LaFeber implies; see also Chomsky's interview with Bill Moyers, PBS video).

★ CLUSTER, DICK, ED., *They Should Have Served That Cup of Coffee*, South End Press, Boston, 1979 (clear and concise oral testimonies of seven radicals of the 1960s, especially good ones on the activity of the Black Panthers and the growth of the women's movement).

★★★ D'EMILIO, JOHN, *Sexual Politics, Sexual Communities*, University of Chicago Press, 1984 (comprehensive history of the gay rights movement; the transformation of homosexual behavior before World War II and the emergence of a homosexual identity after World War II).

★★ DUBOIS, ELLEN C., AND RUIZ, VICKI L., EDS., *Unequal Sisters*, Routledge, New York, 1990 (sophisticated articles about specific events and issues affecting women in American history. An excellent text for a women's history elective).

★ DUIKER, WILLIAM J., *Introduction to Vietnam, History and Culture*, The Lessons of the Vietnam War Series, Pittsburgh Center for Social Studies Education, 1991 (very readable, concise but not simplistic chronology of the war)

★★★ EHRENREICH, BARBARA, *Fear of Falling*, Harper Perennial, New York, 1990 (a socioeconomic study of American history since World War II, with a particularly excellent analysis of labor and women; a provocative twist to Zinn's paradigm).

★★ GOODWYN, LAWRENCE, *The Populist Moment*, Oxford University Press, New York, 1978 (a detailed analysis of the growth of the Grange and Alliance movements culminating in the Democratic Convention of 1896; the story of a courageous grassroots, biracial movement whose leaders were co-opted and whose power was in the end eviscerated by the power elites).

★ GORNICK, LARRY, *The Cartoon History of the United States*, Harper Perennial, New York, 1991 (it is always good to add humor, but "to get" some of the jokes one must already be familiar with the material; having students explain what's so funny would be a legitimate test of their knowledge of the actual history).

★ GORNICK, VIVIAN, *The Romance of American Communism*, Harper-Collins, New York (unfortunately, it is out of print; it is an eloquently written book detailing why people became, remained and no longer were communists; the reasons transcend theory, worth tracking down in libraries or used book stores).

★ HEIMOWITZ AND WEISSMAN, *Women in American History*, Bantam, New York, 1990 (a popular way to introduce women's history to high school students).

★ HERTZBERG, ARTHUR, *The Jews in America*, Touchstone, New York, 1990 (a good overview; some nice detail).

★★ HOFSTADER, RICHARD, *The American Political Tradition*, Vintage, New York, 1974 (cited often by Zinn; a series of biographies of presidents who presided over watershed periods in American history; the first chapter is especially good at providing evidence that the last thing the Founding Fathers wanted to create was a democracy; compelling biographies of Andrew Jackson and the two Roosevelts).

★ KOVIC, RON, *Born on the Fourth of July*, Pocket Books, New York (the memoir on which the Oliver Stone / Tom Cruise movie was based).

★★★★ LaFEBER, WALTER, *America, Russia and the Cold War*, McGraw-Hill, New York, 1996 (incredible detail supporting his thesis that the United States created the cold war in order to convince the American people to financially support a foreign policy that would guarantee world markets for American goods).

★★ LOEWEN, JAMES W., *Lies My Teacher Told Me: Everything Your American History Textbook Got Wrong*, HarperCollins, New York An iconoclastic look at the errors, misrepresentations, and omissions in the leading American history textbooks.

★ MARTINEZ, ELIZABETH, *500 Years of Chicano History*, Albuquerque Southwest Organizing Project, 1991 (photos and text; indispensable for filling this gap in traditional history).

★★★ MERCHANT, CAROLYN, *The Death of Nature*, Harper San Francisco, 1990 (an analysis of the development of a European worldview arising out the Scientific Revolution, which explains why Europeans wanted to explore the New World and could massacre its innocent and peaceful people).

★★★★ MORGAN, EDMUND, *American Slavery, American Freedom* , W. W. Norton and Company, New York, 1996 (cited by Zinn; a beautifully constructed argument with persuasive detail; an in-depth analysis of why and how indentured servants were used as labor by the Virginian Company and why indentured servants were replaced with African slaves; a close look at how class prejudice and then racism were deliberately created as a divide and conquer technique).

★★ MORGAN, EDMUND, *The Puritan Dilemma*, HarperCollins, New York, 1987 (biography of John Winthrop, using his life and writings as a microcosm to explore the dynamics of Puritan society and ideology; excellent chapters on Anne Hutchinson and Roger Williams; explodes the Puritan myth created by Hawthorne).

★ NASH, GARY, *Red, White, and Black*, Prentice Hall, Englewood Cliffs, New Jersey, 1991 (a look at the development of the English colonies in North America as a dynamic among Indians, Europeans, and Africans).

★★ SALE, KIRKPATRICK, *The Conquest of Paradise* , NAL/Dutton, New York, 1991 (Columbus was not the great sailor Morison has made him out to be; Spain knew exactly what they were doing in sending Columbus to the New World; interesting connections made between European conditions at the time and the voyages and experiences of Columbus as well as the English in Virginia).

★ SCHIRMER, DANIEL AND SHALOM, STEPHEN, EDS., *The Philippines Reader*, South End Press, Boston, 1987 (a compendium of original sources; useful, and unusually concrete information about the Filipino experience under Spanish rule; excellent source material for studying the Spanish-American War).

★★ STAMPP, KENNETH, *The Era of Reconstruction*, Random House, New York, 1967 (explores and explodes the myths of the traditional version of Southern history from 1865 to 1877 established by William A. Dunning and D. W. Griffith).

★ TAKAKI, RONALD T., *Strangers from a Different Shore*, Viking Penguin, New York, 1990 (the Asian influence and role of Asian immigrants and their progeny in American history; a story given short shrift even in Zinn's text).

★ TERKEL, STUDS, *American Dreams: Lost and Found*, Ballantine Books, New York, 1985 (another of Terkel's oral histories; excellent evidence of all that Zinn describes; see other titles by Terkel).

★★★ WOOD, PETER, *Black Majority*, W. W. Norton and Company, New York, 1996 (the story of the creation of racism in Charleston, South Carolina; an interesting contrast to how it developed in Jamestown, Virginia; a very close study of slavery in colonial America).

Articles

★★ AJAMI, FOUAD, "The Other 1492," *The New Republic*, April 6, 1992 (connects the expulsion of the Jews from Spain with Columbus's mission).

★★ CHOMSKY, NOAM, "Media Control," *Open Magazine*, pamphlet 10 (how the media engineer public opinion).

★★★★ HAYS, SAMUEL, "The Politics of Reform in Municipal Government in the Progressive Era," In eds. Dinnerstein, Leonard, and Kenneth T. Jackson, *American Vistas*, Oxford University Press, New York, fourth edition (detailed account, with plenty of evidence, of how the municipal reforms of the Progressives succeeded in eliminating the influence of the working class in city government; connects well with *Who Will Tell the People?* and *The Times of Harvey Milk*; at large elections versus ward representation, as well as with Chomsky's "Media Control").

★★★★ JACKSON, KENNETH T., "Race, Ethnicity, and Real Estate Appraisal," In eds. Dinnerstein, Leonard, and Kenneth T. Jackson, *American Vistas*, Oxford University Press, New York, fourth edition (an analysis of the New Deal programs HOLC and FHA; how their policies set the stage for redlining—segregated housing according to race and ethnicity; the effects of these policies can be seen in the PBS/Frontline video *Crisis on Federal Street*; this article is also an excellent companion piece to Bell's Faces).

Videos: *Documentaries*

Attica (a vivid account of the 1971 prison uprising, giving a powerful picture of prison conditions in our society).

Before Stonewall (a history of the creation of the gay and lesbian community from the 1920s until 1965; John D'Emilio would call it the description of the transformation from homosexual behavior to homosexual identity).

Broken Rainbow (an exposé of the supposed border dispute between the Navajo and Hopi tribes in the 1970s; the film reveals the roles that the Peabody Coal Company and the U.S. government played in taking away the land and livelihood of the Indians).

Crisis on Federal Street (PBS/*Frontline*: a history of public housing projects and welfare in Chicago; reveals the racial politics of the projects and describes the grassroots activism that has emerged to combat the problems created by federal housing policy).

Grenada (PBS/*Frontline* investigation into the reasons for the invasion of Grenada and the results of the invasion; a microcosm of American foreign policy).

Harlan County U. S. A. (documentary of the 1977 coal miners' strike in Kentucky; reveals the complex interplay of union politics and practices, the role of women, Wall Street, and the policies and tactics of the Peabody Coal company; Peabody Coal figures prominently in *Broken Rainbow*).

Metropolitan Avenue (an oral history and documentary footage of the grassroots activism in opposing the building of the Brooklyn-Queens Expressway; the effect of the needs and power of suburbia on the culture of an urban neighborhood in Brooklyn).

Out of the Depths: A Miner's Story (a Bill Moyers/PBS oral history of the events preceding, during, and following the Ludlow Massacre).

Roger and Me and its sequel *Pets or Meat* (the complexity of class prejudice and discrimination; the damage done by the layoff of automobile workers in the late 1970s; heartbreaking story told with humor).

Rosie the Riveter (oral history of women who worked in the factories during World War II; how they were seduced and betrayed).

Seeing Red (an oral history of the American Communist movement from the 1930s through the 1950s; excellent documentary footage of the depression era and the McCarthy hearings; follow-up interviews and footage as to what these old communists are doing today; a video version of Vivian Gornick's book).

The Gulf War (a PBS/*Frontline* investigation of the causes and effects of the Persian Gulf War).

The Times of Harvey Milk (an award-winning chronicle of how the first openly gay public official in the United States got elected; an exploration of why he was shot; evidence of the power of grassroots organization and the temporary overcoming of the power elite's divide and conquer methods; a connection to Hays's article on municipal reform—Milk was able to be elected when elections for seats on the Board of Supervisors once again were ward-based instead of at-large).

The War at Home (a long valuable documentary on the growth of the anti-Vietnam war movement; uses the University of Wisconsin at Madison as the microcosm of the larger movement; incredible footage of hearings, interviews, riots, and demonstrations).

Union Maids (Several women who were labor organizers in the 1930's recall the struggle of those years).

Who Will Tell the People? (a PBS/*Frontline* production of William Greider's book of same title; Greider argues that politics has become less democratic in the last thirty years; embroiders on Zinn's bipartisan consensus theory; lots of compelling detail).

With Babies and Banners (the GM strike in Flint, Michigan, with attention to the crucial role played by women).

The Wrath of Grapes (the social and environmental impact of mass production of grapes; includes the successful attempts to organize workers and boycotts by the United Farm Workers and the effects of pesticides on those who live near grape farms).

Videos: *Fiction*

Matewan (John Sayles's account of a 1920s strike which highlights the difficulties and successes of organizing a multiethnic workforce for the purposes of collective bargaining).

Normae Rae (A moving account of textile workers in the south).

Panther (the beginning and end of the Black Panther organization; most of the story takes place in Oakland; critical of both the Panthers and the U.S. government).

Straight Out of Brooklyn (the obstacles in trying to get out of the ghetto in the 1980s—in this instance, Red Hook, Brooklyn).

X (Spike Lee's biography of Malcolm X).

The Grapes of Wrath (a good accompaniment to the *Wrath of Grapes*— stars Henry Fonda).

The Mission (Jeremy Irons and Robert DeNiro; post-Columbian colonial expansion by Spain in South America; conflict between Portugal and Spain over boundaries in the American colonies).

Appendix D

Bloom's Taxonomy

Kathy Emery

I have adapted the following from Benjamin S. Bloom's Taxonomy of Educational Objectives, *a Longman publication, 1984. Bloom believes that the taxonomy defined below can help teachers teach their students the skills needed for the highest levels of thinking. He categorizes cognitive skills into six categories: knowledge, comprehension, application, analysis, synthesis, and evaluation.*

The taxonomy is hierarchical; skills in one category are likely to be built on skills in preceding categories. The skill categories are arranged in order of complexity (the number of prerequisite cognitions and skills) but need not imply increasing difficulty for students. With the proper content, students at all grade levels can exhibit behaviors at all six levels. The degree of difficulty can be manipulated or determined within each category by such factors as:

  ★ student's readiness

  ★ student's ability

  ★ amount of data given for task

  ★ number of steps involved in the task

  ★ time constraints on the task

  ★ mode of presentation to the students

  ★ student's prior experience

  ★ how concrete or abstract the content is

  ★ student's attitude

  ★ quantity of work given

Level One: Knowledge

Description
Knowledge of specifics, of ways or means of dealing with specifics, of the universals and abstractions in a field; ability to remember (recognition or recall) facts, names, places, trends, methods, sequence, categories, and previously learned generalizations or theories.

Verbs for Writing Objectives
Tell, list, cite, choose, arrange, find, group, label, select, match, locate, name, offer, omit, pick, quote, repeat, reset, say, show, sort, spell, touch, write, underline, point to, tally, transfer, underline, recite, identify, hold, and check.

Level Two: Comprehension

Description
Comprehension by translation (changing information into one's own words), interpretation (reordering ideas, and establishing relationships), extrapolation (making appropriate inferences based on given data); ability to know what is being communicated.

Verbs for Writing Objectives
Translate: change, reword, construe, render, convert, expand, transform, alter, vary, retell, qualify, moderate, restate.
Interpret: infer, define, explain, construe, spell out, outline, annotate, expound, account for.
Extrapolate: project, propose, advance, contemplate, submit, offer, calcu late, scheme, contrive.

Level Three: Application

Description
Using general ideas, rules, procedures, or generalized methods; ability to transfer learning, to solve problems by remembering and applying concepts, generalizations, and appropriate skills with little or no direction given.

Verbs for Writing Objectives
Relate, utilize, solve, adopt, employ, use, avail, capitalize on, consume, exploit, profit by, mobilize, operate, ply, handle, manipulate, exert, exercise, try, devote, handle, wield, put in action, put to use, make use of, and take up.

Level Four: Analysis

Description
Studying of elements and their relationships or organizational principles; ability to break down an idea into its component parts and examine the relationship or organization of the parts to the whole.

Verbs for Writing Objectives
Break down, uncover, look into, dissect, examine, take apart, divide, simplify, reason, include, deduce, syllogize, check, audit, inspect, section, canvass, scrutinize, sift, assay, test for, survey, search, study, check, and screen.

Level Five: Synthesis

Description
By communicating, developing a plan, proposing a set of operations, developing a set of abstract relations; ability to put together parts to form a whole, to solve a problem using creative thinking that produces an end result not clearly there before.

Verbs for Writing Objectives
Create, combine, build, compile, make, structure, reorder, reorganize, develop, produce, compose, construct, blend, yield, breed cause, effect, generate, evolve, mature, make up, form, constitute, originate, conceive, and formulate.

Level Six: Evaluation

Description
Ability to make a judgment or assessment of good or bad, right or wrong according to external or internal standards/criteria.

Verbs for Writing Objectives
Judge, decide, rate, appraise, assay, rank, weight, accept, reject, determine, assess, reject, and criticize.

Examples of Objectives

Knowledge
Given background information, students will list the characteristics of each of the three branches of the federal government.

Comprehension
1. Translation: Students will explain the main functions of each of the three branches of the federal government.
2. Interpretation: Given a data revival chart of the characteristics of the three branches of the federal government, students will identify the similarities and differences of each.
3. Extrapolation: Given a discussion of the similarities and differences between the three branches of federal government, students will write two generalizations concerning the need for these similarities and differences.

Application
Given background information on the role of the Constitution as it relates to the government, students will develop as a group a classroom Constitution.

Analysis
Given three articles written about present presidential candidates, students will distinguish the bias of each author.

Synthesis
Students will design, prepare, organize, and conduct a survey related to the role of government in America.

Evaluation
Given background information, students will prepare a debate either pro or con concerning the amount of control the federal government should exert on the citizens of the country.

Examples of Questions

Knowledge
1. Who was the president during the Civil War?
2. List the major rivers of China.

Comprehension
1. Translation: Explain the changes that have taken place in Japan since World War II.
2. Interpretation: Compare the systems of government in the United States and the Soviet Union. How are they alike? Different?
3. Extrapolation: Given the data on immigration from 1880–1980, what trend do you see emerging? What do you predict will happen as a result of this trend?

Application

1. Using the map of the United Sates, how would you plan a car trip from Summit to San Francisco? Include in your plan estimated costs and a time line.
2. How would you show that the period in U.S. history from 1855–60 is similar or dissimilar to the period from 1964–69?
3. Now that you have read about the Middle Ages, how would you develop a plan for building a model of a castle?
4. After interviewing your classmates concerning their ethnic origins, how would you illustrate your finding?

Analysis

1. Third World Countries, particularly in Africa, that cannot afford to pay for oil imports are running out of supplies of firewood. Forests, the most important source of traditional energy, are being depleted at an average of six million acres a year. This situation is especially serious in Africa where it's hastening the spread of deserts. To correct this situation these countries need money to pay for reforestation, domestic oil and gas production, and other energy resources. Is the last sentence a correct conclusion? Why?
2. What motives influenced attempts by the United States to reestablish diplomatic ties with Communist China?
3. Sally has lived in more states than Sha-Ron. Sha-Ron has lived in fewer states than Maria. Who has lived in more states?

Synthesis

1. Political violence in Central America continues to spread. In Guatemala, for example, violence on both the left and the right has polarized society. What possible plans for bringing together these groups can you propose?
2. If Thomas Jefferson could return, how would he view America today?
3. Economic development in developing nations of the world has been slow. You are a member of the United Nations General Assembl;, what plan for a restructured world economy can you propose that will provide for the accelerated and sustained economic development of these countries?

Evaluation

1. The young people of Summit have indicated that they would like Roosevelt School to be converted to a skating rink. How do you evaluate this proposal in terms of cost and community acceptance?
2. What characteristics do you feel a superior president should have? Have the last two presidents been superior?
3. For what reasons would you favor or disfavor an Equal Rights Amendment to the Constitution?

Bibliography

Howard Zinn

This book, written in a few years, is based on twenty years of teaching and research in American history, and as many years of involvement in social movements. But it could not have been written without the work of several generations of scholars, and especially the current generation of historians who have done important work in the history of blacks, Indians, women, and working people of all kinds. It also could not have been written without the work of many people, not professional historians, who were stimulated by the social struggles around them to put together material about the lives and activities of ordinary people trying to make a better were, or just trying to survive.

To indicate every source of information in the text would have meant a book impossibly cluttered with footnotes, and yet I know the curiosity of the reader about where a startling fact or pungent quote comes from. Therefore, as often as I can, I mention in the text authors and titles of books for which the full information is in this bibliography. Where you cannot tell the source of a quotation right from the text, you can probably figure it out by looking at the asterisked books for that chapter. The asterisked books are those I found especially useful and often indispensable.

I have gone through the following standard scholarly periodicals: *American Historical Review, Mississippi Valley Historical Review, Journal of American History, Journal of Southern History, Journal of Negro History, Labor History, William and Mary Quarterly, Phylon, The Crisis, American Political Science Review, Journal of Social History.*

Also, some less orthodox but important periodicals for a work like this: *Monthly Review, Science and Society, Radical America, Akwesasne Notes, Signs: Journal of Women in Culture and Society, The Black Scholar, Bulletin of Concerned Asian Scholars, The Review of Radical Political Economics, Socialist Revolution, Radical History Review.*

Chapter 1
Columbus, the Indians, and Human Progress

BRANDON, WILLIAM. *The Last Americans: The Indian in American Culture.* New York: McGraw-Hill, 1974.

*COLLIER, JOHN. *Indians of the Americas.* New York: W. W. Norton, 1947.

*DE LAS CASAS, BARTOLOMÉ. *History of the Indies.* New York: Harper & Row, 1971.

*JENNINGS, FRANCIS. *The Invasion of America: Indians, Colonialism, and the Cant of Conquest.* Chapel Hill: University of North Carolina Press, 1975.

*KONING, HANS. *Columbus: His Enterprise.* New York: Monthly Review Press, 1976.

*MORGAN, EDMUND S. *American Slavery, American Freedom: The Ordeal of Colonial Virginia.* New York: W. W. Norton, 1975.

MORISON, SAMUEL ELIOT. *Admiral of the Ocean Sea.* Boston: Little, Brown, 1942.

————. *Christopher Columbus, Mariner.* Boston: Little, Brown, 1955.

*NASH, GARY B. *Red, White and Black: The Peoples of Early America.* Englewood Cliffs, N.J.: Prentice-Hall, 1970.

VOGEL, VIRGIL, ED. *This Country Was Ours.* New York: Harper & Row, 1971.

Chapter 2
Drawing the Color Line

*APTHEKER, HERBERT, ED. *A Documentary History of the Negro People in the United States.* Secaucus, N.J.: Citadel, 1974.

BOSKIN, JOSEPH. *Into Slavery: Radical Decisions in the Virginia Colony.* Philadelphia: Lippincott, 1966.

Bibliography

CATTERALL, HELEN. *Judicial Cases Concerning American Slavery and the Negro.* 5 vols. Washington: Negro University Press, 1937.

DAVIDSON, BASIL. *The African Slave Trade.* Boston: Little, Brown, 1961.

DONNAN, ELIZABETH, ED. *Documents Illustrative of the History of the Slave Trade to America.* 4 vols. New York: Octagon, 1965.

ELKINS, STANLEY. *Slavery: A Problem in American Institutional and Intellectual Life.* Chicago: University of Chicago Press, 1976.

FEDERAL WRITERS PROJECT. *The Negro in Virginia.* New York: Arno, 1969.

FRANKLIN, JOHN HOPE. *From Slavery to Freedom: A History of American Negroes.* New York: Knopf, 1974.

*JORDAN, WINTHROP. *White Over Black: American Attitudes Toward the Negro, 1550–1812.* Chapel Hill: University of North Carolina Press, 1968.

*MORGAN, EDMUND S. *American Slavery, American Freedom: The Ordeal of Colonial Virginia.* New York: W. W. Norton, 1975.

MULLIN, MICHAEL, ED. *American Negro Slavery: A Documentary History.* New York: Harper & Row, 1975.

PHILLIPS, ULRICH B. *American Negro Slavery: A Survey of the Supply, Employment and Control of Negro Labor as Determined by the Plantation Regime.* Baton Rouge: Louisiana State University Press, 1966.

REDDING, J. SAUNDERS. *They Came in Chains.* Philadelphia: Lippincott, 1973.

STAMPP, KENNETH M. *The Peculiar Institution.* New York: Knopf, 1956.

TANNENBAUM, FRANK. *Slave and Citizen: The Negro in the Americas.* New York: Random House, 1963.

Chapter 3
Persons of Mean and Vile Condition

ANDREWS, CHARLES, ED. *Narratives of the Insurrections 1675–1690.* New York: Barnes & Noble, 1915.

*BRIDENBAUGH, CARL. *Cities in the Wilderness: The First Century of Urban Life in America.* New York: Oxford University Press, 1971.

Bibliography

HENRETTA, JAMES. "Economic Development and Social Structure in Colonial Boston." *William and Mary Quarterly*, 3rd ser., vol. 22, January 1965.

HERRICK, CHEESMAN. *White Servitude in Pennsylvania: Indentured and Redemption Labor in Colony and Commonwealth*. Washington: Negro University Press, 1926.

HOFSTADTER, RICHARD. *America at 1750: A Social History*. New York: Knopf, 1971.

HOFSTADTER, RICHARD, AND MICHAEL WALLACE, EDS. *American Violence: A Documentary History*. New York: Knopf, 1970.

MOHL, RAYMOND. *Poverty in New York, 1783–1825*. New York: Oxford University Press, 1971.

*MORGAN, EDWARD S. *American Slavery, American Freedom: The Ordeal of Colonial Virginia*. New York: W. W. Norton, 1975.

*MORRIS, RICHARD B. *Government and Labor in Early America*. New York: Harper & Row, 1965.

*NASH, GARY B., ED. *Class and Society in Early America*. Englewood Cliffs, N.J.: Prentice-Hall, 1970.

*———. *Red, White, and Black: The Peoples of Early America*. Englewood Cliffs, N.J.: Prentice-Hall, 1974.

*———. "Social Change and the Growth of Prerevolutionary Urban Radicalism." In *The American Revolution*, ed. Alfred Young. DeKalb: Northern Illinois University Press, 1976.

*SMITH, ABBOT E. *Colonists in Bondage: White Servitude and Convict Labor in America*. New York: W. W. Norton, 1971.

*WASHBURN, WILCOMB E. *The Governor and the Rebel: A History of Bacon's Rebellion in Virginia*. New York: W. W. Norton, 1972.

Chapter 4
Tyranny Is Tyranny

BAILYN, BERNARD, AND N. GARRETT, EDS. *Pamphlets of the American Revolution*. Cambridge: Harvard University Press, 1965.

BECKER, CARL. *The Declaration of Independence: A Study in the History of the Political Ideas*. New York: Random House, 1958.

BROWN, RICHARD MAXWELL. "Violence and the American Revolution." In *Essays on the American Revolution*, ed. Stephen G. Kurtz and James H. Hutson. Chapel Hill: University of North Carolina Press, 1973.

COUNTRYMAN, EDWARD. "'Out of the Bounds of the Law': Northern Land Rioters in the Eighteenth Century." In *The American Revolution: Explorations in the History of American Radicalism*, ed. Alfred F. Young. DeKalb: Northern Illinois University Press, 1976.

ERNST, JOSEPH. "'Ideology' and an Economic Interpretation of the Revolution." In *The American Revolution: Explorations in the History of American Radicalism*, ed. Alfred F. Young. DeKalb: Northern Illinois University Press, 1976.

FONER, ERIC. "Tom Paine's Republic: Radical Ideology and Social Change." In *The American Revolution: Explorations in the History of American Radicalism*, ed. Alfred F. Young. DeKalb: Northern Illinois University Press, 1976.

FOX-BOURNE, H. R. *The Life of John Locke*, 2 vols. New York: King, 1876.

GREENE, JACK P. "An Uneasy Connection: An Analysis of the Preconditions of the American Revolution." *Essays on the American Revolution*, ed. Stephen G. Kurtz and James H. Hutson. Chapel Hill: University of North Carolina Press, 1973.

HILL, CHRISTOPHER. *Puritanism and Revolution*. New York: Schocken, 1964.

*HOERDER, DIRK. "Boston Leaders and Boston Crowds, 1765–1776." In *The American Revolution in the History of American Radicalism*, ed. Alfred F. Young. DeKalb: Northern Illinois University Press, 1976.

LEMISCH, JESSE. "Jack Tar in the Streets: Merchant Seamen in the Politics of Revolutionary America." *William and Mary Quarterly*. July 1968.

MAIER, PAULINE. *From Resistance to Revolution: Colonial Radicals and the Development of American Opposition to Britain, 1765–1776*. New York: Knopf, 1972.

Chapter 5
A Kind of Revolution

APTHEKER, HERBERT, ED. *A Documentary History of the Negro People in the United States*. Secaucus, N.J.: Citadel Press, 1974.

BAILYN, BERNARD. "Central Themes of the Revolution." In *Essays on the American Revolution*, ed. Stephen G. Kurtz and James H. Hutson. Chapel Hill: University of North Carolina Press, 1973.

Bibliography

———. *The Ideological Origins of the American Revolution.* Cambridge, Mass.: Harvard University Press, 1967.

*BEARD, CHARLES. *An Economic Interpretation of the Constitution of the United States.* New York: Macmillan, 1935.

BERLIN, IRA. "The Negro in the American Revolution." In *The American Revolution: Explorations in the History of American Radicalism*, ed. Alfred F. Young. DeKalb: Northern Illinois University Press, 1976.

BERTHOFF, ROWLAND, AND JOHN MURRIN. "Feudalism, Communalism, and the Yeoman Freeholder." In *Essays on the American Revolution*, ed. Stephen G. Kurtz and James H. Hutson. Chapel Hill: University of North Carolina Press, 1973.

BROWN, ROBERT E. *Charles Beard and the Constitution.* New York: W. W. Norton, 1965.

DEGLER, CARL. *Out of Our Past.* Harper & Row, 1970.

HENDERSON, H. JAMES. "The Structure of Politics in the Continental Congress." In *Essays on the American Revolution*, ed. Stephen G. Kurtz and James H. Hutson. Chapel Hill: University of North Carolina Press, 1973.

*HOFFMAN, RONALD. "The 'Disaffected' in the Revolutionary South." In *The American Revolution: Explorations in the History of American Radicalism*, ed. Alfred F. Young. DeKalb: Northern Illinois University Press, 1976.

JENNINGS, FRANCIS. "The Indians' Revolution." In *The American Revolution: Explorations in the History of American Radicalism*, ed. Alfred F. Young. DeKalb: Northern Illinois University Press, 1976.

LEVY, LEONARD W. *Freedom of Speech and Press in Early American History.* New York: Harper & Row, 1962.

*LYND, STAUGHTON. *Anti-Federalism in Dutchess County, New York.* Chicago: Loyola University Press, 1963.

———. *Class Conflict, Slavery, and the Constitution.* Indianapolis: Bobbs-Merrill, 1967.

———. "Freedom Now: The Intellectual Origins of American Radicalism." In *The American Revolution: Explorations in the History of American Radicalism*, ed. Alfred F. Young. DeKalb: Northern Illinois University Press, 1976.

MCLOUGHLIN, WILLIAM G. "The Role of Religion in the Revolution." In *Essays on the American Revolution*, ed. Stephen G. Kurtz and James H. Hutson. Chapel Hill: University of North Carolina Press, 1973.

Bibliography

MORGAN, EDMUND S. "Conflict and Consensus in Revolution." In *Essays on the American Revolution*, ed. Stephen G. Kurtz and James H. Hutson. Chapel Hill: University of North Carolina Press, 1973.

MORRIS, RICHARD B. "We the People of the United States." Presidential address, American Historical Association, 1976.

*SHY, JOHN. *A People Numerous and Armed: Reflections on the Military Struggle for American Independence*. New York: Oxford University Press, 1976.

SMITH, PAGE. *A New Age Now Begins: A People's History of the American Revolution*. New York: McGraw-Hill, 1976.

STARKEY, MARION. *A Little Rebellion*. New York: Knopf, 1949.

VAN DOREN, CARL. *Mutiny in January*. New York: Viking, 1943.

*YOUNG, ALFRED F., ED. *The American Revolution: Explorations in the History of American Radicalism*. DeKalb: Northern Illinois University Press, 1976.

Chapter 6
The Intimately Oppressed

BARKER-BENFIELD, G. J. *The Horrors of the Half-Known Life*. New York: Harper & Row, 1976.

*BAXANDALL, ROSALYN, LINDA GORDON, AND SUSAN REVERBY, EDS. *America's Working Women*. New York: Random House, 1976.

*COTT, NANCY. *The Bonds of Womanhood*. New Haven: Yale University Press, 1977.

————, ED. *Root of Bitterness*. New York: Dutton, 1972.

FARB, PETER. "The Pueblos of the Southwest." In *Women in American Life*, ed. Anne Scott. Boston: Houghton Mifflin, 1970.

*FLEXNER, ELEANOR. *A Century of Struggle*. Cambridge, Mass.: Harvard University Press, 1975.

GORDON, ANN, AND MARY JO BUHLE. "Sex and Class in Colonial and Nineteenth-Century America." In *Liberating Women's History*, ed. Berenice Carroll. Urbana: University of Illinois Press, 1975.

*LERNER, GERDA, ED. *The Female Experience: An American Documentary*. Indianapolis: Bobbs-Merrill, 1977.

SANDOZ, MARI. "These Were the Sioux." In *Women in American Life*, ed. Anne Scott. Boston: Houghton Mifflin, 1970.

Bibliography

SPRUILL, JULIA CHERRY. *Women's Life and Work in the Southern Colonies*. Chapel Hil:. University of North Carolina, 1938.

TYLER, ALICE FELT. *Freedom's Ferment*. Minneapolis: University of Minnesota Press, 1944.

VOGEL, LISE. "Factory Tracts." *Signs: Journal of Women in Culture and Society*. Spring 1976.

WELTER, BARBARA. *Dimity Convictions: The American Woman in the Nineteenth Century*. Athens, Ohio: Ohio University Press, 1976.

WILSON, JOAN HOFF. "The Illusion of Change: Women in the American Revolution." In *The American Revolution: Explorations in the History of American Radicalism*, ed. Alfred F. Young. DeKalb: Northern Illinois University Press, 1976.

Chapter 7
As Long as Grass Grows or Water Runs

DRINNON, RICHARD. *Violence in the American Experience: Winning the West*. New York: New American Library, 1979.

FILLER, LOUIS E., AND ALLEN GUTTMANN, EDS. *The Removal of the Cherokee Nation*. Huntington, N.Y.: R. E. Krieger, 1977.

FOREMAN, GRANT. *Indian Removal*. Norman: University of Oklahoma Press, 1972.

*McLUHAN, T. C., ED. *Touch the Earth: A Self-Portrait of Indian Existence*. New York: Simon & Schuster, 1976.

*ROGIN, MICHAEL. *Fathers and Children: Andrew Jackson and the Subjugation of the American Indian*. New York: Knopf, 1975.

*VAN EVERY, DALE. *The Disinherited: The Lost Birthright of the American Indian*. New York: Morrow, 1976.

VOGEL, VIRGIL, ED. *This Country Was Ours*. New York: Harper & Row, 1972.

Chapter 8
We Take Nothing by Conquest, Thank God

*FONER, PHILIP. *A History of the Labor Movement in the United States*. 4 vols. New York: International Publishers, 1947–1965.

GRAEBNER, NORMAN A. "Empire in the Pacific: A Study in American Continental Expansion." In *The Mexican War: Crisis for American Democracy*, ed. Archie P. McDonald. Lexington, Mass.: D. C. Heath, 1969.

————, ED. *Manifest Destiny*. Indianapolis: Bobbs-Merrill, 1968.

JAY, WILLIAM. *A Review of the Causes and Consequences of the Mexican War*. Boston: B. B. Mussey & Co., 1849.

MCDONALD, ARCHIE P., ED. *The Mexican War: Crisis for American Democracy*. Lexington, Mass.: D. C. Heath, 1969.

MORISON, SAMUEL ELIOT, FREDERICK MERK, AND FRANK FRIEDEL. *Dissent in Three American Wars*. Cambridge, Mass.: Harvard University Press, 1970.

O'SULLIVAN, JOHN, AND ALAN MECKLER. *The Draft and Its Enemies: A Documentary History*. Urbana: University of Illinois Press, 1974.

PERRY, BLISS, ED. *Lincoln: Speeches and Letters*. Garden City, N.Y.: Doubleday, 1923.

*SCHROEDER, JOHN H. *Mr. Polk's War: American Opposition and Dissent 1846–1848*. Madison: University of Wisconsin Press, 1973.

*SMITH, GEORGE WINSTON, AND CHARLES JUDAH, EDS. *Chronicles of the Gringos: ?The U.S. Army in the Mexican War 1846–1848*. Albuquerque: University of New Mexico Press, 1966.

*SMITH, JUSTIN. *The War with Mexico*. 2 vols. New York: Macmillan, 1919.

*WEEMS, JOHN EDWARD. *To Conquer a Peace*. New York: Doubleday, 1974.

WEINBERG, ALBERT K. *Manifest Destiny: A Study of Nationalist Expansion in American History*. Baltimore: Johns Hopkins Press, 1935.

Chapter 9
Slavery Without Submission, Emancipation Without Freedom

ALLEN, ROBERT. *The Reluctant Reformers*. New York: Anchor, 1975.

*APTHEKER, HERBERT. *American Negro Slave Revolts*. New York: International Publishers, 1969.

*————, ED. *A Documentary History of the Negro People in the United States*. New York: Citadel, 1974.

————. *Nat Turner's Slave Rebellion*. New York: Grove Press, 1968.

BOND, HORACE MANN. "Social and Economic Forces in Alabama Reconstruction." *Journal of Negro History*. July 1938.

CONRAD, EARL. *Harriet Tubman*. Middlebury, Vt.: Eriksson, 1970.

COX, LAWANDA AND JOHN, EDS. *Reconstruction, the Negro, and the Old South*. New York: Harper & Row, 1973.

DOUGLASS, FREDERICK. *Narrative of the Life of Frederick Douglass*, ed. Benjamin Quarles. Cambridge, Mass.: Harvard University Press, 1960.

DU BOIS, W. E. B. *John Brown*. New York: International Publishers, 1962.

FOGEL, ROBERT, AND STANLEY ENGERMAN. *Time on the Cross: The Economics of American Negro Slavery*. Boston: Little, Brown, 1974.

FONER, PHILIP, ED. *The Life and Writings of Frederick Douglass*. 5 vols. New York: International Publishers, 1975.

*FRANKLIN, JOHN HOPE. *From Slavery to Freedom*. New York: Knopf, 1974.

*GENOVESE, EUGENE. *Roll, Jordan, Roll: The World the Slaves Made*. New York: Pantheon, 1974.

*GUTMAN, HERBERT. *The Black Family in Slavery and Freedom, 1750–1925*. New York: Pantheon, 1976.

———. *Slavery and the Numbers Game: A Critique of "Time on the Cross."* Urbana: University of Illinois Press, 1975.

HERSCHFIELD, MARILYN. "Women in the Civil War." Unpublished paper, 1977.

*HOFSTADTER, RICHARD. *The American Political Tradition*. New York: Knopf, 1973.

KILLENS, JOHN O., ED. *The Trial Record of Denmark Vesey*. Boston: Beacon Press, 1970.

KOLCHIN, PETER. *First Freedom: The Response of Alabama's Blacks to Emancipation and Reconstruction*. New York: Greenwood, 1972.

*LERNER, GERDA, ED. *Black Women in White America: A Documentary History*. New York: Random House, 1973.

LESTER, JULIUS, ED. *To Be a Slave*. New York: Dial Press, 1968.

*LEVINE, LAWRENCE J. *Black Culture and Black Consciousness: Afro-American Folk Thought from Slavery to Freedom*. New York: Oxford University Press, 1977.

*LOGAN, RAYFORD. *The Betrayal of the Negro: From Rutherford B. Hayes to Woodrow Wilson*. New York: Macmillan, 1965.

*MACPHERSON, JAMES. *The Negro's Civil War*. New York: Pantheon, 1965.

*———. *The Struggle for Equality*. Princeton: Princeton University Press, 1964.

Bibliography

*MELTZER, MILTON, ED. *In Their Own Words: A History of the American Negro*. New York: T. Y. Crowell, 1964–1967.

MULLIN, MICHAEL, ED. *American Negro Slavery: A Documentary History*. New York: Harper & Row, 1975.

OSOFSKY, GILBERT. *Puttin' On Ole Massa*. New York: Harper & Row, 1969.

PAINTER, NELL IRVIN. *Exodusters: Black Migration to Kansas After Reconstruction*. New York: Knopf, 1977.

PHILLIPS, ULRICH B. *American Negro Slavery: A Survey of the Supply, Employment and Control of Negro Labor as Determined by the Plantation Regime*. Baton Rouge: Louisiana State University Press, 1966.

RAWICK, GEORGE P. *From Sundown to Sunup: The Making of the Black Community*. Westport, Conn.: Greenwood Press, 1972.

*ROSENGARTEN, THEODORE. *All God's Dangers: The Life of Nate Shaw*. New York: Knopf, 1974.

STAROBIN, ROBERT S., ED. *Blacks in Bondage: Letters of American Slaves*. New York: Franklin Watts, 1974.

TRAGLE, HENRY I. *The Southmapton Slave Revolt of 1831*. Amherst, Mass.: University of Massachusetts Press, 1971.

WILTSE, CHARLES M., ED. *David Walker's Appeal*. New York: Hill & Wang, 1965.

*WOODWARD, C. VANN. *Reunion and Reaction: The Compromise of 1877 and the End of Reconstruction*. Boston: Little, Brown, 1966.

WORKS PROGRESS ADMINISTRATION. *The Negro in Virginia*. New York: Arno Press, 1969.

Chapter 10
The Other Civil War

BIMBA, ANTHONY. *The Molly Maguires*. New York: International Publishers, 1970.

BRECHER, JEREMY. *Strike!* Boston: South End Press, 1979.

*BRUCE, ROBERT V. *1877: Year of Violence*. New York: Franklin Watts, 1959.

BURBANK, DAVID. *Reign of Rabble: The St. Louis General Strike of 1877*. Fairfield, N.J: Augustus Kelley, 1966.

*CHRISTMAN, HENRY. *Tin Horns and Calico*. New York: Holt, 1945.

*COCHRAN, THOMAS, AND WILLIAM MILLER. *The Age of Enterprise*. New York: Macmillan, 1942.

COULTER, E. MERTON. *The Confederate States of America 1861–1865*. Baton Rouge: Louisiana State University Press, 1950.

DACUS, JOSEPH A. "Annals of the Great Strikes of the United States." In *Except to Walk Free: Documents and Notes in the History of American Labor*, ed. Albert Fried. New York: Anchor, 1974.

*DAWLEY, ALAN. *Class and Community: The Industrial Revolution in Lynn*. Cambridge, Mass.: Harvard University Press, 1976.

*FELDSTEIN, STANLEY, AND LAWRENCE COSTELLO, EDS. *The Ordeal of Assimilation: A Documentary History of the White Working Class, 1830's to the 1970's*. New York: Anchor, 1974.

FITE, EMERSON. *Social and Industrial Conditions in the North During the Civil War*. New York: Macmillan, 1910.

*FONER, PHILIP. *A History of the Labor Movement in the United States,*.4 vols. New York: International Publishers, 1947–1964.

*————, ED. *We, the Other People*. Urbana: University of Illinois Press, 1976.

FRIED, ALBERT, ED. *Except to Walk Free: Documents and Notes in the History of American Labor*. New York: Anchor, 1974.

*GETTLEMAN, MARVIN. *The Dorr Rebellion*. New York: Random House, 1973.

GUTMAN, HERBERT. "The Buena Vista Affair, 1874–1875. In *Workers in the Industrial Revolution: Recent Studies of Labor in the United States and Europe*, ed. Peter N. Stearns and Daniel Walkowitz. New Brunswick, N.J.: Transaction, 1974.

————. *Work, Culture and Society in Industrializing American*. New York: Random House, 1977.

————. "Work, Culture and Society in Industrializing America, 1815–1919." *American Historical Review* June 1973.

HEADLEY, JOEL TYLER. *The Great Riots of New York, 1712–1873*. Indianapolis: Bobbs-Merrill, 1970.

*HOFSTADTER, RICHARD, AND MICHAEL WALLACE, EDS. *American Violence: A Documentary History*. New York: Knopf, 1970.

*HORWITZ, MORTON. *The Transformation of American Law, 1780–1860*. Cambridge, Mass.: Harvard University Press, 1977.

KNIGHTS, PETER R. *The Plain People of Boston 1830–1860: A Study in City Growth*. New York: Oxford University Press, 1973.

MEYER, MARVIN. *The Jacksonian Persuasion*. New York: Vintage, 1960.

MILLER, DOUGLAS T. *The Birth of Modern America*. Indianapolis: Bobbs-Merrill, 1970.

Bibliography

MONTGOMERY, DAVID. "The Shuttle and the Cross: Weavers and Artisans in the Kensington Riots of 1844." *Journal of Social History*. Summer 1972.

*MYERS, GUSTAVUS. *History of the Great American Fortunes*. New York: Modern Library, 1936.

PESSEN, EDWARD. *Jacksonian America*. Homewood, Ill.: Dorsey, 1969.

————. *Most Uncommon Jacksonians*. Albany: State University of New York Press, 1967.

REMINI, ROBERT V. *The Age of Jackson*. New York: Harper & Row, 1972.

SCHLESINGER, ARTHUR M., JR. *The Age of Jackson*. Boston: Little, Brown, 1945.

STEARNS, PETER N., AND DANIEL WALKOWITZ, EDS. *Workers in the Industrial Revolution: Recent Studies of Labor in the United States and Europe*. New Brunswick, N.J.: Transaction, 1974.

TATUM, GEORGIA LEE. *Disloyalty in the Confederacy*. New York: A.M.S. Press, 1970.

*WERTHEIMER, BARBARA. *We Were There: The Story of Working Women in America*. New York: Pantheon, 1977.

WILSON, EDMUND. *Patriotic Gore: Studies in the Literature of the American Civil War*. New York: Oxford University Press, 1962.

YELLEN, SAMUEL. *American Labor Struggles*. New York: Pathfinder, 1974.

ZINN, HOWARD. "The Conspiracy of Law." In *The Rule of Law*, ed. Robert Paul Wolff. New York: Simon & Schuster, 1971.

Chapter 11
Robber Barons and Rebels

ALLEN, ROBERT. *Reluctant Reformers: Racism and Social Reform Movements in the United States*. New York: Anchor, 1975.

BELLAMY, EDWARD. *Looking Backward*. Cambridge, Mass.: Harvard University Press, 1967.

BOWLES, SAMUEL, AND HERBERT GINTIS. *Schooling in Capitalist America*. New York: Basic Books, 1976.

BRANDEIS, LOUIS. *Other People's Money*. New York: Frederick Stokes, 1914.

BRECHER, JEREMY. *Strike!* Boston: South End Press, 1979.

Bibliography

CARWARDINE, WILLIAM. *The Pullman Strike.* Chicago: Charles Kerr, 1973.

*COCHRAN, THOMAS, AND WILLIAM MILLER. *The Age of Enterprise.* New York: Macmillan, 1942.

CONWELL, RUSSELL H. *Acres of Diamonds.* New York: Harper & Row, 1915.

CROWE, CHARLES. "Tom Watson, Populists, and Blacks Reconsidered." *Journal of Negro History.* April 1970.

DAVID, HENRY. *A History of the Haymarket Affair.* New York: Collier, 1963.

FELDSTEIN, STANLEY, AND LAWRENCE COSTELLO, EDS. *The Ordeal of Assimilation: A Documentary History of the White Working Class, 1830's to the 1970's.* Garden City, N.Y.: Anchor, 1974.

*FONER, PHILIP. *A History of the Labor Movement in the United States.* 4 vols. New York: International Publishers, 1947–1964.

————. *Organized Labor and the Black Worker 1619–1973.* New York: International Publishers, 1974.

GEORGE, HENRY. *Progress and Poverty.* New York: Robert Scholkenbach Foundation, 1937.

GINGER, RAY, *The Age of Excess: The U.S. from 1877 to 1914.* New York: Macmillan, 1975.

*————. *The Bending Cross: A Biography of Eugene Victor Debs.* New Brunswick, N.J.: Rutgers University Press, 1949.

*GOODWYN, LAWRENCE. *Democratic Promise: The Populist Movement in America.* New York: Oxford University Press, 1976.

HAIR, WILLIAM IVY. *Bourbonism and Agrarian Protest: Louisiana Politics, 1877–1900.* Baton Rouge: Louisiana State University Press, 1969.

HEILBRONER, ROBERT, AND AARON SINGER. *The Economic Transformation of America.* New York: Harcourt Brace Jovanovich, 1977.

HOFSTADTER, RICHARD, AND MICHAEL WALLACE, EDS. *American Violence: A Documentary History.* New York: Knopf, 1970.

*JOSEPHSON, MATTHEW. *The Politicos.* New York: Harcourt Brace Jovanovich, 1963.

*————. *The Robber Barons.* New York: Harcourt Brace Jovanovich, 1962.

MASON, ALPHEUS T., AND WILLIAM M. BEANEY. *American Constitutional Law.* Englewood Cliffs, N.J.: Prentice-Hall, 1972.

*MYERS, GUSTAVUS. *History of the Great American Fortunes.* New York: Modern Library, 1936.

PIERCE, BESSIE L. *Public Opinion and the Teaching of History in the United States*. New York: DaCapo, 1970.

POLLACK, NORMAN. *The Populist Response to Industrial America*. Cambridge, Mass.: Harvard University Press, 1976.

SMITH, HENRY NASH. *Virgin Land*. Cambridge, Mass.: Harvard University Press, 1970.

SPRING, JOEL H. *Education and the Rise of the Corporate State*. Boston: Beacon Press, 1973.

WASSERMAN, HARVEY. *Harvey Wasserman's History of the United States*. New York: Harper & Row, 1972.

*WERTHEIMER, BARBARA. *We Were There: The Story of Working Women in America*. New York: Pantheon, 1977.

*WOODWARD, C. VANN. *Origins of the New South*. Baton Rouge: Louisiana State University Press, 1972.

*————. *Tom Watson, Agrarian Rebel*. New York: Oxford University Press, 1963.

*YELLEN, SAMUEL. *American Labor Struggles*. New York: Pathfinder, 1974.

Chapter 12
The Empire and the People

APTHEKER, HERBERT, ED. *A Documentary History of the Negro People in the United States*. New York: Citadel, 1973.

BEALE, HOWARD K. *Theodore Roosevelt and the Rise of America to World Power*. New York: Macmillan, 1962.

BEISNER, ROBERT. *Twelve Against Empire: The Anti-Imperialists, 1898–1902*. New York: McGraw-Hill, 1968.

*FONER, PHILIP. *A History of the Labor Movement in the United States,*.4 vols. New York: International Publishers, 1947–1964.

————. *The Spanish-Cuban-American War and the Birth of American Imperialism*. 2 vols. New York: Monthly Review Press, 1972.

FRANCISCO, LUZVIMINDA. "The First Vietnam: The Philippine-American War, 1899–1902." *Bulletin of Concerned Asian Scholars,*.1973.

*GATEWOOD, WILLARD B. *"Smoked Yankees" and the Struggle for Empire: Letters from Negro Soldiers, 1898–1902*. Urbana; University of Illinois Press, 1971.

Bibliography

LAFEBER, WALTER. *The New Empire: An Interpretation of American Expansion.* Ithaca, N.Y.: Cornell University Press, 1963.

PRATT, JULIUS. "American Business and the Spanish-American War." *Hispanic-American Historical Review.* 1934.

SCHIRMER DANIEL BOONE. *Republic or Empire: American Resistance to the Philippine War.* Cambridge, Mass.: Schenkman, 1972.

WILLIAMS, WILLIAM APPLEMAN. *The Roots of the Modern American Empire.* New York: Random House, 1969.

———. *The Tragedy of American Diplomacy.* New York: Dell, 1972.

WOLFF, LEON. *Little Brown Brother.* Garden City, N.Y.: Doubleday, 1961.

YOUNG, MARILYN. *The Rhetoric of Empire.* Cambridge, Mass.: Harvard University Press, 1968.

Chapter 13
The Socialist Challenge

*APTHEKER, HERBERT. *A Documentary History of the Negro People in the United States.* New York: Citadel, 1974.

*BAXANDALL, ROSALYN, LINDA GORDON, AND SUSAN REVERBY, EDS. *America's Working Women.* New York: Random House, 1976.

BRAVERMAN, HARRY. *Labor and Monopoly Capital: The Degradation of Work in the Twentieth Century.* New York: Monthly Review Press, 1975.

BRODY, DAVID. *Steelworkers in America: The Non-Union Era.* Cambridge, Mass.: Harvard University Press, 1960.

CHAFE, WILLIAM. *Women and Equality: Changing Patterns in American Culture.* New York: Oxford University Press, 1977.

COCHRAN, THOMAS, AND WILLIAM MILLER. *The Age of Enterprise.* New York: Macmillan, 1942.

DANCIS, BRUCE. "Socialism and Women." *Socialist Revolution,* January–March 1976.

DUBOFSKY, MELVYN. *We Shall Be All: A History of the Industrial Workers of the World.* New York: Quadrangle, 1974.

DU BOIS, W. E. B. *The Souls of Black Folk.* New York: Fawcett, 1961.

FAULKNER, HAROLD. *The Decline of Laissez Faire 1897–1917.* White Plains, N.Y.: M. E. Sharpe, 1977.

Bibliography

*FLEXNER, ELEANOR. *A Century of Struggle*. Cambridge, Mass.: Harvard University Press, 1975.

FLYNN, ELIZABETH GURLEY. *The Rebel Girl*. New York: International Publishers, 1973.

FONER, PHILIP, ED. *Helen Keller: Her Socialist Years*. New York: International Publishers, 1967.

———. *A History of the Labor Movement in the United States*. 4 vols. New York: International Publishers, 1947–1964.

GILMAN, CHARLOTTE PERKINS. *Women and Economics*. New York: Harper & Row, 1966.

*GINGER, RAY. *The Bending Cross: A Biography of Eugene Victor Debs*. New Brunswick, N.J.: Rutgers University Press, 1969.

GOLDMAN, EMMA. *Anarchism and Other Essays*. New York: Dover, 1970.

GREEN, JAMES. *Grass-Roots Socialism: Radical Movements in the Southwest, 1895–1943*. Baton Rouge: Louisiana State University Press, 1978.

HAYS, SAMUEL. "The Politics of Reform in Municipal Government in the Progressive Era." *Pacific Northwest Quarterl*. October 1964. (Reprinted by New England Free Press.)

HAYWOOD, BILL. *The Autobiography of Big Bill Haywood*. New York: International Publishers, 1929.

JAMES, HENRY. *The American Scene*. Bloomington: Indiana University Press, 1968.

HOFSTADTER, RICHARD. *The American Political Tradition*. New York: Random House, 1954.

JONES, MARY. *The Autobiography of Mother Jones*. Chicago: Charles Kerr, 1925.

KAPLAN, JUSTIN. *Mr. Clemens and Mark Twain: A Biography*. New York: Simon & Schuster, 1966.

*KOLKO, GABRIEL. *The Triumph of Conservatism*. New York: Free Press, 1977.

*KORNBLUH, JOYCE, ED. *Rebel Voices: An I.W.W. Anthology*. Ann Arbor: University of Michigan Press, 1964.

*LERNER, GERDA, ED. *Black Women in White America*. New York: Random House, 1973.

*———. *The Female Experience: An American Documentary*. Indianapolis: Bobbs-Merrill, 1977.

LONDON, JACK. *The Iron Heel*. New York: Bantam, 1971.

NADEN, CORINNE J. *The Triangle Shirtwaist Fire, March 25, 1911*. New York: Franklin Watts, 1971.

Bibliography

SANGER, MARGARET. *Woman and the New Race.* New York: Brentano's, 1920.

SCHOENER, ALLON, ED. *Portal to America: The Lower East Side, 1870–1925.* New York: Holt, Rinehart & Winston, 1967.

SINCLAIR, UPTON. *The Jungle.* New York: Harper & Row, 1951.

SOCHEN, JUNE. *Movers and Shakers: American Women Thinkers and Activists, 1900–1970.* New York: Quadrangle, 1974.

STEIN, LEON. *The Triangle Fire.* Philadelphia: Lippincott, 1965.

WASSERMAN, HARVEY. *Harvey Wasserman's History of the United States.* New York: Harper & Row, 1972.

*WEINSTEIN, JAMES. *The Corporate Ideal in the Liberal State, 1900–1918.* Boston: Beacon Press, 1968.

*WERTHEIMER, BARBARA. *We Were There: The Story of Working Women in America.* New York: Pantheon, 1977.

WIEBE, ROBERT H. *The Search for Order, 1877–1920.* New York: Hill & Wang, 1966.

*YELLEN, SAMUEL. *American Labor Struggles.* New York: Pathfinder, 1974.

ZINN, HOWARD. *The Politics of History.* Boston: Beacon Press, 1970.

Chapter 14
War Is the Health of the State

BARITZ, LOREN, ED. *The American Left.* New York: Basic Books, 1971.

*CHAFEE, ZECHARIAH, JR. *Free Speech in the United States.* New York: Atheneum, 1969.

DOS PASSOS, JOHN. *1919.* New York: Signet, 1969.

DU BOIS, W. E. B. "The African Roots of War." *Atlantic Monthly,* May 1915.

FLEMING, D. F. *The Origins and Legacies of World War I.* Garden City, N.Y.: Doubleday, 1968.

*FUSSELL, PAUL. *The Great War and Modern Memory.* New York: Oxford University Press, 1975.

*GINGER, RAY. *The Bending Cross: A Biography of Eugene Victor Debs.* New Brunswick, N. J.: Rutgers University Pres, 1969.

GOLDMAN, ERIC. *Rendezvous with Destiny.* New York: Random House, 1956.

Bibliography

GRUBER, CAROL S. *Mars and Minerva: World War I and the Uses of Higher Learning in America.* Baton Rouge: Louisiana State University Press, 1975.

JOUGHIN, LOUIS, AND EDMUND MORGAN. *The Legacy of Sacco and Vanzetti.* New York: Quadrangle, 1964.

KNIGHTLEY, PHILIP. *The First Casualty: The War Correspondent as Hero, Propagandist, and Myth Maker.* New York: Harcourt Brace Jovanovich, 1975.

KORNBLUH, JOYCE, ED. *Rebel Voices: An I.W.W. Anthology.* Ann Arbor: University of Michigan Press, 1964.

LEVIN, MURRAY. *Political Hysteria in America.* New York: Basic Books, 1971.

MAYER, ARNO J. *The Politics and Diplomacy of Peace-Making 1918–1919.* New York: Knopf, 1967.

*PETERSON, H. C., AND GILBERT C. FITE. *Opponents of War, 1917–1918.* Seattle, University of Washington Press, 1968.

SIMPSON, COLIN. *Lusitania.* Boston: Little, Brown, 1973.

SINCLAIR, UPTON. *Boston.* Cambridge, Mass.: Robert Bentley, 1978.

WEINSTEIN, JAMES. *The Corporate Ideal in the United States, 1900–1918.* Boston: Beacon Press, 1969.

Chapter 15
Self-help in Hard Times

ADAMIC, LOUIS. *My America, 1928–1938.* New York: Harper & Row, 1938.

*BAXANDALL, ROSALYN, LINDA GORDON, AND SUSAN REVERBY, EDS. *America's Working Women.* New York: Random House, 1976.

BELLUSH, BERNARD. *The Failure of the N.R.A.* New York: W. W. Norton, 1976.

BERNSTEIN, BARTON, J., ED. *Towards a New Past: Dissenting Essays in American History.* New York: Pantheon, 1968.

BERNSTEIN, IRVING. *The Lean Years: A History of the American Worker, 1920–1933.* Boston: Houghton Mifflin, 1960.

———. *The Turbulent Years: A History of the American Worker, 1933–1941.* Boston: Houghton Mifflin, 1969.

BORDEN, MORTON, ED. *Voices of the American Past: Readings in American History.* Lexington, Mass.: D.C. Heath, 1972.

BOYER, RICHARD, AND HERBERT MORAIS. *Labor's Untold Story*. United Front, 1955.

*BRECHER, JEREMY. *Strike!* Boston: South End Press, 1979.

BUHLE, PAUL. "An Interview with Luigi Nardella." *Radical History Review*. Spring 1978.

*CLOWARD, RICHARD A., AND FRANCES F. PIVEN. *Poor People's Movements*. New York: Pantheon, 1977.

CONKIN, PAUL. *F.D.R. and the Origins of the Welfare State*. New York: Crowell, 1967.

CURTI, MERLE. *The Growth of American Thought*. New York: Harper & Row, 1943.

*FINE, SIDNEY. *Sit-Down: The General Motors Strike of 1936–1937*. Ann Arbor: University of Michigan Press, 1969.

GALBRAITH, JOHN KENNETH. *The Great Crash: 1929*. Boston: Houghton Mifflin, 1972.

GENERAL STRIKE COMMITTEE. *The Seattle General Strike*. Charlestown, Mass.: gum press, 1972.

*HALLGREN, MAURITZ. *Seeds of Revolt*. New York: Knopf, 1934.

*LERNER, GERDA, ED. *Black Women in White America: A Documentary History*. New York: Random House, 1977.

LEWIS, SINCLAIR. *Babbitt*. New York: Harcourt Brace Jovanovich, 1949.

LYND, ALICE AND STAUGHTON, EDS. *Rank and File: Personal Histories by Working-Class Organizers*. Boston: Beacon Press, 1974.

LYND, ROBERT AND HELEN. *Middletown*. New York: Harcourt Brace Jovanovich, 1959.

MANGIONE, JERRE. *The Dream and the Deal: The Federal Writers Project, 1935–1943*. Boston: Little, Brown, 1972.

MILLS, FREDERICK C. *Economic Tendencies in the United States: Aspects of Pre-War and Post-War Changes*. New York: National Bureau of Economic Research, 1932.

OTTLEY, ROI, AND WILLIAM J. WEATHERBY. "The Negro in New York: An Informal History." In *Justice Denied: The Black Man in White America*, eds. William Chace and Peter Collier. New York: Harcourt Brace Jovanovich, 1970.

PAINTER, NELL, AND HOSEA HUDSON. "A Negro Communist in the Deep South." *Radical America*. July–August 1977.

RENSHAW, PATRICK. *The Wobblies*. New York: Anchor, 1968.

*ROSENGARTEN, THEODORE. *All God's Dangers: The Life of Nate Shaw*. New York: Knopf, 1974.

STEINBECK, JOHN. *The Grapes of Wrath*. New York: Viking, 1939.

Bibliography

SWADOS, HARVEY, ED. *The American Writer and the Great Depression.* Indianapolis: Bobbs-Merrill, 1966.

*TERKEL, STUDS. *Hard Times: An Oral History of the Great Depression in America.* New York: Pantheon, 1970.

WRIGHT, RICHARD. *Black Boy.* New York: Harper & Row, 1937.

ZINN, HOWARD. *La Guardia in Congress.* Ithaca, N.Y: Cornell University Press, 1959.

Chapter 16
A People's War?

ALPEROVITZ, GAR. *Atomic Diplomacy.* New York: Vintage, 1967.

ARONSON, JAMES. *The Press and the Cold War.* Indianapolis: Bobbs-Merrill, 1970.

BARNET, RICHARD J. *Intervention and Revolution: The U.S. and the Third World.* New York: New American Library, 1969.

BLACKETT, P. M. S. *Fear, War and the Bomb: Military and Political Consequences of Atomic Energy.* New York: McGraw-Hill, 1948.

BOTTOME, EDGAR. *The Balance of Terror: A Guide to the Arms Race.* Boston: Beacon Press, 1972.

BUTOW, ROBERT. *Japan's Decision to Surrender.* Stanford: Stanford University Press, 1954.

CATTON, BRUCE. *The War Lords of Washington.* New York: Harcourt Brace, 1948.

CHOMSKY, NOAM. *American Power and the New Mandarins.* New York: Pantheon, 1969.

DAVIDSON, BASIL. *Let Freedom Come: Africa in Modern History.* Boston: Little, Brown, 1978.

FEINGOLD, HENRY L. *The Politics of Rescue: The Roosevelt Administration and the Holocaust.* New Brunswick, N.J.: Rutgers University Press, 1970.

FREELAND, RICHARD M. *The Truman Doctrine and the Origins of McCarthyism.* New York: Knopf, 1971.

GARDNER, LLOYD. *Economic Aspects of New Deal Diplomacy.* Madison: University of Wisconsin Press, 1964.

GRIFFITH, ROBERT W. *The Politics of Fear: Joseph R. McCarthy and the Senate.* Rochelle Park, N.J.: Hayden, 1971.

HAMBY, ALONZO L. *Beyond the New Deal: Harry S. Truman and American Liberalism.* New York: Columbia University Press, 1953.

IRVING, DAVID. *The Destruction of Dresden*. New York: Ballantine, 1965.

KAHN, HERMAN. *On Thermonuclear War*. New York: Free Press, 1969.

*KOLKO, GABRIEL. *The Politics of War: The World and United States Foreign Policy, 1943–1945*. New York: Random House, 1968.

LEMISCH, JESSE. *On Active Service in War and Peace: Politics and Ideology in the American Historical Profession*. Toronto: New Hogtown Press, 1975.

MAILER, NORMAN. *The Naked and the Dead*. New York: Holt, Rinehart & Winston, 1948.

MILLER, DOUGLAS, AND MARION NOWAK. *The Fifties: The Way We Really Were*. New York: Doubleday, 1977.

MILLER, MARC. "The Irony of Victory: Lowell During World War II." Unpublished doctoral dissertation. Boston University, 1977.

MILLS, C. WRIGHT. *The Power Elite*. New York: Oxford University Press, 1970.

MINEAR, RICHARD H. *Victor's Justice: The Tokyo War Crimes Trial*. Princeton, N.J.: Princeton University Press, 1973.

OFFNER, ARNOLD. *American Appeasement: U.S. Foreign Policy and Germany, 1933–1938*. New York: W. W. Norton, 1976.

ROSTOW, EUGENE V. "Our Worst Wartime Mistake." *Harper's*. September 1945.

RUSSETT, BRUCE. *No Clear and Present Danger*. New York: Harper & Row, 1972.

SAMPSON, ANTHONY. *The Seven Sisters: The Great Oil Companies and the World They Shaped*. New York: Viking, 1975.

SCHNEIR, WALTER AND MIRIAM. *Invitation to an Inquest*. New York: Doubleday, 1965.

*SHERWIN, MARTIN. *A World Destroyed: The Atom Bomb and the Grand Alliance*. New York: Knopf, 1975.

STONE, I. F. *The Hidden History of the Korean War*. New York: Monthly Review Press, 1969.

UNITED STATES STRATEGIC BOMBING SURVEY. *Japan's Struggle to End the War*. Washington: Government Printing Office, 1946.

WEGLYN, MICHI. *Years of Infamy: The Untold Story of America's Concentration Camps*. New York: William Morrow, 1976.

WITTNER, LAWRENCE S. *Rebels Against War: The American Peace Movement, 1941–1960*. New York: Columbia University Press, 1969.

*ZINN, HOWARD. *Postwar America: 1945–1971*. Indianapolis, Bobbs-Merrill, 1973.

————. *The Pentagon Papers*. 4 vols. Boston: Beacon Press, 1973.

Chapter 17

"Or Does It Explode?"

ALLEN, ROBERT. *Black Awakening in Capitalist America*. Garden City, N.Y.: Doubleday, 1969.

BONTEMPS, ARNA, ED. *American Negro Poetry*. New York: Hill & Wang, 1974.

BRODERICK, FRANCIS, AND AUGUST MEIER. *Black Protest Thought in the Twentieth Century*. Indianapolis: Bobbs-Merrill, 1971.

CLOWARD, RICHARD A., AND FRANCES F. PIVEN. *Poor People's Movements*. New York: Pantheon, 1977.

CONOT, ROBERT. *Rivers of Blood, Years of Darkness*. New York: Morrow, 1968.

CULLEN, COUNTEE. *On These I Stand*. New York: Harper & Row, 1947.

HERNDON, ANGELO. "You Cannot Kill the Working Class." In *Black Protest*, ed. Joanne Grant. New York: Fawcett, 1975.

HUGGINS, NATHAN I. *Harlem Renaissance*. New York: Oxford University Press, 1971.

HUGHES, LANGSTON. *Selected Poems of Langston Hughes*. New York: Knopf, 1959.

LERNER, GERDA, ED. *Black Women in White America: A Documentary History*. New York: Random House, 1977.

MALCOLM X. *Malcolm X Speaks*. New York: Meret, 1965.

NAVASKY, VICTOR. *Kennedy Justice*. New York: Atheneum, 1977.

PERKUS, CATHY, ED. *COINTELPRO: The FBI's Secret War on Political Freedom*. New York: Monad Press, 1976.

WRIGHT, RICHARD. *Black Boy*. New York: Harper & Row, 1937.

ZINN, HOWARD. *Postwar America: 1945–1971*. Indianapolis: Bobbs-Merrill, 1973.

————. *SNCC: The New Abolitionists*. Boston: Beacon Press, 1964.

Chapter 18
The Impossible Victory: Vietnam

*Branfman, Fred. *Voices from the Plain of Jars*. New York: Harper & Row, 1972.

Green, Philip, and Sanford Levinson, eds. *Power and Community: Dissenting Essays in Political Science*. New York: Pantheon, 1970.

Hersch, Seymour. *My Lai 4: A Report on the Massacre and Its Aftermath*. New York: Random House, 1970.

Kovic, Ron. *Born on the Fourth of July*. New York: McGraw-Hill, 1976.

Lipsitz, Lewis. "On Political Belief: The Grievances of the Poor." In *Power and Community: Dissenting Essays in Political Science*, ed. Philip Green and Sanford Levinson. New York: Pantheon, 1970.

Modigliani, Andrew. "Hawks and Doves, Isolationism and Political Distrust: An Analysis of Public Opinion on Military Policy." *American Political Science Review*. September 1972.

Pike, Douglas. *Viet Cong*. Cambridge, Mass.: MIT Press, 1966.

Schell, Jonathan. *The Village of Ben Suc*. New York: Knopf, 1967.

Zinn, Howard. *Vietnam: The Logic of Withdrawal*. Boston: Beacon Press, 1967.

———. *Pentagon Papers*. 4 vols. Boston: Beacon Press, 1971.

Chapter 19
Surprises

Akwesasne Notes. *Voices from Wounded Knee, 1973*. Mohawk Nation, Rooseveltown, N.J.: Akwesasne Notes, 1974.

Baxandall, Rosalyn, Linda Gordon, and Susan Reverby, eds. *America's Working Women*. New York: Random House, 1976.

Benston, Margaret. "The Political Economy of Women's Liberation. *Monthly Review*, fall 1969.

Boston Women's Health Book Collective. *Our Bodies, Ourselves*. New York: Simon & Schuster, 1976.

Brandon, William. *The Last Americans*. McGraw-Hill, 1974.

Bibliography

*Brown, Dee. *Bury My Heart at Wounded Knee.* New York: Holt, Rinehart & Winston, 1971.

Brownmiller, Susan. *Against Our Will: Men, Women and Rape.* New York: Simon & Schuster, 1975.

Coles, Robert. *Children of Crisis.* Boston: Little, Brown, 1967.

Cottle, Thomas J. *Children in Jail.* Boston: Beacon Press, 1977.

The Council on Interracial Books for Children, ed. *Chronicles of American Indian Protest.* New York: Fawcett, 1971.

Deloria, Vine, Jr. *Custer Died for Your Sins.* New York: Macmillan, 1969.

———. *We Talk, You Listen.* New York: Macmillan, 1970.

Firestone, Shulamith. *The Dialectics of Sex.* New York: Bantam, 1970.

Friedan, Betty. *The Feminine Mystique.* New York: W. W. Norton, 1963.

Gaylin, Willard. *Partial Justice.* New York: Knopf, 1974.

Jackson, George. *Soledad Brother: The Prison Letters of George Jackson.* New York: Coward McCann, 1970.

Lerner, Gerda, ed. *Black Women in White America: A Documentary History.* New York: Random House, 1977.

Lifton, Robert Jay, ed. *The Woman in America.* Boston: Beacon Press, 1967.

Lynd, Robert and Helen. *Middletown.* New York: Harcourt Brace Jovanovich, 1959.

*McLuhan, T. C. *Touch the Earth: A Self-Portrait of Indian Existence.* New York: Simon & Schuster, 1976.

Mann, Eric. *Comrade George: An Investigation into the Life, Political Thought, and Assassination of George Jackson.* New York: Harper & Row, 1974.

*Mitford, Jessica. *Kind and Usual Punishment: The Prison Business.* New York: Knopf, 1973.

Morgan, Robin, ed. *Sisterhood Is Powerful: An Anthology of Writings from the Women's Liberation Movement.* New York: Random House, 1970.

The Prison Research Project, Urban Planning Aid. *The Price of Punishment: Prisons in Massachusetts.* Cambridge, Mass.: Urban Planning Aid, 1974.

Rich, Adrienne. *Of Woman Born.* New York: Bantam, 1977.

Rothman, David J. and Sheila, eds. *Sources of American Social Tradition.* New York: Basic Books, 1975.

Steiner, Stan. *The New Indians.* New York: Harper & Row, 1968.

WICKER, TOM. *A Time to Die*. New York: Quadrangle, 1975.

*WITT, SHIRLEY HILL, AND STAN STEINER. *The Way: An Anthology of American Indian Literature*. New York: Knopf, 1974.

ZINN, HOWARD, ED. *Justice in Everyday Life*. New York: Morrow, 1974.

Chapter 20
The Seventies: Under Control?

BLAIR, JOHN M. *The Control of Oil*. New York: Pantheon, 1977.

DOMMERGUES, PIERRE. "L'Essor du conservatisme Americain." *Le Monde Diplomatique*. May 1978.

*EVANS, LES, AND ALLEN MYERS. *Watergate and the Myth of American Democracy*. New York: Pathfinder Press, 1974.

FRIEDEN, JESS. "The Trilateral Commission." *Monthly Review*. December 1977.

GARDNER, RICHARD. *Alternative America: A Directory of 5000 Alternative Lifestyle Groups and Organizations*. Cambridge, Mass.: Richard Gardner, 1976.

GLAZER, NATHAN, AND IRVING KRISTOL. *The American Commonwealth 1976*. New York: Basic Books, 1976.

NEW YORK TIMES. *The Watergate Hearings*. Bantam, 1973.

*U.S. CONGRESS, SENATE COMMITTEE TO STUDY GOVERNMENTAL OPERATIONS WITH RESPECT TO INTELLIGENCE ACTIVITIES. *Hearings*. 94th Congress. 1976.

Chapter 21
Carter-Reagan-Bush: The Bipartisan Consensus

BARLETT, DONALD, AND JAMES STEELE. *America: What Went Wrong?*. Kansas City: Andrews & McMeel, 1992.

———. *America: Who Really Pays the Taxes?* New York: Simon & Schuster, 1994.

CHOMSKY, NOAM. *World Orders Old and New*. New York: Columbia University Press, 1994.

CROTEAU, DAVID, AND WILLIAM HOYNES. *By Invitation Only: How the Media Limit the Political Debate*. Monroe, Me: Common Courage Press, 1994.

Bibliography

DANAHER, KEVIN, ED. *50 Years Is Enough: The Case Against the World Bank*. Boston: South End Press, 1994.

DERBER, CHARES. *Money, Murder, and the American Dream*. Boston: Faber & Faber, 1992.

EDSALL, THOMAS AND MARY. *Chain Reaction*. New York: W. W. Norton, 1992.

EHRENREICH, BARBARA. *The Worst Years of Our Lives*. New York: HarperCollins, 1990.

GREIDER, WILLIAM. *Who Will Tell the People?* New York: Simon & Schuster, 1992.

GROVER, WILLIAM F. *The President as Prisoner*. Albany: State University of New York, 1989.

HELLINGER, DANIEL, AND DENNIS JUDD. *The Democratic Facade*. Pacific Grove, Calif.: Brooks/Cole, 1991.

HOFSTADTER, RICHARD. *The American Political Tradition*. New York: Vintage, 1974.

KOZOL, JONATHAN. *Savage Inequalities: Children in America's Schools*. New York: Crown, 1991.

PIVEN, FRANCES FOX, AND RICHARD CLOWARD. *Regulating the Poor*. New York: Vintage, 1993.

ROSENBERG, GERALD N. *The Hollow Hope*. Chicago: University of Chicago Press, 1992.

SAVAGE, DAVID. *Turning Right: The Making of the Rehnquist Supreme Court*. New York: John Wiley & Sons, 1992.

SEXTON, PATRICIA CAYO. *The War on Labor and The Left*. Boulder: Westview Press, 1991.

SHALOM, STEPHEN. *Imperial Alibis*. Boston: South End Press, 1993.

Chapter 22
The Unreported Resistance

EWEN, ALEXANDER, ED. *Voice of Indigenous Peoples*. Santa Fe, N.M.: Clear Light, 1994.

GROVER, WILLIAM, AND JOSEPH PESCHEK, EDS. *Voices of Dissent*. New York: HarperCollins, 1993.

LOEB, PAUL. *Generations at the Crossroads*. New Brunswick, N.J.: Rutgers University Press, 1994.

LOFLAND, JOHN. *Polite Protesters: The American Peace Movement of the 1980s*. Syracuse, N.Y.: Syracuse University Press, 1993.

Bibliography

LYND, STAUGHTON AND ALICE. *Nonviolence in America: A Documentary History.* Maryknoll, N.Y.: Orbis, 1995.

MARTINEZ, ELIZABETH, ED. *500 Years of Chicano History.* Albuquerque: Southwest Organizing Project,1991.

PIVEN, FRANCES, AND RICHARD CLOWARD. *Why Americans Don't Vote.* New York: Pantheon, 1988.

VANNEMAN, REEVE, AND LYNN CANNON. *The American Perception of Class.* Philadelphia: Temple University Press, 1987.

Note:
Much of the material in this chapter comes from my own files of social action by organizations around the country, from my collection of news clippings, and from publications outside the mainstream, including: *The Nation, In These Times, The Nuclear Resister, Peacework, The Resist Newsletter, Rethinking Schools,* and *Indigenous Thought.*

Chapter 23
The Coming Revolt of the Guards

BRYAN, C. D. B. *Friendly Fire.* New York: Putnam, 1976.

LEVIN, MURRAY B. *The Alienated Voter.* New York: Irvington, 1971.

WARREN, DONALD I. *The Radical Center: Middle America and the Politics of Alienation.* Notre Dame, Ind.: University of Notre Dame Press, 1976.

WEIZENBAUM, JOSEPH. *Computer Power and Human Reason.* San Francisco: Freeman, 1976.

Afterword:
On the Clinton Presidency

SMITH, SAM. *Shadows of Hope: A Freethinker's Guide to Politics in the Time of Clinton.* Bloomington: Indiana University Press, 1994.

SOLOMON, NORMAN. *False Hope: The Politics of Illusion in the Clinton Era.* Monroe, Me.: Common Courage Press, 1994.

The State of America's Children: Yearbook 1994. Washington, D.C.: Children's Defense Fund, 1994.

Index

C

Books of related interest
from The New Press

MALAIKA ADERO
*Up South: Stories, Studies, and Letters
of This Century's African American Migrations*
(PB, $12.95, 1-56584-168-9, 238 PP.)
Primary sources from the greatest migration in American history.

IRA BERLIN AND LESLIE S. ROWLAND, EDITORS
*Families and Freedom: A Documentary History
of African American Kinship in the Civil War Era*
(HC, $25.00, 1-56584-026-9, 304 PP.)
A sequel to the award-winning *Free at Last*, moving letters from freed
slaves to their families.

IRA BERLIN AND BARBARA J. FIELDS, ET AL.
*Free at Last: A Documentary History
of Slavery, Freedom, and the Civil War*
(HC, $27.50, 1-56584-015-1; PB, $15.95, 1-56584-120-4, 608 PP.)
A winner of the 1994 Lincoln Prize, some of the most remarkable and
moving letters ever written by Americans, depicting the drama of
Emancipation in the midst of the nation's bloodiest conflict.

AMERICAN SOCIAL HISTORY PROJECT
*Freedom's Unfinished Revolution:
An Inquiry into the Civil War and Reconstruction*
(PB, $17.95, 1-56584-198-0, 320 PP.)
From the award-winning authors of *Who Built America?*,
a groundbreaking high school level presentation of the Civil War and
Reconstruction.

IRA BERLIN
Slaves without Masters: The Free Negro in the Antebellum South
(PB, $14.95, 1-56584-028-3, 448 PP.)
A vivid and moving history of the quarter of a million free blacks who
lived in the South before the Civil War.

JAMES W. LOEWEN
Lies My Teacher Told Me:
Everything Your American History Textbook Got Wrong
(HC, $24.95, 1-56584-100-fl, 384 PP.)
The best-selling, award-winning, iconoclastic look at the errors, misrepresentations, and omissions in the leading American history textbooks.

JAMES W. LOEWEN
The Truth about Columbus: A Subversively True Poster Book
for a Dubiously Celebratory Occasion
(PB WITH POSTER, $12.95, 1-56584-008-9, 48 PP.)
A provocative educational poster and booklet that draws on recent scholarship to debunk the myths and discover the man.

STEPHEN J. ROSE
Social Stratification in the United States:
The American Profile Poster Revised and Expanded
(PB, $14.95, 1-56584-021-6, 48 PP.)
A graphic presentation of the distribution of wealth in America.

VIRGINIA YANS-MCLAUGHLIN, MARJORIE LIGHTMAN,
AND THE STATUE OF LIBERTY-ELLIS ISLAND FOUNDATION
Ellis Island and the Peopling of America: The Official Guide
(PB, $15.00, 1-56584-364-9, 224 PP.)
A primary source reader and resource guide to Ellis Island and issues of immigration.

HOWARD ZINN AND GEORGE KIRSCHNER
A People's History of the United States: The Wall Charts
(PORTFOLIO, $25.00, 1-56584-171-9, 48-PAGE BOOKLET
WITH TWO POSTERS)
Two oversized posters based on Zinn's best-selling social history.

To Order, call W.W. NORTON at 1-800-